STO

ACPL ITEM
DISCARDED

S0-ATG-070

61

Type A behavior

DO NOT REMOVE
CARDS FROM POCKET

ALLEN COUNTY PUBLIC LIBRARY

FORT WAYNE, INDIANA 46802

You may return this book to any agency, branch, or bookmobile of the Allen County Public Library.

DEMCO

TYPE A
Behavior

Edited by Michael J. Strube

Originally published as a special issue of the
Journal of Social Behavior and Personality

SAGE PUBLICATIONS
The International Professional Publishers
Newbury Park London New Delhi

Allen County Public Library
Ft. Wayne, Indiana

Copyright © 1991 by Select Press

All rights reserved. No part of this book may be reproduced or utilized in any form or by any means, electronic or mechanical, including photocopying, recording, or by any information storage and retrieval system, without permission in writing from the publisher.

For information address:

SAGE Publications, Inc.
2455 Teller Road
Newbury Park, California 91320

SAGE Publications Ltd.
6 Bonhill Street
London EC2A 4PU
United Kingdom

SAGE Publications India Pvt. Ltd.
M-32 Market
Greater Kailash I
New Delhi 110 048 India

Printed in the United States of America

Library of Congress Cataloging-in-Publication Data

Main entry under title:

Type A behavior / edited by Michael J. Strube.
p. cm.
"Originally published as a special issue of the Journal of social behavior and personality."
Includes bibliographical references and indexes.
ISBN 0-8039-4089-0. — ISBN 0-8039-4090-4 (pbk.)
1. Type A behavior. 2. Coronary heart disease—Psychosomatic aspects. I. Strube, Michael J.
RC685.C6T956 1991
616.1'2308—dc20

90-24163
CIP

FIRST SAGE PRINTING, 1991

Sage Production Editor: Diane S. Foster

Contents

Special Populations

Measurement and Prediction Refinements

Work Settings

Medical and Psychological Refinements and Extensions

Intervention

Foreword

After some 20 years of intensive research, Type A behavior was designated a risk factor for coronary heart disease (CHD) in 1981 by a review panel sponsored by the National Heart, Lung and Blood Institute (NHLBI). The designation was based primarily on the prospective Western Collaborative Group Study, a reanalysis of the Framingham data, and evidence from coronary angiographic studies. Recent evidence has compromised the seeming unequivocality of these data. The Type A area is, in my judgment, an exemplar of research into biobehavioral mechanisms whereby social and psychological events culminate in physical disease, or at least potentiate disease. Nevertheless, the evidence in support of Type A as a risk factor remains sufficiently compelling, in my judgment, to suggest that something important is out there. Continuing efforts should, therefore, be expended on the study of Type A behavior and its component elements.

Over eight years have elapsed since the NHLBI designation and research on Type A has, indeed, continued unabated. Many of the papers in this volume typify the nature of this research and reflect directions being taken by contemporary investigators. Thus, we see efforts to (1) isolate the so-called "toxic" elements in the Type A behavior pattern such as cynical hostility and anger, (2) delineate gender differences and similarities in Type A behavior and its association with CHD, (3) determine the heritability, if any, of the behavior pattern and its principal components, (4) specify developmental antecedents of the behavior pattern, as well as the reliability of assessing the pattern in children, and (5) develop and evaluate programs aimed at altering Type A behavior.

Of greater importance, perhaps, are the studies based upon theoretical models of the behavior pattern. Such research is a refreshing breath of fresh air. These studies attempt to answer such fundamental questions as what gives rise to Type A behavior and what factors appear to sustain it. Little attention, unfortunately, has been given to conceptualizing Type A behavior over the past two decades. We now see a change that promises to provide an important foundation for understanding the psychological mechanisms underlying the behavior pattern.

Several papers in this volume are noteworthy in this regard, including Strube's self-appraisal model, my own control theory as extended and amplified in, for example, the work of Lawler and her colleagues, and Rhodewalt's conceptual approach to medical noncompliance. We also see in this volume some interesting efforts to look at the role of attentional style in Type A children, and I applaud the paper by Fontana et al. for its systematic approach to Scherwitz's self-involvement hypothesis as an explanation for differences in the evidence suggesting greater physiological reactivity in As compared to Bs.

These research developments are most gratifying to someone who has repeatedly pointed to the relative absence of conceptual models and theoretically-based research in the Type A area. I would hope that this emphasis on conceptualization will be extended to the question of mediating physiological mechanisms. My own hunch is that catecholaminergic and related sympathetic nervous system activity are prime candidates for the mediator role.

I am also struck by the pervasiveness of research indicating a central role for the control variable in cardiovascular disease and, for that matter, in the pathogenesis of a variety of diseases. Taken together with accumulating data on the effects of uncontrollability on catecholamine changes, we may have the beginnings of important insights into the physiological mechanisms underlying the association between psychological variables and Type A behavior. This is, therefore, a nice illustration of exciting theory construction.

It is essential that this area develop coherent and empirically tested models that will stand up to the most rigorous scientific scrutiny. I believe progress is being made in this direction. Such theoretical development, coupled with a solid data base, will go a long way towards addressing the concerns of clinicians by providing them with a foundation for interventions aimed at altering the behavior pattern. In the final analysis, treatment and prevention procedures based upon systematic scientific knowledge are the best rationale for public health policy.

David C. Glass
State University of New York at Stony Brook

PREFACE

From its simple beginnings as a descriptive label characterizing individuals at apparent risk for coronary problems, the Type A pattern has matured into a theory-based variable with applications extending beyond the prediction of coronary endpoints. This diversity is reflected in current research which varies considerably in scope and level of analysis. For example, intense efforts are underway to refine the prediction of coronary disease and to specify the pathophysiological processes. Currently in vogue are attempts to dissemble the Type A pattern in the hopes of identifying the "toxic" subcomponents. Likewise, investigations with special populations (e.g., women, children) have attempted to identify the generality of risk conferred by the Type A pattern, and to identify its developmental antecedents. The Type A pattern also has been found to be useful in understanding noncoronary medical problems, and numerous extensions beyond the medical realm to ordinary social behavior exist. These latter extensions have been justified by recent attempts to understand the psychological underpinnings of Type A behavior. Theory development remains the most critical issue in the Type A area, although the recent emergence of compelling conceptual models augurs well for the future health of this research area. Only through sound theory will investigators be able to place the pattern in a broader, integrative context, embark on more programmatic efforts, and develop a common language for the many different levels of analysis.

This collection of articles brings together a representative cross-section of leading scholars and research programs devoted to the study of Type A behavior. The works attest to the vitality of the area, and the many advances that are being made. The research reported here spans levels of analysis from the physiological to the socio-historical, and covers topics that range widely across the medical and psychological terrains. The discourse varies from the solidly empirical to the conceptually speculative. In short, there is something here for everyone, and the sum total provides an exciting glimpse at the current state of affairs in Type A research.

Michael J Strube
Washington University, St. Louis, MO

Type A Behavior Pattern: A Personal Overview

Ray H. Rosenman, M.D.
Director of Cardiovascular Research, Health Sciences Program
SRI International, Menlo Park, CA 94025

Dr. Strube, Guest Editor for this issue of the journal, has kindly asked me to write an overview-type of lead article and I accepted his flattering invitation. Some of the following is by way of review, and some is a personal overview.

Although the concept of risk factors for coronary heart disease (CHD) is well established, there are many reasons (Rosenman, 1986) to indicate that they only partially explain historical changes of CHD incidences, gender differences, geographical heterogeneity among population groups, or the varying rate of progression of coronary atherosclerosis. Moreover, it is not clear that interventions on these risk factors have significantly reduced either primary or secondary rates of CHD.

Considerable evidence (Rosenman, 1986) links the CHD incidence with urbanization, population densification, and industrialization. Thus, the reported association between CHD and risk factors are strongly mediated by the ambient situations in which individuals live and work, as well as by other psychosocial factors that distinguish one individual from another. Since the relationships of risk factors to CHD incidence are based on statistical findings, they do not provide absolute levels of risk or explain the individual specificity of associated risk. Pathogenicity for CHD is not given solely by the level of one or combination of risk factors, since it is the individual with the risk factor who suffers CHD, but at highly variable levels of such factors.

Development of Type A

Such considerations, along with direct observation of patients with CHD, led to the formulation of the Type A behavior pattern (TABP) and its component behaviors (Rosenman, 1986; Rosenman, Swan & Carmelli, 1988). Initial studies appeared to link TABP with the preva-

© 1990 Select Press

lence of CHD in both sexes (Friedman & Rosenman, 1959; Rosenman & Friedman, 1961). However, these studies were not epidemiologically sound and it was therefore believed necessary to do a carefully controlled, prospective study in order to test the hypothesis that TABP is associated with the incidence of CHD. This was done in the Western Collaborative Group Study (WCGS) (Rosenman, Friedman, Straus, et al., 1964). The large number of subjects and its design necessitated a new method for assessment of TABP. Self-report biases were found to make the use of questionnaires inadequate for this purpose and a structured interview (SI) was developed (Rosenman et al., 1964; Rosenman, 1978a).

The TABP was defined as an action-emotion complex involving behavioral dispositions such as ambitiousness, aggressiveness, competitiveness, and impatience; specific behaviors such as muscle tenseness, alertness, rapid and emphatic vocal stylistics, and accelerated pace of activities; and emotional responses such as irritation, hostility, and increased potential for anger. The SI was designed to allow observation of these behaviors during the interview, and to provide challenges to evoke their manifestations. The converse Type B behavior pattern was conceived as the relative absence of Type A behaviors in individuals who exhibit a different coping style that is characterized by a relative lack of time urgency, impatience, and hostile responses. TABP was not considered to be either a stressor situation or distressed response, and, therefore, not synonymous with stress, or to equate with anxiety, worry, fear, depression, or neurosis.

The WCGS provided strong evidence that TABP is associated with the incidence of CHD (Rosenman, Brand, Sholtz, & Friedman, 1976) and with the severity of coronary atherosclerosis (Friedman, Rosenman, Straus, et al., 1968). Jenkins, Rosenman, and Friedman (1968) found evidence for replicability of the SI-assessment of TABP, as well as for its stability over short periods of time. A search was made for possible biological mechanisms that might explain the CHD risk associated with TABP (Rosenman & Friedman, 1974). It was found that male subjects with well-defined TABP exhibited greater noradrenergic responses than did paired Type B subjects, both during a competitive, cognitive task (Friedman, Byers, Diamant, & Rosenman, 1975), and in their daily occupational milieus (Friedman, St. George, Byers, & Rosenman, 1960). Explorations were made for interventions on TABP, using both psychological (Rosenman & Friedman, 1977) and pharmacological methods (Rosenman, 1978b).

During the course of the WCGS, several psychologists became interested in TABP. Caffrey (1968) studied relationships of TABP with various measures of personality and behavior. Jenkins, Zyzanski, and

Rosenman (1979) developed a questionnaire for self-report assessment of TABP, the Jenkins Activity Survey (JAS), and Bortner and Rosenman (1967) developed a different type of scale, later shortened by Bortner (1969). The Framingham Type A Scale was developed much later (Haynes, Feinleib, & Kannel, 1980). A scale from the Adjective Checklist (ACL) and the Activity Scale of the Thurstone Temperament Schedule were found to correlate with TABP (Rosenman, Rahe, Borhani, & Feinleib, 1976) and this was subsequently confirmed (Rosenman, 1986).

The above only highlights some early history of TABP, described elsewhere in greater detail (Rosenman, 1986; Rosenman, Swan, & Carmelli, 1988). In the 15 years since these early studies, a large literature has appeared, dealing both with psychological implications of TABP as will as its associations with cardiovascular disorders.

Management Issues

Byrne, Rosenman, Schiller, and Chesney (1985), and others found that self-report questionnaires developed for TABP assessment appear largely to measure attitudes rather than the behaviors that are observed and assessd by the SI. These self-report scales fail to assess some of the most important elements of TABP and exhibit only weak correlations among themselves or with the SI. By including judgments of actual Type A behaviors observed during its administration, the SI extends the breadth and scope of assessments to fit the construct of TABP as a set of overt behaviors that occur in association with, and in response to, relevant situational stressors (Matthews, 1982; Byrne, et al. 1985). As reviewed elsewhere (Rosenman, 1986), various methods have been developed to assess TABP in adult females, college students, and in children (Matthews & Siegel, 1982). TABP also has been assessed from a videotaped, modified SI in order to provide quantization of its component behaviors (Friedman & Powell, 1984). However, this method has not been validated by other investigators, nor has its interrater agreement, test-retest reliability, or usefulness for prediction of CHD yet been demonstrated. Different methodologies also have been developed to assess certain components of TABP from the SI (Dembroski, MacDougall, Shields, et al., 1978; Hecker, Chesney, Black, & Frautschi, 1988).

Construct validation of the TABP concept proceeded along several lines. Under appropriate stimulus conditions, Type A subjects have generally been found (Rosenman et al, 1988) to be more likely than Type B counterparts to exhibit competitiveness, impatience, aggressiveness, irritation, and hostility. Regardless of the problems with self-report measures for TABP assessment, there is remarkable consistency with the TABP construct in the cluster of traits that are measured by such scales (Rosenman, 1986; Rosenman,et al., 1988). Moreover, this consistency in the pattern of interrelationships among Type A behaviors and self-reports prevails in different samples that vary by age, sex, geographical distribution, and by different interviewers, raters, and sites of administration (Matthews, 1982; Matthews, Krantz, Dembroski, & MacDougall, 1982).

During exposure to a wide variety of physical and mental stressors in the laboratory setting, Type As also tend to exhibit greater autonomic neural and associated cardiovascular responses compared to Type B counterparts (Krantz & Manuck, 1984; Manuck & Krantz, 1986). Taken together, the results of a large number of studies (Rosenman, et al., 1986) lend strong construct validation for the TABP concept. These and other studies also have confirmed that TABP does not equate with anxiety, neuroticism, stress, or psychopathology. Moreover, recent studies (Kahn, Gully, Cooper, et al., 1987; Schneider, Julius, Moss, et al., 1987; de Quattro, 1988) confirmed earlier findings (Friedman et al., 1960, 1975) that Type A subjects exhibit enhanced noradrenergic responses in their daily milieus.

Type A and Heart Disease

The relationship of TABP to CHD and to severity of coronary artery disease has been assessed in a number of studies since the WCGS. Matthews and Haynes (1986) and Haynes and Matthews (1988) found inconsistent results in their elegant reviews. However, they point out that, on balance, population-cohort studies have found that TABP is indeed a risk factor for CHD, while intervention studies on high-risk persons are less consistent with regard to a relationship of TABP either to primary or recurrent rates of CHD. This is somewhat paradoxical since they noted that the relationship of TABP to CHD in the Framingham Heart Study was strongest when levels of other risk factors were elevated.

Considerable attention has been given to a recent finding in a 22-year follow-up of WCGS subjects accomplished from a mailed questionnaire and death certificate data. In this study, Ragland and Brand (1988) found that TABP did not indicate an adverse prognosis for CHD mortality among patients with CHD. These conclusions solely pertained to mortality from recurring CHD events during the 12 year follow-up experience after CHD already was manifest. During this time it is highly probable that major changes occurred in many risk factors, including TABP. The study findings were based on intake data and on a difference of 13 deaths between Type A and Type B patients over a 22 year period.

Booth-Kewley and H.S. Friedman (1987) used meta-analysis to organize findings in a superb review of the relationships between psychosocial variables and CHD. They found the strongest associations to be with TABP, particularly in cross-sectional studies. Haynes and Matthews (1988) noted that the later studies were performed during years in which a decline of CHD mortality was occurring and during which there was widespread use of possibly protective beta-adrenergic blocking drugs for treatment of hypertension and post-infarction subjects. The negative Type A-CHD associations found in recurrent infarction studies, such as the Aspirin Myocardial Infarction Study (Shekelle, Gale, & Norusis, 1985) and that by Case, Heller, Case, & Moss (1985), are particularly open to question because both studies used the JAS for assessment of TABP, now clearly demonstrated to have major inaccuracies for this purpose (Matthews et al., 1982; Byrne et al., 1985). The study by Case et al. (1985) gave the questionnaire to subjects shortly after suffering acute myocardial infarction, obviously at a time when TABP might be least manifest. Moreover, the JAS notably fails to assess the hostility component of TABP (Abbott, Peters, & Vogel, 1988), which has important relevance for the association of TABP with CHD (Rosenman, 1985).

Haynes and Matthews (1988) considered other factors that might be related to reported inconsistencies, including small sample sizes, the distribution of Type A and B subjects in the samples, low incidence of CHD, as well as drift changes in the administration and assessment of the SI, when this was used. The importance of the latter is emphasized in a series of arduous studies by Scherwitz and Canick (1989). They carefully auditioned the audiotaped intake SIs from CHD cases and control subjects in the WCGS and MRFIT studies and compared interviewer styles, finding marked differences in this regard. It should be recalled that the interviewers in the WCGS had been trained over a long period of time and had ongoing regular follow-up throughout the intake period, while those in the MRFIT Study had only a brief period of training and almost no follow-up (Rosenman, 1986).

In more recent studies, Scherwitz and Brand (unpublished paper) found significant differences in the TABP-CHD risk ratios for various interviewers in the WCGS. These findings strongly suggest that the proficiency of SI interviewers may have confounding effects on the association of TABP with CHD.

Several other factors not considered in the cited reviews might be of even greater importance in the negative results of studies such as MTFIT (Shekelle, Billings, Neaton, et al., 1985). The first concerns the type of subject who is apt to volunteer for multifactorial intervention to prevent primary or recurrent CHD. Study populations are highly selected. Thus, Werko (1976) found that, in a city population, cardiovascular mortality is several times higher among those not answering an invitation for health examination than in participants, presumed to indicate the latter's interest in health problems. It is not likely that time-urgent, competitive, hostile, coronary-prone Type A males often volunteer for intervention studies in which regular and relatively frequent clinic visits are required of participants, and which seek full compliance with major life-style changes of diet and other risk factors. It has further been shown that subjects who volunteer for such studies are often the "worried well," i.e. those with risk factors and no disease (Criqui, Austin, & Barrett-Connor, 1979). The markedly lower than predicted CHD incidence that occurred during follow-up in the MRFIT Study indeed suggests that the participants were biased by health consciousness and other factors that, despite high levels of classic risk factors, were associated with an unexpectedly low rate of CHD.

Another factor of major relevance concerns rates of intervention study dropouts. There is strong evidence that the CHD incidence may be much higher in subjects who drop out of a study compared to those who remain during many years of follow-up (Bruce, Frederick, Bruce, & Fisher, 1979). Almost half of the subjects in the Ontario Rehabilitation study dropped out during follow-up. The consistent predictors of dropout were smoking and blue collar occupation (Oldridge, Donner, Buck, et al., 1982). The MRFIT Study may exemplify these problems. Thus, the observed incidence of CHD during long follow-up in this large group of subjects at highest risk by reason of the three classical risk factors was markedly lower than that predicted by the Framingham Heart Study experience. Certainly the MRFIT experience confirms the point made by Werko (1976) that the results of the Framingham Heart Study are applicable only to those who took part in it, and cannot be used as representative of other populations in the U.S.A. or elsewhere.

The same factors doubtless relate to inconsistencies in studies of the relationship of TABP to angiographic severity of coronary atherosclerosis (Booth-Kewley & Friedman, 1987; Haynes & Matthews, 1988). Pickering (1985) also reviewed such studies and pointed out that they differed in methodologies, lacked normal control of subjects, showed poor correlation of coronary artery disease with the risk factors, often had small sample sizes, and lacked appropriate endpoints. The role of selection bias in angiography studies is well shown by the finding that those suspected of having CAD not confirmed by angiography have a higher prevalence of risk factors than do subjects without suspected CAD (Pearson, Gordis, Achuff, et al., 1982).

Some confusion about an association of TABP with severity of coronary artery disease (CAD) was introduced by an emphasis on studies with negative findings (Williams, Barefoot, & Shekelle, 1985). However, using the SI method of TABP assessment, Blumenthal, Williams, Konig, et al. (1978) and Williams, Haney, Lee, et al. (1980) had observed positive relationships. In their recent analysis of 2,289 patients referred by diagnostic angiography, they again confirmed this relationship

(Williams, Barefoot, Haney, et al., 1988), however, finding it to be stronger in relatively younger subjects. They emphasized that prospective studies generally found that most risk factors exhibit a greatly diminished predictive relationship for both severity of CAD and incidence of CHD with increasing age. Finally, in their reviews of prior studies of the association of TABP with CAD, they point out that those with negative findings had small sample size, failed to consider an age-interaction, and had used self-report questionnaires for assessment of TABP.

Other Data

Aside from relationships to severity of CAD and incidence of CHD, a large literature has developed on other aspects of TABP. Its moderate stability over time has been confirmed (Carmelli, Rosenman, & Chesney, 1987; Abbott et al., 1988; Rosenman et al., 1988). Global TABP does not appear to exhibit significant heritability, although some of its components may have small heritable aspects (Rosenman et al., 1976; Carmelli, Rosenman, Chesney, et al., 1987). The concept of TABP appears to be valid in children (Matthews & Woodall, 1988). It particularly emerges when relevant milieu conditions elicit Type A behaviors in susceptible persons, implying an important role of sociological and socioeconomic factors in an interaction with a subject's personality (Rosenman, 1986). It is therefore not surprising that childhood antecedents of TABP are mainly ascribed to parental and environmental influences that engender learned behaviors (Matthews & Siegel, 1982; Matthews & Woodall, 1988). However, gender and individual differences in active and passive behaviors are apparent even in infancy. This suggests that there are genetic predispositions for TABP that may reside in the distribution and density of hypothalamic nuclei and in other unknown factors that are genetically determined (Rosenman, 1985), but to which little attention has been given.

Self-referencing in the SI was found to be related to TABP, anger, hostility, blood pressure reactivity, severity of CAD, and the primary and secondary rates of CHD in some, if not all studies (Scherwitz, Graham, Grandits, et al., 1986), it was not similarly found by these researchers in the WCGS (Graham, Scherwitz, & Brand, unpublished parer).

Interventions

Levenkron and Moore (1988) recently reviewed issues associated with interventions on TABP. Pharmacological intervention with beta-adrenergic-blocking agents (Rosenman, 1978b, 1983) has been pursued by Schmieder, Friedrich, Neus, et al. (1985) and Krantz, Contrada, La Riccia, et al. (1987). Cognitive methodologies have been developed (Rosenman & Friedman, 1977; Roskies, 1987; Price, 1988), but the endpoints are not well defined. The results of one study of modification of TABP for secondary CHD prevention (Friedman, Thoresen, Gill, et al., 1986) are made difficult by finding almost all subjects to exhibit TABP, changes in evaluating results, a high rate of dropouts, and other methodological problems. Levenkron and Moore (1988) point out that there is a need to clarify conceptual issues that distinguish behavioral versus physiological reactivity and to gather evidence of the health benefits of treatment, despite demonstrated feasibility of TABP intervention. The subject of intervention on TABP was superbly reviewed by Price (1988).

The conceptual issue is a major problem. Booth-Kewley & Friedman (1987) state that "every researcher working in the Type A domain has his or her own conceptualization and accompanying operational definitions of the Type A construct," emphasizing conceptual confusion and that "the psychological dimensions underlying the Type A behavioral characteristics have not been identified" (Matthews, 1982). TABP was conceptualized as an overt behavioral style of living that is neither a personality trait nor a standard reaction to challenges, but rather is the reaction of a predisposed person to a situation which is perceived as a threat or challenge, emphasizing the interaction of a subject and the environmental milieu. Glass (1977) viewed TABP as a characteristic style of response to environmental stressors that threaten an individual's control over the environment. Type A behaviors appear to be an enhanced performance to assert and maintain control over the environment, whenever this is challenged or threatened.

Matthews (1982) proposed that TABP involves a strong need for productivity. The association of TABP with industrialization and Western culture is well recognized (Rosenman, 1986; Helman, 1987). Type A behaviors may reside in inappropriate coping skills (Glass, 1977; Helman, 1987), with the implication that TABP may be associated with CHD risk only when combined with low coping skills and inappropriate defenses (Vickers, Hervig, Rahe, & Rosenman, 1981), or a depressive response that is labelled as "vital exhaustion" (Falger, Schouten, & Appels, 1988). Sibilia, Francioni, Borgo, and Arca (unpublished paper) emphasize that few studies have addressed the systematic assessment of clinically-observed cognitions underlying or associated with TABP or its links with other well-studied forms of emotional disorders and personality dimensions. They find that Type As may hold some beliefs and attitudes that lead to fear and depression that not only may play a role in maintaining TABP but also help to explain the role of depression in precoronary as well as postinfarction patients.

A recent meta-analysis of the literature on the relationship of TABP to anxiety, depression, and neuroticism found that it is positively correlated with psychological disorders (Suls & Chi, 1988). Considering the interest of many psychologists in TABP, it is surprising how little attention has been given to the conceptual issues surrounding the Type A construct and, particularly, to its motivational antecedents.

Physiological Reactions

Some researchers (Dembroski et al., 1978) suggest that the most important aspect of TABP lies in physiologic reactivity. Cardiovascular reactivity has repeatedly been measured in laboratory responses, with the hypothesis that exaggerated reactivity plays a pathogenetic role in the development of essential hypertension and coronary artery disease. A remarkably large literature has dealt with differences of reactivity in Type A and B subjects (Krantz & Manuck, 1984; Manuck & Krantz, 1986; Rosenman, 1987; Contrada & Krantz, 1988; Houston, 1988).

Janisse and Dyck (1988) attempted to integrate physiological and psychological dimensions of TABP. During exposure to a wide variety of stressors in the laboratory setting, Type A-B differences in catecholamine and cardiovascular responses have often, if not consistently, been found (Manuck & Krantz, 1986; Contrada & Krantz, 1988). The largest differences tend to occur during tasks that are associated with more rapid pace of activity, greater task difficulty, and when subjects are challenged to perform more difficult tasks in a competitive manner under time pressure (Ward, Chesney, Swan, et al., 1986; Rosenman, 1987). However, the pattern of these differences and lack of consistency (Krantz & Manuck, 1984) suggest that Type A and B individuals do not have any intrinsic differences of reactivity, but only that a heightened Type A perception of relevant stressors as individually challenging is associated with a more active coping that increases sympathetic neural and associated cardiovascular responses (Light, 1981). Despite the tendency of Type As to exhibit heightened sympathetic responses to perceived relevant challenges in both the laboratory setting and natural environment, neither Type As in general not those with exaggerated cardiovascular reactivity exhibit either higher levels of resting blood pressure or increased prevalence of essential hypertension (Rosenman, 1987). This is of greater significance considering that Type As tend to exhibit higher anger/hostility dimensions, characteristics which are believed to be related to higher blood pressure, heightened reactivity, and increased blood pressure variability.

Cardiovascular Reactivity

There is a rapidly changing concept of cardiovascular reactivity, and this is reviewed elsewhere (Rosenman & Ward, 1988). Among many reasons for this are consistent findings that laboratory stress tests do not predict blood pressure variability in the natural environment and that such variability is not greater either in borderline or established hypertensives than in normotensives (Julius, Weder, & Hinderliter, 1986; Harshfield, James, Schlussel, et al., 1988). The specificity of exaggerated laboratory responses in some borderline hypertensives to mental but not to physical or other stressors is believed to be improperly interpreted to mean that behaviorally-induced blood pressure reactivity is the mechanism by which hypertension develops (Julius et al., 1986). Careful scrutiny of appropriate studies shows three things. First, blood pressure regulation in hypertensive subjects is normal. Second, cardiovascular reactivity cannot explain the development of hypertension or the shifting hemodynamic pattern from borderline to established hypertension. Third, behaviorally-induced blood pressure responses in the laboratory setting and natural environment do not contribute to the pathogenesis of hypertension (Harshfield et al., 1968; Julius, 1988).

These conclusions are strongly supported by the results of a large number of studies of the effects of antihypertensive therapy (Rosenman & Ward, 1988). These have consistently found that effective therapy with a wide variety of medications does not decrease laboratory stressor responses or diminish ambulatory blood pressure variability in the natural environment. The differential effects of such antihypertensive therapy can be explained by the fact that they are under a dual system of regulation, with different anatomic central areas and pathways that regulate basal or tonic and reactive blood pressures. These are to a large extent independently controlled (Reis & LeDoux, 1987).

Cardiovascular reactivity also has been implicated in the pathogenesis of coronary artery disease (Clarkson, Manuck, & Kaplan, 1986). It is plausible that enhanced noradrenergic activity in Type A subjects (Friedman et al., 1960, 1975; Kahn et al., 1987; Schneider et al., 1987; DeQuattro, in press) may play a pathogenetic role in the relationships of TABP to severity of CAD and incidence of CHD. However, reactivity has not been found to be related to the severity of CAD (Schiffer, Hartley, Schuman, & Abelmann, 1976; Krantz et al., 1981). Moreover, blood pressure variability in the natural environment is not a predictor of cardiovascular structural damage (Sokolow, Werdegar, Kain, & Hinman, 1966), and this hypothesis lacks support from animal research (Julius et al., 1986). Nor does reactivity predict cardiovascular morbidity in hypertensive subjects (Pickering & Devereaux, 1987). Thus, although behaviorally-induced elevations of blood pressure may contribute to structural damage, this is not the mechanism by which such damage is conferred (Julius, et al., 1986; Julius, 1988). It finally is important to point out that a large number of studies consistently find that anxiety disorders are related to relative freedom from CAD and low incidence of CHD

(Lantinga, Sprafkin, McCroskery, et al., 1988). But subjects with such disorders exhibit normal responses to laboratory stressors (Mantysaari, Antila, & Peltonen, 1988).

Hostility

The last topic of this overview is perhaps too easily labelled as hostility. There has been a reconceptualization of coronary-proneness that focuses on the hostility construct, confirming that TABP and coronary-proneness are not synonymous. Of course, the majority of individuals, even with a combination of risk factors, do not develop CHD, and those with TABP are no exception. Regardless of this, it may be that only certain aspects of TABP engender coronary-proneness, and early findings from the WCGS provided underpinnings for this evolution.

The first analysis of Type A components from the intake SIs (Jenkins et al., 1966) indicated that hostility was significantly related to the prior occurrence of silent myocardial infarction. This led Bortner to systematically score the TABP components from SIs of subjects who had developed CHD during the initial five-year follow-up and from paired control subjects. The later analysis of Bortner's component scoring (Matthews, Glass, Rosenman, & Bortner, 1977) found that it was competitive drive, impatience. and potential for hostility that particularly identified subjects as coronary-prone. An unpublished reanalysis of Bortner's scores by Spielberger revealed that anger/hostility dimensions were the dominant coronary-prone Type A behaviors in this group of subjects. Hecker et al. (1988) used a new methodology for component-scoring of intake SIs for 250 subjects who developed CHD during the nine-year WCGS follow-up and 500 paired controls. The results strongly confirmed earlier findings. Using a different methodology for scoring SI components (Dembroski et al., 1978), Type A behavioral hostility was found to have predictive associations for both the severity of CAD in angiographic studies and the incidence of CHD in other studies (Dembroski, MacDougall, Williams, et al., 1985; Dembroski & Costa, 1987, 1988).

TABP and behavioral hostility were found to be independently related to the extent of CAD in one study (Williams et al., 1980). Associations were found for SI hostility ratings and either extent of CAD or incidence of CHD in other studies, in which no associations were found for global TABP (Dembroski et al., 1985; MacDougall, Dembroski, Dimsdale, & Hackett, 1985). However, these findings are paradoxical, since behavioral hostility is a major component of global TABP (Rosenman et al., 1988). Vigorous speech stylistics manifested during the SI are an important basis for scoring global TABP (Rosenman et al., 1964). The majority of studies reviewed by Contrada and Krantz (1988) found that such vigorous speech stylistics and behavioral hostility are significantly interrelated. Thus, the findings in the cited studies of relationships between behavioral hostility and extent of CAD and incidence of CHD, in which no relationships were found for global TABP in the same samples, may raise questions about drift in the global TABP assessments by these investigators.

MMPI Hostility Ho

Considerable impetus for a relationship between hostility dimensions and CHD was purportedly given by the results of studies in which the MMPI had been given for various purposes and its Cook and Medley Hostility (Ho) Scale (1954) later analyzed in the context of occurrence of CHD. Barefoot, Dahlstrom, & Williams (1983) found that Ho scores were predictively related to incidence of CHD in 255 physicians who had been followed over a period of 25 years. Similar findings were observed in another data set by Shekelle, Gale, Ostfeld, and Paul (1983). Williams et al. (1980) also found that Ho scores were correlated with the severity of CAD in one angiographic study. However, subsequent studies failed to confirm these findings. Siegman, Dembroski, and Ringel (1987) found a negative association between the experience of hostility and the severity of CAD. Helmer, Ragland, and Syme (1988) did not find the Ho Scale to be correlated with angiographic severity of CAD in either sex. Moreover, scores on the Ho Scale did not predict the incidence of CHD in a 25-year follow-up of 478 physicians (McCranie, Watkins, Brandsma, & Sisson, 1986), in a 30-year follow-up of 280 men (Leon, Murray, Finn, & Bailey, 1988) or in a 33-year follow-up of 1,399 male, university students (Hearn, Murray, & Luepke, 1988).

SI measures of behavioral hostility were sometimes found to be related to cardiovascular reactivity (Dembroski et al., 1978; Contrada & Krantz, 1988). Other studies consistently failed to find a relationship between the Ho Scale and reactivity (Sallis, Johnson, Trevorrow et al., 1987; Smith & Frohm, 1985; Suarez, Williams, & McRae, 1988), unless subjects experience harassment (Suarez et al., 1988).

These findings underlie the need to define the construct of the Cook and Medley Ho Scale. Experts have pointed out that the interpretation given to this measure has not been supported by construct validation for the belief that it measures hostility or anger dimensions, and that there is much evidence to the contrary (Megargee, 1985; Shipman, 1985). It is stated that the Ho Scale assesses the quality and quantity of social supports (Barefoot et al., 1983; Shekelle et al., 1983), and that it is a measure of cynicism and paranoid alienation (Costa, Zonderman, McCrae, & Williams, 1986). Watkins, Fisher, Southard, and Ward (1988) found it to be related to psychosocial and physical distress. Smith, Allred, and Frohm (1988) found it to be a measure of cynical distrust, neuroticism, and general psychopathology, confirming their earlier findings that it measures cynical distrust of others but not overtly aggressive behavior (Smith & Frohm, 1985).

The Ho Scale shows age-related changes and moderate stability over time (Carmelli, Swan, & Rosenman, unpublished paper). There is little evidence for any heritable aspects except for its cynicism subscale (Carmelli, Rosenman, & Swan, 1988). The psychological correlates of behavioral hostility and of the Ho Scale were recently investigated in systematic manner (Swan, Carmelli, & Rosenman, 1989; Swan, Carmelli, & Rosenman, in press). It was found that scores on the Ho Scale were correlated with anxiety, neuroticism, and the tendency to "fake good." Behavioral hostility was not correlated with indices of neuroticism or "fake good," but with measures of dominance, vigor, and self-confidence. The two Ho subscales were found to mirror the intercorrelation pattern found for the full scale, and were negatively correlated with MMPI and other scales that assess constructs that involve paranoia and hostility. The association of Ho Scale scores with neuroticism and psychopathology in these analyses confirm the findings of Costa et al. (1986), and raise further questions about whether the Ho Scale measures hostility (Rosenman, Swan, & Carmelli, 1988a).

Swan et al. (in press) also found that the Ho Scale measures different dimensions from global TABP, as well as from its behavioral hostility component. The psychological correlates of the TABP were found to be congruent with Type A construct, but these were generally different from correlates of the Ho Scale.

It is significant that the findings of Williams and associates (1985) with regard to relationships of the Cook and Medley Ho Scale to severity of CAD and incidence of CHD have not been confirmed by other investigators. In the incidence studies of Barefoot et al. (1983) and Shekelle et al. (1983), the Ho Scale scores were not only predictively related to mortality from CHD, but similarly to mortality from all causes, including cancer. This important issue has not received attention, and may be given a different interpretation. Since the leading causes of death are coronary heart disease and cancer, the findings strongly suggest that the Ho Scale, if associated with mortality from all causes, is not specifically predictive of CHD. Moreover, the subsequent studies not only failed to show any relationship of the Ho Scale to incidence of CHD, but also failed to confirm a relationship to all cause mortality (McCranie et al., 1986; Leon et al., 1988; Hearn et al., 1988). In contrast to the early findings regarding the Ho Scale, TABP has not been found to be a general risk factor for illness (Suls & Sanders, 1988) or to be significantly related to all cause mortality (Yakubovich, Ragland, Brand, & Syme, 1988).

The reasons for discrepancies between early and later studies are unknown. However, it cannot be stated that the findings in regard to the Ho Scale support a relationship between hostility and CHD. Indeed, this would not a priori be expected, since it is a measure of anxiety and neuroticism, and these dimensions are not related to CHD (Bass, Cawley, & Wade, 1983; Costa, 1986; Lantinga et al., 1988).

It is perhaps unfortunate that so much recent attention has been given to "hostility," before its construct is clarified, particularly in the context of any relationship to CHD. It is immediately apparent that interpretations of anger/hostility dimensions are markedly different (Williams et al., 1985; Spielberger, Krasner, & Solomon, 1988). Siegman et al. (1987) differentiated between neurotic and nonneurotic hostility, finding that the former is inversely related to CAD, while the latter is positively related. Assessments of hostility by Dembroski et al. (1978) and Hecker et al. (1988) are behavioral, and both are measured from the SI. However, only the former is directly based on the original Type A components and construct. In view of the strength of the relationship of components assessed by Hecker et al. (1988) to incidence of CHD in the WCGS, it is now important to clarify their construct and meaning.

Competitiveness

In this author's opinion, increasing attention should be given to the competitiveness component of TABP (Rosenman et al., 1964) in underlying its relationship to CHD. This is based on my belief that it has seminal importance for Type A behaviors such as aggressive drive,.accelerated pace of activities, enhanced potential for hostility/anger dimensions, and covert hostility. It also related to self-referencing (Scherwitz & Canick, 1988), and the Type A needs to assert and maintain control over the environment (Glass, 1977), and for productivity (Matthews, 1982). This is a somewhat different type of competitiveness from that which overtly occurs during athletic competition. Its importance might be suspected from the consistency of its relationship to CHD in analyses of data form the WCGS by Jenkins (1966), Matthews et al. (1977), and in univariate analyses by Hecker, et al. (1988).

There are gender differences in competitiveness that may contribute to the sex differential for CHD that occurs in younger ages, as well as for cardiovascular reactivity differences in the laboratory setting (Frankenhaeuser, 1982). It is significant that Type A-B differences in reactivity in males are particularly associated with stressors that are perceived competitively by Type A subjects (Contrada & Krantz, 1988; Dembroski et al., 1978). This Type A component may underlie "cynical distrust" of others (Smith & Frohm, 1985). It is doubtless associated with the enhanced noradrenergic responses of Type A subjects in competitive laboratory tasks (Friedman et al., 1960), and otherwise in their natural environments (Kahn et al., 1987).

Competitiveness may underlie some of the correlations of TABP with self-report psychological dimensions (Rosenman et al., 1976; Rahe, Hervig, & Rosenman, 1978), and probably is a major factor underlying spousal relationships to the occurrence of CHD (Price, 1988). There is a tendency in studies of TABP to separate various components in order to determine their "toxic" elements. However, it seems unlikely that the emotional and behavioral aspects of a human being can ever satisfactorily be subdivided into component parts, which inevitably are intercorrelated.

The Type A competitive dimension probably has both genetic (Rosenman et al., 1976; Rahe, Hervig, & Rosenman, 1978) and learned, environmental (Matthews & Woodall, 1988) influences. An underlying basis may be a covert and deep-seated anxiety. Byrne and Rosenman (1986) noted that the Type A behavioral scales that are predictively related to CHD are correlated with measures of anxiety. But it is the behavioral rather than attitudinal components of TABP which dominate this pattern of intercorrelations. However, it was emphasized that the anxiety which accompanies TABP is independent of neuroticism, in the latter's psychiatric construct. There is evidence that such behavioral anxiety is predictively related to the incidence of CHD during a 35-year follow-up of 126 former Harvard students (Russek, Russek, Russek, & King, 1988). A recent study appears to indicate that peripheral noradrenergic activity is a measure of sympathetic nervous system stimulation by anxiety, and that it reflects rather than causes anxiety (Starkman, Cameron, Nesse, & Zelnik, 1988).

Future Research

An overview would not be complete without some considerations for future research. It is apparent that clarifications are sorely needed for constructs of anxiety, competitiveness, and hostility dimensions as they specifically relate to CHD, as well as for definitions and validation of methodological assessments of such psychological dimensions. Although there is continuing discussion of methods for assessment of TABP (Dembroski & Costa, 1988), it is likely that these will be replaced by quantitation of adrenergic-receptor density and function (Kahn et al., 1987).

There is ongoing faith in the role of cardiovascular reactivity (Contrada & Krantz, 1988; Krantz, Contrada, Robin-Hill, & Friedler, 1988), despite increasing doubt about its value by cardiologists (Pickering & Devereux, 1987; Harshfield, et al., 1988; Julius, 1988; Rosenman &

Ward). The concept of the "hot reactor" (Dembroski, MacDougall, Eliot, & Buell, 1984) is a popular one but "the simple notion of a singular 'hot' versus 'cold' cardiovascular reactor may be oversimplified" (Krantz & Manuck, 1984). Indeed, a recent review of this concept (Eliot, 1988) fails to present factual data for its predictive importance in any follow-up studies.

More population-based studies have been suggested to clarify relationships of TABP to CHD (Haynes & Matthews, 1988). However, it seems probable that future research would be more productively aimed at clarifying relationships of psychosocial variables to platelet and noradrenergic vasoconstrictive factors (Helmstrom, 1982), which are increasingly being identified as having primary pathogenetic relevance for coronary atherogenesis, clinical CHD. and sudden cardiac death. The importance of behavioral factors in this regard is emphasized by the finding that perceived mental stress can induce coronary arterial vasoconstriction and silent myocardial ischemia (Rozanski, Bairey, Krantz, et al., 1987). This may occur more frequently in Type A subjects (Freeman & Nixon, 1988).

Graham (1988) emphasized the need for innovative ideas in this field, quoting the statement by Einstein that "To raise new question, new possibilities, to regard old problems from a new angle, requires creative imagination and marks real advances in science. The problem is how to enhance the production of creative works in our field."

In this overview, it can be seen that there is perhaps less confusion about TABP than sometimes promulgated. There is a real need for clarifications about many issues. It seems likely that these will only come from innovative research rather than, for example, from still more laboratory studies of cardiovascular reactivity in Type A and B subjects. I will close with an apology for citing various review articles. It was possible to cite only some of the extensive literature that has accumulated in this field.

REFERENCES

Abbott, A.V., Peters, R.K., & Vogel, M.E. (1988). Temporal stability and overlap of behavioral and questionnaire assessments of Type A behavior in coronary patients. *Psychosomatic Medicine, 50*, 123-138.

Barefoot, J.C., Dahlstrom, G., & Williams, R.B., Jr. (1953). Hostility, CHD incidence, and total mortality: A 25-year follow-up study of 255 physicians. *Psychosomatic Medicine, 45*, 59-63.

Bass, C., Cawley, R., & Wade, C. (1983). Unexplained breathlessness and psychiatric morbidity in patients with normal and abnormal coronary arteries. *Lancet, 1*, 605-609.

Blumenthal, J., William, R., Konig, Y., Schanberg, S., & Thompson, L. (1978). Type A behavior and angiographically documented coronary disease. *Circulation, 58*, 634-639.

Booth-Kewley, S., & Friedman, H.S. (1987). Psychological predictors of heart disease: A quantitative review. *Psychological Bulletin, 101*, 342-362.

Bortner, R.W. (1969). A short rating scale as a potential measure of Pattern A behavior. *Journal of Chronic Diseases, 22*, 87-91.

Bortner, R.W., & Rosenman, R.H. (1967). The measurement of Pattern A behavior. *Journal of Chronic Diseases, 20*, 525-533.

Bruce, E.M., Frederick, R., Bruce, R.A., & Fisher, L.D. (1976). Comparison of active participants and dropouts in CAPRI cardiopulmonary rehabilitation programs. *American Journal of Cardiology, 37*, 53-62.

Byrne, D.G., & Rosenman, R.H., Schiller, E., & Chesney, M.A. (1985). Consistency and variation among instruments purporting to measure Type A behavior pattern. *Psychosomatic Medicine, 47*, 242-261.

Byrne, D.G., & Rosenman, R.H. (1986). Type A behavior and the experience of effective discomfort. *Journal of Psychosomatic Research, 30*, 661-672.

Caffrey, B. (1968). Reliability and validity of personality and behavioral measures in a study of coronary heart disease. *Journal of Chronic Diseases, 21*, 191-204.

Carmelli, D., Rosenman, R.H., Chesney, M.A. (1987). Stability of the Type A structured interview and related questionnaires in a 10-year follow-up of an adult cohort of twins. *Journal of Behavioral Medicine, 5*, 513-525.

Carmelli, D., Rosenman, R.H., Chesney, M.A., Fabsitz, R., Lee, M., & Borhani, N. (1988). Genetic heritability and shared environmental influences of Type A measures in the NHLBI Twin Study, *American Journal of Epidemiology, 127*, 1041-1052.

Carmelli, D., Rosenman, R.H., & Swan, G.E. (1988). The Cook and Medley HO Scale: A heritability analysis in adult male twins. *Psychosomatic Medicine, 50*, 165-174.

Carmelli, D., Swan, G.E., & Rosenman, R.H. (1985). The relationship between wives' social and psychologic status and their husband's coronary heart disease. *American Journal of Epidemiology, 122*, 90-100.

Carmelli, D., Swan, G.E., & Rosenman, R.H. (1990). Age-related changes in the Cook and Medley Hostility Scale. *Journal of Social Behavior and Personality, 5*, 263-276.

Case, R.B., Heller, S.S., Case, N.B., & Moss, A.J. (1985). Type A behavior and survival after acute myocardial infarction. *New England Journal of Medicine, 312*, 737-741.

Clarkson, T.B., Manuck, S.B., & Kaplan, J.R. (1986). Potential role of cardiovascular reactivity in atherogenesis. In K.A. Matthews, S.M. Weiss, T. Detre, T.M. Dembroski, B. Falkner, S.M. Manuck, R.B. Williams, Jr. (Eds.) *Handbook of stress reactivity and cardiovascular disease* (pp. 35-36). New York: Wiley.

Contrada, R.J., & Krantz, D.S. (1988). Stress, reactivity, and Type A behavior: Current status and future directions. *Annals of Behavioral Medicine, 10*, 64-70.

Cook, W. & Medley, D. (1954). Proposed hostility and pharisaic-virtue scales for the MMPI. *Journal of Applied Psychology, 38*, 414-418.

Costa, P.T., Zonderman, A.B., McCrae, R.R., & Williams, R.B. (1986). Cynicism and paranoid alienation in the Cook and Medley HO Scale. *Psychosomatic Medicine, 48*, 283-285.

Costa, P.T. (1986). Is neuroticism a risk factor for CAD? Is Type A a measure of neuroticism? In T. Schmidt, T. Dembroski, & G. Blumchen, (Eds.). *Biological and Psychological Factors in Cardiovascular Disease*, pp. 85-95. New York: Springer-Verlag.

Criqui, M.H., Austin, M., & Barrett-Connor (1979). The effect of nonresponse on risk ratios in a cardiovascular disease study. *Journal of Chronic Diseases, 32*, 633-638.

Dembroski, T.M., & Costa, P.T. (1987). Coronary-prone behavior: Components of the type A pattern and hostility. *Journal of Personality, 55*, 211-236.

Dembroski, T.M., & Costa, P.T. (1988). Assessment of coronary-prone behaviors: A current overview. *Annals of Behavioral Medicine, 10*, 60-63.

Dembroski, T.M., MacDougall, J.M., Eliot, R.S., & Buell, J.C. (1984). Moving beyond Type A. *Advances, 1*, 16-25.

Dembroski, T.M., MacDougall, J.M., Shields, J.L., Pettito, J., & Lushene, R. (1978). Components of the Type A coronary-prone behavior pattern and cardiovascular responses to psychomotor performance challenge. *Journal of Behavioral Medicine, 1*, 159-176.

Dembroski, T.M., MacDougall, J.M., Williams, R.B., Haney, T., & Blumenthal, J.A. (1985). Components of Type A hostility, and anger-in: Relationships to angiographic findings. *Psychosomatic Medicine, 47*, 219-233.

DeQuattro, V.L. (in press) Physiological aspects of stress — impact on catecholamine release and blood pressure. Presented at Satellite Symposium, *A New Focus for Noradrenergic Protection*, American Society of Hypertension, New York, June 21, 1988.

Eliot, R.S. (1988). The dynamics of hypertension—an overview. Present practices, new possibilities, and new approaches. *American Heart Journal, 116*, 583-589.

Falger, P.R.J., Schouten, E.G.W., & Appels, A.W. (1988). Relationship between age, Type A behavior, life changes over the life-span, vital exhaustion, and first myocardial infarction: A case-referent study. *Proceedings of Society of Behavioral Medicine*, Boston, MA, April 27-30, p. 26.

Frankenhaeuser, M. (1982). The sympatho-adrenal and pituitary-adrenal response to challenge: Comparison between the sexes. In T.M. Dembroski, T.H. Schmidt, & G. Blumchen (Eds.). *Biobehavioral bases of coronary heart disease* (pp. 91-105). Basel: Karger.

Freeman, L.J., & Nixon, P.G.F. (1988). The effect of the Type A behavior pattern on myocardial ischemia during daily life. *International Journal of Cardiology, 17*, 145-154.

Friedman, M., Byers, S.O., Diamant, J., & Rosenman, R.H. (1975). Plasma catecholamine response of coronary-prone subjects (Type A) to a specific challenge. *Metabolism, 24*, 205-210.

Friedman, M., & Powell, L.H. (1984). The diagnosis and quantitative assessment of Type A behavior: Introduction and description of the Videotaped Structured Interview. *Integrative Psychiatry, 2*, 123-136.

Friedman, M., & Rosenman, R.H. (1959). Association of specific overt behavior pattern with blood and cardiovascular findings. *Journal of the American Medical Association, 169*, 1286-1296.

Friedman, M., Rosenman, R., Straus, R., Wurm, M., & Kositchek, R. (1968). The relationship of behavior pattern A to the state of coronary vasculature. *American Journal of Medicine, 44*, 525-537.

Friedman, M., St. George, S., Byers, S.O., & Rosenman, R.H. (1960). Excretion of catecholamines, 17-ketosteroids, 17-hydroxycorticoids, and 5-hydroxyindole in men exhibiting a particular behavior pattern (A) associated with high incidence of clinical coronary artery disease. *Journal of Clinical Investigation, 39*, 758-764.

Friedman, M., Thoresen, C.E., Gill, J.J., Ulmer, D., Powell, L.H., Price, V.A., Brown, B., Thompson, L., Rabin, D.D., Breall, W.S., Bourg, E., Levy, R., & Dixon, T. (1986). Alteration of Type A behavior and its effect on cardiac recurrences in post-myocardial infarction patients: Summary results of the Recurrent Coronary Prevention Project. *American Heart Journal, 11*, 653-665.

Glass, D.C. (1977). *Behavior Patterns, Stress and Coronary Disease*, Hillsdale. New Jersey: Erlbaum.

Graham, L.E., Scherwitz, L., & Brand, R. (unpublished paper). Self-reference and coronary heart disease incidence in the Western Collaborative Group Study.

Graham, S. (1988). Enhancing creativity in epidemiology. *American Journal of Epidemiology, 128*, 249-253.

Harshfield, G.A., James, G.D., Schussel, Y., Yee, L.S., Blank, S.G., & Pickering, T.G. (1988). Do laboratory tests of blood pressure reactivity predict blood pressure changes during everyday life? *American Journal of Hypertension, 1*, 168-174.

Haynes, S.G., Feinleib, M., & Kannel, W. (1980). The relationship of psychosocial factors to coronary heart disease in the Framingham study: III, 8-year incidence of CHD. *American Journal of Epidemiology, 111*, 37-58.

Haynes, S.G., & Matthews, K.A. (1988). Review and methodologic critique of recent studies on Type A behavior and cardiovascular disease. *Annals of Behavior Medicine, 10*, 47-59.

Hearn, M.D., Murray, D.M., & Luepke, R.V. (1988). Hostility, coronary heart disease, and total mortality: A 33-year follow-up study of university students. *Proceedings of Society of Behavioral Medicine*, Boston, MA, April 27-30, p. 129.

Hecker, M.H.L., Chesney, M.A., Black, G.W., & Frautschi, N. (1988). Coronary-prone behaviors in the Western Collaborative Group Study. *Psychosomatic Medicine, 50*, 153-164.

Helman, C.G. (1987). Heart disease and the cultural construction of time: Type A behavior pattern as a Western culture-bound syndrome. *Social Science and Medicine, 25*, 969-979.

Helmer, D.C., Ragland, D.R., & Syme, L. (1988). Hostility and prevalence of angiographically-documented coronary artery disease. *CVD Newsletter, 43*, 9.

Helmstrom, H.R. (1982). The injury-spasm ischemia-induced hemostatic vasoconstrictive and vascular autoregulatory hypothesis of ischemic disease. *American Journal of Cardiology, 49*, 802-810.

Houston, B.K. (1988) Cardiovascular and neuroendocrine reactivity, global Type A, and components of Type A behavior. In B.K. Houston, & C.R. Snyder, (Eds.) *Type A behavior pattern*, pp. 22-252. New York: Wiley.

Janisse, M.P., & Dyck, D.G. (1988). The Type A behavior pattern and coronary heart disease: Physiological and psychological dimensions. In M.P. Janisse, (Ed.) *Individual Differences, Stress, and Health Psychology*, pp. 57-71. New York: Springer-Verlag.

Jenkins, C.D., Rosenman, R.H., & Friedman, M. (1966). Components of the coronary-prone behavior pattern: their relation to silent myocardial infarction and blood lipids. *Journal of Chronic Diseases, 19*, 599-606.

Jenkins, C.D., Rosenman, R.H., & Friedman, M. (1968). Replicability of rating the coronary-prone behavior pattern. *British Journal of Preventative Social Medicine, 10*, 47-59.

Jenkins, C.D., Zyzanski, S.J., & Rosenman, R.H. (1979) *The Jenkins Activity Survey*. New York: Psychological Corp.

Julius, S. (1988). The blood pressure-seeking properties of the central nervous system. *Hypertension, 6*, 177-185.

Julius, S., Weder, A.B., & Hinderliter, A.L. (1986). Does behaviorally induced blood pressure variability lead to hypertension? In K.A. Matthews, S.M. Weiss, T. Detre, T.M. Dembroski, B. Falkner, S.B. Manuck & R.B. Williams, Jr. (Eds.) *Handbook of stress, reactivity, and cardiovascular cisease* (pp. 71-84). New York: Wiley.

Kahn, J.P., Gully, R.J., Cooper, T.B., Perumal, A.S., Thomas, T.M., & Klein, D.F. (1987). Correlation of Type A behavior with adrenergic density: Implications for coronary artery disease pathogenesis. *Lancet, 2*, 937-939.

Krantz, D.S., Contrada, R.J., La Riccia, P.J., Anderson, J.R., Durel, L.A., Dembroski, T.M., & Weiss, T. (1987). Effects of beta-adrenergic stimulation and blockade on cardiovascular reactivity, affect, and Type A behavior. *Psychosomatic Medicine, 49*, 146.

Krantz, D.S., Contrada, R.J., Robin-Hill, D., & Friedler, E. (1988). Environmental stress and biobehavioral antecedents of coronary heart disease. *Journal of Consulting and Clinical Psychology, 56*, 333-341.

Krantz, D.S., & Manuck, S.B. (1984). Acute psychophysiologic reactivity and risk of cardiovascular disease: A review and methodology critique. *Psychological Bulletin, 96*, 435-464.

Krantz, D.S., Schaeffer, M.A., Davia, J.E., Dembroski, T.M., MacDougall, J.M., & Shaffer, R.T. (1981). Extent of coronary atherosclerosis, Type A behavior, and cardiovascular response to social interaction. *Psychology, 18*, 654-664.

Lantinga, L.J., Sprafkin, R.P., McCroskery, J.H., Baker, M.T., Warner, R.A., & Hill,.N.E. (1988). One-year psychosocial follow-up of patients with chest pain and angiographically normal coronary arteries. *American Journal of Cardiology, 62*, 209-213.

Leon, G.R., Murray, D., Finn, S.E., & Bailey, J.M. (1988). Inability to predict cardiovascular disease form hostility scores on MMPI items related to Type A behavior. *Journal of Consulting and Clinical Psychology, 56*, 597-600.

Levenkron, J.C., & Moore, G. (1988). The Type A behavior pattern: Issues for intervention research. *Annals of Behavioral Medicine, 10*, 78-83.

Light, K.C. (1981). Cardiovascular responses to effortful active coping: Implications for the role of stress in hypertension development. *Psychophysiology, 18*, 216-225.

MacDougall, J.M., Dembroski, T.M., Dimsdale, J.E., & Hackett, T.P. (1985). Components of Type A hostility, and anger-in: Further relationship to angiographic findings. *Health Psychology, 4*, 137-152.

Manuck, S.B., & Krantz, D.S. (1986). Psychophysiologic reactivity in coronary heart disease and essential hypertension. In K.A. Matthews, S.M. Weiss, T. Detre, T.M. Dembroski, B. Falkner, S.B. Manuck & R.B. Williams, Jr. (Eds.) *Handbook of stress, reactivity, and cardiovascular disease* (pp. 11-34). New York: Wiley.

Mantysaari, M.J., Antila, K.J., & Peltonen, T.E. (1988). Blood pressure reactivity in patients with neurocirculatory asthenia. *American Journal of Hypertension, 1*, 132-139.

Matthews, K.A. (1982). Psychological perspectives on the Type A behavior pattern. *Psychological Bulletin, 91*, 293-323.

Matthews, K.A., Glass, D.C., Rosenman, R.H., & Bortner, R.W. (1977). Competitive drive, pattern A, and coronary heart disease: A further analysis of some data from the Western Collaborative Group Study. *Journal of Chronic Diseases, 30*, 489-498.

Matthews, K.A., Krantz, D.S., Dembroski, T.M., & MacDougall, J.M. (1982). Unique and common variance in Structured Interview and Jenkins Activity Survey assessment of the Type A behavior pattern. *Journal of Personality and Social Psychology, 42*, 303-313.

Matthews, K.A., & Haynes, S.G. (1986). Type A behavior and coronary disease risk. *American Journal of Epidemiology, 123*, 923-960.

Matthews, K.A., & Siegel, J.M. (1982). The Type A behavior pattern in children and adolescents: Assessment, development, and associated coronary-risk. In A. Baum, & J. Singer (Eds.). *Handbook of Psychology and Health, Vol 2*, Hillsdale, New Jersey: Erlbaum.

Matthews, K.A., & Woodall, K.L. (1988). Childhood origins of overt Type A behaviors and cardiovascular reactivity to behavioral stressors. *Annals of Behavioral Medicine, 10*, 71-77.

McCranie, E.W., Watkins, L.O., Brandsma, J.M., & Sisson, B.D. (1986). Hostility, coronary heart disease (CHD) incidence, and total mortality: Lack of association in a 25-year follow-up study of 478 physicians. *Journal of Behavioral Medicine, 9*, 119-125.

Megargee, E.I. (1985). The dynamics of aggression and their application to cardiovascular disorders. In M.A. Chesney, R.H. Rosenman (Eds.) *Anger and hostility in Cardiovascular and behavioral disorders* (pp. 31-38). New York: Hemisphere.

Oldridge, N.B., Donner, A.P., Buck, C.W., Jones, N.L., Andrew, G.M., Parker, J.O., Cunningham, D.A., Kavanagh, T., Rechnitzer, P.A., & Sutton, J.R. (1982). Predictors of dropout from cardiac exercise rehabilitation-Ontario Exercise-Heart Collaborative Study. (1982). *American Journal of Cardiology, 51*, 70-74.

Pearson, T., Gordis, L., Achuff, S., Bulkley, B., & Kwiterovich, P. (1982). Selection bias in persons undergoing angiography. *American Journal of Epidemiology, 116*, 568.

Pickering, T.G. (1985). Should studies of patients undergoing coronary angiography be used to evaluate the role of behavioral risk factors for coronary heart disease? *Journal of Behavioral Medicine, 8*, 203-213.

Pickering, T.G., & Devereaux, R.B. (1987). Ambulatory monitoring of blood pressure as a predictor of cardiovascular risk. *American Heart Journal, 114*, 925-928.

Price, V.A. (1988). Research and clinical issues in treating Type A behavior. In B.K. Houston & C.R. Snyder (Eds.), *Type A behavior patterns: Research, theory and intervention.* (pp. 275-311), New York: Wiley-Interscience.

Ragland, D.R., & Brand, R.J. (1988). Type A behavior and mortality from coronary heart disease. *New England Journal of Medicine, 318*, 65-69.

Rahe, R.H.,, Hervig, L., & Rosenman, R.H. (1978). Heritability of Type A behavior. *Psychosomatic Medicine, 40*, 478-486.

Reis, D.J., & LeDoux, J.E. (1987). Some central neural mechanisms governing resting and behaviorally coupled control of blood pressure. *Circulation, (Suppl.), 76,* S1-S9.

Rosenman, R.H. (1978a). The interview method of assessment of the coronary-prone behavior pattern. In T.M. Dembroski, S.M. Weiss, J.I. Shields, S.G. Haynes, & M. Feinleib (Eds.) *Coronary-prone behavior* (pp. 55-67). New York: Springer-Verlag.

Rosenman, R.H. (1978b). The role of the Type A behavior pattern in ischemic heart disease: modification of its effects by beta-blocking agents. *British Journal of Clinical Practice, (Suppl. 1), 32,* 58-66.

Rosenman, R.H. (1983). Coronary-prone and coronary heart disease: Implications for the use of beta-blockers for primary prevention. In R.H. Rosenman (Ed.) *Psychosomatic riskfactors and coronary heart disease; indications for specific preventive therapy* (pp. 9-14). Bern: Huber.

Rosenman, R.H. (1985). Health consequences of anger and implications for treatment. In M.A. Chesney & R.H. Rosenman (Eds.), *Anger and behavior in cardiovascular and behavioral disorders* (pp. 103-126). New York: Hemisphere.

Rosenman, R.H. (1986). Current and past history of Type A behavior pattern. In T.H. Schmidt, T.M. Dembroski, & G. Blumchen (Eds.), *Biological and psychological factors in cardiovascular disease* (pp. 15-40). Heidelberg: Springer-Verlag.

Rosenman, R.H. (1987). Type A behavior and hypertension. In S. Julius & D.R. Bassett (Eds.), *Handbook of hypertension: Behavioral factors in hypertension (Vol 9)* (pp. 141-148). Amsterdam: Elsevier.

Rosenman, R.H., Brand, R.J., Sholtz, R.I. & Friedman, M. (1976). Multivariate prediction of coronary heart disease during 8.5 year follow-up in the Western Collaborative Group Study. *American Journal of Cardiology, 37,* 903-910.

Rosenman, R.H. & Friedman, M. (1961). Association of specific behavior pattern in women with blood and cardiovascular findings. *Circulation, 24,* 1173-1184.

Rosenman, R.H., Friedman, M., Straus, R., Wurm, M., Kositchek, R., Hahn, W., & Werthessen, N.T. (1964). A predictive study of coronary heart disease: The Western Collaborative Group Study. *Journal of the American Medical Association, 189,* 15-22.

Rosenman, R.H. & Friedman, M. (1974). Neurogenic factors in pathogenesis of coronary heart disease. *Medical Clinics of North America, 58,* 269-279.

Rosenman, R.H. & Friedman, M. (1977). Modifying Type A behavior pattern, *Journal of Psychosomatic Research, 21,* 323-331.

Rosenman, R.H., Rahe, R.H., Borhani, N.O., & Feinleib, M. (1976). Heritability of personality and behavior. *Acta Genetica Medicae et Gemellologiae, 25,* 221-224.

Rosenman, R.H., Swan, G.E., & Carmelli, D. (1988). Definition, assessment, and evolution of the Type A behavior pattern. In B.K. Houston & C.R. Snyder (Eds.). *Type A behavior pattern: Research, theory and intervention* (pp. 8-31). New York: Wiley-Interscience.

Rosenman, R.H., Swan, G.E., & Carmelli, D. (1988a). Some recent findings relative to the relationship of Type A behavior pattern to coronary heart disease. In S. Maes, C.D. Spielberger, P.D. Defares, & I.F. Sarason (Eds.). *Topics in health psychology* (pp. 21-29). Chichester: Wiley.

Rosenman, R.H., & Ward, M.M. (1988). The changing concept of cardiovascular reactivity. *Stress Medicine*, 4, *241-251*.

Roskies, E. (1987) *Stress management for the healthy Type A: Theory and practice*. New York: Guilford Press.

Rozanski, A., Bairey, C.N., Krantz, D.S., Friedman, J., Resser, K.J., Morrel, M., Milton-Chafen, S., Hestrin, L., Bientendorf, J., & Berman, D.S. (1988). Mental stress and the induction of silent myocardial ischemia in patients with coronary artery disease. *New England Journal of Medicine*, *318*, 1005-1012.

Russek, L.G., Russek, B.A., Russek, M.D., & King, S.H. (1988). The mastery of Stress Study: Psychophysiological arousal in the prediction of future health or disease. *Psychosomatic Medicine*, *50*, 9-13.

Sallis, J.F., Johnson, C.C., Trevorrow, T.R., Kaplan, R.M., & Hovell, M.F. (1987). The relationship between cynical hostility and blood pressure reactivity. *Journal of Psychosomatic Research*, *31*, 111-116.

Scherwitz, L., & Brand, R. (1989). Interviewer behaviors in the WCGS and MRFIT Structured Interviews.

Scherwitz, L., & Canick, J. (1988). Self-reference and coronary heart disease risk. In K. Houston & C.R. Snyder (Eds.), *Type A behavior pattern: Research, theory, and intervention*, (pp. 145-167). New York: Wiley.

Scherwitz, L., Graham, L.E., Grandits, G., Buehler, J.F., & Billings, J. (1986). Self-involvement and coronary heart disease incidence in the Multiple Risk Factor Intervention Trial. *Psychosomatic Medicine*, *48*, 187-199.

Shekelle, R.B., Billings, J.H., Neaton, J.D., Billings, J.H., Borhani, N.O., Gerace, T.A., Jacobs, D.R., Lasser, N.L., Mittlemark, M.B., & Stamler, J. (1985). The MRFIT behavior pattern study, II. Type A behavior and incidence of coronary heart disease. *American Journal of Epidemiology*, *122*, 559-570.

Shekelle, R.B., Gale, M., & Norusis, M. (1985). Type A score (Jenkins Activity Survey) and risk of recurrent coronary heart disease in the Aspirin Myocardial Infarction Study. *American Journal of Cardiology*, *56*, 221-225.

Shekelle, R.B., Gale, M., Ostfeld, A.M., & Ogelsby, P. (1983). Hostility, risk of coronary heart disease, and mortality. *Psychosomatic Medicine*, *45*, 109-114.

Schiffer, F., Hartley, L.H., Schuman, C.L., & Abelmann, W.H. (1976). The quiz electrocardiogram, A new diagnostic and research technique for evaluating the relation between emotional stress and ischemic heart disease. *American Journal of Cardiology*, *37*, 41-47.

Schmieder, F., Friedrich, G., Neus, H., Ruddel, H., & von Eiff, S. (1985). The influence of beta-blockers on cardiovascular reactivity and Type A behavior pattern in hypertensives. *Psychosomatic Medicine*, *45*, 417-432.

Schneider, R.H., Julius, S., Moss, G.E., Dielman, T.E., Zweifler, A.J., & Karunas, R. (1987). New markers for Type A behavior: Pupil size and platelet epinephrine. *Psychosomatic Medicine*, *49*, 579-590.

Shipman, W.G., (1965). The validity of MMPI hostility scales. *Journal of Clinical Psychology*, *21*, 186-190.

Sibilia, L., Francioni, G., Borgo, S., & Arca, M. (unpublished paper). Assessment of dysfunctional beliefs associated with Type A behavior pattern

Siegman, A.W., Dembroski, T.M., & Ringel, N. (1987). Components of hostility and severity of coronary artery disease. *Psychosomatic Medicine*, *49*, 127-135.

Smith, T.W., Allred, K.D., & Frohm, K.D. (1988). Components of the Cook and Medley HO Scale. Proceedings of Society of Behavioral Medicine, Boston, MA, April, 27-30, p. 155.

Smith, T.W., & Frohm, K.D. (1985). What's so unhealthy about hostility? Construct validity and psychosocial correlates of the Cook and Medley HO Scale. *Health Psychology, 4*, 503-520.

Sokolow, M., Werdegar, D., Kain, H.K., & Hinman, A.T. (1966). Relationship between level of blood pressure measured casually and by portable recorders and severity of complications in essential hypertension. *Circulation, 34*, 297-298.

Spielberger, C.D., Krasner, S.S., & Solomon, E.P. (1988). The experience, expression, and control of anger. In M.P. Janisse (Ed.), *Individual differences, stress, and health psychology* (pp. 89-108). New York: Springer-Verlag.

Starkman, M.N., Cameron, O.G., Nesse, R., & Zelnik, T. (1988). Catecholamine levels and symptoms of anxiety. *Psychosomatic Medicine, 50*, 192.

Suarez, E.C., Williams, R.B., & McRae, A.R. (1988). High scores on the Cook and Medley Hostility Scale predict increased Cardiovascular responses to harassment. *Psychosomatic Medicine, 50*, 192.

Suls, J., & Choi, K.W. (1988). Coronary-prone behavior and its relationship to neuroticism, depression, and anxiety: a meta-analysis. Proceedings of Society of Behavioral Medicine, Boston, MA, April 27-30, pp. 167-168.

Swan, G.E., Carmelli, D., & Rosenman, R.H. (1989). The Cook and Medley Ho Scale: Identification of biobehavioral correlates. *Psychosomatics*.

Vickers, R., Hervig, L.K., Rahe, R.H., & Rosenman, R.H. (1981). Type A behavior pattern and coping and defense. *Psychosomatic Medicine, 43*, 381-396.

Ward, M.M., Chesney, M.A., Swan, G.E., Black, G.W., Parker, S.F., & Rosenman, R.H. (1986). Cardiovascular responses in Type A and B men to a series of stressors. *Journal of Behavioral Medicine, 9*, 43-49.

Watkins, F.L., Fisher, E.B., Southard, D.R., & Ward, C.H. (1988). Comparison of hostility and Type A behavior as cardiovascular disease risk factors within a worksite screening program. *Proceedings of Society of Behavioral Medicine*, Boston, MA, April 27-30, p. 148.

Werko, L. (1976). Risk factors and coronary heart disease—facts of fancy? *American Heart Journal, 91*, 87-98.

Williams, R.B., Barefoot, J.C., Haney, T.L., Harrell, F.E., Blumenthal, J.A., & Pryor, D.B., (1988). Type A behavior and angiographically documented coronary atherosclerosis in a sample of 2,289 patients. *Psychosomatic Medicine, 50*, 139-152.

Williams, R.B., Barefoot, J.C., & Shekelle, R.B., (1985). The health consequences of hostility. In M.A. Chesney & R.H. Rosenman (Eds.), *Anger and behavior in cardiovascular and behavioral disorders* (pp. 173-186). New York: Hemisphere.

Williams, R.B., Haney, T.L., & Lee, K.L. (1980). Type A behavior, hostility, and coronary atherosclerosis. *Psychosomatic Medicine, 42*, 539-549.

Yakubovich, I.S., Ragland, D.R., Brand, R.J., & Syme, S.L. (1988). Type A behavior pattern and health status after 22 years of follow-up in the Western Collaborative Group Study. *American Journal of Epidemiology, 128*, 579-588.

Type A Behaviour and Coronary Heart Disease: The Third Stage

H. J. Eysenck
Institute of Psychiatry, University of London
De Crespigney Park, Denmark Hill, London SE5 8AF England

Research on Type A behaviour has shown that assessment and psychometric properties are questionable in terms of reliability, validity, and concordance. The effectiveness of Type A intervention projects is not proven, and contradictory results have been reported as far as prediction is concerned. The studies here reported revert to earlier theories linking personality and coronary heart disease in terms of anger, hostility and aggressiveness, and demonstrate that coronary heart disease can be predicted with considerable accuracy, in terms of personality theory, incorporating these traits into a wider stress-related model of personality. It is also shown that a special type of behaviour therapy designed to alter the coronary heart disease-prone types of behaviour can prevent deaths from this particular disease with considerable success. It is suggested that the theory here presented has taken from Type A theory those elements most directly related to CHD, while eliminating those elements which have not proved relevant.

Introduction

Clinical observation of coronary heart disease patients has linked this disease for a long time with certain personality traits of impatience, hyperalertness,aggressiveness and proneness to anger (Osler, 1910; Kemple, 1945; Menninger & Menninger, 1936). These observations were put together into the concept of Type A behaviour by two cardiologists (Friedman & Rosenman, 1959), who reported that the majority of CHD patients showed a set of behaviour patterns and emotions similar to that shown in previous clinical observations (Price, 1982). In addition to the Type A personality pattern, stress and tension have been advanced as psychosocial causes of coronary heart disease (McGuigan, Sime & Wallace, 1984; Kaplan, 1983). Much research in the past thirty years has attempted to build on these foundations.

The Western Collaborative Group Study (Rosenman, Brand, Jenkins

© 1990 Select Press

et al., 1975) was the first major prospective study designed to examine the coronary risk of Type A probands. In this study, 3154 employed men free of CHD were followed for eight and a half years. The final follow-up report showed that by the end of the study probands assessed by the Structured Interview at entry as Type A had a risk ratio of 2 to 1 for development of coronary heart disease compared with Type Bs. In the Framingham Heart Study, 1674 male and female subjects were followed up. It showed that Type A behaviour was an independent predictor of CHD for both men and women of 45 to 64 years of age in some subgroups. (Haynes, Feinleib & Kannel, 1980). A third large scale study, the Belgian-French Pooling Project (1984) used the Bortner (1969) rating scale to assess Type A behaviour, and found double the incidence of CHD in probands in the highest quarter of the scale as compared with probands in the lowest quarter. The French and Belgian populations had to be combined in this study to reach statistical significance.

Not all studies, however, have been positive in their findings of predictive accuracy for the Type A concept. The largest study so far done was the Multiple Risk Factor Intervention Trial. It used a population of 12,700 men who were CHD-free at entry, and who were followed for an average of 7 years and showed that Type A behaviour was unrelated to the 7-year incidence of CHD, a failure observed both for the Structured Interview and the Jenkins' Questionnaire (Shekelle, Hulley, Neaton, et al., 1985). (Those findings were based on a highly selected "high risk" population that did not in fact turn out to be at high risk.) Similar negative results were found in the Aspirin Myocardial Infarction Study, where it was found that in survivors of a first myocardial infarction, Type A men were at no greater risk of a second myocardial infarction, or coronary death, than their Type B counterparts (Ruberman et al., 1984), although we may doubt the value of the particular questionnaire used. Both positive and negative results are neatly balanced to show that as a predictor Type A behaviour is of doubtful value, and may be quite useless. Weighting the results by numbers of participants, it is doubtful if the total can be regarded as significant in a socially meaningful rather than a statistical sense.

Some of the problems with Type A behaviour as a concept are probably due to the psychometric properties of the scales which have been used (Booth-Kewley and Friedman, 1987). As Eysenck & Fulker (1983) have shown, inter alia, the concept is not unidimensional but breaks down into a number of factors, and indeed it appears largely to consist of a combination of neuroticism and extraversion. It is of interest that epidemiological and experimental studies (e.g. Slaby, Horvath and Frantik, 1981; Floderus, 1974) have shown that important differences in performance and illness, relevant to cardiovascular disorders, can be found when Type

A subjects are subdivided into those high and low, respectively, on N; differences in N may be more important than Type A-Type B differences in relation to CHD (Lichtenstein et al., in press). Floderus (1974) in fact suggests, and provides some evidence for the suggestion that angina pectoris, hypertension and tachycardia may be related to high N and I, while mycardial infarction and hyperlipidemia may be related to high N and E. The relation between E and myocardial infarction has also been demonstrated by Bendien and Groen (1963). Many other studies (e.g. Baer, Collins, Bourianoff & Ketchel, 1979; Frankenhaeuser, Lundberg & Forsman, 1980; Innes, 1980; Jenkins, Zyzanski, Ryan, Flessas & Tannenbaum, 1977; and Nowack & Sassenrath, 1980) clearly indicate the relevance of N and E to the assessment of coronary-prone behaviour.

Another problem with the concept of Type A behaviour is that it seems to be related particularly to the working environment, whereas work on stress has suggested the importance of interpersonal relations, particularly within the family. Thus the concepts developed by Eysenck (1985, 1987) and Grossarth-Maticek (Grossarth-Maticek, Bastiaans & Kanazir, 1985; Grossarth-Maticek, Kanazir, Vetter & Jankovic, 1983; Grossarth-Maticek, Schmidt, Vetter & Arndt, 1984; Grossarth-Maticek, Eysenck, & Vetter, 1988) have attempted to combine those elements in the description of personality which have been found most predictive of coronary heart disease. The concept of stress involves in the main interpersonal relations, such as the loss of a loved one, either by death or by abandonment. We have attempted to demonstrate the predictive accuracy of the resulting personality descriptions in three large scale prospective studies. We have also attempted to demonstrate the prophylactic possibilities of altering the coronary heart disease-prone personality in the direction of a more healthy personality in preventing coronary heart disease.

In this prophylactic study we have tried to improve on the weak effects of modifying behaviour in healthy Type As (Roskies, 1987; Wright, 1988), and with patients in the Recurrent Coronary Prevention Project (Friedman, Thoresen, Gill et al., 1984). We believe that intervention trials of this kind are the best evidence for the causal importance of psychosocial factors, such as personality and stress. We believe that our theories constitute a third stage in the investigations of the relation between disease and personality. The first or anecdotal stage was one of careful, systematic observation, going back over hundreds or even thousands of years. The second stage was that of the Type A - Type B distinction, incorporated in questionnaire and interview form. The third stage has attempted to combine the most valuable elements of stages 1 and 2 into an improved instrument.

In selecting the most relevant, i.e. predictive, traits from the variegated groups assembled under the "Type A" label, we anticipated the results of the meta-analysis carried out by Booth-Kewley and Friedman (1987) and selected hopelessness-helplessness (depression) and anger/hostility/aggression. We also anticipated their conclusion that "the picture of coronary-proneness revealed...is not one of a hurried, impatient workaholic but instead is one of a person with one or more negative emotions." (p. 343). Booth-Kewley and Friedman (1987) go on to say that the concept of the coronary-prone personality be broadened to encompass psychological attributes additional to those associated with Type A behavior, and narrowed to eliminate those components shown to be unimportant. This is what we have tried to do, and the result may be said to be a Type A, Mark Two.

Three Prospective Studies: Personality Typology

The three studies here reported are all prospective, in the sense that personality, health, smoking habits, drinking habits, etc. were ascertained at the beginning of the study, and death and cause of death were ascertained after a ten year period. Our special interest was in the possibility of identifying a cancer-prone and a coronary heart disease-prone type of personality. Our assumption was that these two types of personality would be quite different, and, in turn, quite different from healthy types of personality.

Personality was ascertained in two ways. Both are self-report based, and hence limited by the respondent's insight and openness, factors which themselves may be systematically related to the risk process. In the first place a 109 item questionnaire was administered, which contained a number of scales. There were a number of questions which related to adverse life events or situations leading to long lasting hopelessness/helplessness, a personality trait assumed to be predictive of cancer. Another group of questions related to adverse life events or situations leading to anger and/or hostility, a personality trait believed to be prognostic of coronary heart disease (Dembroski & Costa, 1987; Matthews & Haynes, 1986). Other traits investigated were rationality and anti-emotionality; harmonious interpersonal relationship; lack of positive emotional relationship; acquiescence; and finally, absence of self-reported pathological symptoms, especially anxiety.

The risk ratios associated with increasing degrees of years of the duration of an emotional state are shown in Figure 1. The population in question consisted of a sample of 1,353 subjects, recruited in Yugoslavia, by selecting the oldest person in every second household in a small town with a population of 14,000 inhabitants. (In addition, a number of highly

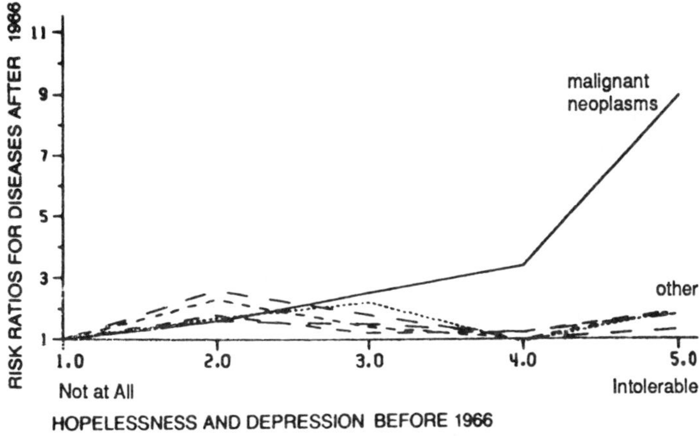

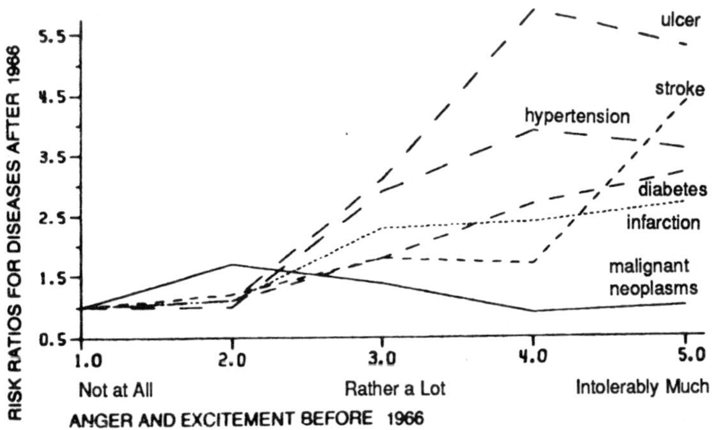

FIGURE 1 Risk Factors for Different Diseases Associated With Two Personality Variables. (Grossarth-Maticek, Frentzel-Beyme, Becker & Schum, 1984)

stressed probands were included who were the oldest in a given household.) Most of the subjects were between 59 to 65 years old. This design was adopted because coronary heart disease and cancer tend to occur most frequently in elderly people, so that a high rate of deaths from cancer and coronary heart disease might be expected in this group (Eysenck, 1988; Grossarth-Maticek, Frentzel-Beyme, Becker & Schum, 1984).

It will be seen that the risk of malignant neoplasms increases drastically as ratings of 4.0 and 5.0 for hopelessness and depression are considered, as compared with lower ratings of 1.0 to 3.0. Conversely, anger and excitement ratings of 3.0, 4.0 and 5.0 give low risk ratios for malignant neoplasms, but high ones for stroke, hypertension and infarction. Summing risk ratios for levels 4 and 5, and comparing them with mean ratios for levels 1, 2 and 3, malignant neoplasms give significantly higher risk ratios for hopelessness and depression, but not for anger and excitement. Stroke, hypertension and infarction give the opposite pattern ($p < .01$ in each case.) These data are in good agreement with the original observation of Osler and others linking anger and excitement with coronary heart disease. (Matthews & Haynes, 1986; Lichtenstein et al., in press.)

An alternative method of assessing a personality type along more holistic lines, is described by Grossarth-Maticek, Eysenck & Vetter (1988). What is given there is a typology containing four types, two of which are respectively predictive of cancer (Type 1) and coronary heart disease (Type 2), whereas Types 3 and 4 are predictive of longevity and health. This system of typology does not claim universal validity, but is specifically geared to the prediction of cancer and cardiovascular disease in people who experience certain types of stress and react in certain ways to this stress. As a consequence, it is specifically the *occurrence* of this stress, and the particular reaction of the different types to the stress, which are important. Detailed descriptions of these types are given in the paper by Grossarth-Maticek, Eysenck and Vetter (1988). The types were developed conceptually prior to the research described here.

Type 1: *Understimulation*

Persons of this type show a permanent tendency to regard an emotionally highly valued object as the most important condition for their own wellbeing and happiness. The stress produced by the continued withdrawal or absence of this object is experienced as an emotionally traumatic event. Type 1 individuals fail to distance themselves from the object and remain dependent upon it. Thus individuals of this type do not achieve success in reaching the object, and remain distant and isolated from this highly valued and emotionally important object. Great stress is produced by this failure to achieve nearness to the highly valued person, success in the highly valued occupation, or whatever. This type shows a lack of *autonomy.*

Type 2: *Overarousal*

Persons of this type show a continued tendency to regard an emotionally highly important object as the most important cause for their particular distress and unhappiness. Rejection by the object (if a person), or failure to reach it (as in the case of occupational success) is experienced as an emotional trauma, but persons of this type fail to achieve disengagement from the object; rather, they feel more and more dependent on the object. Thus persons of this type remain in constant contact with these negatively valued and emotionally disturbing people and situations, and fail to distance themselves and free themselves from dependence on the disturbing object. Where persons of Type 1 keep on seeking nearness to the object of their desires, and experience their failure in terms of hopelessness and helplessness, persons of Type 2 fail to disengage themselves from the object, and experience a reaction of anger, aggression and arousal.

Type 3: ***Ambivalence***

Persons of this type show a tendency to shift from the typical reaction of Type 1 to the typical reaction of Type 2, and back again. As Grossarth-Maticek (1986) put it: "This type shows a permanent tendency to regard an emotionally highly valued object alternately as the most important condition for his own wellbeing, and as the main cause for his own unhappiness". (p.27). Thus in individuals of this type, we have an alternation of feelings of hopelessness/helplessness and of anger/arousal.

Type 4: ***Personal Autonomy***

The typical reactions of Types 1, 2 and 3 indicate a dependence on the highly valued object and their reactions are characterized by constant contradiction between expected consequences and the actual consequences of their actions. For persons of Type 4 there is a strong tendency to regard their own autonomy, and the autonomy of the persons with whom they wish to be in contact, as the most important condition for their own wellbeing and happiness. This enables persons of Type 4 to experience realistically the approach or avoidance behaviour of the object of their desires, and thus enables them to accept the autonomy of the object. In other words, persons of Types 1 and 2 show a dependence on important objects which engage their emotions, but cannot remain autonomous when these emotional objects withdraw or remain unattainable; it is this that constitutes the stress which according to the theory leads to cancer or coronary heart disease. Persons of Type 4 are able to deal with this situation by virtue of their autonomy-preserving ability, and thus avoid the stress reaction.

In terms that will be more familiar to English-speaking psychologists, failure in relation to emotionally highly valued people and/or life goals is experienced by persons of Type 1 and 2 as *unavoidable*, whereas persons of Type 4 possess the ability to cope with the situation, and hence the stress is *avoidable*. Unavoidable stress is closely related to disease,

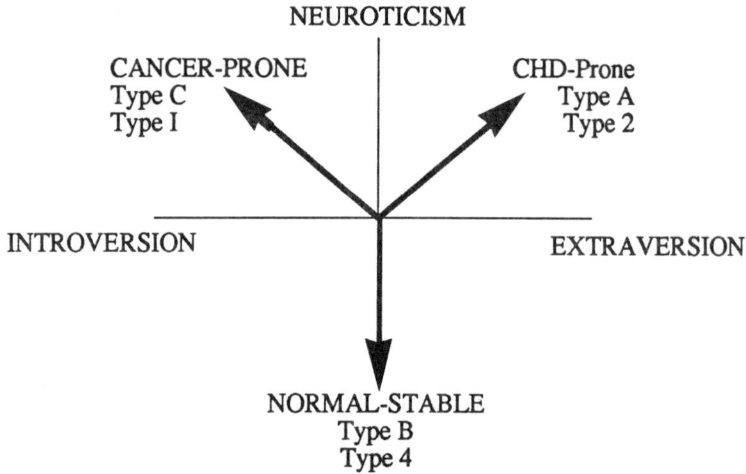

FIGURE 2 Hypothetical Relation Between Types 1, 2 and 3, A, B and C, and E and N.

whereas avoidable stress is not (Sklar & Anisman, 1979, 1981; Brown & Siegel, 1988; Breier et al., 1987). Thus, Type 4 should be less likely to suffer from cancer and heart disease than Types 1 or 2. Type 3 may also be protected to some extent by changing its reaction to the stressful situation from behaviour typical of Type 1 to behaviour typical of Type 2, and back. In this way persons of Type 3 avoid to some extent the build-up of behaviour patterns related to cancer or coronary heart disease respectively.

How are types 1, 2, 3 and 4 related to more widely known typologies? If we may regard the cancer-prone personality as a "Type C", to take its place with "Type A" (CHD-prone) and "Type B" (normal, not disease-prone), as suggested by Greer and Morris (1980), then we may suggest a picture rather like that shown diagramatically in Fig. 2. This also suggests the relation between these types and extraversion-introversion and neuroticism-stability. Type 3 is not shown; it is suggested that this type is associated with the personality variable of psychoticism (Eysenck & Eysenck, 1985), which is orthogonal to both E and N.

This identification of types 1 and 2 with neuroticism presents some problems, in that cancer in particular has usually been found in conjunction with *low* N scores (Kissen & Eysenck, 1962; Eysenck, 1985). The suggestion is that we are dealing here with *repressed* emotions, and that the psychometric patterns appropriate for this hypothesis would be that of the *repressor;* i.e. low N scores but high lie scores (Gudjonsson, 1981). Evidence confirming or refuting this hypothesis is urgently required.

Population Samples Used

The detailed questionnaire used in these studies is given by Grossarth-Maticek, Eysenck & Vetter, (1988). It will clarify any question that might arise with respect to these four types. Here we will not go into details regarding the types but rather look at the predictive values they may have for the populations tested. The first population has already been described. It consisted of the oldest inhabitants in a certain small Yugoslav town, as well as a number of stressed but younger individuals.

Another randomised sample was studied in Heidelberg in the years 1972-1982. (The Yugoslav study was carried out between 1965 and 1976). Here the investigators specified certain age and sex controls, but otherwise subjects were selected on a random basis. The sample was constituted of 1026 persons, 54% of whom were male, with 90% being between the ages of 40 and 60. The sample is thus considerably younger than the Yugoslav one, and would be expected to have many fewer deaths at follow up. The third sample was selected by members of the normal Heidelberg sample, who nominated friends and relatives who were "highly stressed"; the sample contained 1537 persons, 50% of whom were male, with ages ranging from 42 - 63 in 90% of the sample. From both the Heidelberg samples there were losses due to the discovery of chronic disease in some members. There were also losses at follow up due to leaving the town, leaving 872 for the normal sample and 1273 for the highly stressed sample.

In addition, 231 cases in the highly stressed sample were used for an intervention study using behaviour therapy, some acting as controls, others being included in the experimental group, and these must be subtracted from the sample, leaving a total of 1042 persons. We thus have three samples differing in sex composition, age and amount of stress experienced. We would expect on theoretical grounds that a higher proportion of those in the Yugoslav and the highly stressed Heidelberg samples would die of cancer and coronary heart disease, the former because of the higher age, the latter because of the stress experienced, as compared with the normal Heidelberg sample. Our interest was specifically in the relationship between typology in each of these three groups, and the death rate from cancer and coronary heart disease, the expectation being that persons of Type 1 would die more frequently of cancer, persons of Type 2 more frequently from coronary heart disease, with persons of Type 3 and 4 relatively protected against both.

Concerning age and sex, the composition of the three groups relating to Types 1, 2, 3 and 4, is closely similar, with the exception of the Heidelberg normal sample where the percentage of females is higher for Type 1, and lower for Type 4.

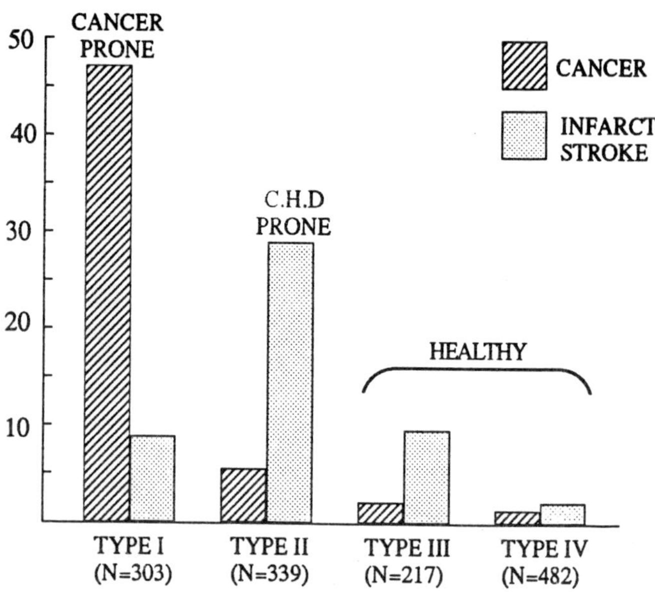

FIGURE 3 Percentage Deaths From Cancer and CHD In Probands of Different Personality Types: Yugoslav Study. (Eysenck, 1987)

Type 4. *Three prospective studies: Results*

Results are based on follow-up interviews, telephone discussions with probands, and finally search for death certificates. All three methods had to agree before the final result was accepted. Tables showing the detailed comparisons are given in the paper by Grossarth-Maticek, Eysenck & Vetter (1988). In this paper, we will give the results in three figures. In each, we show the number of cancer-prone, coronary heart disease-prone, and "healthy" types, as well as the percentage of each type who died of cancer or coronary heart disease. Figure 3 shows the results of the Yugoslav study. It will be obvious that persons of Types 1 and 2 show a much higher death rate than persons of Types 3 and 4, and it will be equally obvious that of Type 1 the great majority died of cancer, rather than of coronary heart disease, whereas of Type 2 the great majority died of coronary heart disease, rather than of cancer. All these results are very highly significant, even when differences in age, sex, smoking, etc. are controlled. Our personality typology appears to have a very much higher predictive accuracy than any of the studies using the Type A-Type B typology.

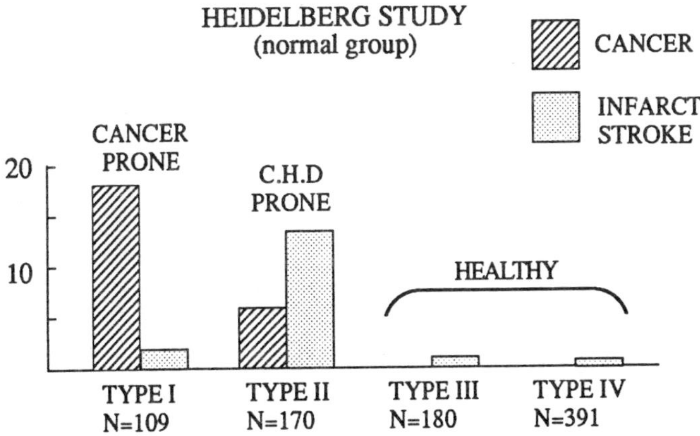

FIGURE 4 Percentage Deaths From Cancer and CHD in Probands of Different Personality Types: Heidelberg Study. (Eysenck, 1987)

Figure 4 shows the results for the Heidelberg normal group, and it is obvious that the number of probands dying in this group is very much smaller, as would have been expected from the lower age. Again, however, persons of Types 1 and 2 show a much higher death rate than persons of Types 3 and 4, and again persons of Type 1 die almost exclusively of cancer, those of Type 2 largely of coronary heart disease, as predicted.

Finally, Figure 5 shows the results for the Heidelberg stress group. It is notable that this group, comparable with the Heidelberg normal group in such features as age, sex composition, smoking, etc. shows a roughly 40% higher death rate, which is most probably due to the difference in stress between the two groups. It must of course be remembered that the "normal" group is a random group of people containing inevitably a proportion of persons who were in fact stressed; the two "stressed" types, Type 1 and Type 2) actually make up a third of the normal group. In the "stressed" Heidelberg group, Types 1 and 2 make up 77% of the total. (It will be remembered that the members of the stress sample were nominated by the members of the normal sample. Although our interviewers considered a proportion of the "stressed" sample not to be really correctly subsumed under that category, we did not exclude any of the people nominated; hence 23% of the so-called "stressed" group might be considered "non-stressed"). We may thus say that the 40% increase in death rate due to stress is an underestimate, and that if the normal group had been selected for absence of stress, and the stress group for presence of stress, the difference would have been considerably greater.

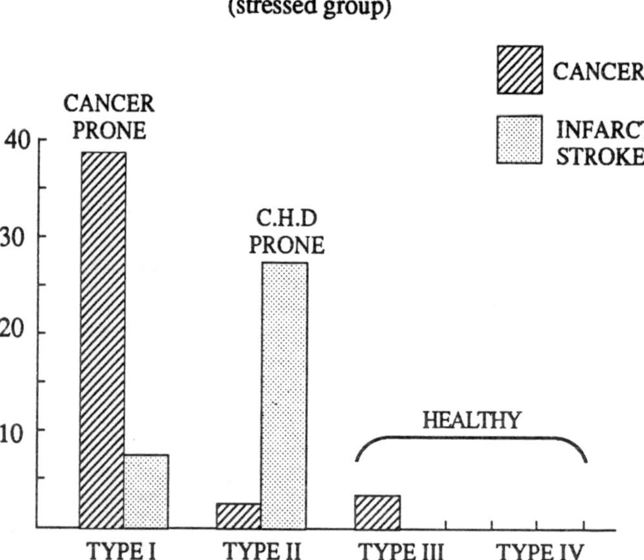

FIGURE 5 Percentage Deaths From Cancer and CHD in Probands of Different Personality Types: Heidelberg Stressed Study. (Eysenck, 1987)

Behaviour Therapies and Prophylaxis

The correlations shown in the above figures are impressive and suggest causal relations, but there is always a danger in interpreting correlations in a causal manner. To make the relationships more convincing, an intervention study would seem necessary. As already mentioned, such an intervention study was indeed carried out on a group of 100 cancer-prone and a group of 92 coronary heart disease-prone probands, diagnosed in terms of their personality characteristics (Eysenck, 1988). Identification of probands and their allocation to treatment or control groups was deposited prior to ascertainment of survival with two independent University departments. Death certificates were checked by an independent expert from the Karlsruhe Statistical Institute. Although some probands had moved from Heidelberg, all probands could be followed up successfully.

TABLE 1 Deaths From Cancer and CHD in Control and Therapy Groups

	Cancer-prone Group:			
	Still alive	*Died of Cancer*	*Died of other causes*	*Total*
Control	19	16	15	50
Therapy	45	0	5	50
Total	64	16	20	100

	Coronary Heart Disease-pron Group:			
	Still alive	*Died of C.H.R.*	*Died of other causes*	*Total*
Control	17	16	13	46
Therapy	37	3	6	46
Total	54	19	19	92

The treatment aimed at changing their behaviour patterns away from the characteristics of Types 1 and 2, respectively, towards that characteristic of Type 4. The method of *creative novation behaviour therapy*, a kind of cognitive behaviour therapy combining novel features with familiar methods of desensitization, teaching of coping mechanisms, social skills training, etc. has been described elsewhere (Grossarth-Maticek & Eysenck, in press). We are here mainly concerned not so much with the methods used, but rather with the prophylactive effects of the method. Table 1 shows the comparison between the therapy and the control group for both the cancer-prone and the coronary heart disease-prone probands. These were allocated to control or therapy on a random basis, and followed up over a period of 13 years. Previous analyses have only been able to give the results of a partial follow up over 10 years (Eysenck, 1988).

It will be clear from these tables that in the cancer-prone groups, the majority of those who died, died of cancer. In the coronary heart disease-prone group, the majority of those who died, died of coronary heart disease, although in each case quite a large number also died of other causes. It is of course well known that diagnoses derived from death certificates are very unreliable, and quite possibly a correction for unreliability, had this been possible, would have reduced the proportion of those who were diagnosed as having died of other causes (Eysenck, 1986).

To avoid the subjectivity inherent in the use of death certificates, it may be useful simply to look at the number of survivors and the number of dead in the therapy groups and the control groups respectively. These totals are given in Table 2, and it will be seen that over four times as many

TABLE 2 Survival of Cancer-Prone and CHD-Prone Probands With and Without Behavior Therapy

	Prophylactic Effects of Therapy		
	Live	*Dead*	*Total*
Therapy Groups	82	14	96
Control Groups	36	60	96
Total	118	74	192

died in the control groups as in the therapy groups, a result which, like those given in Table 1, is well beyond the requisite probability levels usually given. There appears to be no doubt that a behavioural treatment geared to changes in personality structure related to cancer and coronary heart disease can in fact fulfil a prophylactic role.

As the data indicate, our results have a much higher predictive accuracy than had been found to be associated with Type A interviewing procedures or questionnaire data. Similarly, the method of prophylactic treatment here used has been significantly more effective than any found in the literature.

Predictive Accuracy of Psychosocial Factors and Physical Factors

One last comparison may be of interest, namely the predictive accuracy of psychosocial factors of the kind incorporated in our questionnaires, and physical predictors like smoking, blood pressure, etc. A number of tables has been given in Eysenck (1988), and in Grossarth-Maticek, Eysenck & Vetter (1988) which summarize large amounts of data to indicate that the importance of smoking as a predictor of lung cancer and coronary heart disease is very much smaller than that of personality and stress. Thus, in one study, multiple correlations, corrected for bias, between disease and different types of predictors showed that for infarcts the correlation was 0.20 for physical predictors, 0.36 for psychosocial predictors. For apoplexy, the predictive accuracy of physical predictors was 0.23, and of psychosocial predictors 0.32. A more detailed comparison is offered in Table 3, which looks at the influence of risk factors like systolic blood pressure, diastolic blood pressure, blood cholesterol, and cigarettes per day, in groups of Types 1, 2, 3 and 4 in the three studies, where such measures have been taken. These data leave no doubt about the much greater importance of psychosocial factors as compared with the physical factors considered.

TABLE 3 Importance for Survival of Physical and Personality Variables. (Grossarth-Maticek, Eysenck & Vetter, 1988)

		Mean			*b*			*Mort. (percent)*		
	Type	*Y*	*H1*	*H2*	*Y*	*H1*	*H2*	*Y*	*H1*	*H2*
rf: systolic blood pressure	1	151.0	—	174.2	0.056	—	0.024	7.6	—	7.2
dis: infarc/stroke mortality	2	160.7	—	207.6	0.084*	—	0.108	27.2	—	23.7
	3	148.3	—	186.3	0.005	—	0.010	7.7	—	2.3
	4	144.6	—	185.8	0.003	—	0.021	1.8	—	5.0
	all	150.7	—	187.7	0.035	—	0.041	11.1	—	9.1
Significance of differences		0.0000	—	0.0000	0.0004	—	0.0011	<0.0001	—	<0.0001
rf: diastolic blood pressure	1	90.0	—	85.8	0.026	—	0.019	5.1	—	7.2
dis: infarct/stroke mortality	2	93.7	—	93.5	0.093	—	0.071	26.8	—	24.5
	3	88.6	—	88.9	0.020	—	0.004	8.5	—	2.5
	4	86.8	—	89.0	0.014	—	0.007	2.1	—	5.5
	all	89.6	—	88.8	0.038	—	0.025	10.6	—	9.9
Significance of differences		0.0000	—	0.0000	0.0137	—	0.0494	<0.0001	—	<0.0001
rf: blood cholesterol	1	255.6	217.5	258.3	0.011	0.004	0.037	8.3	3.2	8.5
dis infarct/stroke mortality	2	250.4	254.4	305.1	0.036	0.054	0.046	29.4	9.7	24.7
	3	245.8	216.8	282.6	0.027	0.000	0.003	9.2	1.8	1.8
	4	245.5	217.9	280.5	0.001	0.001	0.000	1.8	0.8	3.5
	all	249.1	224.9	277.8	0.019	0.014	0.020	12.2	3.9	9.6
Significance of differences		0.0330	0.0000	0.0000	NS	NS	0.0486	<0.0001	0.0008	0.0000
rf: cigarettes per day	1	15.7	13.0	16.9	0.000	0.003	0.000	7.7	4.1	6.9
dis infarct/stroke mortality	2	10.4	18.8	14.4	0.038	0.050	0.161	29.8	12.0	27.6
	3	11.6	8.9	12.2	0.021	0.016	0.007	8.3	2.5	1.7
	4	10.8	8.2	10.9	0.002	0.008	0.011	1.8	1.2	3.5
	all	11.9	11.1	15.0	0.005	0.019	0.045	11.9	5.0	9.9
Significance of differences		0.0000	0.0000	0.0000	NS	NS	0.0000	<0.0001	0.0002	0.0001
rf: blood cholesterol	1	15.7	13.0	16.9	0.075	0.019	0.044	8.2	3.6	8.3
dis infarct/stroke mortality	2	10.4	18.8	14.4	0.020	0.010	0.003	2.5	2.5	1.5
	3	11.6	8.9	12.2	0.003	0.015	0.007	1.3	2.4	1.7
	4	10.8	8.2	10.9	0.002	0.008	0.011	0.6	1.2	3.5
	all	11.9	11.1	15.0	0.025	0.013	0.016	3.1	2.4	3.7
Significance of differences		0.0000	0.0000	0.0000	0.0001	NS	0.0113	<0.0001	NS	0.0000

For Yugoslavia, the organic variable represent a single measurement taken in 1966 (cholesterol: 1969).

For Heidelberg, the organic variable are the average of up to 7 measurements taken in 1972

*largest (abs.) value is underlined

Abbreviations: rf = risk factor dis = disease mean = mean of organic varible within type groups b = regression coefficient of the dependent variable on the organic with type groups mort. = mortality (the dependent varible) within type groups, adjusted fro the organic variable Y = Yugoslavia HI = Heidelberg representative H2 = Heidelberg stressed NS means p> 0.05

Summary and Conclusions

What can we say, on the basis of our own studies, about the importance of personality and stress for the occurrence of strokes, infarcts, and other coronary heart disorders? There appears to be strong evidence that interpersonal stress is a very important factor in promoting disease and death, whether of cancer or coronary heart disease. The difference in death rate of 40% between unselected and "stressed" samples of similar age and sex composition, and similar smoking habits, is difficult to explain on any other grounds than those of greater stress in one group as compared with the other.Errors in assignment, which are of course unavoidable in studies of this kind, suggest that stress increases the death rate by between 50% and 60%. This is an enormous difference, but as the studies were prospective it appears to be a reasonable estimate based on quite large samples.

Differences in personality, leading to different reactions to interpersonal stress, appear to lie at the basis of the two alternative causes of death we have concentrated on, namely cancer and coronary heart disease. Where cancer is more closely related to feelings of hopelessness\helplessness and depression as a reaction to stress, coronary heart disease appears to be more closely related to reactions of anger and excitement. The personality types associated with these reactions appear to die disproportionately frequently of cancer (Type 1) and coronary heart disease (Type 2). The more normal types (Types 3 and 4) appear to be relatively protected from these two great killers. Obviously the possibility exists that later on even probands of Types 3 and 4 may die of cancer and coronary heart disease. Nevertheless, even a delay of twenty years of so before these diseases manifest themselves would be regarded as well worth having by most people. Ultimately, of course, we all die, but stress makes us die much earlier than necessary, and it does so in terms of either cancer or coronary heart disease, depending on genetic and constitutional factors determining our personality and reactions to stress. (A detailed study of the genetic factors in personality can be found in Eaves, Eysenck & Martin, 1989).

In spite of any genetic predisposition, however, clearly there are strong environmental factors determining the occurrence or non-occurrence of interpersonal stress. Equally, the reaction of the individual is not entirely determined by genetic factors, but may be altered by such factors as social support (Ganster & Victor, 1988), advice and therapy. Our original hypothesis was that behavioural therapy, based on the differential reactions to stress of cancer-prone and coronary heart disease-prone probands, would enable people of Type 1 or Type 2 to change their behaviour in such a way as to resemble that of people of Type 4, the "healthy" type, and thus avoid the dangers inherent in their usual behaviour and life style. Our data suggest that this is in fact true, and that considerable prophylactic value adheres to the type of behaviour therapy used in our studies. It is possible to avoid, or at least postpone, death from coronary heart disease by changing one's reactions to stress away from those characteristic of Type 2; this is an important finding.

Much has been published on the topic of psychosomatic disease, suggesting the necessity of a profound reconsideration of the body-mind relationship. Physicists have found it necessary to give up the notion of space and time as separate entities, but rather consider a space-time continuum. So too, psychologists will have to give up the Cartesian notion of body and mind as separate substances, and conceive of a body-mind continuum. This notion, of course, has a respectable ancestry. Four thousand years ago in the Indian Mahabharta, it was written that: "There are two classes of disease - bodily and mental. Each arises from the other, and neither can exist without the other. Mental disorders arise from physical ones, and likewise, physical disorders arise from mental ones" (Santi Parve, XVI, 8-9).

The consequences of such a realignment are considerable. As far as medicine is concerned, they suggest that psychology is an essential foundation science for the teaching and practice of medicine. For clinical psychology, it means a realignment to take into account its bearing on physical disease, rather than a concentration on psychiatric disorders. Such an integration between psychology and medicine will be difficult to achieve, but is clearly desirable. (Eysenck & Rachman, 1973.)

Even more important from many points of view is the possibility of avoiding physical disease by psychological treatment, i.e. by some kind of cognitive behaviour therapy (Eysenck & Martin, 1987). This possibility suggests a complete change in the practice of modern medicine, bringing it back to the alleged habits of the ancient Chinese of paying their physicians for keeping them healthy and not paying them for treatment once they were ill. Prevention rather than cure as a principle of medical treatment would certainly involve great social changes. Such a practice would lead to a considerable saving of money, not to speak of the considerable contribution that might thus be made to the sum total of human happiness.

The observations of patients suffering from cancer and coronary heart disease which led to the postulation of personality differences leading to disease, going back over thousands of years, have now found support in methodologically well conceived and statistically properly analysed studies. It would seem that paying attention to careful observations of well-trained physicians, even though these might not be considered methodologically adequate by modern standards, may nevertheless repay the time and trouble taken. Not all such observations are necessarily erroneous, simply because they were made in a form and reported in a manner not nowadays acceptable.

REFERENCES

Baer, P.E., Collins, F.H., Bourianoff, G.G., & Ketchel, M.F. (1979). Assessing personality factors in essential hypertension with a brief self-report instrument. *Psychosomatic Medicine,41*, 321-330.

Barefoot, J.C., Dahlstrom, G., & Williams, R.B. Hostility, (1983). CHD incidence and total mortality: a 25-year follow-up study of 255 physicians. *Psychosomatic Medicine, 45*, 59-63.

Belgian-French Pooling Project. Assessment of Type A behaviour by the Bortner scale and schemic heart disease. (1984) *European Heart Journal, 5*, 440-446.

Bendien, J., & Groen, J.(1963). A psychological-statistical study of neuroticism and extraversion in patients with myocardial infarction. *Journal of Psychosomatic Research,7*, 11-14.

Booth-Kewley, S., & Friedman, H.S. (1987). Psychological predictors of heart disease: A quantitative review. *Psychological Bulletin, 101*, 343-362.

Bortner, R.W.(1969). A short rating scale as a potential measure of patterns of behaviour. *Journal of Chronic Diseases, 22*, 87-91.

Breier, A., Albin, M., Pickar, D., Zahn, T., Wolkowitz, O.M., & Paul, S.M.(1987). Controllable and uncontrollable stress in humans: Alterations in mood and neuroendocrine and psychophysical functions. *American Journal of Psychiatry, 44*, 1419-1425.

Brown, J.P., & Siegel, J.M.(1988). Attributions for negative life events and depression: The role of perceived control. *Journal of Personality and Social Psychology, 54*, 310-322.

Dembroski, T.M., & Costa, P.T.(1987). Coronary-prone behavior: Components of the Type A patterns and hostility. *Journal of Personality, 55*, 211-235.

Eaves, L., Eysenck, H.J., & Martin, N.G.(1989). *Genes, culture and personality: an empirical approach.* New York: Academic Press

Eysenck, H.J.(1985). Personality, cancer and cardiovascular disease: A causal analysis. *Personality and Individual Differences, 5*, 535-557.

Eysenck, H.J.Smoking and Health. In: R.D. Tollison (Ed.), *Smoking and society.* (pp. 17-88). Lexington: Lexington Books

Eysenck, H.J.(1987). Personality as a predictor of cancer and cardiovascular disease and the application of behaviour therapy in prophylaxis. *European Journal of Psychiatry, 1*, 29-41.

Eysenck, H.J. (1988). The respective importance of personality, cigarette smoking and interaction effects for the genesis of cancer and coronary heart disease. *Personality and Individual Differences, 9*, 453-464.

Eysenck, H.J., & Eysenck, M.W. (1985). *Personality and individual dfferences: A natural science approach.* New York: Plenum.

Eysenck, H.J., & Fulker, D. (1983). The components of Type A behaviour and its genetic determinants. *Personality and Individual Differences, 4*, 499-505.

Eysenck, H.J., & Martin, I. (Eds.). (1987). *Theoretical foundations of behaviour therapy.* New York: Plenum Press.

Eysenck, H.J., & Rachman, S. (1973). The future of clinical psychology. *Bulletin of the British Psychological Society, 20*, 113-116.

Floderus, B. (1974). Psycho-social factors in relation to coronary heart disease and associated risk factors. *Nordisk Hygienisk Tidskrift*, Supplementum 6, Stockholm.

Frankenhaeuser, M., Lundberg, V., & Forsman, L. (1980) Note on arousing Type A persons by depriving them of work. *Journal of Psychosomatic Medicine, 24*, 45-47.

Friedman, M., & Rosenman, R.H. (1959). Association of specific overt behaviour patterns with blood and cardiovascular findings. *Journal of the American Medical Association, 169*, 1286-1296.

Friedman, M., Thoreson, C.E., Gill, J.J., Powell, L., Ulmer, D., Thompson, L., Price, V.A., Rabin, D.P., Breall, W.S., Dixon, T., Levy, R.A., & Bourg, E. (1984). Alteration of Type A behaviour and reduction of cardiac recurrence in post-myocardial infarction patients. *American Heart Journal, 108*, 237-298.

Ganster, D.C. & Victor, B. The impact of social support on mental and physical health. *British Journal of Medical Psychology, 61*, 17-36.

Grossarth-Maticek, R., Bastiaans, J., & Kanazir, D.T. Psychosocial factors as strong predictors of mortality from cancer, ischaemic heart disease and stroke: The Yugoslav prospective study. *Journal of Psychosomatic Research, 29*, 167-176.

Grossarth-Maticek, R. & Eysenck, H.J. (in press). Novational therapy with cancer patients. *Behaviour Research and Therapy.*

Grossarth-Maticek, R., Eysenck, H.J., & Vetter, H. (1988). Personality type, cancer and coronary heart disease. *Personality and Individual Differences, 9*, 479-495.

Grossarth-Maticek, R., Frentzel-Beyne, R., Becker, N., & Schum, D. (1984). Cancer risks associated with life events and conflict solutions. *Cancer Detection and Prevention, 7*, 201-209

Grossarth-Maticek, R., Kanazir, D.T., Vetter, H. & Jankovic, M. (1983). Smoking as a risk factor for lung cancer and cardiac infarct as mediated by psychosocial variables. *Psychotherapy and Psychosomatics, 39*, 94-105.

Grossarth-Maticek, R., Schmidt, P., Vetter, H., & Arndt, S. (1984). Psychotherapy research in oncology. In: A. Steptoe & A.M. Matthews (Eds.), *Health care and human behaviour*. (pp. 325-340), London: Academic Press.

Gudjonsson, G.H. (1981). Self-reported emotional disturbance and its relation to electrodurmal reactivity, defensiveness and trait anxiety. *Personality and Individual Differences, 2*, 47-52.

Haynes, S.G., Feinleib, M., & Kannel, W.B. (1980). The relationship of psychosocial factors to coronary heart disease in the Framingham Study, III: Eight-year incidence of coronary heart disease. *American Journal of Epidemiology, 111*, 37-58.

Innes, J.M. (1980). Impulsivity and the coronary-prone behaviour pattern. *Psychological Report, 7*, 976-978.

Ivancevich, J.M., & Matteson, M.T. (1988). Type A behaviour and the healthy individual. *British Journal of Medical Psychology, 61*, 37-56.

Jenkins, C.D., Zyzanski, S.J., Ryan, T.J., Flessas, S., & Tannenbaum, S.Z. (1977). Social insecurity - and coronary-prone Type A responses as identifiers of severe atherosclerosis. *Journal of Consulting and Clinical Psychology, 45*, 1060-1067.

Kaplan, H.B. (Ed.). (1983). *Psychosocial stress*. New York: Academic Press.

Kemple, L. (1945). Rorschach method and psychosomatic diagnosis: Personality traits of patients with rheumatic disease, hypertension, cardiovascular disease, occlusions and fracture. *Psychosomatic Medicine, 7,* 85-89.

Kissen, D.M., & Eysenck, H.J.(1962). Personality in male lung cancer patients. *Journal of Psychosomatic Research, 6,* 123-137.

Lichtenstein, P., Pedersen, N.L., Olomin, R., de Faire, U., & MacCann, C.E (in press). Type A behaviour patterns, related personality traits and self-reported coronary heart disease. *Personality and Individual Differences.*

Matthews, K.A., & Haynes, S.G. (1986). Type A behavior patterns and coronary disease risk—update and critical evaluation. *American Journal of Epidemiology, 123,* 923-960.

McGuigan, F.J., Sime, W.E., & Wallace, G.M. (Eds.).(1984). *Stress and tension control.* New York: Plenum Press.

Menninger, R.A., & Menninger, W.C. (1936). Psychosomatic observations in cardiac disorders. *American Heart Journal, 11,* 10-21.

Morris, T., & Greer, S. A (1980). "Type C" for cancer? Low trait anxiety in the pathogenesis of breast cancer. *Cancer Detection and Prevention, 3,* Abstract No. 102.

Nowack, K.M., & Sassenrath, J.M. (1980). Coronary-prone behaviour, locus of control, and anxiety. *Psychological Reports, 47,* 359-364.

Osler, W. (1910). Lecture on Angina Pectoris. *Lancet, 1,* 839-844.

Price, V.A. (1982). Type A Behaviour. New York: Academic Press.

Rosenman, R.H., Brand, R.J., Jenkins, C.D., et al. (1979). Coronary heart disease in the Western Collaborative Group Study: Final follow-up experience of 8 1/2 years. *Journal of the American Medical Association, 233,* 872-877.

Roskies, E. (1987). Stress Managements for the Healthy Type A. New York: Guilford Press.

Ruberman, W., Weinblatt, E., Goldberg, J., & Chaudhury, B. (1984). Psychosocial influences on mortality after myocardial infarction. *New England Journal of Medicine, 311,* 552-559.

Shekelle, R.B., Gayle, M., Ostfeld, A.M., & Paul, O. (1983). Hostility, risk of coronary heart disease, and mortality. *Psychosomatic Medicine, 45,* 109-114.

Shekelle, R.B., Hulley, S.B., Neaton, J.D., et al. (1985). The MRFIT behavior pattern study. III: Type A behavior and incidence of coronary heart disease. *American Journal of Epidemiology, 122,* 559-570.

Sklar, L.S., & Anisman, H.(1979). Stressed coping factors influence tumour growth. *Science, 205,* 513-515.

Sklar, L.S., & Anisman, H. (1981). Stress and cancer. *Psychological Bulletin, 89,* 309-406.

Slaby, A., Horvath, M., & Frantik, E. (1981). Cardiovascular response in stress testing related to some personality characteristics. *Activitas Nervosa Superior, 23,* 64-66.

Williams, R.B. (1984). Type A behaviour and coronary heart disease: Something old, something new. *Behavioral Medicine Update,* 629-633.

Williams, R.B., Barefoot, J.C., & Shekelle, R.B.(1985). The health consequences of hostility. In: M.A. Chesney & R.N. Rosenman (Eds.), *Anger, hostility, and behavioral medicine.* New York: Hemisphere/McGraw-Hill.

Wright, L. (1988). The Type A behavior pattern and coronary artery disease. *American Psychologist, 43, 113,* 2-14.

A "Success Trap" Theory of Type A Behavior: Historical Background

Lawrence F. Van Egeren
Department of Psychiatry
Michigan State University, East Lansing, MI 48824

Type A behavior is paradoxical because it is so unsatisfying and yet so persistent. The present theory argues that Type A behavior is paradoxical because it is "trapped" by the contradictory consequences of success striving. Rewarding consequences of success striving cause it to be persistent. Punishing consequences cause it to be unsatisfying. The contradictory nature of the consequences causes it to be paradoxical. Historical trends in the values of three historical eras (medieval, modern, postmodern) were described to illustrate the development of contradictions from which success traps can emerge.

INTRODUCTION

The Type A behavior pattern (TABP) is at once familiar and disturbing. The central elements of the behavior—the fierce competitiveness, the preoccupation with success, the staking of self-worth on success, the inner tyranny of unreasonable expectations for self and others—are common in our society. Despite an uncompromising drive to succeed, the Type A person usually ends up failing to gain those things that matter most in life: happiness, self-acceptance, and peace of mind. That is what is disturbing. Worldly success is pursued with such single-minded passion that much of what is truly human and valuable (reflectiveness, creativity, social feeling) becomes impoverished (Friedman & Rosenman, 1974; Friedman & Ulmer, 1974).

Type A behavior theory has been unnecessarily narrow and barren, and key aspects of the behavior remain incomprehensible because we have not considered the behavior in the context of underlying social and economic realities. Theories of the TABP have attempted to identify the central motive force behind the behavior—the urge to control one's sur-

Author's Note: I wish to thank colleagues and friends who reviewed an earlier draft of this paper, especially Nathanael Mullener, Mary Davis, David Garner, Thomas Stachnik, Gerald Osborn, and Peter Manning.

© 1990 Select Press

roundings, to reach unrealistic or ambiguous goals, to clarify ambiguous goals, and so on. There is some evidence to support each motive (Strube, 1987).

Two key questions remain unanswered by available theories. First, how is it that the Type A person does not "correct" his or her faulty success goals; for instance, abandon fruitless efforts to control the uncontrollable or to reach the unreachable? Second, how is it that tens of millions of Americans try so desperately to control their surroundings and adopt unrealistic and ambiguous goals? What is it about the reinforcement structure of American society which fosters such futile, ill-fated behavior?

Type A behavior is paradoxical because it is so unsatisfying and yet so persistent. Rewards in the modern industrial society can account for why the behavior persists but not why it is unsatisfying and paradoxical. How can the Type A behavior paradox be explained?

The answer given by the current theory is that someone possessing Type A behavior is "trapped" by an inconsistent reward system; but what, specifically, does this mean? What are the traps, and how did they originate? This paper deals with the broad historical-cultural origin of the success traps. The nature of the traps themselves and the mechanisms by which they operate will be considered elsewhere. My goal here is to sketch in background materials, to provide contours, not details, to present what is plausible, not what is proven. I hope that this will encourage a new and broader mode of thought about Type A behavior.

THE THEORY IN BRIEF

The present theory argues that the Type A mode of success striving—individualistic, competitive, aggressive—is entrapping because the behavior produces multiple consequences, some of which are rewarding and others of which are punishing. Rewarding consequences of the success striving cause it to be persistent; punishing consequences cause it to be unsatisfying. The contradictory nature of the consequences causes it to be paradoxical.

I am proposing specifically that the TABP (a) was rewarded lavishly in the 1800's but is poorly adaptive today, (b) is paradoxical (persistently unrewarding), (c) because it entraps the individual in patterns of success striving, (d) which are aimed at increasing self-esteem, which (e) in the adult-as-child was associated with success by parental conditional love and (f) today is threatened by a reward system that favors Type B behavior.

During the 1800's, America's developing economy rewarded productive industrial work. Work was deified—in sermons, lectures, books, newspapers, and down to the standard McGuffey reader (Huber, 1987; Wyllie, 1954). Public rewards shaped and maintained as industrial "virtues" hard work, frugality, sobriety, punctuality, perseverance, loyalty, and obedience (Fromm, 1955). The "self-made man" and the "rugged individualist" were the celebrated ideals of the Victorian Age. Type A behavior is an expression of such ideals.

During the 1900's, a maturing economy and growing socioeconomic interdependence accompanying ever-increasing urbanization, bureaucratization, and specialization shifted rewards away from economic production and individualism, and toward economic consumption and persuasive salesmanship (Gotshalk, 1958). More so than before, rewards favored those who could master what Huber (1987) called the "personality ethic," Riesman (1961) called "other directedness," and Fromm (1976) called the "marketing character, " which means being attractive, popular, pleasing, and in demand as a "consumer product" in a mass public market. The Type B person, who is less hostile and abrasively competitive than the Type A person, is better suited to the current reward environment.

Radical transformation of values in the West over the past five hundred years (Brinton, 1963; Gotshalk, 1958; Ortega y Gasset, 1961; Riesman, 1961) caused cataclysmic upheavals and jarring incongruities in reinforcement systems. Nested within these incongruities, according to the current theory, "traps" for behavior that specifically allure Type A persons developed. I will review the strikingly inconsistent, potentially entrapping, value systems of three historical periods here: medieval, modern (defined as the years 1500 to 1900), and postmodern (1900 to the present). Elsewhere I will argue that the Type A person is entrapped between the modern and postmodern value systems in specific ways.

The approach-avoidance conflict model is often applied to illuminate a contradictory reinforcement system. When the positive ("approach") consequences are known and the negative ("avoidance") consequences are hidden or unknown, the reinforcement pattern can be usefully viewed as a "trap," a term used by Cross and Guyer (1980). Traps "seduce" a person, or an animal, to act in ways that, on the whole, end up being unrewarding or punishing. The trap model will be applied to the TABP.

Traps arise from self-contradictory reinforcement patterns (systems of values). A person falls into a trap by taking what appear to be all the right steps but consistently ends up in the wrong place — a behavioral and emotional cul de sac. A mousetrap illustrates the essentials of behavioral traps. A mousetrap presents two reinforcers, one positive and sought by the mouse (cheese, the "bait") and the other negative and unexpected (the deadly bar). A mousetrap is a two-part reward system. The mouse seeks one part, and is "surprised" by the the second part.

The current theory claims that (a) success traps exist in our society, (b) the traps have been institutionalized, (c) the traps are "baited" for, or seductively attractive to Type A individuals, and (d) a specific ontogenetic learning mechanism creates the bait-behavior link.Were the traps not institutionalized, i.e., woven into the reinforcement structure of major American institutions, how could tens of millions of Americans be trapped? Were the traps not specifically attractive to Type As, would they not as likely snare Type Bs? Were the traps lacking a plausible learning mechanism, how could Type A 'victims' respond so dependably to the success seductions society offers?

HISTORICAL TRENDS IN WESTERN VALUES

Institutionalized rewards of any society act as guiderails for behavior. The rewards create "behavioral paths" winding through society. Type A behavior is viewed here as a competitive-aggressive response to the success paths in our society. On these roads are traps and pitfalls that have accumulated throughout our history. The traps are fashioned out of inconsistent ideals and values which direct one to do opposed things. I will review some major clashes in Western values that form the groundwork of specific success traps.

During Western history the ideals about fundamentals (the true, the good, the beautiful, the useful), which people live by, changed radically (Brinton, 1963; Gotshalk, 1958; Ortega y Gasset, 1961; Riesman, 1961). The ideas were also ideals or values. As new ideals were added, the old ones did not disappear but were subordinated to the new. The older ideals often performed rearguard actions in shaping human behavior and institutions. The attempt to fit the nineteenth century capitalist spirit to the harness of medieval morality is an example. Protestant clergy tried to adapt the inequalities of the capitalistic economy to a Christian purpose. They looked upon great wealth as part of God's plan for the industrial world; however, wealth was to be used benevolently. The primary mechanism was the principle of stewardship—the injunction to use one's wealth to benefit others, to do well in order to do good (Huber, 1971; Wyllie, 1954).

As much as possible, I will cast the values dominating the medieval, modern, and postmodern periods in behavioral terms, so that the behavioral trap model can be applied more directly. In order to pursue a goal, people must *want* something (drive), must *see* something (cue), must *do* something (response), and must *get* something (reinforcement). Then we can ask of each major historical era the following questions. What do people expect to "get" as an overall reward? What counts as knowledge or correct "seeing"? What counts as morals or correct "wanting"? What are the obstacles to satisfaction?

Medieval Period. The superordinate human goal in the medieval system was to narrow the gap between God and man (Brinton, 1963). The goal was blissful union with divinity (beatitude). The primary obstacle to the goal was sin, which caused guilt. Progress toward the goal was measured in terms of grace. Correct "seeing" was faith through which God was revealed. Correct "wanting" was virtue (i.e., wanting what God desired of humanity), by which people expressed God's plan. In the "supernatural spirit" of the medieval system the ideal human being was the "saint."

Modern Period. The Renaissance stood the medieval value hierarchy (spiritual > material; virtue > desire) on its head (Gotshalk, 1958). Life on earth was valued for its own sake. The Enlightenment promised that the team of Reason, Science, and Industry, by understanding and mastering nature, would lead to inevitable Progress for everyone. We could all have heaven on earth. The primary goal had become to narrow the gap between man and nature by founding society on 'natural' rights and desires. Nature grasped by reason, rather than God's will revealed by faith, became the blueprint for society.

The "natural spirit" celebrated the natural powers of the individual, especially reason (man being the "rational animal"). Natural passions of greed (Adam Smith) and ambition (Machiavelli), and later of aggression (Darwin) and sexuality (Freud), were released from the grip of medieval virtue and honor, fostered by a despotic clergy and monarchy.

The release of natural human energies led to a burst of creativity and productivity — the beginning of the modern "human potential" movement. But there were problems. What would prevent new despots from arising? What would keep greed and ambition within bounds? How could society satisfy and yet contain the selfish people within it? The answer, given by Adam Smith and Montesquieu among others, was the division and opposition of powers, setting greed against greed, ambition against ambition. Like a Gothic cathedral, a stable society would be built out of opposed forces, the very forces (greed and ambition) which threatened social stability.

The disciplining mechanism in the liberal democratic society was free-wheeling competition. Following head-to-head competition in the marketplace, the least greedy merchant would get the sale, the leader with the most enlightened ambition would serve in public office. Rousseau (1964) warned ominously that society could not tolerate the tensions of unbridled individualism and brawling competition, that social feeling would be destroyed by the divisive scramble for social power.

Competition was lavishly celebrated in America of the 1800's as rugged individualism and the philosophy of Social Darwinism (Hofstadter, 1955), which were part of the "naturalism" of that period. Darwin's theory of evolution meant, it was thought, that the earth was changing, evolving, toward something good, humankind itself. There was reason for optimism: progress was built into nature. The pain and suffering from struggle and competition were to be accepted because they were part of the 'perfecting' mechanism of nature. The heaven for superior people who succeeded on earth and the hell for inferior people who failed were what they should be—justice, delivered by nature in its own infallible way. Any attempt to interfere with this process would block Progress and be 'unnatural.'

Struggle, competition, and *success striving*— three cornerstones of the TABP— were honored as primary means of ascent to higher states of perfection and as keys to a 'natural' plan for society. A bright future beckoned to the rugged and the energetic who, with Calvinist insight, faced up to the hardness of life, the impossibility of easy solutions, and the necessity of hard work and self-denial (Hofstadter, 1955).

Daily newspapers of the time dispel any notion that Social Darwinism was merely an isolated preoccupation of intellectual theorists. New York lectures by Thomas Huxley (Darwin's "Bulldog") in the 1870's were "reprinted and discussed in the *Tribune*, and his visit was treated as ceremoniously as that of royalty" (Hofstadter, 1955, p. 26). Social Darwinism was discussed regularly in such popular magazines as *Atlantic Monthly*. American sales of books by the philosopher Herbert Spencer, who wrote extensively on Social Darwinism, came to some 368,755 volumes between the 1860's and 1903 (Hofstadter, 1955).

Protestantism and Social Darwinism combined to provide the laissez faire capitalism of the 1800's with much needed credentials and respectability. Capitalism's wealthiest beneficiaries were thought to be vindicated *intellectually*, as triumphant examples of nature's own way of 'becoming,' *morally*, as divinely anointed and blessed, and *esthetically*, as the highest exemplars of human perfection and excellence. It was a powerful elixir of ideas guiding everyday American life and richly rewarding someone possessing the TABP in the 1800's.

In *The Lonely Crowd*, Riesman (1961) refers to the character type who was best adapted to the "modern" period as the "inner-directed" person. The inner-directed person is someone guided by personal principles, rather than by tradition (as in the medieval era) or by others' opinions (as in the era I label "postmodern"). They are "rational," hard working people who value scientific and technical skills over social skills. They tend to moralize, to be opinionated, to harshly criticize incompetence, to tyrannize themselves and others with uncompromising inner "shoulds" (absolute standards), and to hide personal failures.

Inner-directedness represents the supremacy of social power over social feeling, assertion of self over integration with others, willfulness over willingness, and competition over cooperation. Riesman's "inner-directed" character type has many obvious similarities to the TABP.

It is worth noting that the modern era was dominated by the print media — books, magazines, newspapers (Burke, 1985). Ideas set in print seem to possess 'objectivity' verifiable by facts. Once set in print, ideas acquire stability and can contribute to cumulative knowledge. Print media are ideal for storing the facts and theories of science, which was greatly honored in the modern period. Enlightenment thinkers expected that cumulative scientific knowledge would impart a stable, progressive direction to an ever-more-perfect human life on earth.

Now to summarize the modern period. Just as the medieval system of ideals was God-centered, so the modern system was nature-centered. The superordinate human goal in the "natural spirit" was to possess natural beauty, a harmonious balance of natural forces. Correct "seeing" was truth, the conformity of ideas to the 'nature of things' as grasped by reason. Correct "wanting" was natural goodness, a propensity for natural beauty in one's life. People were called by their ideals to satisfy a double imperative of the Enlightenment — one had to be good (the social imperative), but what was good had to be 'human,' which meant 'natural to' human beings (the biological imperative) (Ortega y Gasset, 1961). The primary obstacles to satisfaction were the demons of sloth and ignorance. The ideal human type was the creative "genius" — at first the Renaissance Man and later the innovative entrepreneur. Failure to realize one's natural human potential, to reach worldly goals, caused shame more than guilt.

Postmodern Period. Sweeping changes beginning around the turn of this century altered radically the reinforcement structure of our society. What is "new" in the socioeconomic organization of the postmodern period is the intensity of *social interdependence* (Gotshalk, 1958). Growing dependency on others, and a corresponding drop in self-sufficiency, resulted from the increased density of living conditions (urbanization), the growth in size of organizations (bureaucratization), the narrowing of life-support skills (specialization), and the reduced concreteness and self-evident necessity of work. Greater dependency on others means that the value of one's work — and one's 'worth,' to the degree one's self-worth hinges on achievement — depends more on the recognition and approval of other people. Self-promotional skills (charm, persuasiveness, friendliness, a winning smile), no less than competence, determine success on the job and in the marketplace.

Just as the modern era was nature-centered, the postmodern world becomes human-centered. With striking speed and intensity, world-wide advances in mass communication, mass transportation, and mass production in this century envelop people more deeply and thoroughly in other people — their ideas, their products, themselves. The environment, and the reward structure, become more human and less natural. Technological innovations accelerate the pace of change, and deepen and widen social interdependence. The focus of the economy changes from scarcity and *production* to affluence and *consumption* (Galbraith, 1958). The technological problem of how to build a mousetrap is replaced by the problem of how to sell thousands of mousetraps piling up in the warehouse. Insufficient consumer demand during the Great Depression was calamitous. Human perversity, more than the unruliness of nature, becomes the obstacle to human satisfaction.

Frontier living came to an end in the late 1800's. People had to settle down to a life of dependence upon one another. The percentage of people who worked for themselves or who lived on farms dropped dramatically. Rewards shifted from the competitive-aggressive individualist to the sensitive negotiator, the team player, the socially smooth person who could 'manage' people and their moods, eliminate hostility and conflict and achieve the harmony that is required in a complex organization. The emphasis shifted from morality to morale, from character to personality, from being "right" to feeling "good" (Riesman, 1961). Affluence and the superfluity of goods turned attention to the pleasures — and to the economic necessity — of consumption.

The postmodern society is dominated by the electronic media. Radio and television are ideal for communicating simple events immediately, as "news of the day" (Postman, 1985). Fragmentary and noncumulative electronic messages about "happenings" here and now increase the value of novelty and unpredictability, as opposed to more stable, cumulative information systems like science. News "flashes" about the world *now* create a mercurial atmosphere. Ideas and ideals communicated by the electronic media can seem disposable — intellectual and moral "fashions of the day" — rather than the stable 'absolutes' of earlier times.

Surrounded by great rapidity of change, it becomes more difficult to know where one stands in the world. It pays less to look to the future, which is impossible to know in advance, or to the past, which is irrelevant, for guidance. One must find guidance elsewhere, by looking *outward* to other people, to see what is happening here and now. Consequently, social verification of reality plays a new and expanded role in the regulation of behavior. Beliefs and values can be checked against public opinion and public taste to see whether one understands today's world 'correctly' and is in step with the times.

Social interdependence in the postmodern environment, then, is epistemological as well as economic. Public consensus becomes the authority on the fundamentals of life. More so than before, human agreement, John Locke's "social contract," creates not only society and government, but truth and values. At the limits of this social determinism, people do not agree because something is true (or good); something is true (or good) because people agree. Human consensus, not 'objective' reality, is the arbiter. Not only beauty but truth is in the eye of the beholder. There is a tendency for "truth" to come to mean little more than "opinion," and for "beauty" to be equivalent to "good taste."

Given the dominating influence of public opinion, it is not surprising that a postmodern industry arose to track and manipulate it. George Gallup began polling public opinion in the 1930's. Advertising and public relations firms began to influence public opinions and values. The public's opinion became a priceless prize.

The economy of the postmodern age changed not only objectively but subjectively. People's perception of it changed. The economy seemed more like a self-regulating organism, a law and a world unto itself, monstrous during depressions and recessions and beatific during booms. It seemed to be more self-justifying, and more an end in itself than in earlier times (Galbraith, 1987). It no longer needed legitimation from above (God) or below (nature). It could dispense with the moral, intellectual, and esthetic credentials the nineteenth century apologists of capitalism assiduously accorded it. Worldly success no longer needed to conform to some 'higher' principle, like the principle of stewardship, to become respectable. The economy 'works,' produces a general prosperity; its success became justification enough (Friedman & Friedman, 1980).

This new understanding of the economy, and the worldly success it encompasses, is reflected in books on success published in this century. Compared to the 1800's, the focus is less on stewardship and more on success, wealth, and luxury goods as ends in themselves (Huber, 1987). The huge popularity of some of the books (Dale Carnegie's *How to Win Friends and Influence People*, published in 1936, sold over 8,000,000 copies and has been translated into thirty languages) suggests that this new meaning of success became widespread.

The explosiveness of change during the postmodern period has been economically beneficial, but psychologically and socially costly. The fixed reference points of the medieval and modern systems, God and nature, became unreliable mariner's needles, and consequently: "The man of the West is undergoing a process of radical disorientation because he no longer knows by what stars he is to guide his life" (Ortega y Gasset, 1961, p. 79).

Riesman (1961) labeled the dominant form of behavior in the twentieth century "other-directedness." The "other-directed" person is sensitive to other people, tolerant, cooperative, and ready to change. The person values social skills over technical skills. Consumption, more so than work, organizes one's social life. Shared likes and dislikes in fads, fashions, and people are primary bases of intimacy and friendship. Being popular and well-liked and keeping up with the Joneses in the competition to consume are major bases of worry. Shallowness, insincerity (utilitarian smiling), docility, and suppression of standards of excellence are special dangers. Riesman's other-directed person is similar to the Type B person.

Now to summarize the commercially- and socially-centered affluent postmodern period. The "social spirit" inverted the value hierarchy of the naturalism of the previous age (natural > social, individual > group). The superordinate goal is to narrow the gap between self and others by being socialized and sociable. The challenge is to be 'in,' 'with it,' tuned into other people, part of the latest fashion trends in food, clothing, and entertainment. Conforming to the group and pleasing others — being whatever the public, the ruling authority desires — is richly rewarded. The end is "luxury," i.e., being or possessing whatever the public desires most. Popularity is a key measure of success. The hero in this era is the "celebrity," whom the public prizes.

Knowledge or correct "seeing" is majority opinion. Morals or correct "wanting" is good taste, that is, wanting what elite consumers value highly. The primary obstacle to personal goals is being different from people whose beliefs and values one admires most, being a nonconformist. The price of not fitting in, the unbearable feeling in our times, is loneliness.

Summary of the Three Periods. Medievalism, modernism, and postmodernism differed radically in total way of life. One might say, in simplistic terms, that the reward system evolved from domination by 'the Fall' (loss of spiritual paradise; humankind sinned earlier, and must pay now) in the Middle Ages, to 'the Rise' (dedication to earthly human progress; pay now, enjoy later) in modern times, to 'the Eden' (arrival of earthly consumer paradise; enjoy now, pay later, if commercial credit runs out) in the postmodern present. There was a change from preoccupation with the inner spiritual struggle, to the struggle against nature, to no struggle at all (present cult of effortlessness). The reward system, which

Domain	Values		
	Medieval	**Modern**	**Postmodern**
Knowlege	Faith	Truth	Opinion
Morals	Virtue	Goodness	Taste
Ends	Beatitutde	Beauty	Luxury
Authority	Revelation	Reason	Consensus
Theory	Theism	Rationalism	Relativism
Hero	Saint	Genius	Celebrity

FIGURE 1 Values Describing Three Historical Eras

provided for conformity, aimed at molding one's life to the purpose and plan, first of God (revealed, divine law), then of nature (discovered, natural law), and finally of the public (created, consensual law) as the final authority.

Figure 1 summarizes values during the medieval, modern, and postmodern epochs. There was a shift in what counts as knowledge (correct "seeing") from spiritual *faith*, to nature-rooted 'objective' *truth*, to socially constructed *opinion*. There was a shift in morals (correct "wanting") from *virtue*, to natural *goodness*, to socially formed *taste*. There was a shift in the end of life (ultimate correct "getting") from spiritual *beatitude*, to natural *beauty*, to man-made *luxury*. There was a shift in cosmology, the basis of understanding the world, including human beings, from *theism*, to *rationalism*, to *relativism*. Finally, there was a shift in the ideal human type, the culture's "hero," from the saint (possessing ample grace), to the *genius* (ample reason, creativity), to the *celebrity* (ample popularity, public appeal). The new authority for the social order is "democratic" — rule by a majority, by consensus — not divinity, or the rule of reason. The sweeping overall change is that the human world is no longer spiritually ordered and justified, or naturally ordered, but socially and commercially constructed.

The historian Irvin Wyllie offers an apt warning. "Men who search for meaning in history know that it is difficult to divine the central tendency of an age or discover the ruling spirit of a people. Tendencies and spirits are as varied as men themselves, and the records which embody them are confused, faulty, and fragmentary. Occasionally, however, the record is very clear" (1954, p. 3). The historical record outlined above is not "very clear," but it seems clear enough for my limited purpose.

CONCLUSIONS

What is striking in this brief historical sketch is the enormous diversity and contradictoriness of Western values today. All three 'spirits' — the supernatural, the natural, and the social — with their different and often opposed ends, moral injunctions, and ways of knowing, are simultaneously present and active, with the social spirit dominant. All three patterns of rewards shape behavior, often contradictorily, in these incomprehensible and bewildering times. There are ample opportunities for entrapped behavior in our fragmented society.

The specific relevant success traps emerging from antinomies in the postmodern reward system will be considered elsewhere. Here I will simply indicate the general direction the analysis will take.

Success striving during the modern age was a sacred and noble 'cause.' The great achievers, and the would-be-great achievers, had in common a sense of mission, a sense of belonging to something that was going to go beyond their own lives and even beyond anything human beings had ever known before. There was an adventurous, conquering, fresh emotional faith in material Progress. Work derived its whole dignity from the necessity it served (Ortega y Gasset, 1961). Success striving *integrated* economic, religious, intellectual, and civic values. All of these values pointed in the same direction — toward a divine, 'natural,' justifiable success goal.

All of this changed when the public reward system was split apart by changes in the economy: a) its secularization, or 'de-Christianization,' b) the shift from production to consumption, and c) mass consumption of luxurious, superfluous, and trivial goods (Corwin, 1986). Worldly success was no longer self-evidently good and necessary; consequently, more urgently than ever it needed social affirmation and validation — from the new (postmodern) authority, the public. Needing the approval of the same people the Type A person is trying to competitively dominate is inherently entrapping. Needing to make choices in a confused and fragmented success-reward system is potentially entrapping. Staking something as essential as self-esteem on something as nonessential as the making and marketing of luxury goods is likewise potentially entrapping.

During this century rewards for success lost much of the internal consistency, the convincing character, the broad attractive force, and the imperative vigor they had in the 1800's.Consequently, the pursuit of one value can more easily annul others, or be too narrowly satisfying of human needs. Antagonisms between major ideals — such as between those of Christianity and capitalism, production and consumption, and luxury consumption and necessary consumption, — are the raw materials of success traps. The reinforcement structure of worldly success-as-an-end-in-itself has not only shrunk, e.g., by no longer compelling religious loyalty, but has become more perilous. These changes place in greater jeopardy the Type A person's self-esteem, so heavily dependent on the rewards of success (Friedman & Ulmer, 1984).

SOME IMPLICATIONS

Stress is typically viewed as an environmental challenge requiring behavioral and biological adjustments. The current theory shifts attention from a "challenge" to a "contradiction" as the primary cause of serious distress. Contradictory reinforcers, i.e., traps, enmesh one in pointless, *meaningless* sacrifices — in behavior lacking a worthwhile purpose (Frankl, 1984). Traps disorganize behavior because the reinforcements which maintain the behavior are divisive. Antonovsky (1979) and Krystal (1988) also view distress as an outgrowth of behavioral disorganization.

Challenges and traps differ psychologically as well as behaviorally. Traps are *hopelessly* challenging, and produce helplessness. One may feel betrayed and misled, either by a destructively organized world or by one's own desires (after all, one walked into the trap 'voluntarily' and is therefore partly responsible). Someone or something must be "blamed" for a trap; it is neither right nor fair. Unlike justifiable challenges, traps are apt to evoke feelings of anger, resentment, and indignation.

This century has seen a sharp rise in coronary heart disease rates. The growth in industrial pressures, and in the incidence of Type A behavior as a response to those pressures, may have contributed to the increase (Rosenman & Chesney, 1982). Trap theory suggests another possibility: Type A behavior has become more *maladaptive* (entrapped, self-defeating, counterproductive), rather than more common, because of a major shift in the socioeconomic reward system in this century. In this view, we do not live in an "Age of Type A Behavior," which, if anything, was the Victorian Age, but in an "Age of Type B Behavior" requiring greater taming of extreme aggression and rugged individualism. It is precisely the poor fit of Type A behavior to the current reward system that makes it behaviorally maladaptive and physiologically damaging.

Contradiction and ambiguity are persistent features of human behavior; however, when the level of irony and perplexity surpasses some critical level of tolerance, behavior may become so fragmented and disintegrated as to become biologically destructive.

REFERENCES

Antonovsky, A. (1979). *Health, stress, and coping*. San Francisco: Jossey-Bass.

Brinton, C. (1963). *Ideas and men*. Englewood Cliffs, NJ: Prentice-Hall.

Burke, J. (1985). *The day the universe changed*. Boston: Little, Brown, and Co.

Corwin, N. (1986). *Trivializing America*. Secaucus, NJ: Lyle Stuart,Inc.

Cross, J.G. & Guyer, M.J. (1980). *Social traps*. Ann Arbor: The University of Michigan Press.

Frankl, V. (1984). *Man's search for meaning*. New York: Simon & Schuster.

Friedman, M. & Freidman, R. (1980). *Free to choose*. New York: Harcourt Brace Javanovich.

Friedman, M. & Rosenman, R.H. (1974). *Type A behavior and your heart*. New York: Alfred A. Knopf.

Friedman, M. & Ulmer, D. (1984). *Treating type A behavior—and your hart*. New York: Alfred A. Knopf.

Fromm, E. (1955). *The sane society*. New York: Fawcett World Library.

Fromm, E. (1976). *To have or to be?* New York: Bantam Books.

Galbraith, J.K. (1976). *The affluent society*. Boston: Houghton Mifflin.

Galbraith, J.K. (1987). *Economics in perspective*. Boston: Houghton Mifflin.

Gotshalk, D.W. (1958). *The promise of modern life*. Yellow Springs, OH: The Antioch Press.

Hofstadter, R. (1955). *Social Darwinism in American thought*. Boston: Beacon Press.

Huber, R.M. (1987). *The American idea of success*. New York: McGraw-Hill.

Krystal, H. (1988). *Integration and self-healing*. Hillsdale, NJ: The Analytic Press, Inc.

Ortega y Gasset, J. (1961). *The modern theme*. New York: Harper & Row.

Postman, N. (1985). *Amusing ourselves to death*. New York: Viking.

Rosenman, R.H. & Chesney, M.A. (1982). Stress, type A behavior, and coronary disease. In L. Goldberger & S. Brenznitz, *Handbook of stress*. New York: MacMillan.

Riesman, D. (1961). *The lonely crowd*. New Haven, CT: Yale University Press.

Rousseau, J.J. (1964). *Jean Jacques Rousseau, His education theories selected from Emile, Julie and other writings*. Edited by R.L. Archer. Woodbury, NY: Barron's Educational Series.

Strube, M.J. (1987). A self-appraisal model of the type A behavior pattern. *Perspectives in personality*, Vol. 2, 201-250. Greenwich, CT: JAI Press, Inc.

Wyllie, I.J. (1954). *The self-made man in America*. New Brunswick, NJ: Rutgers University Press.

Type A Behavior, Self-Appraisals, and Goal Setting: A Framework For Future Research

James S. Phillips
Sara M. Freedman
John M. Ivancevich
Michael T. Matteson
Department of Management, University of Houston
Houston, TX 77004

The present paper presents a research framework and corresponding propositions describing the reactions of Type As and Bs to externally-mediated goal setting. The framework is based on recent conceptualizations of the goal commitment process and on Strube's (1987) self-appraisal model of Type A behavior. At its core is a belief that goal commitment is primarily a function of the degree to which participants perceive that goal attainment is instrumental for satisfying salient task-related needs. The self-appraisal model predicts, however, that Type As and Bs have different degrees of the need to assess their task-related competencies. Thus, when an organizationally-sponsored goal setting program is designed in ways that allow Type As to fulfill this need, they should be more committed to the goals and, therefore, also perform better than Type Bs.

Although a majority of the early research on the coronary-prone behavior pattern (Friedman & Rosenman, 1974) was designed to examine its relationship with coronary artery disease, research has demonstrated that the constellation of tendencies typically assessed by questionnaires that purport to measure Type A behavior are also important social psychological influences in many other contexts. Much of the current interest in the cognitive/perceptual bases of Type A behavior has, in fact, been generated independently of its apparent health-related consequences, and, has stemmed more from these other aspects of behavior.

TYPE A BEHAVIOR IN ORGANIZATIONAL SETTINGS

One domain in which Type A behavior continues to elicit not only an interest in health-related issues but also in many of these other facets of

© 1990 Select Press

behavior is in organizational settings. By its very nature, work tends to accentuate many of the behavioral tendencies typically associated with the Type A behavior pattern including competitiveness, an achievement orientation, and, a chronic sense of time. Thus, work settings logically should serve as a highly relevant context in which to study the existence of cognitive/perceptual differences between Type As and Bs.

Goal Setting

In organizational settings, one is pressed to find a single model of performance that has received more extensive empirical examination and support than goal setting (Locke, 1968). Both narrative and meta-analytic reviews have found that specific, difficult goals lead to higher levels of task performance than either "do your best" or no goal conditions (Locke, Shaw, Saari, & Latham, 1981; Mento, Steele, & Karren, 1987; Tubbs, 1986). The strength of effect that goals have on performance does, however, vary considerably across studies (Jackson & Zedeck, 1982). Substantial proportions of variance in task participants' affective responses to externally-mediated goal setting also remain unexplained; research has found that goal setting can have detrimental effects on intrinsic motivation and satisfaction for otherwise interesting tasks (Amabile, DeJong, & Lepper, 1976; Jackson & Zedeck, 1982; Mossholder, 1980; Reader & Dollinger, 1982; Shalley & Oldham, 1985). Moreover, satisfaction varies with numerous salient characteristics of the goal setting context (Jackson & Zedeck, 1982).

The variability of performance effects and the occasional incidence of negative affective task reactions have each served as an impetus for many contemporary studies to explore individual differences that might exist in participants' cognitive interpretations of goal setting (e.g., Bandura, 1982; Campion & Lord, 1982; Freedman & Phillips, in press; Hollenbeck & Williams, 1987; Locke, Frederick, Lee, & Bobko, 1984) Although these efforts differ in many important ways, there has been at least one integrative theme to emerge from them. Research in this vein now suggests that individual differences related to the perceived instrumentality of an externally-mediated goal and its attainment may be an important determinant of participants' goal commitment and subsequent reactions to its presence (Hollenbeck & Klein, 1987; Hollenbeck & Williams, 1987; Locke, Latham, & Erez, 1988; Phillips & Freedman, 1988; Freedman & Phillips, in press). In other words, it seems that people are more likely to be committed to a goal if the goal is seen as a direct or indirect mechanism for attaining desired intrinsic or extrinsic rewards.

An important implication of this view of goal commitment is that the effectiveness of goal setting will be, in large part, determined by task participants' cognitive assessments of the most salient aspects of the goals vis-a-vis their instrumentality for attaining desired outcomes. These perceptions should be determined, in turn, by participants' needs, values, abilities, and task-related attitudes. Thus, any systematic differences between participants on the personal characteristics that affect perceptions of goal instrumentality should be reflected in differing levels of goal commitment and performance.

Type A Behavior and Goal Setting

There undoubtedly are many individual differences that might influence task participants' goal- related instrumentality perceptions. Of these possibilities, however, there are several compelling reasons to believe that Type A behavior may be an especially important one. Foremost is a remarkable similarity between existing cognitive models of Type A behavior and the conceptual foundations of goal setting as it has been applied in organizational settings. That is, many of the most salient parameters of goal setting should be perceived in systematically different ways by Type As and Bs. To the extent that goal commitment and performance are, in fact, determined by such perceptions, we would also expect to find predictable differences between Type As' and Bs' reactions to externally-mediated goals.

The purpose of the present paper is, therefore, to propose a framework and corresponding propositions that may help guide future research interested in understanding any differences that may exist in the reactions of Type As and Bs to the presence of goals. We feel that such a framework might provide many valuable insights for future studies of Type A behavior in organizations as well as for more general explorations of goal commitment and its relationship to performance and satisfaction.

Although we clearly are not in a position to resolve the construct validity issues that continue to surround questionnaire indices of Type A behavior (see for example, Strube & Boland, 1986), such measures do seem to tap characteristics relevant to the goal setting domain. Thus, for purposes of the present paper, we will view Type A behavior in a fashion similar to many other researchers concerned with its social-psychological consequences. More specifically, we will assume that Type A behavior is a multidimensional construct comprised of many propensities including, but not necessarily limited to, an achievement orientation, a strong competitive desire, and a chronic sense of time urgency.

TYPE A BEHAVIOR AND GOAL SETTING: A RESEARCH FRAMEWORK

Figure 1 graphically depicts our proposed framework for guiding research on Type A behavior and goal setting. It represents a functional

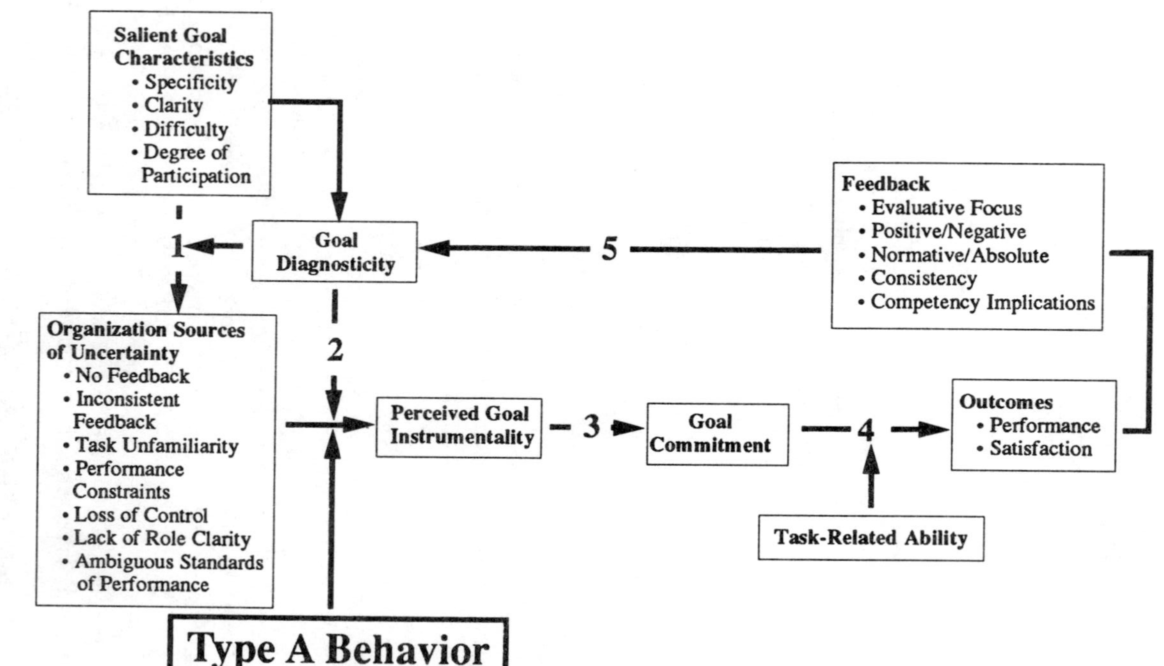

FIGURE 1 Type A Behavior and Goal Setting: A Research Framework

integration of Strube's (1987) self-appraisal model of Type A behavior, goal theory, and recent developments in goal commitment research.

There are currently several cognitively-based models of Type A behavior from which we could have begun the development of this framework, but, we chose to concentrate on the basic premises of the self-appraisal perspective for several reasons. First, rather than being viewed as a new alternative to explaining Type A behavior, the self-appraisal model actually serves as a mechanism for integrating a variety of the major strengths of prior perspectives (Strube, Boland, Manfredo, & Al-Falaij, 1987). Its potential value for understanding Type As' and Bs' reactions to certain aspects of goal setting has also been demonstrated (Freedman & Phillips, 1988). Finally, it provides a seemingly parsimonious explanation for the different instrumentalities that goals might possess for Type As and Bs.

An examination of the framework that we have proposed indicates that it is predicated on two core assumptions, one concerning the need for self-appraisal as an antecedent of Type A behavior and the other on the potential of goal setting to serve as an ability uncertainty reduction mechanism. While there are hopefully a great number of research questions that can be generated from this framework, it is obviously important to first examine its most central propositions. For this reason, we will focus on these two core assumptions as a way of beginning to assess the framework's heuristic value. We do, however, also acknowledge that the research propositions that we have outlined in this paper represent a necessarily limited sample. We would encourage the reader to consider other possibilities as well.

Type A Behavior and the Need for Self-Appraisal

Strube (1987) has recently argued that much of the behavior of Type As can be explained by their need for acquiring information relevant to task-related competency assessments. According to his self-appraisal model, Type As have a greater need than Type Bs for information that either confirms or disconfirms their perceived task-related abilities. Thus, in the face of uncertainty about an important ability, Type As will engage in adaptive behavior designed to provide them with additional diagnostic information. This need is often manifested as the hard-driving competitiveness and sense of time urgency associated with Type As. Strube also suggests, however, that Type As do not have a chronically higher need than Type Bs to acquire accurate information about task-related competencies (Strube et al., 1987). Rather, the need for self-appraisal is elicited by environmental conditions that contribute to uncertainty. This tendency should, therefore, be acute when failure is a distinct possibility as it is in an achievement context such as those exemplified by most work settings.

Studies now suggest that Type As do, in fact, have this greater need than Type Bs to reduce any uncertainty that may exist about salient task-related abilities. Consistent with the self-appraisal model, Strube and Boland (1986) found that Type As persisted longer at a difficult anagram task than Type Bs when the task was low in informational value (causing uncertainty). Thus, their persistence was presumably due to continued efforts to reduce this uncertainty.

Strube et al. (1987) arrived at a similar conclusion. In this latter study, Type As sought and used social comparison information to reduce uncertainty about a salient ability to a significantly greater degree than Type Bs.

A direct extension of Strube's work to organizational settings leads to the first underlying assumption of our framework. Stated as a research proposition, an extrapolation of the self-appraisal hypothesis to organizational settings suggests that:

Proposition 1: Organizational sources of ability uncertainty in a goal setting context will be more salient to Type As than to Type Bs.

As can be seen in the proposed framework, we are suggesting that there are a variety of organizational conditions that may lead to perceptions of ability uncertainty. Many of these are exact replicates of factors already identified by Strube (1987). Others are more specific applications of his conceptualization. Most important for the present paper is the premise that many characteristics of externally-mediated goals can influence ability uncertainty both directly and indirectly through these other organizational sources (linkage #1 in Figure 1). Interestingly, this aspect of our framework also suggests that salient characteristics of the goal setting process can exacerbate or ameliorate perceptions of uncertainty depending on the manner in which they are interpreted by task participants.

Under conditions of uncertainty, the single most important determinant of Type As' cognitive interpretations of these salient goal setting characteristics should be their utility for obtaining highly diagnostic information about important abilities. We have called this property of goal setting "goal diagnosticity". Since it refers to the capability of a goal to provide task participants with information about their competencies, goal diagnosticity is not simply a characteristic of the goal itself. While it is, in part, a property of the goal, it is also dependent on the relationship of the goal to the feedback process in our framework. Thus, goal diagnosticity can best be described as the total potential for acquiring information about a salient ability as a function of one's interactions with the goal setting process.

Goal Diagnosticity, Feedback, and the Reduction of Ability Uncertainty

The concept of goal diagnosticity forms the basis for our second basic proposition. It is the mechanism through which goal setting either conveys or fails to convey information relevant to the reduction of ability uncertainty. Simply stated, goal setting that is high in diagnosticity allows Type As to acquire information relevant to important task-related abilities. Conversely, goal setting that is low in diagnosticity provides little useful information about such abilities.

Although it has not typically been characterized as an issue of goal diagnosticity, existing research does suggest that goals and goal striving can serve as salient standards of performance against which task participants compare their progress, thereby providing them with meaningful information about task-related abilities. Several authors have addressed this informational role of goal setting from a control theory (Powers, 1973) perspective. Campion and Lord (1982) suggested that a performance goal serves as the "thermostatic" device against which progress can be monitored. Whenever performance falls out of tolerance, then corrective action can be taken. Thus, to the extent that goals are accepted, they provide a highly salient feedback mechanism for regulating behavior. In other words, detectable discrepancies between current levels of performance and a priori goal setting provides the feedback necessary for participants to adjust their future behavior.

Hollenbeck and Williams (1987) extended the work of Campion and Lord (1982) by testing the explanatory value of two individual differences in this regulation cycle. They hypothesized and found that goal level would be a function of perceived goal importance and degree of self-focus. The logic of their hypotheses was rather straightforward. Important goals should have attracted and maintained participants' attention and effort more easily than unimportant ones. In addition, individuals high in self-focus should have been more attuned to the regulatory value of goals since they were more interested in monitoring their own behavior than were individuals low in self-focus.

Although Hollenbeck and Williams (1987) were not concerned with the relationship between Type A behavior and goal setting, Type As do seem to be more self-focused than Type Bs (Scherwitz, Berton, & Leventhal, 1978), and, this self-focus is significantly correlated with physiological symptoms of stress (Scherwitz et al., 1983). We are not suggesting that goal setting is an organizational correlate of coronary artery disease, but, the consistency of results across these different studies is nonetheless interesting. At very least, they suggest that our assertion that Type As will view goals primarily as an ability uncertainty reduction mechanism may be correct.

The most direct evidence that goals can vary on their capacity to convey meaningful ability-related information comes from two studies that used cognitive evaluation theory (Deci, 1975; Deci & Ryan, 1980; 1987) as the conceptual basis for exploring the effects of goals on affective task reactions. Manderlink and Harackiewicz (1984) noted that proximal goal setting led to greater reductions in intrinsic motivation than more distal goals. According to the authors, this tendency was related to the relative salience of the competency information and controlling aspects of the goals. More specifically, they argued that during task performance, proximal goals were actually more informative than distal goals. But, because of their implications for more frequent evaluations of performance, the controlling aspect of proximal goals was also greater. Hence, proximal goals were more likely than distal goals to be associated with an overjustification effect.

Using a similar conceptual argument but with a more direct manipulation of competency information, Phillips and Freedman (1988) found that goals which did convey salient competency information resulted in higher task satisfaction than goals which conveyed little information. In terms of our framework, these data collectively suggest the second core research proposition that is represented by linkage #2 in Figure 1.

Proposition 2: Under conditions of uncertainty, goals that convey information about task-related competencies (high goal diagnosticity) will have more perceived instrumentality for Type As than for Type Bs.

Although there is considerable indirect evidence related to the potential informational value of goal setting, we know of only one study that presents data directly relevant to the study of Type A behavior. A laboratory study by Freedman and Phillips (in press) indicated that Type As did perceive significantly greater instrumentality than Type Bs in an externally-mediated goal that provided meaningful social comparison performance information. Unfortunately, their study did not include a direct manipulation of ability uncertainty. Thus, their results are compelling, but, they are also somewhat inconclusive.

The causal flow of our framework indicates that the differences in perceptions of goal utility for Type As and Bs posited by proposition 2 should be systematically related to different levels of goal commitment (linkage #3) and subsequent performance (linkage #4). Moreover, it has been shown that one of the most likely outcomes of uncertainty for Type As is enhanced persistence (a behavioral manifestation of commitment) at a task as they attempt to reduce this uncertainty (Strube, 1987). Thus, a more specific research question that stems directly from our second core proposition is:

Proposition 2a: Type As will show greater goal commitment and subsequent performance than Type Bs under conditions of uncertainty.

The hypothesized existence of such an effect must, however, be further tempered. Strube (1988) has suggested that there is an important distinction between persistence and effort for understanding Type A behavior. Type As are, indeed, expected to persist at a task longer than Type Bs but only when the task is relatively nondiagnostic. The reason is simple—they must persist in the face of a nondiagnostic task in order to acquire enough information for it to meaningfully reduce their uncertainty.

On highly diagnostic tasks, Strube would predict greater initial effort but actually less persistence for Type As than Bs. Once again, the logic is straightforward—where task performance is highly diagnostic, Type As will be willing to exert considerable effort to acquire information about their abilities. But, once having acquired the information, there will be no further utility for them in persisting at the task.

An extrapolation of these notions to a goal setting context should be equally straightforward:

Proposition 2b: Type As will exhibit significantly greater persistence than Type Bs in the presence of relatively nondiagnostic goals. In the presence of highly diagnostic goals, Type As will exert significantly greater initial effort (but not necessarily greater persistence) than Type Bs.

GOAL DIAGNOSTICITY AND THE REDUCTION OF ABILITY UNCERTAINTY: TWO ILLUSTRATIVE CASES

Research has noted that Type As have a significantly greater need than Type Bs to maintain a sense of personal control (Dembroski, MacDougall, & Musante, 1984). Strube (1987) has, in fact, suggested that this need actually stems from the desire to reduce ability uncertainty. That is, one must be capable of controlling his/her environment in order to be able to acquire salient, accurate information about one's task-related competencies. He, therefore, further suggests that a loss of personal control is potentially an extremely important source of ability uncertainty to Type As. Thus, the concept of personal control as a source of ability uncertainty should serve as an illustrative example of how these kinds of organizational sources of uncertainty, goal diagnosticity, and Type A behavior might interface in our framework.

Participation in Goal Setting and Personal Control

In an organizational setting, a loss of personal control might result from any number of conditions such as a lack of job enrichment (Hackman

& Oldham, 1976) or the presence of situational constraints on performance (Peters & O'Connor, 1980). Our framework suggests that each of these is, therefore, a possible influence on Type As' and Bs' reactions in a goal setting context.

Our research framework further suggests that there are many characteristics that can affect the diagnosticity inherent in a particular goal setting program. Since for the moment we are focusing on a loss of personal control as a source of ability uncertainty, one frequently discussed goal characteristic pertinent to diagnosticity in this case should be participation in the goal setting process. Specifically, we would offer the following as the kind of research proposition that can be generated from our framework:

Proposition 2c: In the presence of ability uncertainty, increased participation in goal setting should have a significantly greater effect on the goal commitment and performance of Type As than Type Bs.

One mechanism for this proposed effect that is consistent with the self-appraisal perspective was suggested by Schnake, Bushardt, and Spottswood (1984) who found that participation in the goal setting process was positively related to perceived goal clarity. Consistent with these findings, Dean, Phillips, and Ivancevich (1988) found that participants reported more uncertainty about the meaning of goals when they had been assigned rather than participatively set. Thus, it appeared that ability uncertainty (presumably through an increase in personal control) was being reduced more under conditions of participation in goal setting than it was under an assigned goal.

To follow the logic of this aspect of our framework and, to help resolve some predictable confusion about this particular proposition, it is important to note that goal clarity and goal diagnosticity are not synonymous. Most certainly, clear, specific goals should lead to greater performance increments than ambiguous goals (Locke et al., 1981). Moreover, assigned goals should frequently be more clear than participatively set goals. We are suggesting, however, that the diagnostic value of a goal can vary even within levels of clarity. Thus, an extremely clear assigned goal can still have little diagnostic value. Likewise, a relatively ambiguous participatively set goal might be highly informative.

Interestingly, Dean, et al. (1988) addressed the diagnostic value of goals associated with participation in their study. They did find that Type As performed better under an assigned goal than under a participatively set one despite the fact that their reports of uncertainty about the meaning of the goal had been higher in the assigned condition. Thus, the data were consistent with a self-appraisal interpretation inasmuch as it appeared that the Type As under the assigned goal were struggling to reduce uncertainty through increased efforts to attain their goal. In contrast, the personal control that should have come with participation was apparently reducing uncertainty, thereby eliminating the need for Type As to acquire additional diagnostic information. Since their study was not, however, longitudinal, this causal interpretation about the effects of uncertainty and participation should be viewed with appropriate caution.

Goal Difficulty and Goal Diagnosticity

Goal difficulty is another aspect of goals that has been the subject of considerable research in "traditional" studies of the effectiveness of goal setting. Within our framework, it is another example of a goal characteristic that serves as a direct source of ability uncertainty for organizational members. One of the most well established principles derived from goal setting research is that difficult goals do lead to higher performance than easy goals (Locke et al., 1981). According to goal theory, it must therefore be axiomatic that participants are willing to commit to difficult goals.

The self-appraisal model of Type A behavior and our research framework suggest, however, that Type As should be more readily willing to strive for a difficult goal than Type Bs. The primary utility that goals can possess for Type As ought to be the reduction of ability uncertainty, and, difficult goals should have a greater capability than easy goals of serving as an uncertainty reduction mechanism. Achieving a relatively difficult goal should frequently provide more diagnostic information about competencies than achieving a relatively simple goal. When difficult goals are highly diagnostic, then:

Proposition 2d: Under conditions of ability uncertainty there will be a significantly stronger positive relationship between goal difficulty and goal commitment for Type As than for Type Bs.

While this proposition ought to generally be true in organizational settings, Strube, Lott, Hy, Oxenberg, and Deichmann (1986) warn against erroneously equating task difficulty with task diagnosticity. Such an admonition is warranted for goals as well. That is, difficult goals should generally have a greater diagnostic value for goal setting participants, but, they need not always be more informative than an easier goal.

While Type As' desire to avoid failure might suggest that they would conversely seek to avoid a difficult goal, Strube et al's (1986) results suggested that self-assessment motives were a more important determinant of task choice than self-enhancement motives. Thus, when a difficult goal is highly diagnostic, we would expect Type As to be willing to incur the risk of failure in order to acquire accurate information about task-related abilities. In the presence, however, of nondiagnostic but difficult goals, it is conceivable that Type As would be significantly less willing to commit their efforts to their attainment. For our framework, the implication is clear. While difficult goals do lead to higher levels of performance (Locke et al., 1981; Tubbs, 1986), future research directed at an understanding of commitment and performance requires a more explicit consideration of the relative diagnosticity of the goals in addition to their difficulty.

Feedback, External Evaluations, and Goal Diagnosticity

It should be obvious that a critical feature of the proposed research model is the feedback/corrective loop that exists. For goal setting to be maximally effective, participants need information about their goal progress and about ways to correct performance deficiencies. Moreover, as Type As gather information relevant to their task-related competencies, the degree of uncertainty inherent in the situation should decrease. That is, as is represented by linkage #5 in Figure 1, feedback directly affects goal diagnosticity. Thus, there is a naturally occurring dynamic component to our framework.

The existence of linkage #5 has several implications for the longitudinal effects of goal setting. Noteworthy among these is the frequent lament that goal setting effects seem to "wear off" over time (e.g., Ivancevich, 1977). Our framework suggests that some of this dissipation may be related to a change in the diagnostic value of the goal setting for Type As. Over time and as proficiency increases, Type As might acquire less and less meaningful additional information about their task-related abilities if they continually receive positive feedback about their performance. In conjunction with this feedback, the information value of the goal setting decreases, and, their future commitment and performance should also decrease.

As is further suggested by Figure 1, there are a variety of other characteristics associated with this feedback loop that might affect the way that Type As react to goal setting. For example, research has shown that Type As have a greater desire to acquire social comparison information about performance and competencies (Gastorf, Suls, & Sanders, 1980). In contrast, Type Bs have even demonstrated an apparent aversion to this kind of information in the Freedman and Phillips (in press) study of goal setting and Type A behavior. As a result, one might expect goals that provide social comparison feedback to be maximally diagnostic to Type As.

Another potentially important characteristic of the feedback loop in goal setting contexts was suggested by Harackiewicz and her colleagues. Specifically, their research indicates that implied external evaluations can affect intrinsic motivation independently from feedback (Harackiewicz, Manderlink, & Sansone, in press). Harackiewicz, Abrahams, and Wageman (1987) further suggest that intrinsic motivation will be influenced by the focus of the evaluative contingencies inherent in the task setting. That is, an evaluative contingency refers to the external communications received by task participants about upcoming performance evaluations, and, these contingencies can emphasize either a normative standard (performance vis-a-vis other performers) or the mastery of a task. While either contingency can convey meaningful competency information, they do differ on how "excellence" has been defined.

According to Harackiewicz et al. (1987), the differences between their definitions of excellence leads to the contingencies having predictable effects on intrinsic motivation. Contingencies that focus on normative performance may distract participants from the task or they may be anxiety provoking. Intrinsic motivation is, therefore, expected to decrease since the participants' focus of attention is no longer on the competency implications of task performance. In contrast, if an external evaluation emphasizes task mastery, then participants' focus can still be on the competency implications of performance, thereby maintaining intrinsic interest as predicted by cognitive evaluation theory (Deci & Ryan, 1987).

Harackiewicz et al. (1987) also posited and found evidence that task participants differ in terms of "competence valuation" which refers to the importance that someone attaches to performing well. This disposition, in turn, mediates the relationship between intrinsic motivation and evaluative contingencies. Most interesting for our framework is the apparent similarity of competence valuation and Type As' need for accurate appraisal of their abilities. Logically, Type As should have significantly higher competence valuation (to use Harackiewicz et al.'s term) since they have a greater stake than Type Bs in understanding the meaning of their performance.

Interestingly, Strube et al. (1987) and Freedman and Phillips (in press) each employed social comparison information to operationalize the opportunity for competency assessments in their studies of the self-appraisal model. In both cases, Type As reacted positively and Type Bs reacted negatively to the opportunity. The negative reaction of the Type Bs could have been, however, in response to the obvious implication of an external evaluation focused on normative standards rather than to competency verifications per se. They may simply dislike being evaluated more than Type As.

Type As, on the other hand, should welcome this normatively anchored information. That is, their heightened need for assessing abilities coupled with their desire for social comparison information (Gastorf et al., 1980) should increase the likelihood that Type As will more readily accept a goal than Type Bs under an evaluative contingency that emphasizes normative standards of excellence. Moreover, in applied settings, it is not at all uncommon for goal setting to be intentionally or unintentionally tied to social comparison information. For example, the results of merit pay and other incentive systems are often public knowledge in organizations. Therefore, when such systems are linked with goal setting programs, information about the normative difficulty of goals is also communicated. If participants have this knowledge, then Type As should willingly strive to achieve such goals. Thus, an application to our framework of the conclusions reached by Harackiewicz and her co-workers tempered by an expected difference between Type As and Bs in competence valuation suggests the following:

Proposition 2e: Type As will be more committed to and satisfied with goal setting than Type Bs when existing evaluative contingencies afford them the social comparison information that they desire. In contrast, since the goal commitment of Type Bs might increase when evaluative contingencies emphasize task mastery rather than normative standards of excellence, there may be less of a difference between the goal commitment of Type As and Bs under this latter contingency.

CONCLUSIONS AND RECOMMENDATIONS

Although the issue of the construct validity of questionnaire measures of Type A behavior is far from resolved, research demonstrating the importance of the constellation of behavior tapped by such measures is rapidly accumulating. These behaviors now seem to be important influences on many aspects of behavior relevant to social-psychological and organizational researchers. Thus, we endorse a continued application of them to appropriate research questions and settings.

Goal setting is a motivational technique that promises to be used in organizations for years to come. Its potential for improving productivity is rarely questioned. Moreover, organizations are acutely aware of the need to accommodate the important differences that apparently exist between Type A and B individuals. The model that we have presented in this paper is, therefore, an example of one of those applications that we feel can be highly beneficial.

If research can successfully demonstrate the utility of the self-appraisal model in a goal setting context, knowledge in both of these relevant domains could be enhanced. Verification of the self-appraisal hypothesis as it has been embedded in our research framework would be a contribution to the literature concerned with the social/psychological implications of Type A behavior. And, goal setting researchers should obviously also find such demonstrations to be interesting since they might help to resolve the issue of how to optimally use externally-mediated goals as a motivational technique.

Although it is by no means the only perspective capable of explaining the reactions of Type As and Bs to organizationally sponsored goal setting, our framework appears to be a reasonable conceptual beginning for accomplishing this worthwhile purpose. We would, therefore, encourage researchers interested in either Type A behavior or goal setting to develop methodologically appropriate tests of the research questions that we have raised. While our list is by no means exhaustive, it offers direction and guidance for empirically determining whether the need for self-appraisals and the diagnosticity of goals provide parsimonious explanations for task-related reactions of both Type A and Type B participants to goal setting in an organizational context.

Finally, we think that it is important for researchers who may become interested in our framework to begin devoting more attention to the individual dimensions typically presumed to comprise the Type A behavior pattern. Taylor, Ostrow, and Renard (1988) found that across questionnaire indices of Type A behavior different dimensions of the pattern are represented, and, more important that these dimensions do correlate differentially with various outcome measures. Moreover, recent physiological studies indicate that the negative emotions of anger and hostility associated with Type A behavior may be the most important determinants of coronary artery disease (Booth-Kewley & Friedman, 1987).

It is quite possible, therefore, that certain components of the pattern are more important determinants of Type As' reactions in a goal setting context than other components. It is reasonable to expect the achievement striving and competitive aspects of Type As to be more strongly related to their perceptions of goals than the propensity for hostility. Thus, as did Taylor et al. (1988), we would encourage researchers to investigate relationships between goal setting and Type A behavior at both the holistic and at the dimensional levels to gain more complete insights into our framework.

REFERENCES

Amabile, T. M., DeJong, W., & Lepper, M. R. (1976). Effects of externally imposed deadlines on subsequent intrinsic motivation. *Journal of Personality and Social Psychology, 34*, 92-98.

Bandura, A. (1982). Self-efficacy mechanism in human agency. *American Psychologist, 37*, 122-147.

Booth-Kewley, S., & Friedman, H. S. (1987). Psychological predictors of heart disease: A quantitative review. *Psychological Bulletin, 101*, 343-362.

Campion, M. A., & Lord, R. G. (1982). A control systems conceptualization of the goal-setting and changing process. *Organizational Behavior and Human Performance, 30*, 265-287.

Dean, D. L., Phillips, J. S., & Ivancevich, J. M. (1988). *Type A behavior and goal setting: A field test of the self-appraisal hypothesis.* Paper presented at the 48th annual meetings of the National Academy of Management, Anaheim, August.

Deci, E. L. (1975). Notes on the theory and metatheory of intrinsic motivation. *Organizational Behavior and Human Performance, 15*, 130-145.

Deci, E. L., & Ryan, R. M. (1980). The empirical exploration of intrinsic motivational processes. In L. Berkowitz (Ed.), *Advances in Experimental Social Psychology*, (Vol. 13, pp. 39-80). New York: Academic Press.

Deci, E. L., & Ryan, R. M. (1987). The support of autonomy and the control of behavior. *Journal of Personality and Social Psychology, 53*, 1024-1037.

Dembroski, T. M., MacDougall, J. M., & Musante, L. (1984). Desirability of control versus locus of control: Relationship to paralinguistics in the Type A interview. *Health Psychology, 3*, 15-26.

Erez, M., & Arad, R. (1986). Participative goal setting: Social, motivational and cognitive factors. *Journal of Applied Psychology, 71*, 591-597.

Freedman, S. M., & Phillips, J. S. (in press). Goal utility, task satisfaction, and the self-appraisal hypothesis of Type A behaviorr. *Journal of Personality and Social Psychology.*

Freedman, S. M., & Phillips, J. S. (1985). The effects of situational performance constraints on intrinsic motivation and satisfaction: The role of perceived competence and self-determination. *Organizational Behavior and Human Decision Processes, 35*, 397-416.

Friedman, M., & Rosenman, R. H. (1974). *Type A behavior and your heart.* New York: Knopf.

Gastorf, J. W., Suls, J., & Sanders, G. S. (1980). Type A coronary-prone behavior pattern and social facilitation. *Journal of Personality and Social Psychology, 38*, 773-780.

Hackman, J. R., & Oldham, G. R. (1976). Motivation through the design of work: Test of a theory. *Organizational Behavior and Human Performance, 16*, 250-279.

Harackiewicz, J. M., Abrahams, S., & Wageman, R. (1987). Performance evaluation and intrinsic motivation: The effects of evaluative focus, rewards, and achievement orientation. *Journal of Personality and Social Psychology, 53*, 1015-1023.

Harackiewicz, J. M., Manderlink, G., & Sansone, C. (in press).Competence processes and achievement orientation: Implications for intrinsic motivation. In A. Boggiano & T. S. Pittman (Eds.), *Motivation and achievement: A social-developmental analysis.* New York: Cambridge University Press.

Hollenbeck, J. R., & Klein, H. J. (1987). Goal commitment and the goal-setting process: Problems, prospects, and proposals for future research. *Journal of Applied Psychology, 72,* 212-220.

Hollenbeck, J. R., & Williams, C. R. (1987). Goal importance, self-focus, and the goal-setting process. *Journal of Applied Psychology, 72,* 204-211.

Ivancevich, J. M. (1977). Different goal setting treatments and their effects on performance and job satisfaction. *Academy of Management Journal, 20,* 406-419.

Jackson, S. E., & Zedeck, S. (1982). Explaining performance variability: Contributions of goal setting, task characteristics, and evaluative contexts. *Journal of Applied Psychology, 67,* 759-768.

Locke, E. A. (1968). Toward a theory of task motivation and incentives. *Organizational Behavior and Human Performance, 3,* 157-189.

Locke, E. A., Frederick, E., Lee, C., & Bobko, P. (1984). Effect of self-efficacy, goals, and task strategies on task performance. *Journal of Applied Psychology, 69,* 241-251.

Locke, E. A., Latham, G. P., & Erez, M. (1988). The determinants of goal commitment. *Academy of Management Review, 13,* 23-39.

Locke, E. A., Shaw, K. N., Saari, L. M., & Latham, G. P. (1981). Goal setting and task performance: 1969-1980. *Psychological Bulletin, 90,* 125-152.

Manderlink, G., & Harackiewicz, J. M. (1984). Proximal versus distal goal setting and intrinsic motivation. *Journal of Personality and Social Psychology, 47,* 918-928.

Mento, A. J., Steele, R. P., & Karren, R. J. (1987). A meta-analytic study of the effects of goal setting on task performance: 1966-1984. *Organizational Behavior and Human Decision Processes, 39,* 52-83.

Mossholder, K. W. (1980). Effects of externally mediated goal setting on intrinsic motivation: A laboratory experiment. *Journal of Applied Psychology, 65,* 202-210.

Peters, L. H., & O'Connor, E. J. (1980). Situational constraints and work outcomes: The influences of a frequently overlooked construct. *Academy of Management Review, 5,* 391-398.

Phillips, J. S., & Freedman, S. M. (1988). The task-related competency and compliance aspects of goals: A clarification. *Organizational Behavior and Human Decision Processes, 41,* 34-49.

Powers, W. T. (1973). *Behavior: The control of perception.* Chicago: Aldine.

Reader, M. J., & Dollinger, S. J. (1982). Deadlines, self-perceptions, and intrinsic motivation. *Personality and Social Psychology Bulletin, 8,* 742-747.

Schnake, M. E., Bushardt, S. C., & Spottswood, C. (1984). Internal work motivation and intrinsic job satisfaction: The effects of goal clarity, goal difficulty, participation in goal setting, and task complexity. *Group and Organization Studies, 9,* 201-219.

Scherwitz, L., Berton, K., & Leventhal H. (1978). Type A behavior, self-involvement, and cardiovascular response. *Psychosomatic Medicine, 40,* 593-609.

Scherwitz, L., McKelvain, R., Laman, C., Patterson, J., Dutton, L., Yusim, S., Lester, J., Kraft, I., Rochelle, D., & Leachman, R. (1983). Type A behavior, self-involvement, and coronary atherosclerosis. *Psychosomatic Medicine, 45,* 47-57.

Shalley, C. E., & Oldham, G. R. (1985). The effects of goal difficulty and expected external evaluation on intrinsic motivation. *Academy of Management Journal, 28*, 628-640.

Spector, P. E. (1986). Perceived control by employees: A meta-analysis of studies concerning autonomy and participation at work. *Human Relations, 39*, 1005-1016.

Strube, M. J (1987). A self-appraisal model of the Type A behavior pattern. In R. Hogan & W. Jones (Eds.), *Perspectives in personality theory* (Vol. 2, pp. 201-250). Greenwich, CT.: JAI Press.

Strube, M. J (1988). *Motivational implications of the self-appraisal model of Type A behavior*. Paper presented at the 48th annual meeting of the National Academy of Management, Anaheim, August.

Strube, M. J, & Boland, S. M. (1986). Post performance attributions and task persistence among Type A and B individuals: A clarification. *Journal of Personality and Social Psychology, 50*, 413-420.

Strube, M. J, Boland, S. M., Manfredo, P. A., & Al-Falaij, A. (1987). Type A behavior pattern and the self-evaluation of abilities: Empirical tests of the self-appraisal model. *Journal of Personality and Social Psychology, 52*, 956-974.

Strube, M. J, Lott, C. L., Hy, L. X., Oxenberg, J., & Deichmann, A. K. (1986). Self-evaluation of abilities: Accurate self-assessment versus biased self-enhancement. *Journal of Personality and Social Psychology, 51*, 16-25.

Taylor, M. S., Ostrow, M., & Renard, M. (1988). *The dimensionality of Type A behavior: Its relationship to individual performance and health and group cohesion, process, and performance.* Paper presented at the 48th annual meeting of the National Academy of Management, Anaheim, August.

Tubbs, M. E. (1986). Goal setting: A meta-analytic examination of the empirical evidence. *Journal of Applied Psychology, 71*, 474-483.

Cynical Hostility as a Health Risk:
Current Status and Future Directions

Timothy W. Smith
Mary Katherine Pope
Department of Psychology, University of Utah
Salt Lake City, UT 84112

Recent research has indicated that high scores on the Cook and Medley Ho scale are associated with increased risk of cardiovascular and other diseases. The present paper reviews the evidence of an association between Ho scores and health outcomes, as well as additional research on the construct validity of the scale and its possible links to disease. The evidence suggests that the scale measures anger-proneness, resentment, and mistrust of others, or cynical hostility. Potential links to health include physiological responses to interpersonal conflict, high levels of interpersonal stress and low levels of social support, as well as a dynamic tendency to create conflict and undermine support. Avenues of future research are outlined.

The status of the Type A behavior pattern as a risk factor for coronary heart disease (CHD) is presently controversial. Nearly twenty years of largely confirmatory findings (Review Panel, 1981) have been followed by several notable failures to replicate the relationship between the Type A pattern and CHD (e.g., Case, Heller, Case, & Moss, 1985; Cohen & Reed, 1985; Ragland & Brand, 1988; Shekelle, Gale, & Norusis, 1985; Shekelle, Hulley, et al., 1985). A recent quantitative review of relevant prospective studies (Matthews, 1988) concluded that although Type A behavior is a significant risk factor for the initial development of CHD, this is not true when the Type pattern is assessed with the Jenkins Activity Survey (Jenkins, Rosenman, & Zyzanski, 1974) or in high risk populations. Thus, some of the inconsistencies in this literature are due to differences among Type A assessment devices and the populations studied.

Author's Notes: The authors would like to thank B. Kent Houston for his comments on a previous version of this paper. Address all correspondence to first author.

© 1990 Select Press

Another approach to this inconsistent evidence concerning Type A as a risk factor has been to examine separately the elements within the behavior pattern. Anger and hostility have long been suspected of contributing to the development of CHD (for a review, see Diamond, 1982), and hostility has been an element within the Type A pattern from the time of its initial description (Friedman & Rosenman, 1959). Hostility is presently the leading candidate in the search for the toxic element within the Type A pattern (Dembroski & Costa, 1987). Ratings of the potential for hostility from the Type A structured interview have been found to be related to the development of CHD (Matthews, Glass, Rosenman, & Bortner, 1977; Hecker, Frantschi, Chesney, Black, & Rosenman, 1985) and to the severity of coronary artery disease (CAD) in patients undergoing diagnostic coronary angiography (Dembroski, MacDougall, Williams, Haney, & Blumenthal, 1985; MacDougall, Dembroski, Dimsdale, & Hackett, 1985).

The apparent importance of hostility is also suggested by a series of studies using the Cook and Medley (1954) hostility (Ho) scale. This scale measures a stable characteristic somewhat distinct from the typical descriptions of the Type A pattern, and predicts general mortality as well as CHD incidence. The purpose of this paper is to review the literature on the Ho scale and health, and outline the directions for future research involving this dimension. Such research may extend the original interest in Type A behavior to a focus on a different personality construct and its relationship to general health vulnerability.

STUDIES LINKING HO AND HEALTH

In the initial study of the Ho scale and CHD, Williams et al. (1980) examined the relationship between scores on this 50-item scale from the Minnesota Multiphasic Personality Inventory (MMPI) and CAD in a sample of over 400 patients undergoing coronary angiography. Ho scores were significantly related to the presence of severe CAD, and this relationship was stronger than and independent of the also significant association between SI ratings of Type A and CAD. Two subsequent studies of angiography patients found no association between Ho scores and CAD severity in samples of less than 200 (Dembroski et al., 1985; Seeman, & Syme, 1987). And one recent study found no Ho score differences between CHD case versus control status (Friedman & Booth-Kewley, 1987).

Although obviously important in establishing the potential value of the Ho scale in predicting CHD, cross-sectional angiographic and case-control studies can be criticized on a variety of methodological grounds (cf., Matthews, 1988; Pickering, 1985). Therefore, prospective studies of

Ho and health outcomes are particularly valuable. To date, six such studies have been reported—three with positive results and three with negative findings. In a 25-year follow-up of 255 medical students who had completed the MMPI in medical school, Barefoot, Dahlstrom, and Williams (1983) found that Ho scores predicted the incidence of CHD and death from all causes. Shekelle, Gale, Ostfeld, and Paul (1983) also found that high Ho scores predicted the development of CHD and cardiac deaths at a 10-year follow-up of 1800 men. In the same study, Ho scores predicted total mortality at a 20-year follow-up. Finally, Barefoot, Dodge, Peterson, Dahlstrom, and Williams (1989) found that high Ho scores predicted death from all causes in a 30-year follow-up of 155 lawyers who had taken the MMPI in law school.

One of the three failures to replicate the relationship between Ho and health has been criticized on methodological grounds (Williams, 1987). McCranie, Watkins, Brandsma, and Sisson (1986) found no relationship between Ho scores and CHD or total mortality at a 25-year follow-up of 478 medical students who had taken the MMPI as part of their evaluation for admission to medical school. The low mean scores on the Ho scale and high scores on scales indicating socially desirable responding suggest that concern over the admission process may have produced artificially low and invalid Ho scores. Leon, Finn, Murray, and Bailey (1988) also reported no association between Ho scores and CHD in a 30-year follow-up of 280 men. Compared to samples in which a positive association was found, Ho scores in the Leon et al. (1988) study were relatively low and invariant. The lower, restricted range of Ho scores may have rendered the statistical test of the association less sensitive. Neither criticism applies to the failure to replicate the association between Ho scores and health outcomes in a 33-year follow-up study reported by Hearn, Murray, and Luepke (in press).

Although not using the Ho scale, Barefoot et al. (1987) have reported what might be considered a conceptual replication of the relationship between Ho scores and health. Scores on a scale measuring suspiciousness predicted total mortality over a 15-year follow-up in a sample of 500 older adults. The same measure of suspiciousness was found to predict the development of CHD in a 4.5 year follow-up of approximately 1900 middle-aged men (Ostfeld, Lebovits, Shekelle, & Paul, 1964). As will be discussed below, suspiciousness is quite typical of high scorers on the Ho scale. In spite of several inconsistencies, the available evidence suggests that high scores on the Ho scale may represent increased risk of CHD and other life-threatening illnesses.

CONSTRUCT VALIDITY OF THE HO SCALE

Test-retest reliabilities of the Ho scale are quite high- r = .85 over one year (Barefoot et al., 1983) and r = .84 over four years (Shekelle et al., 1983). Thus, this scale apparently assesses a very stable characteristic. Data concerning the nature of this characteristic has, until recently however, been relatively scarce. Cook and Medley (1954) selected items from a pool that was empirically derived on the basis of discrimination between teachers with good versus bad rapport with students. The final set of 50 MMPI items was selected on the basis of a) good discrimination between groups and b) content judged as reflecting hostility. A subsequent study found that the Ho scale correlated positively with the tendency to view photographs of strangers as unfriendly and potentially dangerous (McGee, 1954). Further, measures of hostility that include Ho scale items have been found to be associated with the delivery of stronger electric shock during a psychology experiment (Hynan, 1982; Youssef, 1968). Because items from other scales were included, however, these studies must be considered cautiously.

Smith and Frohm (1985, Study I) found that the Ho scale correlated significantly more closely with measures of anger proneness than with measures of anxiety and depression. This pattern provides evidence of the convergent and discriminant validity of the Ho scale as a measure of hostility. Regarding the specific type of hostility, Smith and Frohm (1985, Study I) found that the Ho scale correlated quite highly (rs = .60 - .70) with the resentment, suspicion, and irritability subscales of the Buss Durkee Hostility Inventory (BDHI; 1957). The Ho scale was also significantly correlated, but less closely so, with the BDHI subscales reflecting more overt forms of hostility, such as assault and verbal hostility (rs = .41 - .55). The Ho scale was modestly related to measures of Type A behavior (rs = .19 and .39). Finally, the Ho scale was significantly correlated with various measures of cynicism and mistrust.

Smith and Frohm (1985) concluded that this pattern of correlations suggest that high scorers on the Ho scale are, "likely to experience anger often, to be bitter and resentful, and to view others with distrust, ...to view their interpersonal world as an irritating struggle that requires vigilance" (p. 510). They suggested that the scale should be interpreted as a measure of *cynical hostility*. Similarly, Costa et al. (1986) have argued that the primary component of the scale is best labeled *cynicism*, although a smaller second component appears to reflect paranoid alienation. Correlations with other self-report measures of anger-proneness, cynicism, and mistrust have also been reported in recent investigations (Hardy & Smith, 1988; Smith et al., 1988, Study II), and it has been argued recently that the Ho scale may measure aspects of the broader personality trait of agreeableness versus antagonism (Costa, McCrae, & Dembroski, 1989).

Siegman et al. (1987) have recently reported that the Buss Durkee (1957) resentment and suspicion scales were either unrelated or *inversely* related to measures of CAD severity in patients undergoing coronary angiography, while the assault, verbal and indirect hostility subscales were positively correlated with CAD severity. This pattern may reflect the fact that the experience of hostility is an aspect of the broader personality trait of neuroticism, while more overt forms of hostility are not. Neuroticism appears to be associated with somatic complaints, but not actual disease. Costa and McCrae (1987) have argued that this fact explains why neuroticism (and neurotic hostility) is often inversely associated with CAD severity in angiography samples. CAD-free but somatically complaining persons high in neuroticism may undergo angiography along with the patients actually suffering from CAD. Thus, the more neurotic hostility elements of the Ho scale may attenuate its association with CAD and CHD. This suggests that further refinements of this scale may lead to improved prediction of health outcomes (cf. Barefoot et al., 1989).

Very little evidence exists regarding the overt behavioral correlates of the Ho scale. In addition to the studies involving electric shock described above (i.e., Hynan, 1982; Youssef, 1968), Smith, Sanders, and Alexander (1988) recently found that high scores on the Ho scale were associated with higher levels of hostile, antagonistic comments between spouses during discussions of marital disagreements. Interestingly, the Ho scale was not related to hostile, antagonistic behavior when couples discussed low conflict topics.

WHAT LINKS CYNICAL HOSTILITY AND HEALTH?

As the discussion thusfar indicates, there is evidence for a relatively robust and potentially causal relationship between the personality construct of cynical hostility and the development of poor health outcomes, including CHD. The nature of this link, however, is far from certain. Three possible pathways between cynical hostility and health have been proposed: a physiological reactivity pathway, a psychosocial vulnerability pathway, and a transactional view of cynical hostility and health risk. These three pathways will each be discussed in turn, although the reader will note that they are not mutually exclusive and, in fact, are quite complementary.

Increased Physiological Reactivity

The construct validity work done on the Ho Scale indicates that high scorers are suspicious, mistrustful, and resentful of others. Williams,

Barefoot, and Shekelle (1985) have argued that this sort of 'world view' may be accompanied by increased interpersonal vigilance as cynically hostile individuals watch for evidence of impending mistreatment. Such a state of heightened vigilance might be expected to result in increased physiological arousal and reactivity, including elevated levels of norepinephrine and testosterone (Williams et al., 1982). This arousal, as well as the physiological effects of the hostile individual's propensity to anger, might contribute to the development of CHD and other illnesses.

Studies examining this potential link between hostility and physiological arousal have produced mixed results. Two recent studies found no differences in physiological reactivity in response to traditional laboratory stressors (e.g., Stroop color test, mental arithmetic; cf. Krantz, Manuck, & Wing, 1986) between high and low hostile persons (Sallis, Johnson, Trevorrow, & Kaplan, 1987; Smith & Houston, 1987). Other recent studies, however, have found the expected relationship between cynical hostility and blood pressure in response to interpersonal stressors. Hardy and Smith (1988) found that high Ho subjects displayed greater diastolic blood pressure (DBP) reactivity, compared to their low Ho counterparts, during a role play task involving high levels of interpersonal conflict. High and low Ho groups did not differ in a low conflict condition, however. Similarly, Suarez, Williams and McCrae (1988) found that while a stressful word identification task did not produce differences between Ho groups, the addition of insulting comments from the experimenter did elicit greater cardiovascular reactivity in high Ho subjects compared to low Ho subjects. Smith and Allred (1989) found that high Ho subjects displayed higher levels of blood pressure during a debate task than did low Ho subjects.

The apparent inconsistency between these two sets of findings may be at least partially explained by the disparate tasks used to elicit physiological arousal. Those studies that did *not* find an association between hostility and increased physiological reactivity employed relatively *impersonal* laboratory stressors, while the studies finding a positive relationship between hostility and physiological responses utilized stressors of a more interpersonal nature. In light of the interpersonal construct assessed by the Ho scale, these results are perhaps to be expected. While hostile individuals may display increased physiological reactivity in *some* circumstances, the situations that are most likely to elicit this reactivity involve interpersonal conflicts or disagreements. Thus, to truly address this potential link between personality style and illness, further research should include the interpersonal stressors thought to be relevant to cynically hostile individuals.

The other missing aspect of research examining the physiological reactivity link between hostility and health is the lack of inquiry into physiological mechanisms *other* than cardiovascular reactivity. There are as yet, for example, no published studies looking at potential neuroendocrine differences between high and low hostile individuals. In addition, there has been no examination of possible differences between these two groups in terms of immunocompetency, an obvious avenue to explore in the search for a link between personality and general health outcomes. Existing evidence suggests that loneliness and marital conflict are associated with suppressed immune functioning (Kiecolt Glaser et al., 1984; Kiecolt Glaser et al., 1987). In light of what is known about the interpersonal nature of cynical hostility and its psychosocial correlates as discussed below, the immunological correlates of hostility are clearly worthy of research. It should be noted that the Shekelle et al. (1983) found that Ho scores predicted all-cause mortality, including malignant neoplasms.

Psychosocial Vulnerability

The second proposed pathway between hostility and health concerns the cynically hostile individual's apparent psychosocial vulnerability. Such vulnerability is manifested in reports of a relative abundance of psychosocial stressors and a corresponding lack of psychosocial resources.

Several recent studies find that cynically hostile individuals experience greater stress and interpersonal conflict in several domains of their lives. Generally, these persons report a greater frequency and severity of negative life events and daily "hassles" and at the same time report low quality and sometimes even quantity of social support (Houston & Kelly, in press; Smith & Frohm, 1985; Smith et al., 1988; Barefoot et al., 1983). More specifically, these individuals tend to report greater interpersonal conflict and less support in general, and in their family relationships and marriages. Further, high hostile individuals are more likely to report greater stress, less satisfaction, and less social support in the workplace (Houston & Kelly, in press; Smith et al., 1988).

Thus, there is ample evidence to suggest that high hostile individuals live in an interpersonal world perceived to be chronically stressful and lacking in support. Given the particular personality style of such persons, these findings are also to be expected. More importantly, however, each of these individual psychosocial characteristics has been associated with an increased risk of illness and death (Berkman & Syme, 1979; House, Robbins, & Metzner, 1982; Medalie & Goldbourt, 1976; House et al., 1975), as has the combination of high stress and low support (Ruberman et al., 1984).

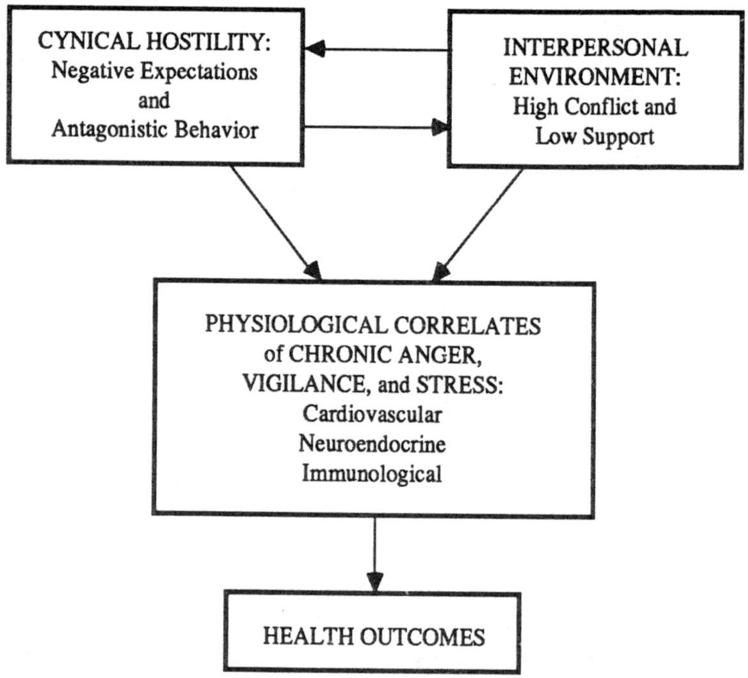

FIGURE 1 Transactional Model of Cynical Hostility and Health.

The Transactional Hypothesis

The final proposed pathway between cynical hostility and poor health outcomes incorporates aspects of both other pathways. It is an extension of interactional or transactional hypotheses concerning the link between the Type A behavior pattern and CHD (Smith, 1989; Smith & Anderson, 1986). This model of coronary-prone behavior proposes that Type As do not simply respond to environmental challenges and demands with increased levels of pathogenic physiological reactivity. Rather, they also *create* such challenges and demands through their thoughts and actions. Thus, the Type A pattern is seen as an on-going process of stress-engendering behavior, reciprocally related to levels of physiologically taxing challenge and demand.

Similar to this view of the Type A pattern, Smith and colleagues (Smith, 1989; Smith & Anderson, 1986; Smith & Frohm, 1985) have suggested that such a transactional process may link cynical hostility and health. This model is presented in Figure 1. Hostile persons appear to expect the worst from others. These negative expectations may, in turn, lead them to behave in an antagonistic manner. Such behavior is likely to elicit unfriendly, disagreeable responses from others, thereby reinforcing or confirming the original cynical expectation and producing a pattern of escalating antagonism. Social psychological research provides evidence of such expectancy confirmation cycles in social interactions in general (for a review, see Darley & Fazio, 1980), and in the particular case of hostile expectations as well (e.g., Snyder & Swann, 1978). Thus, the hostile person is likely to elicit high levels of conflict, and may also undermine potential sources of social support in this untrusting, antagonistic style. This environment, in addition to maintaining the cynic's world view, would also contribute to chronic physiological arousal. An increased level, frequency and perhaps duration of physiological reactions to independently occurring and self-engendered interpersonal stressors would, in turn, facilitate the development of illness.

Clearly, the transactional view complements rather than contradicts the psychophysiological and psychosocial accounts of the link between hostility and health. It also awaits empirical tests.

CONCLUSIONS AND FUTURE DIRECTIONS

Several recent studies have indicated that the Cook and Medley (1954) Ho scale is a useful predictor of CHD and total mortality. Although some contradictory findings have been reported, the evidence is generally consistent. The scale is best viewed as a measure of anger-proneness, resentment, and mistrust of others, or *cynical hostility*. As such, it is somewhat distinct from the usual descriptions of the Type A pattern. Cynical hostility may be linked to health outcomes by a variety of pathways. High Ho persons apparently respond to interpersonal stressors with increased levels of physiological arousal, which could, in turn, lead to illness. Further, cynical hostility is associated with increased levels of interpersonal conflict and decreased levels of social support. This psychosocial profile could also contribute to the high Ho individual's increased risk of illness. Finally, it may be that the cynically hostile individual's negative interpersonal expectations and antagonistic behavior contribute to, and are in turn reinforced by, a stressful, unsupportive interpersonal environment. This reciprocally-determined, *transactional* process may underlie the relationship between hostility and health.

Although this body of research is encouraging, much additional work remains to be done. Additional replications of the relationship between hostility and health are clearly in order. Further evidence regarding the construct assessed by the Ho scale is also needed, particularly evaluating the predicted cognitive and overt behavioral correlates of the scale in interpersonal settings. The physiological correlates of cynical hostility are in need of further research. These efforts should identify the situational characteristics most likely to elicit physiological differences between high and low Ho persons, as well as physiological processes (e.g., immunological functioning) that might account for the general health vulnerability of cynically hostile individuals. In each area of additional research, some attention should be paid to the possibility that not all components of the Ho scale are related to health (Barefoot et al., 1989). Finally, studies of the dynamic, reciprocal relationships between cynical hostility, interpersonal contexts, and physiological responses may help to elucidate the biopsychosocial *process* linking hostility and health.

REFERENCES

Barefoot, J.C., Dahlstrom, W.G., & Williams, R.B., Jr. (1983). Hostility, CHD incidence, and total mortality. A 25-year follow-up study of 255 physicians. *Psychosomatic Medicine, 45*, 59-63.

Barefoot, J.C., Dodge, K.A., Peterson, B.L., Dahlstrom, W.G., & Williams, R.B., Jr., (1989). The Cook-Medley Hostility Scale: Item content amd ability to predict survival. *Psychosomatic Medicine, 51*, 46-57.

Barefoot, J.C., Siegler, I.C., Nowlin, J.B., Peterson, B., Haney, T.L., & Williams, R.B., Jr. (1987). Suspiciousness, health, and mortality: A follow-up study of 500 older adults. *Psychosomatic Medicine, 49*, 450-457.

Berkman, L., & Syme, S.L. (1979). Social networks, host resistance, and mortality: A nine-year follow-up study of Alameda County residents. *American Journal of Epidemiology, 109*, 186-204.

Buss, A.H., & Durkee, A. (1957). An inventory for assessing different kinds of hostility. *Journal of Consulting Psychology, 21*, 342-349.

Case, R.B., Heller, S.S., Case, N.B., & Moss, A.J. (1985). Type A behavior and survival after acute myocardial infarction. *New England Journal of Medicine, 312*, 737-747.

Cohen, J.B., & Reed, D. (1985). The type A behavior pattern and coronary heart disease among Japanese men in Hawaii. *Journal of Behavioral Medicine, 8*, 342-352.

Cook, W.W., & Medley, D.M. (1954). Proposed hostility and pharisaic-virtue scales for the MMPI. *Journal of Applied Psychology, 38*, 414-418.

Costa, P.T., Jr., & McCrae, R.R. (1987). Neuroticism, somatic complaints, and disease: Is the bark worse than the bite? *Journal of Personality, 55*, 299-316.

Costa, P.T., Jr., McCrae, R.R., & Dembroski, T.M. (1989). Agreeableness vs. antagonism: Explication of a potential risk factor for CHD. In A.W. Siegman & T.M. Dembroski (Eds.), *In search of coronary-prone behavior*. New York, Lawrence Erlbaum.

Costa, P.T., Zonderman, A.B., McCrae, R.R., & Williams, R.B., Jr. (1986). Cynicism and paranoid alienation in the Cook and Medley Ho scale. *Psychosomatic Medicine, 48*, 283-285.

Darley, J.M., & Fazio, R.H. (1980). Expectancy confirmation processes arising in the social interaction sequence. *American Psychologist, 35*, 867-881.

Dembroski, T.M., MacDougall, J.M., Williams, R.B., Jr., Haney, T.L., & Blumenthal, J.A. (1985). Components of Type A, hostility, and anger-in: Relationship to angiographic findings. *Psychosomatic Medicine, 47*, 219-233.

Diamond, E.L. (1982). The role of anger and hostility in essential hypertension and coronary heart disease. *Psychological Bulletin, 92*, 410-433.

Friedman, H.S., & Booth-Kewley (1987). Personality, Type A behavior, and coronary heart disease: The role of emotional expression. *Journal of Personality and Social Psychology, 53*, 783-792.

Friedman, M., & Rosenman, R.H. (1959). Association of a specific overt behavior pattern with increases in blood cholesterol, blood clotting, incidence of arcus senilis and clinical coronary artery disease. *Journal of the American Medical Association, 169*, 1286-1296.

Hardy, J.D., & Smith, T.W. (1988). Cynical hostility and vulnerability to disease: Social support, life stress, and physiological response to conflict. *Health Psychology, 7,* 447-459.

Hearn, M.D., Murray, D.M., & Luepke, R.V. (1988). Hostility, coronary heart disease, and total mortality: A 33-year follow-up study of university students. *Proceedings of Society of Behavioral Medicine*, Boston, MA, April 27-30, p. 129.

Hecker, M., Frautschi, N., Chesney, M., Black, G., & Rosenman, R.H. (1985, March). *Components of the Type A behavior pattern and coronary disease.* Paper presented at the meeting of the Society of Behavioral Medicine, New Orleans.

House, J., Robbins, C., & Metzner, H. (1982). The association of social relationships and activities with mortality: Prospective evidence from the Tecumseh Community Health Study. *American Journal of Epidemiology, 116,* 123-140.

House, J., McMichael, A., Wells, J., Kaplan, B., & Landerman, L. (1979). Occupational stress and health among factory workers. *Journal of Health and Social Behavior, 20,* 139-160.

Houston, B.K., & Kelley, K.E. (in press). Hostility in employed women: Relation to work and marital experiences, social support, stress, and anger expression. *Personality and Social Psychology Bulletin.*

Hynan, M.T. (1982). Aggression in a competitive task. *Psychological Reports, 50,* 663-672.

Jenkins, C.D., Rosenman, R.H., & Zyzanski, S.J. (1974). Prediction of clinical coronary heart disease by a test for the coronary-prone behavior pattern. *New England Journal of Medicine, 290,* 1271-1275.

Kiecolt-Glaser, J.K., Fisher, L.D., Ogrocki, P., Stout, J.C., Speicher, C.E., & Glaser, R. (1987). Marital quality, marital disruption, and immune function. *Psychosomatic Medicine, 49,* 13-34.

Kiecolt-Glaser, J.K., Garner, W., Speicher, C.E., Penn, G., & Glaser, R. (1984). Psychosocial modifiers of immunocompetence in medical students. *Psychosomatic Medicine, 46,* 7-14.

Leon, G.R., Finn, S.E., Murray, D., & Bailey, J.M. (1988). The inability to predict cardiovascular disease from hostility scores or MMPI items related to Type A behavior. *Journal of Consulting and Clinical Psychology, 56,* 597-600.

MacDougall, J.M., Dembroski, T.M., Dimsdale, J.E., & Hackett, T.P. (1985). Components of Type A, hostility, and anger-in: Further relationships to angiographic findings. *Health Psychology, 4,* 137-152.

Matthews, K.A. (1988). CHD and Type A behaviors: Update on and alternative to the Booth-Kewley and Friedman quantitative review. *Psychological Bulletin, 104,* 373-380.

Matthews, K.A., Glass, D.C., Rosenman, R.H., & Bortner, R.W. (1977). Competitive drive, Pattern A, and coronary heart disease: A further analysis of some data from the Western Collaborative Study. *Journal of Chronic Diseases, 30,* 489-498.

McCranie, E.W., Watkins, L.O., Brandsma, J.M., & Sisson, B.D. (1985). Hostility, coronary heart disease (CHD), incidence, and total mortality: Lack of association in a 25-year follow-up study of 478 physicians. *Journal of Behavioral Medicine, 9,* 119-125.

McGee, S. (1954). Measures of hostility: A pilot study. *Journal of Clinical Psychology, 10,* 180-182.

Medalie, J., & Goldbourt, V. (1976). Angina pectoris in 10,000 men: II. Psychosocial and other risk factors as evidenced by a multivariate analysis of a five year incidence study. *American Journal of Medicine, 60,* 910-921.

Ostfeld, A.M., Lebovits, B.Z., Shekelle, R.B., & Paul, O. (1964). A prospective study of the relationship between personality and coronary heart disease. *Journal of Chronic Diseases, 17,* 265-276.

Pickering, T.G. (1985). Should studies of patients undergoing coronary angiography be used to evaluate the role of behavioral risk factors for coronary heart disease? *Journal of Behavioral Medicine, 8,* 203-213.

Ragland, D.R., & Brand, R.J. (1988). Type A behavior and mortality from coronary heart disease. *New England Journal of Medicine, 318,* 65-69.

Review Panel (1981). Coronary-prone behavior and coronary heart disease: A critical review. *Circulation, 63,* 1199-1215.

Ruberman, W., Weinblatt, E., Goldberg, J., & Chaudhary, B.S. (1984). Psychosocial influences on mortality after myocardial infarction. *New England Journal of Medicine, 311*, 552-559.

Sallis, J.F., Johnson, C.C., Trevorrow, T.R., Kaplan, R.M., & Hovell, M.F. (1987). The relationship between cynical hostility and blood pressure reactivity. *Journal of Psychosomatic Research, 31*, 111-116.

Seeman, T.E., & Syme, S.L. (1987). Social networks and coronary artery disease: A comparison of the structure and function of social relations as predictors of disease. *Psychosomatic Medicine, 49*, 341-354.

Shekelle, R.B., Gale, M., & Norusis, M. (1985). For the Aspirin Myocardial Infarction Study Research Group: Type A score (Jenkins Activity Survey) and risk of recurrent coronary heart disease in the Aspirin Myocardial Infarction Study. *American Journal of Cardiology, 56*, 221-225.

Shekelle, R.B., Gale, M., Ostfeld, A.M., & Paul, O. (1983). Hostility, risk of coronary heart disease, and mortality. *Psychosomatic Medicine, 45*, 109-114.

Shekelle, R.B., Hulley, S.B., Neaton, J.D., Billings, J.H., Borhani, N.O., Geraco, T.A., Jacobs, D.R., Lasser, N.L., Mittlemark, M.B., & Stamler, J. (1985). The MRFIT behavior pattern study: II. Type A behavior and the incidence of coronary heart disease. *American Journal of Epidemiology, 122*, 559-570.

Siegman, A.W., Dembroski, T.M., & Ringel, N. (1987). Components of hostility and the severity of coronary artery disease. *Psychosomatic Medicine, 49*, 127-135.

Smith, M.A., & Houston, B.K. (1987). Hostility, anger expression, cardiovascular responsivity, and social support. *Biological Psychology, 24*, 39-48.

Smith, T.W. (1989). Interactions, transactions, and the Type A pattern: Additional avenues in the search for coronary-prone behavior. In A.W. Siegman & T.M. Dembroski (Eds.), *In search of coronary-prone behavior*. Hillsdale, NJ: Lawrence Erlbaurm.

Smith, T.W., & Allred, K.D. (1989). Blood pressure responses during social interaction in high and low cynically hostile males. *Journal of Bahavioral Medicine, 11*, 135-143.

Smith, T.W., & Anderson, N.B. (1986). Models of personality and disease: An interactional approach to Type A behavior and cardiovascular risk. *Journal of Personality and Social Psychology, 50*, 1166-1173.

Smith, T.W., & Frohm, K.D. (1985). What's so unhealthy about hostility? Construct validity and psychosocial correlates of the Cook and Medley Ho scale. *Health Psychology, 4*, 503-520.

Smith, T.W., Pope, M.K., Sanders, J.D., Allred, K.D., & O'Keeffe, J. L. (1988). Cynical hostility at home and work: Psychosocial vunerability across domains. *Journal of Research in Personality, 22*, 525-548.

Smith, T.W., Sanders, J.D., & Alexander, J.F. (1988, August). *Cynical hostility in marital interactions*. Paper presented at the American Psychological Association annual meeting, Atlanta.

Snyder, M., & Swann, W.B., Jr. (1978). Behavioral confirmation in social interaction: From social perception to social reality. *Journal of Experimental Social Psychology, 14*, 148-162.

Suarez, E., Williams, R.B., Jr., & McCrae, A. (1988, March). *High Cook Medley scores predict cardiovascular reactivity, but only during harassment*. Paper presented at the American Psychosomatic Society annual meeting, Toronto.

Williams, R.B., Jr. (1987). Psychological factors in coronary artery disease: Epidemiological evidence. *Circulation, 76*, (Supplement I), I177-I123.

Williams, R.B., Jr., Barefoot, J.C., & Shekelle, R.B. (1985). The health consequences of hostility. In M.A. Chesney, & R.H. Rosenman (Eds.)., *Anger and hostility in cardiovascular and behavioral disorders*. New York: Hemisphere.

Williams, R.B., Jr., Haney, T.L., Lee, K.L., Kong, Y., Bluementhal, J. & Whalen, R.E. (1980). Type A behavior, hostility, and coronary atherosclerosis. *Psychosomatic Medicine, 42*, 539-549.

Williams, R.B., Jr., Lane, J.D., Kuhn, C.M., et al. (1982). Type A behavior and elevated physiological and neuroendocrine responses to cognitive tasks. *Science, 218*, 483-485.

Youssef, Z.I. (1968). The role of race, sex, hostility, and verbal stimulus in inflicting punishment, *Psychonomic Science, 12*, 285-286.

Cook and Medley Hostility and the Type A Behavior Pattern: Psychological Correlates of Two Coronary-Prone Behaviors

Gary E. Swan, Ph. D.
Dorit Carmelli, Ph. D.
Ray H. Rosenman, Ph. D.
Health Sciences Program, SRI International
333 Ravenswood Avenue, Menlo Park, CA 94025

The psychological correlates of the Cook and Medley Hostility (Ho) scale and the Type A ratings of the Structured Interview were examined and compared in a sample of adult, middle-aged male participants in a prospective investigation of coronary heart disease risk factors. Although both the Ho scale and the Structured Type A Interview ratings are considered to measure coronary-prone characteristics, the associated patterns of psychological correlates for the two were quite different. High scores on the Ho scale were associated with higher levels of anxiety and neuroticism and lower levels of the tendency to "fake good." Global Type A behavior was not related to indices of neuroticism or to measures of self-presentation but to measures of dominance, self-confidence, and achievement. Despite these differences, there were some correlates common to both Ho and global Type A behavior. These included positive associations with the Hard Driving and Speed and Impatience subscales from the Jenkins Activity Survey, and behavioral rating of potential for hostility. There is a need to understand the similarities and differences between the various behavioral and psychological aspects of the different coronary-prone behaviors so that individuals with high-risk combinations of traits can be identified.

INTRODUCTION

Global determinations of Type A behavior are predictive of later coronary events (Rosenman et al., 1975; Haynes, Feinleib, & Kannel, 1980). They show an association with the presence of coronary athero-

Authors' Notes: This research was supported by Grants HL30801 and HL32795 from the National Heart, Lung, and Blood Institute.

Address reprint requests to the first author.

© 1990 Select Press

sclerosis as determined by angiography studies (Blumenthal, Williams, Kong, Schanberg, & Thompson, 1978; Frank, Heller, Kornfeld, Sporn, & Weiss, 1978; Zyzanski, Jenkins, Ryan, Flessas, & Everist, 1976). Not all data on the Type A-CHD association has been confirmatory. Several recent studies failed to find either a significant prospective association (Shekelle et al., 1985; Case, Heller, Case, Moss, & the Multicenter Post-infarction Research Group, 1985) or a significant association with angiography results (Dimsdale, Hackett, Block, & Hutter, 1978; Dimsdale, Hackett, & Hutter, 1979; Krantz et al., 1981; Scherwitz et al., 1983).

Similarly, the relationship of scores on the Cook and Medley Hostility (Ho) scale of the MMPI (Cook & Medley, 1954) to severity of coronary atherosclerosis was documented by Williams et al. (1980), and to all-cause mortality by Barefoot, Dahlstrom, and Williams (1983) and Shekelle, Gale, Ostfeld, & Paul (1983). McCranie, Watkins, Brandsma, and Sisson (1986), on the other hand, did not confirm the relationship between scores on the Ho scale and either the 25-year incidence of CHD or total mortality in a large group of physicians who were given the MMPI at entrance to medical school. A recently reported study by Leon, Murray, Finn, and Bailey (1988) also could not demonstrate a prospective relationship between Ho and CHD incidence over a 30-year period in a group of males who were middle-aged at intake. Despite these conflicting results, some believe that the Ho scale is measuring an underlying characteristic that is a significant predictor of the severity of coronary atherosclerosis as well as of CHD incidence and mortality (Williams & Barefoot, 1988).

Despite the fact that some recent investigations show Type A behavior and Ho scores to have independent associations with CHD severity (Williams & Barefoot, 1988), relatively little attention has been paid to understanding the similarities and differences between the two traits measured by the Ho scale and the Type A Structured Interview (SI). Only one study to date has attempted to examine the association between Ho and SI Type A ratings; Williams, Barefoot, and Shekelle (1985) reported a significant positive association, which they later described as "weak" (Williams & Barefoot, 1988). Since these authors did not report the actual correlation coefficient, it was of great interest to ascertain the magnitude of this association in the present investigation.

Blumenthal, Barefoot, Burg, and Williams (1987) recently examined several psychological correlates of the Ho scale, but we are aware of no investigation that has examined the psychological correlates of both the Ho scale and the Type A behavior ratings from the Structured Interview simultaneously in the same sample. Such an investigation could lead to a better understanding of the similarities and differences in the traits captured by these measures. Since it is possible that seemingly disparate coronary-prone characteristics can exist within the same individual and that different combinations of coronary-prone characteristics can exist across individuals (Friedman, Hall, & Harris, 1985), the goal of this investigation was to focus on both measures and their correlates rather than to focus on only one.

In the present analysis, we used a data set where both the Ho scale and the Type A Structured Interview were administered. This sample consisted of healthy middle-aged males who were participants in an ongoing investigation of CHD risk factors. A comprehensive array of psychological data was collected at intake, thereby enabling us to conduct a unique comparison of the psychological correlates associated with scores from the Ho scale with those for global Type A behavior ratings based on the Structured Interview.

METHOD

Subjects

Participants from three California centers in the multicenter NHLBI Twin Study constituted the base sample for the present analysis. Subjects were identified through the NAS-NRC Twin Registry (Jablon, Neel, & Gershowitz, 1967). All subjects were born in the United States between 1917 and 1927 and served in the armed forces during World War II or the Korean conflict.They were drawn from different geographic areas of the United States. A cardiovascular examination was conducted from 1969 to 1971 at five centers, three of which were in California, one in Massachusetts, and one in Indiana. The subjects were aged 42 to 56 years (mean = 49.0 years) when first examined.

Psychological Scales

The subjects who were studied in the three California centers were given a battery of psychological tests at the time of their intake into the study (Feinleib et al., 1977). Because a wide variety of psychological and behavioral scales were available, we believed that some sort of selection strategy was needed to reduce the overall number of variables. The framework for the selection strategy was provided by the concept of "construct validity" as formulated by Cronbach and Meehl (1955) and Campbell and Fiske (1959), in which a nomological network guides the selection of variables. This network should include variables that could reasonably be expected to be related to the primary variables of interest in addition to variables that might be unrelated or negatively correlated to the target variables (Wiggins, 1973). Because the original study was not designed as a construct validity investigation, the best we could do here was to construct an "informal" nomological network in which personality variables thought to be related to hostility and the Type A construct were included in the correlational analysis. In addition, other variables found to be associated with CHD were also included (Friedman & Booth-Kewley, 1987; Leon et al., 1988).

Scales included because of their theorized association with the "hostile" personality (Blumenthal et al., 1987) included several of the validity, clinical, and research scales from the MMPI (Dahlstrom, Welsh, & Dahlstrom, 1982), California Psychological Inventory (CPI; Gough, 1980; Megargee, 1977), and the ACL (Gough & Heilbrun, 1980). From the MMPI the selected scales were: L, F, K, Psychopathic Deviate, Hysteria, Paranoia, Psychasthenia, Manifest Anxiety (Taylor, 1953), Welsh Anxiety (Welsh, 1956), Dominance (Gough, McClosky, & Meehl, 1951), Repression (Welsh, 1956), Ego Strength (Barron, 1953), and Ho. From the CPI the selected scales were: Dominance, Tolerance, Well Being, and Anxiety (Leventhal, 1966; Leventhal, 1968). From the ACL the selected scales were Succorance and Counseling Readiness.

Scales selected because of their known or suspected relationship to Type A behavior (Rosenman, Swan, & Carmelli, 1988) included: the Achievement via Conformity and Achievement via Independence scales from the CPI; the Thurstone Temperament Schedule (Thurstone, 1953), the Achievement, Self-confidence, and Type A scales from the ACL (Rahe, Rosenman, Borhani, & Feinleib, 1974; Rosenman, Rahe, Borhani, & Feinleib, 1976), the Jenkins Activity Survey (Jenkins, Zyzanski, & Rosenman, 1979), and several of the behavioral ratings from the SI (see below for a description).

The MMPI Depression scale, and the Extraversion/Introversion scale (Hase & Goldberg, 1967) from the CPI were also included in this analysis. Previous research suggests that these scales measure characteristics related to CHD (Friedman & Booth-Kewley, 1987; Leon et al., 1988).

Behavior Ratings

The Type A Structured Interview (SI; Rosenman, 1978) was administered and tape recorded for later behavioral rating in a subset of subjects. As reported in a previous analysis (Dembroski, MacDougall, Williams, & Haney, 1985), the SI responses for each subject (n = 91) were further coded by two independent raters on 5-point scales. Each subject was scored for a number of variables, including loudness of speech, explosiveness of speech, rapid accelerated speech, latency of responses to SI questions, competition for control with the interviewer, potential for hostility (e.g., subject exhibited many adjudged signs of hostility toward others, including the interviewer), anxiety to complete whatever is unfinished, and hurry. Reliability of the ratings was acceptably high, with Pearson correlations ranging from 0.70 to 0.85 (Dembroski et al., 1985).

Statistical Methods

Depending on the measures employed, all available data were used in the analyses examining the relationships between Ho, Type A behavior, and the psychological variables described previously. Sample size ranged from 224 subjects for the Ho scale to 91 subjects for whom both Ho and Type A behavior ratings were available. (Among the California subjects only the 91 assessed in San Francisco received both the Ho and SI.) For the analysis, the subjects were treated as individuals. A separate analysis examining the heritability of the Ho scale is presented elsewhere (Carmelli, Rosenman, & Swan, 1988). Pearson correlation coefficients were computed between all relevant variables and subjected to two-tailed significance tests. The Type A determination, although usually viewed as a categorical variable (Rosenman, 1978), was assigned a 1 = Type B4 to 5 = Type A1 numerical value for this correlational analysis. Because of the previously reported associations between Ho and the MMPI K validity scale (Shipman, 1965) and the strong association obtained in the present study, an ancillary analysis examined the associations of residual Ho scores after controlling for shared variance with the K scale. It is important to note here that the association between Ho and K does not appear to be attributable entirely to item overlap, the two scales having in common only seven items (9%) out of the total of 80 (50 items for Ho, 30 items for K). The procedure of using standardized residual scores is designed to separate common variance in the Ho scale attributable to the K scale and is distinctly different, conceptually and operationally, from the more traditional "K-correction" approach to scoring the clinical subscales of the MMPI for diagnostic purposes. In the K-correction approach, a fraction of the K-scale score is added to the raw score for a number of clinical scales to provide a more accurate measure of a particular trait. The residualization of K from Ho provides for a more precise adjusted determination of the component of variance attributable to the scale (Rosenman, 1978).

There are at least two ways to view the relationship of K to the Ho scale and our inclusion of psychological correlates of both unresidualized and residualized scores in this analysis. From the first perspective, the strong negative association between Ho and K could indicate that these scales are highly sensitive to a general test-taking attitude—in this case, the tendency to report oneself in an unfavorable light (low scores on K) that is independent of actual hostility. In this view, social desirability is seen as a confounder of the measurement of hostility as first noted by

Shipman (1965). A more recent interpretation of the relationship of K to Ho is that it provides evidence for poor coping skills in hostile individuals. In this view, low scores on K are indicative of a lack of concern with self-presentation (Blumenthal et al., 1987) that has a clinical and conceptual significance. Our perspective is that since both interpretations seem feasible at this early stage, it is justifiable to present our results for K-residualized scores as well. Under the first scenario, residualization simply controls for the confounding response tendency. Under the second scenario, noting the differences between correlational patterns for unresidualized and residualized scores provides a glimpse at the extent to which controlling for coping skill highlights or enhances associated characteristics that may be more fundamental (e.g., biologically determined) than learned behaviors.

To control the probability of a Type I error in the analysis of the association between psychological scales and the Ho scale and Type A behavior ratings, only correlations with a significance level less than or equal to 0.002 will be discussed. This significance level maintains an overall alpha of 0.05 while accounting for the 33 comparisons within each correlational pattern (one for Ho and one for Type A behavior).

RESULTS

Representativeness of the Sample

To characterize the sample of subjects, mean levels on the psychological scales are presented in Table 1. Results indicate values that are entirely within average normal ranges for this age group. This is not surprising, in view of the fact that these men had all been in the military and had qualified for service after passing extensive psychological screening (Feinleib et al., 1977). The mean Ho score in the present study was 17.1, which is somewhat higher than that found for the young medical students in McCranie et al. (1986), but lower than that found by Smith and Frohm (1985) in undergraduate college students. The mean Ho score in this study, however, is quite similar to the mean (16.5) obtained for a sample of noncriminal adults (mean age = 37 years) by Megargee and Mendelsohn (1962). Ratings of the SI's resulted in the following distribution of subjects: 12% A1, 32% A2, 17% B3, and 10% B4. The mean Type A behavioral rating was 3.0 (range = 1 to 5). The differences observed across studies may be due partly to differences in age, in socioeconomic status, and in the demand characteristics of the test-taking situation.

Correlates of Ho and Type A Behavior Ratings

Correlations between the Ho scale and a number of psychological measures were computed. Table 2 reveals that the largest association was

TABLE 1 Psychological Characteristics of Study Sample

	Mean	*Standard Deviation*
MMPI		
Validity Scales		
L	50.3	7.4
F	53.1	6.4
K	56.0	9.6
Clinical Scales[a]		
Depression	57.4	10.5
Psychopathic Deviate	54.1	11.2
Hysteria	56.5	9.0
Hypochondriasis	53.8	10.4
Masculinity/Femininity	57.3	10.2
Paranoia	52.8	7.8
Psychasthenia	53.4	9.8
Research Scales		
Manifest Anxiety	11.7	7.3
Welsh Anxiety	8.5	6.9
Dominance	18.2	3.1
Repression	16.6	4.7
Ego Strength	57.4	9.2
Hostility	17.1	7.7
CPI		
Clinical Scales[a]		
Dominance	50.9	13.1
Tolerance	49.2	9.7
Well Being	51.4	10.1
Achievement via Conformity	50.2	9.4
Achievement via Independence	52.6	10.4
Research Scales		
Leventhal Anxiety	4.2	1.8
Extraversion	16.1	4.9
Thurstone Temperament Schedule		
Activity	10.9	3.7
Vigor	10.9	3.5
Impulsive	10.9	3.6
Stability	11.5	3.5
Sociability	11.0	4.0
Reflectiveness	8.3	3.4
Dominance	8.9	5.2
Adjective Check List[a]		
Achievement	53.5	9.1
Succorance	45.9	7.9
Counseling Readiness	50.5	9.3
Self-confidence	48.2	9.8

(continued on next page)

TABLE 1 *(Continued)*

	Mean	*Standard Deviation*
Type A Measures		
Jenkins Activity Scale[b]		
Speed and Impatience	-1.2	9.2
Job Involvement	-4.1	9.3
Hard Driving	1.4	9.7
Type A score	-0.7	9.2
Adjective Check List		
Type A scale	11.6	3.2
Behavioral Ratings		
Anxious to go	3.8	0.8
Hurry to finish	3.1	1.0
Potential for hostility	2.9	1.0
Latency	3.2	1.0
Loudness	2.9	0.9
Explosiveness	3.0	1.0
Rapid speech	2.9	1.1
Competitiveness	2.5	1.1

[a] *T scores.*
[b] *Standard scores.*

with the MMPI K validity scale (r = -0.80), followed in magnitude by significant associations with the several measures of anxiety (i.e., Manifest Anxiety, r = 0.59; Welsh Anxiety, r = 0.70; Leventhal Anxiety, r = 0.30). However, individuals with higher Ho scores had lower scores on dominance (i.e., MMPI Dominance, r = -0.50; CPI Dominance, r = -0.55); reported less ego strength, well-being, tolerance, and achievement in general; and were less extroverted. Individuals with higher Ho scores also exhibited less stability and more reflectiveness on the Thurstone scales.

Table 2 also shows associations between the Type A behavior rating and the psychological scales. With few exceptions, the correlates of the Type A behavior rating were different from the correlates of the Ho scale. Type A behavior was generally unrelated to indices of psychopathology as reflected in the nonsignificant associations with the MMPI clinical and research scales. On scales from the CPI, Type A behavior was positively related to Dominance and Extraversion. In contrast, Ho scores were related in the opposite direction to these measures. Unlike Ho, however, Type A behavior was not related to lower scores on Well Being. Associations between Type A behavior and scales from the Thurstone Temperament Schedule and Adjective Check List exhibited an interesting pattern

TABLE 2 Correlations Between the Ho Scale, Type A Behavior Ratings, and Psychological Measures

	Cook and Medley Ho Scale		*Type A Behavior Rating*
	Unadjusted	*Adjusted*[a]	
MMPI[b]			
Validity Scales			
L	-0.32*	0.01	0.04
F	0.37*	0.19	-0.02
K	-0.80*	0.00	0.06
Clinical Scales			
Depression	0.10	0.09	0.12
Psychopathic Deviate	-0.26*	0.10	0.11
Hysteria	-0.46*	-0.16	0.15
Hypochondriasis	-0.19	0.10	0.18
Masculinity/Femininity	-0.12	-0.20	0.03
Paranoia	-0.22*	-0.12	0.03
Psychasthenia	-0.16	0.12	0.08
Research Scales			
Manifest Anxiety	0.59*	0.11	0.10
Welsh Anxiety	0.70*	0.15	0.00
Dominance	-0.50*	-0.21*	-0.05
Repression	-0.42*	-0.10	-0.14
Ego Strength	-0.43*	-0.13	0.08
CPI[c]			
Clinical Scales			
Dominance	-0.21*	-0.09	0.24*
Tolerance	-0.69*	-0.32*	-0.08
Well Being	-0.55*	-0.25*	-0.11
Achievement via Conformity	-0.42*	-0.13	-0.05
Achievement via Independence	-0.55*	-0.26*	-0.08
Research Scales			
Leventhal Anxiety	0.30*	0.19	0.00
Extraversion	-0.34*	0.01	0.17*
Thurstone Temperament Schedule[d]			
Activity	0.06	-0.05	0.37*
Vigor	0.08	0.10	0.10
Impulsive	0.12	0.07	0.33
Stability	-0.31*	0.05	-0.06
Sociability	-0.06	0.01	0.21*
Reflectiveness	0.22*	0.10	-0.06
Dominance	-0.11	-0.09	0.27*
Adjective Check List			
Achievement	-0.13	-0.02	0.23*
Succorance	0.14	-0.01	0.02
Counseling Readiness	0.14	-0.06	-0.27*
Self-Confidence	-0.11	0.04	0.29*

[a] *Correlations in the column labeled "Adjusted" are computed with Ho scale scores that have been residualized for their association with the K scale.*

[b] *Correlations between the MMPI and the Ho scale are based on $n = 224$; those between the MMPI and the Type A behavior rating are based on $n = 91$.*

[c] *Correlations between the CPI and the Ho scale are based on $n = 222$; those between the CPI and the Type A behavior rating are based on $n = 336$.*

[d] *Correlations between the Thurstone Temperament Schedule and the Ho scale are based on $n = 159$; those between the TTS and the Type A behavior rating are based on $n = 361$.*

[e] *Correlations between the Adjective Check List and the Ho scale are based on $n = 216$; those between the ACL and the Type A behavior rating are based on $n = 335$.*

* $p < 0.002$.

compared to that exhibited for Ho. Table 2 shows the pattern of intercorrelations for these two coronary-prone characteristics to be, without exception, completely nonoverlapping. Type A behavior was correlated positively with Thurstone Activity, Impulsiveness, Sociability, and Dominance and uncorrelated with Vigor, Stability, and Reflectiveness. Ho, on the other hand, was associated negatively with Stability and positively with Reflectiveness, and uncorrelated with Activity, Vigor, Impulsiveness, Sociability, and Dominance. This pattern of a dissimilar relationship persisted for scales from the ACL. Type A behavior was associated negatively with Counseling Readiness and positively with Self-Confidence and Achievement, and was uncorrelated with Succorance. Ho on the other hand, was not associated with any of the ACL scales.

Intercorrelations Between Ho, Type A Behavior Rating, and Type A Questionnaire Measures

Table 3 presents the correlations between Ho and the Type A behavior rating and questionnaire measures of Type A behavior. The results show that Ho is not correlated with either the Type A behavior rating or the global questionnaire measures of Type A (e.g., JAS Type A score and the ACL Type A scale). Like the Type A behavior rating, however, the Ho scale was positively associated with the JAS Speed and Impatience and Hard Driving subscales. In contrast to the Type A behavior rating, Ho was correlated negatively with the Job Involvement subscale. Correlates in common to Ho and the Type A behavior rating were the Speed and Impatience and Hard Driving subscales from the JAS.

Intercorrelations Between Ho, the Type A Behavior Rating, and Behavioral Component Ratings

Table 4 reveals that the Ho scores tend to be unrelated to specific Type A behavior component ratings. The exception is the positive and significant association between Ho and potential for hostility ($r = 0.29$). As expected, the Type A behavior rating is significantly associated with all of the behavioral component ratings.

Intercorrelations After Controlling for the Association with the MMPI K Scale

As noted earlier, the psychological characteristic with the largest association ($r = -0.80$) with Ho was the MMPI K scale, which measures the tendency to "fake good" (Graham, 1977) or social desirability. From a psychometric perspective, it was important to control for the response set of social desirability to ensure, to the extent possible, Ho scores corrected for this tendency. The effects of K were partialled out from the

TABLE 3 Correlation Between the Ho Scale, Type A Behavior Ratings, and Type A Measures

	Cook and Medley Ho Scale		
Type A Measures	*Unadjusted*	*Adjusted*	*Type A Behavior Rating*
Jenkins Activity Scale			
Speed and Impatience	0.15*[a]	-0.03[a]	0.27*[b]
Job Involvement	-0.15*	-0.09	0.12*
Hard Driving	0.24*	0.09	0.13*
Type A score	0.06	-0.12	0.38*
Adjective Check List			
Type A scale	-0.08[c]	0.02[c]	0.48*[d]
Type A behavior rating	-0.02[e]	-0.13[e]	1.00

[a] *Correlations are based on a sample size of 220.*
[b] *Correlations are based on a sample size of 343.*
[c] *Correlation is based on a sample size of 216.*
[d] *Correlation is based on a sample size of 335.*
[e] *Correlation is based on a sample size of 91.*
* $p < 0.05$.

Ho scale; residual scores were then correlated with all of the scales and measures described earlier. Type A behavior ratings, on the other hand, were not significantly associated with K scale scores and thus were not adjusted. As mentioned earlier, because it is also possible that the K scale measures a "coping style" (Blumenthal et al., 1987), the residualization process would result in scores with this component extracted. In either event, it may be instructive to examine those associations that were only minimally weakened or even strengthened by the residualization process in order to determine correlates that may be more fundamental.

Table 2 reveals that this adjustment substantially reduced the overall strength of the associations that unadjusted Ho had with most psychological measures. Additional findings indicate that residualized Ho scores remained significantly associated in the negative direction with CPI Tolerance (r = -0.32), Well Being (r = -0.25), Achievement via Independence (r = -0.26), and MMPI Dominance (r = -0.21). Table 3 shows that, after adjustment for K, previous associations between Ho and subscales from the JAS as well as Type A speech stylistic became nonsignificant. Table 4 indicates that the adjustment process strengthened the association between Ho and the speech stylistic of loudness and the behavioral rating of hostility.

TABLE 4 Correlation Between the Ho Scale, Type A Behavior Ratings, and Behavioral Component Ratings from the Structured Interview

	Cook and Medley Ho Scale		*Type A Behavior Rating*
	Unadjusted	*Adjusted*	
Speech Stylistics			
Latency	0.08[a]	0.11	0.47*[b]
Loudness	0.11	0.27*	0.41*
Explosiveness	0.02	0.19	0.45*
Rapid speech	-0.06	0.19	0.34*
Competitiveness	-0.10	0.16	0.28*
Behavioral Ratings			
Anxious to go	0.13[a]	0.06	0.19*[b]
Hurry to finish	-0.10	0.02	0.24*
Potential for hostility	0.29*	0.33*	0.42*

[a] *Correlations are based on a sample size of 69.*
b *Correlations are based on a sample size of 318.*
* $p < 0.05$.

DISCUSSION

In this paper we report, for the first time, the association between scores on the Ho scale and Type A behavior as measured by the Structured Interview. In this sample, the two variables are uncorrelated. In other words, full-scale Ho scores are not predictive of the global Type A determination. This finding is at odds with results presented initially by Williams et al. (1985) in graphic format (see their Figure 1, p. 174), which they interpreted as indicating a strong positive association with global Type A (p. 180). These authors, in a later exposition (Williams & Barefoot, 1988) describe these same results as indicating "that Ho scores have been found to be only weakly, albeit significantly, correlated with SI assessments of the global TABP" (p. 195). Our results provide the first specific quantification of this association and seem to be consistent with the later interpretation of their data provided by Williams and Barefoot (1988). Possible reasons for the lack of association will be discussed later in this section.

Review of the findings from the current analysis suggests that individuals scoring high on Ho reported less dominance, repression, ego strength, well-being, achievement in general, stability, and extraversion and higher reflectiveness, need for succorance, and counseling readiness. These results are consistent with previous findings indicating high Ho scores to be characteristic of neurotic individuals with attributes indicative of psychopathology (Wadden, Anderton, Foster, & Love, 1983; Costa, Zonderman, McCrae, & Williams, 1986).

Our findings with regard to correlates of Ho are generally consistent with a recently published investigation of the psychological correlates of the Ho scale in patients undergoing coronary angiography. Blumenthal et al. (1987) concluded that the Ho scale tapped four general dimensions: anger and hostility, coping styles, neuroticism, and social maladjustment. Following their general scheme, one can see in the present study that scores on the Ho scale are strongly related to ineffective coping styles as reflected in low scores on the K, Repression, and Ego Strength scales from the MMPI and the Stability scale from the Thurstone Temperament Schedule, neuroticism as reflected in high positive associations with the Taylor Manifest Anxiety and Welsh Anxiety on the MMPI, Leventhal Anxiety from the CPI, and Counseling Readiness from the ACL and in a negative association with Well-Being from the CPI. Ho's relationship to social maladjustment in the Blumenthal et al. (1987) paper is confirmed by the negative associations with MMPI Dominance, CPI Dominance, Tolerance, Achievement (via Conformity and via Independence), and CPI Extraversion. Thus, even though different scales were used in this analysis, the overall pattern of correlations for the Ho scale is similar to that found by Blumenthal et al. (1987).

Unadjusted scores on the Ho scale were uncorrelated with global Type A scores derived from paper-and-pencil measures and the overall SI. These findings are consistent with previous studies in which no significant associations were found between Ho and global Type A questionnaire scores (Williams et al., 1980; Dembroski et al., 1985; Wadden et al., 1983). This lack of association is not surprising since global Type A measures are not associated with measures of anxiety, neuroticism, or psychopathology (Rahe et al., 1974; Rosenman et al., 1976; Wadden et al., 1983; Chesney, Black, Chadwick, & Rosenman, 1981). Although Smith and Frohm (1985) found a positive association between Ho and JAS Type A, the age of their sample (i.e., college undergraduates) limits the generalizability of their finding, as does the question of the validity of the JAS to measure Type A (Byrne, Rosenman, Schiller, & Chesney, 1985).

Components of JAS Type A, however, were associated with unadjusted scores on Ho. Specifically, subjects with higher Ho scores tended to have higher scores on the JAS Speed and Impatience and Hard Driving subscales and lower scores on Job Involvement. These findings are similar to those showing no association between Ho and the full-scale JAS Type A score and a positive correlation with Speed and Impatience (Wadden et al., 1983).

The Type A behavior rating, on the other hand, appeared to be generally unrelated to indices of psychopathology, as reflected in the non-significant associations with the MMPI clinical and research scales. The behavior rating was related to more dominance and extraversion on the CPI, to indices of temperament, including activity, impulsiveness, sociability, and dominance, and to adjectives indicative of achievement, self-confidence, and lack of counseling readiness. Thus, in contrast with the set of significant psychological correlates for Ho, those of the Type A behavior rating are indicative of a substantially different sort of person: an extraverted, nonanxious, dominant, active, self-confident, achievement-oriented individual who also receives higher ratings on behavioral hostility.

A closer examination of the correlates for the two measures of coronary-prone behavior reveals some points of commonality. Both are related positively to Speed and Impatience (JAS), Hard Driving (JAS), and the potential for hostility. The lack of a significant association between Type A and Ho indicates equal likelihoods of scoring high on Ho and low on Type A behavior as well as scoring low on Ho and high on Type A. This situation may well represent two aspects of coronary-prone behavior: one that is characterized by high levels of anxiety, psychopathology, and hostility, and one that is characterized by high levels of activity, dominance, achievement, and hostility. This formulation is similar to that first proposed by Friedman, Hall, and Harris (1985), in which a high-risk Type A (e.g., repressed, tense, and illness prone) and a high-risk Type B (e.g., submissive, repressed, and tense) were proposed.

The similarities and differences between correlates of Ho and Type A behavior in the present study may be due in part to method variance; Ho, being a paper-and-pencil measure, correlates significantly with other paper-and-pencil measures. This explanation, however, does not account for the fact that Type A behavior is also associated with paper-and-pencil measures (e.g., Thurstone and Adjective Check List). Moreover, the generally nonoverlapping pattern of correlates of Ho and Type A behavior suggest that something more fundamental than method variance is accounting for these results.

As noted previously, the notion of construct validity helped guide this investigation. Even though study limitations prevent us from doing a more formal investigation along the lines suggested by Campbell and Fiske (1959), we are able to make some observations concerning components of validity that can be tested later. We observe first that the Ho scale is correlated significantly with the behavioral hostility measure (see Table 4). This correlation provides evidence for the convergent validity of Ho, especially in view of the fact that two completely different and independent methods of assessment were used (self-report and behavioral ratings). However, it is in the domain of discriminant validity that Ho is likely to encounter the most difficulty as a pure measure of hostility; high associations with measures of anxiety, for example, may dilute its overall specificity. It is interesting that a similar argument about the lack of specificity of Type A behavior has been used to explain the weak association between Ho and Type A behavior (Williams & Barefoot, 1988). It is just as likely, however, that the Ho scale itself has numerous components that diverge from the construct of hostility.

This analysis has several further limitations that should be kept in mind. First, the analysis utilized twins as individuals. Twins are known to be different from the general population on a variety of psychological characteristics (Vogel & Motulsky, 1986); thus, findings from this sample cannot be generalized beyond studies involving twins. Second, as noted previously, the sample size and original study design do not permit a more formal investigation of the construct validity of either Ho or Type A behavior. We note, however, that previous investigations have demonstrated support for the validity of the Type A construct as operationalized here (Rosenman et al., 1988) and hope that future investigations of measures of hostility, including the Ho scale, will include biochemical, psychophysiological, behavioral, and psychometric measures as part of the multimethod, multitrait matrix (Campbell & Fiske, 1959) that needs to be tested. A third limitation is related to our use of univariate tests of association in this analysis. Although multivariate approaches could have been applied here, our intent was to conduct a content analysis of the different covariance structures formed by the wide variety of psychological scales used here in relation to Ho and to Type A. Our hope was to establish a "universe of discourse" rather than to confirm or disconfirm any particular model of hostility or Type A. Future investigations of construct validity with larger sample sizes could well profit from the use of such procedures as LISREL (Joreskog, 1978).

The present investigation studied two purported measures of coronary-prone behavior: one seems to be characterized more by neuroticism and by lower dominance and coping; the other may be characterized more by an active, sociable temperament and higher dominance. They appear to overlap, psychologically and behaviorally, with associations indicative of more speed and impatience, a more hard-driving style, and a greater potential for hostility. The general nonoverlapping of correlates between the two traits suggests that future research in this area could be directed profitably toward understanding high-risk combinations of traits (i.e., high Ho and extreme Type A behavior) rather than toward continuing the search for another unitary phenomenon that may be predictive of CHD.

REFERENCES

Barefoot, J. C., Dahlstrom, W.G., & Williams, R. B. (1983). Hostility, CHD incidence, and total mortality: A 25-year follow-up study of 255 physicians. *Psychosomatic Medicine, 45,* 59-63.

Barron, F. (1953). An ego strength scale which predicts response to psychotherapy. *Journal of Consulting Psychology, 17,* 327-333.

Blumenthal, J.A., Williams, R., Kong, Y., Schanberg, S.M., & Thompson, L.W. (1978). Type A behavior and angiographically documented coronary disease. *Circulation, 58,* 634-639.

Blumenthal, J.A., Barefoot, J., Burg, M.M., & Williams, R.B. (1987). Psychological correlates of hostility among patients undergoing coronary angiography. *British Journal of Medical Psychology, 60,* 349-355.

Byrne, D.G., Rosenman, R.H., Schiller, E., & Chesney, M.A. (1985). Consistency and variation among instruments purporting to measure the Type A behavior pattern. *Psychosomatic Medicine, 47,* 242-261.

Campbell, D.T., & Fiske, D.W. (1959). Convergent and discriminant validation by the multitrait-multimethod matrix. *Psychological Bulletin, 56,* 81-105.

Carmelli, D., Rosenman, R.H., & Swan, G.E. (1988). The Cook and Medley Ho scale: A heritability analysis in adult male twins. *Psychosomatic Medicine, 50,* 165-174.

Case, R.B., Heller, S. S., Case, N.B., Moss, A.J., & the Multi-center Post-infarction Research Group. (1985). Type A behavior and survival after acute myocardial infarction. *New England Journal of Medicine, 312,* 737-741.

Chesney, M.A., Black, G.W., Chadwick, J.H., & Rosenman, R.H. (1981). Psychological correlates of the Type A behavior pattern. *Journal of Behavioral Medicine, 2,* 217-229.

Cook, W., & Medley, D. (1954). Proposed hostility and pharisaic-virtue scales for the MMPI. *Journal of Applied Psychology, 38,* 414-418.

Costa, P.T., Zonderman, A.B., McCrae, R.R., & Williams, R.B. (1986). Cynicism and paranoid alienation in the Cook and Medley Ho scale. *Psychosomatic Medicine, 48,* 283-285.

Cronbach, L.J., & Meehl, P.E. (1955). Construct validity in psychological tests. *Psychological Bulletin, 52,* 281-302.

Dahlstrom, W.G., Welsh, G.S., & Dahlstrom, L.E. (1982). *An MMPI handbook (Vol. 1).* Minneapolis: University of Minnesota Press.

Dembroski, T.M., MacDougall, J.M., Williams, R.B., Jr., & Haney, T. (1985). Components of Type A, hostility, and anger-in: Relationship to angiographic findings. *Psychosomatic Medicine, 47,* 219-233.

Dimsdale, J. E., Hackett, T.P., Block, P.C., & Hutter, A.M. (1978). Type A personality and extent of coronary atherosclerosis. *American Journal of Cardiology, 42,* 583-586.

Dimsdale, J.E., Hackett, T.P., & Hutter, A.M. (1979). Type A behavior pattern and angiographic findings. *Journal of Psychosomatic Research, 23,* 273-276.

Feinleib, M., Garrison, R.J., Fabsitz, R.H., Christian, J.C., Hrubec, Z., Borhani, N.O., Kannel, W.B., Rosenman, R. H., Schwartz, J.T., & Wagner, J O. (1977). The NHLBI Twin Study of cardiovascular disease risk factors: Methodology and summary of results. *American Journal of Epidemiology, 106,* 284-295.

Frank, K.A., Heller, S.S., Kornfeld, D.S., Sporn, A.A., & Weiss, M.B. (1978). Type A behavior pattern and coronary angiographic findings. *Journal of the American Medical Association, 240,* 761-763.

Friedman, H.S., & Booth-Kewley, S. (1987). The "Disease-Prone Personality": A meta analysis of the construct. *American Psychologist, 42*, 539-555.

Friedman, H.S., Hall, J.A., & Harris, M.J. (1985). Type A behavior, nonverbal expressive style, and health. *Journal of Personality and Social Psychology, 48*, 1299-1315.

Gough, H.G. (1980). *Manual for the California Psychological Inventory*. Palo Alto, CA: Consulting Psychologists Press.

Gough, H.G., & Heilbrun, A.L. (1980). *The Adjective Check List manual*. Palo Alto, CA: Consulting Psychologists Press.

Gough, H.G., McClosky, H., & Meehl, P.E. (1951). A personality scale for dominance. *Journal of Abnormal Social Psychology, 46*, 360-366.

Graham, J.R. (1977). *The MMPI: A practical guide*. New York: Oxford University Press.

Hase, H.D., & Goldberg, L.R. (1967). Comparative validity of different strategies of constructing personality inventory scales. *Psychological Bulletin, 67*, 231-248.

Haynes, S.G., Feinleib, M., & Kannel, W.B. (1980). The relationship of psychosocial factors to coronary heart disease in the Framingham study: III. Eight-year incidence of coronary heart disease. *American Journal of Epidemiology, 111*, 37-58.

Jablon, S., Neel, J.V., & Gershowitz, H. (1967). The NAS-NRC Twin Panel: Methods of construction of the panel, zygosity, diagnosis, and proposed use. *American Journal of Human Genetics, 19*, 133-161.

Jenkins, C.D., Zyzanski, S.J., & Rosenman, R.H. (1979). *Manual for the Jenkins Activity Survey*. New York: Psychological Corporation.

Joreskog, K.G. (1978). Statistical analysis of covariance and correlation matrices. *Psychometrika, 43*, 443-477.

Krantz, D.S., Schaeffler, M.A., Davia, J.E., Dembroski, T.M., MacDougall, J.M., & Shaffer, RT. (1981). Extent of coronary atherosclerosis, Type A behavior, and cardiovascular response to social interaction. *Psychophysiology, 18*, 654-664.

Leon, G.R., Murray, D., Finn, S.E., & Bailey, J.M. (1988). Inability to predict cardiovascular disease from hostility scores or MMPI items related to Type A behavior. *Journal of Consulting and Clinical Psychology, 56*, 597-600.

Leventhal, A.M. (1966). An anxiety scale for the CPI. *Journal of Clinical Psychology, 22*, 459-461.

Leventhal, A.M. (1968). Additional technical data on the CPI anxiety scale. *Journal of Counseling Psychology, 15*, 479-480.

McCranie, E.W., Watkins, L.O., Brandsma, J.M., & Sisson, B.D. (1986). Hostility, coronary heart disease (CHD) incidence, and total mortality: Lack of association in a 25 year follow-up study of 478 physicians. *Journal of Behavioral Medicine, 9*, 119-125.

Megargee, E.I. (1977). *The California Psychological Inventory handbook*. San Francisco: Jossey-Bass.

Megargee, E.I., & Mendelsohn, G.A. (1962). A cross-validation of twelve MMPI indices of hostility and control. *Journal of Abnormal and Social Psychology, 65*, 431-438.

Rahe, R.H., Rosenman, R.H., Borhani, N.O., & Feinleib, M. (1974). Heritability and psychologic correlates of behavior pattern types A and B. (Abstract) *American Journal of Epidemiology, 100*, 521-522.

Rosenman, R.H. (1978). The interview method of assessment of the coronary-prone behavior pattern. In T. M. Dembroski, S. M., Weiss, J. L., Shields, S. G., Haynes, & M. Feinleib (Eds.), *Coronary-prone behavior*. New York: Springer-Verlag.

Rosenman, R.H., Brand, R.J., Jenkins, C.D., Friedman, M., Straus, R., & Wurm, M. (1975). Coronary heart disease in the Western Collaborative Group Study: Final follow-up experience of 8 1/2 years. *Journal of the American Medical Association, 233*, 872-877.

Rosenman, R.H., Rahe, R.H., Borhani, N.O., & Feinleib, M. (1976). Heritability of personality and behavior pattern. *Acta Geneticae Medicae Gemellologiae, 25*, 221-224.

Rosenman, R.H., Swan, G.E., & Carmelli, D. (1988). Definition, assessment, and evolution of the Type A behavior pattern. In B. K. Houston, & C. R. Snyder (Eds.), *Type A behavior pattern: Research, theory, and intervention*. New York: Wiley.

Scherwitz, L., McKelvain, R., Laman, C., Patterson, J., Dutton, L., Yusim, S., Lester, J., Kraft, J., Rochelle, D., & Leachman, R. (1983). Type A behavior, self involvement, and coronary atherosclerosis. *Psychosomatic Medicine, 45*, 47-57.

Shekelle, R.B., Gale, M., Ostfeld, A. M., & Paul, O. (1983). Hostility, risk of coronary heart disease, and mortality. *Psychosomatic Medicine, 45*, 109-114.

Shekelle, R.B., Hulley, S.B., Neaton, J.D., Billings, J.H., Borhani, N.O., Gerace, T.A., Jacobs, D.R., Lasser, N.L., Mittlemark, M.B., & Stamler, J., for the Multiple Risk Factor Intervention Trial Research Group (1985). The MRFIT behavior pattern study, Type A behavior and incidence of coronary heart disease. *American Journal of Epidemiology, 122*, 559-570.

Shipman, W.G. (1965). The validity of MMPI hostility scales. *Journal of Clinical Psychology, 21*, 186-190.

Smith, T.W., & Frohm, K.D. (1985). What's so unhealthy about hostility? Construct validity and psychosocial correlates of the Cook and Medley HO scale. *Health Psychology, 4*, 503-520.

Taylor, J.A. (1953). A personality scale of manifest anxiety. *Journal of Abnormal and Social Psychology, 48*, 285-290.

Thurstone, L.L. (1953). *Thurstone Temperament Schedule*. Chicago: Science Research Associates.

Vogel, F., & Motulsky, A.G. (1986). *Human genetics: Problems and approaches*. New York: Springer-Verlag.

Wadden, T.A., Anderton, C.H., Foster, G.D., & Love, W. (1983). The Jenkins Activity Survey: Does it measure psychopathology? *Journal of Psychosomatic Research, 27*, 321-325.

Welsh, G. S. (1956). Factor dimensions A and R. In G.S. Welsh & W.G. Dahlstrom (Eds.), *Basic readings on the MMPI in psychology and medicine*. Minneapolis: University of Minnesota Press.

Wiggins, J.S. (1973). *Personality and prediction: Principles of personality assessment*. Reading, MA: Addison-Wesley.

Williams, R.B. Jr., Barefoot, J.C., & Shekelle, R.B. (1985). The health consequences of hostility. In M.A. Chesney & R.H. Rosenman (Eds.), *Anger, hostility, and behavioral medicine*. New York, Hemisphere.

Williams, R. B. Jr., & Barefoot, J. C. (1988). Coronary-prone behavior: The emerging role of the hostility complex. In Houston, B.K., Snyder, C.R. (Eds.), T*ype A behavior pattern: research, theory, and intervention*. New York: Wiley.

Williams, R.B., Jr., Haney, T.L., Lee, K.L., Kong, Y., Blumenthal, J.A., & Whalen, R. E. (1980). Type A behavior, hostility, and coronary atherosclerosis. *Psychosomatic Medicine, 42*, 539-549.

Zyzanski, S. J., Jenkins, C. D., Ryan, T. J., Flessas, A., & Everist, M. (1976). Psychological correlates of coronary angiographic findings. *Archives of Internal Medicine, 136*, 1234-1237.

The Heritability of the Cook and Medley Hostility Scale Revisited

Dorit Carmelli, Ph.D.
Gary E. Swan, Ph.D.
Ray H. Rosenman, M.D.
Health Sciences Program, SRI International, Menlo Park, CA 94025

In a previous analysis of the heritability of the Cook and Medley Hostility (Ho) scale, we found marginal evidence for a significant genetic component for the Cynicism subscale and no genetic variance for the Paranoid Alienation subscale. Scores on these scales were found to be associated with age, socioeconomic status, zygosity, and the MMPI K scale. In the current analysis the heritability of Ho and its subscales was examined in a larger sample of twins from this cohort assessed 15 years later. This group of twins had mean scores that were significantly lower than the means of Ho scores at intake. Our analyses of these data suggest modest heritability (28%) for the full Ho scale and the Cynicism subscale and no heritability for the Paranoid Alienation subscale. It is speculated that Cynicism taps an enduring trait of moderate stability. Paranoid Alienation, on the other hand, as an index of "weak interpersonal bonds," represents a characteristic that is mostly environmental in nature.

Interest in the genetic determinants of hostility as assessed by the Cook and Medley (1954) Hostility (Ho) scale stems from two independent lines of research. First, hostility, a more specific component of the Type A behavior pattern, has been evaluated independently as a predictor of CHD in a number of studies (Williams et al., 1980; Shekelle, Gale, Ostfeld, & Paul, 1983; McCranie, Watkins, Brandsma, & Sisson, 1986; Leon, Murray, Finn, & Bailey, 1988). More recently, Ho scores have been shown to be even stronger predictors of mortality due to all causes, suggesting that the trait measured by the Ho scale may be a general risk factor for a wide variety of adverse health outcomes. Second, a positive family history of CHD is an established risk factor with origins that have been traced to both genetic and familial influences (Shea, Ottman, Gabrieli, Stein, & Nicholas, 1984; Williams, 1988). Since the mechanisms by

© 1990 Select Press

which Ho is related to adverse health outcomes are likely to involve underlying biological predispositions in each individual, the question of an inherited predisposition to hostile behaviors becomes an important link between these two observations.

In a large-scale study dealing with the construct validity of the Ho scale, Smith and Frohm (1985) concluded that "the scale primarily assesses suspiciousness, resentment, frequent anger, and cynical mistrust of others rather than overtly aggressive behavior or general emotional distress" (p. 503). They also found that persons with high Ho scores report more anger, less hardiness, more frequent and severe hassles, and fewer and less satisfactory social supports. Thus the terms "cynical mistrust" (Costa, Zonderman, McCrae, & Williams, 1986) and "cynical hostility" (Smith & Frohm, 1985; Blumenthal, Williams, Kong, Schanberg, & Thompson, 1987) have been proposed as more accurate descriptors than hostility of the psychological characteristics measured by the Ho scale.

Investigations of psychological and behavioral correlates of the Ho scale in a diverse array of populations, including college students (Smith & Frohm, 1985), middle-aged patients who had undergone diagnostic angiography (Blumenthal, Barefoot, Burg, & Williams, 1987), and a nonclinical cohort of middle-aged twin males, participants in an ongoing investigation of CHD risk factors (Swan, Carmelli, & Rosenman, 1990), generally support the conclusion that the Ho scale is multidimensional in nature. It is variously described as tapping the dimensions of anger/hostility, cynical distrust, neuroticism and psychopathology, coping skills, "hardiness," and social maladjustment.

The two subscales—Cynicism and Paranoid Alienation—proposed by Costa et al. (1986) represent an important attempt to identify the multidimensionality of this scale. Both subscales are said to be related to neuroticism and psychopathology: Cynicism measures an additional element of "contempt for others" while Paranoid Alienation measures "weak interpersonal bonds." Since these represent the only two known subscales of the Ho scale, a genetic analysis on these components may clarify the relative role of genes and environment in the total scores of the Ho scale.

In a previous publication (Carmelli, Rosenman, & Swan, 1988) using intake data on a subgroup of 37 pairs of monozygotic (MZ) and 60 pairs of dizygotic (DZ) twins from the NHLBI Twin Study, we examined the heritability of the Cook and Medley Hostility (Ho) scale and its two subscales, Cynicism and Paranoid Alienation. Marginal evidence for a genetic component was found for the Cynicism subscale, but no evidence was obtained for genetic variance in the Paranoid Alienation subscale. Scores on these scales were found to be associated with age, socioeconomic status, the twinning condition, and the Minnesota Multiphasic

Personality Inventory (MMPI) K scale. Statistical adjustment for these covariates removed differences between the MZ and DZ mean values and weakened MZ intrapair correlations on the Ho scale, but did not change overall conclusions regarding heritability.

The objective of the current study was to extend this investigation to examine the heritability of the Cook and Medley Hostility scale and its two subscales in a larger sample of twins from this cohort. The time frame in the current study from the first assessments of the Ho scale spans 15 years and includes a subgroup of 57 pairs from exam I. Since these twins were between 42 and 56 years old, with mean age of 49 years when recruited to the study in 1970, the current study of the heritability of Ho in twins in their mid-60s represents the first genetic study of Ho in an aging cohort. If age is indeed a significant determinant in self-reports of hostility as measured by the Ho scale, we have the opportunity with the existing data to examine the degree to which estimates of heritability are stable during adulthood.

METHOD

Subjects

The present study was part of a larger multicenter investigation of the demographic, physiologic, psychologic, and metabolic aspects of coronary heart disease (CHD) risk in identical and fraternal twins (Jablon, Neel, & Gershowitz, 1967; Feinleib et al., 1977). All twins participating in these studies were recruited from the NRC-NAS twin registry and were white, male, American veterans of World War II or of the Korean conflict. The five examination sites were: Indianapolis, Framingham, Los Angeles, Davis (California), and San Francisco.

At intake in 1970-71, a subgroup of the California twins from the San Francisco and Davis centers were administered the full MMPI inventory. This group of 221 individual subjects comprised 37 MZ and 60 DZ twin pairs. Their ages ranged from 42 to 56 years at the time of their selection into the study, with a mean age of 49 years for both fraternal and identical pairs (Rahe, Hervig, & Rosenman, 1978).

The analyses reported in the current study are based on follow-up data from a third examination of this cohort that took place during 1987-88. During this follow-up the Cook and Medley Ho scale, consisting of 50 items selected from the MMPI inventory, was given to all returning subjects. The scale was administered to subjects at all participating centers. As a result, we have data on a total of 610 individuals (261 complete pairs). Of these, 156 were individual subjects from the combined San Francisco-Davis centers.

Statistical Methods

The distributions of scores on the Ho scale and its subscales were examined in the total sample and by study center. Center differences in means were tested by a one-way ANOVA and, when significant, by a multiple pairwise test procedure (LSD) at an overall 0.05 significance level (SAS User's Guide, 1982). Differences in means between the combined San Francisco and Davis centers and the rest of the centers were also examined.

In the past, heritability analyses in twins have compared intraclass correlation coefficients in the two zygosity types, predicting a higher correlation in MZ than in DZ twins. The classic estimate of heritability is twice the difference of the intraclass correlation coefficients of MZ and DZ twins, $h^2 = 2(r_{MZ} - r_{DZ})$. Under the assumptions of additive genetic and environmental effects, h represents the proportion of variance attributable to genetic variation. To estimate the genetic component in the Ho scale and its subscales, we used both the classic heritability estimates and an analysis of variance model with the modifications proposed by Christian, Kang, and Norton (1974).

Several assumptions are made in the analysis of variance model, including equality of overall means and variances for MZ and DZ twins, and equality of environmental covariances. When these assumptions are valid, two estimates of genetic variance can be calculated. These are termed the "within-pair" estimate and the "among-pairs" estimate. Because the standard error of the among-pairs estimate is generally much larger than that of the within-pair estimate, the latter is the more powerful and preferable estimate.

To test the assumptions of equal means and variances for MZ and DZ twins, Christian et al. (1974) proposed the two-tailed adjusted t' and F' tests. The among-MZ and among-DZ mean squares are used to estimate variances, assuming a mixed-model nested design, with zygosity being a fixed effect, and twin pairs within each zygosity assumed to be a random sample from a population of such twin pairs. A significant difference between the means of the two types of twins indicates an association of the trait being studied with the twinning condition; therefore, it is possible that all estimates of genetic variance will be biased.

To test for heterogeneity of the total variances, a two-tailed F' test is used. To increase the power of the test, an alpha level of 0.20 is recommended. In the case of significant differences in total variances, the within-pair estimate will overestimate the true genetic variance, while the among-pairs estimate will underestimate it. To compensate for these biases, Christian et al. (1974) proposed combining the two estimates by taking their arithmetic mean. This estimate is known as the "among-components" estimate of genetic variance. The statistical significance of this estimate can be tested by using the approximate F' test.

Equality of environmental covariances for MZ and DZ twins is another important assumption in estimating heritability. Because environments of MZ twins may be more similar to each other than environments of DZ twins, this assumption is frequently violated in twin studies. In this case, all the above estimates of heritability will be spuriously high. This assumption can be tested indirectly by requiring the DZ intraclass correlation to be significantly greater than zero. The rationale for this test is as follows: if DZ twins, who share half of their genes in common, are no more alike than random individuals in the population, it must be suspected that the significant intraclass correlation among MZ twins is due to their greater environmental covariances.

Heritability analysis using the mixed-model nested analysis of variance proposed by Christian et al. (1974) was applied to derive estimates of genetic variance. The underlying assumptions of this procedure were also tested. Genetic estimates for the full Ho scale and its subscales at intake and at 15-year follow-up were derived. For the analysis of exam III data, 261 pairs were used (131 MZ and 130 DZ). For the 57 pairs who had intake data, we did a heritability analysis to examine changes in the estimates over time. The results from these analyses will be reported in a separate publication.

RESULTS

Table 1 shows mean values and standard errors at intake and at 15-year follow-up for the Ho scale and its two subscales by exam center. The mean test score for the full Ho scale in the total San Francisco-Davis sample declined from a value of 17.2 to 12.9. This pattern persisted for the returnees, where the difference in mean scores was 3.1 ($p < 0.001$). Similarly, mean values for both the Cynicism and Paranoid Alienation subscales were lower at follow-up for subjects participating in both exams. No significant difference in Ho was observed between returnees (mean 16.9) and those lost to follow-up (mean 17.8). Multiple test comparisons across centers revealed significant differences, at an overall $p < 0.05$ level, between the Indiana and San Francisco-Davis centers on the full Ho scale and the Cynicism subscale. For the Paranoid Alienation subscale we observed a significantly higher mean in the Framingham sample than in the Los Angeles center.

Spearman rank correlations between the two repeated assessments of the Cook and Medley Hostility scale for the 71% of returning subjects (156 out of 221) were 0.62 for the full Ho scale, 0.64 for Cynicism, and

TABLE 1 Means ± Standard Errors for the Cook and Medley Ho Scale and its Subscales at Exam I and Exam III by Twin Center

	Exam I	*Exam III*			
	SF-Davis (*n* = *221*)	*SF-Davis* (*n* = *183*)	*Los Angeles* (*n* = *112*)	*Framingham* (*n* = *127*)	*Indiana* (*n* = *188*)
Cook-Medley Ho scale	17.19 ± 0.52	12.90 ± 0.67	13.44 ± 0.66	13.94 ± 0.61	14.74 ± 0.58
Cynicism	10.00 ± 0.34	7.82 ± 0.46	8.33 ± 0.48	8.50 ± 0.43	9.22 ± 0.39
Paranoid Alienation	3.08 ± 0.15	2.23 ± 0.20	1.89 ± 0.18	2.49 ± 0.17	2.26 ± 0.14

0.45 for Paranoid Alienation. Test-retest correlations of this order of magnitude over 15 years suggest moderate stability over time.

Table 2 shows mean values, among-pairs mean squares, within-pair mean squares, intraclass correlation coefficients, and corresponding statistics to test for differences in means, total variances, and environmental covariance of MZ and DZ twins for the Ho scale and its two subscales. In addition, the significance levels of the test statistics for the presence of genetic variance are also presented. As seen in Table 2, test statistics comparing MZ and DZ twins' mean values and total variances are not statistically significant for the full Ho scale and the Cynicism subscale. Consequently, the within-pair test of genetic variance for these scales is a valid test. Heritability estimates for the Ho and the Cynicism subscale are 28%. We also noticed in this group of twins that DZ intraclass correlations for Ho and Cynicism are significantly different from zero, precluding greater environmental covariance of MZ as opposed to DZ twins.

Paranoid Alienation shows no evidence of significant genetic variance. DZ twins scored significantly higher on this subscale than MZ twins. Also, a significant difference in total variance between zygosities was observed, and the among-components estimate of genetic variance was not significant.

DISCUSSION

In our previous analysis of the heritability of the Ho scale and its two subscales, using combined intake data from the San Francisco-Davis centers, we found marginal evidence for a significant genetic component for the Cynicism subscale and no genetic variance for the Paranoid Alienation subscale. Scores on these scales were found to be associated with age, socioeconomic status, the MMPI K scale, and zygosity. DZ twins scored higher than MZ twins on the full Ho scale and the Cynicism subscale. Consequently, the significant within-pair estimates of genetic variance for these scales were difficult to interpret. For the Paranoid Alienation subscale, the DZ intraclass correlation was greater than that for MZ pairs, contrary to expectation from a genetic model. An adjustment for age and socioeconomic status removed differences between the MZ and DZ mean values but had only a marginal effect on intrapair similarities. For the Cynicism subscale the among-components estimate of genetic variance was marginally significant.

In the current analysis of the heritability of Ho, a larger sample of twins from this cohort was assessed 15 years later. This group of twins had mean scores that were significantly lower than the means of combined Ho scores at intake in the San Francisco-Davis exam centers, despite the fact that only marginal differences in mean scores were observed between the

TABLE 2 Heritability Analyses for the Ho Scale and its Subscales at 15-Year Follow-up of the NHLBI Twin Cohort

	MZ Twin Pairs					*DZ Twin Pairs*					*Test for Difference in MZ and DZ*		*Heritability*	*Significance*
	N	*X*	*AMS*	*WMS*	*r*	*N*	*X*	*AMS*	*WMS*	*r*	*Means*	*Variance*	*Estimate*	*Level*
Cook-Medley Ho Scale														
Follow-up	131	13.2	63.2	33.9	0.30**	130	14.3	66.7	47.8	0.16*	-1.47	1.17	0.28[a]	0.03
Cynicism														
Follow-up	131	8.3	31.2	15.4	0.34**	130	8.6	32.2	21.5	0.20*	-0.76	1.15	0.28[a]	0.03
Paranoid Alienation														
Follow-up	131	1.9	4.76	2.25	0.36**	130	2.5	5.32	3.83	0.16*	-2.58**	1.31*	0.40[b]	0.16

Note: AMS = among mean squares; WMS = within mean squares.

* $p < 0.05$. ** $p < 0.01$.

[a] *Significance levels were determined by the F' test for the within-pair variances.*

[b] *Significance level for the among-components estimate of genetic variance.*

different centers that participated in the third examination. In addition, no significant differences in the intake Ho scores were observed between returnees and nonreturnees to exam III. Thus, the lower scores observed at follow-up cannot be attributed to selection bias.

Our analyses of these data suggest modest heritability (28%) for the full Ho scale and the Cynicism subscale and no heritability for the Paranoid Alienation subscale. Most important, no differences between zygosities in mean scores on the full Ho scale or the Cynicism subscale were observed in the larger sample 15 years later. Also, DZ intraclass correlations were positive and significantly greater than zero for both the full Ho scale and the Cynicism subscale. The pattern of intraclass correlations fits a model of additive gene effects, and the modest estimate of 28% of genetic variance represents an unbiased estimate under these conditions.

Why does the Cynicism subscale continue to show a heritable component in two separate analyses 15 years apart while Paranoid Alienation does not? If cynicism is a trait that is enduring over the life span from middle to old age (Finn, 1986), it is possible that "contempt for others" taps some fundamental enduring biological characteristics or temperament. As the results of this study show, in spite of the lower scores (i.e., less expression of cynical attitudes), the genetic contribution to the variance of this trait is remarkably stable. Moreover, the confounding effect of environmental variables is diminished with increasing age. Paranoid Alienation, on the other hand, as an index of "weak interpersonal bonds," may represent a characteristic that is more environmental in nature and similar to the dimension of social maladjustment said to be tapped by the Ho scale (Blumenthal et al., 1987). Sociability and paranoia demonstrate only moderate stability from middle to old age; thus, this relative instability may be a result of stronger environmental influences.

Future work in this area could profit from the longitudinal investigation of these traits with a cohort of middle-aged adults and continuing on into old age. The NHLBI Twin Study represented a unique opportunity to do this. One focus of interest in the future could be on individuals who develop a cynical attitude toward others and remain highly cynical over time. Determination of the extent to which tracking is related to adverse health outcomes could provide further clues to the fundamental nature of this trait.

REFERENCES

Blumenthal, J.A., Williams, R.B., Jr., Kong, Y., Schanberg, S.M., & Thompson, L.W. (1978). Type A behavior and angiographically documented coronary disease. *Circulation, 58,* 634-639.

Blumenthal, J.A., Barefoot, J., Burg, M.M., & Williams, R.B., Jr. (1987). Psychological correlates of hostility among patients undergoing coronary angiography. *British Journal of Medical Psychology, 60,* 349-355.

Carmelli, D., Rosenman, R.H., & Swan., G.E. (1988). The Cook and Medley Ho scale: A heritability analysis in adult male twins. *Psychosomatic Medicine, 50,* 165-174.

Christian, J.C., Kang, K.W., & Norton, J.A. (1974). Choice of an estimate of genetic variance from twin data. *American Journal of Human Genetics, 26,* 154-161.

Cook, W., & Medley, D. (1954). Proposed hostility and pharisaic-virtue scales for the MMPI. *Journal of Applied Psychology, 38,* 414-418.

Costa, P.T., Zonderman, A. B., McCrae, R.R., & Williams, R.B., Jr. (1986). Cynicism and paranoid alienation in the Cook and Medley HO scale. *Psychosomatic Medicine, 48,* 283-285.

Feinleib, M., Garrison, R.J., Fabsitz, R.H., Christian, J. C., Hrubec, Z., Borhani, N.O., Kannel, W. B., Rosenman, R.H., Schwartz, J.T., & Wagner, J. O. (1977). The NHLBI Twin Study of cardiovascular disease risk factors: Methodology and summary of results. *American Journal of Epidemiology, 106,* 284-295.

Finn, S.E. (1986). Stability of personality self-ratings over 30 years: Evidence for an age/cohort interaction. *Journal of Personality and Social Psychology, 50,* 813-818.

Jablon, S., Neel, J.V., & Gershowitz, H. (1967). The NAS-NRC Twin Panel: Methods of construction of the panel, zygosity, diagnosis, and proposed use. *American Journal of Human Genetics, 19,* 133-161.

Leon, G.R., Murray, D., Finn, S.E., & Bailey, J.M. (1988). Inability to predict cardiovascular disease from hostility scores or MMPI items related to Type A behavior. *Journal of Consulting and Clinical Psychology, 56,* 597-600.

McCranie, E.W., Watkins, L.O., Brandsma, J.M., & Sisson, B.D. (1986). Hostility, coronary heart disease (CHD) incidence, and total mortality: Lack of association in a 25-year follow-up study of 478 physicians. *Journal of Behavioral Medicine, 9,* 119-125.

Rahe, R.H., Hervig, L., & Rosenman, R.H. (1978). The heritability of Type A behavior. *Psychosomatic Medicine, 40,* 478-486.

SAS User's Guide: Statistics (1982). SAS Institute Inc., Cary, North Carolina.

Shea, S., Ottman, R., Gabrieli, C., Stein, Z., & Nicholas, A. (1984). Family history as an independent risk factor for coronary artery disease. *Journal of the American College of Cardiology, 4,* 793-801.

Shekelle, R.B., Gale, M., Ostfeld, A.M., & Paul, O. (1983). Hostility, risk of coronary heart disease, and mortality. *Psychosomatic Medicine, 45,* 109-114.

Smith, T.W., & Frohm, K.D. (1985). What's so unhealthy about hostility? Construct validity and psychosocial correlates of the Cook and Medley HO scale. *Health Psychology, 4,* 503-520.

Swan, G.E., Carmelli, D., & Rosenman, R.H. (1990). Cook and Medley hostility and the Type A behavior pattern: Psychological correlates of two coronary-prone behaviors. In M.J. Strube (Ed.) (1990). Type A behavior. [Special issue]. *Journal of Social Behavior and Personality,* Vol. 5 (1), 89-106.

Williams, R.B., Jr., Haney, T. L., Lee, K. L., Kong, Y., Blumenthal, J. A., & Whalen, R. E. (1980). Type A behavior, hostility, and coronary atherosclerosis. *Psychosomatic Medicine, 42,* 539-549.

Williams, R.R. (1988). Nature, nurture, and family predisposition. *New England Journal of Medicine, 318,* 769-771.

Women and the Type A Behavior Pattern: Review and Commentary

Carl E. Thoresen
Kathryn Graff Low
School of Education, Stanford University
Stanford, CA 94305-2384

Research on the Type A behavior pattern (TA) and coronary heart disease (CHD) has primarily focused on men because of their greater morbidity and mortality. Because more women currently suffer from CHD, the role of TA and its contribution to heart disease in women deserves careful consideraton. Assessment of TA has been complicated by inadequate validation of instruments, single occasion assessment, global categorical measures, and the fact that women are often socialized to be less overtly competitive or hostile than men. Some studies have linked TA with CHD endpoints, but salient features of TA for predicting CHD have yet to be identified. Studies suggest that time urgency and anger-in may be important contributors to atherosclerosis in women. Prevalence of global TA in women appears to be in the 50-60% range. TA is positively related to SES, educational level and occupational status in women; TA also varies with age, decreasing after age 50. Some evidence suggests TA women show greater physiologic reactivity, but only to certain situations. The role of hostility and anger in CHD development in women remains unclear. Some evidence suggests TA is related to more anxiety, neuroticism, and distress in women. TA appears to interact with sex role and other psychosocial variables in fostering distress and subsequent CHD.

Since the late 1950's, research and clinical studies of the Type A behavior pattern (TA) have focused primarily on white adult males (Houston & Snyder, 1988). Controversy surrounding TA has been largely due to confusion in how best to assess this complex syndrome, coupled with major inadequacies in research design of most published studies (Allan & Scheidt, 1988; Matthews & Haynes, 1986). In recent years, studies of women and children have been reported, (see Baker, Dearborn, Hastings & Hamberger, 1984; Thoresen & Pattillo, 1988). But

© 1990 Select Press

understanding of the TA construct still remains primarily limited to male, middle class men.

Currently the leading cause of death and disability in men and women over 40 is cardiovascular disease (Cleary, 1987). Although some studies have linked TA in women to increased risk of coronary heart disease (CHD) (e.g., Haynes, Feinleib & Kannel, 1980), the theoretical and empirical basis of this relationship remains obscure. Recently, the increasing risk of CHD morbidity and mortality for women has been acknowledged, such that the overall CHD risk for women, while only one-fifth that of men in the middle adult years, sharply increases to approach that of men by age 70 (Mattsen & Herd, 1988). Further, women who suffer myocardial infarctions in their middle adult years are much more likely to die than males. Finally, the distinction between TA and "coronary-prone behavior" remains confused. Some consider the terms synonymous. However, TA is best considered as one of several possible coronary-prone qualities and characteristics (Booth-Kewley and Friedman, 1987).

The original TA construct emerged as a "male model" for good reason, since the growing epidemic of CHD morbidity and mortality in the 1950's and 1960's involved primarily men. The TA concept developed in large part from the clinical and often qualitative observations of male coronary patients (Friedman & Rosenman, 1974). As will be noted, we lack comparable clinically-based observations of women. Simply put, we do not at present have a very clear understanding, scientifically as well as clinically, of TA in women.

Some have conjectured that TA women may experience more depression and anxiety, and exhibit less anger and hostility than TA men. Price (1982), for example, suggests that TA women may become more depressed rather than overtly hostile or angry, a perspective similar to some psychoanalytic observers who have argued that feelings of anger and hostility often may be experienced as anxiety or depression (e.g., Menninger & Menninger, 1936; Alexander, 1950). The Framingham Heart Study also offers some support for this perspective (Haynes & Feinleib, 1980). For example, women working outside the home with higher "anger-in" scores were found to be at greater risk for some forms of CHD. A large scale meta-analysis of coronary prone-behavior and disease outcomes (Booth-Kewley & Friedman, 1987) found that depression measures had an "effect size" comparable to that of global TA (measured by the Structured Interview) in predicting CHD. Anxiety measures were also found to be significant predictors of CHD outcomes.

This paper will selectively review recent literature on TA in women, both theoretical and empirical directions for future work.

SELECTED REVIEW OF LITERATURE

Assessment of Type A in Women

Unfortunately, the research on TA in women has been plagued by inadequate assessment. With rare exception, measures used with women have not been validated against significant outcomes over time in female populations. Most studies have used one of three self-report measures: the Jenkins Activity Survey (JAS), the Framingham Type A Scale (FTAS), and the Bortner Rating Scale. A few have employed the Type A Structured Interview (SI), in part because it allows for assessment of content plus how the person answers questions (e.g., speech stylistics, gestures, facial expressions). Of the self-report measures only the FTAS has been shown to predict CHD outcomes in a prospective study (Haynes, Feinleib & Kannel, 1980).

The SI, acknowledged as the gold standard of TA assessment (see Booth-Kewley & Friedman, 1987; Matthews, 1988), has not been validated prospectively against any major health outcomes for women. The SI has, however, been shown to correlate positively with higher levels of physiologic reactivity as well as with degree of coronary artery disease (atherosclerosis) in women (e.g., Anderson, Williams, Lane, Haney, Simpson, Houseworth, 1987; Blumenthal, Williams, Kong, Schanberg, & Thompson, 1978; Frank, Heller, Kornfeld, Sporn & Weiss, 1978).

Some problems with the SI seem especially relevant to women. These include the global, often dichotomous categorical ratings yielded by the SI (e.g., simply rating women as either A or B). Seldom is the SI used in a way that yields a continuous rating (e.g., scores ranging from 0 to 100). The Videotaped Structured Interview (VSI), uses a continuous scale (Friedman & Powell, 1984) with subscores for Time Urgency and Hostility. However, the VSI still yields an overall global score.

Matthews and Haynes (1986) recently noted some potential problems with the SI and women: "Many of the SI questions are oriented toward work or competitive behavior which may be socially acceptable for working men but not for women, particularly housewives" (p. 925). Results from the Framingham Heart Study with women showed, for example, that women who repressed hostility and who turned their anger inward were at a greater risk of CHD. Such women might score lower on the SI, since the more overt signs of anger and hostility used in SI ratings would be less evident. Further, women commonly differ from men in their speech stylistics, using, for example, less vigorous language. This difference would also contribute to a lower overall SI score.

Coronary Heart Disease, Type A Behavior Pattern, and Women

Since the majority of studies of TA and women have focused upon cardiovascular factors, we will selectively review some of these studies. As noted, while men experience roughly five times more CHD than women during the middle adult years, CHD is still the predominant cause of death in older women (Mattsen & Herd, 1988). Post-menopausal women are at greatest risk, with a dramatic 40-fold increase of CHD in the oldest versus the youngest groups of women (e.g., women in their 30's vs. 70's). Interestingly women report experiencing much more chest pain, possibly angina pectoris, than men but have less than one-half the myocardial infarctions (MI) than men (Eaker & Castelli, 1988). The influence of pregnancy, estrogen, menopause, and other gender-related factors in developing CHD for women remains unclear. What is clear, however, is that CHD risk for women sharply increases after menopause.

Six studies of TA and CHD in women were examined: one longitudinal study, two cross-sectional studies, and three angiographic studies. The Framingham Heart Study offers the only prospective study linking CHD and TA in women (Haynes, Levine, Scotch, Feinleib & Kannel, 1978). This epidemiological study involved roughly 1000 females between 45 and 77, who were assessed for TA using the Framingham Type A Scale (FTAS), a 10-item self-report measure. Diagnoses of MI, coronary insufficiency, and angina pectoris (AP) were studied at eight-year follow-up. Women assessed as TA were at significantly greater risk for CHD and AP, but not for MI; relative risks were 2.1, 3.6 and 1.3, respectively (Haynes, Feinleib & Kannel, 1980). In women working outside the home, TA and suppressed hostility (not discussing anger) were both significant predictors of CHD. Among housewives, TA and self-reported tension symptoms predicted CHD. Further analysis revealed that women in clerical positions with more than three children and a non-supportive boss were at greatest (more than tenfold) CHD risk compared to other women (Haynes & Feinleib, 1980). At ten year follow-up, the relative risk for CHD, angina and MI for TA women compared to non-TA women was 2.0, 2.6, and 1.8 respectively (Haynes & Feinleib, 1981). However, at 14 years, the TA women had twice as much chest pain, but were no longer at significantly greater risk for CHD compared to non-TA women (Eaker & Castelli, 1988). Note, however, that this reduction in risk could be accounted for by a corresponding reduction in TA among women as they become older.

Two cross-sectional studies demonstrated a relationship between TA and coronary heart disease. Rosenman & Friedman (1961) found that TA women assessed by interview had markedly higher serum cholesterol and faster blood coagulation (increased clotting). Also, they experienced five times more diastolic hypertension and four times more clinical heart disease. Keningsberg, Zyzanski, Jenkins, Wardell & Licciardello (1974) also found that women with CHD exhibited higher Type A scores on the Jenkins Activity Survey (JAS) than women without evidence of CHD.

In three angiographic studies with samples including women, a relationship was found between TA (SI) and coronary artery occlusion (Blumenthal et al, 1978; Frank et al, 1978; Williams, Haney, Lee, Kong, Blumenthal & Whalen, 1980). Blumenthal et al. (1978) found a relationship between prevalence of TA (SI) and coronary artery occlusion. TA was highest in the group with greatest artery occlusion.

In a second study, Williams, et al., (1980) assessed 117 women (and 307 men) using the SI. Both TA males and females had significantly more occluded vessels than non-TA patients. In these studies, TA in women, assessed by different measures (FTAS and two types of interview) related positively to CHD markers. These different measures all tap the TA component of time urgent and impatient behaviors. In addition, the Framingham data (Haynes & Feinleib, 1980) also suggests that "anger-in" and contextual factors, such as working for a non-supportive boss, may also contribute to increased coronary risk for TA women.

Coronary Risk Factors and Type A

A number of risk factors for women are associated with CHD, including arterial hypertension, cigarette smoking (e.g., Feinleib & Kovar, 1988; Rosenberg, et al., 1985) family history of CHD (e.g., Colditz, et al., 1986), diabetes mellitus, and use of oral contraceptives, particularly in combination with cigarette smoking or hypertension (Rosenberg et al., 1985). However, the Framingham Study found no relationship between TA (FTAS) and blood pressure, serum cholesterol level, or rate of cigarette smoking in women (Haynes, et al., 1978a). At 14 years, no differences emerged for TA in relation to blood pressure, serum cholesterol or cigarette smoking, but TA women were heavier (body mass index) (Eaker & Castelli, 1988). By contrast, Rosenman and Friedman (1961) found Type A women (clinical interview) had higher serum cholesterol and blood pressure. Blumenthal et al., (1978), in an angiographic study, also found a positive relationship between Type A (SI) and serum cholesterol, while Shekelle, Schoenberger & Stamler (1976) found modest correlations between TA (JAS) and serum cholesterol, blood pressure and cigarette smoking. Finally, Chesney, Black, Frautschi and De Busk (1986) in a study of 942 women found several relationships between TA (assessed by a different self-report measure) and health-related behaviors. TA women were found to be slightly more overweight, less physically active, consume more caffeine daily, and sleep less hours compared to non-TA women. No differences were found for cigarette or alcohol consumption.

Causal relationship between TA and CHD in women remain obscure. Part of the confusion is caused by inadequate or invalid assessment as well as by sampling problems. The evidence reported here suggests that Type A as assessed by interview techniques may be related to elevated serum cholesterol and blood pressure. But assessment based on self-report (FTAS) yields no significant relationships between TA and traditional risk factors. Further, some studies have used highly selected samples of women. We suspect that relationships do exist (e.g., TA and elevated serum cholesterol) but improved assessment strategies, sampling procedures and research designs are needed before such conjectures can be evaluated.

DEMOGRAPHICS OF WOMEN AND TYPE A PREVALENCE

Generally, prevalence data on TA is inconclusive, particularly for women. Estimates for women range from 25 percent to 75 percent of the general population, depending on the measures used. The only well-controlled population-based study (Moss, et al.., 1986) found prevalence of TA (SI) in women to be 64 percent. No differences were found between men and women. However, black adults showed significantly less TA (about 10 percent) than white adults. Chesney et al. (1986) found 59 per cent of a sample of 942 women to be TA (self-report), comparable to the findings of Moss et al. (1986). The greatest TA prevalence in the Chesney et al. sample was among salaried women (69 per cent); the lowest (46 per cent) was among women not working outside of the home. These findings are consistent with other studies using the JAS (Shekelle, et al.., 1976) and the SI (McDougall, Dembroski & Musante, 1979). Prevalence of TA in women in other countries and cultures is currently unknown.

Socioeconomic Status, Education and Occupational Level

In general, TA is positively related to socioeconomic status (SES) educational level, and occupational status (Baker et al., 1984). Kelly and Houston (1985) found TA (JAS) associated with higher occupational levels while Moss et al. (1986) observed that TA (SI) was correlated with income, educational level, and white-collar employment.

Age

In an earlier study, Waldron et al. (1977) found the highest TA values (JAS) for employed women in their 30's. Moss et al. (1986) found an inverted "U" relationship: lowest Type A scores in very young and in older women with highest prevalence in the 40's. Interestingly, Davidson et al. (1980), using the Bortner Scale and the SI, found virtually no TA behavior in a group of female "senior managers" over 60 years old.

What emerges from these limited data is the proposition that elderly women display less TA, despite their increased risk of CHD. One possible explanation is that being more Type A in the middle adult years (roughly 30 to 55) may contribute to increased risk for CHD later in life. Unfortunately, no longitudinal data exist to examine this possibility. We should note that TA also appears to diminish in older men as well (Moss et al. 1986). Without prospective studies that repeatedly assess level of TA over time, the developmental history of TA remains unknown.

PHYSIOLOGICAL REACTIVITY

Type A persons commonly show greater autonomic arousal than non-TAs, but not in all situations. They, for example, produce higher levels of norephinephrine and cortisol under certain conditions than Type B subjects (Williams, 1985). Women, however, are generally less physiologically reactive to "challenging" stimuli than men. They show, for example, less increase in heart rate and blood pressure (Lawler & Schmied, 1986; Matthews & Stoney, 1988).

Some have speculated that this dampened arousal may partially explain why women have a lower incidence of CHD. However, physiologic reactivity studies to date have used a very limited number of so-called challenging tasks (e.g., cold pressor, mental arithmetic). Women may not perceive these particular tasks as especially meaningful or salient and thus not challenging. As with TA assessment, the validity of tasks used to assess physiological reactivity with women remains an open question.

Still, Type A women do demonstrate increased reactivity in some studies and situations. Anderson et al. (1986) found that Black women assessed as TA (SI) showed higher blood pressure changes during the SI but not during a mental arithmetic task. Pfiffner, Elsinger, Nil, Buzzin, Battig (1986) found greater blood pressure changes for TA women during rapid information processing. By contrast, McDougall, Dembroski and Krantz (1981) observed no differences between TA vs. non-TA women in blood pressure and heart rate during a high incentive reaction time task or during a cold pressor test, but significantly greater reactivity during the SI and during a history quiz. Using the JAS, Lawler & Schmied (1986) found no differences in physiological reactivity on a variety of tasks, including "interpersonal, individual, and competitive stressors." Clearly the relationship between TA and physiological changes is largely dependent on how the woman perceives the task and how TA has been measured.

In a review of TA and women, including nine studies on blood pressure reactivity and three that included heart rate changes, Baker et al. (1984) concluded that, "Type A women may be more physiologically reactive to "Type-A-relevant laboratory stressors than Type B women" (p. 484). In general, evidence partially supports a relationship between TA and physiological reactivity in women (Baker, et al. 1984). However, the magnitude of the difference between TA and non-TA women appears to be considerably less than in men (Polefrone & Manuck, 1988). Further, reactivity in women appears to be much more influenced by other factors than in males. Reactivity may also vary with the menstrual cycle (Polefrone & Manuck, 1988), suggesting that in addition to perceived task salience, biological timing can also make a difference. Until TA assessment is refined and gender sensitive situations are used to examine physiological reactivity, the overall relationship with TA will remain ambiguous.

SELECTED PERSONALITY VARIABLES

Hostility

Several studies have linked self-report measures of hostility and CHD in men (e.g., Barefoot, Dahlstrom, & Williams, 1983; Shekelle, Gale & Ostfeld, 1983; Williams et al. 1980). Three studies have suggested that hostility and anger may be related to CHD in women. Note that anger in these studies is viewed primarily as an emotion, episodic in nature. Hostility, by contrast, is primarily attitudinal, assessed as an enduring trait by the Cook-Medley Ho Scale (from the MMPI) as suspiciousness, cynical distrust and resentful thoughts. Dembroski and Costa (1988) have, however, recently challenged this perspective on anger and hostility, arguing for two types of hostility: "neurotic hostility", i.e., experiencing anger as negative emotional state and "antagonistic hostility", i.e., expressing anger toward others in social situations. They view the neurotic kind as unrelated to CHD. However, the role of gender in this conceptualization remains unclear.

Haynes & Feinleib (1980) found a significant relationship in the Framingham Study between Anger-In and CHD. The distinction between constructs like anger-in and hostility in women, however, remains confused. In the Framingham data women found to be at greater risk for CHD reported they were less able to discuss or vent their anger; instead, they appeared to repress their angry emotions. Further analyses suggested a positive link between hostility, tension, anxiety and CHD among these women (Haynes, Feinleib & Kannel, 1980).

In an angiographic study, Williams et al. (1980), found that the Cook-Medley Ho scale predicted degree of coronary occlusion in a sample of over 400 men and women, independent of other risk factors. The relative risk of significant artery occlusion for TA women (SI) who were also above the median on the HO was 3.6 times that of non-Type A women who were below the median on hostility (HO). Of 64 Type A (SI) women above the median on the HO scale, almost 50 percent had serious arterial occlusion compared to less than 15 percent of non-TA women who were low on HO. For women in this sample TA (SI) and HO both independently predicted more coronary artery disease. Note, however, that all these women already suffered from some CHD symptoms, having been referred by physicians for possible coronary artery bypass surgery. Thus, these results may not generalize to women without advanced CHD symptoms.

Overall, the relationship between hostility and CHD in women remains unclear. Anger-in or not openly discussing anger was predictive of CHD in women in one prospective study (Haynes & Feinleib, 1980), while the HO related to degree of atherosclerosis in women who already suffer CHD in a cross-sectional design (Williams et al. 1980). Further data examining relationships between anger, hostility, and CHD in women are essential. Data should look at different ways to assess anger and hostility since they are not simple constructs and may not be readily captured in simple questionnaires.

Anxiety, Neuroticism and Depression

Some evidence suggests that the relationship of TA in women with anxiety, neuroticism and depression may be stronger than in men. In addition, a few studies suggest that anxiety disorders may be linked to CHD mortality in men and women, independent of TA (Crisp & Queenan, 1984; Haines, Imeson, & Meade, 1987). We suspect that being high on TA characteristics and experiencing considerable anxiety may lead to an increased risk of CHD, but the relationship between these two variables has not yet been examined in a prospective design. If the mechanism for atherosclerosis includes increased plasma catecholamine levels, increased blood pressure reactivity and greater changes in cardiac function (e.g., heart rate, stroke volume), as has been suggested, then easily triggered "fight or flight" reactions associated with certain types of anxiety could contribute to CHD in highly aroused TA persons (Wright, 1988).

We know that women assessed as TA (all measures) report more stress and tension, poorer physical health, more daily emotional distress, more frustration, more anxiety, poorer marital adjustment, less self-esteem, more nervousness and greater dysphoria than non-Type A women (Davidson et al, 1980; Dearborn & Hastings, 1987; Haynes &

Feinleib, 1980; Houston & Kelly, 1987; Kelly & Houston, 1985; Waldron, 1978). Booth-Kewley & Friedman (1987) reported evidence from a few studies involving women that depression measures had a statistical "effect size" of 0.27 for predicting CHD in women, comparable to that of the SI. Anxiety measures were also significant in predicting CHD for women. Haynes, Feinleib and Kannel (1980) found that women high on self-reported hostility, tension and anxiety had a higher incidence of CHD. Further, McDougall, Dembroski & Musante, (1979) found significant correlations between the Speed and Impatience scale (JAS) and scales measuring distress in women. Bass (1984) found that the Speed and Impatience Scale (JAS) related to depression scales.

These cross-sectional studies of depression, anxiety and neurotic characteristics in TA women with CHD symptoms may be confounded. Clearly, changes in affect may be the result or a concomitant of CHD or MI, or from medications prescribed to treat CHD, rather than a contributing cause (see Matthews, 1988; Friedman & Booth-Kewley, 1988). Although a number of studies (e.g., Guiry et al. 1987; Trelawny-Ross & Russell, 1987) have prospectively documented changes for male patients after an MI in depression, anxiety, sexual adjustment, and feelings of personal inadequacy, no studies have been reported for post-coronary women.

DeGregorio and Carver (1980) examined the relationship between ratings of masculinity (as assessed by the Bem Sex Role Inventory) and depression in TA subjects. Women characterized as TA and as highly masculine were found to report higher self-esteem and less depression than other women. However, those who were TA and characterized as more feminine experienced more anxiety, depression, and lower self-esteem. These results demonstrate the need to move away from global ratings of TA and, instead, examine interactions between TA and other personality and psychosocial variables. Conceivably, the tension between traditionally "feminine" role behaviors and TA produces for women considerable distress leading to increased disease risk.

Currently, the relationship of TA, depression, anxiety and other neurotic characteristics is ambiguous, due in part to cross-sectional designs involving preselected samples of women. Some degree of anxiety and depression, if not fearfulness, may have always existed within the TA syndrome. It may have gone unrecognized because of limited and oversimplified global assessment methods used to measure TA (Thoresen and Ohman, 1987). Perhaps TA women experience and express more depression and anxiety than men, in part because it has been less acceptable for many of them to express overt anger toward others.

SUMMARY AND COMMENT

A definitive coronary-prone behavior pattern for women is yet to be identified and confirmed via controlled, prospectively designed studies. A tentative picture, however, can be assembled from the existing literature. TA, as currently assessed in women, is related to some but not all CHD markers. For example, no evidence currently links TA to myocardial infarction in women. However, available evidence does suggest that some features of the TA syndrome, such as the time urgent, impatient behaviors, may be predictive of CHD, especially if home and family contexts are taken into account.

Unfortunately, most published data are based on case-control, cross-sectional designs. For example, cross-sectional angiographic evidence is confounded by the fact that features of the TA syndrome may be by-products of CHD and/or MI, or may be the result of stress associated with angiographic procedures. All studies linking TA and CHD are also weakened by inadequate validation of instruments used with women. The only prospective study of TA and women (Framingham Study) has not been replicated to date. Also, no well-controlled prospective studies using the SI have been done with women. Clearly, well-designed prospective studies using validated measures across occasions are needed to clarify relationships between TA, other coronary-prone factors and CHD pathology. Further, studies are needed to explore TA and other physical and social disorders in women.

Type A women, like their male counterparts, typically have larger incomes, tend to be white collar or secretarial-clerical rather than blue collar workers, and, in general, have more formal education than less Type A women. While it is difficult to draw conclusions about psychosocial variables from demographic evidence, data from the Framingham Study suggest that women in clerical positions faced with nonsupportive supervisors, little job mobility, and multiple home and family responsibilities are, not surprisingly, at greatest risk for CHD. In terms of TA prevalence, estimates vary with different measures, but probably slightly over one-half of the female population assessed globally by SI qualifies to some extent as TA.

Age is also a factor. Unfortunately, no data are available on intra-individual changes in TA over time. This is a crucial variable probably confounding interpretations of predictive relationships between TA and CHD factors when TA has been assessed on only one occasion (e.g., Ragland & Brand, 1988; Eaker & Castelli, 1988; Powell, Dennis & Thoresen, 1988). Moss et al. (1986) suggest that TA in women (and men) may begin to diminish gradually after age 55-60. The interaction of TA and age may become important in aging populations, such as women in the Framingham Study. In that study, women over 50 may lower their TA status while, at the same time, increasing their risk for CHD. This inverse relationship may, in part, help explain the gradual decrease in predictive power of TA (measured by the Framingham Scale) over two decades in the Framingham Study population (Eaker & Castelli, 1988). Reasons for decreases in TA score with time remain open to speculation. The multiple demands of the middle years, including family, job, and marriage, may involve more demanding and challenging situations, and thus elicit more TA. Age as a variable clearly deserves more attention.

The relationship of TA to physiological processes remains ambiguous. Some studies show that Type A women experience greater changes in blood pressure and heart rate in response to challenging stimuli. However it is difficult to draw conclusions about physiological reactivity, given the different tasks used in studies, coupled with different TA measures. Further, reactivity in TA women may be affected by other social and physiologic factors, such as menstrual cycle and social-emotional factors. Again, use of challenging tasks with documented salience for women and replication of such studies is essential for understanding the physiological responsiveness of TA women. In addition, prospective designs are needed whereby patterns of physiological change can be documented for women over time and co-variations with psychosocial factors, including TA, can be studied.

Anxiety and depression may play a significant role in disease prone patterns in women, including CHD. Anxiety has been a significant independent predictor of CHD in a few studies, although assessment of anxiety has been inconsistent, at times based on untested instruments. The effect of masculine and feminine roles on affect may be significant in TA individuals, and deserves further attention in light of the fact that single, working women in positions of power appear to have less CHD than women in subordinate clerical positions or housewives. Currently, the role of anger and hostility in atherogenesis in women remains an unresolved issue. The three studies reviewed used globally oriented measures. It is not clear, for example, whether the anger-in described by women in the Framingham Study is simply a manifestation of a hostile and suspicious approach to the world, or is in fact episodic anger that is justified by unreasonable demands or situations. In addition, we lack data on how hostility is actually expressed via direct observation or ratings by others. It may be that women *feel* hostility and thus endorse more globally-oriented self-report items yet may not actually exhibit more behavioral signs of hostility or endorse more behaviorally stated self-report items. Since women are often socialized to be less overtly aggressive and hostile than men, assessment may be confounded by cultural canons that discourage exhibiting hostile or overtly angry reactions (Henry & Stephens, 1977). Could women's hostility, as suggested earlier, be expressed more directly as anxious or depressive behaviors?

A variety of methodological and theoretical problems have slowed the empirical substantiation of a coronary prone pattern in women. One is the prevailing fixed trait orientation of TA measures. Despite a "person by environment" or context-sensitive perspective originally proposed by Friedman & Rosenman (1959), most researchers have conceptualized the TA syndrome as a static, enduring set of behaviors and characteristics. As such, assessment of Type A has often been limited to a single occasion, brief self-report measure, with less attention paid to specific environmental factors which influence the experience and expression of Type A characteristics (Thoresen & Ohman, 1987). Because of this prevailing trait orientation, existing studies of TA in women may seriously underestimate or obscure relationships of TA with various physiological and psychological factors and disorders.

Smith & Anderson (1986), along with others, have argued that TA is best thought of as a dynamic pattern that elicits *and* is elicited by perceived challenge or threat in specific situations. Type As often play an active, "constructivist" role in creating, via their perceptions and expectations, the very situations that they, in turn, often react to with hostile, competitive and/or impatient thoughts and behaviors. This social constructivist perspective has seldom been recognized in the TA literature, yet may be one of the most crucial characteristics of the TA (Thoresen, 1988; Thoresen & Pattillo, 1988). At present we know very little about how Type A women construe reality, in part because assessments have lacked gender-sensitive features that tap how women think about themselves in various situations.

Finally, one can understandably wonder about the possible origins of TA in women. Is it a primarily genetically predetermined biological pattern due to a kind of physiological "prewiring", making the TA woman more susceptible to hyperreacting physiologically and behaviorally to situations (Williams, 1985)? Is it primarily learned early in life as a result of the quality of parent-child interactions, especially the maternal relationship as suggested, for example, by theory and research in infant and early childhood attachment (see Thoresen & Pattillo, 1988)? Or is it in large part created by a dominant American culture that is "time crazy", fiercely competitive and excessively individualistic (Bellah, Madson, Sullivan, Savidler, Tipton, 1985; Rifkin, 1987; Sampson, 1985; Thoresen, 1988), a culture that socially markets the TA style via its institutions, such as education and the media (radio, television and film), as the way to achieve success? Perhaps, it is a blending of each of these and others. Increasing our understanding TA in women will require some thoughtful and patient consideration of possible etiological factors coupled with better ways to assess TA. Especially needed are controlled experimental studies that examine the consequences of changes in TA and related factors to the health and well being of women.

REFERENCES

Alexander, F. (1950) *Psychosomatic medicine.* New York, Norton.

Allan, R. & Scheidt, S. (1988) Is Type-A behavior a risk factor for coronary heart disease? *Cardiovascular Reviews & Reports*, 38-40, 45.

Anderson, N B., Williams, R.B., Jr., Lane, J.D., Haney, T., Simpson, S. & Houseworth, S.J. (1986). Type A behavior, family history of hypertension an cardiovascular responsivity among Black women. *Health Psychology 5*, 393-406.

Baker, L.J., Dearborn, M.J., Hastings, J., & Hamberger, K. (1984). Type A behavior in women: A review. *Health Psychology, 3*, 477-497.

Barefoot, J.C., Dahlstrom, W.G., Williams, W.B. (1983). Hostility, CHD incidence and total mortality: A 25 year follow-up 255 physicians. *Psychosomatic Medicine, 45*, 59-64.

Bass, C. (1984). Type A behavior: Recent developments. *Journal of Psychosomatic Research, 28*, 371-378.

Bellah, R.N., Madson, R., Sullivan, W.M., Savidler, A. & Tipton, S.M. (1985). *Habits of the heart: Individualism and commitment in American life.* Berkeley, CA: University of California Press.

Blumenthal, J.A., Williams, R.B., Jr., Kong, Y., Schanberg, S.M. & Thompson, L.W. (1978). Type A behavior pattern and coronary atherosclerosis. *Circulation, 58*, 634-639.

Booth-Kewley, S. & Friedman, H.S., (1987). Psychological predictors of heart disease: A quantitative review. *Psychological Bulletin, 101*, 343-362.

Chesney, M., Black, G., Frautschi, N. & De Busk, A. (1986). Health behaviors of Type A and Type B women. Paper presented at Society of Behavioral Medicine, Washington, DC.

Cleary, P.D. (1987). Gender differences in stress-related disorders. In R. C. Barnett, L. Biener, G.K. Baruch (Eds.). *Gender and stress*, NY: Free Press, 39-72.

Colditz, G.A., Stampfer, M.J., Willett, W.C., Rosner, B., Speizer, F.E. & Hennekens, C.H. (1986). A prospective study of parental history of myocardial infarction and coronary heart disease in women. *American Journal of Epidemiology, 123*, 48-58.

Crisp, A.H. & Queenan, M. (1984). Myocardial infarction and the emotional climate. *Lancet*, 618-619.

Davidson, M.J., Cooper, C.L. & Chamberlain, D. (1980). Type A coronary prone behavior and stress in senior female mangers and administrators. *Journal of Occupational Medicine, 22*, 801-805.

Dearborn, M.J. & Hastings, J.E. (1987). Type A personality as a mediator of stress and strain in employed women. *Journal of Human Stress, 13*, 53-60.

DeGregorio, E. & Carver, C. (1980). Type A behavior pattern, sex role orientation, and psychological adjustment. *Journal of Personality and Social Psychology, 39*, 286-293.

Dembroski, T.M. & Costa, P.T. (1988). Assessment of coronary-prone behavior: A current overview. *Annuls of Behavioral Medicine, 10*, 60-68.

Eaker, E.D. & Castelli, W.P. (1988). Type A behavior and coronary heat disease in women: Fourteen-year incidence from the Framingham Study. In B.K. Houston & C.R. Snyder (Eds.) *Type A behavior pattern: Research, theory and intervention.* NY: Wiley, 83-97.

Feinleib, M. & Kovar, M.G. (1989). National estimates of the prevalence of risk factors for cardiovascular disease among women in the United States. In. E.D. Eaker, B. Packard, N.K. Wenger, T.B. Clarkson, & H.A. Tyroler (Eds.), *Coronary heart disease in women* (Chapter 6). New York: Haymarket Doyma Inc.

Frank, K., Heller, S., Kornfeld, D., Sporn, A. & Weiss, M. (1978). Type A behavior pattern and coronary angiographic findings. *Journal of the American Medical Association, 240*, 761-763.

Friedman, H. & Booth-Kewley, S. (1988). Validity of the Type A construct: A reprise. *Psychological Bulletin, 104*, 381-384.

Friedman, H.S. & Booth-Kewley, S. (1987). Personality, Type A behavior and coronary heart disease: The role of emotional expression. *Journal of Personality and Social Psychology, 53*, 783-792.

Friedman, M. & Powell, L.H. (1984). The diagnosis and quantitative assessment of Type A behavior: Introduction and description of the Videotaped Structured Interview. *Integrative Psychiatry, 1*, 123-129.

Friedman, M. & Rosenman, R. (1959). Association of specific overt behavior pattern with blood and cardiovascular findings. *Journal of the American Medical Association, 169*, 1286-1296.

Friedman, M. & Rosenman, R. (1974). *Type A behavior pattern and your heart.* NY: Knopf.

Guiry, E., Conroy, K.M., Hickey, N., Mulcahy, R. (1987). Psychosocial response in an acute coronary event and its effect on subsequent rehabilitation and lifestyle change. *Clinical Cardiology, 10*, 256-260.

Haines, A.P., Imeson, J.D. & Meade,T.W. (1987). Phobic anxiety and ischaemic heart disease. *British Medical Journal, 295*, 297-299.

Haynes, S. & Feinleib, M. (1980). Women, work and coronary heart disease: prospective findings from the Framingham Heart Study. American *Journal of Public Health, 70*, 133-141.

Haynes, S. & Feinleib, M. (1981). Type A behavior and the incidence of coronary heart disease in the Framingham Heart Study. In H. Denolin (Ed.), *Advance in vardiology, Vol 29: Psychological problems before and after myocardial infarction.* Basel: S. Karger.

Haynes, S. & Feinleib, M. & Kannel, W. B. (1980). The relationship of psychosocial factors to coronary heart disease in the Framingham Study, III. Eight year incidence of coronary heart disease. *American Journal of Epidemiology, 107*, 362-383.

Haynes, S., Levine, S., Scotch, N., Feinleib, M. & Kannel, W. (1978b). The relationship between psychosocial factors to coronary heart disease in the Framingham Study, II. Prevalence of coronary heart disease. *American Journal of Epidemiology, 107*, 362-383.

Henry, J. & Stephens, P. (1977). *Stress, health, and the social environment*. New York: Springer-Verlag.

Houston, B.K., Kelly, K.E. (1987). Type A behavior in housewives: Relation to work, marital adjustment, stress, tension, health, fear-of-failure and self-esteem. *Journal of Psychosomatic Research, 31*, 55-61.

Houston, B.K., Snyder, C.R. (1988), (Eds.). *Type A behavior pattern: Theory research and intervention*. NY: John Wiley.

Kelly, K. & Houston, B.K. (1985). Type A behavior in employed women: Relation to work, marital and leisure variables, social support, stress, tension and health. *Journal of Personality and Social Psychology, 48*, 1067-1079.

Keningsberg, P., Zyzanski, S.J., Jenkins, C.D., Wardell, W. & Licciardello, A. (1974). The coronary prone behavior pattern in hospitalized patients with and without coronary heart disease. *Psychosomatic Medicine, 35*, 344-351.

Lawler, K.A. & Schmied, L.A. (1986). Cardiovascular responsivity, Type A behavior and parental history of heart disease in young women. *Psychophysiology, 23*, 28-32.

McDougall, J.M., Dembroski, T.M. & Musante, L. (1979). The structured interview and questionnaire methods of assessing coronary-prone behavior in male and female college students. *Journal of Behavioral Medicine, 2*, 71-83.

McDougall, J.M., Dembroski, T.M. & Krantz, D.S. (1981). Effects of types of challenges on [pressor and heart rate responses in Type A and B women. *Psychophysiology, 18*, 1-9.

Matthews, K. A., Haynes, S.G. (1986). Type A behavior pattern and coronary disease risk. *American Journal of Epidemiology, 123*, 923-959.

Matthews, K. & Stoney, C.M. (1988). Influences of sex and age on cardiovascular responses during stress. *Psychosomatic Medicine, 50*, 46-56.

Matthews, K. (1988). *Why are Type A and anger expression related to CHD in women? An alternative hypothesis to reactivity*. Paper presented at the Society of Behavioral Medicine Annual Meeting, Boston, April 30.

Mattsen, M.E. & Herd, J. A. (1988). Cardiovascular disease. In C. Beichman & K. Brownell (Eds.) (pp. 160-174), *Handbook of behavioral medicine for women*. NY: Pergamon.

Menninger, K. A. & Menninger, W. C. (1936). Psychoanalytic observations in cardiac disorders. *American Heart Journal, 7*, 10-21.

Moss, G.E., Dielman, T.E., Campanelli, P. C., Leech, S.L., Harian, W.R., Van Harrison, R. & Horvath, W.J. (1986). Demographic correlates of 51 assessments of Type A behavior. *Psychosomatic Medicine, 48*, 564-574.

Pfiffner, D., Elsinger, P., Nil, R., Buzzin, R. & Battig, K. (1986). Psychophysiological reactivity in Type A and B women during a rapid information processing task. *Experientia, 42*, 126-131.

Polefrone, J.M. & Manuck, S. B. (1987). Gender differences in cardiovascular and neuroendocrine response to stressors. In R. C. Barnett, L. Biener, G.K. Baruch (Eds.), *Gender and stress*, NY: Free Press, 13-38.

Powell, L., Dennis, C. & Thoresen, C.E. (1988). Response to Ragland and Brand, *New England Journal of Medicine, 319*, 114-115.

Price, V. (1982). *Type A behavior pattern: A model for research and practice*. NY: Academic Press.

Ragland, D. & Brand, R. (1988). Type A behavior and mortality from coronary heart disease. *New England Journal of Medicine, 318*, 65-69.

Rifkin, J. (1987). *Time Wars: The primary conflict of human history.* NY: Holt.

Rosenberg, L., Kaufman, D., Helmrich, S., Miller, D., Stolley, P., Shapiro, S. (1985). Myocardial infarction and cigarette smoking in women younger than 50 years of age. *Journal of the Medical Association, 253*, 2965-2969.

Rosenman, R. & Friedman, M. (1961). Association of a specific behavior pattern in women with blood and cardiovascular findings. *Circulation, XXIV*, 1173-1184.

Sampson, E.E. (1985). The decentralization of identity: Toward a revised concept of personal and social order. *American Psychologist, 40*, 1203-1211.

Shekelle, R., Schoenberger, J. A. & Stamler, J. (1976). Correlates of the JAS type A behavior pattern score. *Journal of Chronic Diseases, 29*, 381-394.

Shekelle, R. B., Gale, M., Ostfeld, A. et al. (1983). Hostility, risk of coronary heart disease and mortality. *Psychosomatic Medicine, 45*, 59-64.

Smith, T.W. & Anderson, N. (1986). Models of personality and disease: An interactional approach to Type A behavior and cardiovascular risk. *Journal of Personality and Social Psychology, 50*, 1166-1173.

Thoresen, C.E. (1988). The constructivist concept: Primacy of the obscure. *The Counseling Psychologist, 16*, 249-255.

Thoresen, C.E. & Ohman (1987). The Type A behavior pattern: A person-environment interaction perspective. In D. Magnusson & A. Ohman (Eds.), *Psychopathology: An Interaction Perspective,* NY: Academic Press, 325-246.

Thoresen, C.E. & Pattillo, J.R. (1988). Exploring the Type A behavior pattern in children and adolescents. In B.K. Houston & C.R. Snyder, (Eds.), *Type A behavior pattern: Research, theory and intervention,* NY: Wiley, 98-145.

Trelawny-Ross, C. & Russell, O. (1987). Social and psychological responses to myocardial infarction: Multiple determinants of outcome at six months. *Journal of Psychosomatic Research, 31*, 25-130.

Waldron, I. (1978). The coronary-prone behavior pattern, blood pressure, employment and socio-economic status in women. *Journal of Psychosomatic Research, 22*, 79-87.

Waldron, I., Zyzanski, S.J., Shekelle, R., Jenkins, C.D. & Tannenbaum, S. (1977). The coronary prone behavior pattern in employed men and women. *Journal of Human Stress,* 3, 2-18.

Williams, R.B., Jr., Haney, T., Lee, K., Kong, Y., Blumenthal, J. & Whalen, R.E. (1980). Type A behavior, hostility and coronary atherosclerosis. *Psychosomatic Medicine, 42*, 539-549.

Williams, R.B., Jr. (1985). Neuroendocrine response patterns and stress: Biobehavioral mechanisms of disease. In R.B. Williams, Jr. (Ed.), *Perspectives on behavioral medicine: Neuroendocrine control and behavior.* Orlando, FL: Academic Press.

Wright, L. (1988). The Type A behavior pattern and coronary artery disease: Quest for the active ingredients and the elusive mechanism. *American Psychologist, 43*, 2-15.

Type A Behavior, Desire for Control, and Cardiovascular Reactivity in Young Adult Women

Kathleen A. Lawler
Lori A. Schmied
Cheryl A. Armstead
Julia E. Lacy
Department of Psychology
University of Tennessee, Knoxville, TN 37996

The purpose of this research was to examine the physiological correlates of Type A behavior in young women. Past research has generally failed to discern differential cardiovascular reactivity in Types A and B women, although such differences are frequently reported in studies of male subjects. This paper reviews the literature on physiological correlates of Type A behavior in women and discusses methodological and conceptual issues involved. Two studies are reported with 74 and 67 college-age women, assessed for desire for control and Type A with the Jenkins Activity Survey in experiment one and the Framingham Type A Scale in experiment two. In both, women had their heart rate and blood pressure monitored while resting and performing a reaction time task. Desire for control and Type A classification interacted in both experiments such that high desire for control Type A women had larger increases in heart rate to the task. Post-hoc analyses of women at or above the sample causal mean for systolic blood pressure revealed Type A women were more reactive than Type Bs in experiment one, and high desire for control Type A women were more reactive than low desire for control Type As in experiment two. Desire for control is proposed as a coronary-prone component of the Type A behavior pattern in women.

The Type A behavior pattern consists of a group of behaviors, centered around the themes of time urgency and hostility (Powell, 1984), that has been associated with increased risk of coronary heart disease

Authors' Notes: Gratitude is expressed to Theresa Frazier and Stuart Cowles for their invaluable assistance in carrying out this research.

© 1990 Select Press

(Rosenman, Brand, Jenkins, Friedman, Straus and Wurm, 1975; Rosenman and Friedman, 1961; Haynes, Feinleib, Levine, Scotch and Kannel, 1978). Much of the subsequent work on this topic has focused on identifying mechanisms and mediators that could explain the transition from behavior characteristics to cardiovascular disease. In 1975, Friedman, Byers, Diamant and Rosenman proposed that one physiological mechanism underlying Type A behavior might be excessive sympathetic nervous system response to an acute stressor. This hypothesis remains prominent and viable, though not unquestioned (Krantz & Manuck, 1984; Matthews, Weiss, Detre, Dembroski, Falkner, Manuck & Williams, 1986; Krantz & Durel, 1983; Holmes, 1983). As reviewed by Houston (1983), Houston & Snyder (1988), and Krantz & Manuck (1984), significant studies with male subjects indicate that there are differences between Type A and Type B males in their physiological reactivity to laboratory stressors.

In women, the risk associated with Type A behavior and its relationship to physiological reactivity are much less well established. Only one prospective study associating Type A behavior with coronary heart disease has been carried out (Haynes, et al., 1978). Baker, Dearborn, Hastings and Hamberger (1984) reviewed the literature on Type A behavior in women. Based primarily upon articles published before 1982, they concluded that "Type A women may be more physiologically reactive to Type A - relevant laboratory stressors than Type B women" (p. 486). Since that time, views have become markedly more negative (Eaker & Castelli, 1988; O'Rourke, Houston, Harris, & Snyder, 1988), suggesting that either Type A behavior is not predictive of heart disease in women, that we do not know how to measure Type A behavior in women, that it is not related to physiological reactivity, or some combination of the above. However, these conclusions have been based on a limited number of recent studies, rather than on a thorough assessment of the literature.

Because coronary heart disease is the leading cause of death among women in the United States, it is essential that researchers examine the psychosocial and biological risk factors for this disease in women. The fact that experiments with males and females have produced discrepant results should lead to a more careful examination of methodological as well as conceptual factors that might underlie these differences. Since the review by Baker et al. (1984), at least 22 studies have been published on the physiological reactivity of Type A and Type B women (see Tables 1 and 2). Dividing these studies by age of subjects, one finds 8 articles focusing on adult women and 14 on college-age women.

Type A in Older or Working Women

Description. Of those studies with older women (Lawler, Rixse, & Allen, 1983; Mayes, Sime & Ganster, 1984; Harbin & Blumenthal, 1985; Anderson, Williams, Lane, Haney, Simpson, & Houseworth, 1986; Lawler & Schmied, 1987; Morell, 1988; Weidner, Sexton, McLellarn, Connor & Matarazzo, 1987; Schmied & Lawler, 1988), all but Harbin & Blumenthal (1985) found some differences between Types A and B women in the expected direction. The three studies with the strongest physiological differences between Types A and B women (Lawler et al., 1983; Lawler & Schmied, 1987; Schmied & Lawler, 1988) were obtained by studying one sample of housewives and two samples of clerical workers. Focusing on particular groups of women may be more fruitful than trying to study "women in general." First of all, the Type A literature evolved from the study of middle-class white American men in large companies, not "men in general." Second, studying gender differences *per se* may obscure more important differences within groups of women, such as those of race, social status, age, family history, etc. (Hare-Mustin & Marecek, 1988). Thirdly, more than one study points to the increased coronary heart disease associated with clerical and working-class occupations in women (Orth-Gomer, Hamsten, Perski, Theorell, & deFaire, 1986 ; Bernet, Drivet-Perrin, Blanc, Ebagosti, & Jouve, 1982; Haynes et al., 1978). Thus, the impact of psychosocial variables on cardiovascular responses may be much more apparent in unemployed, clerical, or working-class women. This provides one hypothesis for the general lack of A - B differences found by Morell (1988) who studied faculty and professional women within a university. However, two studies included in Table 1 (Mayes et al., 1984; Anderson et al., 1986) also examined clerical workers and their results were more limited. While the interaction of race and Type A has not been explored sufficiently, the Anderson et al. (1986) study may be affected by a small sample size. While 50 black clerical workers were assessed in a thorough psychophysiological protocol, exclusion due to hypertension or classification as Type X yielded a final sample of seven Type As compared to 18 Type Bs. While not markedly different from other studies of Type A in women (e.g., Lawler et al., 1983), the small number of Type As may have contributed to their lack of differences during the math stressor or using heart rate as a dependent variable. However, they did find that Type A women exhibited larger increases in systolic and diastolic blood pressure during the structured interview. Mayes et al. (1984) examined 63 workers at a social service agency and found no correlations between Type A scores and blood pressure. All results were found with skin temperature, heart rate and skin conductance level. Methodological points may be critical here

TABLE 1 Summary of Recent Studies of Physiological Reactivity and Type A Behavior in Older or Working Women

Reference	*Subjects*	*Type A Assessment*	*Tasks*	*Dependent Variables*	*Results*
Lawler et al. (1983)	21 professional women 20 housewives	JAS	math Ravens Matrice	SBP, DBP, HR, SC	HR: unemployed As > unemployed Bs* mean HR: employed As > unemployed As and Bs SBP: unemployed As > unemployed Bs DBP: unemployed As > employed As, unemployed Bs
Mayes et al. (1984)	63 full-time employees of social service agency	SI, JAS, Bortner, Thurstone	math	HR, SBP, DBP, SCL, skin temperature, urinary catecholamines	Correlations: SI content and % change in HR, skin temperautre, SCL JAS-A and change in skin temperautre. Thurstone and change in skin temperature Bortner and change in skin temperature.
Harbin & Blumenthal (1985)	15 women (27-70 yrs) 34 men (26-74 yrs)	JAS	MFF math	HR, SBP, DBP	HR: As decreased, Bs increased (math) SBP, DBP: Decrease became smaller with age in As, larger in Bs (MFF)
Anderson et al. (1986)	50 black clerical workers	SI JAS	math SI	HR, SBP, DBP	SBP, DBP, A > B (SI only)
Lawler & Schmied (1987)	64 clerical workers	SI JAS	math vigilance SI	HR, SBP, DBP HRV, forehead EMG	mean SBP, DBP: A < B (all tasks) mean HR: high stress A > low stress A (all tasks) change in EMG: A > B ($p < .10$)

(continued)

TABLE 1 (continued)

Reference	*Subjects*	*Type A Assessment*	*Tasks*	*Dependent Variables*	*Results*
Weidner et al. (1987)	182 women 170 men	JAS	fastng blood sample	plasma total cholesterol, HDL, triglycerides	Correlation of Type A score and total cholesterol=.13, p > .06, LDL=.14, p < .06. Multiple regression: interaction of Type A and hostility explained additional variation in plasma total cholesterol and LDL (r = .16). One year follow-up: Type A alone or with hostility unrelated to total cholesterol and LDL.
Morell (1988)	85 faculty and professional staff	JAS	reaction time: high or low stress	HR, PTT, SCL, SCR, respiration	mean HR: high stress A> loow stress A (p<.08)
Schmied & Lawler (1988)	80 secretaries	FTAS E/I locus	concept identification (helplessness task) anagrams	HR, SBP, DBP, HRV	Helplessness/control task: HR: External A > Internal A, External B HRV: External A < Internal A, External B SBP: A > B (helpless only) Anagram task: HRV: A < B (helpless pretreatment only) SBP: A > B (helpless pretreatment only)

**all differences noted are significant at p<.05 level or higher higher unless otherwise reported.Key:*
SI - structured interview
SBP - systolic blood pressure
DBP - diastolic blook pressure
HR - heart rate
SCL/R - skin conductance level/response
HRV - heart rate variability
PTT - pulse transit time
unless otherwise reported.

as well: (1) the stressor was one, 90-second session of mental arithmetic, and (2) the dependent variables were calculated as change from baseline without any examination of baseline levels. It is possible that a lengthier stress protocol and/or evaluation of raw values or adjusted change scores might have produced a different picture.

Analysis. In summary, an examination of Table 1 reveals that studies finding Type A-B differences do not systematically differ from studies without differences on Type A assessment or task protocol. Studies using the Jenkins Activity Survey (JAS), structured interview and Framingham Type A Scale (FTAS) have all found differences between groups, although a direct comparison between the JAS and structured interview in both Anderson et al. (1986), and Lawler & Schmied (1987) found the structured interview to be more strongly associated with A-B physiological differences. Similarly, studies finding differential responses have used mental arithmetic, Ravens matrices, vigilance, verbal interview, reaction time, and a learned helplessness task. Thus, there does not seem to be support for the individual vs. interpersonal task distinction so frequently drawn.

As described above, the clearest difference among studies seems to involve subject sample selection. In our own research, we have focused on clerical workers because of their increased risk for coronary heart disease. In studying this group, we have found that not only does Type A score relate to increased reactivity, but that Type A women who report a lack of powerlessness (Lawler & Schmied, 1987) and Type A women with an external locus of control (Schmied & Lawler, 1988), especially when exposed to a control-relevant task, show the largest increases in sympathetic-like responses. Thus, these two variables of Type A and feelings of lack of control seem to emerge in our analysis of this literature in adult women employed in lower-level occupations. That control is an important variable within the Type A literature has long been hypothesized (Glass, 1977; Strube & Werner, 1985). That it is particularly important for females has been verified by LaCroix and Haynes (1985) who found that female clerical workers with high demands and low control were 5.2 times more likely to develop CHD than other working women.

Type A in College-Age Women

Description. The studies employing college-age women (see Table 2) are both more numerous and heterogeneous in their conclusions (Holmes, Solomon, & Rump, 1982: Ketterer, 1982: Lane, White & Williams, 1984; Lawler, Schmied, Mitchell & Rixse, 1984; Smith, Houston & Zurawski, 1985; Janisse, Edguer, & Dyck, 1986; Jones, Copolov, & Outch, 1986; Lawler & Schmied, 1986; Pfiffner, Elsinger, Nil, Buzzin,

& Battig, 1986; Essau, 1987; Evans & Moran, 1987; Lutz, Holmes & Cramer 1987; Pfiffner, Nil & Battig, 1987; Morrell, 1988). Only four of these studies measured blood pressure (Lawler et al., 1984; Smith et al., 1985 ; Lawler & Schmied, 1986; Lutz et al., 1987), and only Smith et al. (1985) found an A-B difference. They examined males and females, assessed by the FTAS, and measured heart rate, blood pressure and vascular response to verbal interviews administered under high and low challenge. Averaging across genders and challenge conditions, Type As exhibited larger systolic pressure increases.

While twelve studies measured heart rate, in only two did Type A women respond differently from Type B. In Evans & Moran (1987) , female Type As had larger increases in heart rate than Type Bs; however, male As and Bs did not differ from each other on this vigilance, shock-avoidance task. This study also used the FTAS as the assessment device. In Essau (1987), a positive correlation between JAS score and magnitude of heart rate increase to a mental arithmetic task was found. Only two experiments (Lawler et al., 1984; Morrell, 1988) used the same tasks with both a college-age and an adult population, facilitating direct comparisons. Lawler et al. (1984), using mental arithmetic and Ravens matrices, found significant A/B differences in adults, but not in college age subjects. Morell (1988), using a challenging reaction time task, found a tendency for high stress Type As to show larger heart rate increases compared to low stress As in adults, and a significant difference in college-age subjects. There were no A/B differences in either sample.

Analysis. This overall lack of results with college-age women is problematic and has led recent articles to declare that "increases in ... cardiovascular reactivity, tend to characterize Type A men, *but not Type A women...* (italics mine, Matthews & Woodall, 1988, p. 71). However, the fact that Type A females differ from Type B females as children, adolescents (Matthews & Woodall, 1988) and adult women should lead us to examine these studies of college-age women more carefully. As with adults, studies finding A-B differences do not break down clearly with respect to task or Type A assessment procedure, with one exception. Only two studies have used the FTAS and both (Smith et al., 1985: Evans & Moran, 1987) have found differences. This questionnaire deserves further investigation.

Based on the findings with adult women, it is our sense of the literature that studies with college students also suffer from a "gender differences" (Hare-Mustin & Marecek, 1988) bias, that is, that college women represent a generally healthy and low-risk group for heart disease. To allow the contribution of psychosocial factors on cardiovascular

TABLE 2 Summary of Recent Studies of Physiological Reactivity and Type A Behavior in College Women

Reference	*Subjects*	*Type A Assessment*	*Tasks*	*Dependent Variables*	*Results*
Holmes et al (1982)	20 males 19 females (extreme groups)	JAS-student	digit symbol, exercise	HR	females: A = B
Ketterer (1982)	24 females 24 males	JAS	emotion imagery: angry, anxious	SC, EEG desynchronization	SC: A>B* during contentment EEG: During all conditions, R>L for As while L>R for Bs.
Lane et al (1984)	29 females (extreme groups)	JAS-student	math	HR, BP, forearm BF	A=B
Lawler et al. (1984)	37 females	JAS-student SI	math Ravens matrices	HR, SBP, DBP	A=B
Smith et al (1984)	63 males 64 males	FTAS	Interview under high and low challenge	HR, SBP, DBP finger pulse volume	SBP: A>B across gender and challenges
Janisse et al. (1986)	40 females 40 males	JAS-student	anger imagery	HR	HR: B>A HR decrease after anger recall. High anger expression Type As > others, primarily due to males subjects.
Jones et al. (1986)	20 females 20 males	SI	studying, before/after exam	salivary cortisol	No sex effects, data pooled. With successful students, A > B. With unsuccessful students, B > A.

(continued)

TABLE 2 (continued)

Reference	Subjects	Type A Assessment	Tasks	Dependent Variables	Results
Lawler & Schmied (1986)	40 females	JAS-student JAS-N	oral history quiz; Stroop color-word	HR, SBP, DBP	A=B
Pfiffner et al. (1986)	20 females (extreme groups)	German questionnaire**	vigiliance task	HR, HRV, SCR, respiration, finger vasoconstriction, EMG	EMG, vasoconsticiton - finger: A > B (p < .10) Finger pulse variability: A > B
Essau (1987)	30 females	JAS-student	math	HR	Positive correlation (r = .40) for JAS score and HR score.
Evans & Moran (1987)	26 females 22 males	FTAS	monitor/ distractor vigilance task	HR	HR: female A > female B, male A or B HR: female A monitors most reactive group.
Lutz et al. (1987)	71 males 70 females	JAS-student	digit-symbol task; exercise	HR, SBP, DBP	Pooled data: no sex effects A = B
Pfiffner et al. (1987)	9 females 17 males	SI	structured interview; self-disclosure	HR, vascular reactivity, PTT	Correlations: IBI and self-references (r - .40, p < .01) SBP and talking time (r - .31, p < .05), number of words (r - .40, p < .01), self-references (r - .29, p < .05).
Morell (1988)	68 females	JAS-student	Reaction time-high or low stress	HR, PTT, SCL	HR: high stress A > low stress A. SCL: high stress A > high stress B, low stress A

* *correlates .40 with Bortner

Key: *SI - structured interview*; *SBP - systolic blood pressure*; *DBP - diastolic blook pressure*; *HR - heart rate*; *SCL/R - skin conductance level/response*; *HRV - heart rate variability*; *PTT - pulse transit time*

all differences noted are significant at p < .05 level or higher unless otherwise reported.

reactivity to emerge requires some method of narrowing the sample to make it more comparable to adult clerical workers or, at least, to college-age males. In an early study (Lawler et at., 1984) we tried to do that by comparing pre-professional women to education and nursing majors. However, our hypothesis that professional Type As would experience the highest heart disease risk was flawed.

Thus, the present experiments were designed to address both methodological and conceptual factors in understanding the Type A behavior pattern and its potential relationship to cardiovascular reactivity in women. As the studies in Table 2 indicate, a variety of Type A assessment instruments have been used. Rarely has a replication been included affording the opportunity to compare the robustness of results using more than one measure. To permit this comparison, two measures of Type A behavior were administered: in experiment one, the JAS was used, while in experiment two, Type A behavior was assessed using the FTAS. In this way, we are able to compare the predictive validity of two Type A assessment devices in two groups of women to physiological reactivity in a choice reaction-time task with negative feedback, designed to be similar to that used by Morell (1988).

Secondly, the review of the literature suggests that some attempt to restrict the sample of college-age women to one more comparable, in terms of cardiovascular disease risk, to college-age males might facilitate the emergence of psychosocial influences on blood pressure. To this end, *post hoc* analyses were carried out upon women whose casual systolic blood pressure was at or above the sample mean. Thus, in these analyses, casual blood pressure was used as a screening device to select a subset of women whose blood pressure is more comparable to college-age males. Finally, efforts have been made recently to identify the detrimental components of the Type A behavior pattern. Three studies with adult women (Lawler & Schmied, 1987; Schmied & Lawler, 1988; LaCroix & Haynes, 1985) have emphasized the relationship of feelings of lack of control to blood pressure; either independently or in interaction with the Type A behavior pattern. Thus, we decided to examine this concept further by including a measure of desire for control (Burger & Cooper, 1979) in both experiments. Based on our previous studies, it was hypothesized that the combination of Type A behavior and high need for control might identify a subset of young Type A women who would differ from young Type Bs.

EXPERIMENT ONE

Method

Subjects

Seventy-four college-age females volunteered to participate in this research; they ranged in age from 18-23 and all were Caucasian. Subjects were screened for the presence of diagnosed hypertension (n=1) or other medication that could alter physiological reactivity (n=4), and data from those five subjects were not included in the analyses. As an incentive, all subjects received extra credit for their introductory psychology class.

Apparatus

All subjects were tested in the Human Psychophysiology Laboratory, throughout the year, on weekdays between the hours of 12 noon and 4 p.m. Subject room 1 contained a desk and chair where the questionnaires were completed, Subject room 2 contained a recliner chair and the reaction time equipment. This consisted of a lap table and a display of 1 yellow light, 4 red jewel lights, and 4 microswitch buttons displayed in a semi-circle. The equipment room contained a Grass Model 7 polygraph and a SYM-1 microcomputer which controlled stimulus presentation as well as recorded the reaction time data. The polygraph contained the appropriate preamplifier and amplifier for the measurement of heart rate. In addition, the computer activated the signal marker to indicate each warning signal and respond signal. The laboratory also included a Roche Arteriosonde automatic blood pressure monitor.

Procedure

Two subjects were scheduled for each appointment time. After signing informed consent sheets, one subject completed questionnaires while the other began the physiological testing. When the testing was finished the subjects exchanged rooms. Thus, order of activities was counterbalanced across subjects.

In the questionnaire packet were 3 forms: a participant information sheet, the Jenkins Activity Survey Form N for unemployed individuals (available from Psychological Corporation), and the desire for control scale (Burger & Cooper, 1979). The desire for control scale has been reported to have substantial internal consistency (.80) and test-retest reliability (.75). Discriminant validity from measures of locus of control and social desirability have been demonstrated as well as construct validity from studies on learned helplessness, hypnosis, and "illusion of control" (All of this is covered by the Burger & Cooper, 1979 citation.) Jenkins Form N was used, rather than the student form, to facilitate comparison with our own previous studies and with those using the employed adult form. The participant information sheet consisted of 7 questions concerning undergraduate major and career plans, height, weight, medications, smoking status, and family history (both parents and grandparents) for high blood pressure, heart attack, atherosclerosis and stroke.

In the laboratory, three Beckman biopotential electrodes were applied across the midriff for the measurement of heart rate, and the blood pressure cuff was placed on the nondominant arm. After application of the monitoring equipment, subjects were requested to relax for a 15 minute baseline period. At the end of this interval, an experimenter returned to explain the reaction time task. The task was presented as a type of intelligence test measuring sensory-processing capabilities and eye-hand coordination. The subject was informed that it would begin one minute after the experimenter left the room and would last for 3 minutes. For each trial a warning light was illuminated for one second: four seconds after warning light offset, one of the four respond lights was illuminated in a computer-generated random order. Subjects pressed the button corresponding to the illuminated respond light. Intertrial interval varied randomly from 15-25 seconds with a mean of 20 seconds. Subjects were not told that the time interval between warning and respond lights was fixed nor its duration. Three minutes after reaction time task onset, the program was halted and the experimenter returned to the subject room. The experimenter asked the subject whether she understood the instructions or was having difficulties. The subject was informed that her performance was at the 20th percentile and she was urged to try to respond more quickly and try to improve at least to an average speed. The experimenter left and the 2 additional minutes of the task were presented. Physiological responses were monitored for 2 minutes after task offset. At that point the experimenter returned and praised the subject for her improved performance.

Quantification of Data

The testing session was divided into periods of baseline (15 min), task instructions (3-4 mins), pre-task anticipation (1 min), reaction time (RT) 1-3 (3 mins) and RT 4-5 (2 mins). Baseline heart rate was defined as the average of minutes 10, 12 and 14. For the remaining periods, means were calculated as number of R waves during the period divided by its duration. Baseline heart rate was subtracted from these interval means to produce change scores for the following variables: instructions, pre-task, RT 1-3, and RT 4-5. Blood pressure determinations were made during baseline at min 1 (initial), and at mins 4, 9, 11 and 14. Blood pressure measurements were also taken during pre-task anticipation and during mins 1, 3 (RT 1-3), 4 and 5 (RT 4-5). Baseline blood pressure was defined as the mean of mins 9, 11, and 14. This value was subtracted

TABLE 3 Correlation Matrix for Questionnaire Data

	JAS-SI	*JAS JI*	*JAS-HC*	*Desire for Control*
JAS-A	.66*	.51*	.51	.26**
JAS-SI		.23**	.13	.05
JAS-JI			.52*	.34**
JAS-HC				.48*

*$p < .003$
**$p < .05$

from the average of RT mins 1 and 3 and also from the average of RT mins 4 and 5. Thus, change scores were calculated for RT 1-3 and RT 4-6.

Results

Questionnaire Data

The JAS data provide a standard score that is equivalent to a percentile ranking. In this way, one can assess whether the sample is predominantly Type A, B or a balance. This sample had a mean of 49.4 percentile and a median of 50.0th percentile indication that half the subjects were Type A and half were Type B. The range was from the 3rd to the 97th percentile. The same balance held true for the three subscales of hard-driving/competitive, speed-impatience, and job involvement.[1] Using a percentile of 51-100 as Type A and 1-50 as Type B, there were 37 Type As and 32 Type Bs.

The desire for control scale yielded a mean of 101.6 with a range of 70 to 124; this mean is consistent with those presented by Burger and Cooper (1979). Again using a median split, there were 36 high desire for control and 33 low desire for control subjects. Crossing desire for control with JAS-A and -B yielded 23 A-High, 14 A-Lo, 13 B-High and 19 B-low subjects.

A correlation matrix was determined for JAS-Type A score, the JAS components of speed and impatience, hard driving and competitive, and job involvement and desire for control (see Table 3). In summary, the JAS Type A scale is highly intercorrelated with its subscales, and the desire for control scale is positively related to all JAS scales except speed and impatience.

[1] *The questions contributing to the job involvement scale do not necessarily refer to job specifics. Rather they address deadlines, feelings about competition and time. Where they do refer to one's job, Form N has revised those questions to refer to "daily activities," in this case schoolwork and part-time work.*

TABLE 4 Reaction Time Data (msec)

Trials	*Type A*	*Type B*
RT 1-5	1364.9	1453.1
RT 6-9	1274.7	1367.2
RT 10-15	1110.9	1106.6

Examining the participant information sheet, 7 women reported being smokers; of these, 4 were Type As and 3 Bs. Eight women reported taking oral contraceptive medication; of these, 3 were Type As and 5 were Type Bs. With regard to family history, 24 women reported the presence of hypertension and 3 reported heart attack in one parent. Of those with one or more hypertensive parents, 13 were Type A and 11, Type B. Of the three subjects whose fathers had had a myocardial infarction, all were Type A.

Behavioral Data

Reaction time values were obtained for each subject for each trial. These were averaged into blocks of 5 (RT 1-5), 4 (RT 6-9), and 6 (RT 10-15) trials each; all trials in the first two blocks occurred before the interruption and the last block represents the response to the request for improvement. Analyses of variance were conducted on each trial block with two between-groups factors: Type A/B and desire for control. The means by Type are presented in Table 4. Only on RT 1-5 did the main effect of Type ($F(1,65) = 2.49$, $p < .12$) even approach marginal significance. If all 74 subjects were included in the reaction time analysis, the mean for Type Bs during RT 1-5 increased to 1484.5 and the difference between groups then became significant. Thus, if anything, there is only the tendency for Type As to be faster early in the trials: with practice or exhortation, Bs respond as quickly as As. Desire for control bore no relationship to reaction time either as a main effect or in interaction with Type A.

Physiological Data

A repeated measures analysis of covariance was performed on change scores (instructions, pre-task, RT 1-3 and RT 4-5) within the groups of Type A/B and desire for control (high/low), with resting heart rate as the covariate. The triple interaction of Type A/B x Desire for control x Repeated measures was significant ($F(32, 195) = 3.11$, $p < .03$). Follow-up analyses of variance revealed that the interaction was due to a Type A/B x Repeated measures interaction only for high desire for control subjects ($F(3,102) = 3.80$, $p < .01$). The corresponding interac-

TABLE 5 Resting Heart Rate and Change Scores for Types A and B and High Desire for Control Groups

	Repeated Measures			
Type-Control	*Instructions*	*Pre-task*	*RT 1-3*	*RT 4-5*
A - high	10.2	12.4	7.5	13.2
B - high	5.6	4.4	4.3	13.4
A - low	9.6	8.9	5.8	10.7
B - low	7.1	12.2	6.1	11.8

tion term for low desire for control ($F(3,93) = 0.45$) was not significant. These means are presented in Table 5. Within high desire for control Type As, t tests indicated that the increase to instructions, Pre-task and RT 4-5 was higher than to RT 1-3. For Type Bs, the increase to RT 4-5 was higher than the other three intervals. Comparing high desire for control As and Bs directly, As increased their heart rates more than Bs during pre-task and instructions.

Systolic blood pressure: All subjects. Analogous to heart rate, analyses of variance were conducted on systolic blood pressure first on resting levels and then on change scores. Other than the uniformly significant Repeated Measures main effects, there were no significant main effects or interactions involving the grouping variables for either resting levels or change scores.

Systolic blood pressure: Above average casual level subjects. Because casual systolic blood pressure values are strong predictors of subsequent coronary heart disease (Thomas & Greenstreet, 1973; Rosenman, Sholtz & Brand, 1976) another set of analyses were conducted on just those subjects whose casual (initial) systolic blood pressure value was above the sample mean of 116 mmHg (n=32). Baseline values were now found to differ across groups; therefore, the reactivity analyses were tests of covariance with resting systolic blood pressure as the covariate. There was now a highly significant main effect of Type ($F(1,28) = 5.86$, $p < .02$). As shown in Figure 1, Type As increased their systolic blood pressure considerably more than Type Bs. A corresponding analysis of those subjects with casual blood pressures below the sample mean produced no significant grouping factor effects.

Diastolic blood pressure: All subjects. Similar analyses were conducted on diastolic blood pressure for all subjects. Baseline group differences were found (A-high = 62.6, A-low = 67.5. B-high = 65.5, B-low = 61.8 mmHg). These differences are opposite to predictions and further studies using desire for control are needed before this result could be interpreted with confidence. The subsequent change score analysis using

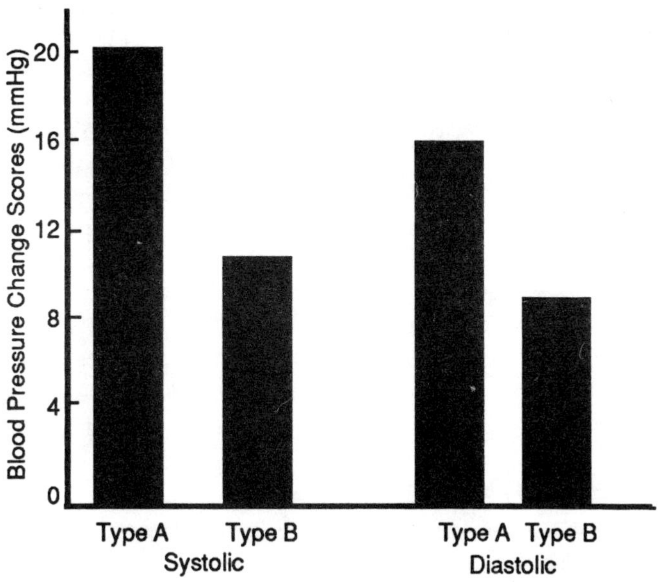

FIGURE 1 Blood Pressure Change Scores for Type A and Type B Women Whose Initial Systolic Blood Pressure Was At or Above the Sample Medians

resting diastolic blood pressure as the covariate produced no significant results.

Diastolic blood pressure: Above average casual level subjects. A second set of analyses was conducted just on those subjects whose casual systolic blood pressure was above the sample mean. Again, analysis of covariance was used to test group reactivity differences, with resting diastolic levels as the covariate. As with systolic blood pressure, a strong main effect of Type A/B emerged ($F(1,28) = 7.27$, $p < .01$) with Type As significantly more reactive than Type Bs (see Figure 1).

EXPERIMENT TWO

Method

Subjects

Sixty-seven college females volunteered to participate in this research; they ranged in age from 18 to 27. Subjects were screened for the presence of diagnosed hypertension or other medication that could alter physiological reactivity (n=4), and data from these four subjects were not included in the analyses. As an incentive, all subjects received extra credit for their introductory psychology class.

Procedure

The apparatus has been described under Experiment One. The procedure was similar to Experiment One, with the following changes. Subjects came to the laboratory singly, rather than scheduling two individuals for the same appointment time. However, appointment times were staggered so that about half the women received the questionnaires first, while the other half received the physiological testing first. The questionnaire packet contained the desire for control scale, the participant information sheet, and the FTAS. The baseline was 15 minutes and the reaction time task was conducted as before. The data were quantified similarly with two exceptions: baseline blood pressure was calculated from readings at minutes 11, 13 and 15 and heart rate was not quantified during task instructions. Thus, means for all variables were obtained for baseline and change scores for pre-task anticipation, RT 1-3 and RT 4-5.

RESULTS

Descriptive Statistics

The FTAS is scored from 0 to 1; the mean was .57 and median was .6. Classifying subjects based on a median split yielded 29 Bs and 34 As. However, the distribution was negatively skewed such that 21 of the 29 Bs had FTAS scores of .4 and .5, with only 8 women scoring 0-.3. There were 13 individuals with an FTAS score of .5; thus, Type A was defined as .6-1.0 (n=34) and Type B as 0.0 -.4 (n=16).

The desire for control score ranged from 71 to 137, with a mean of 102.1. This is similar to the mean found in Experiment One. Using a median split, there were 35 high and 28 low desire for control subjects. Crossing desire for control with FTAS-A and -B yielded 19 A-low, 15 A-high, 11 B-low and 5 B-high subjects. The correlation of FTAS scores with desire for control scores yielded an r=.09, clearly nonsignificant.

The participant information sheets were coded for oral contraceptive use, smoking and parental history of heart disease. Five subjects reported taking oral contraceptives, 2 Type As and 3 Type Bs; only 2 individuals reported smoking, one A and one B. Twenty-one subjects reported parental history of hypertension; 8 Type As and 13 Type Bs; 5 subjects reported parental history of myocardial infarction, one Type 1 and 4 Type Bs.

Reaction Time

Three analyses were conducted to examine the effects of Type A/B and desire for control (high, low) on reaction time: the first on trials 1-5, the second on trials 6-9 and the third on trials 10-15. The third analysis

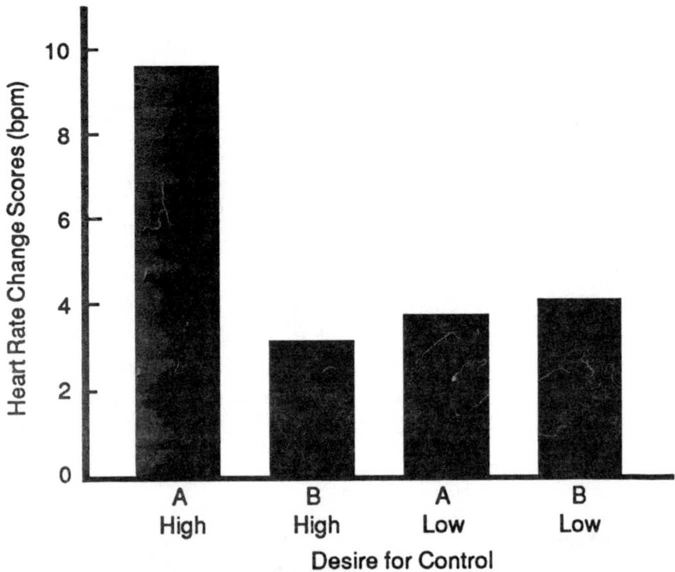

FIGURE 2 Heart Rate Change Scores for Type A and Type B Women Varying on Desire for Control

reflects response time after experimenter exhortation. There were no significant main effects or interactions involving the grouping factors.

Physiological Data

These data were analyzed with two between-subjects variables, Type A-B and Desire for control, and one repeated measures variable with three levels (pre-task anticipation, RT 1-3, and RT 4-5), using the respective baseline variable as covariate.

Heart rate. There were three significant effects: Desire for control (F (1,46)=6.32, p<.02), FTAS by Desire for control (F (1,46)=4.27, p<.04) and repeated measures (F (2.92)=9.93, p<.0001). As illustrated in Figure 2, Type A women who are also high in desire for control are more reactive than any of the other groups (Tukey HSD = 5.43, p<.05). The repeated measures effect means showed an increase of 2.7 bpm to RT 1-3, 4.87 to RT 4-5 and 6.14 to anticipation.

Blood pressure. There were no significant effects for systolic blood pressure. For diastolic, there was a marginal interaction of FTAS type by desire for control (F(1,46)=3.45, p<.07). However, unlike the analysis with heart rate, Type A-high desire for control women were not the most reactive group. All groups were equally reactive, except Type B, low desire for control who were somewhat less reactive than the other three groups (A/high = 2.7, A/low = 4.2, B/high = 4.0, B/low = .03).

In order to compare these data with those presented in Experiment One, all subjects whose initial systolic blood pressure was at or above the median of 117 were retained and the analyses performed again (n=34). For systolic blood pressure, a significant FTAS by Desire for control interaction emerged ($F(1,30) = 5.25$, $p<.03$). The means for Type/Control (A/high = 10.6, A/low = -3.5, B/high = 6.3, B/low = 5.2) indicated that Type A women who were high on desire for control had larger pressor responses than Type As low on desire for control (HSD = 10.1). For diastolic blood pressure, there were no significant effects.

DISCUSSION

The purpose of this research was to investigate the relationship among physiological reactivity, Type A behavior and desire for control in young adult women. In two experiments, women had their heart rate and blood pressure monitored while resting and while performing a difficult reaction time task. In experiment one, Type A was assessed using the JAS questionnaire while the FTAS was used in experiment two. In both experiments, desire for control was also measured. Correlational analyses revealed that while JAS scores and desire for control scores were positively correlated, there was no relationship between control scores and FTAS scores. These correlations are consistent with two prior comparisons (Dembroski, MacDougall, & Musante, 1984; Smith & O'Keeffe, 1985). Analyses of these grouping factors were also carried out on the reaction time data. In experiment one, there was only the barest trend ($p < .12$) for Type As to respond more quickly than Type Bs and then only during the first 5 trials. For thc rcmainder of experiment one and all of experiment two there were no group differences in behavioral performance.

Previous literature with college-aged women has found few differences between Type As and Bs in physiological reactivity. The studies with adult women have suggested that need for control may be an important moderator of Type A effects; however, this factor has not been included in the psychophysiological research on young Type A women. Thus, the present study sought to investigate the hypothesis that high need for control Type A women would be more reactive than other groups. Examining heart rate, there were significant interactions of Type A by desire for control in both experiments. Type A women, measured either by the JAS or the FTAS, who also scored above the median on an instrument designed to assess desire for control, were more reactive to the reaction time stressor than any other group. This increased reactivity was noted only in anticipation of the task when the JAS was used, while it occurred to all intervals equally when the FTAS was used. Thus, for reactivity assessed by heart rate, it may be that desire for control is a coronary-prone component of Type A behavior. Whether this reactivity difference would emerge in response to any task is a question for future research. The reaction time task used here was selected because it is moderately difficult (signalled 4-choice) and involved an interpersonal stressor of negative feedback. These characteristics of the task may have been important in engaging feelings about control in the high desire for control Type A women. We regret that we had not the foresight to question the subjects about their subjective experience of control during the experiment. Such evaluative data would markedly improve our ability to interpret these group differences and will be included in future studies. It should also be noted that Type A assessment method did not markedly affect the results—both the JAS and FTAS Type A women were more reactive when they were also high on desire for control.

The results for the relationship of either psychosocial factor to blood pressure were much less impressive. There were no significant main effects of either variable and only one marginal interaction. Taken together with the other studies on college-aged women, presence of the Type A behavior pattern does not seem to predict increased pressor reactivity in young women. These results are consistent with a meta-analysis of data performed by Stoney, Davis and Matthews (1987). They found, across studies comparing gender differences, that males tended to have higher resting systolic blood pressure and greater increases during challenge, while females tended to have higher resting heart rate and a tendency to greater increases during challenge. This differential reactivity across measures does not remove women from coronary heart disease risk. Kannel, Kannel, Paffenbarger, and Cupples (1987) examined heart rate and cardiovascular mortality in the Framingham study. They note that several prospective studies have found an association between elevated heart rate and cardiovascular morbidity and mortality, and their results were summarized as follows: "In both sexes, at all ages, all-cause, cardiovascular, and coronary mortality rates increased progressively in relation to antecedent heart rate..." (p. 1494). Thus, women with higher heart rates are at greater risk for all illnesses, including cardiovascular, than women with lower heart rates.

As noted earlier, we were also interested in examining the effects of psychosocial variables in a subset of women whose blood pressure values were more comparable to studies using young men. To that end, *post-hoc* analyses were performed on a subset of women whose initial, casual systolic blood pressure values were at or above the sample means of 116-117mmHg. As Stoney et al. (1987) noted, males have higher resting systolic blood pressure values than women and several studies have noted the predictive validity of casual systolic levels for coronary heart disease (see Rosenman et al., 1976 for a discussion). While the samples are reduced, and the results considered only as suggestive, in experiment one Type A women exhibited larger reactivity changes than Type B in both systolic and diastolic responses. Furthermore, the magnitude of these differences was considerable with Type As being approximately twice as reactive. In experiment two, Type A interacted with desire for control and systolic blood pressure scores such that high desire for control Type As were about twice as reactive as the Type B groups and four times as reactive as the low desire for control Type A group.

Taken together, these results suggest that desire for control may be a critical factor linking Type A behavior to physiological reactivity in women. High desire for control women exhibited larger heart rate or blood pressure responses either in anticipation of the task, or throughout all testing intervals. This suggests that their increased reactivity is more likely associated with greater effort or involvement in the task from the outset, rather than a reaction to the threat of loss of control communicated through the negative feedback. In no case were there unique A/B differences connected with the interval following the feedback (RT 4-5). In addition, these data suggest that screening women for initial systolic blood pressure levels of 116-117 mmHg or greater may yield a group of women whose pressure levels are similar to men and for whom the impact of Type A behavior, or other psychosocial factors, on physiological reactivity is more marked.

REFERENCES

Anderson, N.B., Williams, R.B., Lane, J.D., Haney, T., Simpson, S., & Houseworth, S.J. (1986). Type A behavior, family history of hypertension, and cardiovascular responsivity among black women. *Health Psychology, 5,* 393-406.

Baker, L.J., Dearborn, M., Hastings, J.E., & Hamberger, K. (1984). Type A behavior in women: A Review. *Health Psychology, 3,* 477-497.

Bernet, A., Drivet-Perrin, J., Blanc, M.M., Ebagosti, A., & Jouve, A. (1982). Type A behavior pattern in a screened female population. *Advances in Cardiology, 29,* 96-105.

Burger, J.M. and Cooper, H.M. (1979). The desirability of control. *Motivation and Emotion, 3,* 381-393.

Dembroski, T.M., MacDougall, J.M. & Musante, L. (1984). Desireability of control versus locus of control: Relationship to paralinguistics in the Type A interview. *Health Psychology, 3,* 15-26.

Eaker, E.D. & Castelli, W.P. (1988). Type A behavior and coronary heart disease in women: Fourteen year incidence from the Framingham study. In Houston, B.K. & Snyder, C.R. (Eds.) *Type A behavior pattern.* New York: Wiley & sons, pp. 83-97.

Essau, C.A. (1987). Type A personality and discrepancies between self-report and heart rate responses to stress. *Perceptual and Motor Skills, 64,* 544-546.

Evans, P.D. & Moran, P. (1987). The Framingham Type A scale, vigilant coping, and heart rate reactivity. *Journal of Behavioral Medicine, 10,* 311—321.

Friedman, M., Byers, S.O., Diamant, J. & Rosenman, R.H. ,(1975). Plasma catecholamine response of coronary-prone subjects (Type A) to a specific challenge. *Metabolism, 24,* 205-210.

Glass, D.C. (1977). *Behavior Patterns, Stress, and Coronary Disease.* Hillsdale, NJ: Erlbaum.

Harbin, T.J. & Blumenthal, J.A. (1985). Relationships among age, sex, the Type A behavior pattern, and cardiovascular reactivity. *Journal of Gerontology, 40,* 714-720.

Hare-Mustin, R.T. & Marecek, J. (1988). The meaning of difference: gender theory, postmodernism, and psychology. *American Psychologist, 43,* 455-464.

Haynes, S.G., Feinleib, M., Levine, S., Scotch, N.A., & Kannel, W.B. (1978). The relationship of psychosocial factors to coronary heart disease in the Framingham study. II. Prevalence of coronary heart disease. *American Journal of Epidemiology, 107,* 384-402.

Holmes, D.S (1983). An alternative perspective concerning the differential psychophysiological responsivity of persons with the Type A and Type B behavior patterns. *Journal of Research in Personality, 17,* 40-47.

Holmes, D.S., Solomon, S., & Rump, B.S. (1982) Cardiac and subjective response to cognitive challenge and to controlled physical exercise by male and female coronary prone (Type A) and non-coronary prone persons. *Journal of Psychosomatic Research, 26,* 309-316.

Houston, B.K. (1983). Psychophysiological responsivity and the Type A behavior pattern. Journal of Research in Personality, 17, 22-39.

Houston, B.K. & Snyder, C.R. (1988). *Type A behavior pattern.* New York: Wiley & Sons.

Janisse, M.P., Edguer, N. & Dyck, D.G. (1986). Type A behavior, anger expression, and reactions to anger imagery. *Motivation and Emotion, 10,* 371-386.

Jones, K.V., Copolov, D.L. & Outch, K.H. (1986). Type A, test performance and salivary cortisol. *Journal of Psychosomatic Research, 30,* 699-707.

Kannel, W.B., Kannel, C., Paffenbarger, R.S., & Cupples, L.A. (1987). Heart rate and cardiovascular mortality: The Framingham study. *Progress in Cardiology, 113,* 1489-1494.

Ketterer, M.W. (1982). Lateralized representation of affect, affect cognizance and the coronary-prone personality. *Biological Psychology, 15,* 171-189.

Krantz, D.S. and Durel, L.A. (1983). Psychobiological substrates of the Type A behavior pattern. *Health Psychology, 2,* 393-411.

Krantz, D.S., & Manuck, S.B. (1984). Acute psychophysiologic reactivity and risk of cardiovascular disease: A review and methodologic critique. *Psychological Bulletin, 96,* 435-464.

LaCroix, A. & Haynes, S.G. (1985). Occupational exposure to high chronic stress as a factor in psychologic reactivity to challenge. Cited in Haynes,

S.G. (1984). Type A behavior, employment status, and coronary heart disease in women. *Behavioral Medicine Update, 6,* 11-15.

Lane, J.D., White, A.D., & Williams, R.B. (1984). Cardiovascular effects of mental arithmetic in Type A and Type B females. *Psychophysiology, 21,* 39-46.

Lawler, K.A., Rixse, A., & Allen, M.T. (1983). Type A behavior and psychophysiological responses in adult women. *Psychophysiology, 20,* 343-350.

Lawler, K.A. and Schmied, L.A. (1986). Cardiovascular responsivity, Type A behavior and parental history of heart disease in young women. *Psychophysiology, 23,* 28-32.

Lawler, K.A. and Schmied, L.A. (1987). The relationship of stress, Type A behavior and powerlessness to physiological responses in female clerical workers. *Journal of Psychosomatic Research, 31,* 555-566.

Lawler, K.A., Schmied, L.A., Mitchell, V.P., & Rixse, A. (1984). Type A behavior and physiological responsivity in young women. *Psychophysiology, 21,* 197-204.

Lutz, D.J., Holmes, D.S. & Cramer, R.E. (1987). Hard-driving and speed-impatience components of the Type A behavior pattern as predictors of physiological arousal, subjective arousal and challenge seeking. *Journal of Psychosomatic Research, 31,* 713-722.

Matthews, K.A., Weiss, S.M., Detre, T., Dembroski, T.M., Falkner, B., Manuck, S.B., and Williams, R.B. (1986). *Handbook of stress, reactivity, and cardiovascular disease.* New York: Wiley and Sons.

Matthews, K.A. & Woodall, K.L. (1988). Childhood origins of overt Type A behaviors and cardiovascular reactivity to behavioral stressors. *Annals of Behavioral Medicine, 10,* 71-77.

Mayes, B.T., Sime, W.E., & Ganster, D.C. (1984). Convergent validity of Type A behavior pattern scales and their ability to predict physiological responsiveness in a sample of female public employees. *Journal of Behavioral Medicine, 7,* 83-108.

Morell, M.A. (1988, in press). Psychophysiologic stress responsivity in Type A and B community women and female college students. *Psychophysiology.*

O'Rourke, D.F., Houston, B.K., Harris, J.K. & Snyder, C.R. (1988). The Type A behavior pattern: Summary, conclusions, and implications. In Houston, B.K. & Snyder, C.R. (Eds.) *Type A behavior pattern.* New York: Wiley & Sons, pp. 312-334.

Orth-Gomer, K., Hamsten, A., Perski, A.L., Theorell, T. & deFaire, N. (1986). Type A behavior, education, and psychosocial work characteristics in relation to ischemic heart disease—a case control study of young survivors of myocardial infarction. *Journal of Psychosomatic Research, 30,* 633-642.

Pfiffner, D., Elsinger, P., Nil, R., Buzzin, R. & Battig, K. (1986). Psychophysiological reactivity in Type A and B women during a rapid information processing task. *Experientia, 42,* 126-131.

Pfiffner, E., Nil, R., & Battig, K. (1987). Psychophysiological reactivity and speech behavior during the structured Type A interview and a self-disclosure monologue. *International Journal of Psychophysiology, 5,* 1-9.

Powell, L.H. (1984). The Type A behavior pattern: an update on conceptual, assessment, and intervention research. *Behavioral Medicine Update, 6,* 7-10.

Rosenman, R.H., Brand, R.J., Jenkins, C.D., Friedman, M., Straus, R. & Wurm, M. (1975). Coronary heart disease in the Western Collaborative Group Study. *Journal of the American Medical Association, 233,* 872-877.

Rosenman, R.H., & Friedman, M. (1961). Association of a specific overt behavior pattern in females with blood and cardiovascular findings. *Circulation, 24,* 1173-1184.

Rosenman, R.H., Sholtz, R.I., & Brand, R.J. (1976). A Study of comparative blood pressure measures in predicting risk of coronary heart disease. *Circulation, 54,* 51-58.

Schmied, L.A. & Lawler, K.A. (1988). *Control, Type A behavior and cardiovascular responsivity in adult women employed as clerical workers.* Paper presented at Society for Behavioral Medicine, Boston.

Smith, T.W., Houston B.K. & Zurawski, R.M. (1985). The Framingham Type A Scale: Cardiovascular and cognitive behavioral responses to interpersonal challenge. *Motivation and Emotion, 9,* 123-134.

Smith, T.W. & O'Keeffe, J.L. (1985). The inequivalence of self-reports of Type A behavior; Differential relationships of the Henkins Activity Survey and the Framingham Scale with affect, stress and control. *Motivation and Emotion, 9,* 299-311.

Stoney, C.M., Davis, M.C. & Matthews, K.A. (1987). Sex differences in physiological responses to stress and in coronary heart disease: A causal link? *Psychophysiology, 24,* 127-131.

Strube, M.J. & Werner, C.M. (1985). Relinquishment of control and the Type A behavior pattern. *Journal of Personality and Social Psychology, 48,* 688-701.

Thomas, C.B. & Greenstreet, R.L. (1973). Psychobiological characteristics in youth as predictors of five disease states: suicide, mental illness, hypertension, coronary heart disease and tumor. *Johns Hopkins Medical Journal, 132,* 16-43.

Weidner, G., Sexton, G., McLellarn, R., Connor, S.L., & Matarazzo, J.D. (1987). The role of Type A behavior and hostility in an elevation of plasma lipids in adult women and men. *Psychosomatic Medicine, 49,* 136-145.

Type A, Effort to Excel, and Attentional Style in Children: The Validity of the MYTH

Nancy T. Blaney

Department of Psychiatry, University of Miami School of Medicine 1425 N W 10th Ave, Sieron Bldg., Ste. 200, Miami FL 33136

The Matthews Youth Test for Health (MYTH) is emerging as the standard measure for assessing Type A behavior in children, yet there is an absence of replication of the MYTH construct validation findings, or examination of these by the MYTH's two components (competitiveness-achievement and impatience-aggression). Study 1 was conducted to address these issues with third-through sixth grade children. Study 2 was conducted to determine whether the narrowed attentional style characteristic of adult Type As, thought to pose morbidity and mortality risks via symptom underawareness, is evident in children assessed as Type A by the MYTH. The results provide qualified support that the MYTH behavioral validation findings are replicable, and suggest a possible childhood origin for boys of the narrowed attentional focus of Type As. The results also suggested that the negative self-evaluation shown by adult Type As when performance standards are unclear is evident in childhood, in this study appearing as spontaneously-generated behavior.

Research on Type A behavior is at a crucial point. The behavior pattern in adults has been extensively described and research suggests that Type A is an independent risk factor for coronary heart disease (CHD; cf. reviews in Matthews & Haynes, 1986; Siegel, 1984). Recent meta-analyses (Booth-Kewley & Friedman, 1987; Matthews, in press) have refined our understanding of the Type A-CHD link, while also emphasizing the value of studying Type A in terms of its components. Now one task is to learn about the etiology of Type A behavior: where it comes from, and when and how it develops. Hence, the study of Type A behavior in children and adolescents.

Assessing Type A in these age groups has required developing new measures. Those most widely used include the Matthews Youth Test for

Author's Note: The author thanks the administration, teachers and students from West Laboratory Elementary School in Miami, FL, for their participation in and support of these studies; Ofelia Cohen and Mary Ann Vela for gathering the data; and Paul Blaney and anonymous reviewers for their helpful comments.

© 1990 Select Press

Health (MYTH; Matthews & Angulo, 1980) and the Hunter-Wolf A-B Rating Scale (Wolf, Sklov, Wenzl, Hunter & Berenson, 1982), both oriented toward children, and the Adolescent Structured Interview (Siegel & Leitch, 1981) for older youth. Other measures include the recently developed Miami Structured Interview-1 (Gerace & Smith, 1985), the Student Type A Behavior Scale (Kirmil-Gray, Eagleston, Thoresen, et al., 1987), and the Bortner Performance Battery (Bortner & Rosenman, 1967) and Bortner Adjective Rating Scale (Bortner, 1969), both adapted from adult Type A measures. Three recent studies have examined the comparability of several measures of Type A in children to determine their degree of concordance and whether they can be used interchangeably (Bishop, Hailey & Anderson, 1987; Jackson & Levine, 1987; Kirmil-Gray et al., 1987). In all three studies, correlations among the measures were low, and concordance of Type A-B classification was minimal. These findings are not surprising considering that there are many differences among the instruments (cf. Jackson & Levine, 1987). The principal adult measures of Type A are also discrepant (Chesney, Black, Chadwick & Rosenman, 1981). They raise serious concerns that research on the development of Type A behavior in children will be plagued by the same problems (cf. Matthews, 1982) that have hindered the adult research due to lack of clarity in measurement of the Type A construct.

In addressing these concerns, authors in two of the studies (Bishop et. al., 1987; Jackson & Levine, 1987) concluded that, if using multiple Type A measures is not feasible in research with children, investigators should use the MYTH. Since the two most commonly used Type A rating scales for children, the MYTH and the Hunter-Wolf, were the focus of comparison in these two studies, the recommendation to use the MYTH may have considerable impact. This likelihood is enhanced by the fact that neither study effectively replicated the factor structure of the Hunter-Wolf (only partial replication in Jackson & Levine, none at all in Bishop et al.). Both replicated the MYTH factor structure, despite ethnically diverse samples, thereby lending credence to the MYTH.

As it now stands, the MYTH may be poised on the verge of becoming the standard for assessing Type A behavior in children. Indeed, this may be warranted as the MYTH is the most extensively researched of the Type A measures for children and the data demonstrate its validity. For example, construct validation studies have shown numerous parallels between the behavior of Type A adults and MYTH-assessed Type A children. Like adults, grade school Type As evidence Type A behavior when challenged (Matthews & Angulo, 1980), ignore feelings of fatigue and strive to excel (Matthews & Volkin, 1981), make active efforts to exert control when threatened with failure (Matthews, 1979), and show elevated physiological responses to stress under some conditions (Lawler, Allen, Critcher & Standard, 1981; Matthews & Jennings, 1984), although not all (Murray, Blake, Prineas & Gillum, 1985). In preschoolers, MYTH-assessed Type A scores correlate with reaction time on a visual discrimination task as well as with teacher ratings of situation-specific aggression and impatience (Corrigan & Moskowitz, 1983).

However, whereas findings regarding MYTH factor structure (Bishop et al., 1987; Jackson & Levine, 1987; Murray, Bruhn & Bunce, (1983) and reliability (Corrigan & Moskowitz, 1983) have been replicated across studies, there is an absence of replication of the MYTH construct validation findings, or examination of these data by the two components of the MYTH, competitiveness-achievement and impatience-aggression. Demonstrating the replicability of such data could increase our confidence in the soundness of the MYTH. Data exploring the Type A components could enlarge our understanding of the childhood origins of the behavior pattern. In fact, in the adult literature it is research on the components of Type A behavior (rather than the global A-B classification) that has proven crucial for determining which aspects of the behavior pattern are most pathogenic, i.e., most related to cardiovascular pathology (cf. MacDougall, Dembroski, Dimsdale & Hackett, 1985). Comparable analyses in terms of component, rather than global, Type A behaviors are not typical in Type A research in children (for exceptions see Matthews, Stoney, Rakaczky & Jamison, 1986; Murray, Matthews, Blake et al., 1986; Sweda, Sines, Lauer & Clarke, 1986). These are to be encouraged, particularly since individuals can be classed as Type A for different reasons and these may have different developmental antecedents as well as consequences (cf., Siegel, Matthews & Leitch, 1981).

One purpose of the present research, then, is to determine the replicability of previously reported behavioral validation findings for the MYTH with grade school children. These will also be examined in terms of components of Type A behavior in addition to the more commonly reported overall Type A score. The behavioral validations under investigation included performance on a frustrating task (Matthews & Angulo, 1980) and effort to excel (Matthews & Volkin, 1981). The frustrating task (star tracing) was chosen because it provides a useful format for observing a range of Type A-related behaviors, as well as for investigating their occurrence as a function of time elapsed in the task. This factor was not examined in the initial research (Matthews & Angulo, 1980) but would provide additional construct validation if As not only manifest more Type A behaviors than Bs, but do so earlier in the task. How quickly an individual shows frustration may be a discriminating index of impatience. Effort to excel (math task) was chosen because it is an integral part of the view of the Type A individual being in a chronic struggle to master a challenging environment (Glass, 1977).

A second purpose of the present research is to investigate whether the attentional style which differentiates Type A and B adults (Matthews & Brunson, 1979) extends to children as well. This has not been directly examined. The results obtained by Matthews and Volkin (1981) led them to speculate that Type A children may, in fact, have a highly-focused attentional style as do Type A adults. Finding A-B attentional style differences in children assessed with the MYTH would extend behavioral validation of the MYTH to a realm that previous research (Weidner & Matthews, 1978) suggests may be an important behavioral factor in the development of coronary artery disease. To assess attentional style, a second study was conducted with grade school children using the experimental procedure employed by Matthews and Brunson (1979) with adults.

STUDY 1

Method

Subjects and A-B Classification

Participants were 118 predominantly middle-class children in the third through sixth grades at a public elementary school with university research affiliations in Miami, Florida. Of the 125 parental consent forms returned, 120 (96%) approved participation. Two students were eliminated due to absence during the testing periods.

Subjects were classified as Type A or B on the basis of their scores on the MYTH (described below). MYTH total score distributions and medians were determined for each grade separately. These were comparable to those reported by Matthews (Matthews & Angulo, 1980). Since there was a slight increase in Type A with age, the medians were used to determine an overall A/B cutoff such that MYTH scores of students classified as Type A were above the highest median for all grades, and those classified as Type B were below the lowest median for all grades. This ensured that the Type A category would not contain students who would be classified as Type B according to the median of another grade level. The same strategy was used to determine A-B cutoffs for the competitiveness-achievement and impatience-aggression scores of the MYTH. The resulting A/B cutoffs were as follows: MYTH total score—A > 56, B < 52; competitiveness-achievement—A > 30.8, B < 24.5; impatience-aggression—A > 27, B < 21.5.

The final sample contained 94 (47 As, 47 Bs) with the following Grade, Sex and Type breakdown: 32 third-and fourth-graders combined[1], 18 males (8 As, 10 Bs), 14 females (4 As, 10 Bs); 35 fifth-graders, 15 males (9 As, 6 Bs), 20 females (7 As, 13 Bs); and 27 sixth-graders, 15 males (12 As, 3 Bs), 12 females (7 As, 5 Bs). The 24 remaining students were eliminated because of MYTH scores falling between the A/B cutoffs. Race was not included as a variable in analyses due to the small number of Blacks and the unrepresentativeness of the Hispanic population. (Hispanics scored as high as Anglos on the competitiveness subscale of the MYTH and outscored Anglos on the Stanford Achievement Math Tests making generalizations to Hispanics misleading.) Ns for analyses vary slightly due to scheduling problems precluding students participating in or completing one of the tasks, failure to follow instructions, or missing dependent measure data (e.g., student omitting a questionnaire item).

The sample sizes for the three analyses were not identical, since the excluded middle group (i.e., neither A nor B) differed somewhat among them. For the MYTH competitiveness-achievement analyses, the final sample contained 84: 26 third-and fourth-graders, 15 males (6 As, 9 Bs), 11 females (5 As, 6 Bs); 27 fifth-graders, 10 males (5 As, 5 Bs), 17 females (5 As, 12 Bs); and 31 sixth-graders, 15 males (8 As, 7 Bs), 16 females (13 As, 3 Bs). For the MYTH impatience-aggression analyses, the final sample contained 93: 26 third-and fourth-graders, 16 males (11 As, 5 Bs), 10 females (4 As, 6 Bs); 33 fifth-graders, 14 males (9 As, 5 Bs), 19 females (9 As, 10 Bs); and 34 sixth-graders, 16 males (12 As, 4 Bs), 18 females (7 As, 11 Bs).

MYTH Rating Scale

The MYTH contains 17 items indicative of Type A behavior in children (e.g., "gets irritated easily," "does things in a hurry"). Teachers rate how characteristic each statement is of the child's behavior using a scale from 1 (extremely uncharacteristic) to 5 (extremely characteristic).

---

[1] *The rationale for combining third- and fourth-graders in the first study was to create a subject grouping with an N comparable to that of the other two age groups in the study. For convenience, this combined group is called fourth-graders. Fifth- and sixth-graders were retained as separate groups in order to examine whether Type A behaviors evidenced developmental changes (e.g., relatively little Type A behavior in younger children, and more in each successive grade). Results did not suggest that Type A behaviors increased from the fourth through the sixth grade in this sample (i.e., there was no consistent pattern showing fourth graders < fifth graders < sixth graders in Type A behaviors).*

After reverse-coding of three items, scoring yields a total Type A score and subscores for competitiveness-achievement and impatience-aggression. Higher scores represent higher levels of Type A behavior. Previous studies have demonstrated reliability and validity for the MYTH (e.g., Matthews & Angulo, 1980; Matthews & Volkin, 1981).

Task Descriptions

Star Trace. Children were asked to use the Lafayette mirror trace apparatus to trace a star with a pencil held by their preferred hand. The apparatus contains a shield which blocks the child's view of both hand and star, forcing the use of an image in a mirror to guide the tracing effort. Children were given a time limit of four minutes to trace the star. After completing the task, subjects were assured there was no right or wrong to the task, that everybody has trouble doing it, and that the purpose was to see how children of different ages—third through sixth grades—react to something tough the first time they try it. They were told they had done as well as most children their age.

Dependent measures were continuous observations of selected verbal and nonverbal behavior, and time to complete the task. The observation categories tapped behavior shown by Type A adults (Friedman & Rosenman, 1974) that were applicable to the star trace task (e.g., behaviors such as verbal interruptions and emphatic pointing were excluded). These were used by Matthews & Angulo (1980), with the addition of other Type A relevant behaviors (e.g., negative self-statements). Behavior categories included: (1) expiratory sighs; (2) clicking of the tongue; (3) negative self-statements; (4) asking questions; (5) verbal comments; (6) stopping; and indices of restlessness such as (7) repetitive movements (e.g., tapping fingers); (8) forceful movements (e.g., hand/fist hitting table or self); and (9) bodily movements (e.g., squirming).

Interrater reliability for these rating categories was established by having the two experimenters simultaneously observe a sample of subjects (N=19; data not included in star trace analyses). Reliability was computed as the Pearson correlation between the frequencies reported by each observer. Reliability estimates for total behavior as well as for each category are as follows: total behavior, r = .91; clicks, r = .95; questions, r = .94, bodily movements, r = .93, sighs, r = .86; negative self-statements, r = .69; verbal comments, r = .32. Estimates could not be computed for repetitive and forceful movements or stopping due to their absence or scarcity in the reliability sample.

Math Task. After the star task and debriefing, subjects were asked to work on a math task. Each student served as his or her own control, participating in both the no-deadline (first) and deadline (second) conditions.[2] Otherwise, the procedure was identical to that of the Matthews and Volkin (1981) study of efforts to excel among Type A and B children. After the task was explained and subjects worked three practice problems, they were given a sheet containing 72 math problems and told to work as many as they could. In the no-deadline condition, subjects were told that they would be timed but there was no time limit. After four minutes elapsed, subjects were told to stop, the first sheet was collected, and subjects were given a sheet with different but comparable math problems. In this deadline (second) condition, subjects were again told to work as many as they could and that they would be timed, but this time they only had exactly four minutes to do as many problems as they could. After four minutes, subjects were stopped, and the second sheet collected. Subjects then answered a questionnaire on the math task concerning how well they thought they had done, and how challenging the task had been, using a five-point Likert-type scale. Students were debriefed as before, asked if they had any questions, and thanked for their participation.

Procedure

Subjects were tested individually at the elementary school within one month of parental consent and assessment on the MYTH. After filling out a consent slip, subjects participated in the two behavioral tasks just described. Two female experimenters (the author and a graduate student) blind to the MYTH scores administered the two tasks. Only female experimenters were used as they have been shown to elicit superior task performance (Rumenik, Capasso & Hendrick, 1977) and more Type A behavior (Matthews & Angulo, 1980) from children than do male experimenters. When subjects arrived at the testing area, the experimenter greeted them, introduced herself by first name to minimize any apprehension, and asked the subject's name and grade. Subjects were seated at a small table containing the mirror trace apparatus, with the experimenter in a chair positioned to provide a clear view of the subject's face. Subjects wearing watches were requested to remove them, with the explanation that they might interfere with their movement during the first task. The experimenter then told subjects that she wanted them to do two things, trace a star and do some math problems. The subject then proceeded through the two tasks as described above.

---

[2] *This order of presentation was chosen to minimize bias. Counterbalancing the conditions could have resulted in a "sense" of deadline being carried over into the no-deadline condition for half the subjects. This would preclude a valid test of this condition, and it is with this condition that A/B differences would be expected to emerge. Further, placing the deadline condition last ensured that any fatigue effects would not influence the no-deadline condition.*

TABLE 1 Star Trace Behaviors*

FIRST HALF		*MYTH Total Score Analysis*				*Competitiveness-Achievement Analysis*			*Impatience-Aggression Analysis*		
		A	*B*	*p<*		*A*	*B*	*p<*	*A*	*B*	*p<*
Total Behavior		12.60	10.13	(.08)		12.43	10.07	(.06)	12.31	9.76	(.05)
Negative Self Statements		.77	.21	(.02)		.83	.33	(.07)	.56	.24	(.07)
					Grade			(.03)			
					4	1.73	.13				
					5	.30	.41				
					6	.62	.50				
Sighs		.94	.47	(.08)		1.14	.43	(.01)			NS
Verbal Comments		M F	M F	(.05)				NS	3.15	1.80	(.04)
	Grade										
	4	2.00 3.25	3.50 2.50								
	5	3.44 1.57	.67 1.69								
	6	2.58 3.29	4.00 1.00								
Questions				NS				NS	.25	.05	(.05)
Clicks				NS				NS			NS
Stopping				NS	Grade			(.03)			NS
					4	.00	.40				
					5	.20	.06				
					6	.10	.00				
Forceful Movements				NS				NS			NS
Bodily Movements				NS				NS			NS

... included in the table.

TABLE 1 Star Trace Behaviors* (cont'd)

SECOND HALF		MYTH Total Score Analysis				Competitiveness-Achievement Analysis				Impatience-Aggression Analysis		
		A	B	p<		A	B	p<		A	B	p<
Total Behavior				NS				NS				NS
Negative Self Statements		.43	.15	(.02)	Grade			(.07)				NS
					4	.91	.14					
					5	.00	.13					
					6	.54	.38					
Sighs	Grade			(.02)				NS				NS
	4	1.83	1.11									
	5	1.27	.71									
	6	.67	2.75									
Verbal Comments				NS				NS				NS
Questions				NS				NS				NS
Clicks				NS				NS	Sex			(.03)
									M	.55	1.15	
									F	.94	.48	
Stopping		.45	.15	(.03)		.29	.08	(.04)		.46	.06	(.03)
Forceful Movements				NS	Sex			(.02)		M F	M F	(.02)
					M	.41	.11		Grade			
					F	.06	.21		4	.30 .00	.20 .00	
									5	.00 .00	.00 .13	
						M F	M F	(.007)	6	.09 .75	.67 .00	
					Grade							
					4	.50 .20	.13 .00					
					5	.00 .00	.00 .09					
					6	.67 .00	.17 1.50					
Bodily Movements				NS				NS				NS

* *Only those categories for which significant findings emerged in either half of the task are included in the table.*

Results

Star Trace Measures

Data were analyzed separately for the first two minutes and the second two minutes of the task to examine behavior as a function of time spent in a frustrating task, i.e., whether A-B differences emerge early in the task (first two minutes) or only after prolonged exposure (second two minutes). Analyses were performed with subjects' A-B category determined in terms of MYTH total and component scores, and used a least squares solution for unequal cell frequencies. Results of these three analyses will be presented for the first and then the second half of the task for (a) total Type A-related behavior (i.e., collapsed across categories), and (b) frequency of behavior within each category. Independent variables throughout are A-B category, Grade, and Sex.

Total Behavior

As shown by the means in Table 1, in all three analyses As exhibited more Type A-related behavior overall than Bs during the first half of the task. This was marginal for the MYTH total score, $F(1,82) = 3.26$, $p < .08$ and competitiveness-achievement $F(1,72) = 3.76$, $p < .06$, and significant for impatience-aggression, $F(1,81) = 4.30$, $p < .05$. Table 1 means suggest the latter may be due largely to verbal comments. There were no interactions with Grade or Sex and, by the second half of the task, there were no A-B differences in total Type A-related behavior. This was due to Type Bs increasing in overall Type A-related behavior during the second half of the task to the level already shown by As, whose scores remained stable.

Tracing Time

There were no significant differences in tracing time in any of the analyses, thus replicating the pattern reported by Matthews and Angulo (1980) for the MYTH total score.

Category Frequencies: First Half

Negative statements about self occurred more frequently among As than Bs as classified by the MYTH total score, $F(1,82) = 6.47$, $p < .02$. This was marginal for the competitiveness-achievement, $F(1,72) = 3.60$, $p < .07$, and impatience-aggression analyses, $F(1,81) = 3.61$, $p < .07$. A Type x Grade interaction in the competitiveness-achievement analysis showed this was due primarily to fourth-graders, $F(2,72) = 3.83$, $p < .03$. Expiratory sighs were more common among As than Bs as classified by competitiveness-achievement, $F(1,72) = 6.95$, $p < .01$, but not impatience-aggression ($F < .2$). This was marginal for the MYTH total score, $F(1,82) = 3.26$, $p < .08$. Verbal comments also were more characteristic of As, but only those characterized by impatience-aggression, $F(1,81) =$

4.79, $p < .04$. A Type x Grade x Sex interaction for the MYTH total score, $F(2,82) = 3.18$, $p < .05$, showed no consistent pattern in the means. For stopping, although there was a Type x Grade interaction for competitiveness-achievement, the frequency of this behavior was too low during the first half to view this result as meaningful. Type As asked more questions than Bs, as shown in the impatience-aggression analysis, $F(1,81) = 3.99$, $p < .05$. There were no significant A-B main effects or interactions for tongue clicks, repetitive or forceful movements, or bodily movements.

Category Frequencies: Second Half

Results are reported first for variables showing A-B differences during the first-half of the task, followed by A-B differences emerging only during the second half. Ns differ from previous analyses due to the exclusion from analyses of subjects who finished the task in less than three and one-half minutes.

Negative self-statements continued to characterize Type As more than Bs as classified by the MYTH total score, $F(1,70) = 6.36$, $p < .02$. Again a Type x Grade interaction appeared for competitiveness-achievement (this time as a marginal finding), suggesting that this was primarily due to fourth-and sixth-graders, $F(2,60) = 2.90$, $p < .07$. There no longer were differences for the impatience-aggression component.

For expiratory sighs, a Type x Grade interaction in the MYTH total score analysis, $F(2,70) = 4.46$, $p < .02$, showed that sighs were more common among As than Bs in the fourth and fifth grades, the opposite in the sixth. Differences were not obtained as before for competitiveness-achievement, and continued to be absent for impatience-aggression.

Stopping was significantly more common among As than Bs for all three Type A classifications: MYTH total score $F(1,70) = 5.37$, $p < .03$; competitiveness-achievement $F(1,60) = 4.67$, $p < .04$; and impatience-aggression $F(1,68) = 5.44$, $p < .03$. A-B differences no longer appeared for verbal comments or asking questions.

A-B differences not appearing in first-half analyses concerned tongue clicks and forceful movements. Tongue clicks showed a Type x Sex interaction for the impatience-aggression component, $F(1,68) = 5.29$, $p < .03$ (male Bs highest, females As next, with male As and female Bs lower and similar to one another). A Type x Grade x Sex interaction, $F(2,68) = 3.71$, $p < .03$ showed this was due to fifth-and sixth-grade male Bs and fourth-and sixth-grade female As.

Forceful movements were most characteristic of male Type As in the competitiveness-achievement analysis, as shown by a Type x Sex interaction, $F(1,60) = 6.10$, $p < .02$. Although three way interactions appeared for the analyses of both competitiveness-achievement, $F(2,60) = 5.40$, $p < .007$, and impatience-aggression $F(2,68) = 4.42$, $p < .02$, inspection of the

TABLE 2 Math Task Performance

		Competitiveness-Achievement Analysis		
		Type A	*Type B*	*p<*
Total Problems Worked		40.27	31.97	.02
Number Correct		36.87	28.34	.02
Percentage Correct	Grade			.03
No-Deadline	4	88.82	85.33	
	5	91.40	89.25	
	6	95.23	93.92	
Deadline	4	86.73	73.23	
	5	84.60	87.00	
	6	93.31	91.50	

No A-B effects emerged in the MYTH total score or impatience-aggression analyses.

means revealed no consistent pattern. Further, forceful movements were infrequently observed. There were no A-B differences for repetitive or bodily movements, or asking questions.

Math Task Measures

Performance measures on math problems (e.g., total worked, number correct, and percentage correct) were analyzed by a series of analyses in which A-B, Grade, and Sex were treated as between-subject variables and Deadline vs. No-Deadline Conditions were treated as a repeated measure. For the questionnaire items there were no repeated measures. All these analyses were performed with subjects' A-B category determined as before—MYTH total score, and competitiveness-achievement and impatience-aggression components.

As shown by the means in Table 2, for both total number of problems worked and number of problems correct, there were significant A-B main effects in the competitiveness-achievement analysis, $F(1,67) = 6.21$, $p < .02$, and $F(1,67) = 6.89$, $p < .02$. The performance of As surpassed that of Bs for both measures. There were no significant A-B findings for either the MYTH total score or impatience-aggression.

A percentage correct index was calculated to determine if the A-B findings were due to speed (i.e., As working faster). A Type x Grade x Condition interaction, $F(2,67) = 4.06$, $p < .03$, (see means in Table 2) shows that with a correction for speed, As usually did better than Bs, though not strikingly so, except for fifth-graders in the deadline condition. The clearly deviant cell is the combined third/fourth-grade Type Bs in the deadline condition. Since this finding appeared only for the youngest subjects, and since the deadline condition came last, this may also be due to fatigue which Type As are known to suppress (cf. Carver, Coleman &

Glass, 1976). Even so, these means clearly show that substantial A>B discrepancies failed to emerge in the no-deadline condition for any age group, as would be expected based on Burnam, Pennebaker & Glass (1975). Further, deadline condition performance was not superior to the no-deadline condition.

Subsidiary analyses suggest that these A-B differences are not due to differences in mathematical ability. No A-B differences emerged when Stanford Achievement Test math scores were examined by the MYTH total or component scores. There also were no A-B differences in questionnaire items (how well subjects thought they had done, or how challenging the task had been) suggesting that subjects were not differentially motivated.

Discussion

The results of Study 1 provide qualified support that previously reported behavioral validation data for the MYTH (Matthews & Angulo, 1980; Matthews & Volkin, 1981) are replicable: Children assessed as Type A did, in part, evidence more characteristic Type A behavior in a frustrating task and show greater effort to excel in a challenging task than children assessed as Type B. Moreover, the different ways of scoring the MYTH—the total score and its two components, competitiveness-achievement and impatience-aggression—related differently to the two tasks. The MYTH total score and, to a lesser extent, the impatience-aggression score differentiated As and Bs on the frustrating (star) task, and the competitiveness-achievement score on the challenging (math) task.

For the frustrating task, as expected, A-B differences emerged early, suggesting that Type A children (particularly those characterized by impatience-aggression) may respond to such tasks differently than do Bs. During the first half of the task Type A children were more spontaneously self-critical than were Bs and showed a trend toward more Type A-related behavior overall. Those characterized by impatience-aggression made more verbal comments (excluding negative self-statements) and asked more questions, possibly in an attempt to gain a greater sense of control as is characteristic of Type A adults (Glass, 1977) and children (Matthews, 1979). Self criticism (i.e., negative self-statements) was greater among Type As than Bs in all three analyses (marginal for the two components) during the first half of the task and in the total score analysis during the second half.

The self-criticism findings are reminiscent of other research suggesting that, when performance criteria are unclear, Type As manifest a negative cognitive set (Suls, Gastorf & Witenberg, 1979) that extends to self-evaluation (Brunson & Matthews, 1981), a finding also reported for children (Murray et al., 1985). Children's negative self statements in the Murray et al. (1985) study were self-reports on a post-task questionnaire measuring the frequency of specific thoughts during the task. In the present study, the negative self-statements were spontaneously generated during the task without experimenter request. Thus, even though their actual task accomplishment was comparable to that of Bs (there were no A-B differences in tracing time), these Type A children viewed themselves more negatively during this difficult-to-complete task with unclear performance criteria.

During the second half of the task, all three methods of scoring showed that As stopped more than did Bs. While at first appearing to contradict results from Study 2 of Matthews and Volkin (1981), who found As to be more persistent than Bs, in fact the tasks in the two studies are quite different. In the present study, the star-tracing task was frustrating and difficult, fraught with frequent and obvious errors that signaled "poor performance" to the subject. In Matthews and Volkin, the task was simply to hold a weight that was well within each subject's capability and to do so for a "predetermined" amount of time (in actuality, as long as they could). Their task, then, was challenging whereas the present task was quite frustrating. The present findings are reminiscent of previous research on uncontrollability (Glass, 1977) suggesting that, while adult Type As exceed Bs in attempts to control, they also are more likely to give up in the face of failed attempts. Although this pattern is not without criticism as a Type A characteristic (cf. Matthews, 1982), the present study suggests that it may occur in children as well. Further replication of this phenomenon in children is warranted.

During the second half of the star trace task,Type A children also evidenced more frequent verbal stylistics (expiratory sighs and tongue clicks) supposedly characteristic of adult Type As (Friedman & Rosenman, 1974). It is not clear that these findings are particularly informative regarding the development of Type A, however. While expiratory sighs and tongue clicks differentiated As from Bs in early research (Friedman & Rosenman, 1974), these have not continued to be seen as etiologically important since component analyses have shown other attributes of Type A behavior (i.e., hostility; Williams, Haney, Lee, et al., 1980; MacDougall et al., 1985) to be more pathological regarding CHD.

Turning to the math task, the Type A (competitiveness-achievement component) children in this study also evidenced greater effort to excel than did Bs, replicating previous findings with children for math (Matthews & Volkin, 1981) and varied tasks (Wolf et al., 1982). Neither superior ability nor differential motivation could account for these results. Unlike research with adults (Burnam et al., 1975), however, there was a failure to show that As work at maximum capacity even in the absence of a deadline and that Bs respond only to task demands. Matthews and Volkin (1981) and Wolf et al. (1982) also failed to find a Type x Condition interaction to suggest that the superior performance of As occurred only without an explicit deadline. To date, three studies with children have failed to replicate Burnam et al. (1975). Possibly this is because the maladaptive striving aspect of Type A behavior is not as fully developed in children as it is in adults. Alternatively, children may not respond in this manner to the tasks that have been employed and so the question may not have received an adequate test. Clearly a replication study which includes both adults and children with varied tasks is warranted.

In summary, Study 1 suggests that the MYTH behavioral validation findings are replicable for some behaviors, are marginally so for others, and that the MYTH total and component scores differentiate separate aspects of Type A behavior. The MYTH total score and the impatience-aggression component related to behavior during a frustrating task (primarily regarding negative self-statements and stopping) and the competitiveness-achievement component, to effort to excel. Added to the existing literature on the MYTH, these findings lend qualified support to the construct validity of the MYTH and the childhood etiology of Type A behavior in general while also suggesting the need for further replication.

STUDY 2

The childhood etiology of a specific Type A characteristic (i.e., attentional style) which may have important implications for CHD morbidity and mortality is the focus of Study 2. Compared to Bs, adult Type As are characterized by a focused attentional style through which they ignore distracting stimuli which might hinder performance (Humphries, Carver & Neumann, 1983; Matthews & Brunson, 1979), including physical symptoms, This finding is shown for laboratory tasks (Carver et al., 1976; Weidner & Matthews, 1978) as well as in real life (Matthews & Carra, 1982). The concern is that this attentional style may elevate coronary disease risk by causing Type As to ignore symptoms and delay seeking medical attention (Carver, et al., 1976; Matthews & Brunson, 1979). It is of considerable interest to learn if this focused attentional style is merely a consequence, appearing in adulthood, of being a Type A, or whether it has a childhood etiology. Finding A-B attentional style differences among children would constitute evidence for a basic cognitive, not merely behavioral, differentiation of Type As and Bs that is of long standing, as well as extend construct validation of the MYTH.

For these reasons, Study 2 was conducted using the procedure for studying attentional style in adults (Experiment 2 of Matthews & Brunson, 1979). Type A and B children performed the Stroop Color Naming Task (Stroop, 1935) either with or without distraction due to extraneous noise. Noise distraction has been shown to improve Stroop performance (Hartley & Adams, 1974) by causing subjects to inhibit attention to all task-irrelevant cues, including those inherent in the Stroop task. Thus, this paradigm allows a determination of whether As simply attend more to the central task (As would perform similarly in both conditions) or whether they actively inhibit attention to task-irrelevant cues (As would improve with distraction). An A-B attentional style difference was expected to emerge with a Type x Condition interaction showing that Type As outperform Bs with distraction. In the no-distraction condition, As and Bs were expected to perform similarly due to the presence of a time deadline which previous research (Burnam et al., 1975) suggests may nullify A-B performance differences.

Method

Subjects

Subjects were 50 fifth-and sixth-graders[3] selected on the basis of their MYTH scores from the sample of subjects described earlier. Only older children were included in this study because the task complexity was inappropriate for young children. Type A or B classification was determined as described in Study 1 for the MYTH total and component scores.

The final sample contained 50: 23 in the distraction condition, 12 males (7 As, 5 Bs), 11 females (5 As, 6 Bs); and 27 in the no-distraction condition, 13 males (9 As, 4 Bs), 14 females (3 As, 11 Bs). For competitiveness-achievement analyses, the sample contained 47: 22 in the distraction condition, 11 males (6 As, 5 Bs), 11 females (5 As, 6 Bs); and 25 in the no-distraction condition, 12 males (6 As, 6 Bs), and 13 females (5 As, 8 Bs). For impatience-aggression analyses, the sample contained 50: 23 in the distraction condition, 12 males (7 As, 5 Bs), and 11 females (4 As, 7 Bs); and 27 in the no-distraction condition , 13 males (9 As, 4 Bs), and 14 females (4 As, 10 Bs).

Task Description

On the table in front of subjects was a stack of three sheets for the Stroop Color Naming Task (Stroop, 1935) modified by Hartley and Adams (1974). Each sheet contained 31 lines of six color names, each name printed in a color of ink other than its own (e.g., the name "blue"

[3]*Since Study 1 did not show fifth- and sixth-graders to reliably differ on Type A behavior, and since these grades are often combined for instruction at this school, collectively they constituted the subject pool and grade was not retained as an independent variable. These subjects had participated in Study 1.*

printed in red ink). For each line, subjects were to circle names on the right which matched the ink color of the stimulus name on the left. Subjects were given a five-line practice sheet and were allowed to practice until they clearly understood the task. They then performed the Stroop task for five minutes in either the distraction (sound) condition or no-distraction (no sound) condition. All subjects wore headphones to equate across conditions any distraction effect due to wearing headphones.

Procedure

Subjects were tested individually at the same elementary school, within two weeks of the previous study, in the same testing area. A different experimenter (a female graduate student) blind to subjects' MYTH scores conducted the testing, using the same introduction format as before. Subjects were told that this was a study of the effects on task performance of either noise (sound distraction condition) or visual distraction (no sound condition). No-sound (no-distraction) subjects were told the headphones were to block extraneous noise. After the task instructions were given, subjects completed the practice problems. They were then told they would have five minutes for the task, to work as many and as accurately as they could, and to keep working from one sheet to the next until they were told to stop.

Subjects in the sound (distraction) condition were told they would be hearing a tape of various sounds while they performed the Stroop task. The tape was identical to that used by Matthews and Brunson (1979): electronic music interspersed with familiar sounds (e.g., sports broadcast, a ticking clock, brief verbal comments). Average sound intensity was 72dB (A), slightly lower than that of Matthews and Brunson (1979). Pilot subjects in the present study complained of ear pain and discomfort with the 78 dB (A) intensity previously used. Gradual intensity reductions indicated that the 72 dB (A) level was the loudest tolerable intensity. The experimenter installed the headphones, checked the fit and that sound condition subjects were hearing sounds, and told subjects to begin. After five minutes, subjects were stopped and the headphones removed. Subjects then completed a seven-item post-experimental questionnaire about the task (how hard, confusing, or challenging), the sounds (how unpleasant, distracting, or loud), and their performance (how well they had done) using a five-point Likert-type scale for their ratings. After any questions were answered, subjects were debriefed and thanked for their participation.

TABLE 3 Stroop Color Naming Task MYTH Total Score Analyses

	No-distraction		*Distraction*	
	A	*B*	*A*	*B*
Number Correct*				
Males	68.00	67.50	65.57	40.20
Females	66.33	58.27	42.40	60.50
Percentage Correct*				
Males	96%	98%	96%	58%
Females	87%	93%	73%	94%

* $p < .03$
No A-B effects emerged in the competitiveness-achievement or impatience- aggression analyses.

Results

Task performance and postexperimental questionnaire items were analyzed by 2 X 2 X 2 (Type x Condition x Sex) analyses of variance using a least squares solution for unequal cell frequencies.

Stroop Task Performance

Performance on the Stroop Color Naming Task was assessed with three measures—total number of problems worked, number correct, and percentage correct (an accuracy measure incorporating a correction for speed).

Unlike Matthews and Brunson (1979), there were no main effects for Type on any of the performance measures in the MYTH total score analysis. Further, there were no significant differences at all in the competitiveness-achievement or impatience-aggression analyses. There was, however, a Type x Condition x Sex interaction in the MYTH total score analysis for number correct, $F(1,42) = 5.57, p < .03$, and percentage correct, $F(1,42) = 5.53, p < .03$. As the means in Table 3 show, male As and Bs performed similarly without distraction as expected, and in the presence of distraction As clearly outperformed Bs. However, this was not due to a distraction-related improvement for As so much as to a decrement for Bs who made more errors, despite being comparable to As in number of attempts. For females, results were quite different. Performance of female As paralleled that of male Bs (decreased with distraction) whereas female Bs performed more like male As (similar in both conditions).

These results suggest that, although Type A boys may not actively inhibit attention to extraneous stimuli to the degree shown by adult As, there is some evidence for a focused attentional style, as shown by their superiority over Bs in screening out distraction. Note that the present task was brief and the results of Zelson and Simons (1986) suggest that the use of a brief task may result in an underestimate of A-B attentional style differences.

Nevertheless, these findings are discrepant with previous research showing that distraction improves Stroop performance (Hartley & Adams, 1974). It should be noted that the performance decrement of Bs with distraction is not without precedent. Matthews and Brunson (1979) also found a distraction-related performance decrement among Bs in one of their two studies using the Stroop distraction paradigm.

Postexperimental Questionnaire

In all three MYTH analyses, distraction/no-distraction condition main effects served as a manipulation check confirming that the distraction condition was louder, more unpleasant, and more distracting (all p values $< .004$). Although A-B main effects were absent from all three analyses, there were several Type x Sex interactions which showed interesting parallels to the sex differences in the Stroop performance of As and Bs: for the competitiveness-achievement analysis, regarding "how well they had done", $F(1,39) = 16.88$, $p < .001$; for the impatience-aggression analysis regarding how "hard" and "challenging" the task was, $F(1,41) = 8.79$, $p < .005$ and, $F(1,40) = 11.33$, $p < .002$ respectively. In each case, the pattern was the same: male As and female Bs scored similarly and higher than male Bs and female As, although the later rated the sounds as being louder, $F, (1,35) = 4.14$, $p < .05$, in the impatience-aggression analysis.

Discussion

While these results provide partial support for a narrowed attentional style in Type A boys, they should be viewed with caution. Unlike previous research with adults (Matthews & Brunson, 1979), Type As did not outperform Bs in the presence of a distractor and males and females did not perform similarly. Whereas previous replication attempts with adults have confirmed A-B attentional style differences (Stern, Harris & Elverum, 1981; Strube, Turner, Patrick & Perillo, 1983; Zelson & Simons, 1986), this attempt with children leaves some uncertainty regarding the childhood etiology of A-B differences in attentional style. That Type A boys appear to be more successful than Bs in screening out distraction suggests that attentional style differences may have a childhood origin, although this finding warrants replication.

If A-B attentional differences do have a childhood etiology, it would suggest that attentionally-based symptom underawareness may have a long developmental history such that concerns about its long-term effects may be especially warranted. For both children and adults, it would be useful to know how pervasive the A-B attentional style differences are, that is, whether they pertain to a wide range of tasks and experiences. Also important to investigate are the concomitant cardiovascular responses, and how these relate to symptom awareness, particularly during naturalistic environmental challenges (e.g., school or work settings). This would extend our understanding of the functional effect of attentional style vis-a-vis cardiovascular risk, and whether, as suggested by Williams (1975), attentional and perceptual dimensions of Type A constitute a link between Type A and coronary disease pathogenesis.

Further, component analyses in such studies would refine our understanding of whether attentional style differences pertain to Type As overall, or primarily to those who are characterized by one or another component (e.g., hostility). There was no evidence in the present study to suggest that the focused attentional style was associated with either of the Type A components measured (competitiveness-achievement or impatience-aggression), only with the overall Type A score. It may be, however, that Type A components are not sufficiently well developed in children this age for such a differential association to appear with attentional style. The component analyses with adults reported by Carmody, Hollis, Matarazzo et al. (1984) are a step in the right direction.

It is worth noting that, although Carmody et al. found that Type As were more effective than Bs at allocating attention to meet task demands, in contrast to previous research (Humphries et al., 1983; Matthews & Brunson, 1979) they did not show a narrowed attentional focus. However, Carmody et al. used a self-report measure of attentional focus whereas other previous research which found attention narrowed among As, and the present study, used behavioral measures. These may be a more appropriate analogue for how Type As actually behave in response to environmental demands. Hence, these may be more accurate, provided the behaviors tapped are not undertaken at the instigation of others, a problem which undermined the Matthews et al. (1986) study of child-initiated medical care as a measure of symptom awareness.

That limited evidence of narrowed attentional focus emerged only for boys, and not girls, is reminiscent of other studies finding Type A characteristics to differ for boys and girls (Kirmil-Gray et al., 1987; Lundberg, 1986; Steinberg, 1985, 1988). Studies of adults have not shown gender differences in attentional style (Carmody et al., 1984; Matthews & Brunson, 1979; Stern et al., 1981; Zelson & Simons, 1986). Their presence in this study may be due to the gender specificity of the task.Boys may have found it to be challenging in ways that females did not, at least among Type As. Although the postexperimental questionnaire data tend to support this view, it should be pointed out that females performed nearly as well as males in the no-distraction condition. However, since research with adults suggests that challenge may be essential for eliciting attentional focus among Type As (Schlegel, Wellwood, Copps et al., 1980), absence of challenge for the female As in the present study could preclude the emergence of narrowed attentional focus. Alternatively, narrowed attentional style may simply have a different developmental course for females than for males. Both possibilities should be investigated further before it is concluded that Type A girls do not manifest a narrowed attentional focus at this age or that Type B girls do.

CONCLUDING COMMENTS

Taken together, findings from the two studies provide qualified support for replicating behavioral validation of the MYTH. In particular, the self-evaluation and possible attentional style findings call to mind the Steinberg (1985, 1988) suggestion that there may be childhood stylistic precursors of the Type A behavior pattern which facilitate its full development—that "how" a child does something may be more important than "what" he or she does.

That Type A children spontaneously generate negative self-statements about their performance when it is not objectively inferior suggests that even at this early age Type As may experience themselves as failing to meet performance standards. Since previous research has shown that parents of Type A children are more demanding and less positive in their evaluations of their children's performance (Glass, 1977; Matthews, 1977), parental behavior may help foster these negative self-views. Indeed, other recent research suggests that parents do have a key role in the development of Type A behavior in children (Kliewer & Weidner, 1987; Matthews et al., 1986; Sweda et al., 1986), particularly for boys (Kliewer & Weidner, 1987; Matthews et al., 1986). This has not been investigated regarding A-B differences in self-evaluation or attentional style, nor has the age at which these develop in each gender or their stability across time been determined.

Since there is mounting evidence that Type A identified in childhood shows considerable stability across time (Bergman & Magnusson, 1986; Matthews & Avis, 1983; Visintainer & Matthews, 1987), a negative cognitive set may have important physiological implications. Type A children may chronically "create" environmental stressors that repeatedly expose them to heightened physiological reactivity in the manner recently suggested for Type A adults. (For a discussion of Type A behavior as a stress-engendering process rather than a static trait see Smith & Anderson,

1986, and Smith & Rhodewalt, 1986.) And, in fact, blood pressure and catecholamine elevations have been found to characterize Type A children (Lundberg, 1986). If these co-occur with a narrowed attentional focus, thereby reducing awareness of and response to physical symptoms, disease risk could well be elevated, particularly if this occurs over a period of many years, possibly beginning in childhood.

REFERENCES

Bergman, L.R., & Magnusson, D. (1986). Type A behavior: A longitudinal study from childhood to adulthood. *Psychosomatic Medicine, 48,* 134-142.

Bishop, E.G., Hailey, B.J., & Anderson, H.N. (1987). Assessment of Type A behavior in children: A comparison of two instruments. *Journal of Human Stress, 13,* 121-127.

Booth-Kewley, S., & Friedman, H.S. (1987). Psychological predictors of heart disease: A quantitative review. *Psychological Bulletin, 101,* 343-362.

Bortner, R.W. (1969). A short rating scale as a potential measure of Pattern A behavior. *Journal of Chronic Diseases, 22,* 87-91.

Bortner, R.W., & Rosenman, R.H. (1967). The measurement of Pattern A behavior. *Journal of Chronic Diseases, 20,* 525-533.

Brunson, B.I. & Matthews, K.A. (1981). The Type A coronary-prone behavior pattern and reactions to uncontrollable stress: An analysis of performance strategies, affect and attributions during failure. *Journal of Personality and Social Psychology, 40,* 906-918.

Burnam, M.A., Pennebaker, J.A., & Glass, D.C. (1975). Time consciousness, achievement-striving, and the Type A coronary-prone behavior pattern. *Journal of Abnormal Psychology, 84,* 76-79.

Carmody, T.P., Hollis, J.F., Matarazzo, J.D., Fey, S.G., & Connor, W.E. (1984). Type A behavior, attentional style, and symptom reporting among adult men and women. *Health Psychology, 3,* 45-61.

Carver, C.S., Coleman, A.E., & Glass, D.C. (1976). The coronary-prone behavior pattern and the suppression of fatigue on a treadmill test. *Journal of Personality and Social Psychology, 33,* 460-466.

Chesney, M.A., Black, G.W., Chadwick, J.H., & Rosenman, R.H. (1981). Psychological correlates of the Type A behavior pattern. *Journal of Behavioral Medicine. 4,* 217-229

Corrigan, S.A., & Moskowitz, D.S. (1983). Type A behavior in preschool children: Construct validation evidence for the MYTH. *Child Development, 54,* 1513-1521.

Friedman, M., & Rosenman, R. (1974). *Type A behavior and your heart.* New York: Knopf.

Gerace, T.A., & Smith, J.C. (1985). Children's Type A interview: Interrater, test-retest, reliability, and interview effect. *Journal of Chronic Diseases, 38,* 781-791.

Glass, D.C. (1977). *Behavior patterns, stress, and coronary disease.* Hillsdale, N.J.: Lawrence Erlbaum.

Hartley, L.R., & Adams, R.G. (1974). Effect of noise on the Stroop test. *Journal of Experimental Psychology, 102,* 62-66.

Humphries, C., Carver, C.S., & Neumann, P.G. (1983). Cognitive characteristics of the Type A coronary-prone behavior pattern. *Journal of Personality and Social Psychology, 44,* 177-187.

Jackson, C., & Levine, D.W. (1987). Comparison of the Matthews Youth Test for Health and the Hunter-Wolf A-B Rating Scale: Measures of Type A behavior in children. *Health Psychology, 6,* 255-267.

Kirmil-Gray, K., Eagleston, J.R., Thoresen, C.E., Heft, L., Arnow, B., & Bracke, P. (1987). Developing measures of Type A behavior in children and adolescents. *Journal of Human Stress, 13,* 5-15.

Kliewer, W. & Weidner, G. (1987). Type A behavior and aspirations: A study of parents' and children's goal setting. *Developmental Psychology, 23,* 204-209.

Lawler, K.A., Allen, M.T., Critcher, E.C., & Standard, B.A. (1981). The relationship of physiological responses to the coronary-prone behavior pattern in children. *Journal of Behavioral Medicine, 4,* 203-216 .

Lundberg, U. (1986). Stress and Type A behavior in children. Journal of the *American Academy of Child Psychiatry, 25,* 771-778.

MacDougall, J.M., Dembroski, T.M., Dimsdale, J.E., & Hackett, T.P. (1985). Components of Type A, hostility, and anger-in: Further relationships in angiograpic findings. *Health Psychology, 4,* 137-152.

Matthews, K.A. (1977). Caregiver-child interactions and the Type A coronary-prone behavior pattern. *Child Development, 48,* 1752-1756.

Matthews, K.A. (1979). Efforts to control by children and adults with the Type A coronary-prone behavior pattern. *Child Development, 50,* 842-847.

Matthews, K.A. (1982). Psychological perspectives on the Type A behavior pattern. *Psychological Bulletin, 91,* 293-323.

Matthews, K.A. (in press). CHD and Type A behaviors: Update on and alternative to the Booth-Kewley and Friedman quantitative review. *Psychological Bulletin.*

Matthews, K.A. & Angulo, J. (1980). Measurement of the Type A behavior pattern in children: Assessment of children's competitiveness, impatience-anger, and aggression. *Child Development, 51,* 466-475.

Matthews, K.A., & Avis, N.E. (1983). Stability of overt Type A behaviors in children: Results from a one-year longitudinal study. *Child Development, 54,* 1507-1512.

Matthews, K.A., & Brunson, B.I. (1979). Allocation of attention and the Type A coronary-prone behavior pattern. *Journal of Personality and Social Psychology, 37,* 2081-2090.

Matthews, K.A., Carra, J. (1982). Suppression of menstrual distress symptoms: A study of Type A behavior. *Personality and Social Psychology Bulletin, 8,* 146-151.

Matthews, K.A., & Haynes, J.G. (1986). Type A behavior pattern and coronary disease risk. Update and critical evaluation. *American Journal of Epidemiology, 123,* 923-960.

Matthews, K.A., & Jennings, J.R. (1984). Cardiovascular responses of boys exhibiting the Type A behavior pattern. *Psychosomatic Medicine, 46,* 484-497.

Matthews, K.A., Stoney, C.M., Rakaczky, C.J., & Jamison, W. (1986). Family characteristics and school achievements of Type A children. *Health Psychology, 5,* 453-467.

Matthews, K.A., & Volkin, J.I. (1981). Efforts to excel and the Type A behavior pattern in children. *Child Development, 52,* 1283-1289.

Murray, D.M., Blake, S.M., Prineas, R., & Gillum, R.F. (1985). Cardiovascular responses in Type A children during a cognitive challenge. *Journal of Behavioral Medicine, 8,* 377-395.

Murray, D.M., Matthews, K.A., Blake, S.M., Prineas, R.J., & Gillum, R.F. (1986). Type A behavior in children: Demographic, behavioral, and physiological correlates. *Health Psychology, 5,* 159-169.

Murray, J.L., Bruhn, J.G., & Bunce, H. (1983). Assessment of Type A behavior in preschoolers. *Journal of Human Stress, 9* (3),32-39.

Rumenik, D.K., Capasso, D.R., & Hendrick, C. (1977). Experimenter sex effects in behavioral research. *Psychological Bulletin, 84,* 852-877.

Schlegel, R.P., Wellwood, J.K., Copps, B.E., Gruchow, W.H., & Sharratt, M.T. (1980). The relationship between perceived challenge and daily symptom reporting in Type A vs. Type B postinfarct subjects. *Journal of Behavioral Medicine, 3,* 191-204.

Siegel, J.M. (1984). Type A behavior: Epidemiologic foundations and public health implications. *Annual Review of Public Health, 5,* 343-367.

Siegel, J.M., & Leitch, C.J. (1981). Assessment of the Type A behavior pattern in adolescents. *Psychosomatic Medicine, 43,* 45-56.

Siegel, J.M., Matthews, K.A., & Leitch, C.J. (1981). Validation of the Type A interview assessment of adolescents: A multidimensional approach. *Psychosomatic Medicine, 43,* 311-321.

Smith, T.W., & Anderson, N.B. (1986). Models of personality and disease: An interactional approach to Type A behavior and cardiovascular risk. *Journal of Personality and Social Psychology, 50,* 1166-1173.

Smith, T.W., & Rhodewalt, F. (1986). On states, traits, and processes: A transactional alternative to the individual difference assumptions in Type A behavior and physiological reactivity. *Journal of Research in Personality, 20,* 229-251.

Steinberg, L. (1985). Early temperamental antecedents of adult Type A behaviors. *Developmental Psychology, 21,* 1171-1180.

Steinberg, L. (1988). Stability of Type A behavior from early childhood to young adulthood. *Lifespan Development and Behavior, 8,* 129-161.

Stern, G.S., Harris, J. R., & Elverum, J. (1981). Attention to important versus trivial tasks and salience of fatigue-related symptoms for coronary prone individuals. *Journal of Research in Personality, 15,* 467-474.

Stroop, J.R. (1935). Studies of interference in serial verbal reactions. *Journal of Experimental Psychology, 18,* 643-662

Strube, M.J., Turner, C.W., Patrick, S., & Perillo, R. (1983). Type A and Type B attentional responses to aesthetic stimuli: Effects on mood and performance. *Journal of Personality and Social Psychology, 45,* 1369-1379.

Suls, J., Gastorf, J., & Witenberg, S. (1979). Life events, psychological distress and the Type A coronary-prone behavior pattern. *Journal of Psychosomatic Research, 23,* 315-319.

Sweda, M.G., Sines, J.O., Lauer, R.M., & Clarke, W.R. (1986). Familial aggregation of Type A behavior. *Journal of Behavioral Medicine, 9,* 23-32.

Visintainer, P.F., & Matthews, K.A. (1987). Stability of overt Type A behaviors in children: Results of a two-and five-year longitudinal study. *Child Development, 58,* 1586-1591.

Weidner, G., & Matthews, K.A. (1978). Reported physical symptoms elicited by unpredictable events and the Type A coronary-prone behavior pattern. *Journal of Personality and Social Psychology, 36,* 1213-1220.

Williams, R.B. (1975). Physiological mechanisms underlying the association between psychosocial factors and coronary disease. In W.D. Gentry & R.B. Williams, Jr. (Eds.), *Psychological aspects of myocardial infarction and coronary care.* St. Louis, MO: Mosby.

Williams, R.B., Haney, T.L., Lee, K.L., Kong, Y.H., Blumenthal, J.A., & Whalen, R.W. (1980). Type A behavior, hostility, and coronary atherosclerosis. *Psychosomatic Medicine, 42,* 539-549.

Wolf, T.M., Sklov, M.S., Wenzl, P.A., Hunter, S.M., & Berenson, G.S. (1982). Validation of a measure of Type A behavior pattern in children: Bogalusa Heart Study. *Child Development, 53,* 126-135.

Zelson, M.F., & Simons, R.F. (1986). Sustained attention in Type A and Type B subjects: A blink reflex analysis. *Psychophysiology, 23,* 385-392.

Children's Type A Behavior:
The Role of Parental Hostility and Family History of Cardiovascular Disease

Frank A. Treiber, P. Alex Mabe,
William T. Riley, Melissa McDuffie,
William B. Strong, and Maurice Levy
Departments of Pediatrics, Psychiatry, and Health Behavior
Georgia Institute for the Prevention of Human Disease and Accidents
Medical College of Georgia
Augusta, Georgia 30912-3770

This study assessed the influence of parental hostility and family history of coronary heart disease (CHD) upon preschool children's Type A behavior pattern. A county wide screening of 24,882 children's family CHD histories identified 796 intact families with preschool age children. From this sample, 64 low and 52 high CHD risk children were identified based on their family health histories. Results indicated adequate correspondence between mothers' and fathers' ratings of their children's Type A behavior (Matthews Youth Test for Health, MYTH). Collective parental MYTH ratings were found to have a factor structure similar to original MYTH validation studies. Parental measures of verbal and reactive hostility correlated modestly with children's total MYTH scores and impatience/aggression component scores. Further analyses indicated that children's MYTH scores were influenced via an interaction of family CHD history and mothers' verbal hostility levels. Specifically, mother's verbal hostility was associated with MYTH scores in high CHD risk families whereas no relationship between mothers' verbal hostility and MYTH scores was found in low CHD risk families. Component analyses indicated that this relationship held for the impatience/aggression component but not for the competitiveness component of the MYTH. Theoretical explanations for these findings are discussed and directions for future research are recommended.

Authors' Note: This research was supported by funds from the National Institutes of Health: Heart, Lung, and Blood Institute (NIH HL35073 and HL41781).

© 1990 Select Press

INTRODUCTION

The Type A behavior pattern (TABP) in adults has been found to be an independent predictor of coronary heart disease (CHD) in both retrospective and prospective studies (see Cooper, Detre, & Weiss, 1981 and Matthews & Haynes, 1986 for reviews). Although some investigators have not found global TABP to relate to CHD (see Dembroski, 1986), recent findings have shown that components of Type A behavior, (i.e., anger expression and hostility) are predictive of CHD even when global measures are not (Dembroski, MacDougall, Williams, Haney, & Blumenthal, 1985; MacDougall, Dembroski, Dimsdale, & Hackett, 1985; Williams et al., 1980). Thus, hostility appears to be a primary pathogenic component of the TABP (Barefoot, Dahlstrom, & Williams, 1983; Siegman, Dembroski, & Ringel, 1987).

Since the pathogenic process of CHD begins during childhood (Newman et al., 1986; Strong & McGill, 1969) efforts have begun to investigate the developmental antecedents of TABP (Corrigan & Moskowitz, 1983; Matthews, Stoney, Rakaczky, & Jamison, 1986). Evaluation of familial similarities has been one means of assessing environmental and/or genetic influences on the development of the TABP. Twin studies using the Jenkins Activity Scale (JAS) have indicated possible genetic determinants for components of the TABP including hard driving/competitiveness (Factor H; Matthews & Krantz, 1976; Vandenberg, 1962) and speed/impatience (Factor S; Rahe, Hervig, & Rosenman, 1978). Evidence also indicates similarities between parents' TABP (i.e., JAS or Framingham Type A scale) and their children's TABP (i.e., JAS or MYTH) (Matthews et al., 1986; Matthews & Krantz, 1976; Sweda, Sines, Lauer, & Clarke, 1986; Vega-Lahr & Field, 1986).

Only the Vega-Lahr and Field (1986) study used very young children (2 to 4 year olds). Thus, little is known concerning the early relationship of parent-offspring TABP. Sweda et al. (1986) noted that further assessment of the familial aggregation of the TABP is needed with a *focus on* the relationship between *components of the TABP in children* (e.g., impatience/aggression) and *parents' hostility*, since it has been implicated as a primary pathogenic component of the TABP (Dembroski et al., 1985; MacDougall et al., 1985; Siegman et al., 1987; Williams et al., 1980).

Recently, Matthews et al. (1986) found a positive relationship between family history of CHD and TABP in adult males. To our knowledge the only research which has assessed this relationship in young children found no significant relationships except for a trend ($p < .08$) indicating Type A children were more likely to have a grandparent with hypertension (Matthews et al., 1986). However, no assessment was made of potential interactive effects of family CHD history and parental TABP on the offspring's TABP. It may be that children from families with a history of CHD who also have parents with high levels of toxic components of TABP (i.e., hostility) will exhibit the greatest TABP. This hypothesis is supported by the work of Baer, Vincent, Williams, Bourianoff, & Bartlett (1980) who used a family conflict task and found that children whose fathers had hypertension and displayed nonverbal hostility showed higher levels of similar hostility than children whose fathers were normotensive.

The purpose of this study was to assess the relationship between parents' hostility and their young children's global and component TABP scores in families at varying risk for CHD based upon family health history. To our knowledge, this is the first attempt to assess the relationship of the TABP component of parental *hostility* to preschool-age children's global and component TABP scores. This is also the first study in which preschool age children's risk for CHD based upon their family health history has been taken into account in assessing familial relationships of the TABP.

METHOD

Subjects

Subjects were 116 four and five year old children and their biological parents selected as participants in Project SCAN (Study of Children's Activities and Nutrition). The SCAN Project is a five-year, multiple-site assessment of children's and their families' lifestyle behaviors which have been associated with the development of coronary heart disease in adults (i.e., nutrition, eating behaviors, physical activity/fitness, psychosocial variables). The children and their families were selected based upon the child's risk of developing coronary heart disease. Risk status was determined based on a detailed family health history with 64 families classified as lower risk and 52 families classified as higher risk. The lower risk group comprised 48 white children (23 male) and 16 black children (6 male). The higher risk group comprised 41 white children (16 male) and 11 black children (7 male).

Sample Selection Procedures

The Family Health History Questionnaire (FHH; Treiber, Carr, Strong, & Levy, 1989) was distributed to each child in grades 1 through 8 (n = 23,396) in the Richmond County, Georgia Public School System and to all preschoolers (n = 1,486) enrolled in a Richmond County preschool with 20 or more children. The FHH was developed based upon two other family medical history questionnaires which have been successfully used in large epidemiological CHD related studies (Blonde, Webber, Foster, & Berenson, 1981; Prineas, Gillum, Horibe, & Hannan, 1980). The FHH has been found to have adequate psychometric properties including test - retest reliability, construct validity (i.e., young adults CHD risk based upon their FHH associated with various cardiovascular risk factors - resting blood pressure, percent body fat) and verification via physician and/or hospital records (Treiber et al., 1989).

Of the 24,882 FHHs distributed 13,990 (56.2%) were returned. Families were then selected to meet the following criteria: 1) one or more children three or four years of age at time of initial screening), 2) not an adopted child, 3) both biological parents in the home, and 4) parents not students in a college/university or in the military service. The last two criteria were incorporated to decrease the likelihood of attrition over the five-year study. In all, 796 families were found to meet the above criteria.

Assessment of Risk

At this time there are no longitudinal data beginning in childhood which will predict future overt coronary artery disease. However, for purposes of CHD risk assignment, three family history variables associated with CHD risk and available on the FHH questionnaire were used in this study. First, premature myocardial infarction (MI) in first and second degree relatives has been associated strongly with later development of CHD (Barrett-Conner & Knaw, 1984) and with physical CHD risk factors in children (Glueck, Laskarzewski, Rao, & Morrison, 1985; Schrott, Clarke, Wiebe, Conner, & Lauer, 1979). Thus MI at or before 55 years of age for biological parent or grandparent was chosen as the strongest predictor of future heart disease. Two additional predictors: (1) number of family members (i.e., biological parents and biological grandparents) with a reported history of hypertension receiving therapy (HBP) and (2) number of biological parents who are current smokers (SMO) were also chosen because they are well established risk factors for CHD (Fraser, 1986; Kannel, 1981). It should be noted that other risk factors (e.g., serum cholesterol levels) were not accessible via the FHH. In the process of deriving a risk classification equation from these family history variables, history of MI ≤ 55, as the strongest predictor of CHD, was given a weight of 1.0. Risk weights for the remaining risk factors were obtained through regression analysis that determined to what extent HBP and SMO predicted MI ≤ 55. This approach made the assumption that MI ≤ 55 represented the essential feature of high risk of CHD within the confines of the available data, and HBP and SMO represented risk factors only to the extent that they were associated with MI ≤ 55. Using unstandardized regression weights for HBP and SMO, the following risk classification equation was derived: Risk = 1.00 x MI ≤ 55 + (0.04165 x SMO) + (0.02566 x HBP). To be considered high risk, a family had to have a risk score ≤ 1.0 (i.e., had to have at least a history of MI ≥ 55 in a parent or grandparent).

In order to select groups as different as possible, families were recruited into the study beginning with the zero risk scores for the low risk group, and the highest risk scores for the high risk group. All zero risk families were contacted but the sample was below the desired number of subjects for the lower risk group. Therefore, families with the next lowest risk scores from the original screening were contacted. These families had a history of hypertension in one biological grandparent only (risk score = .0256). In all, 61 lower risk families (risk score range = 0 to .0256, m = .013) and 52 higher risk families (risk score range = 1.00 to 1.16, m = 1.07) were recruited which represented participation rates of 53 per cent and 76 per cent, respectively.

Instruments

The following instruments were selected based upon their psychometric properties and collective ability to assess the multidimensional nature of TABP, especially hostility. Since hostility appears to be one of the primary pathogenic components of the TABP (Dembroski et al., 1985; Siegman et al., 1987) three measures of hostility were chosen for the parental assessment. The terminology of Siegman et al. (1987) and Spielberger, Jacobs, Russell, & Crane (1983) was used to define hostility. Hostility is a multi-dimensional construct and refers to an enduring attitudinal state to become angry and remain angry as a result of environmental stressors with concomitant aggressive behavior often occurring. Siegman et al. (1987) conceptualized hostility as comprising two primary factors termed reactive and neurotic hostility based upon Sarason's (1961) factor analysis of the seven subscales of the Buss Durkee Hostility Inventory (Buss & Durkee, 1957). Reactive hostility is the overt expression of anger and annoyance, comprising verbal argumentation and potential for physical assault. In contrast, neurotic hostility involves more of the experience of anger in which individuals often feel resentful, mistreated and suspicious of others' motives and are generally discontent with their life situation. These individuals, however, do not necessarily overtly express their hostility via verbal or physical assault. The neurotic hostility dimension is highly associated with anxiety/neuroticism (Costa, 1986).

Buss Durkee Verbal Hostility Scale (BDVH). (Buss & Durkee, 1957). The BDVH scale comprises 13 true-false items from the 75-item BDHI. The BDVH scale has been found to have adequate reliability with adults (test-retest over a two week period, r = .77). The BDVH has been shown to correlate positively with the Type A Structured Interview factor of "potential for hostility" and negatively with "anger-in" (Musante, MacDougall, Dembroski, & Costa, 1988) which in turn have been associated with severity of CHD (Dembroski et al., 1985).

Buss Durkee Reactive and Neurotic Hostility Scales (BDRH/ BDNH). Siegman et al., 1987). As previously discussed, Sarason (1961) factor analyzed the BDHI and found items loaded on two factors which Siegman et al. (1987) termed neurotic and reactive hostility. The reactive hostility subscale (BDRH) correlated positively and the neurotic subscale (BDNH) negatively with angiographic measures of CHD. To decrease the parents' response burden, only those items with the highest item-total correlations from the reactive and neurotic hostility factors were used (Siegman, personal communication). This resulted in a total of seven true - false items for the BDRH scale and six items for the BDNH scale. The concurrent validity of these modified scales have been substantiated in a previous study (Riley & Treiber, 1989).

Matthews Youth Test for Health (MYTH; Matthews and Angulo, 1980). Children's Type A behavior was assessed using the MYTH since it is the only measure with established validity for preschool age children (Corrigan & Moskowitz, 1983; Vega-Lahr & Field, 1986; Kurdek & Lillie, 1985). It assesses Type A behavior from both a global and subcomponent perspective (Matthews & Avis, 1983). Parents were chosen as raters of the children's TABP since 1) the majority of children were not enrolled in preschool, precluding the use of teacher ratings, 2) for this age group, parents as opposed to teachers' are more likely to observe children across a variety of environmental situations (Achenbach & Edelbrock, 1981; Treiber & Mabe, 1987), and 3) recent studies have found parents' MYTH ratings useful in differentiating children's TABP (Kurdek & Lillie, 1985; Murphy, Alpert, & Somes, 1988; Murray, Bruhn, & Bunce, 1983).

The MYTH is a 17-item Likert rating scale which has primarily been used with teachers of young children (preschool to 6th grade). Factor analyses across studies consistently yield two components: competitiveness, and impatience/aggression (Bishop, Hailey, & Anderson, 1987; Matthews & Angulo, 1980; Matthews & Avis, 1983). Recent studies involving parent MYTH ratings indicate adequate interparent reliability ($r = .65$) (Murphy et al., 1988) and internal consistency (Cronbach's alpha = .83 for total MYTH) (Kurdek & Lillie, 1985). Evidence of construct validity of parent MYTH ratings has also been shown via comparison to children's self report of temperament dimensions, sociometric ratings of likeability and laboratory social cognitive tasks (Kurdek & Lillie, 1985).

Procedure

All families were seen in their homes by a research assistant who was unaware of the family's risk classification. Both parents and the target child had vital and anthropometric measures assessed which included height, weight, skinfold measurements and blood pressure. Findings from these assessments are presented elsewhere (Cho, Treiber, & Pruitt, 1988; Treiber et al., 1988). Collectively, the findings revealed that for the entire sample the significant predictors of children's systolic blood pressure (SBP) included their body mass (Quetelet index) and triceps skinfold thickness but age, race, gender, socioeconomic status, and family CHD history were not significant predictors. Parental variables that predicted the children's SBP included maternal and paternal triceps skinfold measures. Subgroup analyses indicated that children with family histories of essential hypertension had slightly higher SBP than children without such family histories.

Following the completion of the vital anthropometric assesment the parents' were given a brief battery of behavioral questionnaires to complete individually concerning their own lifestyle behaviors as well as those of their child who was involved in the study. The hostility scales as well as the MYTH were among this packet of questionnaires. Total time required to complete the packet ranged from 20 to 28 minutes (mean = 23 minutes). The research assistant was trained to answer any questions the parents had without biasing their responses.

RESULTS

Initial Analyses of Risk Groups

Chi-square analyses revealed no significant differences in the children between the lower and higher risk groups on race or gender ratios. Analyses of variance indicated no significant differences between the groups on all sociodemographic characteristics assessed which included parental age, family size and socioeconomic status based upon the Siegel Prestige Scale (In Featherman & Hauser, 1977). Similar analyses were conducted comparing the participant versus nonparticipant families within risk group with no significant differences noted. In addition, the proportion of whites to blacks recruited was representative of both the population distribution and the CHD morbidity rates for the Richmond County Area.

Parents' MYTH Ratings

Pearson correlations were computed between the mothers' and fathers' ratings for the MYTH total score and the two subcomponents of the MYTH. Results suggested moderately high correspondence between mothers' and fathers' perceptions of TABP in their preschool children with correlations of .54 for the Total MYTH, .50 for the impatience/ aggression component, and .41 for the competitiveness component (all p values < .001). In light of these moderate correlations, it was concluded that mothers' and fathers' ratings on the MYTH could be combined meaningfully into composite scores that represented both shared and unique information regarding their children's TABP. Therefore, all further analyses of the children's MYTH scores will pertain to the average of the mother's and father's score for each child. Separate analyses were conducted of paternal and maternal MYTH ratings which yielded similar findings as those to be presented.

A factor analysis with principal axis extraction and varimax rotation was performed on the mother's and father's average score for the 17 items of the MYTH. Four factors with eigenvalues greater than one initially were extracted and accounted for 32.5, 15.0, 8.4 and 6.3 percent of variance, respectively. This factor structure confirmed the competitiveness subscale but divided the impatience/aggression subscale into separate components of aggression and impatience. The fourth factor loaded significantly on only one item and was not found to be significant based on the scree method of factor selection. More complex factor structures have been found for parent report as opposed to teacher report (e.g., Murray et al., 1983). However, due to the small number of items loading on factors III and IV and previous research which used the combined impatience/aggression factor with parent ratings (e.g., Vega-Lahr & Field, 1986), the MYTH was re-analyzed rotating two factors only. The factor structure from this procedure was found to be similar to that found by Matthews & Angulo (1980) with a coefficient of congruency of .95 for Factor I and .97 for Factor II. These factor structures are compared in Table 1. Due to the high level of congruence between the factor structures and the significant research on the Matthews and Angulo (1980) factor scales, the original factor scales scoring method was used in further analyses.

Association of Parent Hostility and Child TABP

Table 2 presents a correlation matrix examining the relationship between parental hostility scales and children's MYTH scores. Statistically significant correlations were obtained between verbal and reactive hostility scales and the Total MYTH scores as well as the impatience/ aggression component scores. Parental neurotic hostility scale (BDNH) scores failed to yield statistically significant correlations with any of the MYTH scores. Also, none of the parental hostility scale scores were significantly correlated with the MYTH competitiveness component

TABLE 1 Factor Loading for the MYTH Selecting Two Factors and Comparison to the Matthews and Angulo (1980) Loadings

	Present Sample		*Matthews and Angulo Sample*	
Item	*I*	*II*	*I*	*II*
1	.718	.143	.725	.304
2	.592	.288	.449	.095
3	.276	.544	.250	.617
4	.542	.189	.239	.354
5	.138	-.371	-.073	-.546
6	.186	.591	.116	.688
7	.857	-.050	.764	-.045
8	.252	.652	.155	.790
9	.695	.027	.686	.094
10	.321	.605	.270	.763
11	-.011	-.419	-.005	-.594
12	.678	.124	.794	.162
13	.024	-.499	.178	-.500
14	.397	.200	.544	.448
15	.740	-.096	.813	-.187
16	.686	.200	.775	.336
17	.179	.606	.169	.735

scores. Although there appeared to be a trend for the mothers' hostility scores to be more strongly associated with the MYTH scores than the fathers' hostility scores, t-tests for dependent correlations showed none of these differences to be statistically significant.

In order to examine to what extent TABP in young children is a function of parental subcomponents of hostility and the child's risk of developing CHD based upon family history, a 2 X 2 X 2 ANOVA design was used.[1] Median splits for the mother and father scores on Verbal Hostility along with the lower risk/higher risk for CHD categorization using the FHH represented the independent variables. Children's gender was not entered as a separate independent variable since the sample size was judged insufficient for providing reliable results if gender was included among the independent variables. Mother and father verbal hostility scores were chosen over the other hostility measures in these analyses due to the relative correlative strength of verbal hostility with

[1] *These analyses were also conducted using our MYTH factor scale structure. Similar findings were obtained with both factor structures.*

TABLE 2 Intercorrelations of Children's MYTH Scores With Their Parents' Hostility Scores

	Total MYTH	*Impatience/ Aggression*	*Competitiveness*
Verbal Hostility			
Mother	.31**	.35**	.15
Father	.19*	.18*	.12
Reactive Hostility			
Mother	.22**	.29**	.07
Father	.17*	.17*	.10
Neurotic Hostility			
Mother	.12	.08	.12
Father	.03	.14	-.10

* $p < .05$
** $p < .01$

the MYTH scores and the similarity of the verbal hostility to the component of hostility assessed in the Type A structured interview (Musante et al., 1989). This has been identified as one of the primary toxic components of TABP linked to severity of CHD in adults (Dembroski et al., 1985; MacDougall et al., 1985). It should be noted that similar findings were obtained when reactive hostility, which has also been associated with CHD (Siegman et al., 1987), was used as the measure of parental hostility.

The three-way ANOVA for the dependent measure of Total MYTH scores revealed a significant main effect only for the fathers' verbal hostility level with the low group average total MYTH = 53.19 versus 56.24 for the high group ($F(1.108) = 4.99, p < .05$). There was, however, a significant two-way interaction between mothers' verbal hostility scores and children's CHD risk ($F(1,108) = 8.96, p < .01$). Figure 1 presents a graph of the means for the total MYTH scores displayed by mothers' verbal hostility by CHD risk.

Collectively, these findings indicate that: 1) high verbal hostility scores for the father are associated with higher Total MYTH scores for the children irrespective of the mothers' verbal hostility scores or children's CHD risk, 2) the mothers' verbal hostility scores interact with the children's CHD risk such that high verbal hostility scores for the mothers are associated with higher Total MYTH scores for children only when the CHD risk is high, and 3) the mothers' verbal hostility scores and

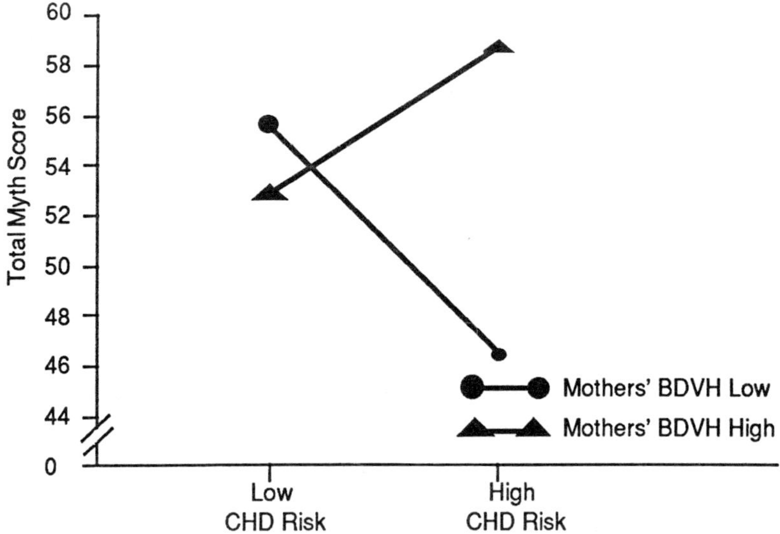

FIGURE 1 Mean Scores for the Total MYTH by Mothers' Verbal Hostility by CHD Risk

children's CHD risk interact in such a way that low verbal hostility scores for the mothers are associated with lower Total MYTH scores for children when their CHD risk is high.

The three-way ANOVA for the dependent measure of impatience/aggression component scores revealed a significant two-way interaction between mothers' verbal hostility scores and children's CHD risk ($F(1,108) = 10.48$, $p < .01$), but no significant main effects. Figure 2 presents a graph of the means for the impatience/aggression component scores displayed by mothers' verbal hostility by children's CHD risk. The pattern of interactions is similar to the interaction pattern noted for the Total MYTH score means indicating that, 1) the mothers' verbal hostility scores interact with CHD risk such that high verbal hostility scores for the mother are associated with higher impatience/aggression component scores for children only when the CHD risk is high, and 2) that the mothers' verbal hostility scores and CHD risk interact in such a way that low verbal hostility scores for the mother are associated with lower impatience/aggression component scores for children when CHD risk is high.

The three-way ANOVA conducted for the dependent measure of the competitiveness component scores failed to yield any significant main effects or interactions, indicating a lack of significant association between this component of the MYTH and parental hostility or CHD risk.

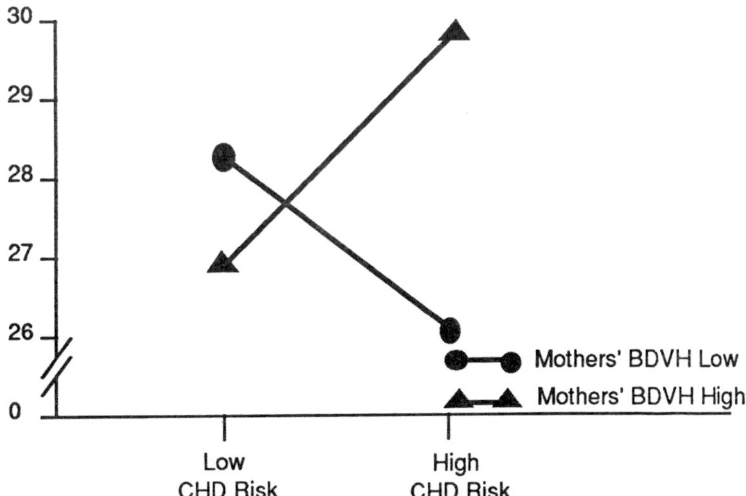

FIGURE 2 Mean Scores for the Impatience/Aggression Component of the MYTH by Mothers' Verbal Hostility by CHD Risk

DISCUSSION

The current findings indicate a positive relationship between measures of parental verbal and reactive hostility and preschool children's global Type A behavior as well as the impatience/aggression component as measured by the MYTH. These findings are similar to other research efforts which have compared children's and parents' TABP (Matthews et al., 1986; Matthews & Krantz, 1976; Sweda et al., 1986; Vega-Lahr & Field, 1986). The principal findings of this study add to the accumulating evidence of familial similarity of the TABP in very young children (i.e., preschool age). They also suggest that this relationship is moderated by family history of CHD. Specifically, it appears that children's TABP may be influenced via an interaction effect of their risk for future development of CHD and their mothers' self report of verbal hostility. That is, although maternal level of verbal hostility was positively associated with TABP in children at high risk for CHD there was no relationship between maternal verbal hostility and the TABP of low CHD risk children. Subcomponent analyses indicated that this relationship was manifested within the impatience/aggression component of the MYTH but not within the competitiveness component.

Our findings and those of Matthews et al. (1986) indicate that young children at increased risk for the development of CHD are not necessarily more likely to develop the TABP. Rather, they are similar to the work of Baer et al. (1980) with families varying in hypertension status. If a predisposition exists for the development of CHD and if the family environment is prone to hostility (e.g., having mothers who report tendencies to become verbally hostile when frustrated or stressed), then this combination may foster the development of similar characteristics in preschool age children. Mothers may play an especially important role in the early developement of their child's TABP since they may be the child's primary role model for early social behavioral development. Given that most of the mothers were housewives and many of the children were not in preschool, mothers may have the greatest amount of contact with their children.

Unexpectedly, the results of this study also suggest that children from high CHD risk families with mothers who report low levels of verbal hostility will have lower levels of TABP. It may be that children with a family history of CHD are generally more reactive to their environment than are children from families of lower CHD risk. Perhaps the sympathetic nervous systems of high CHD risk children are highly responsive to the environment such that they exhibit high levels of impatience/aggression in hostile environments and low levels of impatience/aggression in environments where little hostility is exhibited. Low CHD risk children, in comparison, appear less affected by the level of verbal hostility in the environment.

These findings are similar to those observed in cardiovascular reactivity research in which Type A individuals with a family history of CHD show the greatest levels of autonomic reactivity to various psychological/physical stressors (Katkin, Goldband, & Medine, 1980; Williams et al., 1982). Also, similar are the Baer et al. (1980) findings that following a family conflict task, the greatest blood pressure levels were exhibited by those children who had a father with hypertension and had parents who exhibited greatest frequency of nonverbal hostility. This rationale for the interaction, however, is speculative and deserves further inquiry.

Although a main effect was found for fathers' verbal hostility on the total MYTH, this was not a consistent finding. Specifically, no such effects were obtained for the MYTH components. Nevertheless, further scrutiny of paternal influence on children's TABP is warranted.

Some important limitations of this study should be noted. Generalization of these findings are limited due to the lack of demographic information on those families that did not complete the FHH questionnaire as part of the initial screening (i.e., 44% of the sample). Of those completing the initial screening, however, no differences were noted in participants versus nonparticipants of the study on the demographic variables assessed. A second limitation is the use of parent ratings on the MYTH, a measure validated using predominantly teacher ratings. As noted previously, most of the subjects in this study were not in school, necessitating the use of parents as raters. The significant positive correlations between mother and father ratings and the similarity to the original factor structure (Matthews & Angulo, 1980) in this study support the growing evidence of reliability and validity of parent MYTH ratings (Kurdek & Lillie, 1985; Murphy et al., 1988; Vega-Lahr & Field, 1986). Nevertheless, parents were the only source of information in this study (child TABP, self-report of hostility). Therefore, some of the associations found may have been affected by this method variance. Further studies utilizing independent measures of TABP (e.g., direct observations, collateral ratings, analogue tasks) as well as parent-child interactions (e.g., frustration-inducing tasks) are necessary to confirm these results.

Cognizant of these limitations, the results of this study indicate a relationship between parental hostility and TABP in children as young as 3 and 4. Furthermore, these results offer initial evidence that CHD risk is a moderating factor in this relationship. Prospective studies of familial aggregation of TABP components, especially hostility, are needed which take into account family CHD history along with other variables which have been identified as possible moderators of the TABP. These include sociodemographic factors (e.g., SES, race) and family structural (e.g., family size, birth order) and systemic factors (e.g., family cohesiveness, parent child rearing attitudes) (Amos, Hunter, Zinkgraf, Miner & Berenson, 1987; Matthews, 1986; Shekelle, Schoenberger & Stamler, 1976; Strube & Ota, 1982; Waldron et al., 1980). In this manner a better understanding will be obtained of the early familial antecedents of TABP. These findings could enable the development of family based intervention programs to prevent development of such potentially harmful lifestyle behaviors.

REFERENCES

Achenbach, T.M., & Edelbrock, C.S. (1981). Behavioral problems and competencies reported by parents of normal and disturbed children aged four through sixteen. *Monographs for the Society for Research in Child Development, 46* (serial no. 188).

Amos, C.I., Hunter, S. Zinkgraf, S.A., Miner, M.H., & Berenson, G.S. (1987). Characterization of a comprehensive Type A measure for children in a biracial community: The Bogalusa Heart Study. *Journal of Behavioral Medicine, 10,* 425-439.

Baer, P.E., Vincent, J.P., Williams, B.J., Bourianoff, G.G., & Bartlett, P.C. (1980). Behavioral response to induced conflict in families with a hypertensive father. *Hypertension, 2,* (Supple. I), 70-77.

Barefoot, J.C., Dahlstrom, W.G., & Williams, R.B., Jr. (1983). Hostility, CHD incidence, and total mortality: A 25-year follow-up study of 255 physicians. *Psychosomatic Medicine, 45, 59-63.*

Barrett-Conner, E., & Knaw, K. (1984). Family history of heart attack as an independent predictor of death due to cardiovascular disease. *Circulation, 69,* 1065-1069.

Bishop, E.G., Hailey, B.J., & Anderson, H.N. (1987). Assessment of Type A behavior in children: A comparison of two instruments. *Journal of Human Stress, 15,* 121-127.

Blonde, C.V., Webber, L.S., Foster, T.A., & Berenson, G.S., (1981). Parental history and cardiovascular disease risk factor variables in children. *Preventive Medicine, 10,* 25-37.

Buss, A.H., & Durkee, A. (1957). An inventory for assessing different kinds of hostility. *Journal of Consulting Psychology, 71,* 343-349.

Cho, C., Treiber, F.A., & Pruitt, A.W. (1988). *Blood pressure measurements in 3 and 4 year olds with and without a family history of hypertension.* Presented at the annual meeting of the Southern Society for Pediatric Research, New Orleans, LA, Feb. 1988.

Cooper, T., Detre, T., & Weiss, S.M. (1981). Coronary prone behavior and coronary heart disease: A critical review. *Circulation, 63,* 1199-1215.

Corrigan, S.A., & Moskowitz, D.S. (1983). Type A behavior in preschool children: Construct validation evidence for the MYTH. *Child Development, 54,* 513-521.

Costa, P.T., Jr. (1986). Is neuroticism a risk factor for CAD? Is Type A a measure of neuroticism? In T. Schmidt, T. Dembroski, & G. Blumchen (Eds.) *Biological and Psychological Factors in Cardiovascular Disease.* New York: Springer-Verlag.

Dembroski, T.M. (1986). Overview of classic and stress related risk factors: Relationship to substance effects on reactivity. In K.A. Matthews, S.M. Weiss, T. Detre, T.M. Dembroski, B. Falkner, S.B. Manuck, & R.B. Williams (Eds.), *Handbook of stress, reactivity, and cardiovascular disease; Status and prospects.* New York: Wiley.

Dembroski, T.M., MacDougall, J.M., Williams, R.B., Jr., Haney, T.L., & Blumenthal, J.A. (1985). Components of Type A, hostility and anger-in: Relationship to Angiographic Findings. *Psychosomatic Medicine, 47,* 219-233.

Featherman, D.L., & Hauser, R.M. (1977). Commonalities in social stratification and assumptions about status mobility in the United States. In R. Hauser &

D. Featherman (Eds.), *The process of stratification.* New York: Academic Press.

Fraser, G. E. (1986). *Preventive Cardiology.* New York: Oxford University Press.

Glueck, C.J., Laskarzewski, P.M., Rao, D.C., & Morrison, J.A. (1985). Familial aggregation of coronary risk factors. In W.E. Conner & J.D. Bristow (Eds.) *Coronary Heart Disease—Prevention, Complications and Treatment.* Philadelphia: J.B. Lippincott.

Kannel, W.B. (1981). Hypertension, blood lipids, and cigarette smoking as co-risk factors for coronary heart disease. *New York Academy of Sciences, 304,* 128-139.

Katkin, E.S., Goldband, S., & Medine, B. (1980). Cardiovascular responses to stressful and nonstressful reaction time tasks as a function of family history of cardiovascular disease and Type A behavior. *Psychophysiology, 17,* 318-319.

Kurdek, L.A., & Lillie, R. (1985). Temperament, classmate likability and social perspective coordination as correlates of children's parent-rated Type A behaviors. *Journal of Applied Developmental Psychology, 6,* 73-83.

MacDougall, J.M., Dembroski, T.M., Dimsdale, J.E., & Hackett, T.P. (1985). Components of Type A, hostility, and anger-in: Further relationships to angiographic findings. *Health Psychology, 4,* 137-152.

Matthews, K.A., & Angulo, J. (1980). Measurement of the Type A behavior pattern in children: Assessment of children's competitiveness, impatience - anger and aggression. *Child Development, 51,* 466-475.

Matthews, K.A., & Avis, N.E. (1983). Stability of overt Type A behaviors in children: Results from a one-year longitudinal study. *Child Development, 54,* 1507-1512.

Matthews, K.A., & Haynes, S.G. (1986). Type A behavior pattern and coronary disease risk: Update and critical evaluation. *American Journal of Epidemiology, 123,* 923-960.

Matthews, K.A., & Krantz, D.S. (1976). Resemblances of twins and their parents in Pattern A behavior. *Psychosomatic Medicine, 38,* 140-144.

Matthews, K.A., Stoney, C.M., Rakaczky, C.J., & Jamison, W. (1986). Family characteristics and school achievements of Type A children. *Health Psychology, 515,* 453-467.

Murphy, J., Alpert, B., & Somes, G. (1988). *Children's Type A behavior: Normative data and concordance among family members.* Unpublished manuscript, University of Tennessee, Memphis, TN.

Murray, J.L., Bruhn, J.G., & Bunce, H. (1983). Assessment of Type A behavior in preschoolers. *Journal of Human Stress, 9,* 32-39.

Musante, L., MacDougall, J.M., Dembroski, T.M., & Costa, P.T. (1989). Potential for hostility, and the two dimensions of anger. *Health Psychology, 8,* 343-354.

Newman, W.P. III, Freedman, D.S., Voors, A.W., Gard, P.D., Srinvasan, S.R., Cresanto, J.L., Williamson, G.D., Webber, L.S., & Berenson, G.S. (1986). Serum lipoproteins and systolic blood pressure are related to atherosclerosis in early life: The Bogalusa Heart Study. *New England Journal of Medicine, 314,* 138-144.

Prineas, R.J., Gillum, R.F., Horibe, H., & Hannan, P.J. (1980). The Minneapolis Children's Blood Pressure Study Part II: Multiple determinants of children's blood pressure. *Hypertension, 2* (Supple. I), 118-123.

Rahe, R.H., Hervig, L., & Rosenman, R.H. (1978). Heritability of Type A behavior. *Psychosomatic Medicine, 40,* 478-486.

Riley, W.T., & Treiber, F.A., (1989). Validity of anger scales in normal and psychiatric populations. *Journal of Clinical Psychology,* (in press).

Sarason, I., (1961). Intercorrelations among measures of hostility. *Journal of Clinical Psychology, 17,* 192-195.

Schrott, H.G., Clarke, W.R., Wiebe, D.A., Connor, W.E., & Lauer, R.M.. (1979). Increased coronary mortality in relatives of hypercholesterolemic school children: The Muscatine Study. *Circulation, 59,* 320-326.

Shekelle, R.B., Schoenberger, J.A., & Stamler, J. (1976). Correlates of the JAS Type A behavior pattern score. *Journal of Chronic Diseases, 29,* 381-394.

Siegman, A.W., Dembroski, T.M., & Ringel, N. (1987). Components of hostility and the severity of coronary artery disease. *Psychosomatic Medicine, 49,* 127-135.

Spielberger, C.D., Jacobs, G., Russell, S., & Crane, R. (1983). Assessment of anger: The State-Trait Anger Scale. In J.N. Butcher & C.D. Spielberger (Eds.), *Advances in personality assessment* (Vol. 2). Hillsdale, NJ: Lawrence Erlbaum Associates.

Strong, J., & McGill, H. (1969). The pediatric aspects of atherosclerosis. *Journal of Atherosclerosis Research, 9,* 251-265.

Strube, M.J., & Ota, S. (1982). Type A coronary-prone behavior pattern: Relationship to birth order and family size. *Personality and Social Psychology Bulletin, 8,* 317-323.

Sweda, M.G., Sines, J.O., Lauer, R.M., & Clarke, W.R. (1986). Familial aggregation of Type A behavior. *Journal of Behavioral Medicine, 9,* 23-32.

Treiber, F.A., & Mabe, P.A. (1987). Child and parent perceptions of children's psychopathology in psychiatric outpatient children. *Journal Abnormal Child Psychology, 15*(1), 115-124.

Treiber, F.A., Carr, T., Strong, W.B., & Levy, M. (1989). Development of the family health history questionnaire as a means of assessing cardiovascular risk. Submitted for publication.

Treiber, F.A., Rhodes, T.R., Riley, W.T., Strong, W.B., & Levy, M. (1988). The Role of socioeconomic, vital/anthropometric, family health history and psychosocial variables in predicting biracial preschoolers' systolic blood pressure. In program and abstracts of *The Third International Interdisciplinary Conference on Hypertension in Blacks, p.* 30, April 21-24, Baltimore.

Vandenberg, V.C. (1962). The hereditary abilities study: hereditary components in a psychological test battery. *American Journal of Human Genetics, 19,* 220-237.

Vega-Lahr, N., & Field, T.M. (1986). Type A behavior in preschool children. *Child Development, 57* 1333-1348.

Waldron, I., Hickey, A., McPherson, C., Butensky, A., Gruss, L., Overall, K., Schmader, A., & Wohlmuth, D. (1980). Type A behavior pattern: Relationship to variation in blood pressure, parental characteristics, and academic and social activities of students. *Journal of Human Stress, 6,* 16-27.

Williams, R.B., Jr., Haney, T.L., Lee, K.L., Kong, Y.H., Blumenthal, J.A., & Whalen, R.E. (1980). Type A behavior, hostility, and coronary atherosclerosis. *Psychosomatic Medicine, 42,* 539-549.

Williams, R.B., Jr., Lane, J.D., Kuhn, C.M., Melosh, W., White, A.D., & Schanberg, S.M. (1982). Type A behavior and elevated physiological and neuroendocrine responses to cognitive tasks. *Science, 218,* 483-485.

Type A Behavior in Young Males in a Country of High and a Country of Low Coronary Heart Disease Incidence: The American-Hellenic Heart Study

Terence A. Gerace, Ph.D.
John C. Smith, Ph.D.
George Christakis, M.D.
Department of Epidemiology and Public Health (R-669)
University of Miami School of Medicine, Miami, FL 33101
Anthony G. Kafatos, M.D.
University of Crete School of Medicine
Deanna Trakas, Ph.D.
Laurie Osterweis-Stangos, M.S.W.
Institute of Child Health, Athens, Greece

Miami Structured Intrviews (Gerace & Smith, 1985) were administered to 710 males 7 to 20 years old to test three hypotheses: 1) Prevalence of Type A behavior is greatest in the USA, a country of high coronary heart disease (CHD) incidence, less in mainland Greece, a country of low incidence and least in Crete, a site of very low incidence; 2) Migration from Greece to the USA results in an increased prevalence of Type A; and 3) Urban sites in mainland Greece and Crete have a higher prevalence of Type A than their respective rural regions. Contrary to the first hypothesis, the age-adjusted prevalence of Type A in the USA (Greek-Americans), 44.5 per 100, was lower than that in mainland Greece, 52.1 per 100 (p<.05), and similar to that in Crete, 44.8 per 100 (p>.05). Examining the migration hypothesis revealed Greece-born Americans, 57.0, were more similar to mainland Greeks, 52.1 (p>.05), than to USA-born Greek-Americans, 43.6 (p<.05). These data suggest cultural assimilation in the USA may affect the development of Type A. Rural-urban differences were as predicted for mainland Greece: Athens, 66.6 vs Etoloakarnania, 42.9 (p<.05); but not for Crete: City of Iraklion, 46.8 vs villages of Iraklion, 44.1 (p>.05). If Type A is a risk factor for CHD in Greece, the remarkably high prevalence in Athens may portend a rise in the incidence of CHD four to five decades from now.

Authors' Notes: This research was supported by National Heart, Lung and Blood Institute Grant R01HL23356 and Florida Legislature. We appreciate the helpful comments of the reviewers.

© 1990 Select Press

INTRODUCTION

Type A behavior, characterized by competitiveness, impatience, and hostility, has been related prospectively to coronary heart disease (CHD) in both the USA (Rosenman et al, 1975) and Europe (French-Belgium Collaborative Group, 1982) and related cross-sectionally to coronary atherosclerosis (Blumenthal, Williams, Kong, Shanberg, & Thompson, 1978; Frank, Heller, Kornfield, Sporn, & Weiss, 1978). Its generalizability as a risk factor for CHD, however, has been recently questioned (Bass & Wade, 1982; MacDougall, Dembroski, Dimsdale, & Hackett, 1985; Ragland & Brand, 1988; Shekelle et al., 1985; Shekelle et al., 1988). Finding a positive cross-cultural association between prevalence of Type A and CHD mortality could lend support to Type A behavior as a CHD risk factor. Previously, international comparisons of the prevalence of Type A have not been possible using the Structured Interview (Rosenman, 1978a), perhaps the best behavioral predictor of CHD (Brand, Rosenman, Jenkins, Sholtz, & Zyzanski, 1978). The cross-cultural validity of the Structured Interview has not been established and different raters and interviewers have been used across studies (see Gerace & Smith, 1985).

Since the stability of behavioral type during childhood (Gerace & Smith, 1984) is similar to that during adulthood (Jenkins, Rosenman, & Friedman, 1968), and the relative prevalence of Type A characteristics in youngsters most likely reflects the relative prevalence in the adult population (Kagan & Moss, 1962; see Visintainer and Matthews, 1987), we hypothesized: 1) Prevalence of Type A in young males would be greatest in the USA, a country of high CHD incidence, less in mainland Greece, a country of relatively low incidence, and least on the island of Crete, a site of very low incidence (Keys, 1980); 2) Migration would reveal an increasing prevalence of Type A from mainland Greeks to Greece-born Americans to USA-born Greek-Americans; and 3) Urban sites in mainland Greece and Crete would have a higher prevalence of Type A behavior than rural areas on mainland Greece and Crete, respectively, because Type A characteristics are more likely elicited by competitive, fast-paced urban environments (Rosenman, 1978b).

METHODS

Participants

Participants were 710 males 7 to 18 years old at entry into the American-Hellenic Heart Study, a cross-cultural examination of CHD risk factors (Christakis et al., 1981). Six cohorts were administered the Miami Structured Interview to assess Type A behavior: (1) USA-born Greek-Americans and (2) Greece-born Americans attending primarily Greek parochial schools in New York City (Bronx, Manhattan, Queens) and Orange, New Jersey; and Greek public school students from mainland Greece, i.e., (3) Athens and (4) rural Etoloakarnania, and from the island of Crete, i.e., (5) city of Iraklion and (6) rural villages of Iraklion. The males in the United States were recruited from the Greek Orthodox Archdiocese and participated in the study if they provided the investigators with written parental approval. In Greece, the Minister of Health strongly endorsed the study and therefore nearly all youngsters who were selected, participated in the study. All the Greek-Americans and 40% of the Greeks, by systematic random sampling, received the Miami Structured Interview. The six cohorts were examined in the first third of 1980, 1981, and 1982. Eighty-three percent of the participants were interviewed more than once for a total of 1,692 interviews.

Assessing Type A Behavior

The Miami Structured Interview, similar in format, content, and administration to the Structured Interview for adults (Gerace & Smith, 1985), was conducted in English and Greek, respectively, by two trained interviewers in the USA (T.A.G., J.C.S.) and Greece (D.T., L.S.). The Greek interviewers were trained by T.A.G. and J.C.S. using written, audio taped, and in-person instruction.

Previous studies of the Miami Structured Interview support its interrater and test-retest reliability (Gerace & Smith, 1985), cross-cultural validity (Smith, Gerace, Christakis, & Kafatos, 1985), construct validity (Smith & Gerace, 1987), and comparability of the interviewers within each country (Gerace & Smith, 1983). Specifically, we have reported interrater agreements on the Type A versus not A scale of 73% for Greek-Americans ($k=0.49$, $p<0.01$, $n=88$), 80% for Greek-Americans and non-Greek Americans combined ($k=0.61$, $p<0.01$, $n=69$), and 88% for Greeks ($k=0.76$, $p<0.01$, $n=65$)(Gerace & Smith, 1985). These levels of interrater reliability are similar to those reported for the adult structured interview. In addition, test-retest administrations within ten minutes showed 91% agreement ($k=0.82$, $p<0.01$, $n=44$). The sensitivity was 95%, with only 1 of 21 test As not rated A at retest. This latter finding suggests the Miami Structured Interview can be used more than once with the same person without losing its ability to detect Type A youngsters.

There have been two published studies of the validity of the Miami Structured Interview. In the first, which examined the cross-cultural validity of the Miami Structured Interview, we found that interview determined Type As received higher Matthews Youth Test for Health (MYTH) scores (teacher ratings of Type A), than did non Type As for American and Greek adolescents and Greek preadolescents (Smith et al., 1985). The second study revealed significant correlations between the Miami Structured Interview ratings and the MYTH for Greek-American male preadolescents rated by English teachers (r=.34) and adolescents rated by English (r=.36) and mathematics (r=.39) teachers (Smith & Gerace, 1987). Interview ratings were also related to the factor analytically derived "competitive-leadership" component scale of the MYTH (rs=.32 to .42) for both preadolescents and adolescents, but not to the "impatience-aggression" scale.

In two other studies, we examined the potential effect of the interviewer on behavioral ratings. In the first study, under highly controlled conditions, we detected an interviewer effect (Gerace & Smith, 1985). In the second study, using interviews conducted by two English speaking interviewers (n=373) and interviews administered by two Greek speaking interviewers (n=161), we found no significant association between interviewers and the prevalence of the behavior pattern types for either pair of interviewers (Gerace & Smith, 1983). Taken together these studies suggest that interviewers need to be similarly trained and monitored to insure that they do not differentially effect behavioral ratings.

In the current study, interviews were audio tape recorded for later rating by T.A.G. and J.C.S. (monolingual English) who were trained by Chesney, Eagleston, and Rosenman (1980) to rate and administer the Structured Interview for adults. To minimize bias in ratings due to "drift in calibration" from fatigue or increasing experience of the raters (1) English and Greek language interviews were randomly intermixed with all cohorts proportionately represented within each block of 20 interviews and (2) interrater reliability was checked at regular intervals throughout the rating process using 101 Greek-American interviews and 125 Greek interviews. To minimize spurious interrater agreement resulting from the order of the interviews, each rater listened to the interviews in a different random sequence.

The interviews used for checking interrater reliability were selected at regular intervals from the interviews being assessed by one or the other of the raters. These interviews were rated independently by both raters in blocks of 20 interviews. Following each block of interviews, the raters jointly reviewed, discussed and re-rated interviews on which they disagreed by two categories. For interviews rated during interrater reliability checks, the assessments from rater J.C.S. were assigned to boys with "odd" identification numbers and the assessments from T.A.G. were assigned to boys with "even" identification numbers.

The 1980 interviews were rated first, while 1981 and 1982 interviews were intermixed and rated together. Cumulative results were not compiled during the rating process; 1980 results were, however, known to the raters prior to rating 1981 and 1982 interviews.

Behavioral ratings of Type A were based exclusively on the participants voice stylistics during the Miami Structured Interview. Type As speak faster, respond more quickly to questions, and emphasize words more often then Type Bs. We chose to operationalize Type A using voice stylistics alone because 1) voice stylistics have consistently accounted for the greatest proportion of variance in predicting global Type A scores of adults (see Schucker & Jacobs, 1977; Scherwitz, Berton, & Leventhal, 1977), 2) the raters could more reliably score the interviews by focusing on speech characteristics across cohorts some of whose language the raters did not know (i.e., Greek), and 3) the raters were trained to score audio tape recorded interviews of adults by concentrating on voice stylistics and not the content of the interview (Chesney, Eagleston, & Rosenman, 1980). Interviewees were rated either A1 (nearly all Type A responses), A2 (mostly Type A responses, but with some Type B responses), X (not clearly Type A or B), B3 (mostly Type B responses, but with some Type A responses) or B4 (near absence of Type A responses). For purposes of reporting prevalence of Type A, A1s and A2s were combined.

Analyses

To determine the "best estimate" of the age-adjusted prevalence of Type A for each cohort, we used all 1,692 interviews from 1980, 1981, and 1982. First, for each cohort we created a single frequency distribution of Type As by age categories 7 to 20 years, using interviews from the three years. Eighty-three percent of participants were interviewed in more than one year and thus were represented more than once. Second, for each cohort we calculated the proportion of Type A youngsters at each age. If the proportion of Type A was .00 for an age category or the category did not contain any youngsters, we assigned the mean of the adjacent proportions (i.e., from 1 year younger and 1 year older) or the proportion of the only adjacent age category. This procedure was necessary in 27% (23/84) of cohort by age cells.

Third, we constructed a "standard population" (MacMahon & Pugh, 1970) by summing the total number of youngsters interviewed at each age across all cohorts. Finally, the estimated age-adjusted prevalence for each cohort was determined by 1) multiplying the proportion of Type A at each age for the cohort times the number of youngsters in each age category of the "standard population," 2) summing the products, and 3) dividing by 1,692—the total number of interviews in the "standard population." Differences between cohorts in the age-adjusted prevalence of Type A per 100 were tested using the z test of proportions for independent samples (Fleiss, 1981).

RESULTS

Interrater agreement on the classification of Type A (A1s + A2s) vs not Type A (Xs + B3s + B4s) was similar for the Greek-Americans, 87%, and Greeks, 81% (n=101, Cohen's Kappa=.74, z=7.60, and n=125, Cohen's Kappa=.60, z=6.81, respectively, ps<.001). Two category disagreements were rare, occurring for only 27 of the 226 interviews (12%) used to assess interrater reliability. Each of these disagreements was resolved with a single, joint review session by the raters.

Table 1 summarizes the age-adjusted and unadjusted prevalences of Type A per 100 youngsters for the six cohorts. The age-adjusted and unadjusted prevalences differ only slightly. For purposes of testing the hypothesis regarding the relationship between prevalence of Type A and rate of adult CHD Mortality, the USA was represented by Greek-Americans (USA- and Greece-born). The age-adjusted prevalence of Type A for Greek-Americans was 44.5 per 100, significantly lower than the 52.1 per 100 for mainland Greece (Athens + Etoloakarnania) (z=2.50, p<.05) and similar to the 44.8 per 100 for Crete (Iraklion + villages of Iraklion) (z=0.11, p>.05). The prevalence for mainland Greece exceeded the prevalence for Crete (z=2.40, p<.05).

Regarding the migration hypothesis, Greece-born Americans had a prevalence of Type A more similar to mainland Greeks, 57.0 vs 52.1, respectively, (z=0.86, p>.05) than to USA-born Greek-Americans, 43.6 (z=2.40, p<.05). A posteriori examination revealed Greece-born Americans, (57.0) resembled youngsters in Athens (z=1.59, p>.05), but not youngsters in Etoloakarnania (z=2.33, p<.05).

The prevalence of Type A in Athens, 66.6 per 100, was significantly greater than in rural mainland Greece, Etoloakarnania, 42.9 per 100 (z=5.11, p<.001). In contrast, urban Crete (Iraklion) and rural Crete (villages of Iraklion) had similar prevalences, 46.8 vs 44.1, respectively (z=0.62, p>.05).

DISCUSSION

Greek-Americans in the USA, the site with the greatest incidence of CHD mortality, did not have the predicted highest prevalence of Type A (44.5 per 100) compared to mainland Greece (52.1 per 100) or the island of Crete (44.8 per 100). Three possible explanations for this finding should be considered. First, the influence of Greek family and community traditions on Type A behavior in Greek-Americans may be so strong that these youngsters do not reflect the prevalence of Type A in the general population. The prevalence for the Greek-Americans, however, closely matched that for a group of non-Greek Americans (primarily Irish and Italian Catholics) (Gerace et al., 1986) indicating that the prevalence for

TABLE 1 Estimated Age-Adjusted and Unadjusted Prevalence of Type A Behavior Per 100 in Two Greek-American and Four Greek Cohorts

	Greek-American Cohorts		*Greek Cohorts*			
	USA-born	*Greece-born*	*Mainland*		*Crete*	
	Greek-Americans	*Americans*	*Athens*	*Rural*	*Iraklion*	*Rural*
Age Adjusted Prevalence/100	43.6	57.0	66.6	42.9	46.8	44.1
Unadjusted Prevalence/100	44.1	55.4	66.0	41.1	48.1	40.0
Number of Interviews	600	92	206	265	272	257

Greek-Americans may not be unusual for male youngsters in the USA. Rather than interpreting the prevalence for Greek-Americans as unusually low for American youngsters, it may be more reasonable to think of the prevalence for mainland Greece, specifically Athens, as unexpectedly high.

Second, although the mortality rate from CHD for the USA is one of the highest in the world, there is great variability in rates by region of the country (see Ragland, Selvin, & Merrill, 1988) and ethnic grouping. Greek-Americans may, in fact, have a CHD mortality rate and prevalence of Type A below that of the general population. Cross-cultural comparisons of Type A in the future need to take into account variations in mortality rates by ethnic group within countries. Third, the prevalence for Greek-American youngsters may not have reached its highest level. Since youngsters mature socially and biologically at different rates across countries, it is possible that the prevalence was still rising in the USA while prevalences in mainland Greece and Crete had reached their upper limits. Although this explanation is plausible, it seems unlikely that the prevalence in the USA would ever exceed that of Athens, discussed below.

Mainland Greece, as predicted, had a higher prevalence of Type A behavior than Crete, corresponding to mainland Greece's greater incidence of CHD. This higher prevalence of Type A, however, was completely accounted for by the very high prevalence in Athens, greatest of the six cohorts. Perhaps the high prevalence in Athens should have been expected. Nearly one-third of Greece's population is crowded into metropolitan Athens, the center of Greece's rapid transition since World War II from an agrarian society to an industrialized nation. In this environment young males are pressured by parents and schools to gain admittance to a university and "to achieve academic excellence to compete in the world marketplace" (Bouhoutsos & Roe, 1984, p.57). This competitive atmosphere is also reflected in the fathers of the Athenian youngsters in the present study. For instance, 26% of Athenian fathers graduated from college, more than from any other cohort. Overall in Greece, only 7% of the fathers entered college. In addition, the Athenian fathers contained the highest percentage of executives and professionals relative to the other cohorts.

The very high prevalence of Type A behavior in Athens may help explain its purported increasing rate of CHD mortality (C. Aravanis, personal communication, February 2, 1986; Keys, Alessandro, & Aravanis, 1984) and portend a rise in the incidence of CHD four to five decades from now. A noteworthy parallel to the high prevalence of Type A in Athens is that Athenian adult males now have higher blood cholesterol values, a major risk factor for CHD, than American males and comparable rates of smoking (Moulopoulos et al., 1987). Future studies of the Athenian population should examine how the Type A "life style" influences traditional risk factors such as blood cholesterol and cigarette smoking and explore specific Type A characteristics such as "potential for hostility", a purported atherogenic component of Type A (MacDougall, et al. 1985; Matthews & Haynes, 1986).

Examination of the migration hypothesis revealed Greece-born Americans (57.0 per 100) were more similar to mainland Greeks (52.1 per 100) than to USA-born Greek Americans (43.6 per 100). Specifically, Greece-born Americans resembled youngsters from Athens, not rural mainland Greece. The direction of the trend is opposite to our hypothesis: Migration from Greece to the USA would reveal a rise in the prevalence of Type A. Thus, we expected the USA-born Greek-Americans to have the highest prevalence. The pattern is, however, consistent with the thesis that migration leads to changes in the prevalence of Type A behavior toward the level in the host country. Since the prevalence of Type A for USA-born Greek-Americans resembled that for a group of non-Greek Americans from New York City (Gerace et al., 1986), and the prevalence of Type A for Greece-born Americans resembled that for Athenians, we suggest that cultural assimilation in the USA affects the development of Type A behavior, but its impact takes many years. The above finding might also have occurred if more recent immigrants to the USA, the parents of the Greece-born Americans, tend to be more aggressive, competitive individuals with similar Type A sons (Bortner, Rosenman, & Friedman, 1970) than past immigrants, the parents and grand-parents of USA-born Greek-Americans.

To determine whether duration of exposure to the USA affects behavioral type, we examined the Pearson correlations between length of time in the USA (years) and Type A scores (A1=1, A2=2, etc.) without controlling for age, and then controlling for age in the Greece-born American cohort. The first correlation was r=0.28 (p=.10), suggesting no relationship between exposure time to the USA and behavioral type. The partial correlation, controlling for age, was r=0.23 (p=.20), again indicating that length of time in the USA did not affect the Type A score. The lack of a significant correlation was not due to restricted ranges of the variables. For years in the USA the SD=2.77 and range=11; for Type A scores the SD=1.28 and range=4. One possible explanation for this finding is that the effects of the family and immediate community on Greece-born Americans are more powerful than those of the larger community. A corollary explanation is that the process of assimilation by the larger community takes longer than the mean residence in the USA of approximately seven years for this cohort.

We also conducted a preliminary study to see whether place of birth had a residual effect on the prevalence of Type A in Greece-born Americans. To accomplish this we categorized the youngsters into two groups by population density and found that 53% were born in the largest Greek urban centers (pop. greater than 100,000) and 47% were born in less populated regions. The large urban centers yielded an unadjusted prevalence of Type A of 56 per 100, nearly identical to the less populated regions' yield of 55 per 100, (z=0.08, p>.05). This finding appears to suggest that there was no residual effect of place of birth on Type A behavior for this cohort. But, it should be noted that the Greece-born Americans lived in Greece for slightly less than four years on the average, a period perhaps too short to allow the Greek socio-cultural environment to affect Type A prevalence.

Rural-urban results were as predicted for mainland Greece (i.e., a higher prevalence of Type A for Athens than for Etoloakarnania), but not for Crete (i.e., similar prevalences in Iraklion and villages of Iraklion); Athens (pop. 3,027,331) may differ more sharply from its contrast rural area (pop. 113,942) than does Iraklion (pop. 243,622) from its rural area (pop. 107,440). Athens, being more urbanized and Westernized appears more conducive to fostering Type A behavior than Iraklion. In Greece there is "rapidly accelerating change... in capital and big towns, but much less so... in the rural areas" (Ierodiakonou, Kokantzis, & Fekas, 1979, p. 189). The rural-urban difference on mainland Greece is consistent with that found in children from the USA (Butensky, Faralli, Heebner, & Waldron, 1976) and again supports the thesis that social-environmental factors influence the prevalence of Type A. The like prevalences in rural (economically rich) and urban Crete and rural mainland Greece (economically poor) strongly suggest that simple rural-urban designations cannot predict geographical differences in the distribution of Type A.

Besides their relatively low prevalence of Type A behavior, youngsters in rural and urban Crete had the lowest level of LDL-cholesterol, the primary atherogenic fraction of cholesterol — reflecting the very low mortality rate from CHD in their homeland (Christakis, Fordyce-Baum, Duncan, & Kafatos, 1986). The highest levels of HDL-cholesterol, the so-called "good" cholesterol, were observed in the two rural sites in Greece, Etoloakarnania and rural Crete. Differences in dietary habits most likely contribute to these findings. For example, the four Greek cohorts obtained 22% of their total calories from monounsaturated fatty acids (primarily from olive oil) compared to 13% for Greek-Americans. Monounsaturated fats lower total cholesterol while either raising or not effecting HDL-cholesterol.

SUMMARY

In summary, the current study suggests the following conclusions. The dramatically greater prevalence of Type A behavior in Athens compared to the other three Greek cohorts and the variability of behavior type in all cohorts (i.e., all sites have more than 30% Type Bs) argue against these findings simply being the result of dissimilar cultural voice stylistics such as speed of speech and frequency of emphasis.

Complicated social-environmental factors most likely influence the prevalence of Type A. Support for this conclusion comes from observing: 1) different prevalences of Type A behavior in rural and urban mainland Greece, 2) no difference in prevalence between the more homogeneous urban and rural environments of Crete, and 3) no difference in prevalence between economically poor and rich rural areas on mainland Greece and Crete, respectively. The impact of social-environmental factors was also indicated by the fact that the prevalence of Type A in recently arrived Greece-born Americans was more similar to that of mainland Greeks than that of USA-born Greek Americans whose families have been in the USA for many years.

Finding the prevalence of Type A behavior in Athens was greater than for the two Greek-American cohorts in the New York City area suggests caution in drawing conclusions regarding the impact of large urban centers on the prevalence of Type A behavior. It should be noted that comparing public school students in Athens to private school youngsters in the New York City area may have created a confound since private school students may be more insulated from influences of urban life that may contribute to Type A behavior.

Certainly, hereditary factors and genetic-environmental interactions cannot be ruled out as contributors to the differences in prevalence of Type A found in this study. However, the fact that the prevalence of Type A in Athens far exceeded the prevalence in the four other cohorts from the Greek "gene pool" that reside in their homelands, supports the notion that the Athenian milieu is most conducive to eliciting and reinforcing Type A behavior in its young males. Finally, if Type A is an independent risk factor for CHD in Greece, the remarkably high prevalence of Type A in Athens suggests a greater increase in the incidence of CHD four to five decades from now relative to rural mainland Greece, Crete, and the USA.

REFERENCES

Bass, C., & Wade, C. (1982). Type A behaviour: Not specifically pathogenic? *Lancet, 2*, 1147-1149.

Blumenthal, J.A., Williams, R.B., Kong, Y., Shanberg, S.M., & Thompson, L.W. (1978). Type A behavior and coronary atherosclerosis. *Circulation, 58*, 634-639.

Bortner, R.W., Rosenman, R.H., & Friedman, M. (1970). Familial similarity in pattern A behavior. *Journal of Chronic Disease, 23*, 39-43.

Bouhoutsos, C., & Roe, K.V. (1984). Mental health services and the emerging role of psychology in Greece. *American Psychologist, 39*, 57-61.

Brand, R.J., Rosenman, R.H., Jenkins, C.D., Sholtz, R.I., & Zyzanski, S.J. (1978, March). Comparison of coronary heart disease prediction in the Western Collaborative Group Study using the Structured Interview and the Jenkins Activity Survey assessments of the coronary-prone Type A behavior pattern. *Annual Conference of Cardiovascular Disease Epidemiology*, American Heart Association, Orlando, Florida.

Butensky, A., Faralli, V., Heebner, D., & Waldron, I. (1976). Elements of the coronary prone behavior pattern in children and teenagers. *Journal of Psychosomatic Research, 20*, 439-444.

Christakis, G., Fordyce-Baum, M.K., Duncan, R., & Kafatos, A. (1986). *Demographic and nutritional determinants of coronary heart disease risk factors in U.S. - Greek adolescents*. Unpublished manuscript, University of Miami School of Medicine, Florida.

Chesney, M.A., Eagleston, J.R., & Rosenman, R.H. (1980). The Type A structured interview: A behavioral assessment in the rough. *Journal of Behavioral Assessment, 2*, 255-272.

Christakis, G., Kafatos, A., & Fordyce, M., Kurtz, C., Gerace, T.A., Smith, J.C., Duncan, R., Cassady, J., & Doxiodis, S. (1981). Cultural and nutritional determinants of coronary heart disease risk factors in adolescents: A USA-Greece cross-cultural study, preliminary results, in Nutrition in Health and Disease and International Development: *Symposia from the XII International Congress of Nutrition* (pp. 799-810). New York: Alan R Liss, Inc.

Fleiss, J.L. (1981). *Statistical Methods for Rates and Proportions*. New York: John Wiley.

Frank, K.A., Heller, S.S., Kornfield, D.S., Sporn, A.A., & Weiss, M.B. (1978). Type A behavior pattern and coronary angiographic findings. *Journal of the American Medical Association, 240*, 761-763.

French-Belgian Collaborative Group (1982). Ischemic heart disease and psychological patterns—prevalence and incidence studies in Belgium and France. *Advances in Cardiology, 29*, 25-31.

Gerace, T.A., & Smith, J.C. (1983). Miami Type A interview for preadolescents and adolescents: A third examination of the interviewer effect. *American Heart Association CVD Epidemiology Newsletter, 33*, 16.

Gerace, T.A., & Smith, J.C. (1984). Stability of type A behavior in preadolescent and adolescent males. *American Heart Association CVD Epidemiology Newsletter, 35*, 30.

Gerace, T.A., & Smith, J.C. (1985). Children's type A interview: Interrater, test-retest reliability, and interviewer effect. *Journal of Chronic Diseases, 38*, 781-791.

Gerace, T.A., Smith, J.C., Christakis, G., Kafatos, A.G., Trakas, D., & Osterweis-Stangos, L. (1986). [Prevalence of Type A behavior in the USA and Greece]. Unpublished raw data.

Ierodiakonou, C.S., Kokantzis, N., & Fekas, L. (1979). Stressful factors in Greek life leading to illness. In E.K.E. Gunderson, & R.H. Rahe (Eds.), *Life, Stress and Illness* (pp. 189-194). Springfield, Illinois: Charles C. Thomas.

Jenkins, C.D., Rosenman, R.H., & Friedman, M. (1968). Replicability of rating the coronary-prone behavior pattern. *British Journal of Preventive and Social Medicine, 22*, 16-22.

Kagan, J., & Moss, H.A. (1962). *Birth to Maturity: A Study of Psychological Development*. New York: John Wiley.

Keys, A. (1980). *Seven Countries: A Multivariate Analysis of Death and Coronary Heart Disease*. Cambridge, Massachusetts: Harvard University Press.

Keys, A., Alessandro, M., & Aravanis, C. (1984). The seven countries study: 2,289 deaths in 15 years. *Preventive Medicine, 13*, 141-154.

MacDougall, J.M., Dembroski, T.M., Dimsdale, J.E., & Hackett, T.P. (1985). Components of Type A, hostility and anger-in: Further relationships to angiographic findings. *Health Psychology, 4*, 137-152.

MacMahon, B., & Pugh, T.F. (1970). *Epidemiology: Principles and Methods*. Boston: Little Brown and Company.

Matthews, K.A., & Haynes, S.G. (1986). Type A behavior pattern and coronary disease risk: update and clinical evaluation. *American Journal of Epidemiology, 123*, 923-960.

Moulopoulos, S.D., Adamopoulos, P.N., Diamantopoulos, E.I., Nanas, S.N., Anthopoulos, L.N., & Iliadi-Alexandrou, M. (1987). Coronary heart disease risk factors in a random sample of Athenian adults: the Athens Study. *American Journal of Epidemiology, 126*, 882-892.

Ragland, D.R., & Brand, R.S. (1988). Coronary heart disease mortality in the Western Collaborative Group Study. *American Journal of Epidemiology, 127*, 462-475.

Ragland, K.E., Selvin, S., & Merrill, D.W. (1988). The onset of decline in ischemic heart disease mortality in the United States. *American Journal of Epidemiology, 127*, 516-531.

Rosenman, R.H. (1978a). Introduction. In T.M. Dembroski, S.M. Weiss, J.L. Shields, S.G. Haynes, & M. Feinleib (Eds.), *Coronary-prone Behavior* (pp. i- xvi). New York: Springer Verlag.

Rosenman, R.H. (1978b). The interview method of assessment of the coronary-prone behavior pattern. In T.M. Dembroski, S.M. Weiss, J.L. Shields, S.G.

Haynes, & M. Feinleib (Eds.), *Coronary-prone Behavior* (pp. 55- 69). New York: Springer Verlag.

Rosenman, R.H., Brand, R.J., Jenkins, C.D., Friedman, M., Straus, R., & Wurm, M. (1975). Coronary heart disease in the Western Collaborative Group Study: Final follow-up experience of 8 1/2 years. *Journal of the American Medical Association, 233*, 872-877.

Scherwitz, L., Berton K., & Leventhal, H. (1977). Type A assessment and interaction in the behavior pattern interview. *Psychosomatic Medicine, 39*, 229-240.

Schucker, B., & Jacobs, D.R. (1977). Assessment of behavioral risk for coronary disease by voice characteristics. *Psychosomatic Medicine*, 39, 229- 240.

Shekelle, R.B., Hulley, S.B., Neaton, J.D., Billings, J.H., Borhani, N.O., Gerace, T.A., Jacobs, D.R., Lasser, N.L., Mittlemark, M.B., & Stamler, J. (1985). The MRFIT behavior pattern study II. Type A behavior and incidence of coronary heart disease. *American Journal of Epidemiology, 122*, 559-570.

Shekelle, R.B., Hulley, S.B., Neaton, J.D., Borhani, N.O., Grimm, Jr., R.H., Lasser, N.L., Schoenberger, J.A., & Stamler, J. (1988). Type A behavior [Letter to the editor]. *American Heart Journal, 115*, 1348-1350.

Smith, J.C., & Gerace, T.A. (1987). Validity of the Miami Structured Interview-1 for assessing Type A behavior, competitiveness, and anger in children. *Journal of Psychopathology and Behavioral Assessment, 9*, 369-384.

Smith, J.C., Gerace, T.A., Christakis, G., & Kafatos, A. (1985). Cross-cultural validity of the Miami Structured Interview-1 for Type A in children: The American-Hellenic Heart Study. *Journal of Chronic Diseases, 38*, 793-799.

Visintainer, P.F., & Matthews, K.A. (1987). Stability of overt Type A behavior in children: Results from a two- and five-year longitudinal study. *Child Development, 58*, 1586-1591.

Type A Behavior and Self-Referencing:
Interactive Risk Factors?

Alan F. Fontana
Yale University School of Medicine and NEPEC 182, Veterans Administration Medical Center, West Haven, CT 06516

Roberta L. Rosenberg
Psychology Service 116B, Vetrans Administration Medical Center, West Haven, CT 06516

Matthew M. Burg
Robert D. Kerns
Yale University School of Medicine and Psychology Service 116B, Veterans Administration Medical Center, West Haven, CT 06516

Kathleen L. Colonese
Psychology Service 116B, Veterans Administration Medical Center, West Haven, CT 06516

Previous investigation of the Type A behavior pattern and self-referencing as predictors of cardiovascular reactivity and coronary heart disease has produced a series of apparently inconsistent findings. We reexamined two studies of blood pressure reactivity from our laboratory. By evaluating the Type A behavior pattern and self-referencing in combination with each other and by classifying our sample according to interview style, we were able to demonstrate substantial consistency. From a theoretical perspective, the results are consistent with a model of self-referencing and the Type A behavior pattern as interactive risk factors for coronary heart disease. This model proposes a concern with protecting self-esteem as a critical element in understanding the psychological bases of coronary-prone behavior. Methodologically, the results are consistent with findings from other studies suggesting that variations in the style of administration of the Structured Interview may affect the nature of the findings. The results lend support to the importance that has been attributed to engaging subjects in the interview.

Authors' Notes: We would like to express our appreciation to Larry Scherwitz for his helpful comments on an earlier draft. All errors and omissions are solely the responsibility of the authors.

Address reprint requests to the second author.

© 1990 Select Press

Introduction

The Type A behavior pattern (TABP) is a collection of emotions and behaviors distinguished most importantly by hyperaggressiveness, free-floating hostility, and a sense of time urgency (Friedman & Rosenman, 1974; Rosenman & Chesney, 1980; Friedman & Ulmer, 1984). It has received substantial empirical support as a risk factor for coronary heart disease (CHD) and coronary artery disease (CAD) (Cooper, Detre, & Weiss, 1981). Early robust findings related the TABP to the incidence of CHD (Caffrey, 1969; Friedman & Rosenman, 1959; Rosenman, Brand, Jenkins, Friedman, et al., 1975), to the severity of CAD (Blumenthal, Williams, Kong, Schanberg, & Thompson, 1978; Frank, Heller, Kornfeld, Sporn & Weiss, 1978), and to heightened cardiovascular reactivity (CVR) as a hypothesized mechanism for these endpoints (Houston, 1983; Matthews, 1982). More recently, these results have given way to weaker findings regarding these relationships (Booth-Kewley & Friedman, 1987; Dimsdale, Hackett, Hutter, Block, Catanzano, & White, 1979; Ragland & Brand, 1988; Shekelle, Hulley, Neaton, Billings, et al., 1985).

Two general lines of investigation have been pursued in the examination of these apparent inconsistencies. One approach has been to examine other behavioral variables in conjunction with the TABP in the search for more complete coverage of coronary-prone behaviors. Self-involvement is one such variable. Self-involvement has been defined as the identification with and attachment to a narrowly defined self-representation. It has been described as a combination of self-centeredness and selfishness (Scherwitz & Canick, 1988; Scherwitz & Pavone, 1988). Thus far, self-involvement has typically been measured by the number of self-references (first-person pronouns) uttered by subjects during the Structured Interview (SI), a primary method for assessment of the TABP.

At times, self-references have been found to be related significantly to coronary endpoints when the TABP has not (Scherwitz, McKelvain, Laman, Patterson, et al., 1983; Scherwitz, Graham, Grandits, Buehler, & Billings, 1986). At other times, self-references have been found to be related significantly to cardiovascular reactivity and CHD within Type A's but not within Type B's (Scherwitz, Berton, & Leventhal, 1978; Scherwitz, Graham, & Ornish, 1985). In fact, Scherwitz and his colleagues have suggested that self-involvement interacts with other risk factors for CHD including the TABP, and that the interaction of self-involvement and the TABP can be expected to yield more consistent associations with CHD endpoints than either self-involvement or the TABP alone (Scherwitz, Graham, & Ornish, 1985; Scherwitz & Pavone, 1988).

A second approach has grown out of concern that "drift" has occurred in the style of administration of the SI (e.g., Matthews, 1982; Matthews &

Haynes, 1986; Scherwitz, 1988a). Although the SI is but one method for measuring the TABP, it is the method that has produced the strongest relationships with CHD, CAD, and cardiovascular reactivity (cf., Matthews, 1982; Friedman & Booth-Kewley, 1987). Variations in the style of administration of the SI are important to evaluate because the TABP has been conceptualized as the product of internal tendencies and eliciting situations (Chesney, Eagleston, & Rosenman, 1980; Rosenman, 1978). Thus, the behavior of the interviewer is a critical determinant of the eliciting situation that is the SI.

Scherwitz (1988a) has made an extensive comparison of interview styles in the Western Collaborative Group Study (WCGS) and Multiple Risk Factor Intervention Trial (MRFIT). He found that MRFIT interviewers asked fewer questions, had a shorter latency between questions, interrupted more frequently and more rudely, and conducted shorter interviews overall. This mode of administration is consistent with the belief that the SI has to be challenging in its style of delivery in order to elicit Type A behavior reliably and validly (Chesney, Eagleston, & Rosenman, 1980). Indeed, in addition to hurrying subjects and interrupting them, interviewers have been trained to emphasize key words and to maintain control over the interview. Scherwitz has speculated that the MRFIT interview style failed to engage subjects in the task of disclosing themselves to the interviewer. It could fail to motivate some subjects to respond as completely as they might if they had been engaged. Or it may motivate other especially sensitive or hostile subjects to suppress their responses in passive-aggressive retaliation. In either case, the lack of engagement could have worked against the expression of true coronary-prone behaviors. Therefore, it is possible that the shift in style of interview administration from WCGS to MRFIT served to alter the relationships of the TABP and self-references with CHD incidence.

In summary, both the TABP and self-referencing have received support as prognostic factors for CHD and CAD, but the confidence in each has been diminished by the inconsistency of results. One question that we explore is whether the interaction of the two is more predictive of cardiovascular reactivity than either one alone. In practice, self-referencing has generally been examined within levels of the TABP (Scherwitz, Berton & Leventhal, 1978; Scherwitz, Graham, & Ornish, 1985). We believe, however, that the TABP should be examined within levels of self-referencing as well. In this way, the role of each might be clarified as a condition for the manifestation of the other as a risk factor.

The second question that we explore concerns the method of SI administration. Specifically, and following Scherwitz's (1988a) pioneering work, we explore the effects of different styles of SI administration on relationships considered to be critical to the issue of coronary-proneness. Two studies were conducted. In the first, the TABP was related significantly to cardiovascular reactivity (Fontana, Rosenberg, Kerns, & Marcus, 1986) but self-referencing was not. In a second study, self-referencing was related significantly to cardiovascular reactivity but the TABP was not (data to be reported in this paper). These findings parallel those obtained by the analyses of the WCGS and MRFIT data. In the WCGS, the TABP has been found to be related significantly to CHD incidence (Rosenman, Brand, Jenkins, Friedman, et al., 1975) but self-referencing has not (Graham, Scherwitz, & Brand, 1988). In MRFIT, self-referencing has been found to be related significantly to CHD incidence (Scherwitz, Graham, Grandits, Buehler, & Billings, 1986) but the TABP has not (Shekelle, Hulley, Neaton, Billings, et al., 1985).

This parallelism suggests that if we were able to discover some theoretical and data analytic framework for revealing consistent results across our studies, the same framework might be useful in revealing consistent results across other data sets. In pursuing this goal, we examine the role of the TABP and self-referencing as risk factors in the context of the style of administration of the SI.

METHOD

Subjects

Subjects were medical and surgical patients who were free of a known history of cardiovascular disease, cancer, renal disease, other life threatening diseases, and psychiatric disorders. Typically, these patients had podiatric, orthopedic, gastrointestinal or urologic disorders. Forty-four[1] subjects participated in the first study and 70 subjects participated in the second study. Subjects in the first study averaged 47 years of age, with a range of 23 to 67 years. Socioeconomically, 48% were white-collar (Classes I-III) and 52% were blue-collar (Classes IV-V) according to the Hollingshead Scale (1957). Subjects in the second study averaged 45 years of age, with a range of 30 to 66 years. Thirty-seven percent were white-collar and 63% were blue-collar. Subjects in the two studies did not differ significantly in age or socioeconomic status.

Variables

The TABP was assessed by the SI (Rosenman, 1978). In both studies, it was administered and coded by R.L.R., who received training from Dr. Rosenman and his colleagues. Before beginning data collection, the interviewer attained an agreement of 88% (Kappa = .87) with expert

[1] *The original sample consisted of 50 subjects. Six subjects were dropped for the present analyses because their Structured Interviews were not available for scoring individual behaviors.*

coding on a set of standard tapes. The TABP was coded in four levels: A_1, A_2, X, B. Also, the two groups of A's and the X's and B's were collapsed to form a dichotomous variable as well (Kappa = .66). At the conclusion of the second study, the interviews from the first study were reaudited so that the effects of any drift in coding criteria over time could be minimized. The reexamination of interviews resulted in only minimal change, with the codes from two interviews being changed by one level each.

In addition to being coded for the TABP, the SI was also coded for the following component behaviors: Loudness of Voice, Explosiveness of Speech, Rapidity and Acceleration of Speech, Latency of Response, and Potential for Hostility, according to guidelines developed by Dembroski and MacDougall (1983). One of the authors (A.F.F.) received training from Dr. Dembroski in the scoring of these components. He then trained two of the other authors, eventuating in the following interjudge intraclass reliabilities: Loudness (.93), Explosiveness (.87), Rapidity (.85), Latency (.95), and Potential for Hostility (.92). These coefficients were derived from a model II analysis for fixed effects as described by Bartko (1966).

Self-references (SR) were coded from the entire SI by counting the number of times subjects used the pronouns, "I", "me", "my", and "mine" (cf., Scherwitz, Berton, & Leventhal, 1978). The interjudge intraclass reliability for SR was .96. In addition, self-referencing density (SRD) was examined as a secondary measure of self-involvement. SRD was derived by dividing SR by the total number of clauses spoken (Scherwitz, Graham, Grandits, Buehler, & Billings, 1986). The interjudge intraclass reliability for counting clauses was .97. Scherwitz and his colleagues are divided in their opinion regarding the proper role of the density measure. If quantity of speech is considered to represent a phenomenon separate from self-involvement, then the density measure is an appropriate control for length of speech. If quantity of speech is considered to be one reflection of self-involvement, however, then the density measure inappropriately controls for relevant variance. In practice, the density measure has been found to be inferior to the unadjusted total of self-references in relating to coronary disease endpoints. The density measure was included here for completeness of coverage of the self-referencing measure.

The interviews from the two studies were classified to reflect differences in style of administration. In the first study, a change in interview style was made as a result of the interviewer's experience with two subjects who were interviewed consecutively and who were extremely sarcastic, condescending and controlling of the interview. Based on her training instructions,[2] the interviewer decided that she needed to become more challenging and more stern in her demeanor in order to maintain

[2]*Personal communication from Margaret Chesney and Michael Hecker, March 19, 1982.*

control over the interview. Thus, in subsequent interviews, she became more emphatic by delivering key words more deliberately and more loudly. At the same time, she became less warm by decreasing the frequency of her nonprogrammed responses to subjects' answers that signified her interest in, and comprehension of, what they were saying. We characterize the initial group of interviews in the first study as low in emphasis and moderate in warmth (N = 19); the subsequent group we characterize as moderate in emphasis and low in warmth (N = 25). In the second study, the interviewer increased the emphasis further, by speaking even more loudly and by pausing slightly after the enunication of key words. Warmth was specifically reinstated, however, in response to early reports that MRFIT interviews might not have been sufficiently engaging. Therefore, we characterize the interviews in the second study as high in emphasis and moderate in warmth (N = 70).

As a way of checking on our classifications empirically, we selected ten interviews at random from each interview style. They were coded independently by two judges. However, the judges' familiarity with the interviews precluded blind assessment according to interview condition. We counted the number of words that the interviewer spoke with low, moderate, and high emphasis. Each low emphasis utterance was given a weight of one, each moderate emphasis utterance a weight of two, and each high emphasis utterance a weight of three. These were then summed to create an overall emphasis score. In addition to emphasis, we also assessed warmth by counting the number of times that the interviewer responded to subjects' answers with a phrase signifying acceptance and understanding. Common examples were the phrases, "I see" and "okay," as well as paraphrases of the subjects' answers that were uttered without a questioning inflection and when the meaning was already evident. The interjudge intraclass correlations were .86 for emphasis and .88 for warmth. One-way analyses of variance were performed on each of these scores across the three interview styles. Both emphasis ($F(2,27) = 59.05$, $p<.0001$) and warmth ($F(2,27) = 6.95$, $p<.005$) differed significantly across interview styles. Mean levels of emphasis were 58.10 (SD=14.60), 113.50 (SD=16.03), and 193.80 (SD=43.53) and mean levels of warmth were 5.50 (SD=2.17), 2.40 (SD=1.84), and 7.10 (SD=4.07) for the low emphasis-moderate warmth, moderate emphasis-low warmth, and high emphasis-moderate warmth conditions respectively.

Systolic (SBP) and diastolic (DBP) blood pressure were measured as indices of cardiovascular activity. Assessments were made in the sitting position at heart level. In the first study, assessments were made manually from a portable, standing mercury sphygmomanometer. In the second study, they were made automatically by the Dynamap 845 XT. Prior to beginning the second study, the two methods of assessments were compared and were found to yield equivalent readings. In both studies, an experimenter sat behind the subject and initiated readings to coincide with the same preselected questions.

Procedure

The first study was conducted in two sessions: one in the morning and one in the afternoon of the same day, or one on each of successive days. The SI was the first task administered in the second session. That session began with subjects being asked to relax and sit quietly so that stable baselines could be established for their blood pressures. In all cases, a stable baseline was obtained within five minutes. Five readings were made at fixed times during the SI. Readings were averaged separately for the final two baseline measures and for the five SI measures, and the means were used for data analysis. An examination of demographic variables revealed that age was associated significantly with the blood pressure indices in some of the interview conditions. Therefore, age was controlled statistically in the derivation of blood pressure reactivity (BPR). BPR was derived by regressing blood pressure during the SI on baseline blood pressure and age. The resulting residual score represents the change in blood pressure from baseline to SI, adjusted for baseline level and age.

The second study was conducted in one session. Subjects began by completing a short battery of questionnaires. Baselines were then established for blood pressure, followed by administration of the SI. Assessment of blood pressure and derivation of BPR measures were accomplished as in the first study.

Analytic Strategy For Evaluating Interactions. In order to determine the nature of the interactions and to conduct analyses comparable to those employed in other studies of the TABP and self-referencing (cf., Scherwitz, Berton & Leventhal, 1978; Scherwitz, McKelvain, Laman, Patterson, et al., 1983; Scherwitz, Graham & Ornish, 1985), we elected to treat each variable both continuously and discretely in parallel analyses. That is, each self-referencing variable was treated continuously in combination with discrete levels of the TABP as either A's or B's, and the TABP was treated continuously in combination with discrete levels of the self-referencing variables as highs or lows. Multiple regression analyses were performed first to determine the statistical significance of the interactions. For each significant interaction, the simple main effect of the continuous variable was evaluated for statistical significance correlationally within each level of the discrete variable (cf., Kirk, 1968, pp. 179-182). Thus, each significant interaction was evaluated as a pair of main effects, and the particular member of this pair that was associated significantly with BPR was identified.

RESULTS

Before examining the relationships of the TABP, SR, and SRD with BPR, we wished to determine whether interview style seemed to have any effect upon the level of subjects' behavioral and cardiovascular responses to the SI and upon the correspondence of their behavioral responses to the global TABP code. Therefore, one-way analyses of variance were performed on the TABP, component behaviors, SR, SRD, and blood pressure indices. They revealed that SR ($F(2,111) = 3.35$, $p<.05$) and SRD ($F(2,111) = 7.90$, $p<.001$), as well as Rapidity ($F(2,111) = 4.75$, $P<.01$), Latency ($F(2,111) = 10.10$, $p<.0001$), and Potential for Hostility ($F(2,111) = 3.19$, $p<.05$) differed significantly across interview style. Among the three groups, subjects in the high emphasis-moderate warmth condition were highest in SR and SRD and lowest in Latency and Potential for Hostility. Subjects in the moderate emphasis-low warmth condition were highest in Rapidity, Latency, and Potential for Hostility; and subjects in the low emphasis-moderate warmth condition were lowest in SR and Rapidity. The TABP was not significantly different across groups, either as a four-level variable as in the table or as a dichotomous variable (60% Type A among high emphasis-moderate warmth subjects, 56% Type A among moderate emphasis-low warmth subjects, and 53% Type A among low emphasis-moderate warmth subjects).

Blood pressure indices were found not to differ significantly across interview style. Paired-comparison t-tests indicated, however, that highly significant levels of BPR occurred within each interview style. The least significant BPR occurred for SBP under low emphasis and moderate warmth ($t(18) = 4.63$, $p<.0002$).

Product-moment correlations between the TABP and the component behaviors revealed a similar pattern of significant relationships for the low emphasis-moderate warmth and the high emphasis-moderate warmth interview styles. In both cases, Loudness, Rapidity, Explosiveness, and Latency were associated significantly with the TABP. By contrast, only two component behaviors, Loudness and Latency, were related significantly to the TABP in the moderate emphasis-low warmth interview style.

Product-moment correlations of the TABP and SR with BPR within interview styles revealed that the TABP but not SR was related significantly to DBP reactivity among subjects interviewed with low emphasis and moderate warmth, and SR but not the TABP was related significantly to DBP reactivity among subjects interviewed with high emphasis and moderate warmth. The correlation between the TABP and DBP reactivity in the low emphasis-moderate warmth condition was marginally greater than the correlation between SR and DBP reactivity in

TABLE 1 Means[1] for the Type A Behavior Pattern (TABP), Component Behaviors, Self-References (SR), and Self-Reference Density (SRD) by Interview Style

		Component Behaviors						
Interview Style	*TABP*	*Loudness*	*Rapidity*	*Explosiveness*	*Latency*	*Pot. Hostility*	*SR*	*SRD*
High Emphasis	2.53	3.27	3.49	3.11	2.03	2.93	99.29	0.70
Moderate Warmth (N=70)	(1.02)	(1.08)	(0.90)	(1.52)	(1.01)	(1.40)	(46.96)	(0.14)
Moderate Emphasis	2.60	3.06	3.92	3.44	3.16	3.64	81.20	0.58
Low Warmth (N=25)	(1.08)	(1.16)	(0.89)	(1.16)	(1.14)	(0.99)	(34.65)	(0.16)
Low Emphasis	2.52	2.95	2.95	3.37	2.63	3.34	73.84	0.61
Moderate Warmth (N=19)	(1.35)	(1.27)	(1.58)	(1.46)	(1.42)	(1.00)	(41.42)	(0.13)

[1]*Standard deviations are in parentheses.*

TABLE 2 Blood Pressure Means[1] for Baseline, SI, and Reactivity by Interview Style

	Systolic			*Diastolic*		
Interview Style	*Baseline*	*SI*	*Reactivity*	*Baseline*	*SI*	*Reactivity*
High Emphasis Moderate Warmth (N=70)	124.11 (16.01)	137.46 (17.59)	13.35 (8.80)	77.21 (10.86)	90.86 (13.88)	13.65 (8.19)
Moderate Emphasis Low Warmth (N=25)	126.48 (18.38)	140.96 (25.01)	14.48 (8.19)	75.80 (13.60)	85.88 (14.63)	10.08 (4.98)
Low Emphasis Moderate Warmth (N = 19)	133.63 (17.48)	144.95 (18.73)	11.32 (10.66)	83.26 (13.42)	92.63 (14.86)	9.37 (5.79)

[1] *Standard deviations are in parentheses.*

this condition (Critical ratio = 1.71, p<.10). However, the correlation between SR and DBP reactivity in the high emphasis moderate warmth condition was not significantly greater than the correlation between the TABP and DBP reactivity in this condition (Critical ratio = 1.44, p>.10). No significant relationships with BPR were found either for SRD in any condition or for any variable among subjects interviewed with moderate emphasis and low warmth. The lack of relationships in this latter regard is consistent with the sparse correlation of the TABP with the component behaviors under this interview style.

TABLE 3 Correlations of the Type A Behavior Pattern with Component Behaviors by Interview Style

	Interview Style		
Component Behavior	*Low Emphasis Moderate Warmth N=19*	*Moderate Emphasis Low Warmth N=25*	*High Emphasis Moderate Warmth N-70*
Loudness	.83***	.75***	.48***
Rapidity	.82***	.14	.59***
Explosiveness	.77***	.31	.42***
Latency	.57**	.46*	.35**
Potential for Hostility	.56*	-.04	.22

**p<.05 **p<.01 ***p<.001*

TABLE 4 Correlations of the Type A Behavior Pattern (TABP), Self-References (SR), and Self-Reference Density (SRD) with Blood Pressure Reactivity by Interview Style

		Interview Style		
Reactivity	*Predictor*	*Low Emphasis Moderate Warmth N=19*	*Moderate Emphasis Low Warmth N=25*	*High Emphasis Moderate Warmth N=70*
Systolic	TABP	.34	.23	.19
	SR	-.08	-.21	.12
	SRD	-.09	-.18	.01
Diastolic	TABP	.56*	.09	.05
	SR	.03	-.03	.29*
	SRD	.11	-.04	.20

*$p<.05$

Next, the interaction of the TABP with each of SR and SRD separately was examined for BPR within each interview style. As specified above, the dichotomized version of the TABP was used to define Type A's and B's. SR and SRD scores were dichotomized at the medians of their distributions for each interview style, because SR and SRD had been found to differ significantly across interview styles. Thus, subgroups of SR and SRD were designated as high or low relative to the median level that was elicited by a given interview style.

Hierarchical regression analyses revealed significant interactions between the TABP and high and low SR for SBP reactivity ($F(1,66) = 4.51$, $p<.05$) and DBP reactivity ($F(1,66) = 9.13$, $p<.01$) in the high emphasis-moderate warmth condition, and for DBP reactivity ($F(1,15) = 3.77$, $p=.07$) in the low emphasis-moderate warmth condition. The only interaction that was significant between the TABP and high and low SRD was for DBP reactivity ($F(1,15)=9.30$, $p<.01$) in the low emphasis-moderate warmth condition.

Conversely, SR interacted significantly with Type A's and B's only for SBP reactivity ($F(1,66)=4.95$, $p<.05$) and DBP reactivity ($F(1,66) = 6.11$, $p<.02$) in the high emphasis-moderate warmth condition. SRD did not interact significantly with Type A's and B's at all.

Finally, the simple main effects comprising each interaction for the TABP and SR were evaluated correlationally. No further evaluation was made of SRD, since no main effect and only one interaction was significant. Product-moment correlations revealed only one significant relationship between SR and BPR; namely, within Type A's for DBP reactivity under conditions of high emphasis and moderate warmth. High

TABLE 5 Correlations of Self-References with Blood Pressure Reactivity within Type A's and B's by Interview Style

Reactivity	*Type*	*Interview Style* — *Low Emphasis Moderate Warmth*	*Moderate Emphasis Low Warmth*	*High Emphasis Moderate Warmth*
Systolic	A	-.24 (10)[1]	-.08 (14)	.29 (42)
	B	.02 (9)	-.35 (11)	-.26 (28)
Diastolic	A	.02 (10)	-.18 (14)	.53*** (42)
	B	-.57 (9)	.12 (11)	-.10 (28)

****p<.001*

[1]*N's in parentheses.*

self-referencing was associated with high reactivity. The correlation between SR and DBP reactivity for Type A's was significantly greater than the corresponding correlation between SR and DBP reactivity for Type B's (Critical ratio = 2.68, p<.01). In contrast, three significant relationships were revealed between the TABP and BPR, all within the high level of SR. These were obtained for SBP and DBP reactivity under conditions of high emphasis and moderate warmth, and for DBP reactivity under conditions of low emphasis and moderate warmth. In each case, Type A behavior was associated with high reactivity. These correlations between the TABP and both SBP and DBP reactivity among high self-referencers were significantly greater than the corresponding correlations between the TABP and these reactivity indices among low self-refer-

TABLE 6 Correlations of the Type A Behavior Pattern with Blood Pressure Reactivity within High and Low Self-References by Interview Style

Reactivity	*Self References*	*Interview Style* — *Low Emphasis Moderate Warmth*	*Moderate Emphasis Low Warmth*	*High Emphasis Moderate Warmth*
Systolic	High	.49 (10)[1]	-.15 (13)	.44** (35)
	Low	.22 (9)	.15 (12)	-.05 (35)
Diastolic	High	.74* (10)	-.22 (13)	.40* (35)
	Low	.25 (9)	.34 (12)	-.30 (35)

**p<.05 **p<.01*

[1]*N's in parentheses*

encers in the high emphasis-moderate warmth condition (Critical ratio = 2.13, $p<.05$ for SBP reactivity; and Critical ratio = 3.04, $p<.01$ for DBP reactivity). However, the correlations between the TABP and DBP reactivity in the low emphasis-moderate warmth condition were not significantly different from each other (Critical ratio = 1.25, $p>.10$).

DISCUSSION

It is important to recognize at the outset that the findings reported here resulted from a reexamination of two studies which had yielded apparently inconsistent findings. The classification of interviewer emphasis and warmth as stylistic variables was made post hoc, and the sizes of two of the groups are small. Further, the post hoc nature of the classification did not yield an exhaustive set of combinations of emphasis and warmth. For example, it would have been desirable to see the effects of low warmth in combination with additional levels of emphasis. Replication and extension of our findings is necessary before any definitive conclusions can be drawn. Given these limitations, however, we believe these findings to be sufficiently intriguing in their implications to warrant serious consideration as empirically based hypotheses for exploration with other data sets.

Of major theoretical interest are the findings that the Type A behavior pattern and self-referencing interacted to yield significant relationships with blood pressure reactivity in both instances where one but not the other yielded significant main effects, as well as in a third instance in which neither one yielded a significant main effect. It is possible, therefore, that inconsistent main effects for the Type A behavior pattern and self-referencing among studies of similar methodology might well be reconciled by examination of their interaction.

The theoretical explication of the interaction constitutes a major task for the future. We would like to offer a few thoughts here, however, as a contribution to the beginning of such an endeavor. We start with two propositions. First, there are some people whose attempts to cope with a great many obstacles typically include Type A behavior. These are people who "throw themselves into" coping with much verve and energy, and their coping attempts are generally accompanied by heightened physiological arousal. Secondly, there are also some people who tend to relate success and failure in coping to their self-esteem. These are people who "take everything personally." We agree with Scherwitz and Pavone's (1988) conception of self-involved people as being particularly likely to appraise obstacles as threats to their self-esteem. These appraisals of threat are generally accompanied by anxiety or other forms of emotional distress.

We propose, then, that people who are both Type A and self-involved are more likely to appraise given obstacles, and more obstacles overall, as posing threats to their self-esteem and to attempt to cope with them with more verve and energy than people who possess only one or none of these orientations. Finally, when obstacles are appraised and coped with in this way, a pathogenic physiological pattern of arousal is activated. Thus, the interactional model proposes that Type A behavior is benign under some circumstances; that is, when the potential for failure is not tied to a loss of self-esteem. Also, self-involvement can be expected to be benign under some circumstances; specifically, when a measured and moderately-paced approach is taken to coping with obstacles.

Social psychological theory and research has equated high self-referencing with a high focus of attention on oneself (Buss, 1980; Carver & Scheier, 1981; Davis & Brock, 1975; Duval & Wicklund, 1972). Further, studies have found that a heightened focus of attention on oneself is associated with a lowered level of self-esteem (Brockner, 1979; Ickes, Wicklund & Ferris, 1973; Turner, Scheier, Carver, & Ickes, 1978). Several theoretical formulations of the psychological foundations for the Type A behavior pattern have been offered that have their bases in self-evaluation and self-esteem (Friedman & Ulmer, 1984; Matthews, 1982; Price, 1982; Scherwitz & Pavone, 1988; Strube, Boland, Manfredo, & Al-Falaij, 1987). If subsequent investigation continues to support self-involvement as interactive with the Type A behavior pattern, we may well find that these formulations are particularly salient for deepening and extending our understanding of coronary-prone behavior.

Of major methodological interest are the findings that differences in interview style were related to the expression of different levels of both self-referencing and several component behaviors of the TABP as well as to differences in the strength of the relationships between the component behaviors and the TABP. The major aspect of interviewer style that seemed to be responsible for a general absence of significant relationships was the low frequency of interviewer behaviors directed toward establishing and maintaining rapport in one of the conditions. When the level of warmth was low, the Type A behavior pattern corresponded less closely to the component behaviors of the SI than when the level of warmth was higher. Not only is the sparseness of the low warmth pattern different from the fuller pattern found for moderate warmth in these studies, but it differs from the fuller pattern obtained by other investigators as well (Dembroski, MacDougall, Williams, Haney, & Blumenthal, 1985; MacDougall, Dembroski, Dimsdale, & Hackett, 1985). Further, when the level of warm behaviors was low, neither the Type A behavior pattern nor self-referencing was related significantly to blood pressure reactivity in any of the analyses. The fact that we found differences in subjects' behaviors across interview styles is consistent with other findings that subjects' and interviewers' behaviors covary significantly (cf., Howland and Siegman, 1982; Scherwitz, Graham, Grandits, & Billings, 1987).

These differences and patterns of correlation suggest strongly that the nature of the relationship between subjects and interviewers cannot be ignored in evaluating the meaning of subjects' behaviors. In this regard, Scherwitz (1988a, b) has argued that the stimulus-response model of assessment should be replaced with a transactional model. The implication of his argument is that the methodology for assessment should involve a shift in focus from the interviewer's behaviors alone to the relationship between interviewer and subjects. The relevance of Scherwitz's argument to the present studies can be seen concretely by examining the issues of warmth and emphasis in the context of how they have been viewed traditionally.

In his papers describing the administration of the SI, Rosenman (1978; Chesney, Eagleston, & Rosenman, 1980) has downplayed the need to maintain rapport with subjects and instead has emphasized the need to challenge them behaviorally through the style of delivery of the interview. We believe that this focus has led interviewers to pay insufficient attention to the establishment and maintenance of rapport and to overemphasize the role of stylistic challenge. Also, the lack of clearly stated limits to the amount of challenge may well have fostered the assumption that if some challenge is good, more challenge is better. This is not to say that Type A behaviors can be observed validly under routine, everyday conditions. Rather, what our experience does suggest is that the special, activating conditions that are most necessary for eliciting Type A behaviors validly may be those that establish and maintain rapport with subjects (e.g., Friedman & Powell, 1984; Scherwitz, 1988a, b), rather than those that test their tolerance for being challenged by heavy emphasis and so forth. Rather than standardizing interviewers' behavior across subjects invariantly regardless of the degree of engagement achieved, it may be more desirable to standardize the degree of engagement achieved across subjects by varying interviewers' behavior as necessary.

Reexamination of existing studies can be valuable in identifying the parameters of interviewing style which might affect the validity of assessment. The optimal mix of parameters such as rapport and challenge, however, can only be determined from their systematic manipulation in planned investigations. Such investigations will also, of necessity, produce greater precision in the definition of the parameters than has been the case in the past. All of these corrective processes, although time-consuming and often tedious, promise to bring greater reliability and validity to the assessment of coronary-prone behaviors.

In conclusion, we started by reexamining two studies of blood pressure reactivity which at first appeared to yield inconsistent relationships for the Type A behavior pattern and self-referencing. By examining the interaction of the Type A behavior pattern and self-referencing as risk factors and by classifying our samples according to interview style, we were able to demonstrate substantial consistency of relationships with reactivity. Our success in this regard as well as the parallelism between our seemingly inconsistent results and the inconsistent results reported for CHD incidence in the WCGS and MRFIT suggest that the present approach might be used profitably in the reexamination of these and other data sets.

REFERENCES

Bartko, J.J. (1966). The intraclass correlation coefficient of reliability. *Psychological Reports, 19,* 3-11.

Blumenthal, J.A., Williams, R.B., Kong, Y., Schanberg, S.M., & Thompson, L.W. (1978). Type A behavior and coronary atherosclerosis. *Circulation, 58,* 634-639.

Booth-Kewley, S., & Friedman, H.S. (1987). Psychological predictors of heart disease: A quantitative review. *Psychological Bulletin, 101,* 343-362.

Brockner, J. (1979). The effects of self-esteem, success-failure, and self-consciousness on task performance. *Journal of Personality and Social Psychology, 37,* 1732-1741.

Buss, A.H. (1980). *Self-consciousness and social anxiety.* San Francisco, Freeman & Co.

Caffrey, B. (1969). Behavior patterns and personality characteristics related to prevalence rates of coronary heart disease in American monks. *Journal of Chronic Disease, 22,* 93-103.

Carver, C.S., & Scheier, M.F. (1981). *Attention and self-regulation: A control-theory approach to human behavior.* New York: Springer-Verlag.

Chesney, M.A., Eagleston, J.R., & Rosenman, R.H. (1980). The Type A Structured Interview: A behavioral assessment in the rough. *Journal of Behavioral Assessment,* 2, 255-272.

Cooper, T., Detre, T., & Weiss, S.M. (1981). Coronary-prone behavior and coronary heart disease: A critical review. *Circulation, 63,* 1199-1215.

Davis, D., & Brock, T.C. (1975). Use of first person pronouns as a function of increased objective self-awareness and performance feedback. *Journal of Experimental Social Psychology, 11,* 381-388.

Dembroski, T.M., & MacDougall, J.M. (1983). Behavioral and psychophysiological perspectives on coronary-prone behavior. In T.M. Dembroski, T.H. Schmidt, & G. Blumchen (Eds.), *Biobehavioral bases of coronary heart disease* (pp. 106-129). Basel, Switzerland: Karger.

Dembroski, T.M., MacDougall, J.M., Williams, R.B., Haney, T.L., & Blumenthal, J.A. (1985). Components of Type A, hostility and anger-in: Relationship to angiographic findings. *Psychosomatic Medicine, 47,* 219-233.

Dimsdale, J.E., Hackett, T.P., Hutter, A.M., Block, P.C., Catanzano, D.M., & White, P.J. (1979). Type A behavior and angiographic findings. *Journal of Psychosomatic Research, 23*, 273-276.

Duval, S. & Wicklund, R.A. (1972). *A theory of objective self-awareness*. New York: Academic Press.

Fontana, A.F., Rosenberg, R.L., Kerns, R.D., & Marcus, J.L. (1986). Social insecurity, the Type A behavior pattern, and sympathetic arousal. *Journal of Behavioral Medicine, 9*, 79-88.

Frank, K.A., Heller, S.S., Kornfeld, D.S., Sporn, A.A., & Weiss, M.B. (1978). Type A behavior pattern and coronary angiographic findings. *Journal of the American Medical Association, 240*, 761-763.

Friedman, H.S., & Booth-Kewley, S. (1987). Personality, Type A behavior, and coronary heart disease: The role of emotional expression. *Journal of Personality and Social Psychology, 33*, 783-792.

Friedman, M., & Rosenman, R.H. (1959). Association of specific overt behavior pattern with blood and cardiovascular findings. *Journal of the American Medical Association, 169*, 1286-1296.

Friedman, M., & Rosenman, R.H. (1974). *Type A behavior and your heart*. New York: Knopf.

Friedman, M. & Powell, L.H. (1984). The diagnosis and quantitative assessment of Type A behavior: Introduction and description of the Videotaped Structured Interview. *Integrative Psychiatry, 2*, 123-129.

Friedman, M. & Ulmer, D. (1984). *Treating Type A behavior and your heart*. New York: Fawcett Crest.

Graham, L.E., Scherwitz, L., & Brand, R. (1988). Self-references and CHD incidence in the Western Collaborative Group Study. *Ninth Annual Proceedings, Society of Behavioral Medicine*, p. 58 (Abstract).

Hollingshead, A.B. (1957). *Two-factor index of social position*. New Haven, CT, Yale University.

Houston, B.K.. (1983). Psychophysiological responsivity and the Type A behavior pattern. *Journal of Research in Personality, 17*, 22-39.

Howland, E.W., & Siegman, A.W. (1982). Toward the automated measurement of the Type-A behavior pattern. *Journal of Behavioral Medicine, 5*, 37-54.

Ickes, W.J., Wicklund, R.A., & Ferris, C.B. (1973). Objective self-awareness and self-esteem. *Journal of Experimental Social Psychology, 9*, 202-219.

Kirk, R.E. (1968). *Experimental design: Procedures for the behavioral sciences*. Belmont, CA: Brooks/Cole Publishing Company.

MacDougall, J.M., Dembroski, T.M., Dimsdale, J.E., & Hackett, T.P. (1985). Components of Type A, hostility, and anger-in: Further relationships to angiographic findings. *Health Psychology, 4*, 137-152.

Matthews, K.A. (1982). Psychological perspectives on the Type A behavior pattern. *Psychological Bulletin, 91*, 293-323.

Matthews, K.A., & Haynes, S.G. (1986). Type A behavior pattern and coronary disease risk: Update and critical evaluation. *American Journal of Epidemiology, 123*, 923-960.

Price, V.A. (1982). *Type A behavior pattern: A model for research and practice*. New York: Academic Press.

Ragland, D.R., & Brand, R.J. (1988). Type A behavior and mortality from coronary heart disease. *New England Journal of Medicine, 318*, 65-69.

Rosenman, R.H. (1978). The interview method of assessment of the coronary-prone behavior pattern. In T.M. Dembroski, S.M. Weiss, J.L. Shields, S.G. Haynes, & M. Feinleib (Eds.), *Coronary-prone behavior* (pp. 55-69). New York: Springer-Verlag.

Rosenman, R.H., Brand, R.J., Jenkins, C.D., Friedman, M., Straus, R., & Wurm, M. (1975). Coronary heart disease in the Western Collaborative Group Study: Final follow-up experience of 8 1/2 years. *Journal of the American Medical Association, 233*, 872-877.

Rosenman, R.H., & Chesney, M.A. (1980). The relationship of Type A behavior pattern to coronary heart disease. *Activitas Nervosa Superior, 22*, 1-45.

Shekelle, R.B., Hulley, S.B., Neaton, J.D., Billings, J.H., Borhani, N.O., Gerace, T.A., Jacobs, D.R., Lasser, N.L., Mittlemark, M.B., & Stamler, J. (1985). The MRFIT behavior pattern study. II. Type A behavior and incidence of coronary heart disease. *American Journal of Epidemiology, 122*, 559-570.

Scherwitz , L. (1988a). Interviewer behaviors in the Western Collaborative Group Study and the Multiple Risk Factor Intervention Trial Structured Interviews. In B.K. Houston & C.R. Snyder (Eds.), *Type A behavior pattern: Current trends and future directions*. New York: Wiley & Sons.

Scherwitz, L. (1988b). Type A behavior assessment in the Structured Interview: Review, critique, and recommendations. In A. Siegman (Ed.), *In search of coronary-prone behavior*. Hillsdale, NJ: Erlbaum Press.

Scherwitz, L., Berton, K., & Leventhal, H. (1978). Type A behavior, self-involvement, and cardiovascular response. *Psychosomatic Medicine, 40*, 593-609.

Scherwitz, L., McKelvain, R., Laman, C., Patterson, J., Dutton, L., Yusim, S., Lester, J., Kraft, I., Rochelle, D., & Leachman, R. (1983). Type A behavior, self-involvement, and coronary atherosclerosis. *Psychosomatic Medicine, 45*, 47-56.

Scherwitz, L., Graham, L.E., & Ornish, D. (1985). Self-involvement and the risk factors for coronary heart disease. *Advances, 2*, 6-18.

Scherwitz, L., Graham, L.E., Grandits, G., Buehler, J., & Billings, J. (1986). Self-involvement and coronary heart disease incidence in the Multiple Risk Factor Intervention Trial. *Psychosomatic Medicine, 48*, 187-199.

Scherwitz, L., Graham, L.E., Grandits, G., & Billings, J. (1987). Speech characteristics and behavior-type assessment in the Multiple Risk Factor Intervention Trial (MRFIT) Structured Interviews. *Journal of Behavioral Medicine, 10*, 173-195.

Scherwitz, L. & Canick, J. (1988). Self-reference and coronary heart disease risk. In B.K. Houston & C.R. Snyder (Eds.), *Type A behavior pattern: Research, theory, and intervention*. New York: Wiley.

Scherwitz, L. & Pavone, R. (1988). *The self and the soma: A review and meta-theory of self-processes and coronary heart disease risk factors*. Unpublished manuscript.

Strube, M.J., Boland, S.M., Manfredo, P.A., & Al-Falaij, A. (1987). Type A behavior pattern and the self-evaluation of abilities: Empirical tests of the self-appraisal model. *Journal of Personality and Social Psychology, 52*, 956-974.

Turner, R.G., Scheier, M.F., Carver, C.S., & Ickes, W. (1978). Correlates of self-consciousness. *Journal of Personality Assessment, 42*, 285-289.

Self-Ratings and Perceptions of Type A Traits in Adult Twins

Dorit Carmelli, Ph.D.
Gary E. Swan, Ph.D.
Ray H. Rosenman, M.D.
Health Sciences Program, SRI International, Menlo Park, CA 94025

The present study utilized a large cohort of adult male twins to explore reported perceptions of Type A behavior in twin brothers and examined discrepancies between self-ratings and ratings of brothers as a function of zygosity, twin closeness, and the Type A-Type B pairing. The implications of the findings for heritability estimates of self report Type A ratings were also investigated. The results show that the overall concordance between self report and brother's report was low—of the order of 50%, regardless of zygosity. We observed a consistent tendency to rate one's brother higher than oneself on Type A characteristics, and this tendency was also dependent on the characteristics of who was doing the ratings. When twins were stratified on the extreme low (Type B) and extreme high (Type A) end of their self reports, we observed that Type B individuals rated their brothers consistently higher on Type A behaviors, regardless of whether the brother rated himself as an A or a B. We also found that the twins' reported closeness mediated intra-twin-pair differences of these traits. When examined by twins' reported closeness, the intraclass correlations and heritability estimates were different from the overall values. The implications of these results to self report measures of Type A traits and heritability estimates derived from twins are discussed.

At present, there are two approaches to assessment of the Type A behavior pattern (TABP): behavior ratings based on a structured interview (Rosenman, 1978); and a number of self-administered questionnaires, including the JAS (Jenkins, Zyzanski, & Rosenman, 1979), the Bortner Scale (Bortner, 1969), the Framingham Type A scale (Haynes, Levine, Scotch, et al., 1978), a modified self-report scale taken from the Gough Adjective Checklist (ACL) (Gough & Heilbrun, 1975), and the Eysenck-Fulker Scale (Eysenck, 1985). Both the structured interview and

---

Authors' Note: Supported by the National Heart, Lung, and Blood Institute Contract N01-HC-55029 and Grant HL32795.

© 1990 Select Press

the self-administered questionnaires contain a series of questions seeking the subject's self-report concerning everyday traits and behaviors relevant to the Type A dimension. The structured interview, however, goes farther than just the content of the response by including items intended to elicit and assess specific verbal and nonverbal Type A behaviors within the context of the interview itself.

Self-report measures of TABP are concerned largely with the assessment of perceived attitudes, attributes, and activities rather than being objective measures of behavior (Byrne, Rosenman, Schiller, et al., 1985). Therefore, for Type A questionnaires, as for all questionnaires that rely on the self-report strategy, there may be response bias that diminishes the accuracy of subjects' responses concerning the presence or absence of Type A related behaviors. Many Type As believe that they lack the very qualities (Type A traits) from which they actually suffer a surfeit (Rosenman & Chesney, 1982). Thus, the question of how Type As perceive their own behavioral style relative to how others view them is an issue of considerable importance.

The present study pursued this question through a systematic comparison of self-perceptions of subjects' TABP attributes with those reported by their twin brothers. The choice of the twin design seemed appropriate for several reasons. First, same-sex twins provide a measure of environmental control not otherwise possible with singletons by virtue of sharing such factors as birth rank, parental age and experience, schooling, and nutrition. Second, since the origins of the Type A behavior pattern can be seen largely in the environments in which early learning takes place, the study of TABP in the context of family presents an opportunity to explore such early environmental influences (Matthews, 1981; Kahn, 1984). Third, by studying twins, useful estimates can be obtained of genetic versus environmental factors in the variance of the trait studied.

A second issue examined in the present study is the extent to which twin closeness mediates discrepancies between self-report and brother's report of Type A as a function of zygosity. Since twins' reported closeness may mediate the extent to which twin brothers acknowledge the presence of Type A characteristics in each other, we also present in the current study an approach to ascertain differences in environmental covariances between monozygotic (MZ) and dizygotic (DZ) twins by grouping twins on self reported closeness.

METHODS

The present study was part of a larger investigation of demographic, metabolic, cardiorespiratory, anthropometric, social, and psychological aspects of proneness to coronary heart disease in identical and fraternal twins. All twins participating in these studies were Caucasian, male, and American veterans of World War II and/or the Korean conflict. At intake in 1970-71, 514 twin pairs participated in the first clinical examination of the NHLBI Twin Study. Details of the recruitment process, response rate, determination of zygosity, and examination protocol for this study were published elsewhere (Jablon, Neel, & Gershowitz, 1967; Feinleib, Garrison, Fabsitz, et al., 1977).

During 1981-82, 792 twin subjects returned for a second examination, and during 1987-88, 622 twins participated in a third examination. As part of the third examination, the Adjective Checklist (ACL) Type A scale was administered to all participants in the exam. The analyses reported here were conducted on 266 pairs (134 monozygotic and 132 dizygotic pairs) with complete data.

The ACL Type A scale is a 20-item self-report inventory developed from examining the associations of individual items with ratings of the structured interview (Herman, Blumenthal, Black, et al., 1981). The ACL questionnaires were mailed to the subjects before the examination with instructions to circle the number that seemed to represent best the extent to which each statement was self-descriptive. Examples of Type A adjectives include: aggressive, energetic, dominant, ambitious. Examples of the Type B adjectives are: calm, relaxed, or cautious. Each of these 20 statements was accompanied by a four-point scale, point 1 being labeled "always" and point 4 "never." When twin subjects came to the examination site, they were given the same questionnaire and asked to circle the number for each adjective that best described their twin brother. Since twins were examined separately, the two ratings of self versus brother were done independently. In addition to the ACL ratings, reported twin closeness was assessed. Each subject was asked to rate "closeness" with his twin brother in comparison with ordinary (nontwin) brothers. Possible responses were on a four-point scale (1 = less close, 2 = as close, 3 = somewhat closer, and 4 = much closer). To avoid small sample sizes, we collapsed categories 1 and 2 and categories 3 and 4 to form two categories "as close" and "closer."

Statistical Methods

The distributions of self- and brother's ACL Type A ratings were examined by zygosity, and the corresponding intraclass correlations were calculated. The available data permit three types of comparisons: those based on self-ratings, those based on brother's ratings, and the comparison of self-ratings with ratings of the brother (see Figure 1). For each possible pairing, the twin pair differences and intraclass correlations were calculated. These differences were examined in relation to twins' reported

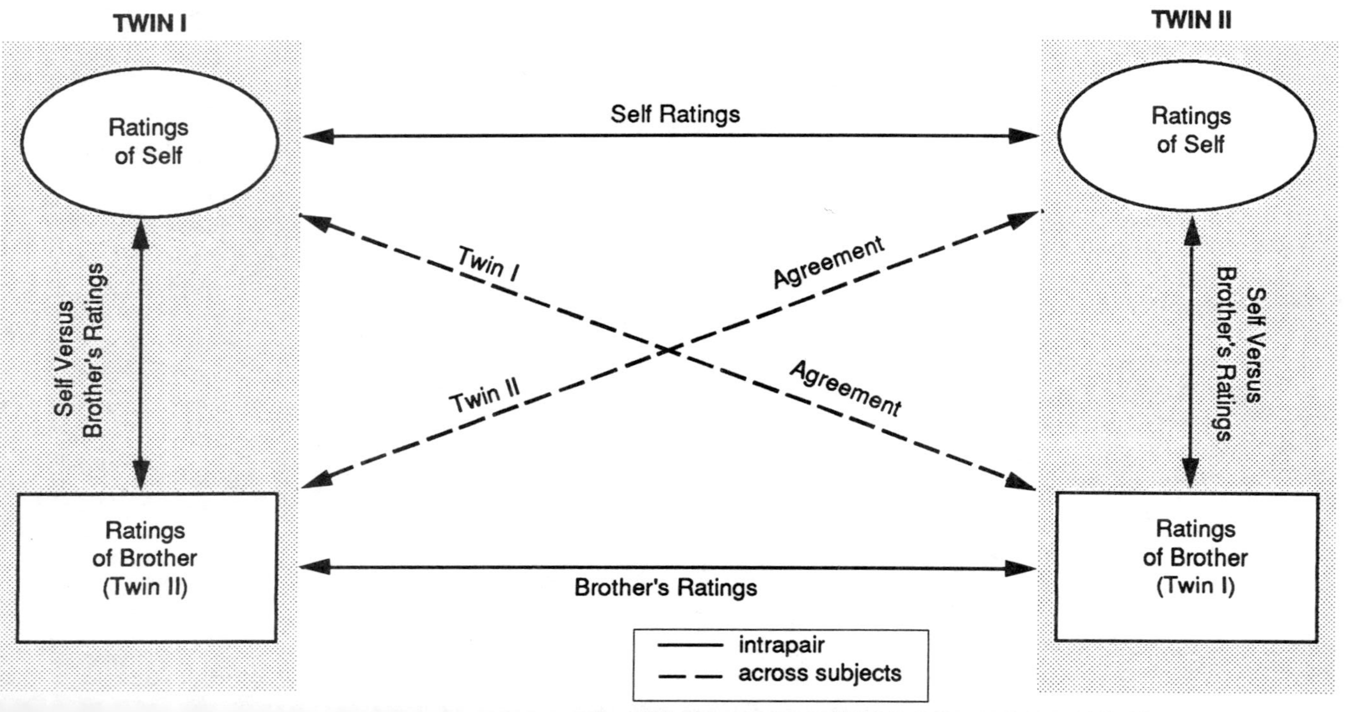
TWIN I
TWIN II
Ratings of Self
Self Ratings
Ratings of Self
Self Versus Brother's Ratings
Twin I
Agreement
Twin II
Agreement
Self Versus Brother's Ratings
Ratings of Brother (Twin II)
Brother's Ratings
Ratings of Brother (Twin I)
intrapair
across subjects

closeness only for pairs who agreed on their closeness ratings. The extreme Type A-Type B pairings were constructed using ACL self-reports. The distribution was divided into thirds with the lower and upper third designated as the Type B and Type A categories, respectively. The joint distribution of these rankings was formed and three groups of pairs were identified on these extremes: both Type A; both Type B; and one Type A, one Type B. For each possible Type A-Type B pairing, the twin pair differences of self-ratings and brother's ratings were calculated. The objective in this analysis was to ascertain the magnitude of differences of self-ratings and brother's ratings on the low versus high end of the distribution (e.g., to what extent are the A-A pairs different in their perception of the brother's characteristics compared to the B-B pairs).

To test heritability, we used two estimates: the classical heritability estimate of Falconer (Henderson, 1982), $2(r_{MZ} - r_{DZ})$, and the Holzinger estimate $(r_{MZ} - r_{DZ})/(1 - r_{DZ})$, where r_{MZ} and r_{DZ} are the intraclass correlation coefficients for monozygotic and dizygotic twin pairs, respectively. To preclude a possible bias in these estimates, the means and total variances of the MZ and DZ twin samples were compared using the corresponding T' and F' tests of Christian et al. (Christian, Kang, & Norton, 1974). In addition, heritability estimates of self- and brother's ACL Type A ratings were examined in twin pairs stratified by their closeness ratings.

RESULTS

We first examined the distribution of self-ratings and brother's ratings in monozygotic (MZ) and dizygotic (DZ) twins (see Table 1). We observed for both zygosities a significant difference in means, ($p < 0.001$) with brother's ratings always higher, indicating a tendency to attribute more Type A traits to the brother than to oneself. This difference persisted for the different percentiles of the distribution and was not present for the variances. Thus a persistent shift in the distribution of brother's versus self-ratings is evident across all subjects. Since higher scores imply more Type A traits, we conclude that, on the average, there is a tendency to attribute more Type A characteristics to one's brother than to oneself.

Table 2 presents intraclass correlations and concordance correlations for self-ratings and brother's ratings. The values below the diagonal describe MZ twins, and the values above describe DZ twins. For both self-ratings and brother's ratings, all possible Twin I by Twin II cross-correlations were calculated. Correlations between ratings of two members of a pair represent an intrapair correlation; correlations between self-report and brother's report for either Twin I or Twin II represent agreements between self and brother's ratings. (See Figure 1.)

TABLE 1 Distribution Characteristics of Self and Brother's ACL Type A Rating by Zygosity

	*MZ (n = 300)**		*DZ (n = 319)**	
	Self-Ratings	*Brother's Ratings*	*Self-Ratings*	*Brother's Ratings*
Mean	47.01	49.32	47.11	48.78
Standard deviation	5.83	5.89	5.08	5.72
Minimum	34	33	35	29
25%	43	45	44	45
Median	47	49	47	48
75%	51	53	50	52
Maximum	67	66	62	69

**The sample sizes represent all the individual participants in exam III of the NHLBI study, including twins that came to the exam without their brothers.*

Two results emerge from examination of the correlations in Table 2. First, the agreement between self-ratings and brother's ratings is about 0.50, independent of zygosity. Second, MZ intrapair correlations are significant and of the same order of magnitude for all pairwise comparisons, ranging from 0.41 to 0.48. For DZ twins the corresponding intratwin correlations are nonsignificant and close to zero. On the assumption that MZ and DZ twin pairs differ in their perceptions of similarities between

TABLE 2 Intraclass Correlations and Reliability in Self-Rating and Brother's Rating by Zygosity

		Self-Report		*Brother's Report*	
		Twin I	*Twin II*	*Twin II*	*Twin I*
Self-Report	Twin I	—	-0.05	0.06	(0.45)
	Twin II	0.45	—	(0.43)	0.05
Brothers' Report	Twin II	0.48	(0.56)	—	0.04
	Twin I	(0.51)	0.45	0.41	—

Note: ( ) represents agreement between self-ratings and brother's ratings. Values above and below diagonal are corresponding DZ and MZ correlations.

TABLE 3 Twin Pair Differences (Mean ± Standard Error) ACL Self-Ratings and Brother's Ratings According to Twins' Reported Closeness[a]

Differences	*As Close as Ordinary Siblings (n = 34)*	*Closer Than Ordinary Siblings (n = 162)*
Self-ratings	2.85 ± 1.18*	-0.09 ± 0.50
Brother's ratings	1.22 ± 1.11	0.01 ± 0.57
Brother's versus self-ratings	1.02 ± 1.20	1.81 ± 0.54**

[a] *Only pairs where both twins agreed on their responses to closeness were included; this criterion excluded 69 pairs.*
* *Significantly different from zero at $p < 0.05$.*
** *Significantly different from zero at $p < 0.01$.*

them, we expected correlations between self-ratings and ratings of brothers to be somewhat larger than those of self-reports, but only a slight positive association was indicated ($r = 0.06$ as compared with $r = -0.05$).

Self- and Brother's ACL Ratings as a Function of Twin Closeness

Anticipating that twin closeness would influence the responses of brother's ratings, we examined intra-pair differences by twins' response to this question. Of the total 264 pairs, 161 pairs (61%) viewed themselves as closer than ordinary brothers, 34 pairs (13%) considered themselves as close as ordinary siblings, and 69 pairs (26%) disagreed regarding closeness. Table 3 describes twin pair differences on self-ratings and brother's ratings for the two groups of twins that agreed on closeness. Twin pairs that disagreed in their responses to closeness were excluded from this analysis.

Examination of twin pair differences by closeness reveals that twins who viewed themselves as closer than ordinary siblings show a pattern similar to that observed in Table 2, i.e., ratings of one's brother being significantly higher than self-ratings; all other differences show no significant trend. For twin pairs who considered themselves as close as ordinary siblings, the within-pair difference for ACL self-reports is significantly different from zero.

The question remains as to how these results influence heritability estimates. We already know from results for the intraclass correlations reported in Table 2 that no matter what combination of twin ratings is used, estimates of heritability will be the same. However, since closeness mediated twin pair differences on self-ratings as compared to brother's ratings and the distributions of these responses differed in MZ and DZ twins, we examined the effect of closeness on estimates of heritability.

Table 4 summarizes the heritability analysis for the sample as a whole and stratified by reported closeness. We first observe that MZ twins rate themselves "closer than ordinary siblings" more often than DZ twins ($p < 0.001$). This group, labeled the "closer" group, consists of 98 MZ and 63 DZ pairs, and the intraclass correlations in MZ and DZ twins show a pattern similar to that observed for the total sample. In the "as close" group, consisting of 9 MZ and 25 DZ pairs, we observe a different pattern. MZ intraclass correlations for self-report, and self-report versus brother's report are of the same order of magnitude as in the closer group (average across ratings = 0.40). The correlations for DZ twins in the group that rated themselves as close as ordinary siblings are positive and approaching significance (average of all ratings = 0.27). The lack of overall statistical significance of the different heritability estimates may be due to reduced sample sizes; however, the pattern of intraclass correlations in the group of twins who rated themselves as close as ordinary siblings does not support a hypothesis of significant gene effects.

Self- and Brother's ACL Type A Ratings as a Function of Type A-Type B Twin Pairings

Table 5 shows intrapair differences on self-ratings, brother's ratings, and self-ratings versus brother's ratings for the extreme Type A-Type B pairs defined by the upper and lower thirds of self-reported ACL adjectives. The striking result from this analysis is the asymmetry in intrapair differences for brother's versus self-ratings in the A-A as compared with the B-B pairs—A-A pairs show a closer match between self-ratings and brother's ratings than B-B pairs. The mean difference in self-ratings versus brother's ratings for A-A pairs is 1.52 (not significantly different from zero); in B-B pairs this difference is 3.81 (more than twice the mean difference in A-A pairs). This asymmetry in self-ratings versus brother's ratings is also reflected in comparing the differences in brother's ratings; the A-A intrapair differences in brother's ratings are larger than the B-B differences, and the differences are in the opposite direction to those observed for self-ratings versus brother's ratings. Finally, no asymmetry in intrapair differences was observed for self-ratings in A-A pairs as compared with B-B pairs.

TABLE 4 Intrapair Correlations and Estimates of Heritability and ACL Type A Source of Rating According to Twin Closeness

Ratings	*Total Sample*				*As Close as Ordinary Siblings*				*Closer Than Ordinary Siblings*			
	MZ	*DZ*	*Heritability Estimates*		*MZ*	*DZ*	*Heritability Estimates*		*MZ*	*DZ*	*Heritability Estimates*	
	(n=134)	*(N=132)*	*F*	*H*[a]	*(n=9)*	*(n=25)*	*F*	*H*	*(n-98)*	*(N-63)*	*F*	*H*
Self-rating	0.45	-0.05	1.00	0.48*	0.39	0.13	0.52	0.30	0.42	-0.07	0.98	0.46*
Brother's rating	0.42	0.04	0.75	0.39*	0.18	0.45	-0.54	-0.49	0.44	-0.09	1.06	0.49*
Self versus	0.48	0.06	0.85	0.45*	0.47	0.25	0.44	0.29	0.45	0.07	0.76	0.41*
brother's rating	0.45	0.05	0.80	0.42*	0.54	0.23	0.62	0.40	0.42	0.04	0.76	0.40*
Average					*0.40*	*0.27*	*0.26*	*0.18*	*0.43*	*-0.01*	*0.88*	*0.44*

[a]*Significance levels for Holzinger H were determined by the F test for the within-pair variances.*

*$p < .01$.

F - Falconer estimate; H - Holzinger estimate.

TABLE 5 Twin Pair Differences (Mean ± Standard Error) in Self-Ratings and Brother's Ratings According to Type A-Type B Twin Pairings

	Type B-Type B *(n = 44)*	*Type A-Type A* *(n = 37)*	*Type B-Type A* *(n = 23)*	*Type A-Type B* *(n = 27)*
Self-ratings	0.89 ± 0.55	0.94 ± 0.61	12.56 ± 0.72*	-10.52 ± 0.89*
Brother's ratings	0.50 ± 1.06	2.10 ± 0.95*	4.70 ± 1.83*	-2.08 ± 1.43
Brother's versus self-ratings	3.81 ± 0.86*	1.52 ± 0.92	8.63 ± 1.36*	-6.39 ± 1.40*

*$p < .01$.

DISCUSSION

The approach taken in the present study derives directly from recent theoretical re-formulations of the Type A construct as a transactional social phenomenon. In this view, coronary-prone behaviors are seen as active inter-personal processes rather than passive traits, and attitudes of individual people (Smith & Rhodewalt, 1986; Rose, 1988). Given the increased recognition being given to the social nature of Type A, we believe that the family and, more specifically, the assumed relationship between twin siblings is a good starting model for testing this hypothesis. Of course, any relationship in which the participants have a history of interaction could serve as an appropriate dynamic model that could, in turn, be used in a similar fashion to that used in the present study.

We viewed this study as an examination of the perceptual differences that exist between the members of dyads who know each other extremely well and who are asked to rate each other on traits descriptive of Type A behavior. The primary objective was to identify the magnitude of dyadic differences in perception of coronary-prone characteristics and the extent to which pair-wise differences are mediated by the "closeness," i.e., the social contact, with which they might occur. Our results suggest that the extent to which members of the dyad are close to each other and share common coronary-prone characteristics is an important determinant of the social and perceptual processes exhibited in the test setting.

The ACL Type A scale was used as a vehicle to study these processes because it is a self (or peer) report instrument. In fact, if we accept that coronary-prone characteristics occur in a social, interpersonal context, then the report by each member of a given dyad about the other member of the dyad seems to be an essential piece of the assessment puzzle. We now report the main findings from our analyses:

(a) There is a consistent tendency to rate one's brother higher on Type A characteristics than oneself, regardless of zygosity. The distribution of scores, while shifted upward, retains basic similarity to that for the self-ratings. These consistent differences between self-ratings and brother's ratings may be attributed to the influence that social desirability is thought to have on ACL responses. Our use of the term "social desirability" to explain mean differences between self ratings and brother ratings refers primarily to the less desirable of the Type A traits. While this is a possible contributor to the mean differences observed here, we believe that previous evidence has shown a tendency for Type A individuals to under-report negative characteristics; a response bias observed specifically for the ACL scale (Herman, Blumenthal, Black, et al., 1981). Whether the response bias results from true lack of insight or a strong tendency to want to present oneself in a positive way remains to be seen. We believe coronary-prone individuals have a strong need to appear good to the outside world in a way that irrevocably influences their social interactions (Scherwitz & Canick, 1988). Understanding this self-perceptual process would represent a true advance in the assessment of coronary-proneness.

(b) Within twin pairs, the tendency to rate the brother higher than oneself on Type A attributes depends on the characteristics of the person doing the ratings. Type B individuals appear to rate their brothers consistently higher on Type A traits, regardless of whether their brothers are A's or B's. When an A twin rates his B brother, the difference in scores is not of the same magnitude as when a B rates an A (-6.39 compared with 8.63). These differences could be explained by two main hypotheses that may interact with the personality pairings: (a) significant underreporting of Type A-related self-characteristics in Type B individuals and (b) overreporting of brother characteristics that is influenced by an increased sensitivity and awareness to such behaviors and their social implications. Thus, for the B-B pairings it is possible that individuals underreport self-characteristics and overreport brother's characteristics so that the difference becomes larger. The results for the A-A pairings suggest that A twins tend to attribute characteristics to their A twin brothers similar to themselves. We speculate that Type B individuals are more accurate in assessing Type A characteristics. This consistent tendency may be related to perceptual/personality makeup unique to Type B's that so far has been overlooked in TABP research.

(c) An important aspect of the current study was to examine the difference that exists between Type A self-ratings and the Type A ratings of a twin brother as a function of the twins' reported closeness. In the current study, pairs who viewed themselves as closer than ordinary siblings showed a significant difference between self-ratings and ratings of brothers. On the other hand, twins who considered themselves to be as close as ordinary siblings showed no difference between self-ratings and ratings of brothers. This mediating effect of perceived closeness can be confounded, as before, by social desirability. To the extent that one is closer to his twin brother, he wishes to rate him in a more desirable light—so that the adjectives on the ACL indicative of strength, aggressiveness, and assertiveness become exaggerated.

Finally, we demonstrated in the current study the relationship between twins' perceived closeness and their effects on heritability estimates of self-reported behaviors. One of the major criticisms of the twin method is that a "mutual effect" operates within twin pairs to bias estimates of heritability (Henderson, 1982). The hypothesis is that the development of a particular behavior in one twin might influence the other twin of a pair to react in a way that might increase or decrease their degree of similarity. This mechanism will operate differently in MZ and DZ pairs. The best examples can be found in those instances where the MZ correlation coefficients are inflated and highly significant, whereas DZ correlations are not significantly different from zero. This pattern of intraclass correlations was evident for all the pairwise ACL Type A ratings: self-self, brother-brother, and self-brother. We therefore suspected from these results that MZ twins have more similar environments than DZ twins. To test this hypotheses we grouped the twins on the basis of self reported closeness. Calculating the average intraclass correlation across ratings, for each group and zygosity, we found that twins who consider themselves as close as ordinary siblings have a higher DZ intraclass correlation than twins who consider themselves as closer than ordinary siblings. In the most extreme case, if we assume that all MZ twins consider themselves as closer than ordinary siblings and all DZ twins as close as ordinary siblings, we would obtain intraclass correlations of 0.43 and 0.27 for MZ and DZ twin pairs, respectively. Thus, failure to take into account the operation of such a mutual effect might lead one to conclude erroneously the presence of a significant genetic variance for ACL self reported Type A traits when the estimate is simply a function of the twin's perceived closeness. In terms of assessing environmental covariance, the question "how close do you feel that you and your twin brother have been, compared to closeness between ordinary brothers" may be a simple but valuable measure of mutual effects and should be considered for inclusion in future twin studies.

The results of this analysis suggest that the study of Type A through self-report measures is likely to lead to an underestimation of the true prevalence of this trait in any given research sample. The downward bias may be as much as one-half standard deviation below the mean for Type A as seen by others; in the present study, the co-twin acted as the observer. This tendency to under-report less than desirable characteristics will become more important as the focus of Type A research moves to more "toxic" components such as hostility (Houston & Snyder, 1988). Hostility, as a psychological trait, would seem to have even fewer socially desirable aspects from the perspective of the person who is asked to complete a questionnaire such as the Ho scale (Cook & Medley, 1954). Thus, we would expect that future studies will find an even larger downward bias in prevalence estimates of "high hostile" people if they rely exclusively on self-report measures. One approach to solving the problem of under-reporting socially undesirable qualities involves the combined use of self-report, peer ratings such as those used in the present study, and independent ratings based on behavioral observation such as those found for the Type A Structured Interview (Rosenman, 1978). In this way, the estimation of the "true" prevalence of coronary-prone hostility could be triangulated. This approach would require the development of new strategies that go beyond present-day methodology.

REFERENCES

Bortner, R.W. (1969). A short rating scale as a potential measure of Pattern A behavior. *Journal of Chronic Diseases, 22*, 87-91.

Byrne, D.G., Rosenman, R.H., Schiller, E., & Chesney, M.A. (1985). Consistency and variation among instruments purporting to measure the Type A behavior pattern. *Psychosomatic Medicine, 47*, 242-261.

Christian, J.C., Kang, K.W., & Norton, H.A. (1974). Choice of an estimate of genetic variance from twin data. *American Journal of Human Genetics, 26*, 154-161.

Cook, W., and Medley, D. (1954). Proposed hostility and pharisaic-virtue scales for the MMPI. *Journal of Applied Psychology, 38*, 414-418.

Eysenck, H.J. (1985). Personality, cancer and cardiovascular disease: A causal analysis. *Personality and Individual Differences, 5*, 535-557.

Falconer, D. S. (1981). *Introduction to quantitative genetics* (2nd ed.). London: Longmans.

Feinleib, M., Garrison, R.J., Fabsitz, R.H., Christian, J.C., Huber, A., Borhani, N.O., Kannel, W.B., Rosenman, R.H., Schwartz, J.T., & Wagner, J. O. (1977). The NHLBI Twin Study of cardiovascular disease risk factors: Methodology and summary of results. *American Journal of Epidemiology, 106*, 284-295.

Gough, H.H., & Heilbrun, A.B. (1975). *The Adjective Checklist*. Palo Alto: Consulting Psychologists Press.

Haynes, S.G., Levine, S., Scotch, N., Feinleib, M., & Kannel, W.B. (1978). The relationship of psychosocial factors to coronary heart disease in the Framingham Study: I. Methods and risk factors. *American Journal of Epidemiology, 107*, 362-383.

Henderson, N.D. (1982). Human behavior genetics. *Annual Review of Psychology, 33*, 403-440.

Herman, S., Blumenthal, J.A., Black, G.W., Chesney, M. A., & Rosenman, R.H. (1981). Self ratings of Type A (coronary-prone) adults: Do Type A's know they are Type A's? *Psychosomatic Medicine, 43*, 405-413.

Houston, B.K., and Snyder, C.R. (1988). *Type A behavior pattern. Research, theory and intervention*. Wiley Series on Health Psychology/ Behavioral Medicine.

Jenkins, C.D., Zyzanski, S.J., & Rosenman, R.H. (1979). *The Jenkins Activity Survey*. New York: Psychological Corporation.

Kahn, A.S. (1984). *Social psychology*. Iowa: W.C. Brown.

Jablon S., Neel, J.V., & Gershowitz, H. (1967). The NAS-NRC Twin Panel: Methods of construction of the panel, zygosity, diagnosis, and proposed use. *American Journal of Human Genetics, 19*, 133-161.

Matthews, K.A. (1981). Antecedents of the Type A coronary-prone behavior pattern. In S. Brehm, S.M. Kassin, & F.X. Gibbons (Eds.). *Developmental social psychology: Theory and research*.

Rose, R.J. (1988). Genes, stress and the heart. *Stress Medicine, 4, 265-271*.

Rosenman, R.H. (1978). The interview method of assessment of the coronary-prone behavior pattern. In T.M. Dembroski, S. M. Weiss, J. L. Shields, S. G. Haynes, & M. Feinleib (Eds.), *Coronary-prone behavior*. New York: Springer-Verlag.

Rosenman, R.H., & Chesney, M.A. (1982). Stress, Type A behavior, and coronary disease. In L. Goldberger & S. Breznitz (Eds.), *Handbook of stress: Theoretical and clinical aspects*. New York: Free Press.

Scherwitz, L., & Canick, J.D. (1988). Self-reference and coronary heart disease risk. In B.K. Houston & C.R. Snyder. (Eds.), *Type A behavior pattern. Research, theory and intervention* (pp. 146-167). New York: Wiley.

Smith, T. W., & Rhodewalt, F. (1986). On states, traits, and processes: A transactional alternative to the individual differences assumptions in Type A behavior and physiological reactivity. *Journal of Research Personality, 20*, 229-251.

The Effect of Self-Consciousness on Type A and Type B Self-Schemata

Julia L. Bienias
Department of Psychology, University of Illinois
603 E. Daniel, Champaign, IL 61820

Michael J Strube
Department of Psychology, Washington University
St. Louis, MO 63130

This study examined the effect of trait private self-consciousness on the self-schema consistency of Type As and Type Bs. Reaction times to Type A and Type B adjectives were assessed twice. Initially, patterns of reaction times were shown to be consistent with schema theory predictions of information-processing advantages for schema-relevant items. A model-fitting approach was then taken to analyze the impact of subject classification (Type A-B, private self-consciousness) on the consistency between the two trait endorsement task trials. Subjects were very consistent in their responses, and the classification variables did not moderate this consistency. It was suggested that future studies into Type A and Type B self-schemata test the use of other tasks to define people as having self-schemata.

The Type A behavior pattern is characterized by a competitive striving for achievement, an exaggerated sense of time urgency, and easily aroused hostility. Its behavioral opposite is the Type B pattern, which is characterized by a relatively relaxed, easy-going, and patient lifestyle (for reviews, see Glass, 1977; Matthews, 1982). The Type A pattern appears to be stable and enduring (Jenkins, 1976). It represents an independent risk factor in the etiology of coronary heart disease (e.g., Cooper, Detre, & Weiss, 1981; Dembroski, Weiss, Shields, Haynes, &

Authors' Notes: This paper is based in part on research conducted in partial fulfillment of the Master of Arts degree by the first author at Washington University. Support was provided by a National Science Foundation Graduate Fellowship and by a grant-in-aid from the Washington University chapter of Sigma Xi, the Scientific Research Society, both to the first author. The authors wish to thank Stanley Wasserman for his helpful comments. Address correspondence to the first author.

© 1990 Select Press

Feinleib, 1978; Haynes, Feinleib, & Kannel, 1980; Rosenman, Brand, Jenkins, Friedman, Straus, & Wurm, 1975). This risk appears to be moderated by assessment procedures (Friedman & Booth-Kewley, 1987).

Although Type As and Bs exhibit some consistency in their behaviors, the patterns do not represent traits in the classic sense. Rather, psychological research indicates that the Type A pattern is best seen as an interactional or transactional variable. That is, Type A behavior is elicited more clearly in some situations than others, suggesting the need to investigate moderators of the display of Type A and B styles.

One such moderator appears to be the possession of a clear, coherent cognitive representation, or self-schema, that closely parallels overt behavior. For example, Strube et al. (1986) have demonstrated that individuals defined as Type A or B according to traditional measurement procedures possess clear self-schemata in the A and B domains. Given that self-schemata are presumed to be linked to overt behaviors, further examination of the cognitive representation of Type A and B patterns may provide insight into the display and stability of Type A and B behaviors.

The purpose of the present study was to further elucidate the self-schema concept associated with Type A behavior and investigate chronic self-awareness as a possible moderator of self-schema stability. Before turning to a discussion of self- awareness as a moderator of stability, a brief review of relevant work on self-schemata will be provided.

Self-Schemata

A schema is a hypothetical cognitive structure that "represents organized knowledge about a given concept or type of stimulus" (Fiske & Taylor, 1984, p. 140; see also Fiske & Linville, 1980; Hastie, 1981; Rumelhart & Ortony, 1977; Taylor & Crocker, 1981). A schema guides information processing. It implies a "theory-driven" or "top-down" method of gathering information about the environment. Knowledge of people and situations organized in this manner aids a person in making sense of new information. In particular, a self-schema is an "easily accessible verbal self- concept that guides information processing about the self" (Fiske & Taylor, 1984, p. 149). This includes information about one's personality, appearances, and behavior. If a person has a schema for a given characteristic or set of characteristics (e.g., those associated with Type A behavior), that person is said to be "schematic" along that dimension; otherwise, the person is called "aschematic." People are schematic "on dimensions that are important to them, on which they think of themselves as extreme, and on which they are certain the opposite does not hold" (Fiske & Taylor, 1984, p. 154; Markus, 1977).

Schema theory holds that self-schemata have several purposes. They channel and guide perception (see Markus & Sentis, 1982, for a review) and speed information processing. Because of this expected processing advantage, a common experimental task involves measuring subjects' reaction times when deciding whether or not a set of adjectives is self-descriptive. Experimental results show that having a schema allows a person to make rapid judgments about the self regarding such trait adjectives (Bargh, 1982). Self-schemata also exert a powerful, often distorting, effect on memory (Kuiper & Rogers, 1979; Rogers, 1981; Rogers, Kuiper, & Kirker, 1977; Rogers, Rogers, & Kuiper, 1979). People are more likely to remember and recall self-relevant information regarding their schemata. This finding has been replicated across diverse areas of study (e.g., Markus, Crane, Bernstein, & Siladi, 1982).

Self-schemata are "stubborn" as well; this is known as the "perseverance effect" (Fiske & Taylor, 1984, p. 171; Markus 1977). If this were not the case, one's self-image would be constantly changing, and there would be no information processing advantage (Ross, Lepper, & Hubbard, 1975). Thus, self-schemata help to stabilize behavior regarding the self.

Previous research in self-schemata has focused on identifying people who consider a certain set of trait adjectives to be self-descriptive and, sometimes, who see that dimension as important to their self-concept, in line with Markus' (1977) definition. These people are invariably labelled "schematic." Various predictions from schema-theory, such as better memory for schema-relevant adjectives and the "false alarms effect" of falsely recognizing schema-relevant adjectives, are often used to determine if the "schematic" group of people are behaving schematically. However, on the basis of the definitional criteria used, it is difficult to separate "schematic" individuals from people who merely have a given personality trait or pattern. Because of this, people who do not have as coherent a cognitive structure regarding the given dimension are aggregated with those who have a very coherent structure, potentially affecting the experimental results. An alternative approach would be to separate people initially into "potentially schematic" subgroups and then examine their performance on a standard task. Further research could examine many such behavioral criteria with the goal of developing a "test" for schematicity, one that would at least involve more criteria than are currently used. Hence, one specific purpose of this study was to further investigate the claim of schematicity and what classification variables might be used to better define it.

Self-Consciousness

A second specific purpose of the study was to examine a personality variable that might moderate behavioral consistency and schema accessibility among Type As and Bs. One such candidate is private self-consciousness, measured by a self-report questionnaire (Fenigstein, Scheier, & Buss, 1975). People who are high in private self-consciousness show "greater responsiveness to their internal states, including their behavioral tendencies and their attitudes" (Fiske & Taylor, 1984, p. 378; Froming & Carver, 1981; Scheier & Carver, 1983). They are "more likely to express attitudes that remain consistent over time" (Fiske & Taylor, 1984, p. 205).

Given that an individual who is high in private self-consciousness spends a great deal of time concentrating on the self, self-consciousness should moderate self-schema accessibility. Consistent with this premise, Hull and Levy (1979, Exp. 1) have shown that chronic self-attention aids encoding of self-relevant information. Private self-consciousness is also positively correlated with the speed of making decisions regarding trait adjectives (Turner, 1978). If self-schemata provide a cognitive counterpart to the behavior patterns of Type As and Bs, and if self-consciousness moderates behavioral consistency by making self-schemata more accessible (cf. Duval & Wicklund, 1972; Carver & Scheier, 1981), then an important determinant of behavioral consistency in Type As and Bs may be the degree to which they are chronically aware of their self-schemata.

Thus, this study focused specifically on private self-consciousness. The expectation was that a person's self-report consistency regarding trait adjectives should be a function of the level of private self-awareness. Highly self-conscious Type A schematic subjects should be more consistent in their responses in the A domain than schematic subjects lower in self-consciousness. A similar pattern should emerge for subjects schematic in the B domain. By contrast, temporal consistency among aschematics (subjects lacking a schema for a domain) should not depend on whether an individual is high or low in self-consciousness, because self-awareness cannot prime a schema that doesn't exist.

METHOD

Subjects

Subjects were 176 college volunteers (99 females and 77 males). The average age was 19.67 years (range, 17-27).

Procedure

Subjects were tested twice, approximately one week apart, in the same room (mean number of days was 7.14, range 7-10), at the same time of day, in what was described as a study examining the relationship between personality and attitudes toward human nature. During the first session they completed a short questionnaire assessing some of their attitudes toward human nature (to enhance the credibility of the cover story), the Jenkins Activity Survey, Form T (a student-adapted measure of the Type A behavior pattern; see Krantz, Glass, & Snyder, 1974), and the Self-Consciousness Scale (Fenigstein, Scheier, & Buss, 1975).

They also completed a reaction time task on a computer that served as part of the measure of Type A and B schematic representation. Adjectives were presented in a random order singly on the screen, and subjects responded by pushing one of two buttons, labelled "like me" and "not like me," indicating whether or not the adjectives described them. Sixty-six adjectives were used to represent each of the following: Type A behavior, Type B behavior, and neutral behavior (22 of each type). Response time was measured unbeknownst to the subjects (see Strube et al., 1986, for extensive discussion of the construction and validation of the word lists; see Markus, 1977, for a further description of this technique). The following week subjects completed the reaction time task again and were fully debriefed.

RESULTS

Following the practice of other researchers (e.g., Markus, 1977), an initial classification of "potential schematicity" was made on the basis of self-reports. That is, a median split was performed on the number of adjectives subjects endorsed during the first test session. The Jenkins Activity Survey (JAS) scores were trichotomized, yielding three approximately equal-sized groups. Only A adjectives were used to classify Type As and B adjectives to classify Type Bs. Isolating subjects who endorsed more than the median number of adjectives and were extreme on the JAS yielded three groups: those classified as A (JAS >= 10, number of A endorsements > 13, N = 45), those classified as B (JAS <= 5, number of B endorsements > 13, N = 36), and those classified as Neutral (all other subjects, N = 95).

The distribution of subjects' scores on the private self-consciousness scale was divided into thirds to ensure that subjects labelled "high" were, in fact, high on the private self-consciousness scale and, presumably, in private self-consciousness. This yielded three groups, those labelled "high" in private self-consciousness (PSC >= 29, N = 69), those labelled "low" (PSC <= 24, N = 54), and those labelled "medium" (N = 53).

Testing for Schematic Responding

In this first analysis, we were interested in testing whether or not subjects classified as "potentially schematic" by using the JAS and the number of adjectives endorsed did, in fact, behave in accord with having a schema.

Schema theory predicts that schema-consistent decisions should be made more quickly than schema-inconsistent decisions. To test this,

TABLE 1 Endorsement Decision Times (seconds) as a Function of Subject Type, Word Type, and Endorsement Type

Subject type/ endorsement type	*Word type*			
	Type A		*Type B*	
Type A (N=43)				
"Like me"	2.03	(0.95)	3.42	(1.70)
"Not like me"	3.24	(1.67)	2.89	(1.11)
Type B (N=35)				
"Like me"	3.04	(1.34)	2.32	(0.67)
"Not like me"	2.57	(0.97)	3.68	(2.26)
Type Neutral (N=95)				
"Like me"	2.69	(1.75)	2.78	(1.33)
"Not like me"	2.99	(1.71)	3.81	(2.11)

Note: Standard deviations are given in parentheses.

reaction time on the computer task was used. The prediction was that a Type A schematic should be able to decide that a given Type A adjective is self-descriptive (choosing "Like me" on the computer task) faster than deciding that a Type A adjective is not self-descriptive (choosing "Not like me"). Other subjects (who are not schematic in the Type A domain) should not exhibit as great a difference in response time to Type A adjectives. The reverse should hold for Type B schematics and Type B adjectives.

To test whether or not subjects classified as "potentially schematic" exhibited this processing advantage, the reaction time data[1] from the first test session were analyzed in a 3 (Subject type: A, B, or Neutral) x 2 (Word type: A or B) x 2 (Endorsement type: "Like me" or "Not like me") ANOVA, with repeated measures on the latter two factors. Because of the different predictions for subjects responding to A adjectives and B adjectives, and because the difference in reaction time between endorsement types was expected only for schematic subjects, a 3-way interaction was predicted. Three cases were excluded because the subjects had 0 endorsements of one type (e.g., 22 "Like me" responses for all A adjectives, no "Not like me" responses), so no mean reaction time could be

[1] *Analyses were performed on the raw, untransformed reaction time data, measured in seconds. Graphs of log transformed data were farther from approximating normality than the raw data. Further, Strube et al. (1986) noted that, in their study, the same pattern of results was found in both raw and log-transformed data.*

computed for that endorsement category. The means and standard deviations of the reaction times for the 12 cells are presented in Table 1. Because of the experimental manipulation[2] and because of possible practice effects, the data from session 2 were not similarly analyzed.

Results indicated that there was a main effect for Word type ($F(2,170) = 18.90, p < .001$) and for Endorsement type ($F(1,170) = 27.75, p < .001$). However, these were superseded by the expected 3-way interaction ($F(2,170) = 21.70, p < .001$). To test whether subjects exhibited the expected differences in reaction time, a priori Scheffe contrasts were conducted (using $MSE = 1.59$ and the 12 cells of the 3-way interaction). Because of the differences between the adjective lists, contrasts were performed within the lists and within the subtypes of people.

As expected, subjects initially classified as Type A responded with "Like me" more quickly than "Not like me" to schema-relevant, or A, words ($F(11,161) = 1.80, p = .06$; see Table 1). Similarly, Type Bs took more time to respond "Not like me" than "Like me" to B adjectives ($F(11,161) = 1.84, p = .05$). Thus, "potentially schematic" subjects were behaving schematically.

Neutral subjects were expected either to exhibit no differences between "Not like me" and "Like me" reaction times, or to take longer to respond "Not like me," as it is a general finding that negative decisions require greater processing time (e.g., Markus, 1977; Strube et al., 1986). For B adjectives, Neutral subjects took longer to respond "Not like me" ($F(11,161) = 2.90, p < .01$); the contrast for A adjectives was not significant. These results were consistent with the predictions and with the results found by Strube et al. (1986).

The Moderating Effect of Private Self-Consciousness

In this second analysis, we were interested in examining whether or not private self-consciousness affected the degree to which subjects were consistent in responding schematically during the two test sessions. In keeping with the above analysis, reaction times were used to represent schematic responding. Based on the above results and analysis (the expectation of differential processing time for the "Like me" and "Not like me" responses), the behavioral performance measure used in the subsequent analyses was differential reaction time, or the difference between the mean reaction time to adjectives not endorsed and the mean reaction

---

[2] *An additional variable, public self-attention, was manipulated by placing a mirror in front of half of the subjects during the second testing session. This variable was found to have no influence on subjects' performance on the reaction time task, so it is not discussed further here.*

time to adjectives endorsed, within each domain.[3] The same classification scheme, based on the number of endorsements and the JAS, was used.

The approach taken in the current study was one of model-fitting. At this exploratory stage, we were interested in determining which variables moderated the consistency (i.e., correlation) between the reaction time difference measure taken at test sessions 1 (RT1) and 2 (RT2). For such an approach, only those variables which are found to significantly moderate the relationship are kept in the model, and the resulting regression can be described and plotted. Model fit is assessed via F-statistics, R-squared, and plots of the predicted and residual values from the model.

To assess what impact, if any, the A/B subject classification scheme and private self-consciousness had on the relationship between RT1 and RT2, dummy codes were created. The subject classification was dummy-coded into 2 variables: Type1 = 1 if subject is Type A, 0 otherwise; Type2 = 1 if subject is Type B, 0 otherwise. The three groups of private self-consciousness were similarly coded: Priv1 = 1 if subject is High, 0 otherwise; Priv2 = 1 if subject is Low, 0 otherwise. Finally, preliminary analyses indicated there might be a cubic component to the relationship between RT1 and RT2, so powers of RT1 were included.

Thus, the model being tested included the dependent variable RT2 and the independent variables RT1, RT1*RT1, RT1*RT1*RT1, Type1, Type2, Priv1, Priv2, the interactions among the classification variables, and the interactions of the classification variables with the continuous variables.[4] It was predicted that schematic subjects should exhibit greater consistency between RT1 and RT2 than aschematic subjects. In terms of the regression analysis, an interaction of the "Type" classification variables and the powers of RT1 was expected. If private self-consciousness moderates this effect, then there should be an interaction of the "Priv" classification variables, the "Type" classification variables, and the powers of RT1.

Because of the inclusion of interaction terms in the model, and because RT1, as a covariate, should be included first in the model, the variables were tested in a pre-planned stepwise (or hierarchical) manner

---

3 *Another possible way to measure consistency is to use the adjective endorsements themselves (provided the endorsements are not used to classify subjects). However, analyses of the number of adjectives endorsed during the two test sessions revealed little; subjects were not particularly variable on such a measure. Analyses of the selection of adjectives endorsed were equally uninformative; subjects were minimally variable and exhibited no clear-cut patterns. Hence reaction time was chosen as a more revealing dependent variable, and adjective endorsements were used to classify subjects.*

4 *Preliminary analyses indicated there were no reliable sex differences, so the results described are collapsed across sex.*

TABLE 2 Hierarchical Significance Tests of Model Parameters

A. Type A Adjectives

Factor	*Sums of Squares*	*df*	*F*	*p*
RT1	13.43	1	12.51	.0005
RT1*RT1*RT1	9.33	1	8.69	.0037
Type1	7.46	1	6.95	.0092
Priv2	3.81	1	3.55	.0613
RT1*Priv1	10.00	1	9.32	.0027
Error	*168.44*	*157*		

B. Type B Adjectives

Factor	*Sums of Squares*	*df*	*F*	*p*
RT1	34.63	1	20.32	.0001
Type1	12.57	1	7.37	.0074
Priv2	5.47	1	3.21	.0752
Type1*Priv1	4.78	1	2.80	.0960
Error	*269.34*	*158*		

Note: Sample size is 163. Type1 refers to the dummy variable representing Type A subjects grouped against all other subjects. Priv1 represents the dummy variable representing High Private Self-Consciousness subjects grouped against all others; Priv2 represents Low Privates grouped against all others.

in the order described above. An alpha level of .10 was used in order that more explanatory variables be included in this exploratory model-fitting approach. Initial analyses revealed several cases were outliers, causing the model fit to be suboptimal. The outliers were from subjects with extreme endorsement patterns (e.g., 20 or more "Like me" responses) and thus the reaction time difference was based on a difference between one reliable mean and an unreliable one for these subjects. Dropping these subjects yielded a sample size of 163.

For the Type A adjectives, the final equation was: RT2 = .2337 + .0841*RT1 + .0339*RT1*RT1*RT1 + .5515*Type1 + .2685*Priv2 - .3945*RT1*Priv1, where the coefficients are unstandardized regression coefficients, or B-weights. This model accounted for 20.72% of the variance in RT2. All of these effects were significant at alpha = .10 when tested using F tests in a hierarchical model (see Part A of Table 2). It should be noted that these significant effects do not necessarily correspond to significant B-weights in the regression equation above, as the B-weights are derived from a simultaneous, rather than hierarchical, regression solution (see Cohen & Cohen, 1983).

To further clarify the significant cubic effect and the interaction of Priv1, the High Private dummy variable, and RT1, a graph of the regression equation separated by level of private self-consciousness is presented in Figure 1. Consistency between RT1 and RT2 is represented as the correlation between the two variables, or the slopes of the curves on the graph. As can be seen in the figure, all subjects with extreme initial differential reaction time scores demonstrate high degrees of consistency (correlation) between their measurements, whereas those with initial differential reaction time scores toward the middle of the range are less consistent. These differences in consistency account for the cubic effect.

The cubic pattern is the same regardless of the level of private self-consciousness, so the prediction that high privates would be more consistent was not supported. Subjects with reaction time scores near 0 are not very consistent. To have a near-0 reaction time difference is to respond at approximately the same speed regardless of the endorsement type (i.e., "like me" or "not like me"). Thus these latter subjects experienced no processing advantage in the endorsement task, and probably do not possess clear self-schemata for the Type A adjectives.

The significant positive contribution of Type1, the dummy variable grouping Type As against all other subjects, reflected the fact that Type As had a higher mean differential reaction time during the second test session that did Type Bs and Neutral subjects, a finding that does not explain much about the nature of the cognitive representation.

For the Type B adjectives, the final equation was: $RT2 = .3625 + .2678*RT1 - .3737*Type1 + .2922*Priv2 - .7141*Type1*Priv1$. This model accounted for 17.58% of the variance in RT2. Sums of squares and F tests are presented in Part B of Table 2. Figure 2 shows a graphical depiction of the Type1*Priv1 interaction. Here, there was no cubic trend, so the interaction reflects the finding that High Private Type As tended to have lower reaction time difference scores during the second testing session than did the other subjects. All subjects were very consistent from the first session to the second.

The specific predictions of an interaction among "Type" and the powers of RT1 and an interaction among "Type," "Priv," and the powers of RT1 were not found.

The finding of a significant cubic effect of RT1 for A adjectives was consistent with the notion that subjects exhibiting large differences between reaction times to adjectives not endorsed and reaction times to endorsed adjectives are behaving schematically and should therefore exhibit more consistency. However, the Type A/B classification scheme used did not shed much light on the relationship between RT1 and RT2.

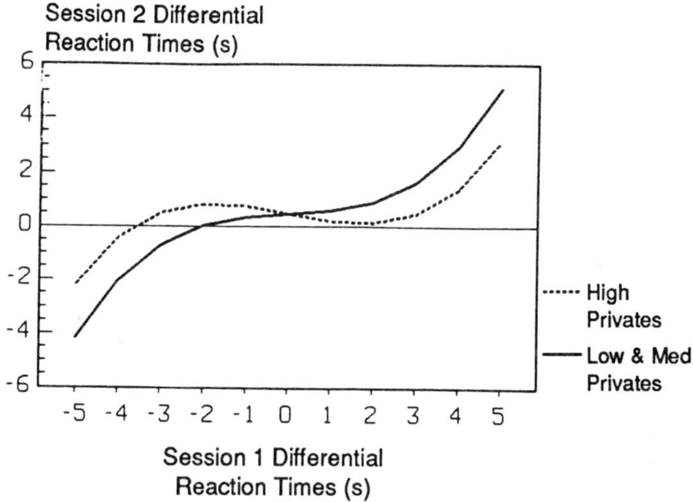

FIGURE 1 "A" Adjective Domain Differential Reaction Times Separated by Level of Private Self-Consciousness

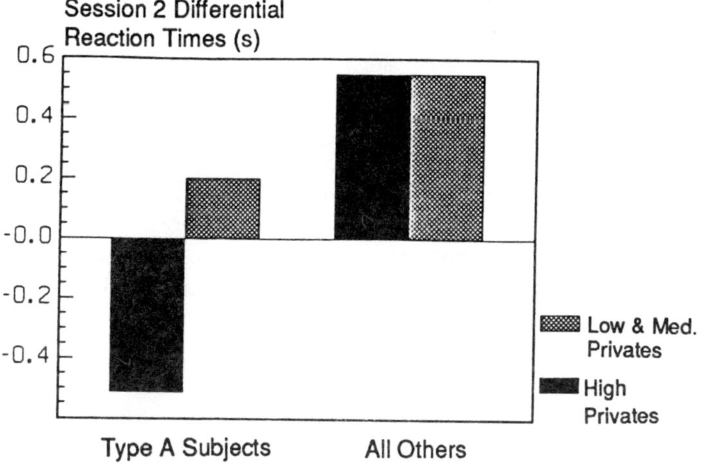

FIGURE 2 "B" Adjective Domain Differential Reaction Times Separated by Type of Subject and Level of Private Self-Consciousness

DISCUSSION

The current study builds upon the previous research by using two variables (JAS and trait endorsements) instead of the JAS alone to classify subjects into the A, B, and Neutral groups, where "Neutral" was used merely to designate people who were not so clearly Type A or Type B. The addition of this third group reflects our contention that schematicity, while undoubtedly representing a continuum of levels of cognitive organization, is only methodologically useful as a more categorical variable. When the data of these "potentially schematic" subjects are analyzed in aggregate form, they should display the processing time advantages predicted from schema theory as compared to other subjects.

In accordance with Strube et al. (1986), these processing advantages were found on the trait endorsement task for subjects classified as "potentially schematic" in the given domain. Thus the new classification scheme (or, set of definitional criteria) used here appears to be a useful one for determining if a person has a schema. Future research could examine several possible variables to be used as definitional criteria. Cutpoints of several variables might be established, preferably defining a person as "schematic" who has critical levels on several measures.

Results here indicated that the "Type B" category was not a significant predictor of consistency between test sessions, whereas the "Type A" category did contribute to the models. The expected interactions were not found, however. It may be that all subjects were too consistent on the computer task for the effect of the category variables to be felt. The cubic effect found for Type A adjectives was consistent with schema theory. Subjects exhibiting the most schematic behavior (greatest discrepancy of reaction times) were most consistent. Perhaps this variable could be used to help define someone as being schematic. In addition, the use of other tasks suggested by predictions from schema theory would help to better understand the behavioral expression of self-schemata.

The role of self-consciousness in moderating behavioral consistency among Type As and Bs deserves more attention in future research. The stability of any behavior may hinge on the degree of chronic private self-consciousness a given subject possesses. That is, people may only act like Type As or Type Bs across many situations if they also possess chronic private self-consciousness. Conversely, the ability to predict the behavior of low self-conscious Type As and Bs can be expected to be hampered. In the current study, the classification of "high" in private self-consciousness contributed to the models fit, whereas "low" and "medium" classifications could be considered together. This is consistent with the notion that private self-consciousness is a more dichotomous trait. There may be a measurable cutpoint past which people can be identified as behaving in accord with being high in private self-consciousness, but below this point such behavior is undetectable.

The present results have several important clinical implications. Because of the demonstrated coronary risk, many attempts have been made to modify the behavior of coronary patients who exhibit the Type A pattern, but few seem to have met with much success (Roskies, this issue). Relaxation training has proven somewhat helpful (Suinn & Bloom, 1978). Other techniques that have been attempted include group therapy and muscle-relaxation training (Roskies, Spevack, Surkins, Cohen, & Gilman, 1978). A successful clinical intervention requires that the Type A person be the primary agent for changing behavior, thus the cognitions of the patient must be taken into account to effect such change (Rosenman & Friedman, 1977). An understanding of how people perceive their own behavior would be an aid in changing that behavior, as Rosenman and Friedman have indicated (1977; see Fiske & Taylor, 1984; Carver & Scheier, 1981). Clearly much more research into the cognitive aspects of Type A and Type B behavior is needed to address these issues.

REFERENCES

Bargh, J. A. (1982). Attention and automaticity in the processing of self-relevant information. *Journal of Personality and Social Psychology, 43,* 425-436.

Carver, C.S., & Scheier, M.F. (1981). *Attention and self-regulation: A control-theory approach to human behavior.* New York: Springer-Verlag.

Cohen, J., & Cohen, P. (1983). *Applied multiple regression/correlation analysis for the behavioral sciences* (2nd ed.). Hillsdale, NJ: Erlbaum.

Cooper, T., Detre, T., & Weiss, S.J. (1981). Coronary-prone behavior and coronary heart disease: A critical review. *Circulation, 63,* 1199-1215.

Dembroski, T.M., Weiss, S.M., Shields, J., Haynes, S., & Feinleib, M. (Eds.) (1978). *Coronary-prone behavior.* New York: Springer.

Duval, S., & Wicklund, R.A. (1972). *A theory of objective self-awareness.* New York: Academic Press.

Fenigstein, A., Scheier, M.F., & Buss, A.H. (1975). Public and private self-consciousness: Assessment and theory. *Journal of Consulting and Clinical Psychology, 43,* 522-527.

Fiske, S.T., & Linville, P.W. (1980). What does the schema concept buy us? *Personality and Social Psychology Bulletin, 6,* 543-557.

Fiske, S.T., & Taylor, S.E. (1984). *Social cognition.* Reading, MA: Addison-Wesley Publishing Company.

Friedman, H. S., & Booth-Kewley, S. (1987). Personality, Type A behavior, and coronary heart disease: The role of emotional expression. *Journal of Personality and Social Psychology, 53,* 783-792.

Froming, W.J., & Carver, C.S. (1981). Divergent influences of private and public self-consciousness in a compliance paradigm. *Journal of Research in Personality, 15,* 159-171.

Glass, D.C. (1977). Behavior patterns, stress, and coronary disease. Hillsdale, NJ: Erlbaum.

Hastie, R. (1981). Schematic principles in human memory. In E.T. Higgins, C.P. Herman, & M.P. Zanna (Eds.), *Social cognition: The Ontario Symposium* (Vol. 1). Hillsdale, NJ: Erlbaum.

Haynes, S.G., Feinleib, M., & Kannel, W.B. (1980). The relationship of psychosocial factors to coronary heart disease in the Framingham study: III. Eight year incidence of coronary heart disease. *American Journal of Epidemiology, 111*, 37-58.

Hull, J. G., & Levy, A. S. (1979). The organizational functions of the self: An alternative to the Duval and Wicklund model of self-awareness. *Journal of Personality and Social Psychology, 37*, 756-768.

Jenkins, C. D. (1976). Recent evidence supporting psychologic and social risk factors for coronary disease. *New England Journal of Medicine, 294*, 987-994, 1033-1038.

Krantz, D. S., Glass, D. C., & Snyder, M. L. (1974). Helplessness, stress level, and the coronary prone behavior pattern. *Journal of Experimental Social Psychology, 10*, 284-300.

Kuiper, N. A., & Rogers, T. B. (1979). Encoding of personal information: Self-other differences. *Journal of Personality and Social Psychology, 37*, 499-514.

Markus, H. (1977). Self-schemata and processing information about the self. *Journal of Personality and Social Psychology, 35*, 63-78.

Markus, H., Crane, M., Bernstein, S., & Siladi, M. (1982). Self-schemas and gender. *Journal of Personality and Social Psychology, 42*, 38-50.

Markus, H. & Sentis, K.P. (1982). The self in social information processing. In J. Suls (Ed.), *Psychological perspectives on the self (Vol. 1)*. Hillsdale, NJ: Erlbaum.

Matthews, K.A. (1982). Psychological perspectives on the Type A behavior pattern. *Psychological Bulletin, 91*, 293-323.

Rogers, T.B. (1981). A model of the self as an aspect of human information processing. In N. Cantor & J. Kihlstrom (Eds.), *Personality, cognition, and social interaction*. Hillsdale, NJ: Erlbaum.

Rogers, T.B., Kuiper, N. A., & Kirker, W.S. (1977). Self-reference and the encoding of personal information. *Journal of Personality and Social Psychology, 35*, 677-688.

Rogers, T.B., Rogers, P. J., & Kuiper, N.A. (1979). Evidence for the self as cognitive prototype: The "false alarms effect." *Personality and Social Psychology Bulletin, 5*, 53-56.

Rosenman, R.H., Brand, R.J., Jenkins, C.D., Friedman, M., Straus, R., & Wurm, M. (1975). Coronary heart disease in the Western Collaborative Group Study: Final follow-up experience of 8.5 years. *Journal of the American Medical Association, 233*, 872-877.

Rosenman, R. H., & Friedman, M. (1977). Modifying Type A behavior pattern. *Journal of Psychosomatic Research, 21*, 323-331.

Roskies, E., Spevack, M., Surkis, A., Cohen, C., & Gilman, S. (1978). Changing the coronary-prone (Type A) behavior pattern in a non-clinical population. *Journal of Behavioral Medicine, 1*, 201-216.

Ross, L., Lepper, M.R., & Hubbard, M. (1975). Perseverance in self-perception and social perception: Biased attribution processes in the debriefing paradigm. *Journal of Personality and Social Psychology, 32*, 880-892.

Rumelhart, D.E. & Ortony, A. (1977). The representation of knowledge in memory. In R.C. Anderson, R.J. Spiro, & W.E. Montague (Eds.), *Schooling and the acquisition of knowledge*. Hillsdale, NJ: Erlbaum.

Scheier, M. F., & Carver, C. S. (1983). Two sides of the self: One for you and one for me. In J. Suls & A.G. Greenwald (Eds.), *Psychological perspectives on the self* (Vol. 2). Hillsdale, NJ: Erlbaum.

Strube, M. J, Berry, J. M., Lott, C. L., Fogelman, R., Steinhart, G., Moergen, S., & Davison, L. (1986). Self-schematic representation of the Type A and B behavior patterns. *Journal of Personality and Social Psychology, 51*, 170-180.

Suinn, R. M., & Bloom, L. J. (1978). Anxiety management training for pattern A behavior. *Journal of Behavioral Medicine, 1*, 25-35.

Taylor, S. E. & Crocker, J. (1981). Schematic bases of social information processing. In E.T. Higgins, C. P. Herman, & M. P. Zanna (Eds.), *Social cognition: The Ontario Symposium* (Vol. 1). Hillsdale, NJ: Erlbaum.

Turner, R.G. (1978). Self-consciousness and speed of processing self-relevant information. *Personality and Social Psychology Bulletin, 4*, 456-460.

Type A Status and Selected Work Experiences Among Male and Female Accountants

Arthur G. Bedeian
Department of Management, Louisiana State University, Baton Rouge, LA 70803-6312

Kevin W. Mossholder
Department of Management, Auburn University Auburn, AL 36849-5241

John Touliatos
Department of Family Studies and Home Economics Texas Christian University, Fort Worth, TX 76129

The relationships between Type A status and selected work experiences were investigated for separate samples of male and female accounting professionals. Using a special-purpose index from the California Psychological Inventory to assess Type A status, it was determined that relationships between Type A status and certain situationally-related work experiences were generally stronger for males than for females. The implications of this finding are discussed, emphasizing the need for further research on gender-based differences connected with Type A phenomena.

Type A Status and Selected Work Experiences Among Male and Female Accountants

Characteristics associated with the *Type A*, or coronary-prone, behavior pattern are widely recognized by both the scientific and lay communities (Strube, 1987). Individuals exhibiting the Type A pattern are characterized as extremely hard driving and competitive, highly achievement-oriented and work-involved, and engrossed in an incessant struggle to accomplish more and more in less and less time, especially in

---

Authors' Note: The helpful comments of Joseph J. Palladino and Caroline C. Wilhelm on an earlier draft manuscript are gratefully acknowledged. Address all manuscript correspondence to the first author. U.S.A. Telephone: (504) 388-6141.

© 1990 Select Press

relation to vocational deadlines (Friedman & Ulmer, 1984). Individuals who are relatively lacking in these characteristics are identified as *Type B*, representing a more relaxed, easygoing lifestyle. The overt manifestations of the Type A pattern include a heightened pace of living, an impatience with slowness, a tendency to challenge and compete with others even in noncompetitive situations, a free-floating hostility, and a sense of time urgency. Strictly defined, Type A is not construed as a trait, but rather as a set of behaviors elicited from "susceptible" individuals by situational factors (Matthews, 1982).

A central element of the Type A pattern is an excessive preoccupation and over-involvement in work. Type As are quite often workaholics with an exaggerated success ethic. Much of their time and effort is directed at vocational pursuits where, in addition to competing with others, they seem obsessed with meeting higher standards of productivity and bettering previous performance. They constantly feel under time pressure, hurry colleagues, and display overt irritability with the efforts of others (Burke & Weir, 1980a; Chesney & Rosenman, 1980; Davidson & Cooper, 1980; Howard, Cunningham, & Rechnitzer, 1977; Sorensen et al., 1987). Not surprisingly, Type A status has been positively related to having heavier work loads (Burke & Weir, 1980b), nonsupportive interactions with co-workers (Sorensen et al., 1987), enhanced feelings of time urgency (Davidson & Cooper, 1980), decreased levels of perceived environmental control (Chesney & Rosenman, 1980), competitiveness and aggression (Van Egeren, Sniderman, & Roggelin, 1982), and interpersonal dominance (Yarnold & Grimm, 1986).

Given the extensiveness of the above findings, it is equally surprising that they are primarily based on studies conducted with all male samples and that previous research, with few exceptions, has neglected to specify the situations that prompt Type A behavior (cf. Chesney et al., 1981). Indeed, the Type A factor has rarely been studied using women, especially those in professional occupations (Ivancevich, Matteson, & Preston, 1982), and only one study has examined the possibility that the sex distribution of Type A characteristics is related to differences in male and female exposure to situationally-related work experiences.

Using data drawn from the Minnesota Heart Survey for 2,512 employed men and women, Sorensen et al. (1987) found high Type A scores positively related in both sexes to long work hours, high occupational mobility, and nonsupportive job-related interactions with co-workers. While Sorensen et al. (1987) found no sex differences in the relationships between Type A status and these work experiences, research has shown that the Type A pattern is more prevalent in men than women (Chesney, Hecker, & Black, in press). This prevalence may well contribute to the well-established gender difference in coronary heart disease (CHD; Waldron, 1976). At present, specific information about the relationship of work experiences to Type A status in men and women remains to be fully developed. Such information is sorely needed, given that CHD is the leading cause of death for both adult males and adult females (Chesney et al., in press).

The higher prevalence of the Type A pattern among men than women may reflect genetic sex differences in aggressiveness, but is more likely due to sex differences in socialization (Waldron, 1976). Such differences appear, according to Waldron (1978a), to be "fostered by parents and schools who have typically pushed boys to achieve in the occupational world and girls to seek success in the less competitive family sphere" (p. 202). Along this same line, both Matteson, Ivancevich, and Gamble (1987) and Sorensen et al. (1987) suggest that the relatively high prevalence of the Type A factor among men may reflect variations in men's and women's work experiences, some of which may serve to facilitate or strengthen Type A characteristics. Accordingly, the purpose of the present exploratory research was to determine if the relationships of work experiences with the Type A pattern are different for men and women. Understanding these relationships is important to stress research and, ultimately, to managers because they can influence the development and maintenance of supportive work experiences that minimize excessive stress.

The simple fact of membership in a work organization can present the occasion for displays of the Type A behavior pattern. This is so because, as previously noted, a central element in the behavior pattern is the excessive preoccupation Type As display with respect to their work (Ivancevich & Matteson, 1988; Matteson, Ivancevich, & Smith, 1984). Curiously though, little attention has been paid to the relationship between Type A characteristics and situationally-related work experiences, except for some research that supports the notion relative to Type Bs, Type As are more hyper-responsive (for a review, see Krantz & Durel, 1983).

In their original Type A research, Rosenman and Friedman (1959) stressed that the onset of the behavior pattern is facilitated by exposure to certain environmental stimuli. This notion has prompted speculation that Type As and Bs may actually thrive in contrasting work environments. In fact, taking an interactionist perspective, Ivancevich and Matteson (1984) have proposed a person-environment fit model of Type A in the workplace. More recently, Smith and colleagues (Smith & Anderson, 1986; Smith & Rhodewalt, 1986), have proposed a similar model. Their model, however, not only presents Type As as responding to stressful situations, but as actively seeking and creating additional challenge and demand in their environment. Thus, while Type As placed in a rich environment would be expected to do several things simultaneously, this model suggests that, when placed in a simple environment, Type As, through their choices, cognitions, and behaviors, will create a more challenging and demanding environment. Empirical support for a dynamic interactional view of Type A that emphasizes person-environment processes is just beginning to appear (Kirmeyer & Biggers, in press).

A limited number of studies conducted in organizational settings provide relevant, but at times ambiguous, data concerning the relationship between work experiences and Type A status. Though some negative findings have been reported, Type A status has been, in general, related to long work hours (e.g., Burke & Weir, 1980b), role conflict (e.g., Howard et al., 1977), role ambiguity (e.g., Keenan & McBain, 1979), and job-related tension (Kelly & Houston, 1985). Given limited findings, the nature of the relationship between Type A status and job satisfaction, however, is yet unclear (Matteson et al., 1984).

Acknowledging conceptual and empirical uncertainties, it is too early to offer a precise theoretical statement that would relate work experiences to the Type A pattern, as well as indicate a rationale for specific predictions. Thus, in this study we suggested that five work experiences may be associated with an individual's Type A status: (a) extensive work hours, (b) role conflict, (c) role ambiguity, (d) job-related tension, and (e) job satisfaction. These work experiences were chosen for examination because of their early identification and apparent pervasiveness as job-related situational contingencies. Given the influence of past socialization practices and documented genetic differences in aggressiveness, it was anticipated that the relationship between the above work experiences and Type A status would not be as strong for females as males. Using measures gauging these work experiences, we asked whether any or all of them were Type A correlates. Accounting professionals were selected as a focal sample because they are employed in a field affording increasing access to both men and women. This access made it possible to study a large, but roughly equal number of male and female subjects, as well as also fill a knowledge gap pertaining to the Type A status of women in professional occupations.

METHOD

Sample

The data analyzed in this study were collected as part of a national survey of accounting professionals. The present sample consisted of 1,086 accountants randomly selected (with a participation rate of 63%)

from the membership lists of the American Society of Certified Public Accountants, National Association of Accountants, American Association of Women Accountants, and Association of Government Accountants (Bedeian, Mossholder, Touliatos, & Barkman, 1986). Inclusion in the present analyses was limited to those accountants who were employed full-time and had complete data on all variables relevant to the national survey. These restrictions reduced the focal sample to 505.

For the male sample (n = 256), 97% were 20 to 59 years old, 62% in the 20-39 age range, and 21% in the 40-49 range. More than 94% were college graduates. Some 80% were married, with 8% divorced, separated, or widowed. Mean job tenure equalled 8.7 years (SD = 7.9). For the female sample (n = 249), 99% were 20 to 59 years old, 71% in the 20-39 age range and 16% in the 40-49 range. Approximately 85% held college degrees. Mean job tenure equalled 5.7 years (SD = 5.1). More than 61% were married, with some 16% divorced, separated, or widowed.

Tests of significance were computed to determine whether men and women respondents differed with respect to age, education, and job tenure (measurement details are given below). Both age and education have been associated with the Type A pattern, in that Type A characteristics have been shown to vary by age group (Davidson & Cooper, 1980) and increase with educational level (Waldron et al., 1977). Job tenure was of interest given its potential impact on role behavior. While occupational status has also been positively related to the Type A pattern (Chesney & Rosenman, 1980), the focal sample's occupational homogeneity controls for this factor. The tests for age and education resulted in chi-squares of 90.88, df = 4, and 20.26, df = 4, respectively, which are both significant at the .001 level. The test for job tenure also resulted in a significant difference (t = 4.94, df = 503, p < .001). These differences suggested the need to partial out the effects of all three variables.

Measures

Demographic variables. The four demographic variables used in the analyses were *age* (coded on a 5-point scale from (1) 20-29 years to (5) above 59 years), *education* (coded on a 5-point scale from (1) less than junior college to (5) graduate degree), *job tenure* (years with present employer), and *sex* (male = 1, female = 2).

Dependent variable. A special-purpose index of the California Psychological Inventory (CPI; Gough, 1987) constituted the Type A measure. Developed by Palladino and Motiff (1981), the validity of this index is based on its ability to discriminate Type As and Type Bs as originally classified by the Jenkins Activity Survey (JAS-Form T; Jenkins, Zyzanski, & Rosenman, 1979). The JAS is perhaps the most widely used questionnaire measure for classifying employed individuals as Type A or B (Matthews, 1982; Matteson et al., 1987).

In the present analysis, the Type A measure was scored by using a linear combination of six CPI scales (in parentheses) weighted as follows: .22 (Dominance) + .62 (Self-Acceptance) + .32 (Responsibility) - .35 (Socialization) - .39 (Achievement via Independence) - .26 (Flexibility). Higher scores were coded to indicate higher Type A status. Designed for use with nonclinical populations, the validity and reliability of the CPI are well established (Gynther & Gynther, 1983). Moreover, the CPI is generally unaffected by demographic variables like age or education (Dyer, Monson, & von Drimmelen, 1971).

Independent variables. Based on both prior research and theory, five work experiences were selected as independent variables. *Work hours* were examined by asking respondents, "On the average, how many hours a week do you work at your present job?" The response categories for this item ranged from (1) 1-39 hours to (5) 60 or more hours. The modal response category for both males (n = 120) and females (n = 114) was 41-48 hours per week.

Role conflict and *role ambiguity* as job stressors were measured using six and eight items, respectively, from the scales developed by Rizzo, House, and Lirtzman (1970). Each scale was scored using a 7-point response format ranging from (1) *very rarely* to (7) *continually.* Responses to both scales were averaged to yield a single score. These scales were chosen because of their established psychometric properties (House, Schuler, & Levanoni, 1983) and widespread use in role theory. Examples of role conflict items are: (a) "I work with two or more groups who operate quite differently," and (b) "I have to break a rule or policy in order to carry out an assignment." Exemplary role ambiguity items include: (a) "I feel certain about how much authority I have," and (b) "I know exactly what is expected of me."

Job-related tension was assessed by a 9-item instrument taken from Lyons (1971). Developed from a longer list used by Kahn, Wolfe, Quinn, Snoek, and Rosenthal (1964), the items gauge the frequency with which subjects report feeling bothered by work-related factors. Seven response categories (coded from 1 to 7) ranged from (1) *very rarely* to (7) *continually.* Items were averaged to yield a single tension score.

Overall job satisfaction was measured by the Minnesota Satisfaction Questionnaire, Short Form (Weiss, Dawis, England, & Lofquist, 1976). For purposes of the present study, only the 20 general satisfaction items were utilized. Response alternatives were scored using a 5-point response mode ranging from (1) *not satisfied* to (5) *extremely satisfied,* and by averaging across all items.

Data Analyses

Hierarchical multiple regression was used to examine the main effects of work experiences on Type A status. Age, job tenure, and education were entered as a functional block and treated as covariates to statistically control for differences between the male and female samples. Respondent Type A scores were then regressed on the set of five independent variables (work hours, role conflict, role ambiguity, job-related tension, and job satisfaction) as a second functional block. Using functional blocks hierarchically controls for variance attributable to causally antecedent, but nonfocal variables. Here, this means controlling the influence of demographic variables before considering the impact of work experiences on Type A status. Regression analyses were conducted for males and females separately. Respective pairs of beta weights for males and females were examined for significant differences using a one-tailed t-test as recommended by Blalock (1967) and Duncan (1975). This procedure was preferable to testing for the overall difference between regression equations, as it provides specific information on the differences between single coefficients.

RESULTS

Table 1 separately presents descriptive statistics for males and females. Coefficient alpha reliability estimates are also shown. Consistent with prior research, male Type A scores were significantly higher than females ($t = 3.60$, $df = 503$, $p < .001$). No other gender differences are evident.

Zero-order correlations among the study variables are displayed in Table 2. Separate correlation matrices were computed for men and women. The overall pattern of relationships within each matrix was similar for the two groups. No significant or systematic differences between males and females were found. The strong positive relationship for both males and females between role conflict and role ambiguity, as well as between each variable individually and job-related tension is consistent with prior research (Bedeian & Armenakis, 1981). Similarly, the high negative relationships for both males and females between role conflict, role ambiguity and job-related tension with job satisfaction is in accord with previously published research and theory (Kemery, Bedeian, Mossholder,& Touliatos, 1985).

The main effects of work experiences on Type A status for males and females are shown in Table 3. Individual beta weights with their standard errors are reported. The beta weights provide a rough estimate of the relative contributions of the five independent variables in predicting the Type A pattern. The calculated t value for determining the presence or

TABLE 1 Descriptive Statistics for Males and Females

		Men			Women		
Variable	*Reliability*	*n*	*M*	*SD*	*n*	*M*	*SD*
Type A status	_a	256	9.72	10.04[b]	249	6.51	9.97[b]
Work hours	_a	256	3.00[c]	.86	249	3.00[c]	.85
Role conflict	.84	253	2.38	.94	248	2.28	1.02
Role ambiguity	.86	255	3.18	1.12	249	3.16	1.19
Job-related tension	.85	255	2.40	1.02	249	2.41	1.07
Job satisfaction	.91	256	3.33	.62	249	3.32	.64

[a]*Not applicable.*
[b]*Means are significantly different, p < .001.* [c]*Median value.*

TABLE 2 Zero-Order Correlations

				r		
Variable	*1*	*2*	*3*	*4*	*5*	*6*
1. Type A status		02	-04	-07	-04	19
2. Work hours	20		10	-08	11	21
3. Role conflict	06	03		55	79	-39
4. Role ambiguity	-12	-04	48		61	-53
5. Job-related tension	01	11	78	54		-48
6. Job satisfaction	11	22	-45	-58	-50	

Note. Decimal points omitted for correlations. Female sample (n = 249) above diagonal; male sample (n = 256) below diagonal, r ≥ .12 , p ≤ .05, two-tailed test.

absence of a statistically significant difference between respective coefficients in the male and female regressions is also shown.

Table 3 shows a positive and significant age covariate score for the female sample, thus confirming the need to control for this variable. Considering the significant relationships between work experiences and Type A status, all but one relationship was stronger for males than females. The relationship between extensive work hours and Type A status was significantly ($t = 2.22$, $p < .05$) stronger for males (β .19, $p < .05$) than females (β -.03, ns). A similar pattern existed for the relationship between role conflict and Type A status (a a for males = .20, $p < .05$; β for females = -.05, ns; $t = 1.76$, $p < .05$). Role ambiguity had a significantly ($t = -1.41$, $p < .10$) stronger negative correlation with Type A status for males (β -.14, $p < .10$), than females (β .03, ns). By contrast, the association between job satisfaction to Type A status was significantly

TABLE 3 Hierarchical Regression Analysis for Type A Status

Variable	*Male (n = 250)*			*Female (n = 247)*			
	Step1 (β_1)	*Step 2 (β_2)*	*SEβ_2*	*Step1 (β_1)*	*Step 2 (β_2)*	*SEβ_2*	*t*
Covariate							
Age	.03	-.01		.15	.16**		
Education	.09	.06		.10	.10		
Tenure	-.01	-.01		-.02	-.03		
Main Effect							
Work hours		.19**	.07		-.03	.07	2.22a
Role conflict		.20**	.10		-.05	.10	1.76a
Role ambiguity		-.14*	.08		.03	.09	-1.41b
Job-related tension		-.08	.11		.11	.11	ns
Job satisfaction		.04	.08		.25**	.08	-1.86b
Total R		.28**			.26**		

Note. Entries are beta weights associated with each independent variable. The beta weight listed for each variable is that obtained after controlling for all other variables.
[a]The difference in beta weights for males and females is significant at $p \leq .05$, one-tailed.
[b]The difference in beta weights for males and females is significant at $p \leq .10$, one-tailed.
$*p < .10$. $**p < .05$.

($t = -1.86$, $p < .10$) stronger for females (β .25, $p < .01$) than for males (β .04, ns). Finally, the relationship between job-related tension and Type A status was nonsignificant for both males (β .08, ns) and females (β .11, ns).

DISCUSSION

This paper examined the relationship of various work experiences to Type A status. The contrast between male and female respondents on a majority of the variables indexing work experience was striking. On the whole, the pattern of results suggests that Type A status is correlated with work experiences of males, but not females.

The relationship of hours worked to Type A status has been examined by other investigators using either all male or female samples. For example, both Jenkins, Rosenman, and Friedman (1967) and Burke and Weir (1980b) reported that Type A male managers work longer hours than their Type B counterparts. Similarly, compared to Type B females, Type A females have been found to work more hours per week (Kelly & Houston, 1985; Waldron, 1978b). This study found, however, that the relationship between extensive work hours and Type A status was significant only for men. Interestingly, Waldron (1978b) reports finding that Type A women do not prefer more hours of employment, but rather work longer hours than they prefer. This suggests the possibility that Type A subjects are less likely to leave a task once they have begun. In contrast, however, Kelly and Houston (1985) found that Type A women actually prefer to work more overtime. Further research is thus needed before any firm conclusions can be drawn in this regard.

The positive association between role conflict and Type A status among males supports the earlier work of Howard et al. (1977). These researchers found that, as compared to Type Bs, Type A male managers report a greater inability to satisfy conflicting work roles. Why, in contrast to previous research (i.e., Kelly & Houston, 1985), a similar pattern does not exist for females is uncertain. It is possible, however, that sex differences in social role expectations (both at and away from work) reinforce a greater effectiveness among females than males in managing stress that arises from conflicting job demands. In this connection, Howard, Rechnitzer, and Cunningham (1975) investigated the techniques used by male Type As to cope with pressures at work. Male Type As were found to rely on the least effective method studied—i.e., changing to a different work activity. Thus, rather than cope with work pressures by diversion or relaxation, Type As continued to work. A similar investigation involving female Type As has yet to be conducted. An examination of the dynamics behind possible gender differences in resolving work pressures that result from role conflict represents a significant area for additional Type A research.

The need for such research is reinforced by a reversal of the preceding gender difference with respect to role ambiguity (see Table 3). In contrast to the female sample which reported virtually no association between role ambiguity and Type A status, these variables were negatively related for males. This finding may be due to sex differences in achievement orientation. That is, in striving for competitive achievement, males may well experience role ambiguity as a greater obstacle to performance than females. Chesney (1983), for one, contends that achievement in terms of Type A characteristics is more consistent with the traditional masculine sex role. It is thus possible that this difference is an additional factor contributing to the higher prevalence of coronary heart disease among men than women. The exact nature of this differential male/female response and its full implications remain to be determined.

Though not on a consistent basis, job dissatisfaction has sometimes been found to be positively associated with coronary heart disease (e.g., House, 1974; Sales & House, 1971). Based on this finding, a negative association between the Type A pattern and job satisfaction would have been expected. Nevertheless, available research (e.g., Burke & Weir, 1980b, Caplan, Cobbs, French, Harrison, & Pinneau, 1975) shows no such relationship, at least for employed males. For the current male sample, job satisfaction and Type A status were only weakly related. In contrast, a moderate, but significant positive relationship between job satisfaction and Type A status emerged for the current female sample. This finding suggests that, at least among females, job satisfaction may reinforce the high achievement orientation associated with the Type A pattern. This gender-based difference may be related to a relative ineffectiveness of males in managing such negative Type A characteristics as impatience, hostility, and aggressiveness.

As with any study, certain caveats need to be mentioned to place this study in proper perspective. The preceding conclusions rely on the use of a special-purpose index of the California Psychological Inventory. As a paper-and-pencil measure, it (like the widely used Jenkins Activity Survey) is susceptible to the biases of self-report and self-appraisal. Moreover, the CPI has been employed only rarely as an instrument to assess Type A status. Further research with this means of identifying Type A individuals will need to be done to insure that the current results are substantive and not method bound. While there are those who only advocate use of measures permitting direct observation of Type A behavior, this alternative is too costly for use in large population studies of the kind reported here (Sorensen et al., 1987). In any instance, no single test can be expected to be a pure exemplar of a construct in all studies that are intended to map the construct's nomological network (Matthews, 1982; Yarnold & Bryant, in press). Thus, the use of alternative measures of the Type A pattern could provide a greater understanding of its antecedents and consequences. Another caveat to note is that the generalizability of the present results is limited by the occupation (accounting profession) of the study's respondents. Though the national character of the sample increases the potential for geographical generalizability, additional research needs to be done with professionals and nonprofessionals alike.

Relatedly, an area for future research involves examining the relationship between Type A status and work experiences across a variety of occupational groups. Although portions of the present findings relating to males are consistent with those reported among other jobholders (Burke & Weir, 1980b; Caplan et al., 1985; Howard et al., 1977), the inclusion of men and women from a range of occupations is necessary to clarify the relationship between Type A status and work experiences in different contexts. This would seem particularly important since environments with excessive and sustained stress place Type As at special risk (Heilbrun & Friedberg, 1987). Furthermore, research by Mettlin (1976) suggests that the Type A pattern is particularly common in competitive occupations having high expectations for the quality and quantity of work performed. In this respect, Mettlin (1976) notes that the Type A pattern is integral to the modern occupational career.

Finally, it is unclear whether Type As select more demanding jobs or merely perceive them as more demanding (Smith & Anderson, 1986; Waldron et al., 1980). To clarify this issue, a longitudinal study that assesses the Type A status of males and females some time before they begin job searches (or certainly before organizational entry) is necessary. Examining characteristics of jobs chosen by participants might reveal if job choice differences correspond with differences in Type A status. In such a study, the complexity/demand level of chosen jobs should be measured by both objective (e.g., Gerhart, 1987) and subjective (Zaccaro & Stone, 1988) means. Gathering both types of measures would permit one to determine whether any job choice differences that occurred were due only to the perceptual biases of Types As or to objective differences in the complexity/demand level of chosen jobs.

It is conceivable that the increased time pressures, competitiveness, and conscientiousness required by a job over time could convert a Type B person into a Type A (Davidson & Cooper, 1980; Dembroski, MacDougall, Herd, & Shields, 1979). Another kind of longitudinal study, sampling job incumbents across a range of jobs possessing different complexity/demand levels, could be performed to address this issue. Multiple measures of Type A status (e.g., JAS, CPI index, Structured Interview technique) would be collected at two or more points in time to track possible changes in Type A status among people holding jobs of the same complexity/demand level across time. Were upward or downward shifts in Type A status registered for jobs of a particular complexity/demand level, especially on more than one Type A measure, the notion that work experience may influence Type A status (or, perhaps more likely, that they exist in a reciprocal relationship) would become credible. Of course, the studies outlined above are but two of many that are possible. In any event, longitudinal studies could provide the next step in augmenting our understanding of interrelationships of Type A status and work experiences.

REFERENCES

Bedeian, A. G., & Armenakis, A. A. (1981). A path-analytic study of the consequences of role conflict and ambiguity. *Academy of Management Journal, 24,* 417-424.

Bedeian, A. G., Mossholder, K. W., Touliatos, J., & Barkman, A. I. (1986). The accountant's stereotype: An update for vocational counselors. *Career Development Quarterly, 35,* 113-122.

Blalock, H. M., Jr. (1967). Causal inferences, closed populations, and measures of association. *American Political Science Review, 61,* 130-136.

Burke, R. J., & Weir, T. (1980a). Personality, value, and behavioral correlates of the Type A individual. *Psychological Reports, 46,* 171-181.

Burke, R. J., & Weir, T. (1980b). The Type A experience: Occupational and life demands, satisfaction, and well being. *Journal of Human Stress, 6,* 28-38.

Caplan, R. D., Cobbs, S., J.R.P. French, Harrison, R. V., & Pinneau, S. R. (1975). *Job demands and worker health.* Publ. No. (NIOSH) 75-160. Washington, D.C.: U.S. Department of Health, Education, & Welfare.

Chesney, M. A. (1983). Occupational setting and coronary-prone behavior in men and women. In T. M. Dembroski, T. H. Schmidt, & G. Blumchen (Eds.), *Biobehavioral bases of coronary heart diesase* (pp. 79-90). New York: Karger.

Chesney, M. A., Hecker, M.H.L., & Black, G. W. (in press). Coronary-prone components of Type A behavior in the WCGS: A new methodology. In B. K. Houston & C. R. Synder (Eds.), *Type A behavior: Current trends and future directions.* New York: Wiley.

Chesney, M. A., & Rosenman, R. H. (1980). Type A behaviour in the work setting. In C. L. Cooper & R. Payne (Eds.), *Current concerns in occupational stress* (pp. 187-212). Chichester, U.K.: Wiley.

Chesney, M. A., Sevelius, G., Black, G. W., Ward, M. M., Swan, G. E., & Rosenman, R. H. (1981). Work environment, Type A behavior, and coronary heart disease risk factors. *Journal of Occupational Medicine, 23,* 551-555.

Davidson, M. J., & Cooper, C. L. (1980). Type A coronary-prone behavior in the work environment. *Journal of Occupational Medicine, 22,* 375-383.

Dembroski, T., MacDougall, J., Herd, J., & Shields, J. (1979). Effects of level of challenge on pressor and heart rate responses in Type A and B subjects. *Journal of Applied Social Psychology, 9,* 209-228.

Duncan, O.D. (1975). *Introduction to structural equation models.* New York: Academic Press.

Dyer, E., Monson, M., & von Drimmelen, J. (1971). Are administrative level, age, and educational preparation reflected in California Psychological Inventory scores? *Psychological Reports, 29,* 1111-1120.

Friedman, M., & Ulmer, D. (1984). *Treating Type A behavior and your heart.* New York: Knopf.

Gerhart, B. (1987). How important are dispositional factors as determinants of job satisfaction? Implications for job design and other personnel programs. *Journal of Applied Psychology, 72,* 366-373.

Gough, H. G. (1987). *Manual for the california psychological inventory* (4th ed.). Palo Alto, CA: Consulting Psychologists Press.

Gynther, M. D., & Gynther, R. A. (1983). Personality inventories. In J. B. Weiner (Ed.), *Clinical methods in psychology* (2nd ed.; pp. 152-232). New York: Wiley.

Heilbrun, A. B., Jr., & Friedberg, E. B. (1987). Type A behavior and stress in college males. *Journal of Personality Assessment, 51,* 555-564.

Howard, J. H., Rechnitzer, P. A., Cunningham, D. A. (1975). Effective and ineffective methods for coping with job tension. *Public Personnel Management, 4 (5),* 317-326.

Howard, J. H., Cunningham, D. A., & Rechnitzer, P. A. (1977). Work patterns associated with Type A behaviors: A managerial population. *Human Relations, 30,* 825-836.

House, J. S. (1974). Occupational stress and coronary heart disease: A review and theoretical integration. *Journal of Health and Social Behavior, 15,* 12-27.

House, R. J., Schuler, R. S., & Levanoni, E. (1983). Role conflict and ambiguity scales: Reality or artifacts? *Journal of Applied Psychology, 68*, 334-337.

Ivancevich, J. M., & Matteson, M. T. (1984). A Type A-B person-work environment interaction model for examining occupational stress and consequences. *Human Relations, 37*, 491-513.

Ivancevich, J. M., & Matteson, M. T. (1988). Type A behaviour and the healthy individual. *British Journal of Medical Psychology, 61*, 37-56.

Ivancevich, J. M., Matteson, M. T., & Preston, C. (1982). Occupational stress, Type A behavior, and physical well being. *Academy of Management Journal, 25*, 373-391.

Jenkins, C. D., Rosenman, R. H., & Friedman, M. (1967). Development of an objective psychological test for the determination of the coronary-prone behavior pattern in employed men. *Journal of Chronic Disease, 20*, 371-379.

Jenkins, C. D., Zyzanski, S. J., & Rosenman, R. H. (1979). *Jenkins Activity Survey manual.* New York: Psychological Corporation.

Kahn, R. L., Wolfe, D. M., Quinn, R. P., Snoek, J. D., & Rosenthal, R. A. (1964). *Organizational stress: Studies in role conflict and ambiguity*. New York: Wiley.

Keenan, A., & McBain, G.D.M. (1979). Effects of Type A behaviour, intolerance of ambiguity, and locus of control on the relationship between role stress and work-related outcomes. *Journal of Occupational Psychology, 52*, 277-285.

Kelly, K. E., & Houston, B. K. (1985). Type A behavior in employed women: Relation to work, marital, and leisure variables, social support, stress, tension, and health. *Journal of Personality and Social Psychology, 48*, 1067-1079.

Kemery, E. R., Bedeian, A. G., Mossholder, K. W., & Touliatos, J. (1985). Outcomes of role stress: A multisample constructive replication. *Academy of Management Journal, 28*, 363-375.

Kirmeyer, S. L., & Biggers, K. T. (in press). Environmental demands and demand engendering behavior: An observational analysis of the Type A pattern. *Journal of Personality and Social Psychology.*

Krantz, D. S., & Durel, L. A. (1983). Psychobiological substrates of the Type A behavior pattern. *Health Psychology, 2*, 393-411.

Lyons, T. F. (1971). Role clarity, need for clarity, satisfaction, tension, and withdrawal. *Organizational Behavior and Human Performance, 6*, 99-110.

Matteson, M. T., Ivancevich, J. M., & Gamble, G. O. (1987). A test of the cognitive social learning model of Type A behavior. *Journal of Human Stress, 13*, 23-31.

Matteson, M. T., Ivancevich, J. M., & Smith, S. V. (1984). Relation of Type A behavior to performance and satisfaction among sales personnel. *Journal of Vocational Behavior, 25*, 203-214.

Matthews, K. A. (1982). Psychological perspectives on the Type A behavior pattern. *Psychological Bulletin, 91*, 293-323.

Mettlin, C. (1976). Occupational careers and the prevention of coronary-prone behavior. *Social Science & Medicine, 10*, 367-372.

Palladino, J. J., & Motiff, J. P. (1981). Discriminant analysis of Type A/Type B subjects on the California Psychological Inventory. *Journal of Social and Clinical Psychology, 1*, 155-161.

Rizzo, J. R., House, R. J., & Lirtzman, S. J. (1970). Role conflict and ambiguity in complex organizations. *Administrative Science Quarterly, 15*, 150-163.

Rosenman, R. H., & Friedman, M. (1959). The possible relationship of the emotions to clinical coronary heart disease. In G. Pincurs (ed.), *Hormones and atherosclerosis*. New York: Academic Press.

Sales, S. M., & House, J. S. (1971). Job satisfaction as a possible risk factor in coronary disease. *Journal of Chronic Disease, 23*, 861-873.

Smith, T. W., & Anderson, N. B. (1986). Models of personality and disease: An interactional approach to Type A behavior and cardiovascular risk. *Journal of Personality and Social Psychology, 50*, 1166-1173.

Smith, T. W., & Rhodewalt, F. (1986). On states, traits, and processes: A transactional alternative to the individual difference assumptions in Type A behavior and physiological reactivity. *Journal of Research in Personality, 20*, 229-251.

Sorensen, G., Jacobs, D. R., Jr., Pirie, P., Folsom, A., Luepker, R., & Gillum, R. (1987). Relationships among Type A behavior, employment experiences, and gender: The Minnesota heart survey. *Journal of Behavioral Medicine, 10*, 323-336.

Strube, M. J. (1987). A self-appraisal model of the Type A behavior pattern. *Perspectives in Personality, 2*, 201-250.

Van Egeren, L. F., Sniderman, L. D., & Roggelin, M. S. (1982). Competitive two-person interactions of Type-A and Type-B individuals. *Journal of Behavioral Medicine, 5* , 55-67.

Waldron, I. (1976). Why do women live longer than men? Part I. *Journal of Human Stress, 2*, 2-13.

Waldron, I. (1978a). Sex differences in the coronary-prone behavior pattern. In T. M. Dembroski, J. M. Weiss, J. L. Shields, S. G. Haynes, & M. Feinleib (Eds.), *Coronary-prone behavior*, (pp. 199-205). New York: Springer-Verlag.

Waldron, I. (1978b). The coronary-prone behavior pattern, blood pressure, employment, and socio-economic status in women. *Journal of Psychosomatic Research, 122* 79-87.

Waldron, I., Hickey, A., McPherson, C., Butensky, A., Gruss, L., Overall, K., Schmader, A., & Wohlmuth, D. (1980). Type A behavior pattern: Relationship to variation in blood pressure, parental characteristics, and academic and social activities of students. *Journal of Human Stress, 6*, 16-27.

Waldron, I., Zyzanski, S., Shekelle, R. B., Jenkins, C. D., & Tannebaum, S. (1977). The coronary-prone behavior pattern in employed men and women. *Journal of Human Stress, 3*, 2-18.

Weiss, R. V., Dawis, G., England, G. W., & Lofquist, L. H. (1976). *Manual of the Minnesota Satisfaction Questionnaire*. Minneapolis: Industrial Relations Center, University of Minnesota.

Yarnold, P. R., & Bryant, F. B. (1988). A note on measurement issues in Type A research: Let's not throw out the baby with the bath water. *Journal of Personality Assessment, 52*, 410-419.

Yarnold, P. R., & Grimm, L. G. (1986). Interpersonal dominance and coronary prone behavior. *Journal of Research in Personality, 20*, 420-433.

Zaccaro, S. J., & Stone, E. F. (1988). Incremental validity of an empirically based measure of job characteristics. *Journal of Applied Psychology, 73*, 245-252.

Type A Behavior, Career Aspirations, and Role Conflict in Professional Women

Esther R. Greenglass
Department of Psychology, York University
Downsview, Ontario, Canada, M3J 1P3

This study investigated relationships between Type A behavior, career aspirations, and role conflict in faculty women. A mail questionnaire was used to collect the data. On the average, this sample was highly Type A. As predicted, Type A scores correlated positively and significantly with role conflict—the higher the Type A, the higher the role conflict in areas involving work and familial roles. The results of a multiple regression predicting Type A behavior in women with children living at home showed that total number of hours spent on home and professional work accounted for a significant proportion of the variance in Type A scores. Implications of these results are discussed.

INTRODUCTION

The coronary-prone or Type A behavior pattern is a hard- driving, aggressive, competitive, job-devoted lifestyle which is associated with a significantly increased risk of coronary heart disease (Jenkins, 1976). The Type A individual has also been described as having a high achievement orientation, a constant sense of time-urgency, an unrelenting drive, hurried speech patterns, an impatient manner, and aggressiveness or free-floating hostility. This is in contrast to the Type B individual who is characteristically more relaxed, less aggressive, and less time urgent.

Other research has shown that the greater the Type A behavior in male administrators, the more hours worked per week, the higher the level of concentration required, the greater the responsibility for things, the greater the quantitative and qualitative overload, the greater the rate of change in one's organization, the greater the stress in communicating, and the greater the total stress from work conditions (Burke & Weir, 1980). The

Authors Note: This research was supported by a research grant from Imperial Oil Ltd. Grateful acknowledgement is due to Mirka Ondrack and the Institute for Social Research for their assistance in the data analyses. Thanks are also due to Fiorella Cribari and Lori Visconti for their assistance in this research.

© 1990 Select Press

same study reports that the greater the Type A, the more individuals reported their jobs having negative effects on home and personal life. Additional research has confirmed similar findings in women. For example, Kelly and Houston (1985) found that middle-class Type A women who were employed full-time outside the home reported more demanding jobs and more daily stress and tension than Type Bs. Similar to results reported for women and men employed full-time, housewives who were Type A have been found to have more stressful work experiences. Also, similar to men, Type A housewives have been reported to have poorer marital adjustment than Type Bs (Houston & Kelly, 1987). In line with these results are the findings reported by Abush & Burkhead (1984) who studied midlife women. The findings were that the greater the woman's Type A personality, the more likely she was to perceive tension at work. Thus, the Type A behavior pattern would appear to have similar psychological and behavioral correlates in women and in men.

The coronary-prone behavior pattern is correlated with the prevalence of coronary heart disease in both sexes (Jenkins, 1976; Haynes et al., 1977; Waldron, 1978). Standard risk factors apparently do not account for much of the risk associated with the coronary-prone behavior. The coronary-prone behavior pattern, as measured by existing instruments, has been reported to be more prevalent among men than among women (Haynes et al., 1978; Waldron et al., 1977; Waldron, 1976).

More recent research indicates that a sex difference may reflect variations in men's and women's job experiences, some of which may increase Type A behavior. For example, Sorensen et al. (1987) found that Type A behavior in both women and men was related to long work hours, high occupational mobility, and nonsupportive interactions with co-workers. In general, men, compared to women, are more likely to have jobs whose characteristics are correlated highly with Type A. In the Sorensen et al. study, when work hours were controlled for, women were more Type A than men. These findings are in line with those of Shekelle et al. (1976) who also found no sex differences on Jenkins-Activity-Scale Type A scores after controlling for socio- economic status. A study by Moss et al. (1986) also found no sex differences in Type A behavior assessed by the Structured Interview (SI) method (Rosenman, 1978) when controlling for income, occupation, marital status, age, race, education or any combination of these variables. The absence of sex differences in Type A behavior, particularly when socio-economic status is controlled for, suggests that these variables should be incorporated into studies of Type A behavior.

On the average, employed women have been found to display more of the coronary-prone behavior pattern than housewives (Haynes et al., 1978; Waldron, 1978). These findings are in line with results of other research with samples of college-educated women that the "need for achievement" is higher among employed women than among housewives (Kriger, 1972; Baruch, 1967; Shelton, 1968). Additional data indicate that women with higher status occupations, i.e., administrative, business proprietor, semi- professional, have higher Type A scores than those with lower status occupations (Waldron, 1978). This suggests that the coronary-prone behavior pattern may be related to upward mobility. These data further suggest that the Type A behavior pattern may be associated with success in the vocational sphere, one which has been traditionally considered more important for men.

The greater prevalence of coronary-prone behavior among employed women may reflect the operation of several factors. For example, it may be that women with the hard-driving coronary-prone behavior pattern may be more likely to seek employment or less likely to leave jobs once they have begun (Waldron, 1980). Also, pressures associated with employment may increase the coronary- prone behavior pattern. For example, employed women are under more time pressure, having one-third less free time daily than housewives (Szalai, 1972). Moreover, Haynes et al. (1980) suggest that the dual role of employment and raising a family may place excessive demands on employed women. At the same time, Haynes and Feinleib (1980) found that coronary heart disease (CHD) rates were almost twice as great among women holding clerical jobs compared to housewives. Clerical workers with children were over three times more likely to develop CHD than non- clerical mothers. Thus, it may be that the lack of autonomy and control associated with blue-collar jobs is related to illness to a greater degree than is Type A behavior which is more predominant among women in white-collar jobs.

Regardless of a woman's employment, she is still seen and likely sees herself as primarily responsible for home and children and as the emotional mainstay of the family. Previous research on dual-career families indicates that conflicts between professional and parental roles are especially stressful for the female spouse (Bryson & Bryson, 1978; Heckman et al., 1977; Holahan & Gilbert, 1979). In their study of dual-career marriages, Holahan and Gilbert (1979) focus on four major life roles and the potential conflict between them. These major roles are Professional, Spouse, Parent, and Self as Self Actualized Person. They constructed six scales to measure the conflict in those areas represented by specific pairs of these roles, i.e., the area of Professional vs. Parent. Table 1 presents the six role-conflict scales developed by Holahan and Gilbert (1979), along with representative items. In their study of 28 dual career couples, Holahan and Gilbert (1979) compared role conflict between parent and non-parent groups. They found that although the parent group reported the

TABLE 1 Representative Items From The Six Role-Conflict Scales

Scale	*No. of Items*	*r*	*Representative item*
Professional vs. Spouse	3	.81	Wanting to be a "good" spouse vs. being unwilling to risk taking the time from your professional work.
Professional vs. Parent	4	.81	Spending most evenings on work-related activities vs. spending most evenings with your family.
Professional vs. Self	4	.86	Wanting to be recognized as a high level professional vs. wanting to maximize your personal development.
Spouse vs. Parent	3	.82	Spending prime time developing and maintaining the relationship with your spouse vs. spending prime time developing and maintaining the relationship with your child.
Spouse vs. Self	4	.75	The life style you prefer vs. the life style preferred by your spouse.
Parent vs. Self	3	.88	Giving priority to your family vs. giving priority to yourself.

Source: Holahan and Gilbert (1979), p.455.

highest role conflict on the Professional vs. Self Scale, this conflict was matched by that of Professional vs. Parent and Parent vs. Self. Thus, the addition of the parent role provides additional conflict with each of the roles in the area of most conflict, Professional vs. Self.

Previous research has indicated that Type A behavior is associated with perceived role conflict. For example, nurses classified as Type A have been found to perceive greater role conflict, receiving incompatible requests to do some job related activity (Ivancevich et al., 1982). And, research has also indicated that female faculty members classified as medium and high Type A perceived more interrole conflict involving demands of work and family/home roles (Eberhardt & Eberhardt, 1983). The latter study assessed interrole conflict using a single scale based on four items which assessed job versus non-job conflict.

The present study investigates the relationship between Type A behavior and specific types of role conflict involving work and familial roles using Holahan and Gilbert's (1979) six role conflict scales. In this way a more precise statement may be made as to the specific areas in which

TABLE 2 Demographic Characteristics of Female Faculty Sample

Highest degree	*N*	%
B.A.	4	5
M.A.	20	25
Ph.D.	54	67.5
Other	2	2.5
Total	*80*	*100.0*
Marital Status		
Married	51	64.0
Single	9	11.0
Separated/Divorced	16	20.0
Widowed	1	1.0
Other	3	4.0
Total	*80*	*100.0*
Presence/Absence of children		
Children at home	47	59.0
Children left home	11	14.0
No children	22	27.0
Total	*80*	*100.0*
Rank		
Full	7	9
Associate	46	57
Assistant	15	19
Lecturer	6	7.5
Other (Associate Lecturer, etc.)	6	7.5
Total	*80*	*100.0*
Number with Children		
Yes	58	72.5
No	22	27.5
Total	*80*	*100.0*

the Type A woman experiences role conflict, i.e., Professional vs. Parent, Professional vs. Spouse, etc. Related goals of the present study involve exploring the factors associated with Type A behavior. In this regard, the relationship between Type A behavior and career aspirations was explored as well as the relationship between Type A behavior and number of hours worked in the home and professionally. Because the parental role has been found to provide additional conflict with each of the roles of Professional and Self (Holahan & Gilbert, 1979), the relationship between Type A behavior and hours spent working at home and professionally was analyzed among respondents with children living at home.

METHOD

Subjects

Respondents were 80 full-time female faculty members at a large Canadian university. Most of the respondents held a Ph.D., were at the assistant or associate professorial rank, and were married and had children living at home. The average age of respondents was 43.87 years (S.D. = 7.65, n = 79,[1] range: 28 to 64). Table 2 presents the demographic characteristics of the sample.

Procedure

A mail questionnaire was used to collect the data. The procedure involved sending the questionnaire with a covering letter which explained the purpose of the study and informed prospective respondents that their participation was voluntary and that their responses would be completely anonymous. Three weeks later, another questionnaire and a reminder letter were sent out asking the respondent to complete and return her questionnaire if she had not already done so. Of the 150 questionnaires that were sent out, 84 were returned giving a response rate of 56%. Four respondents were deleted from the sample because of incomplete questionnaires leaving a sample of 80 female faculty members.

Measures

The Jenkins Activity Survey (Jenkins et al., 1979), was used to assess Type A behavior and three components of this broader construct— Speed and Impatience, Job Involvement, and Hard Driving and Competitive factors.

Role conflict between various life roles was assessed using Holahan and Gilbert's (1979) role conflict measure. As mentioned earlier, this measure yields six scales which assess conflict between four major roles—Professional, Spouse, Parent and Self. The six role conflict scales are based on three or four items which ask respondents to indicate on a 5-point scale how much conflict is caused by each type of item. The items comprise the following types of role conflict: Professional vs. Self, Professional vs. Parent, Spouse vs. Parent, Spouse vs. Self, Parent vs. Self, and Professional vs. Spouse. Table 1 lists each of the six role confict scales, a representative item of the scale and the internal reliability coefficients for each scale. Almost all of the scales had a reliability coefficient of .80 or greater. Another measure of role conflict included for study was a single item (separate from the above-mentioned role conflict scales) which asked respondents to indicate on a 5-point scale how much

---

[1] *One respondent did not report her age.*

total role conflict in general they experienced. Three measures of career motivation were employed. They included self-ratings of the degree to which the respondent wanted to be a full professor, her perceived chances of becoming a full professor, and how high the respondent rated her aspirations for career recognition and achievement.

RESULTS

Level of Type A Behavior and Age

Scores on the Jenkins Activity Survey scales were computed for the whole sample and then compared with norms provided by Jenkins et al. (1979). Mean Type A scores[2] for this sample ($\bar{X}$ = 6.4, S.D. = 8.4, n = 79) fell at the 70th percentile, mean Speed and Impatience scores ($\bar{X}$ = 3.0, S.D. = 9.1, n = 78) fell at the 65th percentile, mean Job Involvement scores ($\bar{X}$ = 5.6, S.D. = 6.1, n = 79) fell at the 70th percentile, and mean Hard Driving and Competitive scores ($\bar{X}$ = -2.6, S.D. = 8.9, n = 79) fell at the 45th percentile.

Results of a correlation between age and Type A behavior indicated a significant negative relationship between these variables ($r = -.30$, $df = 76$, $p < .01$). A breakdown of mean Type A scores in three age groups showed the following: between ages 28 and 39, the mean Type A score was 8.73 (n = 27, S.D. = 6.32); between ages 40 and 46, the mean Type A score was 6.58 (n = 24, S.D. = 7.81), and between ages 47 and 64, the mean was 4.32 (n = 27, S.D. = 10.16).

Type A and Role Conflict Scales

Table 3 presents a correlation matrix with the four Jenkins Activity Survey scales and the six role conflict scales as well as scores on "total role conflict" experienced. Scores on Type A and Speed and Impatience scales correlated significantly and positively with role conflict scales especially involving the respondent's role as a professional. Further results were that scores on the Type A and Speed and Impatience scales correlated significantly and positively with role conflict involving spousal and parental roles and with "total role conflict".

Type A scores correlated positively and significantly with Speed and Impatience, Job Involvement and Hard Driving and Competitive scores—an expected finding given that Type A behavior is defined especially in terms of these dimensions. Job Involvement was independent of Speed and Impatience scores, which in turn were moderately related to Hard Driving and Competitive Scores. Data indicated that scores on the Job Involvement and Hard Driving and Competitive Scales were also moder-

---

[2] *One respondent did not fill out the Jenkins Activity Survey Scale. A second respondent omitted more than one item used to score the Speed and Impatience Scale thus resulting in the loss of one more respondent in this scale mean.*

TABLE 3 Correlation Matrix for Jenkins Activity Survey and Role Conflict Scales[1]

	Pr.vs.Self	*Pr.vs.Par.*	*Sp.vs.Par.*	*Sp.vs.Self*	*Par.vs.Self*	*Pr.vs.Sp.*	*Total role Conf.*	*Type A*	*Sp.& Imp.*	*Job Inv.*	*Hard Dr. & Comp.*
Pr. vs. Self	–										
Pr. vs. Par.	.77*** (44)[2]	–									
Sp. vs. Par.	.58*** (36)	.74*** (35)	–								
Sp. vs. Self	.52*** (50)	.54*** (36)	.35* (32)	–							
Par. vs. Self	.61*** (47)	.70*** (44)	.65*** (35)	.60*** (36)	–						
Pr. vs. Sp.	.62*** (56)	.79*** (38)	.51** (34)	.66*** (48)	.66*** (38)	–					
Total Role Conf.	.67*** (68)	.78*** (44)	.55*** (36)	.62*** (51)	.64*** (46)	.73*** (54)	–				
Type A	.13 (73)	.37** (45)	.33* (35)	.13 (51)	.24 (47)	.28 (56)	.20** (71)	–			
Sp. & Imp.	.26* (73)	.37** (45)	.35* (35)	.09 (51)	.21 (47)	.36** (56)	.30** (71)	.59*** (78)	–		
Job Inv.	-.03 (73)	-.04 (45)	-.12 (35)	.04 (51)	-.29* (47)	-.05 (56)	-.11 (71)	.27** (78)	.04 (77)	–	
Hard Dr. & Comp.	.09 (73)	.24 (45)	.02 (35)	.14 (51)	.17 (47)	.17 (56)	.11 (71)	.63*** (78)	.20* (77)	.29** (78) *	–

*p < .05 **; p < .01 ***; p < .001*

[1]*The n's for the correlations were variable for the following reasons. First, 78 repondents filled out the entire Jenkins Activity Survey Scale. Secondly, only respondents who were married or living with a member of the opposite sex answered items involving spousal conflict. Third, only women who were mothers responded to items related to maternal conflict. A total of 69 respondents answered the question assessing self-reported total role conflict; 73 respondents answered all items in the measure of Pr. vs. Self conflict; 57 answered all items in the measure of Pr. vs. Sp. conflict. A total of 51 respondents answered all items in the Sp. vs. Self conflict measure and 46 answered the Pr. vs. Par. conflict items; 48 respondents answered all the items in the Par. vs. Self conflict scale, and 36 respondents answered all items relating to conflict beteen Sp. vs. Par.*

[2]*(n)*

TABLE 4 Mean Hours Working in the Home, at Professional Work, and Overall for three groups of women

	*Home**			*Professional Work*			*Overall***		
Group	*N*	*Mean*	*S.D.*	*N*	*Mean*	*SD*	*N*	*Mean*	*SD*
Children at home	47	44.2	16.8	47	42.0	16.4	47	86.2	24.2
Children left home	11	25.1	13.6	11	43.8	8.6	11	68.9	17.3
No children	22	21.1	8.0	22	52.4	14.9	22	73.1	19.7

* *hours in the home = housework hrs. + childcare hrs. + maintenance hrs.+ finance hrs.*
** *overall hours = home hrs. + professional work hrs.*

ately related. Correlations among the role conflict scales showed highly significant relationships.

Hours Worked at Home and Professionally and Jenkins Activity Survey Scores

Table 4 presents average hours worked in the home, professionally, and overall (total hours working in the home and at work) for three groups: Women with children living at home, women whose children have grown up and left home, and women who have never had children. Hours spent working in the home include the sum of hours doing housework, childcare, household maintenance activities, and financial or bookkeeping tasks. The results of an analysis of variance of hours spent working in the home showed a significant effect due to the presence of children variable ($F = 22.17$, $df = 2, 77$, $p < .001$). Results of Duncan Multiple Range tests indicated that women with children at home spent significantly more hours working in the home than either women with children who had left home or those with no children ($df = 77$, $p < .05$). A significant effect due to the presence of children variable was also found in an analysis of variance of hours spent at professional work ($F = 3.40$, $df = 2, 76$, $p < .05$): Women with no children were working more hours at their profession than women with children at home and women whose children have left home.

A multiple regression analysis was conducted in which hours spent working in the home and at professional work were regressed (used as multiple regression predictors) on Type A scores. Six variables were entered into the equation. These were: Hours spent at housework, childcare, household maintenance tasks, financial and bookkeeping activities, professional work, and age. The results of the analysis are presented in Table 5. Forty- three percent of the variation in Type A scores was predicted by a combination of these variables. Of these, the most important variables predicting Type A scores were: Hours spent in childcare, home maintenance activities and professional work. Thus, the more hours

TABLE 5 Multiple Regression for Type A Scores for Women With Children Living at Home

Analysis of variance: Source	DF	SS	MS	F
Regression	6	1282.1	213.7	4.39**
Residual	35	1703.4	48.7	
R square = 0.43				

Variables in the equation Variable	B	Std. Error	T
Housework hrs.	-0.11	0.14	-0.76
Childcare hrs.	0.35	0.11	3.02**
Maint. hrs.	0.71	0.31	2.21*
Finance hrs.	-0.67	0.83	-0.82
Work hrs.	0.17	0.08	2.25*
Age	0.18	0.24	0.72
Constant	-13.69	12.61	-1.09

* $p < .05$ ** $p < .01$

spent in childcare, home maintenance, and professional work, the higher the Type A scores.

Career Motivation and Type A Behavior

Mean ratings on three measures of career motivation were computed. These were self-ratings on the degree to which the respondent wanted to be a full professor, her perceived chances of becoming a full professor, and how high the respondent rated her aspirations for career recognition and achievement. On average, these ratings were relatively high. For example, the mean response to the question, "Do you want to be a full professor?" was 2.8 (S.D. = 1.7, n = 65)[3] on a scale ranging from 1 (yes) to 7 (no). And, when asked what they thought were their chances of being a full professor some day, the mean response was 2.8 (S.D. = 1.3, n = 65)[3] on a scale that ranged from 1 (100%) to 5 (0%). Finally, when asked to indicate how high their career aspirations were, the average response was 5.7[4] (S.D. = 1.3, n = 77) on a scale that ranged from 1 (very low) to 7 (very high).

Table 6 presents correlations of the four Jenkins Activity Survey scales with the three measures of career motivation. Nine of the twelve correlations reached statistical significance—only the Speed and Impatience scale did not significantly correlate with career motivation. The results showed that the higher the Type A scores, the more the respondent

[3] *Fifteen respondents did not respond to the items asking them if they wanted to be a full professor and to indicate their chances of being a full professor some day. Some of these were already full professors and thus the questions did not apply to them. Others did not answer these items because being a full professor was not part of their career aspirations.*

[4] *Three respondents did not answer this item.*

TABLE 6 Correlations Between Four Jenkins Activity Survey Scales and Career Motivation Measures

Jenkins Activity Survey	*Want Full Prof.*[1]	*Chances of Full Prof.*[2]	*Career Aspirations*[3]
Type A	-.33**	-.31**	.28**
Speed and Impatience	-.23	-.02	-.02
Job Involvement	-.30*	-.38**	.22*
Hard Driving and Competitive	-.27*	-.26*	.25*

[1] *definitely yes = 1, definitely no = 7*
[2] *100% = 1, 0% = 5*
[3] *very low = 1, very high = 7*
* $p < .05$; ** $p < .01$; *** $p < .001$

wanted to be a full professor, the greater her perceived chances of becoming one, and the higher her career aspirations for career recognition and achievement. The Job Involvement and Hard Driving and Competitive scales showed similar significant relationships with career motivation measures.

DISCUSSION

This sample of faculty women was highly Type A. These results are in line with previous research showing that higher levels of Type A behavior are found in women who occupy higher status occupations (Waldron, 1978). Further, results in the present research confirm the relationship of a high achievement orientation to Type A in women. Thus, a woman who exhibited high Type A behavior was more likely than her less Type A counterpart to want to be a full professor, to perceive a greater likelihood of being a full professor, and to score higher on self-rated career aspirations. These results parallel those of previous research by Glass (1977a; 1977b) in which Type A's demonstrated a greater manifest orientation toward achievement. Moreover, additional research (Rosenman et al., 1974) has found positive correlations between Type A behavior and several adjective scales including achievement, as assessed by Gough's Adjective Check List (1952). Putting these results together, Type A behavior in men as well as in women is correlated with a high achievement orientation and a strong desire for career recognition.

The present results showed highly significant relationships among the various role conflict scales thus suggesting considerable overlap in the role conflict assessed. Thus, high role conflict appears to suggest conflict among the four major roles—spouse, parent, professional and "self as a self actualized person." Moreover, the data showed that each of the six role conflict scales correlated significantly with the self-report measure of "total role conflict" experienced. Thus, it may be that when individuals experience a great deal of conflict (in general), they are more likely to report that they experience conflict among specific roles. It is also likely that when individuals experience a great deal of conflict between two specific roles, this conflict may spread to other roles thus resulting in greater overall or total role conflict experienced.

The present findings that role conflict correlated positively with Type A behavior confirm and extend findings of previous research (Eberhardt & Eberhardt, 1983) which employed a different measure of Type A behavior—a nine-item scale developed by Caplan et al. (1975). Specifically, the present results showed that in addition to experiencing more total role conflict, higher Type A women were experiencing more role conflict between their familial roles (Spouse vs. Parent) and between their professional role and each of their familial roles (Professional vs. Parent, Professional vs. Spouse). Speed and Impatience scores were similarly correlated with role conflict, with one additional result—the higher the Speed and Impatience, the higher the conflict between being a professional and being a self actualized person. Thus, the higher the role conflict among various life roles, the higher the Type A behavior and the higher the Speed and Impatience.

An explanation of these results can be found in the Type A woman's expectations of herself. Pressures to perform on the job are greater for the Type A woman, given her high professional achievement orientation. Demands associated with spousal and parental roles probably also contribute to Type A behavior, as has been suggested in the past (Waldron, 1978; 1980). In attempting to meet all of these demands, the Type A woman experiences greater time pressures and as a result, greater conflict. Moreover, the data suggest that a woman who is high on Speed and Impatience not only experiences role conflict among her various work and familial role but also between demands of her work role and her needs for self development. Thus, with higher Speed and Impatience and the associated time urgency, a professional woman with children is likely having difficulty making time for herself and her own personal needs.

Clearly, the combination of the parental role with that of the professional role involves a considerable commitment on the part of women, in terms of energy and time. Faculty women with children living at home are spending an average of 20 hours per week more working in the home (mainly in childcare activities) than either women with no children or those whose children have left home. Despite their heavy home responsibilities, women with children living at home do not appear to be working significantly less hours professionally than women whose children have left home. Moreover, the data suggest that women who have *no* children are working longer hours professionally than women in the other two groups. Results showing that women with children living at home are working more hours, overall, suggest that this is due primarily to their heavy time commitment to childcare. Thus, women with children at home are working an average of 86 hours per week both professionally and in the home. This figure is less than that reported for a comparable sample of female faculty in a large U.S. Midwestern university—107 hours worked professionally and at home (Yogev, 1982). Moreover, despite their heavy workload, women in this study did not consider themselves overworked. Not only did they not acknowledge that they were overworked, they also took for granted that they ought to be able to accept their dual role without complaint. In not admitting they were overworked, these women felt they could and should be able to be feminine, successful in their careers, good mothers, and have happy marriages—all that without feeling overloaded. Taken together, these results suggest that professional women with children living at home appear to have very high standards about combining career and family. Moreover, data from the present study suggest that this would hold even more for Type A women, given their hard-driving approach to work.

Results of the multiple regression analysis predicting to Type A behavior suggest that Type A behavior is associated with number of hours spent working, particularly the number of hours spent on childcare, home maintenance activities, and professional work. The positive relationship between Type A behavior and number of working hours parallels previous research which has reported a similar relationship, primarily among malc workers (Burke and Weir, 1980; Howard et al., 1977). Moreover, number of hours spent working in the home and professionally accounted for a significant proportion (43%) of the variation in Type A scores.

The multiple regression analysis also indicated that age was not a significant predictor of Type A behavior when other variables were controlled for. However, results of a correlation between age and Type A behavior showed a significantly negative relationship: As age increased, there was a decrease in Type A scores. A breakdown of Type A scores according to three age groups showed a decline in Type A scores from 8.73 in the 28 to 39 age range, to 4.32 in the higher age group which ranged from 47 to 64 years old. The tren for Type A scores to decline after mid years coincides with the findings by Moss et al. (1986) who report an inverted V-shaped relationship beteen age and Type A behavior. While the present results also suggest that Type A behavior declines with age, particularly in the middle years, the age factor would appear to be a less important predictor of Type A behavior than hours spent in various home and work-related activities.

CONCLUSIONS

While the Jenkins Activity Survey Scale (JAS) is the most widely-used measure of Type A behavior, it is important to be aware of some of its limitations. Although a relationship between CHD in women and Type A behavior, as measured by the JAS, has been reported in the research literature (Kenigsberg et al., 1974), research has not yet established the validity of the JAS for predicting CHD in women. Nevertheless, there is evidence for the face validity of the JAS as a measure of Type A behavior given the reported significant and positive correlation between Type A scores, using this measure, and occupational status (Waldron, 1978). This suggests that the coronary-prone behavior pattern is related to upward mobility in women. Also, research has indicated that anger and hostility are significant predictors of CHD (Matthews & Haynes, 1986; Williams, Haney, Lee, Kong, Yi-Hong, Blumenthal & Whalen, 1980). However, while the Jenkins Activity Survey Scale assesses Type A behavior, it does not include many items which assess anger and hostility.

Previous research on dual-career families confirms that conflicts between professional and parental roles are especially stressful for the female spouse (Bryson & Bryson, 1978; Heckman et al., 1977; Holahan & Gilbert, 1979). Research has also shown a relationship between role conflict and health. For example, Greenglass (1985) reports significant correlations among managerial women between job/family conflict or interference, and scores on psychosomatic measures such as depression, irritation and job anxiety. There is evidence from previous research that professional women may not even acknowledge that they are overworked (Yogev, 1982). It is likely that they will not take measures to alleviate the pressure until they acknowledge that a problem exists.

REFERENCES

Abush, R., & Burkhead, E.J. (1984). Job stress in midlife working women: Relationships among personality type, job characteristics, and job tension. *Journal of Counseling Psychology, 31*, 36-44.

Baruch, R. (1967). The achievement motive in women: Implications for career development. *Journal of Personality and Social Psychology, 5*, 260-267.

Bryson, J.B. and Bryson, R.A. (1978). Dual-career couples. *Psychology of Women Quarterly, 3*, whole issue.

Burke, R.J. & Weir, T. (1980). The Type A experience: Occupational and life demands, satisfaction, and well- being. *Journal of Human Stress, 6*, 28-38.

Caplan, R.D., Cobb, S., French, J.R.P., Harrison, R.V., & Pinneau, S.R. (1975).

Job demands and worker health. U.S. Government Printing Office: HEW Publication No. (NIOSH) 75- 160.

Eberhardt, B.J., and Eberhardt, M.J. (1983). *The prevalence and effects of the Type A behavior pattern in men and women: A direct comparison.* Paper presented at the 43rd National Meeting of the Academy of Management, Dallas, Texas.

Glass, D.C. (1977a). *Behavior patterns, stress, and coronary disease.* Erlbaum, Hillsdale, N.J.

Glass D.C. (1977b). Stress, behavior patterns, and coronary disease. *American Scientist, 65,* 177-187.

Gough, H.G. (1952). *The adjective check list.* University of California Press, Berkeley.

Greenglass, E.R. (1985). Psychological implications of sex bias in the workplace. *Academic Psychology Bulletin, 7,* 227-240.

Haynes, S., Feinleib, M., Levine, S., Scotch, N.A., & Kannel, W.B. (1977). *Psycho-social factors and CHD prevalence–the Framingham Heart Study.* Talk presented at the Conference on Cardiovascular Disease Epidemiology, San Diego, California.

Haynes, S.G., Feinleib, M., Levine, S., Scotch, N.,& Kannel, W.B. (1978). The relationship of psychosocial factors to coronary heart disease in the Framingham Study II. Prevalence of coronary heart disease. *American Journal of Epidemiology, 107,* 384-402.

Haynes, S.G., Feinleib, M., & Kannel, W.B. (1980). The relationship of psychosocial factors to coronary heart disease in the Framingham Study III. Eight year incidence of coronary heart disease. *American Journal of Epidemiology, 111,* 37-58.

Heckman, N.A., Bryson, R., & Bryson, J.B. (1977). Problems of professional couples: A content analysis. *Journal of Marriage and the Family, 39,* 323-330.

Holahan, C.K., & Gilbert, L.A. (1979). Conflict between major life roles: Women and men in dual career couples. *Human Relations, 32,* 451-467.

Houston, B.K., & Kelly, K.E. (1987). Type A behavior in housewives: Relation to work, marital adjustment, stress, tension, health, fear-of-failure and self esteem. *Journal of Psychosomatic Research, 31,* 55-61.

Howard, J.H., Cunngham, D.A., & Rechnitzer, P.A. (1977). Work patterns associated with Type A behavior. A managerial population. *Human Relations, 30,* 825-836.

Ivancevich, J.M., Matteson, M.T., & Preston, C. (1982). Occupational stress, Type A behavior, and physical well being. *Academy of Management Journal, 25,* 373-391.

Jenkins, C.D. (1976). Recent evidence supporting psychologic and social risk factors for coronary heart disease. *New England Journal of Medicine, 294,* 1033-1038.

Jenkins, C.D., Zyzanski, S.J. & Rosenman, R.H. (1979). *Jenkins Activity Survey Manual.* The Psychological Corporation, New York.

Kelly, K.E., & Houston, B.K. (1985). Type A behavior in employed women: Relation to work, marital, and leisure variables, social support, stress, tension, and health. *Journal of Personality and Social Psychology, 48,* 1067-1079.

Kenigsberg, D., Zyzanski, S.J., Jenkins, C.D., Wardwell, W.I. & Licciardello, A.T. (1974). The coronary-prone behavior pattern in hospitalized patients with and without coronary disease. *Psychosomatic Medicine, 36,* 344-351.

Kriger, S.F. (1972). n Ach and perceived parental child- rearing attitudes of career women and homemakers. *Journal Of Vocational Behavior, 2,* 419-432.

Matthews, K.A. & Haynes, S.A. (1986). Type A behavior pattern and coronary disease risk: Update and critical evaluation. *American Journal of Epidemiology, 123,* 923-960.

Moss, G.E., Dielman, T.E., Campanelli, P.C., Leech, S.L., Harlan, W.R., Harrison, V., & Horvath, W.J. (1986). Demographic correlates of SI assessments of Type A behavior. *Psychosomatic Medicine, 48,* 564-574.

Rosenman, R.H. (1978). The interview method of assessment of the coronary-prone behavior pattern. In T.M. Dembroski, S.M. Weiss, J.L. Shields, S.G. Haynes, & M. Feinleib (Eds.) *Coronary-Prone Behavior.* New York: Springer.

Rosenman, R.H., Rahe, R.H., Borhani, N.O., and Feinleib, M. (1974). Heritability of personality and behavior pattern. Proceedings of the First International Congress on Twins, Rome.

Shekelle, R.B., Schoenberger, J.A., & Stamler, J. (1976). Correlates of the JAS Type A behavior pattern score. *Journal of Chronic Diseases, 29,* 381-394.

Shelton, P.B. (1968). Achievement motivation in professional women, *Dissertation Abstracts, 28,* (10-A), 4274.

Sorensen, G., Jacobs, D.R., Jr., Pirie, P., Folsom, A., Luepke, R., & Gillum, R. (1987). Relationships among Type A behavior, employment experiences, and gender: The Minnesota Heart Survey. *Journal of Behavioral Medicine, 10* (4), 323- 336.

Szalai, A. (Ed.) (1972). *The use of time.* Mouton, The Hague.

Waldron, I. (1976). Why do women live longer than men? *Social Science and Medicine, 10,* 349-362.

Waldron, I. (1978). Type A behavior pattern and coronary heart disease in men and women. *Social Science and Medicine, 12,* 167-170.

Waldron, I. (1980). Employment and women's health: An analysis of causal relationships. *International Journal of Health Services, 10,* 435-454.

Waldron, I., Zyzanski, S., Shekelle, R.B., Jenkins C.D., & Tannenbaum, S. (1977). The coronary-prone behavior pattern in employed men and women. *Journal of Human Stress, 3,* 2-18.

Williams, R.B., Haney, T.L. Lee, K.L., Kong, Y., Blumenthal, J.A. & Whalen, R.E. (1980). Type A behavior, hostility and coronary atherosclerosis. *Psychosomatic Medicine, 42,* 539- 549.

Yogev, S. (1982). Are professional women overworked? Objective versus subjective perception of role loads. *Journal of Occupational Psychology, 55,* 165-169.

An Alternative Approach to Type A Behavior and Health: Psychological Reactance and Medical Noncompliance

Frederick Rhodewalt
Marita Fairfield
Department of Psychology, University of Utah
Salt Lake City, UT 84112

The Type A/Reactance model of medical noncompliance is reviewed and supporting evidence is summarized (Rhodewalt & Strube, 1985; Rhodewalt & Marcroft, 1988; Fairfield & Rhodewalt, 1988). The model specifies that self-evaluative processes associated with Type A behavior lead Type As to be more likely to perceive threats to behavioral freedom and respond with exaggerated attempts to reestablish control. Many health disabilities and treatment regimens pose control threats to Type As. As a consequence, Type As are often noncompliant with treatment in the service of reestablishment of perceived control. Additional findings suggest that Type A treatment compliance can be enhanced by providing Type As with perceived choice within the treatment setting. Discussion focuses on unanswered questions and future research directions for the Type A/Reactance model of medical noncompliance including issues involved with compliance promoting interventions.

It has been almost thirty years since Friedman and Rosenman (1959) first offered their clinically based description of the Type A behavior pattern. They maintained that the tendency to exhibit extreme competitiveness, ambition, time urgency, and easily evoked hostility placed one at risk for premature coronary heart disease (CHD). Their observations spawned three decades of research on Type A and biobehaviorally mediated risk for CHD. A wealth of data now exists with which one can evaluate Friedman and Rosenman's clinically derived speculations.

CURRENT STATUS OF TYPE A BEHAVIOR AND CHD RISK

Recently, enthusiasm for the Type A construct has waned primarily because epidemiological findings have failed to show a consistent pattern of association between Type A and clinical endpoints of CHD (Manuck,

Author Notes: We wish to acknowledge the creative and empirical contributions of Michael Strube and Marina Marcroft to our thinking. Address correspondence to the first author.

© 1990 Select Press

Kaplan, & Matthews, 1986; Matthews & Haynes, 1986). Several recent qualitative (Matthews & Haynes, 1986) and quantitative reviews (Booth-Kewley & Friedman, 1987; Matthews, 1988) lead to the conclusion that Type A behavior as indexed by the Structured Interview (SI) is a reliable predictor of CHD incidence but, that Type A behavior as assessed by the Jenkins Activity Survey (JAS, Jenkins, Rosenman, & Zyzanski, 1974), the most frequently employed paper and pencil measure of Type A, is not associatied reliably with CHD. Moreover, the conclusion regarding SI-CHD risk appears most true for population based studies in which the sample is not at risk for CHD because of the presence of other factors like hypertension, smoking, or previous myocardial infarction (Matthews, 1988).

The issues involved in interpreting null effects in these epidemiological studies are very complex. For example, Matthews (1988) notes that many of the high risk sample studies have a prevalence of Type A patients which restricts the range of Type A-B behavior and possibly the ability to detect behavior pattern–CHD associations. Other investigations have failed to find evidence for their main hypotheses making tests of subsidiary predictions concerning Type A less sensitive. These interpretive difficulties not withstanding, the best evidence suggests that JAS Type A is not significantly associated with CHD. A recent meta analysis in which only prospective studies were included failed to find a significant association between the JAS and CHD across eleven investigations (Matthews, 1988; see also Friedman & Booth-Kewley, 1988).

Smith and Rhodewalt (1986) have argued that the relationship between Type A behavior and episodes of cardiovascular reactivity, the presumed biobehavioral pathway to CHD, is more complex than is assumed by current epidemiological models. Smith and Rhodewalt contend that the various methods of Type A assessment differ in the extent to which they tap cardiovascular reactivity versus what they term "stress engendering behavior". The SI appears to be the superior measure of reactivity to challenge. In contrast, the JAS according to Smith and Rhodewalt is a measure of stress engendering behavior. JAS Type As through their choice of situations, self-appraisals, interpersonal relationships, and cognitive and behavioral coping strategies create many more frequent, intense, and often longer duration stressful encounters than do their Type B counterparts (see Smith & Rhodewalt, 1986 for review of supporting empirical literature). It is perhaps the presence of both JAS and SI Type A behavior in the same individual that elevates his or her risk for CHD as a function of social context.

It is interesting to note that while the role of Type A behavior in the genesis of CHD has been sharply questioned, the reduction of Type A behavior appears to have reduced new morbidity and mortality in a sample of CHD survivors. M. Friedman et al. (1986) report that over one third of the patients assigned to a Type A behavioral intervention group showed a marked reduction in Type A behavior. Moreover, this group displayed a cumulative CHD recurrence rate of approximately half (12.9%) that of a group receiving only cardiological counseling (21.2%) or a group receiving no treatment (28.2%). Nonetheless, confusion in the area has led some to suggest that global Type A be abandoned in favor of a search for the "toxic" components of coronary-prone behavior such as hostility as measured by the Cook-Medley Scale (Barefoot, Dahlstrom, & Williams, 1983) or Potential for Hostility as gleaned from a rescoring of the SI (Dembroski & Costa, 1987).

AN ALTERNATIVE APPROACH TO TYPE A AND HEALTH RISK

To summarize the preceding section, it is quite clear that the relation between Type A behavior and risk for CHD is not as straightforward as once assumed. This is most apparent for JAS defined Type A and calls into question its status as a useful predictor of CHD (Dembroski & Costa, 1988). Does this mean that JAS Type A should be relegated to a footnote in the annals of health psychology? We suggest not. One consequence of the intensive research effort in the area is that JAS Type A has emerged as a social/cognitive personality variable of great interest. Numerous laboratory investigations demonstrate that Type As and Bs differ in their self-regulatory behavior (O'Keeffe & Smith, 1988; Strube, Boland, Manfredo, & Al-Falaij, 1987), use of social comparison information (Gastorf, Suls, & Sander, 1980), appraisal of threat (Carver, 1980; Rhodewalt & Comer, 1982; Rhodewalt & Davison, 1984), cognitive coping strategies, (Pittner & Houston, 1980), and evaluations of performance (Cooney & Zeichner, 1985).

We propose that these differences in self-appraisal and self-regulatory processes have a direct impact on health related behaviors and, consequently the health of Type A and B individuals. In the remainder of this article we review evidence, collected primarily in our laboratory, that ties Type A-B differences in social/cognitive processes to health outcomes. Specifically, this research indicates that JAS defined Type A behavior becomes a more general health risk factor whenever adherence to medical treatment is a determinant of a positive health outcome. We then review research in which we attempted to channel Type A self-regulatory behavior to increase treatment compliance. Finally, we conclude with a discussion of the current status of the Type A-Reactance model of noncompliance and outline directions for future research.

THE PSYCHOLOGY OF THE TYPE A INDIVIDUAL

In his seminal monograph on Type A behavior, Glass (1977) concluded that the core motivational dynamic of the Type A individual is effective control. Glass portrayed the Type A behaviors of time urgency, competitiveness, achievement striving, aggressiveness, and hostility as collectively representing a set of control mastery coping responses elicited by perceived threats to control. Subsequent research has supported this characterization. In most cases (see Lovallo & Pishkin, 1980 for an exception), Type As respond to challenge or threats to control with increased efforts to regain control.

Additional studies have elaborated the antecedents and consequences of the control dynamic in Type As. Of central importance to the present discussion are laboratory investigations showing that Type As, relative to Type Bs, are more likely to perceive coercive intent (Carver, 1980) and display reactance in response to a threatened behavioral freedom (Rhodewalt & Comer, 1982; Rhodewalt & Davison, 1983; Snyder & Frankel, 1975; Strube & Werner, 1985).

Since the publication of the Glass (1977) monograph several additional theoretical frameworks have been developed to account for the psychology of Type A behavior (Matthews & Siegel, 1982, Price, 1982; Scherwitz, Berton, & Levonthal, 1978; Scherwitz & Canick, 1988; Strube, 1987). While all of these perspectives are distinct from one another in important ways, they share the common theme of Type As and Bs differing in how they appraise and cope with challenging, self-relevant outcomes.

Consistent with these views, our research has demonstrated that self-appraisal biases underlie both Type As' lower thresholds to perceive threat and their effortful coping responses. For instance, Rhodewalt and Davison (1983) provided evidence that Type As' elevated reactance responses are mediated by their self-attributions for why they expected to exercise a behavioral freedom in the first place. Type As tended to assume that possession of a behavioral freedom was attributable to factors under their control while Type Bs were more likely to recognize factors in the situation controlling their behavior. Consequently, when a behavioral freedom was threatened, Type As responded with reactance while Type Bs did not. Moreover, an experimental induction designed to lead subjects to believe they had earned a behavioral freedom (self-attribution) produced elevated reactance responses in both Type A and B participants when that freedom was threatened. In contrast, when subjects were induced to believe they had been randomly assigned to a condition in which they were allowed to exercise a behavioral freedom, neither Type As nor Bs displayed reactance when that freedom was threatened. These latter findings highlight the role of self-attributional processes in the experience of reactance (see also Wortman & Brehm, 1975).

Other studies corroborate the finding that Type As and Type Bs differ in the causal inferences they draw about their outcomes (Brunson & Matthews, 1981; Musante, MacDougal, & Dembroski, 1984; Rhodewalt, 1984; Rhodewalt, Strube, Hill, & Sansone, 1988; Strube, 1985). For example, Rhodewalt et al. (1988) asked Type A and B participants to imagine themselves in a series of positive and negative situations and to provide attributions for those imagined events. For each event subjects gave an open-ended attributional statement followed by scalar ratings of the internality-externality, stabilty-unstability, globality-specificity of the cause. The negative events were constructed to vary the extent to which they constituted a threat to control or a threat to self-esteem. When negative event attributions were compared to positive event attributions, both Type As and Bs were self-serving in that they attributed positive outcomes to themselves and negative outcomes to the situation (see also Strube, 1985). Type As offered slightly more stable attributions for positive outcomes and slightly more unstable attributions for negative outcomes than did Type Bs.

These attributional differences are clarified when one examines attributions for negative events that posed either a threat to self-esteem or control. These data indicate that Type As differed from Type Bs mainly in their attributions for negative events that posed a great threat to their control. Type As attributed such events to internal-unstable causes while Type Bs attributed the same events to external-stable causes. Rhodewalt et al. interpreted their data to indicate that when Type As encounter negative outcomes, particularly ones that threaten their control, they are more than ready to conclude that the cause of the outcome is internal and modifiable. Rhodewalt et al. suggest that such attributions justify the control mastery behaviors so often displayed by Type As in challenging situations. What emerges from the work described in the preceding paragraphs is a profile of Type As as being hyperresponsive to perceived threats to control because of the propensity to view themselves as causal or responsible for the unwanted outcomes. These causal interpretations, in turn, mandate increased effort in an attempt to reestablish and maintain control and behavioral freedom.

TYPE A BEHAVIOR, REACTANCE, AND TREATMENT COMPLIANCE

The literature summarized in the preceding section suggests that Type As possess a general tendency to construe threats to behavioral freedom as events requiring active responding in order to restore their sense of control. This characterization of the Type A prompted Rhodewalt and Strube (1985) to question how Type As might respond when the threat to behavioral freedom was a health problem or its treatment. This question seemed important because several researchers have commented on the importance of personal control in the psychological context of the health care setting. Taylor (1979) has outlined the ways in which hospitalization can lead to reactant or helpless behavior and the consequences of such behavior for the course of treatment. Krantz (1980) and Krantz & Schulz (1980) have suggested that the more a health event is perceived as predictable and controllable, the less disruptive that event will be. In many instances injury, illness, treatment, and the depersonalization of hospitalization can all contribute to the perception of reduced behavioral freedom. Such events should have greater impact on Type As than Type Bs because of Type As' concerns with personal control.

How might Type As respond to threatened behavioral freedoms in a health care setting? Several courses of action appear open to Type As which would appease their concerns about control. Type As might engage in rigidly compliant behavior in order to facilitate recovery and thus restore their feelings of control. However, in most instances compliance entails relinquishing control to the health care practitioner. Several studies indicate that Type As are unlikely to relinquish control to another even when it is in their best interest to do so (Strube & Werner, 1985). The other path open to the control-threatened Type A is maladaptive reactant behavior in the service of restoring perceived control.

How might reactance be displayed in a health care setting? Rhodewalt and Strube (1985) cataloged an array of mechanisms the reactant patient can employ to restore perceived freedom. Most obviously, reactant individuals can engage in the forbidden behaviors such as failing to control their diets or ceasing smoking. Often, reactant individuals display anger and aggression toward the freedom threatening agent, in this case the health care provider or perhaps the health problem itself (Taylor, 1979). Rhodewalt and Strube reasoned that reactant anger and aggression would be likely in Type As because of their tendency to respond to interpersonal threat in this way (Carver & Glass, 1978; Strube, Turner, Cerro, & Stevens, & Hinchey, 1984). Finally, the threatened behavior can become more desirable, a demonstrated propensity in Type As (Rhodewalt & Comer, 1982; Rhodewalt & Davison, 1983).

These factors led Rhodewalt and Strube (1985) to examine the prediction that Type A individuals would be more likely than Type Bs to exhibit reactance motivated noncompliant behavior in response to treatment. A sample of Type A and B recreational runners who were undergoing treatment for running related foot injuries were surveyed at the time of their initial visit to the physician's office for treatment. In addition to completing the JAS, patients responded to a battery of questionnaires designed to assess their perceptions of, and reactions to their injury. The measure of patient compliance was a physician's evaluation of each patient's rate of progress to recovery from much worse than expected to much better than expected. In support of our predictions, six of the seven patients rated by the physician as noncompliant were Type A (11 Type As and 14 Type Bs were judged as compliant by the physician, $t(30) = 2.24$, $p < .05$).

In order to determine if the noncompliant Type As were displaying reactance we compared their questionnaire data to compliant Type As and compliant Type Bs. While noncompliant Type As did not differ from the other groups in terms of age, extremity of Type A behavior, or severity of injury, they did differ in their perceptions of and reactions to the running injury. As one can see in Figure 1, noncompliant Type As were significantly more likely than compliant Type As and compliant Type Bs to feel responsible for the injury, view the injury as an entity to be fought, and be angry about it (all F's$(2,28) > 7.00$, p's $< .001$). At the same time, they expressed no preference for behavioral involvement with treatment. It is interesting to note that follow-up data from the patients indicated that both compliant and noncompliant Type As were less satisfied with their rate of recovery than were Type Bs ($F(2,19) = 3.38$, $p < .06$).

Thus we have initial evidence that some Type As relative to Type Bs are more likely to self-attribute their injury, be angry about it, and be viewed as noncompliant with treatment by their physician. Admittedly several inferential leaps of faith were required to reach this conclusion. We could only assume that nonadherence to proscribed treatment led to the physician's assessment of unsatisfactory recovery. Of course, as Rhodewalt and Strube noted, it could be that those who were most angry and upset about their injury or rate of recovery communicated their anger to the physician and this influenced his judgment. At minimum, Type As appeared to be differentially sensitive to some aspect of the health care setting which, in turn, led them to be evaluated negatively by their physician.

One question raised by the Rhodewalt and Strube study is why only some Type As and not others experienced reactance in response to treatment? One possibility is that some other individual difference variable not shared by all Type As predisposes some and not others to reactance engendered medical noncompliance. Rhodewalt and Strube conjectured that perhaps only Type As with a clear bias to self-attribute negative outcomes experience reactance in treatment settings. This speculation plus the limitations in the measurement of compliance indicated additional research was in order.

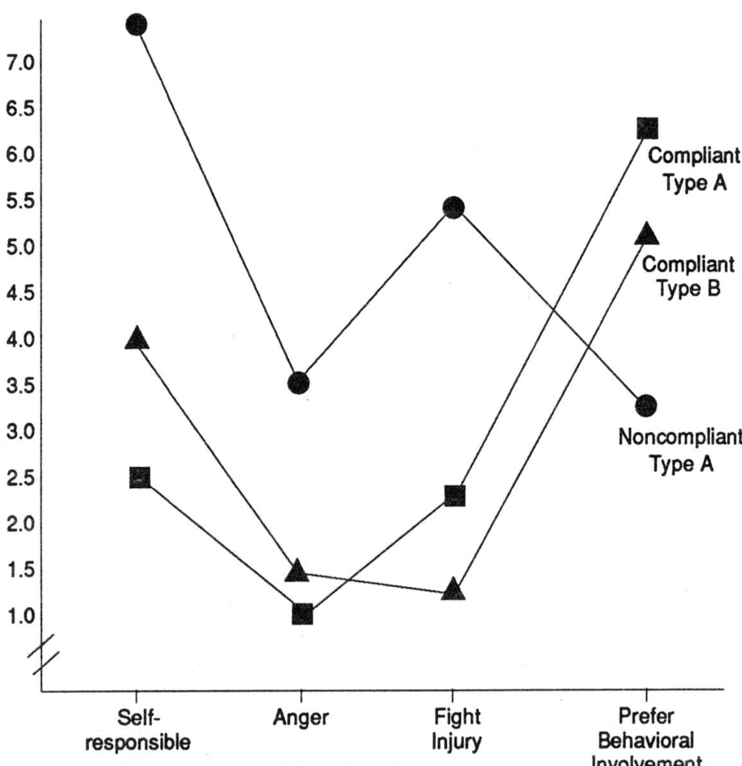

FIGURE 1 Recreational Runners' Reactions to Injury Adapted from Rhodewalt & Strube (1985)

Rhodewalt and Marcroft (1988) attempted to address some of the questions raised in the Rhodewalt and Strube study by investigating treatment compliance in Type A and B diabetes mellitus (Type 1) patients. Diabetes mellitus is a condition of chronic hyperglycemia (elevated blood glucose) that often can be controlled by diligent patient monitoring of diet, glucose levels, and self-administration of insulin. Rhodewalt and Marcroft surmised that this patient population would be an appropriate one in which to test the Type A - noncompliance hypotheses because of the high level of imposition involved in treatment and the fairly unambiguous means measuring compliance. Accordingly, thirty-nine patients completed the same battery of questionnaires (JAS, reactions to illness, preference for involvement with treatment) included in the Rhodewalt and Strube investigation as well as additional measures tapping general concerns about control (Desirability of Control, Burger & Cooper, 1979) and general self-attributional style (Attributional Style Questionnaire,

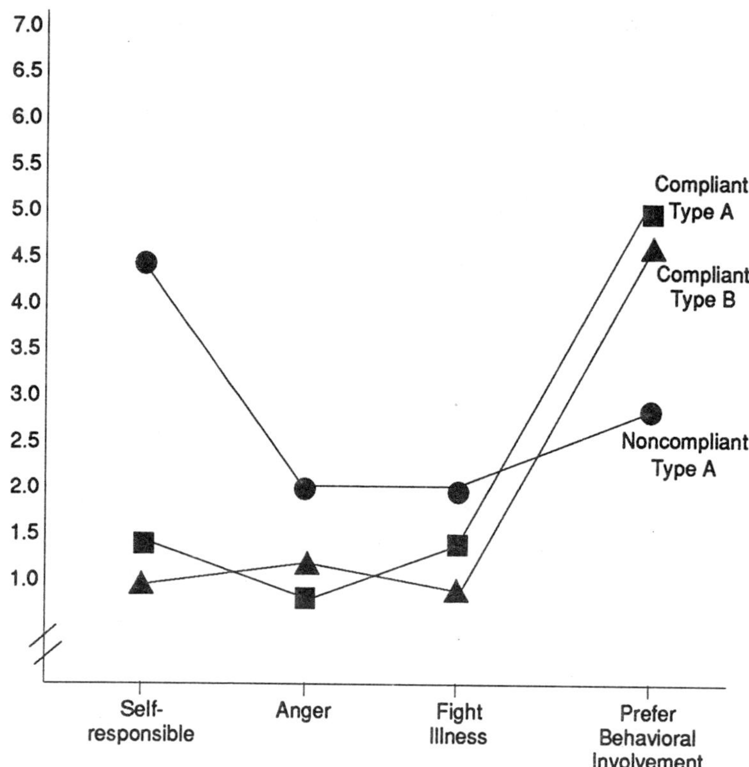

FIGURE 2 Diabetes Mellitus Patients' Reactions to Illness Adapted from Rhodewalt & Marcroft (1988)

Peterson, Semmel, von Baeyer, Abramson, Metalsky, & Seligman, 1982). Patients also responded to a single item asking them how much their diabetic condition interfered with their lifestyle. The measure of treatment complicance was degree of glucose control inferred from blood assays of glycosylated hemoglobin (Hb A1c). Glucose becomes attached to Hb A1c, a process that is ongoing during the two month life span of a red blood cell thus providing a relatively long term measure of glucose regulation. An independent laboratory collected the blood samples, conducted the Hb A1c analyses, and translated the Hb A1c scores into ranges labeled optimal glucose control, adequate glucose control, and poor glucose control.

Consistent with predictions, Type As had significantly higher Hb A1c levels than did Type Bs indicating overall poorer glucose regulation ($t(35) = 2.11$, $p < .05$). More informative however, are the numbers of patients judged to be in poor glucose control. Eight of the thirty-nine patients were rated in this range, seven of whom were Type A (Fisher's Exact $p < .025$).[1]

Again we examined the self-report data for compliant Type Bs, compliant Type As, and noncompliant Type As respectively and found a pattern of data strikingly similar to Rhodewalt and Strube (1985). As one can observe in Figure 2, noncompliant Type As viewed themselves as responsible for their diabetes, were angry about it, and viewed it as an enemy to be battled (all F's$(2,33) > 3.75$, p's $< .04$). While both groups of Type As endorsed statements such as "it is something I must overcome myself," only noncompliant Type As expressed no interest in behavioral involvemnt with treatment (F $(2,33) = 5.84$, p. $< .02$). Rhodewalt and Marcroft suggest these findings indicate that poor glucose control in Type As is not a passive response to treatment but rather an active response consistent with reactance motivation. Consistent with this interpretation is the finding that noncompliant Type As complained that their diabetes interfered more with their lives than did compliant Type As or compliant Type Bs ($F(2,33) = 5.02$, $p < .02$).

One purpose of the Rhodewalt and Marcroft investigation was to determine if noncompliance could be predicted by Type A in combination with some other reactance relevant individual difference. Unfortunately, neither individual differences in desire for control nor attributional style reliably discriminated noncompliant from compliant Type As. The only hint of a difference was that noncompliant Type As tended to view themselves as more responsible for negative outcomes in general than did their compliant counterparts. Thus, we again have evidence of the Type A - reactance model's selectivity or ability to identify at risk individuals. But, to date we have not been able to improve on its specificity. If one relies solely on Type A as a predictor of noncompliance then many compliant individuals will be labeled as at risk. We will return to these issues in our concluding comments.

REDUCING REACTANCE, PROMOTING COMPLIANCE

One implication of the model is that if treatment settings pose a potential threat to behavioral freedom which, in turn, engenders reactance motivated noncompliance in many Type As, then by reducing such threats

[1] *Rhodewalt and Marcroft (1988) tested a second hypothesis. Because research has shown that sympathetic arousal is related to glucose regulation (Surwit, Feinglos, & Scovern, 1983), Type As who experience frequent episodes of sympathetically mediated cardiovascular reactivity might have more difficulty controlling blood glucose for reasons unrelated to treatment adherence. A measure of life change was included as a crude test of this possibility. However, amount of recent life change (i.e. stress) was unrelated to Hb A_1c levels in their data. It is possible that the SI assessment of Type A which appears to be more closely tied to sympathetic reactivity might be a useful predictor of glucose regulation.*

one should be able to promote compliance. There are many strategies one might pursue to reduce the coercive aspects of treatment recommendations such as the employment of referent power or the social power one possesses because he or she is respected and liked (Rodin & Janis, 1979 see also DiMatteo & DiNicola, 1982). Cognitive dissonance theory (Wicklund & Brehm, 1976) in particular provides an abundance of experimental manipulations that in motivating dissonance should reduce reactance. For example, Cooper and Axsom (1982; Axsom & Cooper, 1984) have employed both induced compliance and effort justification manipulations to promote treatment effectiveness. These investigations indicate that patients who believe they freely chose to engage in effortful behavior (treatment) displayed greater treatment gains than did patients who believed they had no choice or who did not expend effort. With regard to Type A behavior, any aspect of the treatment setting that enhances the Type A's perception of freedom should also reduce reactance and treatment nonadherence.

Fairfield and Rhodewalt (1988) tested this hypothesis by using an adapted version of an experimental weight reduction therapy developed by Axsom and Cooper (1984). JAS defined Type A and B female undergraduates who were from six to forty-four percent overweight served as participants. They were informed that the research was investigating the relative effectiveness of three recently developed weight loss procedures. Each involved performing different sets of mental exercises in combination with a diet. Through pilot testing we designed descriptions of three bogus weight loss therapies that appeared equally desirable and highly plausible. Choice was manipulated by permitting half the experimental subjects to select which therapy they wanted while the other half were randomly assigned to one of the therapies. In actuality, all subjects were engaged in the same tasks for four "treatment sessions" over a two week period. In addition, a control group was also run in which subjects' weights were taken over the same two week span. A variety of measures were collected including weight loss, self-reports of expended effort, attributions for treatment outcomes, and, as a measure of dissonance/reactance, their evaluations of the treatment received versus the other allegedly available treatment options.

Fairfield and Rhodewalt predicted an interaction between manipulated choice and Type A-B behavior. We expected low choice Type As to be more reactant and therefore less compliant than low choice Type Bs. In contrast, we predicted that in the high choice condition Type As would respond most positively to treatment and consequently lose the most weight. We reasoned that because issues of behavioral freedom are more salient to Type As, they would be more affected by their choice to perform

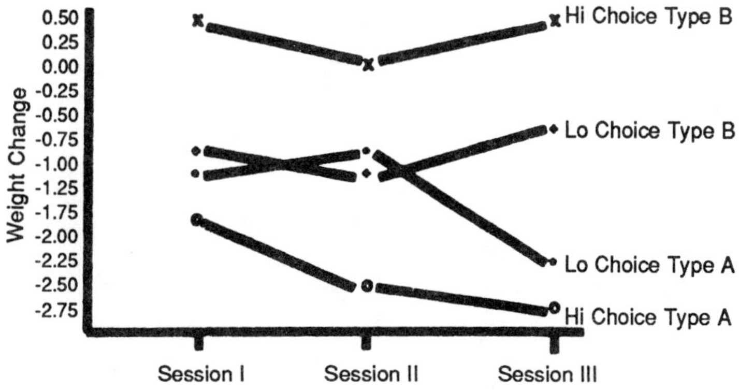

FIGURE 3 Weight Loss for Type A and B Subjects as a Function of Choice over Weight Loss Program. Subjects' initial percent over ideal weight is covaried from change scores. Sessions are approximately one week apart (Fairfield & Rhodewalt, 1988)

a highly effortful venture and, therefore experience the most dissonance. Weight loss of course would be the most salient way to reduce their dissonance. We predicted Type Bs would be less responsive to the dissonance manipulation because concerns about personal control are not as paramount to them as they are to Type As.

The results provided partial support for our predictions. Checks on the manipulation indicated that both Type A and B high choice subjects perceived greater chioce and flexibility in their treatment program than did low choice subjects ($F(1,45) = 16.91$, $P < .001$). Although the choice by Type A-B interactions failed to reach significance, Type As responded more positively to high choice than did Type Bs. High choice Type As, compared to their Type B counterparts, felt they were more successful at meeting the treatment requirements, reported exerting more effort throughout the study, and consistently lost more weight (there were few differences between Type As and Bs in the low choice condition). Interestingly, while there were no A-B differences in attrition rate, by the end of the study all remaining Type As regardless of choice condition lost significantly more weight ($F(1,35) = 7.59$, $p < .01$), perceived they had exerted more effort ($F(1,35) = 9.06$, $p < .01$), and attributed their progress in the program more to their desire to lose weight than did Type Bs (Type A = -2.45 lbs., Type B = -.21 lbs., $F's(1,35) = 16.03$, $p's < .001$). Although the choice by Type A-B interaction on weight loss was not significant, planned comparisons revealed that high choice Type As lost significantly more weight than the other groups combined ($p < .01$). These findings can be seen in Figure 3.

The failure to support the reatance predictions is less surprising when one examines the choice manipulation checks collected at the end of the first treatment session shortly after the administration of the choice manipulation. Although these measures indicated that we were successful in manipulating subjects' perceptions of choice within the treatment setting, absolute scale values suggest that all subjects believed they had a high degree of choice in the study. The choice manipulation was in all likelihood attenuated by procedures such as the volunteer nature of participation and the administration of informed consent. Although we did not find different dropout rates for Type A and B participants, it is possible that Type As who remained in the study where those for whom the volunteer aspect of the study was most salient. We have no way of evaluating this hypothesis, thus, the findings are best thought of as preliminary and requiring replication. However, these results do suggest that medical compliance can be enhanced in Type As by highlighting for them their personal choice in the treatment setting.

IMPLICATIONS AND FUTURE DIRECTIONS

In the previous sections we have detailed the theory and research linking Type A behavior and medical noncompliance. Although the research described is provocative and appears to be consistent with the Type A - reactance model, many questions remain unanswered. We turn now to the several paths future research might follow in addressing issues of Type A behavior and medical compliance.

An intriguing question asks why some Type As and not others engage in counterproductive treatment responses. One direction would be to continue the approach taken here and seek out other individual differences that combine with Type A to foster noncompliance. Our research (Rhodewalt & Marcroft, 1988) hints that differences in the tendency to engage in self-blame for illness and injury might be one fruitful avenue.

The role of self-blame has been examined by others with very mixed results. Taylor, Lichtman, and Wood (1984) found self-blame to be associated with good adjustment in some breast cancer patients and poor adjustment in others. Bulman and Wortman (1977) reported better adjustment in patients with spinal cord injuries who engaged in self-blame than those who did not. It may be that self-blame operates differently as a function of the health event. The beneficial effects of self-blame observed by Bulman and Wortman (1977) may be limited to discrete, irreversible events such as spinal cord injuries. In such cases, self-blame is beneficial because it permits the individual to find meaning in the event (Taylor et al., 1984). In other cases where the health problem is recurrent (such as a Myocardial Infarction) or chronic (such as diabetes) self-blame may promote noncompliance because the individual feels compelled to undo or compensate for the reduced behavioral freedom imposed by the disability.

A second focus would be to examine interactions between Type A sensitivities to control threat and features of specific health care situations. It is possible that the same Type A individual may respond constructively to one treatment regimen and reactantly to another. If this is the case then we will need finer grained analyses of the control contingencies of the health care setting [and the potential threats posed by various illnesses, injuries, and their treatments.] Control contingencies include variables such as physician-patient relationships, patient involvement in treatment, the availability of information, and life-style circumstances. It may be that Type As typically respond to any control threat with reactance. If they locate the threat to control in the health problem then they will adhere to the treatment but if the threat to control is located in the treatment then they will be noncompliant. The motivation in both instances is the same, only in the former case it promotes constructive behavior while in the latter it promotes self-harming behavior.

Another possibility noted by Rhodewalt and Strube (1985) is that perhaps initially all Type As are reactant to the reduced freedom imposed by their disability and/or treatment yet they attempt to follow treatment proscriptions. However, if their experiences do not match with their expectancies for recovery, they become frustrated and cease adherence. Type A self-evaluation processes may also contribute to violated expectancies and nonadherence to treatment. That is, even when Type As have clear expectations about the course of treatment and recovery, their selective attention to negative feedback (Cooney & Zeichner, 1985) and their tendency to set high standards for success and be self-critical (O'Keeffe & Smith, 1988) might foster frustration and reduced motivation to comply.

Another approach would be to examine the time course of Type A responses to health related threats to behavioral freedom. Our analysis of Type A and reactance bears many similarities to Wortman and Brehm's (1975) integration of reactance theory and the learned helplessness model. They argue that reactance is the initial response to uncontrollability in those individuals who expect to have control (perhaps Type As). However, after prolonged exposure these same individuals give up and become helpless. Similarly, Glass (1977) argues that the Type A's initial reaction to uncontrollability is hyperresponsiveness in an attempt to regain control but that after prolonged exposure to uncontrollability the Type A becomes hyporesponsive and gives up or withdraws effort (see Strube, 1987).

Both hyperresponsiveness (reactance) and hyporesponsiveness (helplessness) can lead to medical noncompliance. Thus, interventions designed to promote treatment compliance will need to consider the current motivational state underlying the noncompliant behavior. Procedures designed to counter reactance (e.g. enhanced perceptions of choice) should be ineffective in motivating the helpless individual just as procedures designed to counter helplessness (e.g. attributions to lack of effort) should be ineffective or even counterproductive in promoting compliance in the reactant individual.

The preceding discussion highlights the many avenues along which research on the Type A - reactance model of medical noncompliance might proceed. This discussion also suggests that attempts to promote compliance will need to be sensitive to the subtle complexities of the social psychological context of the health care setting as well as individual characteristics of the patient. We suggest that variables as subtle as perceived choice can diminish the Type A propensity to display reactance. There are undoubtedly other interventions that can be studied. It is unlikely that one control intervention or combination of interventions will be appropriate for all health problems and treatments.

As we noted at the outset, there are several recent reports of successful attempts to reduce Type A behavior and attendant CHD risk (Friedman et al., 1984, 1986; Gill et al., 1985). These studies have employed broad-based, multifaceted interventions administered over relatively long durations. The findings indicate that these multi-component interventions can lead to significant reductions in Type A behavior and, that reduction in Type A behavior is related to both decreased serum cholesterol (Gill et al., 1985) and CHD mortality (Friedman et al., 1986). Although these intervention programs appear promising, their effectiveness is no doubt limited by Type A-reactance mediated noncompliance. Participants are asked to invest large amounts of time in therapy and to acquire new ways of thinking about and responding to familiar situations. Only some Type As respond favorably to treatment. Friedman et al. (1984) reported that after three years only 18% of those who entered treatment displayed clear evidence of reduction in Type A behavior, another 27% presented some evidence of change, but more important, 21% displayed no evidence of change and 34% dropped out. There is no evidence that the no change Type As and the drop outs were manifesting reactance engendered noncompliance, but it is clear that the majority of Type As did not respond to treatment. Thus, the Type A intervention trials are consistent with our findings (Rhodealt & Marcroft, 1988; Rhodewalt & Strube, 1985) that many Type As fail to benefit from treatment. It is likely then, that attempts to alter Type A behavior and, ultimately, reduce CHD risk could be improved by attending to features of the treatment protocol that elicit reactance and noncompliance.

At the same time it is noteworthy that although the Type A's striving for control is considered maladaptive there may be occasions when such concerns are beneficial. Fairfield and Rhodewalt's findings suggest that Type A control mastery behaviors can be channeled toward adaptive behaviors in the health care environment. These observations have implications for those attempts to reduce CHD risk by modifying the Type A characteristics of the individual (Friedman et al., 1986). In order to improve the Type As adherence to recommendations for reducing CHD risk factors (diet, smoking, exercise, and the like) it may be more productive to change the terms under which the recommendations are presented (see also Baile & Engel, 1978). If medical recommendations and the health care environment reinforce the Type As' perception of behavioral freedom in the health care setting and prompt the individual to locate the threat to freedom in the health problem, we argue that Type As will respond with medically compliant behavior, thereby rendering Type A a positive factor in health outcomes.

SUMMARY AND CONCLUSIONS

In this article we have summarized the Type A - Reactance model of medical noncompliance and presented supporting research. Type As, because of their self-appraisal biases, are sensitive to threats to their behavioral freedom and respond to such threats with attempts to reestablish perceptions of control. These attempts to reestablish control are often manifested as noncompliance with treatment in health care settings. We then discussed additional data that indicates Type As' concerns about control can be channeled to promote treatment compliance. Finally we suggested issues for future research.

If continued research leads to the conclusion that Type A behavior is not the independent risk for CHD once thought, our research suggests that JAS Type A is still an important health related individual difference. Other researchers have demonstrated that Type As and Bs differ in how readily they perceive and label physical symptoms (Matthews & Siegal, 1983; Schlegel, Wellwood, Copps, Gruchow, & Sharratt, 1980; Weidner & Matthews, 1978). One implication of this is that Type As may often delay in seeking beneficial and needed treatment. Thus, they may gravely compound or exacerbate a health problem such as delaying treatment of the symptoms of an impending myocardial infarction (Matthews & Siegel, 1983). In addition, heightened sympathetic reactivity, perhaps as indexed by the SI measure of Type A, can also aggravate existing conditions such as glucose control in diabetics (Surwit et al., 1983). Taken together, these findings suggest that in the future Type A behavior might be more usefully conceived as a social/cognitive individual difference that through a variety of self-regulatory processes influences many aspects of physical well-being.

REFERENCES

Axsom, D., & Cooper, J. (1984). Reducing weight by reducing dissonance. In E. Aronson (Ed.), *Reading about the social animal,* (4th Ed. pp. 164-177). New York: Freeman and Company.

Baile, W. F., & Engel, B. T. (1978). A behavioral strategy for promoting treatment compliance following myocardial infarction, *Psychosomatic Medicine, 40,* 413-419.

Barefoot, J., Dahlstrom, W. G., & Williams, R. B. (1983). Hostility and CHD incidence, and total mortality: A 25 year follow-up study 225 physicians. *Psychosomatic Medicine, 45,* 59-64.

Booth-Kewley, S., & Friedman, H. S. (1987). Psychological predictors of heart disease: A quantitative reeview. *Psychological Bulletin, 101,* 343-362.

Brunson, B. I., & Matthews, K. A. (1981). The Type A coronary-prone behavior pattern and reactions to uncontrollable to stress: A analysis of performance strategies, affect, and attributions during failure, *Journal of Personality and Social Psychology, 40,* 906-918.

Bulman, R. J., & Wortman, C. B. (1977). Attributions of blame and coping in the "real world": Severe accident victims react to their lot. *Journal of Personality and Social Psychology, 35,* 351-363.

Burger, J. M., & Cooper, H. M. (1979). The desirability for control. *Motivation and Emotion, 3,* 381-393.

Carver, C. S. (1980). Perceived coersion, resistance to persuasion, and the Type A behavior pattern. *Journal of Research in Personality, 14,* 467-481.

Carver, C. S., & Glass, D. C., (1978). The coronary-prone behavior pattern and interpersonal aggression. *Journal of Personality and Social Psychology, 36,* 361-366.

Cooney, J. L., & Zeichner, A. (1985). Selective attention to negative feedback in Type A and Type B individuals. *Journal of Abnormal Psychology, 91,* 110-112.

Cooper, J., & Axsom, D. (1982). Effort justification in psychotherapy. In G. Weary and H. Mirels (eds.), *Integrations of clinical and social psychology,* London: Oxford University Press.

Dembroski, T., & Costa, P. (1987). Coronary-prone behavior: Components of the Type A behavior pattern and hostility. *Journal of Personality, 55,* 211-235.

Dembroski, T. M., & Costa, P. (1988). Assessment of coronary-prone behavior: A current overview. *Annals of Behavioral Medicine, 10,* 60-63.

DiMatteo, M. R., & DiNicola, D. D. (1982). *Achieving patient compliance: The psychology of the medical practitioner's role.* New York: Pergamon Press.

Fairfield, M.L., & Rhodewalt, F. (1988). *Perceived choice and response to treatment in Type A and B individuals.* Manuscript in preparation University of Utah.

Friedman, H.S. & Booth-Kewley, S. (1988). Validity of the Type A construct: A reprise. *Psychological Bulletin, 104,* 381-384.

Friedman, M., & Rosenman, R.H. (1959). Association of specific overt behavior pattern with blood and cardiovascular findings. *Journal of the American Medical Association, 159,* 1286-1296.

Friedman, M., Thoreson, C.E., Gill, J.J., Ulmer, D., Thompson, L., Price, V. A., Rabin, D.D., Breall, W.S., Dixon, T., Levy, R., & Bourg, E. (1984). Alteration of Type A behavior and reduction of cardiac recurrences in post-myocardial infarction patients. *American Heart Journal, 108,* 237-248.

Friedman, M., Thoresen, C.E., Gill, J.J. , Ulmer, D., Powell, L.H., Price, V.A., Brown, B., Thompson, L., Rabin, D.D., Breal, W.S., Bourg, E., Levy, R., & Dixon, T. (1986). Alteration of Type A behavior and its effect on recurrences in post-myocardial infarction patients: Summary results of the recurrent coronary prevention project. *American Heart Journal, 112,* 653-665.

Gastorf, J. W., Suls, J., & Sanders, G. S. (1980). Type A coronary-prone behavior pattern and social facilitation. *Journal of Personality and Social Psychology, 38,* 773-780.

Gill, J.J., Price, V.A., Friedman, M., Thoresen, C.E., Powell, L.H. Ulmer, D., Brown, B., & Drews, F.R. (1985). Reduction of Type A behavior in healthy middle-aged American military officers. *American Heart Journal, 110,* 503-514.

Glass, D.C. (1977). *Behavior patterns, stress, and coronary disease.* Hillsdale, NJ: L. A. Erlbaum.

Jenkins, C.D., Zyzanski, S.J., & Rosenman, R. (1971). Progress toward validation of a computer-scored test for the Type A coronary-prone behavior pattern. *Psychosomatic Medicine, 33,* 193-202.

Krantz, D.S. (1980). Cognitve processes and recovery from a heart attack: A review and theoretical analysis. *Journal of Human Stress, 6,* 27-38.

Krantz, D.S., & Schulz, R. (1980). A model of life crisis, control, and health outcomes: Cardiac rehabilitation and relocation of the elderly. In A. Baum and J. Singer (Eds.), *Advances in environmental psychology,* (Vol. 1, pp. 23-57). Hillsdale, N.J.: Laurence Erlbaum.

Lovallo, W.R., & Pishkin, V. (1980). Type A behavior, self-involvement, autonomic activity, and the traits of neuroticism and extraversion. *Psychosomatic Medicine, 42,* 329-334.

Manuck, S. B., Kaplan, J. R., & Matthews, K. A. (1986). Behavioral antacedents of coronary heart disease and artereosclerosis. *Artereosclerosis, 6,* 2-14.

Matthews, K. A. (1988). CHD and Type A Behaviors: Update on and Alternative to the Booth-Kewley and Friedman Quantitative Review. *Psychological Review, 104,* 373-380.

Matthews, K.A., & Haynes, S.G. (1986). Type A behavior pattern and coronary risk: Update and critical evaluation. *American Journal of Epidemeology, 123,* 923-960.

Matthews, K.A., & Siegel, J.M. (1982). Type A behavior pattern in children and adolescents. In A. Baum & J. E. Singer, (eds.), *Handbook of psychology and health* (Vol. 2, pp. 99-118). Hillsdale, N. J.: Erlbaum.

Matthews, K.A., Siegal, J.M., Kuller, L.H., Thompson, M., & Verat, M. (1983).

Determinants of decisions to seek treatment by patients with acute myocardial infarction symptoms. *Journal of Personality and Social Psychology, 44,* 1144-1156.

Musante, L. McDougall, J. M., & Dembroski, T. (1984). The Type A behavior pattern and attributions for success and failure. *Personality and Social Psychology Bulletin, 10,* 544-553.

O'Keeffe, J. L., & Smith, T. W. (1988). Self-regulation and Type A behavior. *Journal of Research in Personality, 22,* 232-251.

Peterson, C. Semmel, A., von Baeyer, C., Abramson, L. Y., Metalsky, G., & Seligman, M. E. P. (1982). The attributional style questionnaire. *Cognitive Therapy and Research, 6,* 287-299.

Pittner, N., & Houston, B.K. (1980). Response to stress, cognitive coping strategies, and the Type A behavior pattern. *Journal of Personality and Social Psychology, 39,* 147-157.

Price, V.A. (1982). *The Ttpe A behavior pattern: A model for research and practice.* Orlando, FL: Academic Press.

Rhodewalt, F. (1984). Self-attribution, self-involvement, and the Type A coronary-prone behavior pattern. *Journal of Personality and Social Psychology, 47,* 662-670.

Rhodewalt, F., & Comer, R.J. (1982). Coronary-prone behavior and reactance: The attractiveness of an eliminated choice. *Personality and Social Psychology Bulletin, 8,* 152-158.

Rhodewalt, F., & Davison, J. (1984). Reactance and the Type A coronary-prone behavior pattern: The role of self-attribution in response to reduced behavioral freedom. *Journal of Personality and Social Psychology, 44,* 220-228.

Rhodewalt, F., & Marcroft, M. (1988). Type A behavior and diabetic control: Implications of psychological reactance for health outcomes. *Journal of Applied Social Psychology, 18,* 139-159.

Rhodewalt, F., & Strube, M. (1985). A self-attribution reactance model of recovery from injury in Type A individuals. *Journal of Applied Social Psychology, 15,* 330-344.

Rhodewalt, F., Strube, M., Hill, C.A., & Sansone, C. (1988). Strategic self-attribution and Type A behavior. *Journal of Research in Personality, 22,* 60-74.

Rodin, J., & Janis, I. L. (1979). The social power of health care pratitioners as agents of change. *Journal of Social Issues, 35,* 60-81.

Scherwitz, L., Berton, K., & Levonthal, H. (1978). Type A behavior, self-involvement, and cardiovascular response. *Psychosomatic Medicine, 40,* 593-609.

Scherwitz, L., & Canick, J. D. (1988). Self-Reference and coronary heart disease risk. In B.K. Houston & C.R. Snyder (Eds.), *Type A behavior pattern: Research, theory, and intervention* (pp. 146-167). New York: John Wiley & Sons.

Schlegel, R.P., Wellwood, J.K., Copps, B.E., Gruchow, W.H., & Sharratt, M.T. (1980). The relationship between perceived challenge and daily symptom reporting in Type A versus Type B postinfarct patients. *Journal of Behavioral Medicine, 3,* 191-204.

Smith, T.W. & Rhodewalt, F. (1986). On states, traits, and processes: A transactional alternative to the individual difference assumptions in Type A behavior and physiological reactivity. *Journal of Research in Personality, 20,* 229-251.

Snyder, M. L., & Frankel, A. (1975). Reactance and the Type A. Unpublished manuscript, Dartmouth College. Strube, M. (1985). Attributional style and the Type A behavior pattern. *Journal of Personality and Social Psychology, 49*, 500-509.

Strube, M. (1987). A self-appraisal model of the Type A behavior pattern. In R. Hogan & W. H. Jones (Eds.), *Perspectives in personality* (Vol.2 pp. 201-250). Greenwich, CN: JAI Press.

Strube, M., Boland, S. M., Manfredo, P. A., & Al-Falaij, A. (1987). Type A behavior pattern and the self-evaluation of abilities: Empirical tests of the self-appraisal model. *Journal of Personality and Social Psychology, 52*, 956-974.

Strube, M., J, Turner, C.W., Cerro, D., Stevens, J.H., & Hinchey, F. (1984). Interpersonal aggression and the Type A coronary-prone behavior pattern: A theoretical distinction and practical implications. *Journal of Personality and Social Psychology, 47*, 839-387.

Strube, M.J, & Werner, C.M. (1985). Relinquishment of control and the Type A behavior pattern. *Journal of Personality and Social Psychology, 48*, 688-701.

Surwit, R.S., Feinglos, M.N., & Scovern, A.W. (1983). Diabetes and behavior: A paradigm for health psychology, *American Psychologist, 38*, 255-262.

Taylor, S.E. (1979). Hospital patient behavior: Reactance, helplessness or control. *Journal of Social Issues, 35*, 156-184.

Taylor, S.E., Lichtman, R.R., & Wood, J.V. (1984). Attributions, beliefs about control, and adjustment to breast cancer. *Journal of Personality and Social Psychology, 46*, 489-502.

Wicklund, R.A., & Brehm, J. (1976). *Perspectives on cognitive dissonance.* Hillsdale, N. J.: Erlbaum.

Weidner, G., & Matthews, K.A. (1978). Reported physical symptoms elicitd by unpredictable events and the Type A coronary-prone behavior pattern. *Journal of Personality and Social Psychology, 36*, 1213-1220.

Wortman, C. B., & Brehm, J. (1975). Responses to uncontrollable outcomes: An integration of reactance theory and the learned helplessness model. In L. Berkowitz (Ed.), *Advances in experimental social psychology* (Vol. 8). New York: Academic Press.

Wright, L. (1988). The Type A behavior pattern and coronary artery disease: Quest for the active ingredients and the illusive mechanism. *American Psychologist, 43*, 2-14.

Cognitive, Cardiovascular and Haematological Responses of Type A and Type B Individuals Prior to and Following Examinations

Janice Abbott

Department of Community Medicine, University of Manchester Manchester, M13 9PT, England

Colin Sutherland

School of Applied Biology, Lancashire Polytechnic Preston, England

Type A and Type B male students were assessed on cognitive, cardiovascular and haematological dimensions over a twelve-week period, whilst preparing for and following academic examinations. Type A individuals demonstrated greater elevations in heart rate, systolic and diastolic blood pressure, epinephrine, norepinephrine, the anticoagulant antithrombin III, and faster platelet aggregation (although percentage aggregation decreased similarly for both groups). No differences emerged between the two groups regarding anxiety and depression. Type As as compared with Type Bs, however, reported greater feelings of hostility over an eight week period. Differences in coping strategies (perception of challenge, alcohol consumption, smoking, GP visiting, medication taking, and symptom reporting) emerged between the two groups and are discussed within the framework of Lazarus (1966). When faced with life challenge, the Type A coping strategy coupled with a greater magnitude and duration of cardiovascular and haematological responses, may have potential importance in the development of cardiovascular pathology.

In a recent critical review of the epidemiological Type A studies, Matthews and Haynes (1986) reached the same conclusion as did the Biomedical Review Panel in 1981—that the Type A behavior pattern is a risk factor for coronary heart disease (CHD). Recent research has been directed towards investigating psychophysiological responses whilst

---

Authors' Notes: This research was supported by the Research and Consultancy Committee of Lancashire Polytechnic.

Address requests for reprints to the first author.

© 1990 Select Press

Type A and Type B individuals are subjected to a variety of challenges. Many studies of this kind have revealed that, although not differing in baseline values, under challenging situations Type As, as compared with Type Bs, demonstrate greater elevations in heart rate and systolic blood pressure (e.g., Dembroski, MacDougall & Shields, 1977; Van Schijndel, De May & Naring, 1984). They also demonstrate greater increases in plasma catecholamines (Contrada, Glass, Krakoff, Krantz, Kehoe, Isecke, Collins & Elting, 1982; Glass, Krakoff, Contrada, Hilton, Kehoe, Mannucci, Collins, Snow & Elting, 1980; Williams, Lane, Kuhn, Melosh, White & Schanberg, 1982).

The major assumption underlying these studies is that Type A individuals who respond to laboratory challenge with enhanced cardiovascular responses, respond in the same way to everyday life events and hassles, and that this frequent cardiovascular upheaval is associated with the development of atheroma and the onset of clinical CHD. Therefore, the enhanced cardiovascular responses observed in the laboratory are assumed to reflect the state of vascular contractility and intravascular coagulation. Coronary heart disease takes many years to develop, however, yet the laboratory psychophysiological experiment on which the behavior-disease assumption is based, lasts only hours or minutes. For these studies to be of predictive validity, therefore, it is necessary to demonstrate that responses to laboratory tasks can reliably predict the cardiovascular reactions of individuals in their everyday lives. To test this prediction, a naturalistic, longitudinal study, employing Type As and Type Bs was undertaken.

Although Type A behavior is a recognised significant risk factor for CHD, the presumptions made regarding the possible mechanisms which mediate the behavior-disease relationship, have, at present, little support. Type As may respond with greater cardiovascular arousal, but reactivity per se has not been linked extensively with the development of atheroma or CHD. In the only prospective study, however, the magnitude of diastolic blood pressure responses emerged as a predictor of the disease (Keys, Taylor, Blackburn, Brozek & Anderson, 1971).

The most consistent evidence to date emerges from studies in which Type As, relative to Type Bs, demonstrated not only enhanced cardiovascular responses but also increased plasma catecholamines. These amines can facilitate intravascular coagulation by increasing platelet activity (e.g., Ardlie, McGuiness & Garrett, 1985). Platelet adhesion and aggregation are the initial factors in the formation of a thrombus, which may contribute to the subsequent arterial narrowing, impeded blood flow and eventually, total occlusion of the lumen. In view of this, it is essential to investigate whether individuals who respond to challenging situations with increased cardiovascular arousal show a greater risk of developing atheroma. In addition to the measurement of cardiovascular (HR, SBP and DBP), catecholamine (epinephrine and norepinephrine), and platelet activity (percentage and speed of aggregation), the body's major anticoagulant, the heparin co-factor, antithrombin III (ATIII) was evaluated.

ATIII is one of the most important defences against intravascular coagulation, through its inhibitory effects on thrombin and other factors of the coagulation cascade (Rosenberg & Damus, 1973). Consequently, it has been suggested that plasma levels of ATIII may mirror the degree of hypercoagulability of the blood (Yue, Gertler & Starr, 1976). However, recent animal work has indicated that increased catecholamines facilitated an increased production of ATIII, which may enable the body to deal more effectively with any tendency towards intravascular coagulation (Abbott, Sutherland & Watt, 1984).

It was predicted that individuals who show elevated cardiovascular responses should be more likely to demonstrate enhanced catecholamine activity and have a greater tendency toward platelet aggregation. Type As were expected to demonstrate the greater tendency towards intravascular coagulation (greater increases in HR, SBP, DBP, epinephrine, norepinephrine, percentage and speed of platelet aggregation). The possible 'protection effect' of ATIII was investigated, although no Type A-Type B predictions were made.

Although field studies lack the rigid experimental controls made possible in the laboratory, investigations concerning the day-to-day living of Type A and Type B persons offer a promising approach for understanding the behavior-disease association. As a whole, the findings of the few previous studies are inconsistent and confusing. Manuck, Course & Winkelman (1979) reported higher peak levels and greater day to day variability of systolic and diastolic blood pressure, over a six-week period in Type A lawyers compared to their Type B counterparts. Consistent with this work, Type A male students have shown elevated blood pressure during academic stress (Waldron, Hickey, Butensky, Gruss, Overall, Schmader & Wohlmuth, 1980). A study employing air traffic controllers, however, failed to demonstrate an A-B difference (Rose, Jenkins & Hurst, 1978), and unexpectedly, under commuting stress, Type Bs demonstrated the greater overall systolic pressure, although Type As had the greater peak values (Stokols, Novaco, Stokols & Campbell, 1978). Evidence for higher urinary catecholamine levels in Type As compared with Type Bs during the working day was provided by Friedman and his colleagues (1960), although de Backer, Kornitzer, Kittle, Bogaert, Van Durme, Vincke, Rustin, Degre & De Schaepdrijver (1979) were unable to replicate these findings.

Elevated cardiovascular activity in Type As is only observed in the laboratory under conditions that are perceived as challenging or stressful to the individual. The every day occurrences in previous studies may not have been appraised as stressful or challenging by the person, but rather as the hassles of every day living. This is of the utmost importance, as it is not the event per se which is stressful. It is the individual's perception of that event as undesirable and/or uncontrollable, which triggers enhanced cardiovascular arousal, and increased reports of psychological distress (MacFarlane, Norman, Streiner, Roy & Scott, 1980; Suls & Mullen, 1981). Given that the behavior-disease association may be moderated, in part, by coping styles, in addition to cardiovascular and haematological parameters, the study examined behavioral coping strategies (the perception of challenge, cigarette smoking, alcohol consumption, physical symptoms, medication taking and visits to the doctor) and the affective states (anxiety, hostility and depression) of Type As and Type Bs over a three month period, whilst they were preparing for, and sitting final year examinations.

METHOD

Behavior Pattern Classification

To ensure that subjects were typed as accurately as possible, both the Bortner Scale (Bortner, 1969) and the Thurstone Activity Scale (Thurstone, 1949) were employed. The Bortner Scale has been shown to have both prospective (French-Belgian Collaborative Group, 1982) and retrospective validity (Koskenvuo, Kaprio, Langinvainio, Romo & Sarna, 1981; Heller, 1979). It has been more highly correlated with the Structured Interview than has the Jenkins Activity Survey (Johnson & Shaper, 1983; Rustin, Dramaiz, Kittle, Degre, Komitzer, Thiely & de Backer, 1976). In addition, the Thurstone Activity Scale, although not developed as a measure of Type A behavior, shows greater agreement with the Structured Interview than any Type A questionnaire (MacDougall, Dembroski & Musante, 1979; Rosenman, Rahe, Borhani & Feinleib, 1976). Not only did the subject's two scores have to be congruent (e.g., both Type A), but only those subjects were employed whose scores were half a standard deviation above (Type A) or below (Type B) the mean on both Scales.

Subjects

Prior to being employed in the study, potential subjects underwent an assessment which involved obtaining cardiovascular measures, and information regarding their past and present health status. Subjects were excluded from participating in the study if any of the following were

TABLE 1 Bimonthly Assessments Over the 12-Week Experimental Period

	Assessments					
	1	*2*	*3*	*4*	*5*	*6*
Number of Weeks Prior to The Examination	8	6	4	2	All Subjects Assessed Within 36 Hrs Prior to The First Examination	All Subjects Assessed Within 48 Hrs After The Last Examination

applicable to them; (1) systolic blood pressure greater than 140 mmHg; (2) diastolic blood pressure greater than 90 mmHg; (3) reported a history of cardiovascular disease; (4) diabetes mellitus; (5) renal or haematological disorders; (6) were obese; and (7) smoked more than ten cigarettes per day. Subjects were asked to abstain from consuming alcohol for a least eighteen hours prior to the experiment and to refrain from eating and drinking, tea, coffee, cocoa or coca cola and smoking for four hours prior to the assessment. If a subject admitted smoking or consuming food or any of these liquids they were asked to return to the laboratory on the following day. Rigorous questioning regarding the taking of medication was carried out.

Given the double classification procedure and exclusive criteria, from a pool of two-hundred and sixteen male students, only 30 Type As and 30 Type Bs, preparing for final year examinations, were eligible and agreed to take part in the study. Their mean age was 22.40 years (range 20 to 23 years, SD = ±0.95), and 23.08 years (range from 21 to 25 years, SD = ±1.02) respectively. The study relied heavily on the appointment keeping of the students, and due to insufficient attendance (mostly immediately prior to or following the examinations) data from only twenty-six Type As and twenty-seven Type Bs were incorporated in the cardiovascular and behavioral analyses. At recruitment seven Type As and eight Type Bs smoked up to ten cigarettes per day. As the smokers were not included in the haematological analysis (due to the effects of nicotine on the parameters being measured) blood was analysed from 19 Type As and 16 Type Bs (3 non-smoking Type Bs refused venipuncture). None of the subjects had been employed in an earlier Type A investigation. They were informed that the study was investigating the long-term stability of physiological factors in young men.

Cardiovascular Measures

At each assessment (see Table 1), measures of baseline heart rate, systolic and diastolic blood pressure were obtained. Heart rate (HR) was monitored continuously as digital pulsation by use of a photocell plethysmograph attached to the subject's ear. The photocell plethysmograph was interfaced to a BBC microcomputer for 'on line analysis.' The computer averaged the heart rate over each 30 second period. HR was monitored for at least twenty minutes or until ten consecutive readings were within ±3 bpm. The mean of these ten readings gave the baseline value for each subject. Systolic (SBP), and diastolic blood pressure (DBP), measurements were obtained using a Copal autoinflation digital sphygmomanometer (UA-231). The compression cuff was placed over the brachial artery of the subject's dominant arm. SBP and DBP were taken every two minutes until the readings were within ±3 mm Hg on four successive measures. The mean of these readings gave the baseline value for each subject. On average, the adaptation period took between twenty and thirty minutes. Occasionally, subjects took up to forty minutes to adapt given the criteria which had been imposed.

Haematological Measures

Provided the subject had not taken any medication within the past ten days, 15 cm^3 of blood was collected, and centrifuged immediately. The ratio of blood to anticoagulant (10 mmol dm^{-3} trisodium citrate solution) was 9:1. 1.5 cm^3 of the sample was centrifuged at 250 x g for 10 minutes to obtain platelet-rich plasma, the remainder was spun at 2,000 x g for 15 minutes to provide platelet-poor plasma. 0.70 cm^3 of the supernatant was taken from both samples for use in the platelet aggregation tests, which were performed within 30 to 45 minutes of blood collection. The remaining platelet-poor plasma was equally divided into three microcentrifuge tubes, and frozen at -20°C for the subsequent assays of epinephrine, norepinephrine and antithrombin III.

The amount of plasma ATIII was determined by absorbance spectrophotometry according to the Chromozym method of Röka (1978). Reagents were obtained in kit form from Boehringer Mannheim. Three analyses were performed on each sample, of which the mean was taken as the experimental value. The levels of epinephrine and norepinephrine were measured by the fluorimetric method of Von Euler and Floding (1955). The method permits the quantification of plasma epinephrine and norepinephrine by the different oxidation speeds at different pH values. Again, three analyses of each sample were performed, the mean of which was taken as the experimental value. ATIII and catecholamine assays were performed approximately one week and four weeks respectively, following plasma preparation and storage. The within sample variance provides accuracy/sensitivity data by calculating the variance between the assay values obtained from the same plasma sample. The baseline within sample variance was 6.48%, 5.76%, and 5.80%, for ATIII, epinephrine and norepinephrine respectively. The variance between each subject's mean value was; ATIII (12.69% - As = 10.72%, Bs = 15.83%); epinephrine (23.09% - As = 24.13%, Bs = 21.90%); and norepinephrine (12.77% - As = 12.47%, Bs = 13.14%). Intra-assay variations for Peak reactivity (assessment five) were 5.73% (ATIII), 7.78% (epinephrine), and 4.61% (norepinephrine). The between subject variance immediately prior to the examinations was; ATIII (12.84% - As = 11.40%, Bs = 14.50%); epinephrine (23.00% - As = 18.83%, Bs = 28.77%); and norepinephrine (40.04% - As = 33.86%, Bs = 50.91%).

The percentage and speed of platelet aggregation, in response to collagen, was evaluated by the method of optical density (Born, 1962; O'Brien, 1962). Collagen lyophilized with buffer salts was obtained from Sigma (stock number 881-5). Platelet-rich plasma was stirred whilst the percentage transmission of light through the platelet suspension was determined on an EEL photometer and recorded on a Tekman chart recorder (Tekman Ltd., England). Therefore a continuous recording of platelet aggregation was obtained. 0.05 cm^3 of 0.002cm^{-3} was found to be the threshold concentration of the collagen suspension, which when added to platelet-rich plasma produced an aggregation curve which gave a transmission not less than 80% of that given by platelet-poor plasma. The percentage aggregation and the speed or reaction time (RT) of aggregation was defined as the interval (as percent transmission or seconds) between the addition of the collagen until the completion of aggregation (when there was no further decrease of the slope).

Cognitive Measures

Reported anxiety, hostility and depression were measured by the Multiple Affect Adjective Checklist (MAACL) (Zuckerman & Lubin, 1965). In addition, a questionnaire was designed to evaluate the subject's perception of how stressful their life was at that particular time, the taking of medication, visits to the doctor, alcohol consumption and cigarette smoking patterns. Kobasa's (1982) Physical Symptom Scale was also included. At each assessment they were asked to reflect on the behavioral and cognitive aspects of their life over the previous two weeks.

Procedure

Subjects were required to attend for assessment on six occasions over the twelve-week period. Throughout the study, each volunteer was individually assessed at the same time during the morning so as to avoid the diurnal variations of the parameters under study. At each assessment the individual was seated comfortably, and questioned regarding any medication they had taken during the past two weeks. A photocell plethysmograph was attached to their ear and a sphygmomanometer cuff was placed over the brachial artery of their dominant arm. Baseline heart rate, systolic and diastolic blood pressure were evaluated. If venipuncture was to be performed, blood was obtained from the non-dominant arm at this stage, after which baseline cardiovascular parameters were measured again. This timely procedure was undertaken to ensure that subjects were as relaxed as possible prior to venipuncture, following which, a more accurate cardiovascular baseline measure could be obtained. After recording the cardiovascular measures, the questionnaires were completed.

Design and Analysis

For the purpose of between group analyses, change scores were calculated by subtracting the subject's baseline value from the values of the five subsequent assessments. All cardiovascular, haematological and cognitive variables were separately analysed in 2 x 5 ANOVA's with repeated measures (A-B x Assessments). In order to pinpoint the differences, post-ANOVA independent t-tests were performed on the data.

BMDP2V was employed to analyse all the analyses of variance data. Violation of the sphericity assumption tends to occur in psychophysiological repeated measures designs, since the cardiovascular measures are usually highly correlated, especially those taken nearer together in time. It has been proposed, therefore, that corrections are made for analysis of variance terms derived from degrees of freedom accumulated across several repeated measures (e.g., Fridlund, 1987; Vasey & Thayer, 1987). The significance of an ANOVA term is calculated by employing degrees of freedom reduced by multiplication with the weighting factor Greenhouse-Geisser epsilon corrected degrees of freedom have been employed. The normally accepted degrees of freedom together with the correction factor and adjusted p values are given (for example $F(5,150) = 7.36$, $\hat{e} = 0.89$, $p < 0.001$).

RESULTS

Baseline Data: Cardiovascular and Haematological Measures

The results of the first assessment were taken as baseline values, against which subsequent data were compared. Independent t-tests were performed on the mean baseline values of heart rate (HR), systolic blood

TABLE 2 Mean Baseline Values of Cardiovascular and Haematological Parameters for Type A's and Type B's (Standard Deviation in Parenthesis)

	Type As	*Type Bs*
HR(bpm)	75.00 (7.46) n=26	75.63 (8.22) n=27
SBP(mmHg)	111.96 (8.79) n=26	112.41 (7.95) n=27
DBP(mmHg)	74.69 (5.66) n=26	73.85 (5.86) n=27
E(pg cm^{-3})	53.00 (9.26) n=19	55.38 (9.10) n=16
Ne(pg cm^{-3})	292.16 (31.48) n=19	285.00 (31.52) n=16
% PA	76.72 (10.94) n=16	75.00 (14.49) n=12
RT-PA (sec)	151.77 (40.41) n=16	157.93 (38.96) n=12
ATIII(%)	96.74 (8.55) n=19	97.56 (10.36) n=16

pressure (SBP), diastolic blood pressure (DBP), epinephrine (E), norepinephrine (NE), percentage platelet aggregation (%PA), speed (or reaction time) of aggregation (RT-PA), and antithrombin III (ATIII), between the groups of Typc A and Type B subjects. No significant differences emerged. Mean baseline values are given in Table 2.

Cardiovascular Measures

Changes in HR, SBP and DBP are illustrated in Figure 1. The HR ANOVA yielded an A-B, $F(1,51) = 8.59$, $p < .005$, and an Assessments main effect, $F(4,204) = 129.68$, $\hat{e} = .67$, $p < .001$. Together with a significant A-B x Assessments interaction, $F(4,204) = 2.91$, $\hat{e} = .67$, $p < .05$, the results suggest that Type As, compared with Type Bs, demonstrated greater HR responses during the three month period. Specifically, differences between Type As and Type Bs emerged immediately prior to (assessment 5, $t = 2.82$, $df = 51$, $p < .01$) and following the examinations ($t = 2.25$, $df = 51$, $p < .05$). The ANOVA performed on the SBP data generated an A-B, $F(1,51) = 5.97$, $p < .002$, and an Assessment main effect, $F(4,204) = 147.35$, $\hat{e} = .72$, $p < .001$, together with an A-B x

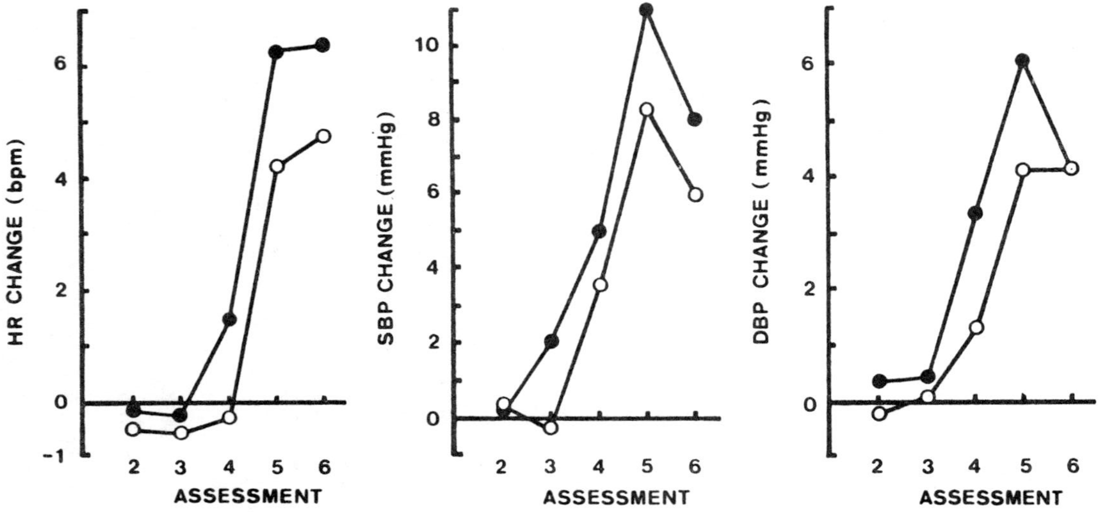

FIGURE1 Mean Changes in Heart Rate, Systolic and Diastolic Blood Pressure, During the Experimental Period (●—● = Type A's; ○—○=Type B's)

Assessments interaction, $F(4,204) = 5.41$, $\hat{e} = .72$, $p < .002$. The findings indicate that Type As demonstrated greater increases in systolic pressure than Type Bs during the experimental period. Differences between the two groups emerged four weeks before the examinations and were still apparent immediately prior to them (assessment 3, $t = 4.10$, $df = 51$, $p < .001$; assessment 4, $t = 1.74$, $df = 51$, $p < .05$; assessment 5, $t = 2.10$, $df = 51$, $p < .05$). Similarly, the DBP ANOVA yielded an A-B effect, $F(1,51) = 7.07$, $p < .01$, and an Assessments main effect, $F(4.204) = 130.71$, $\hat{e} = .68$, $p < .001$. The A-B x Assessments interaction was also significant, $F(4,204) = 5.50$, $\hat{e} = .68$, $p < .002$. In accordance with the HR and SBP findings, DBP arousal was also greater for Type As than for Type Bs whilst male students were preparing for and sitting examinations. Specifically, A-B differences emerged two weeks before (assessment 4, $t = 4.81$, $df = 51$, $p < .001$) and immediately prior to the examinations (assessment 5, $t = 3.39$, $df = 51$, $p < .001$).

Smoking and Cardiovascular Measures. As smoking may have an effect on cardiovascular parameters, 2 x 5 ANOVAs with repeated measures were separately performed on the HR, SBP and DBP data of smokers and non-smokers, Type A smokers and Type A non-smokers, and Type B smokers and Type B non-smokers. No significant results emerged from the data.

Haematological Measures

Plasma Catecholamines. The E ANOVA yielded an A-B, $F(1,33) = 17.30$, $p < .001$, and an Assessments main effect, $F(4,132) = 170.73$, $\hat{e} = 0.37$, $p < .001$, together with an interaction of these two factors $F(4,132) = 7.76$, $\hat{e} = 0.37$, $p < .003$. The results indicated that Type As, relative to Type Bs, demonstrated greater increases in epinephrine. Specifically, A-B differences emerged four weeks prior to the event and were still apparent following the examinations (assessment 3, $t = 2.17$, $df = 33$, $p < .05$; assessment 4, $t = 2.90$, $df = 33$, $p < .01$; assessment 5, $t = 3.69$, $df = 33$, $p < .001$; assessment 6, $t = 3.01$, $df = 33$, $p < .01$). Similarly, Type As compared with Type Bs exhibited greater norepinephrine responses. An A-B, $F(1,33) = 20.89$, $p < .001$, and an Assessment main effect emerged, $F(4,132) = 97.25$, $\hat{e} = 0.33$, $p < .001$, together with the A-B x Assessment interaction, $F(4,132) = 14,97$, $\hat{e} = .33$, $p < .001$. A-B differences emerged two weeks prior to the examinations, and were maintained until the end of the experimental period (assessment 4, $t = 5.26$, $df = 33$, $p < .001$; assessment 5, $t = 3.96$, $df = 33$, $p < .001$, and assessment 6, $t = 4.33$, $df = 33$, $p < .001$).

Platelet Activity. Plasma from 3 Type As and 4 Type Bs was not suitable for tests of platelet aggregation. A general decrease in the percentage of platelet aggregation occurred throughout the experimental

TABLE 3 Cardiovascular and Haematological Correlations Among Type A's (Upper Value) and Type B's (Lower Value)

Variables	*SBP*	*DBP*	*E*	*NE*	*ATIII*	*%PA*	*RT-PA*
HR	.24 .32	.17 .12	.20 .06	.07 -.03	.11 .11	-.21 .26	-.13 .08
SBP		.59** .31	.67** .56*	.54* .08	.35 -.11	-.49* -.39	-.35 -.19
DBP			.55* .19	.47* .02	.07 .04	-.51* -.52*	-.47* -.29
E				.49* .32	.52* .17	-.58* -.39	-.42 -.32
NE					.39 .24	-.81*** -.84***	-.76*** -.21
ATIII						.03 -.01	-.39 -.22
%PA							.23 .80***

*All tests are two-tailed *p<0.05, **p<0.01, ***p<0.001.*

period, F (4,104) = 25.26, ê = .48, p < .001. There was an increase in the speed at which platelets aggregated, F (4,104) = 39.25, ê = .54, p < .001. An A-B x Assessment interaction, F (4,104) = 3.85, ê = .54, p < .02 indicates that Type As tended to show a greater decrease of in vitro platelet reaction time than Type Bs at certain times during the study period. An A-B difference only emerged immediately prior to the examinations (assessments 5, t = 2.14, df = 26, p < .05).

Plasma Antithrombin III. Two main effects emerged from the ATIII ANOVA. A-B, F(1,33) = 14.87, p < .001, and Assessments, F (4,132) = 22.46, ê = 0.73, p < .001. The A-B x Assessments interaction was also significant, F (4,132) = 3.05, ê = .73, p < 0.05, suggesting that Type As demonstrated greater increases in ATIII during the experiment than Type Bs. Specifically, Type As demonstrated greater increases immediately prior to (assessment 5, t = 4.78, df = 33, p < .001) and following the examination period (assessment 6, t = 2.29, df = 33, p < .05). Catecholamine, antithrombin III and platelet responses are presented in Figure 2.

Cardiovascular and Haematological Intercorrelations

Relationships were examined among all variables on the change

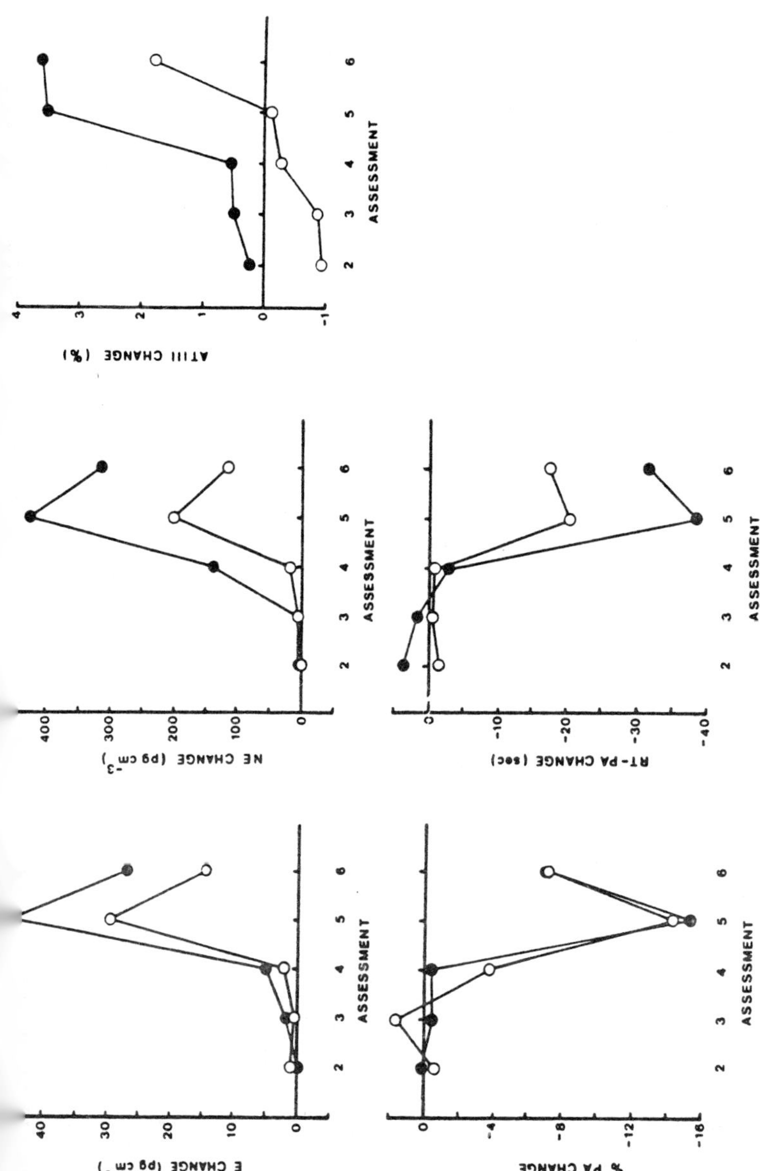

FIGURE 2 Mean Changes in Catecholamines, Platelet Activity and Antithrombin III, During the Experimental Period (●–● = Type A's; ○–○ = Type B's)

scores for peak responses (assessment 5). Product-moment correlations between these scores were computed separately for Type As and Type Bs. Several coefficients are of particular interest (see Table 3). For Type As SBP and DBP were significantly correlated with E, NE, %PA and RT-PA (DBP only). Additionally, E was related to NE, ATIII and %PA, whereas NE was correlated with %PA and RT-PA. Fewer significant associations emerged between the variables for the Type B group. SBP was correlated with E, and DBP was related to NE and %PA. %PA and RT-PA showed a strong relationship to each other.

Cognitive Measures

Data Reduction and Baseline Data. In addition to completing the Multiple Adjective Checklist which measures anxiety, hostility and depression, subjects were asked to indicate on an eleven point scale how stressful/challenging their life had been over the past two weeks. Kobasa's Physical Symptom Scale asks subjects to indicate, on a four point scale, the extent to which they were bothered by sixteen stress-related symptoms (e.g., loss of appetite, trouble sleeping). Alcohol consumption was measured by asking subjects to recall the number of pints of beer/lager/cider, or pub measures of wine or spirits that they had drunk over the past week. This information was translated into units of alcohol. One unit is equivalent to a half pint of ordinary strength beer/lager/cider, or a single pub measure of wine or spirits. These alcohol units were used in the data analysis. A measure of cigarette smoking was obtained by asking the subjects to report the average number of cigarettes smoked per day. Where subjects relied heavily on memory (the alcohol and smoking data), they were urged to keep a diary, although approximately 17% of subjects reported that they had not conformed to this procedure. The values obtained from assessment one were taken as baseline measures. Independent t-tests performed on the mean baseline values, demonstrated no differences between Type As and Type Bs, for all these self-reported variables.

The perception of the situation. The ANOVA yielded an A-B main effect, $F(1,51) = 4.52$, $p <.01$, and an Assessments effect, $F(4,204) = 167.41$, $\hat{e} = .69$, $p < .001$. The A-B x Assessments interaction was also significant, $F(4,204) = 5.42$, $\hat{e} =.69$, $p < .01$, indicating that Type As, relative to Type Bs, perceived the situation as more stressful throughout the experimental period (assessment 3, $t = 2.29$, $df = 51$, $p < .05$; assessment 4, $t = 1.83$, $df = 51$, $p < .05$; assessment 5, $t = 2.81$, $df = 51$, $p < .01$). Changes in all the cognitive variables are illustrated in Figure 3.

Physical symptoms, GP consultation and medication. The physical symptoms ANOVA revealed only an Assessments main effect, $F(4,204) = 53.81$, $\hat{e} = .37$, $p < .001$, reflecting a similar increase in symptom

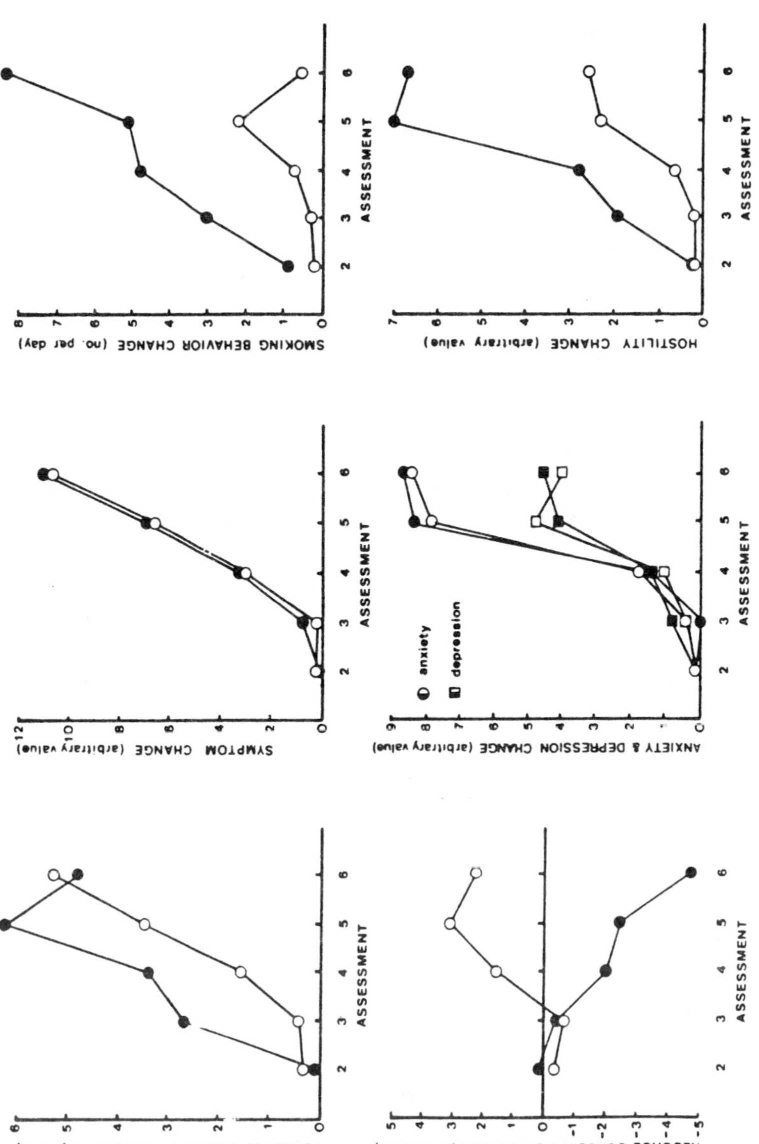

FIGURE 3 Mean Changes in the Perception of the Situation as Stressful, Reported Physical Smyptoms, Smoking Behavior, Alcohol Consumption, Anxiety, depression, and Hostility, During the Experimental Period (●–● and ■–■ = Type A's; ○–○ and □–□ = Type B's)

reporting over the three month period for both Type As and Type Bs. Over the twelve-week period, Type Bs were more likely to visit their GPs than were Type As, $X^2 = 8.00$, df = 1, $p < .01$ (out of sixteen consultations, twelve involved Type Bs). The two groups did not differ regarding the amount of reported medication taking.

Alcohol consumption and smoking behavior. An A-B main effect, F (1,51) =14.64, $p < 0.001$, emerged from the alcohol consumption data in addition to an A-B x Assessments interaction, F (4,204) = 8.05, ê = .71, $p < .001$, indicating that Type B individuals increased their alcohol intake in comparison with Type As. Specifically, A-B differences emerged two weeks prior to the examinations and remained until the end of the experimental period (assessment 4, t = 2.47, df = 51, $p < .05$; assessment 5, t = 4.18, df = 51, $p < .001$; assessment 6, t = 5.45, df = 51, $p < .001$). In contrast, the ANOVA performed on the smoking behavior generated an A-B effect, F (1,13) = 9.81, $p < .01$, and an Assessments main effect, F (4,52) = 7.57, ê = .67, $p < .001$, together with an A-B x Assessments interaction, F (4,52) = 5.39, ê = .67, $p < .01$. These findings suggest that Type As, relative to Type Bs, increased their smoking behavior immediately following the examinations (assessment 6, t = 2.37, df = 13, $p < .05$).

Anxiety, Hostility and Depression. Only an anxiety Assessments main effect emerged, F (4,204) = 236.24, ê = .42, $p < .001$ indicating similar increases in reported anxiety over the challenging period for both groups. The hostility ANOVA yielded an A-B effect, F (1,51) = 46.34, $p < .001$, and an Assessments main effect, F (4,204) = 168.22, ê = .59, $p < .001$, together with an interaction of these factors, F (4,204) = 35.15, ê = .59, $p <.001$. These findings suggest that Type As, compared with Type Bs, reported greater hostility four weeks prior to the examinations and throughout the remainder of the experimental period (assessment 3, t = 5.20, df = 51, $p < .001$; assessment 4, t = 4.81, df = 51, $p < .001$; assessment 5, t = 7.62, df = 51, $p < .001$; assessment 6, t = 7.76, df = 51, $p < .001$). Similar increases in depression were reported by Type As and Type Bs over the twelve weeks, F (4,204) = 34.11, ê = 0.63, $p < .001$.

DISCUSSION

Cardiovascular and Haematological Parameters

The academic examination situation was perceived as stressful/challenging by all subjects, although more so by Type As. In this respect, it was not the event per se but the perception of the situation which was evaluated. The findings clearly indicate that both Type As and Type Bs demonstrated tonic cardiovascular and haematological adjustments, leading up to and during the challenging period. Although increases in HR, SBP, and DBP were observed for both groups, the prediction that Type As, relative to Type Bs, would demonstrate greater cardiovascular arousal during a real-life situation was confirmed. Compared with Type Bs, Type A subjects exhibited greater elevations in SBP and DBP, four weeks, and two weeks prior to the examinations respectively. The A-B pressor response difference was still evident immediately prior to the examinations. Increases in HR were not demonstrated until immediately prior to and following the event, with Type As exhibiting the greater increase. The different temporal patterns which have emerged for HR and BP arousal during a natural situation must question the findings (or lack of findings) in some laboratory studies. For example, if HR is the only cardiovascular variable under study a failure to observe an anticipation effect may result. The findings amplify the negligence of employing the cardiovascular variables as interchangeable indices.

The prediction that increased cardiovascular responses would be associated with concomitant increases in catecholamines and platelet function, in the direction of hypercoagulability, was given only partial support. A-B differences emerged for epinephrine and norepinephrine, four weeks and two weeks prior to the examinations respectively, and remained throughout the experimental period. Findings which are inconsistent with the general pattern of intravascular coagulation emerged from the platelet function tests and ATIII assays. Both groups showed similar platelet response patterns: a decrease in both the reaction time and the percentage of aggregation. An A-B difference was observed in the speed of aggregation immediately prior to the examinations, indicating that the platelets from Type As aggregated more quickly to a collagen challenge, than platelets from Type Bs. An increase in circulating antithrombin III was demonstrated by both groups towards the end of the experiment although Type As demonstrated the greater increase immediately before and following the examinations.

The A-B cardiovascular differences observed in a naturalistic setting provide laboratory findings with a degree of external validity. The findings are consistent with Lovallo, Pincomb, Edwards, Bracket and Wilson (1986a) who reported a greater rate pressure product in Type As, compared with Type Bs, on exam days and non-exam days during the same week. Moreover, basal plasma epinephrine, norepinephrine, total cholesterol, and low density lipoproteins were elevated one week prior to examinations, in medical students (O'Donnel, Meara, Owens, Johnson, Collins & Tomkin, 1987). The anticipation affect of the cardiovascular and catecholamine parameters, is comparable with the findings of Jorgensen and Houston (1981), who observed greater SBP in subjects who scored high on the hard-driving component of the JAS, compared with low scorers. The authors propose that the high scorers were more threatened by anticipating a stressful situation in which they may fail to maintain control. Indeed, Gastorf and Teevan (1980) reported an association between fear of failure and the hard-driving component of the JAS.

An increase in the speed of aggregation prior to the examinations, especially for Type As, may reflect a hypercoagulable state. The percentage aggregation results, however, appear incongruent with this conclusion. The decrease in percentage aggregation is in accordance with O'Brien, Etherington and Jamieson (1981) and Arkel, Haft, Kreutner, Sherwood and Williams (1977). O'Brien et al. (1971) recorded a reduction in the aggregation response to ADP and collagen during surgery. Arkel et al. (1977) demonstrated a similar effect in medical students which lasted for at least twenty-four hours, following a case presentation. Furthermore, Simpson, Olewine, Jenkins, Ramsey, Zyzanski, Thomas and Hames (1974) recorded a slight reduction in the aggregating response in Type B subjects after an exercise task. The demonstration of a possible 'protection effect' during a challenging situation has not been reported by all researchers. Increases in platelet aggregation have been demonstrated on hospital admission and following a bicycle ergonometer test (Fleischman, Bierenbaum & Stier, 1976; Jenkins, Thomas, Olewine, Zyzanski, Simpson & Hames, 1975).

Physiological levels of circulating epinephrine and norepinephrine have been shown to be capable of inducing platelet aggregation (Ardlie, Cameron & Garrett, 1984; Ardlie et al., 1985). Given the increases in circulating catecholamines in the present study and in other experiments which have recorded decreased platelet aggregation, this effect merits further consideration. An explanation which has received some attention is that platelet refractoriness is due to prior in vivo aggregation and release, facilitated by enhanced circulating catecholamine levels (Rozenberg & Holmsen, 1968; Arkel et al., 1977). When the partially aggregated platelets are subjected to subsequent in vitro challenge, an apparent reduction in the percentage of platelet aggregation is recorded. If the release reaction had occurred in vivo, a reduction in the ADP and ATP contents of the platelet would be recorded. Arkel et al. (1977) however, found an increase in the nucleotides which they were unable to explain. They did, however, offer an alternative explanation for the reduction in aggregation. They proposed that during the stressor situation catecholamines partially blocked platelet receptor sites, rendering the platelets less sensitive to later in vitro challenge. Mills and Roberts (1967), however, had previously demonstrated that the exposure of platelets to small quantities of epinephrine, augmented the aggregation response to ADP.

Both the in vivo aggregation and receptor blocking hypotheses attempt to uncover the apparent 'protection effect' of decreased aggregation as an artifact, produced by a prior in vivo interaction. This reflects the expectations of researchers, as the conditions are ideal for an increase in platelet aggregation to occur. Not only would enhanced circulating catecholamines induce platelet aggregation, but an increase in lipoprotein concentrations and thrombin would be expected to potentiate the effect (Burstein, Berns, Heldenberg, Kahn, Werbin & Tamir, 1978). Three explanations may be offered, however, to explain the decrease in platelet function in this present study. Firstly, the effect may have been due to blood collection and handling procedures. This is unlikely given that the procedure was identical throughout the study, and a decrease in aggregation only occurred at the time of the examinations. Secondly, although not consistent with current conjecture, platelet activity may actually decrease during long-term natural stressor situations. This decrease may be facilitated by increased ATIII and other anticoagulatory compounds, counteracting the aggregatory effects of thrombin and possibly epinephrine and norepinephrine. Alternatively, factors which as yet remain undocumented may inhibit platelet aggregation. Finally, and perhaps most likely, partial aggregation may have occurred in vivo, rendering platelets less sensitive to a later in vitro collagen challenge. Occasionally, platelet-rich plasma had to be discarded and the responses eliminated from the analysis as spontaneous aggregation occurred (11 samples–7 Type As and 4 Type Bs– taken at assessments 4, 5 and 6). In other words, the platelets were aggregating prior to the addition of the collagen. Although speculative, this observation may lend support to the in vivo aggregation hypothesis. As platelet function is largely controlled by the aggregatory action of thromboxane A2 and the inhibitory action of prostacyclin (Moncada & Vane, 1978), the balance between these prostaglandins may help to explain the aggregation discrepancy.

The ATIII results are consistent with the findings of previous animal work as an increase in catecholamines was followed by an increase in ATIII (Abbott et al., 1984). During shape change the platelet membrane becomes a catalytic surface which promotes the formation of thrombin (Spaet & Cintron, 1965). Therefore, an increase in ATIII to combat the increased thrombin formation is rational. Although it seems that ATIII offers a degree of protection against intravascular coagulation, a direct evaluation of this would have to incorporate a quantitative measure of thrombin. Only by assessing the thrombin-antithrombin III ratio could a conclusion regarding a state of protection or hypercoagulability be made. The increases in ATIII may or may not be sufficiently potent to buffer the coagulatory activity of thrombin. Further work on ATIII and thrombin within a behavior pattern-CHD framework may be valuable. Given that the half-life of ATIII is longer than that of epinephrine or norepinephrine, ATIII levels may be a better long-term measure of physiological variation.

Behavior and Affect

Different coping styles have a common denominator: that of providing the individual with a sense of control over the situation. Three differences in coping between Type As and Type Bs emerged leading up to and during the challenging examinations. Firstly, although Type As and Type Bs reported a similar proportion of minor ailments and medication taking, Type As were less likely to have been prescribed the medication by a doctor. Secondly, Type Bs increased their alcohol intake whereas Type As reduced the amount. Thirdly, of the individuals who smoked, those who were Type A increased the number of cigarettes smoked per day, whereas no change was reported by the Type Bs. Given that only subjects who smoked less than ten cigarettes per day were employed in the study, findings concerning smoking as a coping strategy are likely to be restrictive.

The reluctance of Type As, compared with Type Bs, to visit their GPs when experiencing minor ailments is intriguing. Possibly, Type As adopt a more internal locus of control, whereas Type Bs tend to adopt an external approach. If this is so, Type As would view their health as being in their own hands and would therefore take the necessary steps to treat themselves. Visiting their GP may also be viewed as an interruption to their work. The more external approach adopted by Type Bs would be to view their health in the hands of others, and in this respect seek the advice of a doctor. Burke and Weir (1980) reported no difference in psychosomatic symptom reporting between Type As and Type Bs, although contrary to this study, they found that Type As were more likely than Type Bs to be taking medication. The self-reported behaviors in Burke and Weir's study, however, did not occur during a time-pressured,challenging situation.

The finding that Type Bs increased their alcohol intake, whilst Type As became almost abstinent, is very interesting. The finding does not support the work of Folsom, Hughes, Buehler, Mittlemark, Jacobs and Grimm (1985) who reported that Type As consumed more alcohol and drank more frequently than Type Bs. Indeed, middle-aged Type A men report that they drink twice as much as Type Bs (Camargo, Vranizan, Thoresen and Wood, 1986). Consistent with the present findings, however, O'Donnel et al. (1987) reported a decrease in alcohol consumption in medical students prior to examinations. Perhaps during a long-term challenging situation male Type A students adapt behaviorally, to meet the situational demands. Although the study provides no direct evidence as to why these differences emerged, one hypothesis may be that spending time socialising may distract from the task in hand.

In this respect a distinction between Type A and Type B behavior may fit into the coping framework proposed by Lazarus (1966), who draws a distinction between active and palliative coping strategies. Type As engaging in active coping would face the challenging situation by rigorously preparing for it. The increased smoking behavior of Type As is unlikely to distract from the immediate challenge, and may even serve as a palliative action. Type Bs, on the other hand, may cope better by trying to erase the threat from their minds, at least for a short time, which may be accomplished by social drinking. This line of reasoning would agree with the finding that Type As and Type Bs differ in their attributions of success and failure. Type As generally attribute failure to internal factors, rather than external factors as Type Bs tend to do (Musante, MacDougall & Dembroski, 1984).

Although the Type As' coping style may provide them with a degree of control over the situation, the physiological consequences of such a strategy may be detrimental, especially for the Type A individuals who are smokers. Interestingly, Lombardo and Carreno (1987) reported that although the smoking behavior of Type As and Type Bs did not differ in the number of puffs taken or puff volume, the inhalation duration was 70% longer in Type As than Type Bs. This may increase their CHD risk. The Type A consummatory response pattern is consistent with their striving to obtain the most from their environment in the shortest possible time. Nicotine has been shown to reduce negative affect resulting from frustration (Gilbert, 1979; Fleming & Lombardo, 1987). Type As may inhale longer in order to improve their performance which would reduce performance related frustration (Wesnes & Warburton,1983). Moderate alcohol drinkers appear to have a lower rate of CHD and live longer than non-drinkers or heavy drinkers (e.g., Hennekens, Willett, Rosner, Cole, & Mayrent, 1979; LaPorte, Cresanta & Kuller, 1980). Besides aiding in relaxation, alcohol increases high density lipoproteins which have been inversely associated with CHD (LaPorte, et al., 1980), and decreases platelet aggregation and coagulation (Baum-Baicker, 1981). The apparent decrease in percentage aggregation in the present study, however, was not correlated with alcohol consumption (at assessment 5, Type As, $R = .02$; Type Bs - $R = .10$). Moderate alcohol intake may, to some extent, act as a buffer in the behavior-disease relationship. The Type B coping style may serve as a CHD buffer, whereas the Type A strategy may only serve to augment the Type A-CHD association. Indeed, Barboriak (1984) claims that the cardioprotective effect of alcohol is sufficient to warrant its use as a treatment for CHD.

The finding that Type As, compared with Type Bs, do not report higher levels of anxiety, even though they reported greater perceived challenge and demonstrated greater cardiovascular and catecholaminergic responses, is consistent with laboratory studies (e.g., Carver, Degregorio & Gillis, 1981; Matthews & Volkin 1981). Reports of greater increases in hostility by Type As is also consistent with laboratory findings (e.g., Siegel & Leitch, 1981; Dembroski, MacDougall & Lushene, 1979). Faced with a challenging situation, Type A students may attempt to control it by denying various elements of the situation (e.g. negative effect), and perhaps reappraising the situation in a more positive way. In exerting additional behavioral and cognitive efforts to control the situation, however, Type As may be exerting greater and more prolonged strain on their cardiovascular system. They demonstrated the greater magnitude and duration of cardiovascular, catecholaminergic, and to some extent, platelet function responses.

REFERENCES

Abbott, J.M., Sutherland, C.J., & Watt, D.A.L. (1984). The effects of catecholamines on circulating levels of antithrombin III in the rat. *Thrombosis and Haemostasis, 52,* 367.

Ardlie, N.G., Cameron, H.A., & Garrett, J.J. (1984). Platelet activation by circulating levels of hormones: A possible link in coronary heart disease. *Thrombosis and Haemostasis, 36,* 315-322.

Ardlie, N.G., McGuiness, J.A., & Garrett, J.J. (1985). Effect on human platelets of catecholamines at levels achieved in the circulation. *Atherosclerosis, 58,* 251-259.

Arkel, Y.S., Haft, J.I., Kreutner, W., Sherwood, J., & Williams, R. (1977). Alteration in second phase platelet aggregation associated with an emotionally stressful activity. *Thrombosis and Haemostasis, 38,* 552-561.

Barboriak, J.J. (1984). Alcohol, lipids and heart disease. *Alcohol, 1,* 341-345.

Baum-Baicker, C. (1985). The health benefits of moderate alcohol consumption: A review of the literature. *Drug and Alcohol Dependence, 15,* 207-227.

Biomedical Convened Panel (1981). Coronary-prone behavior and coronary heart disease: A critical review. *Circulation, 63,* 1199-1215.

Born, G.V.R. (1962). Quantitative investigations into the aggregation of blood platelets. *Journal of Physiology, 162,* 67-68.

Bortner, R.W. (1969). A short rating scale as a potential measure of pattern A behavior. *Journal of Chronic Diseases, 22,* 87-91.

Burke, R.J., & Weir, T. (1980). The Type A experience: Occupational and life demands, satisfaction and well-being. *Journal of Human Stress, 6,* 28-38.

Burstein, Y., Berns, L., Heldenberg, D., Kahn, Y., Werbin, B.Z., & Tamir, I. (1978). Increase in platelet aggregation following a rise in plasma free fatty acids. *American Journal of Haematology, 4,* 17-22.

Camargo, C.A.,Vranizan, K.M., Thoresen, C.E., & Wood, P.D. (1986). Type A behavior pattern and alcohol intake in middle-aged men, *Psychosomatic Medicine, 48,* 575-581.

Carver, C.S., Degregorio, E., & Gillis, R. (1981). Challenge and Type A behavior among intercollegiate football players. *Journal of Sports Psychology, 31,* 140-148.

Contrada, R.J., Glass, D.C., Krakoff, L.R., Krantz, D.S., Kehoe, K., Isecke, W., Collins, C., & Elting, E. (1982). Effects of control over aversive stimulation and Type A behavior on cardiovascular and plasma catecholamine responses. *Psychophysiology, 19,* 408-419.

De Backer, G., Kornitzer, M., Kittle, F., Bogaert, M., Van Durme, J.P., Vincke, J., Rustin, R.M., Degre, C., & De Schaepdrijver, A. (1979). Relation between coronary-prone behavior pattern, excretion of urinary catecholamines, heart rate and heart rhythm. *Preventive Medicine, 8,* 14-22.

Dembroski, T.M., MacDougall, J.M., & Lushene, R. (1979). Interpersonal interaction and cardiovascular response in Type A subjects and coronary patients. *Journal of Human Stress, 5,* 28-36.

Dembroski, T.M., MacDougall, J.M., & Shields, J.L. (1977). Physiologic reactions to social challenge in person evidencing the Type A coronary-prone behavior pattern. *Journal of Human Stress, 3,* 2-9.

Flesichman, A.I., Bierenbaum, M.L., & Stier, A. (1976). Effects of stress due to anticipated minor surgery upon in vivo platelet aggregation in humans. *Journal of Human Stress, 2,* 33-37.

Fleming, S.F., & Lombardo, T.W. (1987). Effects of cigarette smoking on phobic anxiety. *Addictive Behaviors, 12,* 195-198.

Folsom, A.R., Hughes, J.R., Buehler, J.F., Mittlemark, M.B., Jacobs, D.R., & Grimm, R.H. (1985). Do Type A men drink more frequently than Type B men? Findings in the Multiple Risk Factor Intervention Trial (MRFIT). *Journal of Behavioral Medicine, 8,* 227-235.

French-Belgian Collaborative Group (1982). Ischemic heart disease and psychological patterns. *Advances in Cardiology, 29,* 25-31.

Fridlund, A.J. (1987). Alternatives in analyzing repeated measures. *Psychophysiology, 24,* 477-478.

Friedman, M., St. George, S., Byers, S.O. & Rosenman, R.H. (1960). Excretion of catecholamines, 17-ketosteroids, 17-hydroxy-corticoids and 6-hydroxyindole in men exhibiting a particular behavior pattern (A) associated with high incidence of clinical coronary artery disease. *Journal of Clinical Investigations, 39,* 758-764.

Gastorf, J.W., & Teevan, R. (1980). Type A coronary-prone behavior pattern and fear-of-failure. *Motivation and Emotion, 4,* 71-76.

Gilbert, D.G. (1979). Paradoxical tranquilizing and emotion-reducing effects of nicotine. *Psychological Bulletin, 86,* 643-661.

Glass, D.C., Krakoff, L.R., Contrada, R., Hilton, W.F., Kehoe, K., Mannucci, E.G., Collins, C., Snow, B., & Elting, B. (1980). Effect of harassment and competition upon cardiovascular and plasma catecholamine responses in Type A and Type B individuals. *Psychophysiology, 17,* 453-463.

Heller, R.F. (1979). Type A behavior and coronary heart disease. *British Medical Journal, 11,* 368.

Hennekens, C.H., Willett, W., Rosner, B., Cole, D.S., & Mayrent, A.L. (1979). Effects of beer, wine and liquor in coronary deaths. *Journal of the American Medical Association, 242,* 1973-1974.

Jenkins, C.D., Thomas, G., Olewine, D., Zyzanski, S.J., Simpson, M.T. & Hames, C.G. (1975). Blood platelet aggregation and personality traits. *Journal of Human Stress, 1*, 34-46.

Johnston, D.W., & Shaper, A.G. (1983). Type A behavior in British men: Reliability and intercorrelation of two measures. *Journal of Chronic Diseases, 36*, 203-207.

Jorgensen, R.S., & Houston, B.K. (1981). The Type A behavior pattern, sex differences, and cardiovascular responses to and recovery from stress. *Motivation and Emotion, 5*, 201-214.

Keys, A., Taylor, H.L., Blackburn, H., Brozek, J., & Anderson, J.T. (1971). Mortality and coronary heart disease among men studied for twenty-three years. *Archives of Internal Medicine, 128*, 201-205.

Kobasa, S.C. (1982). Commitment and coping in stress resistance among lawyers. *Journal of Personality and Social Psychology, 42*, 707-717.

Koskenvuo, M., Kaprio, J., Langinvainio, H., Romo, M., & Sarna, S. (1981). Psychosocial and environmental correlates of coronary-prone behavior in Finland. *Journal of Chronic Diseases, 34*, 331-340.

LaPorte, R.E., Cresanta, J.L., & Kuller, L.H. (1980). The relationship of alcohol consumption to atherosclerotic heart disease. *Preventive Medicine, 9*, 22-40.

Lazarus, R.S. (1966). *Psychological Stress and Coping Process.* McGraw-Hill: New York.

Lombardo, T., & Carreno, L. (1987). Relationship of Type A behavior pattern in smokers to carbon monoxide exposure and smoking topography. *Health Psychology, 6*, 445-452.

Lovallo, W.R., Pincomb, G.A., Edwards, G.L., Bracket, D.J., & Wilson, M.F. (1986a). Work pressure and the Type A behavior pattern. Exam stress in male medical students. *Psychosomatic Medicine, 48*, 125-133.

Lovallo, W.R., Pincomb, G.A., & Wilson, M.F. (1986b). Heart rate reactivity and Type A behavior as modifiers of physiological response to active and passive coping. *Psychophysiology, 23*, 105-112.

MacDougall, J.M., Dembroski, T.M. & Musante, L. (1979). The SI and questionnaire methods of assessing coronary-prone behavior in male and female college students. *Journal of Behavioral Medicine, 2*,71-83.

MacFarlane, A., Norman, G., Streiner, D., Roy, R., & Scott, D. (1980). A longitudinal study of the influence of psychosocial environment on health status: A preliminary report. *Journal of Health and Social Behavior, 21*, 124-133.

Manuck, S.B., Course, C.D., & Winkelman, P.A. (1979). Behavioral correlates of individual differences in blood pressure reactivity. *Journal of Psychosomatic Research, 2*, 281-288.

Matthews, K.A., & Haynes, S.G. (1986). Type A behavior pattern and coronary disease risk. Update and critical evaluation. *American Journal of Epidemiology, 123*, 923-960.

Matthews, K.A., & Volkin, J.I. (1981). Efforts to excel and the Type A behavior pattern in children. *Child Development, 52*, 1283-1289.

Mills, D.C.B., & Roberts, G.C.K. (1967). Effects of epinephrine on human blood platelets. *Journal of Physiology, 193*, 443-453.

Moncada, S. & Vane, J.R. (1978). Unstable metabolites of arachidonic acid and their role in haemostasis and thrombosis. *British Medical Bulletin, 34*, 129-132.

Musante, L., MacDougall, J.M. & Dembroski, T.M. (1984). The Type A behavior pattern and attributions for success and failure. *Personality and Social Psychology Bulletin, 10*, 544-553.

O'Brien, J.R. (1962). Platelet aggregation. 1. Some results from a new method of study. *Journal of Clinical Pathology, 15*, 452-455.

O'Brien, J.R., Etherington, M,. & Jamieson, S. (1971). Refractory state of platelet aggregation with major operations. *Lancet, 2*, 741-743.

O'Donnel, L., Meara, N., Owens, D., Johnson, A., Collins, P., & Tomkin, G. (1987). Plasma catecholamines and lipoproteins in chronic psychological stress. *Journal of the Royal Society of Medicine, 80*, 339-342.

Röka, L. (1978). *Antithrombin. Diagnosis Today*. Boehringer Mannheim GmbH Mannheim.

Rose, R.M., Jenkins, C.D., & Hurst, M.W. (1978). Air traffic controller health change study. *Report to the Federal Aviation Administration.*

Rosenberg, R.D., & Damus, P.S. (1973). The purification and mechanism of action of human antithrombin III-heparin cofactor. *Journal of Biological Chemistry, 248*, 6490-6505.

Rosenman, R.H., Rahe, R.H., Borhani, N.O., & Feinleib, M. (1976). Heritability of personality and behavior. *Acta-Geneticae Medicae et Genellogagiae, 25*, 221-224.

Rozenberg, M.C., & Holmsen, H. (1968). Adenosine nucleotide metabolism of blood platelets. IV. Platelet aggregation response to exogenous ATP and ADP. *Biochemica et Biophysica Acta,, 157*, 280-282.

Rustin, R.M., Dramaiz, M., Kittle, F., Degre, C., Kornitzer, M., Thiely, C., & de Backer, G. (1976). Validation of the techniques used to evaluate the Type A behavior pattern. *Revue Epidemiologie et Sante Publique, 24*, 497-507.

Siegel, J.M., & Leitch, C.A. (1981). Assessment of the Type A behavior pattern in adolescents. *Psychosomatic Medicine, 43*, 45-56.

Simpson, M.T., Olewine, D.A., Jenkins, C.D., Ramsey, F.H., Zyzanski, S.J., Thomas, G., & Hames, C.G. (1974). Exercise-induced catecholamines and platelet aggregation in the coronary-prone behavior pattern. *Psychosomatic Medicine, 36*, 476-487.

Spaet, T.H., & Cintron, J. (1965). Studies on platelet factors bio-availability. *British Journal of Haematology, 11*, 269-274.

Stokols, D., Novaco, R.W., Stokols, J., & Campbell, J. (1978). Traffic congestion, Type A behavior, and stress. *Journal of Applied Psychology, 63*, 467-480.

Suls, J., & Mullen, B. (1981). Life change and psychological distress: The role of perceived control and desirability. *Journal of Applied Social Psychology, 11*, 379-389.

Thurstone, L.L. (1949). Thurstone Temperament Schedule. *Science Research Associates*, Chicago.

Van Schijndel, M., De May, H., & Naring, G. (1984). Effects of behavioral control and Type A behavior on cardiovascular responses. *Psychophysiology, 21*, 501-509.

Vasey, M.W., & Thayer, J.F. (1987). The continuing problem of false positives in repeated measures ANOVAS in psychophysiology: A multivariate solution. *Psychophysiology, 24*, 479-486.

Von Euler, U.S., & Floding, I. (1955). A fluorimetric micromethod for differential estimation of epinephrine and norepinephrine. *Acta Physiologica Scandinavica, 118,* 45-56.

Waldron, I., Hickey, A., Butensky, A., Gruss, L., Overall, K., Schmader, A., & Wohlmuth, D. (1980). Type A behavior pattern: Relationship to variation in blood pressure, paternal characteristics, and academic and social activities of students. *Journal of Human Stress, 5,* 16-27.

Wesnes, K., & Warburton, D.M. (1983). Smoking, nicotine and human performance. *Pharmacology and Therapeutics, 21,* 189-208.

Williams, R.B., Lane, J.D., Kuhn, C.M., Melosh, W., White, A.D., & Schanberg, S.M. (1982). Type A behavior and elevated physiological and neuroendocrine responses to cognitive tasks. *Science, 218,* 483-485.

Yue, R.H., Gertler, M.M., Starr, T., & Koutrouby, R. (1976). Alteration of plasma antithrombin III levels in ischemic heart disease. *Thrombosis and Haemostasis, 35,* 598-606.

Zuckerman, M., & Lubin, B. (1965). *Manual for the Multiple Affect Adjective checklist.* Edits, San Diego, California.

The Impact of Type A Behavior on Subjective Life Quality: Bad for the Heart, Good for the Soul?

Fred B. Bryant
Department of Psychology, Loyola University of Chicago
Sheridan Road, Chicago, IL 60626

Paul R. Yarnold
Northwestern University Medical School and
University of Illinois at Chicago, Chicago, IL 60611

Two studies investigated whether Type As and Type Bs differ in the subjective quality of their lives. Subjective life quality was defined as self-evaluations of subjective experience comprised of both a "trait"-like component referred to as subjective adjustment, and a "state"-like component, referred to as mood. In Study 1, a six-factor model of self-evaluation was used to compare mean levels of subjective adjustment reported by Type A and Type B college students (n=456). Whereas As reported higher levels of positive experience (i.e., happiness, gratification, and self-confidence) than Bs, As and Bs did not differ in reported levels of negative experience (i.e., strain, vulnerability, and uncertainty). This pattern of results suggests that Type A behavior (TAB) provides a heightened sense of instrumentality that functions more as a source of positive experience than as a means of reducing negative experience. In Study 2, a six-factor profile measure was used to contrast mean levels and reliabilities of mood states reported by Type A and Type B college students (n=147) in relation to daily events over a two-week period. Intersubject and intrasubject analyses revealed that TAB was unrelated to negative moods, but was significantly related to feelings of psychological vigor. Considered together, these two studies provide converging evidence that, despite its possible negative impact on cardiovascular health, TAB in young adults is associated with positive psychological outcomes. Recommendations are provided for improving the quality of theory and research in this area.

Authors' Notes: The authors contributed equally to this manuscript and are listed alphabetically. Appreciation is extended to Liz Sanders for assistance in data coding for Study 1, to Don Kindwald, Gayle Mann, and Tom Russell for assistance in data collection for Study 2, to the editor and anonymous reviewers for thoughtful criticisms, and to Janet Goranson for assistance in preparing the manuscript. Preliminary versions of Study 1 were presented at the annual meeting of the Midwestern Psychological Association (Chicago, May, 1987), and at the annual meeting of the American Psychological Association (Atlanta, August, 1988). Preliminary versions of Study 2 were presented at the annual meeting of the American Association for the Advancement of Science (Chicago, February, 1987) and at the annual meeting of the Midwestern Psychological Association (Chicago, May, 1987). Reprint requests should be addressed to the first author.

© 1990 Select Press

Type A behavior (TAB), elicited by either perceived threat to one's control over salient events (Glass, 1977) or uncertainty about one's abilities created by situational demands (Strube, Boland, Manfredo, & Al Falaij, 1987), is characterized by hard-driving competitiveness and hostility. Type Bs' response to such "control-challenges," on the other hand, is characterized by a more relaxed and easy-going orientation (Friedman & Rosenman, 1974). Although much research has investigated the impact of TAB on physical health—e.g., increased rates of cardiovascular disease (Booth-Kewley & Friedman, 1987)—relatively little research, in contrast, has explored how TAB influences the subjective quality of people's lives. One might well expect, however, that the subjective quality of As' and Bs' lives would differ as a consequence of their divergent lifestyles.

Imagine, for example, a hypothetical Type A individual who confronts another individual, on whose behavior the Type A is dependent. A "stereotypic" Type A response to such a contingency would include suspicion of the other person's ability (Yarnold & Bryant, 1987) and a preference for maintaining personal control (Strube & Werner, 1985). Failure on the other person's part might well trigger hostile/dominant responding from the Type A—a reaction referred to as "free-floating hostility," in the case of extreme Type As (Friedman & Ulmer, 1985). This characteristic interpersonal style could lead to smaller, less developed "social networks" and, consequently, to fewer resources for both celebrating good fortune and coping with distress (Pilisuk & Parks, 1986). Type Bs, in contrast, are less suspicious of others, are more willing to delegate control (and are less upset by the thought of failure), and are less likely to exhibit hostility or dominance toward others. These characteristic responses to control-challenges could facilitate the Type B's integration into and involvement with social support networks.

Accordingly, the purpose of the present research was to systematically examine whether Type A and Type B college students differ in the subjective quality of their lives. In the following sections, we first describe the origins of research on subjective life quality, we define subjective life quality as self-evaluations of subjective experience comprised of both a "trait"-like component (which we examine in Study 1) and a "state"-like component (which we examine in Study 2), and we argue that a better understanding of subjective life quality may advance our conceptual understanding of TAB. We then review past research on TAB and subjective adjustment in developing hypotheses for Study 1.

The Origins of Research on Subjective Life Quality

Self-report measures of subjective life quality originally evolved from the use of quantitative indexes to monitor objective social conditions. Sociologists and public administrators initially studied "social indicators," such as aggregate statistics reflecting unemployment rates and economic status, to gauge how economic, social, and political changes affect the objective quality of life (Bauer, 1966; Carley, 1981; Gross & Straussman, 1974; Verwayen, 1984). As this research progressed, however, investigators began to recognize the importance of also considering individuals' own evaluations of the subjective quality of life, including perceived needs and satisfaction in various life domains (Campbell, 1976). Similarly, health-care evaluators initially focused on objective health indicators, such as mortality rates and functional status, to assess the impact of medical treatments on the quality of life (Berg, 1977; Blau, 1977); but this objective focus has since been expanded to include patients' own thoughts and feelings about their lives (Alexander & Willems, 1981; Chubon, 1987; Freed, 1984).

Self-evaluations of subjective life quality are intended to complement, rather than to replace, social indicators of objective circumstances (Campbell, Converse, & Rodgers, 1976; Rossi & Gilmartin, 1980). These subjective self-assessments are, however, unlike self-reports of objective psychopathology (e.g., Dohrenwend, Yager, Egri, & Mendelsohn, 1978; Langner, 1962), which epidemiologists use to identify people at psychiatric risk. In contrast to psychiatric screening devices, subjective self-evaluations entail "a global assessment of a person's quality of life according to his own chosen criteria" (Shin & Johnson, 1978, p.478). (For reviews of research on subjective life quality, see Campbell, 1980, Diener, 1984, Larson, 1978, and Wilson, 1967).

Definition and Measurement of Subjective Life Quality

As the literature on self-evaluations of subjective life quality has grown, numerous terms have been used to denote the underlying construct being studied. Different researchers have given their dependent measures different labels, including perceived life quality (Andrews & Withey, 1974), self-reported well-being (Andrews & Crandall, 1976), subjective well-being (Wan & Livieratos, 1978), psychological well-being (Warr, 1978), mental well-being (Beiser, 1974), psychological adjustment (Reid & Ziegler, 1980), subjective adjustment (Veroff, Feld, & Gurin, 1962), subjective welfare (McKennell, 1974), and subjective mental health (Bryant & Veroff, 1984). This confusion of terminology reflects the fact that the concept of subjective life quality has no universally accepted definition and has been used so generally as to be nearly useless (cf. Bloom, 1975; Gehrmann, 1978; Lawton, 1983; McNeil, Stones, & Kozma, 1986).

Reflecting the lack of conceptual agreement in the literature, social researchers have used many different kinds of outcome measures to assess subjective life quality. Measures of morale (Lawton, 1975), life satisfaction (Adams, 1969), psychophysical symptoms (Cox, Thirlaway, Gotts, & Cox, 1983), happiness (Shin & Johnson, 1978), mood (Cameron, 1975), and the balance between positive and negative affect (Bradburn, 1969), for example, have been used in past studies to operationally define subjective life quality. More recently, researchers (e.g., Andrews & McKennell, 1980; Bryant & Veroff, 1984; Padilla & Grant, 1985; Veit & Ware, 1983) have used theoretical models to develop instruments that tap subjective life qualify along multiple dimensions, including affective and cognitive self-evaluations of both positive and negative experience. Despite these theoretical and empirical advances, however, there still exists no general agreement about the meaning or measurement of subjective life quality.

In the present research, we define subjective life quality as having at least two basic, self-evaluative components. The first component we will refer to as *subjective adjustment,* which involves an integrated, global self-evaluation of all aspects of one's life along multiple dimensions, including satisfaction as well as positive and negative affect (Andrews & Withey, 1976; Bryant & Veroff, 1982; Campbell, 1980; Diener, 1984). We view subjective adjustment as representing a relatively stable, "trait"-like characteristic of the subjective quality of one's life. The second component of subjective life quality we will refer to as *mood,* which involves a short-term self-evaluation of positive and negative affects experienced in response to daily life (Fiske & Taylor, 1984; Leventhal, 1984; Watson, 1988). We view mood as representing a relatively transitory, "state"-like characteristic of the subjective quality of one's life. Evidence that (a) everyday moods can influence self-assessments of subjective adjustment (Cohen, Towbes, & Flocco, 1988; Schwarz & Clore, 1983; Schwarz & Strack, 1985) and (b) measures of subjective adjustment can be used to accurately predict the duration of self-reported daily moods (Larsen, Diener, & Emmons, 1985) further underscores the importance of considering these two constructs as separate, but related, components of subjective life quality.[1]

---

[1] *Our distinction between subjective life quality as a relative trait (subjective adjustment) versus a relative state (mood) has several precedents in the literature on emotions. With respect to positive emotions, for example, Diener (1984) has argued that happiness is both a trait (i.e., one's predisposition to experience certain levels of affect) as well as a state (i.e., one's mood at a particular moment). With respect to negative emotions, Speilberger, Gorsuch, and Lushene (1970) have presented evidence that anxiety has both trait and state components. And with respect to emotions in general, Watson (1988) has suggested that affects can be measured either as traits (i.e., persistent differences in general affective level) or as states (i.e., transient fluctuations in mood).*

Refinements in the definition and measurement of subjective life quality are important not only in improving research on subjective life quality, but also in advancing our conceptual understanding of TAB. A better understanding of *negative* subjective experience, for example, may improve our knowledge of how TAB leads to coronary-artery heart disease (CAHD), by helping to identify specific negative affects or cognitions that may exert a direct or indirect influence on CAHD. In addition, a better understanding of positive subjective experience may help pinpoint specific sources of reinforcement that contribute to the development and maintenance of TAB; and this knowledge could make it easier to extinguish TAB by replacing it with healthier alternative behaviors that provide the same rewards without the increased risk of CAHD. Furthermore, the relationship between TAB and subjective life quality is worthy of investigation regardless of whether or not TAB leads to CAHD. Indeed, TAB may well predispose individuals to dissatisfaction and depression in later years (Friedman & Ulmer, 1985; Price, 1982; Strube, Berry, Goza, & Fennimore, 1985)—risks worth studying in their own right.

This article reports the results of two studies on the relationship between TAB and subjective life quality. In Study 1, we examine how TAB relates to the "trait"-like component of subjective life quality, using a multidimensional model of self-evaluations (Bryant & Veroff, 1984) to operationally define subjective adjustment. In Study 2,we examine how TAB relates to the "state"-like component of subjective life quality, using a multidimensional mood profile (McNair, Lorr, & Droppleman 1971) to operationally define mood. We turn now to past research on TAB and subjective adjustment in developing hypotheses for Study 1.

STUDY 1

Type A Behavior and Subjective Adjustment

Research relating TAB to subjective adjustment has been sporadic and has produced mixed results. In some studies, As have reported greater subjective adjustment than Bs (e.g., Strube et al., 1985); in other studies, Bs have reported greater subjective adjustment than As (e.g., Suls, Becker, & Mullen, 1981); and in still other studies, As and Bs have shown no differences in subjective adjustment (e.g., Caffrey, 1970). Moreover, individual studies that have used multiple measures (e.g., Burke & Weir, 1980) have often found inconsistent results, with As reporting greater subjective adjustment on some measures and Bs reporting greater subjective adjustment on others. Thus, there is little agreement concerning how TAB influences subjective adjustment.

In trying to resolve these inconsistent findings, previous researchers have concentrated primarily on identifying additional "moderator" variables that may interact with A/B lifestyle to determine whether As or Bs report greater subjective adjustment. For example, DeGregorio and Carver (1980) found that As with a sex-role orientation low in masculinity reported the lowest level of self-esteem and the highest levels of anxiety and depression. Investigating another possible moderator variable, Strube et al. (1985) found that As, relative to Bs, reported greater adjustment in younger age groups, but lower adjustment in older groups. Other work suggests that excessive self-preoccupation (Heilbrun & Friedberg, 1987) and reliance on repressive coping strategies (Heilbrun & Renert, 1986) interacts with TAB to increase reported stress.

The present research took a different approach to resolving the inconsistent differences in subjective adjustment that have been found between As and Bs. Whereas previous efforts to understand the mixed results have focused on improving the specificity of the *independent* variables involved, the present study, in contrast, was aimed at improving the specificity of the *dependent* variables under consideration. Inspection of the measures used in past Type A research reveals a general lack of theoretical clarity in measuring subjective adjustment—a reflection of the conceptual disarray in the broader literature on subjective adjustment. A wide variety of outcome measures—including life satisfaction (Burke & Weir, 1980; Theorell & Rahe, 1972), self-esteem (DeGregorio & Carver, 1980; Leak & McCarthy 1984), depression (Caplan & Jones, 1975), anxiety (Blumenthal, Thompson, Williams, & Kong, 1979; Burke & Weir, 1980), social insecurity (Jenkins, Zyzanski, Ryan, Flessas, & Tannenbaum, 1977; Suls et al., 1981), and psychiatric symptomology (Rhodewalt & Agustsdottir, 1984; Somes, Garrity, & Marx, 1981)—has been used in different Type A studies without conceptual distinctions being made among these various measures. Virtually no attention has been paid to (a) the ways in which these various dependent measures are similar to or different from one another and (b) the implications these similarities and differences have for obtained results. Thus, past researchers in this area have typically used an *ad hoc* "piecemeal" approach in selecting measures of subjective adjustment, without a formal theoretical framework for understanding the constructs being assessed and their interrelationships.

This conceptual chaos is especially critical because whether As or Bs report greater subjective adjustment may well depend on the particular outcome measure that is used (cf. Bryant & Veroff, 1982). Indeed, research strongly suggests that subjective adjustment is multidimensional and that these different dimensions represent separate self-evaluations of subjective experience (Andrews & Withey, 1976; Bryant &

Veroff, 1982, 1984; Campbell, 1980; Diener, 1984; McKennell & Andrews, 1980). Clearly, research on TAB and subjective adjustment could be improved by using a formal theoretical model of subjective adjustment as a guide in selecting dependent measures, so as to enhance the construct validity of outcome measures and to clarify how these measures relate to one another.

Accordingly, the present study used a recently developed multidimensional model of self-evaluations (Bryant & Veroff, 1984, 1986) to conceptualize and measure subjective adjustment. Based on confirmatory factor analyses of 25 indices of subjective adjustment included in Veroff, Douvan, and Kulka's (1981) nationwide "Study of Modern Living," this model is comprised of six dimensions that represent different kinds of cognitive and affective evaluations of positive and negative experience: *happiness* (an affective evaluation of positive experience in terms of past, present, and future happiness); *gratification* (a cognitive evaluation of positive experience in terms of satisfaction and value fulfillment in current role relationships); *strain* (an affective evaluation of negative experience in terms of psychophysical and behavioral reactions to stress); *vulnerability* (a cognitive evaluation of negative experience in terms of personal susceptibility to stress); *self-confidence* (a cognitive and affective evaluation of the self in terms of zest, self-esteem, and perceived control); and *uncertainty* (a cognitive and affective evaluation of the future in terms of pessimism and worrying). Evaluations of *positive* experience (happiness, gratification, and self-confidence) are referred to as dimensions of *well-being*; and evaluations of *negative* experience (strain, vulnerability, and uncertainty) are referred to as dimensions of *distress*. This six-factor model has been validated in a national sample of adults and has been shown to explain the responses of both men and women equally well (Bryant & Veroff, 1984). The model has been used to operationally define subjective adjustment in past research on occupational complexity (Adelman, 1987), marital status (Weingarten & Bryant, 1987), intimacy motivation (McAdams & Bryant, 1987), and educational attainment (Bryant & Marquez, 1986).

Research Hypotheses

In formulating *a priori* hypotheses, the inconsistency in past findings and the absence of a formal theory relating TAB to specific dimensions of subjective adjustment made it difficult to build strong predictions. Several alternatives, however, seemed plausible. First, based on Strube et al.'s (1985) argument that TAB is adaptive at younger ages, the present college-aged sample might be expected to show a positive relationship between TAB and subjective adjustment, regardless of the particular dependent measures involved. If this is so, then As should report greater levels of positive experience (or well-being) as well as lower levels of negative experience (or distress), relative to Bs.

A second possibility is that As will report not only greater levels of well-being, but also greater levels of distress than Bs. This prediction is based on the notion that TAB brings positive rewards through productivity and achievement (Friedman & Rosenman, 1974; Price, 1982), but that it also has a cost in terms of increased stress (Suls et al., 1981). If this is so, then As should report greater happiness, gratification, and self-confidence as well as greater strain, vulnerability, and uncertainty, relative to Bs.

A third possibility, based on a study by Burke and Weir (1980), is that TAB affects levels of well-being, but not levels of distress. In Burke and Weir's (1980) research, TAB was unrelated to levels of psychosomatic symptoms, but was associated with greater life satisfaction, greater self-esteem, and less depression. In explaining their results, Burke and Weir (1980) argued that TAB not only provides individuals with psychological gratification, but also diverts attention from stressful stimuli and thereby masks psychological distress. This interpretation suggests that As will report greater levels of positive experience (i.e., happiness, gratification, and self-confidence) than Bs, but equal levels of negative experience (i.e., strain, vulnerability, and uncertainty).

METHOD

Subjects and Procedure

Subjects were 456 undergraduates (231 males, 178 females, and 47 for whom information about gender was missing) who participated in exchange for course credit. As a measure of TAB, subjects first completed the short form of the Student Jenkins Activity Survey (SJAS; Bryant & Yarnold, 1989; Yarnold & Bryant, 1988; Yarnold, Bryant, & Grimm, 1987). This short form contains only the 21 "scored" items, and not the 23 "filler" items, from the original SJAS (Krantz, Glass, & Snyder, 1974). The short form of the SJAS is temporally reliable and internally consistent (Yarnold, Mueser, Grau, & Grimm, 1986), yields factors that are more consistent with hypothesized structure than the original form (Bryant & Yarnold, 1989; Yarnold et al., 1987), and demonstrates relatively high cross-cultural generalizability (Yarnold, Bryant, & Litsas, in press).[2]

After completing the SJAS, subjects then filled out a questionnaire

[2] *Unfortunately, only SJAS total scores were available for subjects in both Studies 1 and 2, so that analysis by SJAS subscale (Bryant & Yarnold, 1989) could not be performed.*

containing the measures of subjective adjustment. These measures were extracted from Veroff et al.'s (1981) survey instrument in the original order of appearance and were phrased identically.[3] Responses to these measures were used to create factor scores for happiness, gratification, self-confidence, strain, vulnerability, and uncertainty, following Bryant and Veroff's (1984) original procedures.

RESULTS

Table 1 presents the internal consistency (i.e., Cronbach's α) and intercorrelations of the six dimensions of subjective adjustment. As expected, each subscale showed a reasonable degree of internal consistency for the college sample (cf. Magnusson, 1967). Consistent with this finding, confirmatory factor analyses have demonstrated that this six-factor model provides an equivalent degree of fit for both the national sample with which it was originally developed and a random sample of college undergraduates comparable to subjects in the present study (Bryant, in press).

Multivariate analysis of variance (MANOVA) was used initially to examine the impact of TAB on the six dimensions of subjective adjustment. A median-split of SJAS scores (Glass, 1977) was used to dichotomize subjects into groups of As (SJAS > 7, $n = 234$) and Bs (SJAS < 7, $n = 178$), with subjects who scored exactly at the median (SJAS = 7, $n = 44$) deleted from the analysis. This procedure yielded a final sample of 143 male As, 90 female As, 88 male Bs, and 88 female Bs. Factor scores for each of the six subscales of subjective adjustment were entered as dependent measures in the MANOVA.

This MANOVA revealed a significant multivariate main effect of A/B Type on subjective adjustment, $F(6,265) = 2.0$, $p < .05$. (The degrees of freedom for the error-term is lower than those for univariate analyses, due to case-wise deletion of missing data.) Although gender and the A/B Type x gender interaction were also examined, neither of these terms was significantly related to subjective adjustment; thus they were excluded in subsequent analyses. Additional analyses indicated that the nonsignificant A/B Type x gender interaction was not due to restric-

---

[3] *The one exception to this rule involved the indices of role adjustment that comprise the gratification factor. To measure gratification in the original national survey, adults were asked to indicate how much satisfaction and how much value fulfillment they had gotten from work, marriage, parenting, and leisure activities (see Appendix A of Bryant & Veroff, 1984). Because the present college-aged sample was predominantly single, the items regarding marriage and parenting were re-phrased to address relationships with members of the opposite sex and with one's family and friends. The wording of all other items remained identical. Copies of the scoring protocol are available upon request.*

TABLE 1 Reliabilities and Intercorrelations for the Six Subscales of Subjective Adjustment[a]

	Happiness (1.40)	*Gratification (3.50)*	*Self-Confidence (1.10)*	*Strain (1.40)*	*Perceived Vulnerability (2.33)*	*Uncertainty (1.17)*
Happiness	0.70[b]	—	—	—	—	—
Gratification	0.20**	0.86[b]	—	—	—	—
Self-Confidence	0.50**	0.49**	0.56[b]	—	—	—
Strain	-0.25**	-0.21**	-0.45**	0.63[b]	—	—
Perceived Vulnerability	-0.18**	-0.07	-0.33**	0.41**	0.80[b]	
Uncertainty	-0.07	-0.13*	-0.34**	0.50**	0.23**	0.65[b]

Note: $* = p < 0.05$, $** = p < 0.0005$. *The number in parentheses under subjective adjustment subscales is the multiplying constant "n" for the Spearman-Brown "prophecy formula" (see note b below).*

[a]*Exact ns for intercorrelations varied from 347 to 395, depending on missing data for some subjects.*
[b]*Cronbach's α, provided along the diagonal, represents a reliability coefficient of internal consistency (Magnusson, 1967). Reliabilities have been corrected for attenuation due to differences in the number of items across subscales, using the Spearman-Brown "prophecy formula" (Magnusson, 1967). This adjustment procedure involves first determining the number of items in the largest subscale (i.e., self-confidence) and then using the prophecy formula to calculate the reliabilities that each of the other subscales would have shown had they contained the same number of items as this largest subscale. That is,* $\alpha_{corrected} = n\alpha_{uncorrected}/[1 \pm (n-1)\alpha_{uncorrected}]$, *where n = (number of items in the largest subscale)/(number of items in the subscale for which* $\alpha_{corrected}$ *is being computed). We used the Spearman-Brown prophecy formula because α is a function of the number of items that constitute the particular subscale, and the range of items constituting our subscales (i.e., 2-7) was large relative to the number of items constituting the largest subscale (i.e., 7). Under these conditions, estimates of α for the theoretical dimensions will be highly influenced by the number of items in the particular subscale—a problem that the Spearman-Brown formula is specifically designed to correct (Magnusson, 1967). These corrected αs reflect the internal consistencies that each of the subscales would have shown had they not been confounded by differences in breadth of measurement. Reading down the diagonal from upper left to lower right, the uncorrected αs for each subscale were as follows: 0.64, 0.58, 0.56, 0.56, 0.60, 0.58.*

tion in the range of SJAS scores for either gender. Specifically, there was no significant gender difference either in the mean, $F(1,396) = 1.0$, n.s., or in the variance, F max $(187,255) = 1.1$, n.s., of SJAS scores.

Based on the results of the MANOVA, separate multiple regression analyses were then used to relate SJAS scores to each subscale of subjective adjustment. These analyses involved regressing each subjec-

TABLE 2 Results of Multiple Regression Analyses for Each Subjective Adjustment Subscale

Dimension of Subjective Adjustment[b]	*Results of Multiple Regressions*[a]		
	F	*df*[c]	*Direction of Effect*
Happiness (present happiness past happiness, future morale)	4.7*	1,393	Type As > Type Bs
Gratification (life satisfaction, role fulfillment)	12.1**	1,423	Type As > Type Bs
Self-Confidence (zest score[d], self-esteem, perceived control)	6.9**	1,375	Type As > Type Bs
Strain (psychophysical and behavioral symptoms of stress)	<1	1,382	—
Perceived Vulnerability (frequency of feeling overwhelmed, feeling of nervous breakdown, frequency of bad things)	<1	1,394	—
Uncertainty (frequency of worrying, satisfaction with time use, pessimism)	<1	1,404	—

*$p<.05$; **$p<.001$.

[a] *Based on analyses regressing each subjective adjustment subscale separately on total SJAS scores.*

[b] *Based on Bryant and Veroff's (1984) six-factor model of subjective adjustment.*

[c] *Degrees of freedom vary because some subjects did not complete all of the items necessary to receive scores on all six subscales of subjective adjustment. For each regression analysis, all subjects with scores on both the SJAS and the indicated subscale of subjective adjustment are included.*

[d] *Zest was measured by six items adapted by Veroff et al. (1981) from the Zung Depression Inventory (Zung, 1965). These items were phrased so that high scores reflected an endorsement of positive experience and low scores reflected a rejection of positive experience.*

tive adjustment subscale separately on total SJAS scores (including subjects who scored at the median). The results of these regression analyses are displayed in Table 2.

Confirming predictions based on research by Burke and Weir (1980), As reported greater happiness, gratification, and self-confidence than did Bs, but As and Bs showed no significant differences in reported levels of strain, vulnerability, and uncertainty.[4]

DISCUSSION

The most important finding of Study 1 is that whether or not Type As report greater subjective adjustment than Type Bs depends on the particular dependent measure used. Whereas As reported greater happiness, gratification, and self-confidence than Bs, As and Bs did not differ in strain, perceived vulnerability, or uncertainty. Thus, when self-evaluations of *positive* experience (well-being) are considered, As show higher levels of subjective adjustment than do Bs; but when self-evaluations of *negative* experience (distress) are considered, As and Bs show no differences in levels of subjective adjustment. This pattern of results suggests that, for college students, TAB functions more as a source of positive experience than as a means of reducing negative experience.

Past research corroborates the conclusion that TAB is rewarding. Relative to Bs, for example, As typically achieve greater success in school (Glass, 1977; Waldron, Hickey, McPherson, Butensky, Gruss, Overall, Schmader, & Wohlmuth, 1980), attain greater scientific distinction (Matthews, Helmreich, Beane, & Lucker, 1980), and reach higher occupational status (Mettlin, 1976; Waldron, 1978). Other research (e.g., Grimm & Yarnold, 1985) has found a strong positive relationship between TAB and "psychological instrumentality." This evidence supports the notion that TAB provides individuals with a heightened sense of mastery and personal competence. This feeling of efficacy may well be a source of positive affect, satisfaction, value fulfillment, and self-confidence in people's lives, and may therefore make the Type A lifestyle particularly difficult to quit (Burke & Weir, 1980; DeGregorio & Carver, 1980; Friedman & Ulmer, 1985).

But why was TAB unrelated to levels of distress? One possibility is

---

[4] *When limiting the sample to individuals with absolute SJAS scores at least one standard deviation from the mean (to increase the reliability of classification into A/B types; Yarnold & Mueser, 1989), results remained essentially the same. Although extreme As and extreme Bs showed no differences in reported levels of distress, i.e., strain, vulnerability, and uncertainty (all F's < 1, n.s.), extreme As reported more happiness* $[F(1,132) = 4.0, p < 0.05]$*, more self-confidence* $[F(1,132) = 9.4, p < 0.01]$*, and marginally more gratification* $[F(1,132) = 3.2, p < 0.10]$ *than extreme Bs.*

that the hard-driving, competitive achievement orientation central to the Type A lifestyle is indeed stressful, but that Type As do not actually perceive it as such (Burke & Weir, 1980; Friedman & Rosenman, 1974; Glass, 1977). This conclusion is consistent with evidence that As find stressful life events less distressing (Burke & Weir, 1980; Somes et al., 1980) and are better able to suppress negative feeling states (Carver, Coleman, & Glass, 1976; Matthews, 1982) than Bs. Thus, perceived instrumentality may serve as both a source of positive experience as well as a means of preventing increases in negative experience for Type As. This interpretation suggests that a reduction in perceived level of personal competence may not only diminish As' levels of subjective well-being, but may also increase their levels of subjective distress, relative to Bs. This may help to explain why actual or threatened loss of control is so devastating to Type As (cf. Brunson & Matthews, 1981; Dimsdale, Hackett, Block, & Hutter, 1978; Rhodewalt & Davison, 1983). Furthermore, evidence that perceived efficacy declines in later years (Schulz, 1980, 1982) supports the notion that perceived loss of control underlies the decreasing levels of subjective adjustment observed among Type As over the lifespan (cf. Strube et al., 1985).

One alternative explanation for the present results is that higher scores on measures of subjective adjustment, and indeed higher scores on measures of TAB, may reflect nothing more than a desire to present oneself in a favorable light. This "social desirability" explanation implies that Type As are more motivated than Type Bs to present themselves positively. Furnham (1986) presents evidence, however, that As and Bs are equally sensitive to the influence of social desirability. In addition, a straightforward social desirability explanation suggests that As should have reported not only higher levels of well-being, but also lower levels of distress, relative to Bs. Yet, As reported only higher levels of well-being and not lower levels of distress. Considered together, this evidence suggests that social desirability does not explain the present findings.

Study 1 sheds light on the relationship between TAB and subjective adjustment, the "trait"-like component of subjective life quality, but it leaves unanswered the question of how TAB relates to mood, the "state"-like component of subjective life quality. Accordingly, Study 2 was designed to examine and compare the mood states of As and Bs in relation to everyday life. We turn now to past research on TAB, emotions, and naturally-occurring mood, in developing hypotheses for Study 2.

STUDY 2

Type A Behavior and Negative Emotions

A wealth of research, largely independent of research concerning TAB, has examined the role of negative emotions (e.g., anger, anxiety, and depression) in the etiology and ontogenesis of illness in general (e.g., Baker, 1987; Johnson & Broman, 1987; Pilisuk & Parks, 1986; Watson, 1988) and of CAHD in particular (e.g., Byrne, 1987; Jenkins, 1971; Keith, 1966). This research has typically conceived of negative emotions in the context of personality traits (i.e., implying a lasting disposition toward responding to situations with negative affect), and a recent quantitative review of the literature suggests that individuals generally predisposed toward negative affect are at greater risk for CAHD (Booth-Kewley & Friedman, 1987). Accordingly, researchers have begun exploring the role of negative emotions in the expression of TAB, and as a potential mediating variable in the relationship of TAB to CAHD.

Research investigating the relationship between TAB and negative emotions has focused primarily on anger and hostility (e.g., Dembroski, MacDougall, Williams, Haney, & Blumenthal, 1985; Shekelle, Gale, Ostfeld, & Paul, 1983) and on hostile and instrumental forms of interpersonal aggression (e.g., Strube, Turner, Cerro, Stevens, & Hinchey, 1984; Yarnold & Grimm, 1988). This research emphasizes the interaction between specific threatening situations and *TAB manifest as negative emotional reactivity* (i.e., the person-by-environment interaction hypothesized by Glass's control theory and Strube's self-appraisal theory). The focus of this research is often on behavioral (Strube et al., 1984; Yarnold & Grimm, 1988), cognitive (Furnham, Borovoy, & Henley, 1986; Price, 1982; Smith & Brehm, 1981), and physiological (Graboys, 1984; Williams, 1987) concommitants of negative emotions. One recent study (Friedman, Hall, & Harris, 1985) suggests that Type As predisposed to respond with negative affect are at particularly high risk for CAHD and that Type Bs similarly predisposed are also at greater risk.

Research examining TAB and negative emotions has been based almost entirely upon experimental methodology with contingencies designed to elicit TAB from susceptible individuals (i.e., Type As). Thus, for example, when placed in a laboratory situation where progress towards completion of a salient task is threatened by another person, a Type A typically responds with irritability, time-urgency, controlling-behaviors (e.g., dominance), and/or hostility. However, the relative frequency with which Type As express negative emotions under more naturalistic conditions, where direct provocations may be relatively infrequent, has not yet been studied. Consequently, it is unknown whether Type As and Type Bs differ in their characteristic emotional responses to the unique challenges experienced in their everyday lives. In order to address this issue, it is first necessary to define the nature of the emotional responses to be considered.

Prior research concerning trait-predispositions toward negative affect has employed measures such as the MMPI that are highly insensitive to the rapidly-changing situations that comprise day-to-day life, and which are thus unsuitable for assessing individuals' short-term naturally-occurring emotional responses. Alternatively, prior research examining emotional responses of As and Bs in relation to specific challenging situations may be unrepresentative of naturally-occurring daily life events. Thus, methods used in previous research are unsuitable for the purposes of contrasting As' and Bs' naturally-occurring emotionality.

Type A Behavior and Naturally-Occurring Mood

The approach we adopted involved assessing individuals' short-term (i.e., weekly) mood states. As discussed by Leventhal (1984), emotions appear and disappear very rapidly, whereas moods may be sustained for relatively long periods of time. Emotions are quantitatively more intense than moods, and are qualitatively different than moods since emotions generally involve phasic automatic expressive-motor activity (Leventhal, 1984). Whereas emotional responses to specific events may serve to interrupt one's behavior during the emotional episode (Carver & Scheier, 1982; Simon, 1982), moods have pervasive effects on behavior and judgment (e.g., affecting the content and valence of inferences regarding one's experiences, influencing automatic versus controlled cognitive processing, and affecting one's decision-making style; see Fiske & Taylor, 1984). Research suggests that the pervasive effect of mood on behavior may be attributable to "priming" of similarly toned material in memory (i.e., a positive mood results in positive associations in memory, and *vice versa*; e.g. Blaney, 1986; Bower, 1981; Wright & Mischel, 1982). Acute emotional episodes are largely related to specific experiences (including perceptual phenomena such as imagery; Lazarus, 1980), and are accompanied by clearly discriminable short-term phasic activity in common neurochemical systems (Leventhal, 1984). Moods, which may be elicited by a specific event, are generally non-specific and appear to be related to tonic levels of neurotransmitters such as monamines and neuropeptides (e.g., Iversen, 1982; Leventhal 1984; van Praag, 1982). There is the potential, therefore, for mood states to result in chronically elevated tonic levels of neurotransmitters (such as noradrenalin) that are risk-factors for CAHD, as well as in a lower level of general immunological defense (Pilisuk & Parks, 1986).

The only study we have found that contrasted the mood states of As and Bs in relation to their general life experiences was conducted by Dimsdale, Hackett, Block, and Hutter (1978), who administered the self-report Profile of Mood States (McNair et al., 1971; see Method) to a sample of patients awaiting cardiac catheterization. Dimsdale et al. (1978) reported that TAB is associated with more negative moods (i.e., high levels of subjective tension, depression, and anger). It is unclear, however, whether these findings would generalize to non-clinical Type As and Bs, since it is known that the onset of illness leads to an increase in negative affect (e.g., Finn, Mulcahy, & Hickey, 1974; Lebovits, Shekelle, Ostfeld, & Paul, 1967; Shekelle, Ostfeld, Lebovits, & Paul, 1970). Chesney, Black, Chadwick, and Rosenman (1981), for example, found no relationship between TAB and measures of psychological distress (e.g., state and trait anxiety, depression, and neuroticism) for a non-clinical sample of adults. Similarly, in Study 1 we found that for a non-clinical sample of college undergraduates, TAB was related to self-evaluations of well-being (i.e., happiness, gratification, and self-confidence), but not to self-evaluations of distress (i.e., strain, vulnerability, and uncertainty). This latter evidence suggests that for non-clinical samples TAB should be related to *positive moods* in relation to one's everyday experiences, and thus that TAB may actually have some utility in *reducing* risk for CAHD *vis-a-vis* the generally positive affect with which it is correlated. These latter studies, however, employed measures of affect that are relatively insensitive to changes in daily life events. Accordingly, the present study asked a non-clinical sample of college undergraduate As and Bs to provide ratings of their moods in relation to events occurring over two contiguous weeks of their lives.

Research Hypotheses

We adopted an intersubject/intrasubject methodology (Watson, 1988) in contrasting As' and Bs' mood states. This particular design allows one to compare responses *between* independent groups (intersubject), as well as *within* individuals over time (intrasubject). The *intersubject* hypothesis concerns whether Type As, considered as a group, characteristically report more negative moods than Type Bs in response to the naturally-occurring events in their lives (thus, the intersubject hypothesis represents an attempted replication of Dimsdale et al., 1978, using a non-clinical sample). Based on the findings of prior research employing trait measures of subjective distress and well-being with non-clinical samples (e.g., Burke & Weir, 1980; Chesney et al., 1981) and on the results of Study 1, it was hypothesized that TAB would be unrelated to negative moods and positively related to positive moods (the only positive mood assessed by the POMS is Vigor).

The *intrasubject* hypothesis concerns the temporal stability of individuals' week-to-week mood states. Individuals who consistently react to daily life with negative moods should be at higher risk for CAHD than individuals who respond with less consistent negative moods or with more positive moods (e.g., Friedman et al., 1985). Unfortunately, prior research has neither examined nor compared the short term temporal stability of Type A's and Type B's moods in relation to naturally-occurring life experiences. Therefore, this was the second purpose of the present study.

METHOD

Subjects and Procedure

Subjects were introductory psychology undergraduates who voluntarily participated in exchange for class credit. They were selected from the tails of a distribution of 1,284 individuals who were tested in large groups ($n \geq 125$) on the short form of the SJAS. The final sample consisted of 35 male and 38 female extreme Type As (SJAS total score > 10) and 46 male and 28 female extreme Type Bs (SJAS total score < 5; see Yarnold, 1987, for normative values).

Subjects actually participated in an unrelated study (in which they kept records of their sleep patterns via structured diaries) that began one week after the TAB screening and that required two meetings scheduled seven days apart. At the outset of each of these meetings, subjects completed the Profile of Mood Stages (POMS), a state measure that is highly sensitive to short-term variations in mood (McNair et al., 1971). The POMS assesses six moods including *Tension* (symptoms of anxiety and heightened musculoskeletal tension), *Depression* (a depressed mood and sense of personal inadequacy), Anger (anger and antipathy toward others), *Fatigue* (a mood consisting of weariness and inertia), *Confusion* (characterized by bewilderment, cognitive inefficiency, and a disorienting mood state), and (the only positive mood) *Vigor* (a mood of vigorousness, ebullience, and high energy). These moods are assessed in relation to the events of one's last week. There was a 12% dropout rate between the two measurements. No subjects reported any acute or chronic medical problems over the two-week span of the study.

RESULTS

Significance Levels

Because Study 2 involved a large number of tests of statistical hypotheses, we employed the Bonferroni procedure of alpha adjustment to avoid capitalizing on Type I errors (see Kleinbaum, Kupper, & Muller, 1988). Since there were a total of 275 tests of statistical hypotheses [12 involving comparisons of means (analyses of variance), 120 involving intercorrelations among POMS subscales (Table 3), 104 involving test-retest reliabilities of the POMS subscales (Table 4), and 39 involving the heterogeneity of test-retest reliability coefficients (Table 4)], we divided our desired alpha (0.05) by the total number of statistical hypotheses evaluated (275) in order to obtain a new (Bonferroni-adjusted) alpha criterion. To achieve an actual alpha level of 0.05 for Study 2, we thus used $p < 0.0002$ as a criterion for establishing statistical significance with the present data. Although this procedure is conservative, the large number of statistical tests performed in Study 2 would otherwise facilitate identification of spurious effects.[5]

Mean Levels of Moods

Table 3 presents descriptive statistics and intercorrelations of the six POMS subscales, separately by A/B Type and gender. To determine whether male and female As and Bs differed in their mean levels of moods (the first intersubject hypothesis), a 2(A/B Type) x 2(gender) x 2(testing period) multivariate analysis of variance with repeated measures was performed: the six POMS subscale scores composed the multivariate dependent profile, and testing period was treated as the within-subjects factor (Winer, 1971). Casewise deletion for subjects missing POMS data (n = 11) resulted in a final sample of $n = 136$. The only statistically significant multivariate effect to emerge was the main effect of A/B Type, $F(6,129) = 4.6, p < 0.0002$ [all other $F(6,129)$'s < 2.3, p's > 0.05]. Subsequent contrasts using analyses of variance revealed that Type As reported being significantly more Vigorous than Type Bs, $F(1,134) = 13.5, p < 0.0002$ [all other $F(1,134)$'s < 5.2, p's > 0.02]. Thus, only when the mean level of moods of As and Bs was compared,

---

5 *Study 1 involved a relatively modest number of statistical tests in comparison to Study 2 (requiring only 10.5% as many). Indeed, the "test size" of Study 1 is relatively modest in an absolute sense, representing two fewer tests than would be necessary to evaluate the unique off-diagonal correlations in a matrix involving eight variables (for which 28 statistical tests would be necessary). Furthermore, the results of Study 1 were robust, with 24 of the 26 (or 92%) of the findings reported in Tables 1 and 2 (including the MANOVA) remaining consistent after applying the Bonferroni criterion. The 17 statistically significant effects reported in Study 1 represent 1172% as many as would be expected given chance alone.*

TABLE 3 Descriptive Statistics and Intercorrelations of Six POMS Subscales, for Two Testings, by A/B Type and Gender

A/B		First Testing									Second Testing							
Type		T	D	A	V	F	C	$\bar{X}_M$	sd_M		T	D	A	V	F	C	$\bar{X}_M$	sd_M
T	T		.78*	.82*	-.46	.50	.77*	1.17	.83	T		.76*	.72*	-.38	.62*	.72*	1.04	.88
Y	D	.61*		.70*	-.36	.44	.78*	.56	.66	D	.76*		.78*	-.30	.61*	.71*	.44	.56
P	A	.59*	.80*		-.23	.28	.70*	.62	.61	A	.72*	.77*		-.18	.52	.52	.49	.60
E	V	-.18	-.19	-.06		-.61*	-.55*	2.29	1.01	V	-.03	.06	.19		-.54	-.55	2.35	.86
	F	.62*	.50	.33	-.54		.48	.87	.69	F	.35	.35	.14	-.57*		.60*	.64	.67
A	C	.65*	.69*	.54	-.39	.68*		.36	.63	C	.67*	.84*	.61*	-.08	.43		.30	.65
	$\bar{X}_F$	1.02	.46	.76	2.52	.62	.31			$\bar{X}_F$	1.06	.56	.87	2.23	.74	.33		
	sd_F	.71	.55	.73	.79	.58	.68			sd_F	.79	.67	.88	.85	.65	.67		
T	T		.54*	.51*	-.05	.46	.63*	1.00	.71	T		.65*	.60*	-.36	.59*	.75*	1.10	.77
Y	D	.66*		.83*	-.22	.60*	.76*	.53	.61	D	.66*		.74*	-.45	.65*	.82*	.62	.64
P	A	.75*	.59		-.08	.52*	.65*	.45	.60	A	.85*	.74*		-.19	.37	.65*	.57	.73
E	V	-.01	-.27	.12		-.31	-.14	1.83	.91	V	.06	-.15	.15		-.43	-.40	1.84	.88
	F	.38	.65*	.62*	-.20		.61*	.75	.55	F	.44	.66*	.35	.24		.61*	.72	.65
B	C	.81*	.91*	.68*	-.22	.59		.46	.55	C	.79*	.86*	.74*	-.21	.49		.56	.71
	$\bar{X}_F$	1.03	.74	.67	1.84	.84	.61			$\bar{X}_F$	.98	.64	.55	1.93	.85	.54		
	sd_F	.62	.61	.56	.81	.59	.71			sd_F	.58	.65	.61	.72	.74	.70		

Note: T = Tension, D = Depression, A = Anger, V = Vigor, F = Fatigue, C = Confusion. For each correlation matrix, coefficients above the diagonal are Pearson correlations between indicated POMS subscales for males, and coefficients below the diagonal are for females. Similarly, descriptive statistics on the row marginals are for males, and descriptive statistics on the column marginals are for females (indexed by M and F, respectively). An asterisk (*) indicates $p < 0.05$ at the Bonferroni-adjusted criterion.

collapsing across time, was there a statistically significant effect. In this regard, Type As reported feeling more Vigorous than Type Bs. Mean scores on the POMS subscales did not vary as a function of main or interactive effects of gender and testing period, nor as a function of these variables crossed by A/B Type.

The Temporal Reliability of Moods

The absence of a main or interactive effect of testing period in the preceding analysis suggests that male and female As and Bs—considered *in aggregate*—did not have variable POMS subscale scores over testings. In order to determine whether POMS subscale scores were temporally reliable for individuals (an intrasubject hypothesis), test-retest reliability coefficients (Pearson correlations) for each POMS subscale were computed separately for each combination of A/B Type and gender (see Table 4). As seen in Table 4, the test-retest reliabilities for Type As and Bs, and for males and females, are predominantly statistically significant, particularly when attenuation-corrected estimates are considered. However, whereas one-week reliabilities are statistically significant, their practical significance is suspect. That is, considering the six POMS subscales *individually*, the median R-squared (i.e., the percentage of variance in a POMS subscale that remains constant over the seven-day retest period) is 0.54, and the mean R-squared is 0.32. (These values are based upon uncorrected reliability estimates, since the scales upon which data are based were not corrected for attenuation). Thus, on average, the POMS subscales showed only 32% stable variance over one week. Considering all six POMS subscales *simultaneously*, the median R-squared was 0.69, and the mean R-squared was 0.49, such that on average only 49% of the variance of the POMS profile is stable over one week. When extended over a longer retest interval, these estimated effect strengths would be expected to diminish even further (cf. Heise, 1975).

Finally, the second intersubject hypothesis concerns whether the groups formed by crossing A/B Type and gender have statistically heterogeneous (i.e., noncomparable) test-retest reliabilities on each of the six POMS subscales (or on the POMS profile). As seen in Table 4, however, no test of the heterogeneity of variance of reliability estimates, corrected for attenuation or uncorrected, met the Bonferroni-adjusted criterion for statistical significance. Thus, POMS subscales (and profiles) were statistically homogeneous (i.e., comparably unreliable) for Type As versus Type Bs, for males versus females, and for the four separate groups in the factorial design.

TABLE 4 One-Week Test-Retest Reliabilities (Pearson *r*'s) of Six POMS Subscales and Total Profile, Including Correction for Attenuation, by A/B Type and Gender

A/B			*Tension* (1.67)		*Depression* (1.0)	*Anger* (1.25)		*Vigor* (1.88)		*Fatigue* (2.14)		*Confusion* (2.14)		*Total POMS*	
Type	*Gender*	*N*	*r*	r_{SB}	*r*	*r*	r_{SB}	*r*	r_{SB}	*r*	r_{SB}	*r*	r_{SB}	*r*	r_{SB}
A	Male	35	.50	.63*	.53	.43	.49	.65*	.78*	.64*	.79*	.67*	.81*	.73*	.82*
A	Female	38	.34	.46	.76*	.79*	.82*	.24	.37	.35	.54	.68*	.82*	.69*	.77*
B	Male	46	.32	.44	.54	.58*	.63*	.46	.62*	.49	.67*	.47	.65*	.64*	.77*
B	Female	28	.76*	.84*	.73*	.76*	.80*	.37	.52	.56	.73*	.73*	.85*	.79*	.85*
	Q(df=3)		8.1	14.1	4.5	10.2	8.4	2.5	7.6	1.1	11.4	3.5	4.7	1.6	1.2
A	Both	73	.40	.53*	.63*	.57*	.62*	.35	.50*	.45*	.64*	.68*	.82*	.68*	.77*
B	Both	74	.42*	.55*	.60*	.64*	.69*	.42*	.58*	.52*	.70*	.55*	.72*	.69*	.78*
	Q(df=1)		< 1	< 1	<1	<1	<1	<1	<1	<1	<1	1.5	3.7	<1	<1
Both	Male	81	.38	.51*	.54*	.50*	.56*	.53*	.68*	.55*	.72*	.54*	.72*	.67*	.77*
Both	Female	66	.45*	.58*	.75*	.78*	.82*	.28	.42*	.58*	.52*	.70*	.83*	.72*	.80*
	Q(df=1)		< 1	< 1	4.7	8.4	9.4	3.1	5.0	<1	1.4	2.4	2.7	<1	<1

Note: The number in parentheses under POMS subscales is the multiplying constant "n" for the Spearman-Brown "prophecy formula" (see note b in Table 1). Tabled on the left for each POMS subscale (except Depression) is the Pearson product-moment correlation between corresponding POMS subscales completed seven days apart (r); tabled on the right is the estimated one-week temporal reliability corrected for attenuation using the prophecy formula (r_{SB}). Since Depression was the subscale with the largest number of items (15), its multiplying constant is 1.0, and no correction for attenuation is made. Tabled under Total POMS is the profile reliability coefficient (Yarnold, 1984), representing the one-week temporal reliability of classifications made using all six POMS subscales. Estimated reliabilities for combined groups were calculated using the method of maximum-likelihood (Hedges & Olkin, 1985, pp. 232-234). The test statistic Q is a test of the heterogeneity of the reliability estimates in the corresponding column, and is distributed as chi-square with the indicated degrees of freedom (Hedges & Olkin, 1985, ps. 234-236). An asterisk (*) indicates $p < 0.05$ at the Bonferroni-adjusted criterion.

DISCUSSION

Considered together, the results of Study 2 suggest that: (a) when examined in aggregate, Type As, relative to Bs, have significantly greater feelings of Vigor from one week to the next (the first intersubject hypothesis); (b) for all groups of subjects, the temporal reliability of moods was of little practical significance (the intrasubject hypothesis); and (c) moods were comparably unreliable for all groupings of subjects (the second intersubject hypothesis). Thus, although Type As felt significantly more vigorous than Type Bs when considered in aggregate, individual Type As are not reliably vigorous from one week to the next, so that different Type As are highly vigorous from one testing to another.

The finding that As, in aggregate, feel more *psychologically* vigorous in relation to (one week of) their everyday lives than Bs is consistent with research that suggests that, in aggregate, As are more *behaviorally* vigorous (e.g., hard-driving and competitive; time-urgent) than Bs (Friedman & Rosenman, 1974). Behavioral vigor has traditionally been considered a risk factor for negative health consequences. For example, research involving randomly sampled individuals suggests that behavioral vigor is associated with increased cardiovascular function and variability (Smith, Allred, Morrison, & Carlson, in press), lower immunological function (Curti, Radice, Cesana, Zanettini, & Grieco, 1982), and greater symptom reporting (Jones, Brantley, & Gilchrist, 1988). However, research also suggests that for Type As scoring at high levels on hard-driving subscales, the enhanced instrumentality associated with psychological vigor may have positive concommitants such as *lower* stress responses during episodes of both behavioral vigor (Lutz, Holmes, & Cramer, 1987) and rest (Lambert, MacEvoy, Klackenberg-Larsson, Karlberg, & Karlberg, 1987). Indeed, there is some evidence that inhibiting behavioral vigor of Type As may *increase* their stress responses (Frankenhaeuser, Lundberg, & Forsman, 1980), including inducing hostile aggression against others (Carver & Glass, 1978), although the manifestation of hostile aggression may be mediated by the perceived efficacy of alternative instrumentally aggressive responses (Strube et al., 1984; Yarnold & Grimm, 1988). Considered together, this research suggests that behavioral vigor may be more stressful for Type Bs than for Type As (cf. Weidner & Matthews, 1978).

Given the importance of psychological and behavioral manifestations of Vigor in discriminating As from Bs, and in light of their uncertain relationships with stress reactions, future research should explore in greater detail these facets of TAB. Particularly interesting issues include the conditions under which behavioral vigor can be expected to occur (e.g., Strube et al., 1987, and Yarnold, Mueser, & Lyons, 1988, report evidence that concern over one's abilities may be the salient agent), and the association of "frustrated vigor" (e.g., unsuccessful behavior) to perceived distress (cf. Seligman, 1975). The role of the aging process, which progressively limits one's capacity for exhibiting behavioral vigor, should also be further examined as a mediator of the relationship between TAB and both short- and long-term measures of subjective life quality.

The finding that As are more psychologically vigorous than Bs is also consistent with the findings of Study 1, insofar as psychological vigor may be considered a positive generalized affect.[6] That is, both studies found no relationship between TAB and subjective distress, and both studies suggested a positive relationship between TAB and subjective well-being. This latter conclusion must be tempered because "positive affect" is not very well measured by the POMS Vigor scale. Furthermore, the brief measurement period and collection of only two assessments limits the generalizability of the findings. Future work should examine a wider range of both positive and negative moods (see, e.g., Russell, 1980) in a population experiencing a larger number of salient, challenging events with the potential for chronically taxing the resources of Type As. Such a procedure would provide a more robust assessment of the relationship between TAB and subjective mood.

In addition to increasing the sensitivity of the mood assessments, future research should employ a more comprehensive assessment of TAB than the present studies. For example, it is surprising that a statistically significant positive relationship between the SJAS and the Anger subscale did not emerge in the present study, since aggression/hostility is one of the defining characteristics of the TAB pattern (Friedman & Rosenman, 1974). However, since the SJAS has only one item that assesses anger/hostility, the lack of a correlation between Anger and the SJAS may be a result of poor measurement of this domain by the SJAS (Yarnold et al., 1986). The use of a TAB measure that assesses predisposition toward anger more comprehensively would provide a more powerful test of the association between anger and TAB, and would help rule

---

[6] *One might argue that positive mood is the opposite of negative mood and that, therefore, the greater vigor found for Type As should have been paralleled by lower negative mood(s) for Type As. As the data in Table 3 indicate, however, positive mood is not simply the inverse of negative mood. Although 34 of the 40 correlations between Vigor and the 5 negative POMS subscales were negative, only 3 (7.5%) of these correlations were statistically significant. Thus, Vigor appears to be somewhat antagonistic with the negative POMS subscales but this inverse relationship is far from perfect. The notion of relative independence between positive and negative affect is further supported by past theory and research on subjective adjustment (e.g., Andrews & Withey, 1976; Bradburn, 1969; Bryant & Veroff, 1982, 1984; Campbell, 1980).*

out measurement inadequacy as an explanation for failure to find anticipated effects (Yarnold & Bryant, 1988).

Finally, the preceding discussion has considered the mood states of As and Bs in relation to the (unspecified) events of their everyday lives. In a sense, it does not matter what the nature of the events comprising As' and Bs' lives might be, but rather simply how As and Bs respond to their unique situations, since ultimately it is the naturalistic functioning of these responses that determines clinical outcome. That is, if one assumes that the week-long "slice of life" we sampled is representative of the comparative lives of As and Bs, then the results should generalize over the near-term lifespan. However, without information regarding the nature of the life events to which As and Bs were exposed, it is impossible to determine whether different types/levels of life events were responsible for the As enhanced psychological vigor, or whether As and Bs were exposed to similar life events which they perceived differently. Whereas generalized responses to life events (irrespective of their content) may serve to explain cardiovascular disorders, understanding responses to specific life events should help uncover avenues for specific interventions to enhance subjective life quality.

CONCLUSIONS

Considered together, these two studies suggest that TAB is associated with enhanced psychological vigor and that this positive mood may generalize to global self-assessments of happiness, gratification, and self-confidence. The absence of A-B differences in negative moods and in negative domains of subjective adjustment suggests that, for college students, TAB entails more cognitive and affective benefits than it does costs. This evidence supports the notion that TAB makes college students more vigorous, more self-confident, and happier, and makes their lives more satisfying and fulfilling—rewards that may underlie the development and maintenance of the coronary-prone behavior pattern.

There are, however, several important limitations to these conclusions. First, using only college students as subjects restricts the external validity of our research. For example, our results may only hold for younger populations and may not generalize to older groups. Indeed, evidence suggests that the costs of TAB, in terms of dissatisfaction and depression, outweigh its benefits for older adults (Strube et al., 1985). Similarly, our findings may not generalize to clinical populations, such as post-myocardial infarction patients, who may be particularly prone to depression and anxiety (Follick, Gorkin, Smith, Capone, Visco, & Stablein, 1988; Mayou, Foster, & Williamson, 1978; Stern, Pascale, & Ackerman, 1977).

Second, our results may be unique to the particular measure of TAB that we used (i.e., the SJAS). Research comparing the relationship of subjective distress to different measures of TAB has yielded inconsistent findings. There is, on the one hand, evidence that different measures of TAB show *different* relationships with subjective distress. Smith, Houston, and Zurawski (1983), for example, found that scores on the Framingham Type A Scale (FTAS; Haynes, Feinleib, & Kannel, 1980) correlated positively with trait anxiety, whereas scores on the SJAS were uncorrelated with trait anxiety. And Byrne and Rosenman (1986) found that scores on the adult version of the JAS (AJAS; Jenkins et al., 1977) correlated positively with the report of stressful life experiences, whereas A-B classifications based on the Structured Interview (SI; Rosenman, Friedman, & Strauss, 1964) were unrelated to the report of stressful life experiences. But there is also, on the other hand, evidence that different measures of TAB show the *same* relationships with subjective distress. Smith (1984), for example, found that scores on both the AJAS and the FTAS correlated positively with trait anger. And, consistent with the present results, Byrne, Rosenman, Schiller, and Chesney (1985) found that five different measures of TAB—the AJAS, the FTAS, the SI, the Bortner Scale (Bortner & Rosenman, 1967), and the Vickers Scale (Vickers, Hervig, Rahe, & Rosenman, 1981)—were all unrelated to both trait anxiety and state anxiety. The conclusion to be drawn here is that researchers should be cautious in generalizing results found using any one, particular measure of TAB. Obviously, using just the SJAS to measure TAB restricts the construct validity of the independent variable in the present research (cf. Cook & Campbell, 1978; Yarnold & Bryant, 1988). This same criticism, of course, applies to our use of the POMS as the exclusive measure of mood.

Third, because we did not measure the actual life events that As and Bs experienced, the causal mechanism underlying our results remains unspecified. Without information about the specific events encountered, we have no way of knowing whether observed A-B differences in subjective adjustment and in mood are due to objectively different life experiences or to different subjective perceptions of similar life experiences. Past research (e.g., Dimsdale et al., 1978; Rhodewalt & Agustsdottir, 1984; Rhodewalt, Hays, Chemers, & Wysocki, 1984; Witenberg 1979) suggests that As encounter a greater number of life events than Bs. Clearly, future work in this area should include measures of the life events experienced by As and Bs, as well as the perceived salience, desirability, and controllability of these events, to clarify the source of differences in subjective life quality.

Fourth, subjects in our research did not complete measures of subjective adjustment and of mood in the context of a salient "real world" situation (e.g., during work or while socializing), but rather completed these measures in a setting removed from their everyday lives. As Rhodewalt et al., (1984) have noted, one would not necessarily expect A-B differences in subjective distress under low stress conditions. Perhaps As would have reported more subjective distress than Bs had we assessed subjective adjustment and mood during actual work experiences or during competitive, interpersonal interactions.

Future Directions

Several recommendations seem warranted for future research in this area. First, TAB investigators should pay closer attention to the selection and interpretation of measures of subjective life quality. The present results demonstrate the utility of distinguishing measures of positive experience (well-being) from measures of negative experience (distress). Clearly, the quality of research in this area can be improved if researchers (a) use theoretical models of subjective adjustment to guide their choice and conceptualization of dependent measures and (b) avoid "lumping together" multiple indicators of adjustment.

Second, the specificity and scope of quality-of-life measures should be improved (cf. Gehrmann, 1978). Most research, including the present study, has used measures of subjective adjustment that are largely global and not particularly fine-grained. Respondents are typically asked to reflect on the overall quality of their lives (e.g., morale, happiness) or on the general quality of specific role relationships (e.g., role fulfillment, life-facet satisfaction), but are not required to specify the particular aspects of their lives that they find pleasant or troublesome. In addition, little work has studied As' and Bs' use of leisure time or the quality and quantity of their social activities and friendships. For example, do As spend less time than Bs simply relaxing and enjoying themselves? Do As actually find leisurely relaxation stressful (cf. Frankenhaeuser et al., 1980) or less enjoyable (cf. Becker & Byrne, 1984)? Do As spend less time than Bs reminiscing about the past (cf. Friedman & Ulmer, 1985)? Do As procrastinate enjoyment and celebration of their successes in pursuit of unreached goals (Friedman & Rosenman, 1974) or in pursuit of rewards they derive from the achievement *process* (Davis, Grover, Sadowski, Tramill, & Kleinhammer-Tramill, 1986)? Perhaps including these types of additional measures would reveal previously "hidden" costs of TAB for young age-groups.

Third, researchers should adopt a multidimensional perspective not only in assessing subjective adjustment, but also in assessing TAB (Blumenthal, O'Toole, & Haney, 1984; Bryant & Yarnold, 1989; Musante, MacDougall, Dembroski, & Van Horn, 1983; Yarnold &

Bryant, 1988). Although the SJAS is the most commonly used measure of TAB (Davis & Cowles, 1985), it includes only one item measuring hostility (Yarnold et al., 1986), a dimension which may well be the most important determinant of cardiovascular risk for Type As (Williams, 1987). Improved measures of TAB are needed that allow researchers to quantify separately such dimensions as hostility, competitiveness, impatience, polyphasic thought, future orientation, and distrustfulness. These refinements would better enable investigators to pinpoint the specific components of TAB that are associated with differences in life quality and would improve our understanding of the mechanisms underlying these effects.

Future research should also adopt a more rigorous perspective on mood. For example, an interesting question not addressed by the present research is whether the quantitative/qualitative nature of the naturally-occurring negative affect of Type As' is greater than that typically observed in experimental studies. That is, researchers attempting to threaten Type As' sense of control are constrained by ethical considerations to limit the salience of experimental manipulations. Such constraints are not present in naturalistic situations, however, and naturally-occurring challenges may be significantly more salient than experimentally-induced challenges (see, e.g., Larsen, Diener, & Emmons, 1986). In addition, whereas the present study considers the stability of mood levels, the stability of mood variability (e.g., Larsen, 1987) represents another interesting consideration for future research.

A final, related recommendation is that TAB research should focus more directly on *processes* and less exclusively on *outcomes* in studying subjective adjustment. Review of the literature indicates an absence of longitudinal studies on TAB and subjective adjustment, with cross-sectional surveys being the predominant methodology (a weakness shared by the present study). While it is clear that As and Bs often react differently to life events (Rhodewalt et al., 1984; Suls et al., 1979), we currently know very little about the ways in which life events are translated into different subjective experiences for As and Bs. Longitudinal field research is needed that examines the daily lives of As and Bs at a detailed, molecular level, with an emphasis on ongoing activities and on cognitive, behavioral, and affective stimuli and responses to everyday life. Experience-sampling methods (Csikszentmihalyi & Larson, 1987; Hormuth, 1986) and diary techniques (Wrightsman, 1981) seem promising in this regard. Although this recommendation is relevant for life-quality research in general, it is especially critical if TAB research is to identify the specific thoughts and behaviors of As that contribute to the subjective quality of their lives.

REFERENCES

Adams, D.L. (1969). Analysis of a life satisfaction index. *Journal of Gerontology, 24,* 470-474.

Adelman, P.K. (1987). Occupational complexity, control, and personal income: Their relation to psychological well-being in men and women. *Journal of Applied Psychology, 72,* 529.537.

Alexander, J.L., & Willems, E.P. (1981). Quality of life: Some measurement requirements. *Archives of Physical Medicine and Rehabilitation, 62,* 261-265.

Andrews, F.M., & Crandall, R. (1976). The validity of measures of self-reported well-being. *Social Indicators Research, 3,* 1-19.

Andrews, F.M., & McKennell, A.C. (1980). Measures of self-reported well-being: Their affective, cognitive, and other components. *Social Indicators Research, 8,* 127-155.

Andrews, F.M., & Withey, S.B. (1976). *Social indicators of well-being: Americans' perceptions of life quality.* New York: Plenum Press.

Baker, G.H.B. (1987). Psychological factors and immunity. *Journal of Psychosomatic Research, 31,* 1-10.

Bauer, R. (Ed.) (1966). *Social indicators.* Cambridge, MA: MIT Press.

Becker, M.A., & Byrne, D. (1984). Type A behavior and daily activities of young married couples. *Journal of Applied Social Psychology, 14,* 62-68.

Beiser, M. (1974). Components and correlates of mental well-being. *Journal of Health and Social Behavior, 15,* 320-327.

Berg, O. (1975). Health and quality of life. *Acta Sociologic, 18,* 3-22.

Blaney, Ph.H. (1986). Affect and memory: A review. *Psychological Bulletin, 99,* 229-246.

Blau, T.H. (1977). Quality of life, social indicators, and predictors of change. *Professional Psychology, 8,* 464-473.

Bloom, M. (1975). Discontent with contentment scales. *Gerontologist, 15,* 99.

Blumenthal, J.A., O'Toole, L.C., & Haney, T. (1984). Behavioral assessment of the Type A behavior pattern. *Psychosomatic Medicine, 46,* 415-423.

Blumenthal, J.A., Thompson, L.W., Williams, R.B., & Kong, Y. (1979). Anxiety-proneness and coronary heart disease. *Journal of Psychosomatic Research, 23,* 17-21.

Booth-Kewley, S. & Friedman, H.S. (1987). Psychological predictors of heart disease: A quantitative review. *Psychological Bulletin, 101,* 343-362.

Bortner, R.W. & Rosenman, R.H. (1967). The measurement of pattern A behavior. *Journal of Chronic Diseases, 20,* 525-533.

Bower, G.H. (1981). Mood and memory. *American Psychologist, 36,* 129-148.

Bradburn, N.M. (1969). *The structure of psychological well-being.* Chicago: Aldine.

Brunson, B.I., & Matthews, K.A. (1981). The Type A coronary-prone behavior pattern and reactions to uncontrollable stress: An analysis of performance stategies affect, and attributions during failure. *Journal of Personality and Social Psychology, 40,* 906-918.

Bryant, F.B. (in press). A four-factor model of perceived control: Avoiding, coping, obtaining, and savoring. *Journal of Personality.*

Bryant, F.B., & Marquez, J.T. (1986). Educational status and the structure of subjective well-being in men and women. *Social Psychology Quarterly, 49,* 142-153.

Bryant, F.B. & Veroff, J. (1982). The structure of psychological well-being: A sociohistorical analysis. *Journal of Personality and Social Psychology, 43*, 653-673.

Bryant, F.B., & Veroff, J. (1984). Dimensions of subjective mental health in American men and women. *Journal of Health and Social Behavior, 25*, 116-135.

Bryant, F.B., & Veroff, J. (1986). Dimensions of subjective mental health in American men and women. In F. M. Andrews (Ed.), *Research on the quality of life* (pp. 117-146). Ann Arbor, MI: Institute for Social Research.

Bryant, F.B., & Yarnold, P.R. (1989). A measurement model for the short form of the Student Jenkins Activity Survey. *Journal of Personality Assessment, 53*, 188-191.

Burke, R.J., & Weir, T. (1980). The Type A experience: Occupational and life demands, satisfaction and well-being. *Journal of Human Stress, 6*, 28-38.

Byrne, D.G. (1987). Personality, life events and cardiovascular disease. *Journal of Psychosomatic Research, 31*, 661-671.

Byrne, D.G., & Rosenman, R.H. (1986). The Type A behaviour pattern as a precursor to stressful life-events: A confluence of coronary risks. *British Journal of Medical Psychology, 59*, 75-82.

Byrne, D.G., Rosenman, R.H., Schiller, E., & Chesney, M.A. (1985). Consistency and variation among instruments purporting to measure the Type A behavior pattern. *Psychosomatic Medicine, 47*, 242-261.

Caffrey, B. (1970). A multivariate analysis of sociopsychological factors in monks with myocardial infarction. *American Journal of Public Health, 60*, 452-458.

Cameron, P. (1975). Mood as an indicator of happiness: Age, sex, social class, and situational differences. *Journal of Gerontology, 30*, 216-224.

Campbell, A. (1976). Subjective measures of well-being. *American Psychologist, 31*, 117-124.

Campbell, A. (1980). *The sense of well-being in America*. New York: McGraw-Hill.

Campbell, A., Converse, P.E. & Rodgers, W.L. (1976). *The quality of American life: Perceptions, evaluations and satisfactions*. New York: Russell Sage Foundation.

Caplan, R.D. & Jones, K.W. (1975). Effects of work load, role ambiguity, and Type A personality on anxiety depression, and heart rate. *Journal of Applied Psychology, 60*, 713-719.

Carley, M. (1981). *Social measurement and social indicators*. London: Allen and Unwin.

Carver, C.S., Coleman, A.E., & Glass, D.C. (1976). The coronary-prone behavior pattern and the suppression of fatigue on a treadmill test. *Journal of Personality and Social Psychology, 33*, 460-466.

Carver, C.S., & Glass, D.C. (1978). Coronary-prone behavior pattern and interpersonal aggression. *Journal of Personality and Social Psychology, 36*, 361-366.

Carver, C.S., & Scheier, M.F. (1982). Control theory: A useful conceptual framework for personality-social, clinical, and health psychology. *Psychological Bulletin, 92*, 111-135.

Chesney, M.A., Black, G.W., Chadwick, J.H., & Rosenman, R.H. (1981). Psychological correlates of the Type A behavior pattern. *Journal of Behavioral Medicine, 4*, 217-229.

Chubon, R.A. (1987). Development of a quality-of-life rating scale for use in health-care evaluation. *Evaluation and the Health Professions, 10*, 186-200.

Cohen, L.H., Towbes, L.C., & Flocco, R. (1988). Effects of induced mood on self-reported life events and perceived and received social support. *Journal of Personality and Social Psychology, 55*, 669-674.

Cook, T.D., & Campbell, D.T. (1978). *Quasi-experimentation: Design and analysis issues for field settings*. Chicago: Rand McNally.

Cox, T., Thirlaway, M., Gotts, G., & Cox, S. (1983). The nature and assessment of general well-being. *Journal of Psychosomatic Research, 27*, 2353-2359.

Csikszentmihalyi, M., & Larson, R. (1987). Validity and reliability of the Experience-Sampling Method. *Journal of Nervous and Mental Diseases, 175*, 526-536.

Curti, R., Radice, L., Cesana, G.C., Zanettini, R., & Grieco, A. (1982). Work stress and immune system: Lymphocyte reactions during rotating shift work (Preliminary results). *Medicina del Lavoro, 6*, 564-570.

Davis, C., & Cowles, M. (1985). Type A behavior assessment: A critical comment. *Canadian Psychology, 26*, 39-42.

Davis, S.F., Grover, C.A., Sadowski, C.J., Tramill, J.L., & Kleinhammer-Tramill, P.J. (1986). The relationship between the Type A behavior pattern and process versus impact achievement motivation. *Bulletin of the Psychonomic Society, 24*, 441-443.

DeGregorio, E., & Carver, C.S. (1980). Type A behavior pattern, sex role orientation, and psychological adjustment. *Journal of Personality and Social Psychology, 39*, 286-293.

Dembroski, T.M., MacDougall, J.M., Williams, R.B. et al. (1985). Components of Type A, hostility, and anger in: Relationship to angiographic findings. *Psychosomatic Medicine, 47*, 219-233.

Diener, E. (1984). Subjective well-being. *Psychological Bulletin, 95*, 542-572.

Dimsdale, J.E., Hackett, T.P., Block, P.C., & Hutter, A.M. (1978). Emotional correlates of Type A behavior pattern. *Psychosomatic Medicine, 40*, 580-583.

Dohrenwend, B.P., Yager, T.J., Egri, G., & Mendelsohn, F.C. (1978). The Psychiatric Status Schedule as a measure of dimensions of psychopathology in the general population. *Archives of General Psychiatry, 35*, 731-737.

Finn, F., Mulcahy, R., & Hickey, N. (1974). The psychological profiles of coronary and cancer patients, and of matched controls. *Irish Journal of Medical Science, 143*, 176-178.

Fiske, S.T., & Taylor, S.E. (1984). *Social cognition*. Reading, MA: Addison.

Follick, M.J., Gorkin, L., Smith, T.W., Capone, R.J., Visco, J., & Stablein, D. (1988). Quality of life post-myocardial infarction: Effects of a transtelephonic coronary intervention system. *Health Psychology, 7*, 169-182.

Frankenhaeuser, M., Lundberg, V., & Forsman, L. (1980). Note on arousing Type A persons by depriving them of work. *Journal of Psychosomatic Research, 24*, 45-47.

Freed, M.M. (1984). Quality of life: The physician's dilemma. *Archives of Physical Medicine and Rehabilitation, 65*, 109-111.

Friedman, H.S., Hall, J.A., & Harris, M.J. (1985). Type A behavior, nonverbal expressive style, and health. *Journal of Personality and Social Psychology, 48*, 1299-1315.

Friedman, M. & Rosenman, R.H. (1974). *Type A behavior and your heart*. New York: Alfred Knopf.

Friedman, M. & Ulmer, D. (1985). *Treating Type A behavior and your heart.* New York: Alfred Knopf.

Furnham, A. (1986). The social desirability of the Type A pattern. *Psychological Medicine, 16,* 805-811.

Furnham, A., Borovoy, A., & Henley, S. (1986). Type A behaviour pattern, the recall of positive personality information and self-evaluations. *British Journal of Medical Psychology, 59,* 365-374.

Gehrmann, F. (1978). "Valid" empirical measurement of quality of life? *Social Indicators Research, 5,* 73-109.

Glass, D.C. (1977). *Behavior patterns, stress, and coronary disease.* Hillsdale, NJ: Lawrence Erlbaum Associates.

Graboys, T.B. (1984). Stress and the aching heart (To the Editor). *The New England Journal of Medicine, 311,* 594-595.

Grimm, L.G., & Yarnold, P.R. (1985). Sex typing and the coronary-prone behavior pattern. *Sex Roles, 12,* 171-178.

Gross, B.M., & Straussman, J.D. (1974). The social indicator movement. *Social Policy,* September/October, 43-54.

Haynes, S.G., Feinleib, M., & Kannel, W.B. (1980). The relationship of psychosocial factors to coronary heart disease in the Framingham Study. III. Eight-year incidence of coronary heart disease. *American Journal of Epidemiology, 111,* 37-58.

Hedges, L.V., & Olkin, I. (1985). *Statistical methods for meta-analysis.* Orlando, FL: Academic Press.

Heilbrun, A.B., & Friedberg, E.B. (1987). Type A behavior and stress in college males. *Journal of Personality Assessment, 51,* 555-564.

Heilbrun, A.B., & Renert, D. (1986). Type A behavior, cognitive defense, and stress. *Psychological Reports, 58,* 447-456.

Heise, D.R. (1975). *Causal analysis.* New York: Wiley.

Hormuth, S.E. (1986). The sampling of experiences in situ. *Journal of Personality, 54,* 262-293.

Iversen, L.L. (1982). Neurotransmitters and CNS disease: An introduction. *Lancet, 2,* 914-918.

Jenkins, C.D. (1971). Psychologic and social precursors of coronary disease. *The New England Journal of Medicine, 284,* 244-255.

Jenkins, C.D., Zyzanski, S.J., Ryan, T.J., Flessas, A., & Tannenbaum, S.Z. (1977). Social insecurity and coronary-prone Type A responses as identifiers of severe atherosclerosis. *Journal of Consulting and Clinical Psychology, 45,* 1060-1062.

Johnson, E.H., & Broman, C.L. (1987). The relationship of anger expression to health problems among black Americans in a national survey. *Journal of Behavioral Medicine, 10,* 103-116.

Jones, G.N., Brantley, P.J., & Gilchrist, J.C. (1988, August). *The relation between daily stress and health.* Paper presented at the annual convention of the American Psychological Association, August, Atlanta, GA.

Keith, R.A. (1966). Personality and coronary heart disease: A review. *Journal of Chronic Disease, 19,* 1231-1243.

Kleinbaum, D.G., Kupper, L.L., & Muller, K.E. (1988). *Applied regression analysis and other multivariable methods (2nd Ed.).* Boston, MA: PWS-Kent.

Krantz, D.S., Glass, D.C., & Snyder, M.L. (1974). Helplessness, stress level, and the coronary-prone behavior pattern. *Journal of Experimental Social Psychology, 10,* 284-300.

Lambert, W.W., MacEvoy, B., Klackenberg-Larsson, I., Karlberg, P., & Karlberg, J. (1987). The relation of stress hormone excretion to Type A behavior and to health. *Journal of Human Stress, 13,* 128-135.

Langner, T.S. (1962). A twenty-two item screening score of psychiatric symptoms indicating impairment. *Journal of Health and Social Behavior, 3,* 169-276.

Larsen, R.J. (1987). The stability of mood variability: A spectral analytic approach to daily mood assessments. *Journal of Personality and Social Psychology, 52,* 1195-1204.

Larsen, R.J., Diener, E., & Emmons, R.A. (1985). An evaluation of subjective well-being measures. *Social Indicators Research, 17,* 1-17.

Larsen, R.J., Diener, E., & Emmons, R.A. (1986). Affect intensity and reactions to daily life events. *Journal of Personality and Social Psychology, 51,* 803-814.

Larson, R. (1978). Thirty years of research on the subjective well-being of older Americans. *Journal of Gerontology, 33,* 109-125.

Lawton, M.P. (1975). The Philadelphia Geriatric Center Morale Scale: A revision. *Journal of Gerontology, 30,* 85-89.

Lawton, M.P. (1983). The varieties of well-being. *Experimental Aging Research, 9,* 65-72.

Lazarus, R.S. (1980). The stress and coping paradigm. In C. Eisdorfer, D. Cohen, A. Klienman et al. (Eds.), *Theoretical bases for psychopathology.* New York, NY: Spectrum.

Leak, G.K., & McCarthy, K. (1984). Relationship between Type A behavior subscales and measures of positive mental health. *Journal of Clinical Psychology, 40,* 1406-1408.

Lebovits, B.Z., Shekelle, R.B., Ostfeld, A.M., & Paul, O. (1967). Prospective and retrospective psychological studies of coronary heart disease. *Psychosomatic Medicine, 29,* 165-272.

Leventhal, H. (1984). A perceptual-motor theory of emotion. In L. Berkowitz (Ed.), *Advances in experimental social psychology (Vol. 17).* Orlando, FL: Academic Press.

Lutz, D.J., Holmes, D.S., & Cramer, R.E. (1987). Hard-driving and speed-impatience components of the Type A behavior pattern as predictors of physiological arousal, subjective arousal and challenge seeking. *Journal of Psychosomatic Research, 31,* 713-722.

Magnusson, D. (1967). *Test theory.* Reading, MA: Addison-Wesley.

Matthews, K.A. (1982). Psychological perspectives on the Type A behavior pattern. *Psychological Bulletin, 91,* 293-323.

Matthews, K.A., Helmreich, R.L., Beane, W.E., & Lucker, G.W. (1980). Pattern A, achievement striving and scientific merit: Does Pattern A help or hinder? *Journal of Personality and Social Psychology, 39,* 962-967.

Mayou, R., Foster, A., & Williamson, B. (1978). Psychosocial adjustment in patients one year after myocardial infarction. *Journal of Psychosomatic Research, 22,* 447-453.

McAdams, D.P., & Bryant, F.B. (1987). Intimacy motivation and subjective mental health in a nationwide sample. *Journal of Personality, 55,* 1-19.

McKennell, A. (1974). Surveying subjective welfare: Strategies and methodological considerations. In B. Strumpel (Ed.), *Subjective elements of well-*

being (pp. 45-72). Paris: Organization for Economic Development and Cooperation.

McKennell, A.C. & Andrews, F.M. (1980). Models of cognition and affect in perceptions of well-being. *Social Indicators Research, 8,* 257-298.

McNair, D., Lorr, M., & Droppleman, L. (1971). *Profile of mood states.* San Diego, CA: Educational and Industrial Testing Services.

McNeil, J.K., Stones, M.J., & Kozma, A. (1986). Subjective well-being in later life: Issues concerning measurement and prediction. *Social Indicators Research, 18,* 35-70.

Mettlin, C. (1976). Occupational careers and the prevention of coronary-prone behavior. *Social Sciences and Medicine, 10,* 367-372.

Musante, L., MacDougall, J.M., Dembroski, T.M., & Van Horn, A.E. (1983). Component analysis of the Type A coronary-prone behavior pattern in male and female college students. *Journal of Personality and Social Psychology, 45,* 1104-1117.

Padilla, G.V., & Grant, M.M. (1985). Quality of life as a cancer nursing outcome variable. *Advances in Nursing Science, 8,* 45-60.

Pilisuk, M. & Parks, S.H. (1986). *The healing web: Social networks and human survival.* Hanover, MA: University Press of New England.

Price, V.A. (1982). *Type A behavior pattern: A model for research and practice.* New York: Academic Press.

Reid, D.W., & Ziegler, M. (1980). Validity and stability of a new desired control measure pertaining to psychological adjustment in the elderly. *Journal of Gerontology, 35,* 395-402.

Rhodewalt, F. & Davison, J., Jr. (1983). Reactance and the coronary-prone behavior pattern: The role of self-attribution in response to reduced behavioral freedom. *Journal of Personality and Social Psychology, 44,* 220-228.

Rhodewalt, F. & Agustsdottir, S. (1984). On the relationship of hardiness to the Type A behavior pattern: Perceptions of life events versus coping with life events. *Journal of Research in Personality, 18,* 212-223.

Rhodewalt, F., Hays, R.B., Chemers, M.M., & Wysocki, J. (1984). Type A behavior, perceived stress and illness: A person-situation analysis. *Personality and Social Psychology Bulletin, 10,* 149-159.

Rosenman, R.H., Friedman, M., & Strauss, R. (1964). A predictive study of coronary heart disease: The Western Collaborative Group Study. *Journal of the American Medical Association, 182,* 15-26.

Rossi, R.J., & Gilmartin, K.J. (1980). *The handbook of social indicators: Sources, characteristics, and analysis.* New York: Garland.

Russell, J.A. (1980). A circumplex model of affect. *Journal of Personality and Social Psychology, 39,* 1161-1178.

Schwarz, N., & Clore, G.L. (1983). Mood, misattribution, and judgments of well-being: Informative and directive functions of affective states. *Journal of Personality and Social Psychology, 45,* 513-523.

Schwarz, N., & Strack, F. (1985). Cognitive and affective processes in judgments of subjective well-being: A preliminary model. In H. Brandstaetter & E. Kirchler (Eds.), *Economic psychology* (pp. 439-447). Linz, Austria: Trauner.

Seligman, M.E.P. (1975). *Human helplessness.* San Francisco: Freeman.

Shekelle, R.B., Gale, M., Ostfeld, A.M., & Paul, O. (1983). Hostility, risk of coronary heart disease, and mortality. *Psychosomatic Medicine, 45,* 109-114.

Shekelle, R.B., Ostfeld, A.M., Lebovits, B.Z., & Paul, O. (1970). Personality traits and coronary heart disease: A re-examination of Ibrahim's hypothesis using longitudinal data. *Journal of Chronic Disease, 23*, 33-38.

Shin, D.C., & Johnson, D.M. (1978). Avowed happiness as an overall assessment of the quality of life. *Social Indicators Research, 5*, 475-492.

Schulz, R. (1980). Aging and control. In J. Garber & M.E.P. Seligman (Eds.), *Human helplessness: Theory and applications* (pp. 261-277). New York: Academic Press.

Schulz, R. (1982). Emotionality and aging: A theoretical and empirical analysis. *Journal of Gerontology, 37*, 42-51.

Simon, H.A. (1982). Comments. In M.S. Clark & S.T. Fiske (Eds.), *Affect and cognition: The 18th Annual Carnegie Symposium on Cognition*. Hillsdale, NJ: Erlbaum.

Smith, T.W. (1984). Type A behaviour, anger and neuroticism: The discriminant validity of self-reports in a patient sample. *British Journal of Clinical Psychology, 23*, 147-148.

Smith, T.W., Allred, K.D., Morrison, C.A., & Carlson, S.D. (in press). Cardiovascular reactivity and interpersonal influence: Active coping in a social context. *Journal of Personality and Social Psychology*.

Smith, T.W., & Brehm, S. (1981). Cognitive correlates of the Type A coronary-prone behavior pattern. *Motivation and Emotion, 5*, 215-223.

Smith, T.W., Houston, B.K., & Zurawski, R.M. (1983). The Framingham Type A Scale and anxiety, irrational beliefs, and self-control. *Journal of Human Stress, 9*, 32-37.

Somes, G.W., Garrity, T.F., & Marx, M.B. (1980). The relationship of coronary-prone behavior to the health of college students at varying levels of recent life change. *Journal of Psychosomatic Research, 25*, 565-572.

Speilberger, C.D., Gorsuch, R.L., & Lushene, R.E. (1970). *STAI: Manual for the State-Trait Anxiety Inventory*. Palo Alto, CA: Consulting Psychologists Press.

Stern, M.J., Pascale, L., & Ackerman, A. (1977). Life adjustment post-myocardial infarction. *Archives of Internal Medicine, 137*, 1680-1685.

Strube, M.J., Berry, J.M., Goza, B.K., & Fennimore, D. (1985). Type A behavior, age and psychological well-being. *Journal of Personality and Social Psychology, 49*, 203-218.

Strube, M.J., Boland, S.M., Manfredo, P.A., & Al-Falaij, A. (1987). Type A behavior pattern and the self-evaluation of abilities: Empirical tests of the self-appraisal model. *Journal of Personality and Social Psychology, 52*, 956-974.

Strube, M.J., Turner, C.W., Cerro, D., Stevens, J., & Hinchey, F. (1984). Interpersonal aggression and the Type A coronary-prone behavior pattern: A theoretical distinction and practical implications. *Journal of Personality and Social Psychology, 47*, 839-847.

Strube, M.J. & Werner, C.M. (1985). Relinquishment of control and the Type A behavior pattern. *Journal of Personality and Social Psychology, 48*, 688-701.

Suls, J., Becker, M.A., & Mullen, B. (1981). Coronary-prone behavior, social insecurity, and stress among college-aged adults. *Journal of Human Stress, 15*, 27-34.

Suls, J., Gastorf, J.W., & Witenberg, S.H. (1979). Life events, psychological distress and the Type A coronary-prone behavior pattern. *Journal of Psychosomatic Research, 23,* 315-319.

Theorell, T. & Rahe, R.H. (1972). Behavior and life satisfaction characteristics of Swedish subjects with myocardial infarction. *Journal of Chronic Disease, 25,* 139-147.

van Praag, H.M. (1982). Neurotransmitters and CNS disease: Depression. *Lancet, 2,* 1259-1264.

Veit, C.T., & Ware, J.E., Jr. (1983). The structure of psychological distress and well-being in general populations. *Journal of Consulting and Clinical Psychology, 51,* 730-752.

Veroff, J., Douvan, E., & Kulka, R. (1981). *The inner American.* New York: Basic Books.

Veroff, J., Feld, S., & Gurin, G. (1962). Dimensions of subjective adjustment. *Journal of Abnormal and Social Psychology, 64,* 192–205.

Verwayen, H. (1984). Social indicators: Actual and potential uses. *Social Indicators Research, 14,* 1-28.

Vickers, R., Hervig, L.K., Rahe, R.H., & Rosenman, R.H. (1981). Type A behavior pattern and coping and defense. *Psychosomatic Medicine, 43,* 381-395.

Waldron, I. (1978). The coronary-prone behavior pattern, blood pressure, employment and socio-economic status in women. *Journal of Psychosomatic Research, 22,* 79-87.

Waldron, I., Hickey, A., McPherson, C., Butensky, A., Gruss, L., Overall, K., Schmader, A., & Wohlmuth, D. (1980). Type A behavior pattern: Relationships to variation in blood pressure, parental characteristics, and academic and social activities of students. *Journal of Human Stress, 6,* 16-26.

Wan, T.H., & Livieratos, B. (1978). Interpreting a general index of subjective well-being. *Health and Society, 56,* 531-556.

Warr, P. (1978). A study of psychological well-being. *British Journal of Psychology, 69,* 111-121.

Watson, D. (1988). Intraindividual and interindividual analyses of positive and negative affect: Their relation to health complaints, perceived stress, and daily activities. *Journal of Personality and Social Psychology, 54,* 1020-1030.

Weidner, G., & Matthews, K.A. (1978). Reported physical symptoms elicited by unpredictable events and the Type A coronary-prone behavior pattern. *Journal of Personality and Social Psychology, 36,* 1213-1220.

Weingarten, H., & Bryant, F.B. (1987). Marital status and the meaning of subjective well-being: A structural analysis. *Journal of Marriage and the Family, 49,* 883-892.

Williams, R.B. (1987). Refining the Type A hypothesis: Emergence of the hostility complex. *American Journal of Cardiology, 60,* 27j-32j.

Wilson, W. (1967). Correlates of avowed happiness. *Psychological Bulletin, 67,* 294-306.

Winer, B.J. (1971). *Statistical principles in experimental design* (Second Edition). New York: McGraw-Hill.

Wright, J., & Mischel, W. (1982). Influence of affect on cognitive social learning and person variables. *Journal of Personality and Social Psychology, 43,* 901-914.

Wrightsman, O.S. (1981). Personal documents as data in conceptualizing adult personality development. *Personality and Social Psychology Bulletin, 7,* 376-385.

Yarnold, P.R. (1984). The reliability of a profile. *Educational and Psychological Measurement, 44,* 49-59.

Yarnold, P.R. (1987). Norms for the Glass model of the short student version of the Jenkins Activity Survey. *Social and Behavioral Sciences Documents, 16,* 60 (MS# 2777).

Yarnold, P.R. & Bryant, F.B. (1987). Dimensions of social insecurity and their relations to coronary-prone behavior in college undergraduates. *Psychological Medicine, 17,* 715-725.

Yarnold, P.R. & Bryant, F.B. (1988). A note on measurement issues in Type A research: Let's not throw out the baby with the bath water. *Journal of Personality Assessment, 52,* 410-419.

Yarnold, P.R., Bryant, F.B., & Grimm, L.G. (1987). Comparing the short and long versions of the Student Jenkins Activity Survey. *Journal of Behavioral Medicine, 10,* 75-90.

Yarnold, P.R., Bryant, F.B., & Litsas, F.. (in press). Type A behavior and psychological androgyny among Greek college students. *European Journal of Personality.*

Yarnold, P.R. , & Grimm, L.G. (1988). Interpersonal dominance of Type As and Bs during involved group discussions. *Journal of Applied Social Psychology, 18,* 787-795.

Yarnold, P.R. & Mueser, K.T. (1989). Meta analysis of the reliability of Type A behaviour measures. *British Journal of Medical Psychology, 63,* 43-50.

Yarnold, P.R., Mueser, K.T., Grau, B.W., & Grimm, L.G. (1986). The reliability of the Student version of the Jenkins Activity Survey. *Journal of Behavioral Medicine, 9,* 401-414.

Yarnold, P.R., Mueser, K.T., & Lyons, J.S. (1988). Type A behavior, accountability, and work rate in small groups. *Journal of Research in Personality, 22,* 353-360.

Zung, W.W.K. (1965). A self-rating depression scale. *Archives of General Psychiatry, 12,* 63-70.

Self-Reliance and Desire for Control in the Type A Behavior Pattern

Laura K. Clark
Virginia Polytechnic Institute and State University
Blacksburg, VA 24061
Suzanne M. Miller
Department of Psychology, Temple University
Philadelphia, PA 19122

We explored differential preferences for control among Type A and B individuals, in a work-analog, interpersonal context. Subjects were presented with a nonaversive interviewing task and were allowed to choose whether to accomplish it alone or with a partner. Partners were perceived to be either of similar or superior competence. The results indicated that Type As chose to work alone significantly more often than did Type Bs, who were more likely to choose cooperation. Further, in explaining their work choices, Type As were more likely than Type Bs to want all the responsibility themselves. Finally, Type As were no more willing to work with a superior than an equally competent partner, and generally indicated that the partner would not be helpful to them. The results suggest the possibility that Type As have an extensive desire for control that is readily activated and, in addition, see no particular advantage in cooperating with another individual.

The Type A pattern, characterized by excessive achievement-striving, hard-driving competitiveness, potential for hostility, and a sense of time urgency, has been implicated as a risk factor for coronary heart disease (CHD) (Jenkins, 1988). While one body of research has focused primarily on aspects of the Type A pattern that appear to be related to health risks, a second focus has been on illuminating the psychological mechanisms involved and their implications for social behaviors. One major conceptualization suggests that Type A individuals are driven by a

Authors' Notes: We are indebted to A. Bandura and D. Kipnis for their invaluable comments on an earlier draft of this paper. We also thank A. Birnbaum, D. Durbin, and F. Quintos for their help. This research was partially supported by the Robert Wood Johnson Foundation and by Temple University Research Incentive Fund, Grant-In-Aid of Research, and Biomedical Support Research Grant.

Requests for reprints should be sent to the second author.

© 1990 Select Press

need to maintain control over their environments (Glass, 1977). The present study tested this notion by directly examining preference for control in an interpersonal, work-analog setting.

Correlational studies have demonstrated a link between Type A and desire for control, as indicated by moderate associations between the two constructs (Dembroski, MacDougall, & Musante, 1984; Burger, 1985). Studies involving actual behaviors, rather than self-report measures, have generally focused on reactions to the loss of control. Under certain conditions, Type As react more strongly to this loss than do Type Bs (those people who show an absence of the pattern) (Glass, 1977). More recent work suggests that under aversive conditions, Type As (versus Bs) also have a greater preference for control when given the choice of retaining or relinquishing it (Miller, Lack & Asroff, 1985; Strube & Werner, 1985). This work has typically presented subjects with a challenging situation (such as a negative comparison of the person's own performance on a task relative to that of a confederate) and/or an aversive outcome (such as being subjected to noise bursts) for poor performance. The individual is then offered the choice of retaining control or relinquishing it to a partner.

The present study sought to extend previous work by examining desire for control and the reasons for it among Type As and Bs in a relatively nonaversive setting. The setting was one where the individual's sense of competence was not so directly challenged, and where potential outcomes did not involve explicitly aversive consequences (neither threats to physical comfort nor self-esteem). Rather than using more traditional operationalizations of retaining or yielding control, desire for control was operationalized as preference for self-reliance (working alone) versus cooperation (working together). While this operationalization may tap a more "indirect" form of control, working cooperatively does involve shared decision-making and responsibility. One must be willing to allow the other person to influence both the task process and its outcome. A strong desire for control should therefore lead to a preference for avoiding cooperation, since it is difficult to work together without yielding some degree of control to one's partner. Further, important real-life decisional contexts most often involve a choice between retaining and sharing (rather than completely yielding) control. The present paradigm allowed us to capture this situation and thereby extend previous work.

Offering subjects a choice between cooperation and self-reliance—rather than between cooperation and competition—enabled us to explore whether Type As prefer control and resist cooperation, even in settings that may actually elicit cooperativeness from Type Bs. While several studies suggest that Type As may prefer competition over cooperation (Gotay, 1981; Van Egeren, 1979) and that they will choose to work alone rather than in the presence of others while under stress (Dembroski & MacDougall, 1978), preference for working cooperatively versus alone has not been directly examined. To test this, Type As and Bs were faced with a nonaversive, work-analog task ("interviewing") and offered a choice of accomplishing it alone or with a partner.

One possible explanation for Type As' choice to remain in control is that they believe it will ensure the best possible outcome. That is, control minimizes the maximum aversiveness (or maximizes the minimum positivity) of the situation (Miller, 1979, 1980). Data from Miller et al. (1985) do not support a minimax explanation. There, Type As chose to have control even when it meant risking a more aversive outcome for themselves and their partner, who had been shown to be more competent at the task. An alternative explanation concerns the desirability of control for more internal reasons: that is, individuals may be more concerned with achieving a sense of personal satisfaction and/or may have a desire for control in and of itself.

These two explanations were compared by offering some subjects the opportunity to work with a highly experienced partner, while other subjects were offered the opportunity to work with a merely competent partner. If Type As retain control mainly in order to guarantee the most positive outcome possible, they should be less concerned about retaining control when a more competent partner is available. However, if Type As prefer control for internality reasons, then providing a more competent partner should not weaken their preferences. If anything, describing the partner as superior might cause Type As to feel more competitive and thereby strengthen their desire to complete the task alone.

Thus, the study explored whether Type As show greater preference for control than Bs in a nonaversive setting, as seen in Type As' greater desire to avoid cooperation by working alone. As a secondary aim, we examined whether Type As desire control mainly because they are concerned that sharing it would reduce the likelihood of a good outcome (minimax explanation), or whether they desire control in order to be able to attribute outcomes to themselves (internality explanation).

METHOD

Subjects

One hundred ninety volunteer undergraduate subjects were asked to fill out a 9-item "survey on student lifestyles" (questions 6, 9, 11, 18, 19, 21, 31, 41, 44 from the Jenkins Activity Survey: items used by Smith and Brehm, 1981, for a similar screening purpose; Jenkins, Zyzanski, &

Rosenman, 1971; Krantz, Glass, & Snyder, 1974). Volunteers were told that they might or might not be called, depending upon how many people were needed for the interviewing study. Those scoring 3 or below, or 6 and above, on the screening measure were called and invited to participate in the study. As compensation, participants were told that they would have their names put into a lottery. Four names would be drawn at the end of the study, and each of those people would be awarded $30.00.

One hundred twenty-three subjects were later administered the complete student version of the Jenkins Activity Survey (JAS), Form T, and only the data from those scoring above or below 8 (the median) were retained for analysis (Jenkins et al., 1971; Krantz et al., 1974). Although the JAS is not as strongly linked with disease endpoints as other measures of Type A (Williams, Haney, Lee, Kong, Blumenthal, & Whalen, 1980), it has been the instrument most commonly used in laboratory studies of social interactions. Therefore, it was chosen in the present study to provide comparability with previous work.

Eight subjects were discarded because they were much older than the other subjects, did not complete the JAS, or indicated on the suspicion probes that they did not believe the cover story. The final sample consisted of fifty-two Type A and fifty-three Type B subjects. Subjects ranged in age from 17 to 35 (M = 22.24, SD = 4.49) and scored between 0 and 18 on the JAS, inclusive (M = 8.26, SD = 4.23). Those scoring 9 and above were considered to be Type As (M = 11.90, SD = 2.46), while those scoring 7 or below were considered to be Type Bs (M = 4.68, SD = 1.88). The proportion of males and females of each Type (A/B) was roughly equivalent across each of the four experimental conditions.

Procedure

Subjects were run in small groups of two to seven people, since having other subjects present lent credibility to the cover story that they would be performing the task with one to two other people. Subjects were first seated in individual cubicles, where they could see the experimenter but not each other. They were told that this was a study of the interview process, and that they would be playing the role of an interviewer or an applicant for one interview session. Subjects were asked to complete some background information on their previous interview experience, which requested them to estimate the number of times they had been involved in an interview, either as an applicant or as an interviewer. They also completed a questionnaire on their "general lifestyle" (actually the JAS).

Following this, subjects were given more detailed information about the interviewing task. Being in an interview was described as a common but interesting experience that is also "slightly unpredictable." The task was described as "slightly unpredictable" to ensure a moderate level of subject involvement. The experimenter played audiotapes of two "sample interviews" that involved undergraduates supposedly discussing a student activities job. All subjects heard the same two tapes, one with two interviewers, and another with one interviewer. The order of presentation for the tapes was counter-balanced across conditions.[1] The interview samples were brief and did not specify any outcomes for either the applicant or the interviewer(s).

After receiving the manipulations (see below), all subjects participated in a sham drawing that "randomly" assigned them to the role of interviewer or applicant (actually, all subjects drew numbers designating them as interviewers). Subjects were given a short account of the ways in which interviews may differ, including degree of formality, type of setting, and number of interviewers present. Subjects then indicated whether they wished to interview the applicant alone or with the partner and completed several questionnaires. They were debriefed, thanked, and asked to keep the study's nature and purpose confidential. No subject actually went on to carry out an interview.

Manipulations. Subjects were randomly assigned to one of three "responsibility conditions." Responsibility was manipulated by describing the task as mainly influenced by the interviewer (High Responsibility Focus), as mainly influenced by the applicant (Low Responsibility Focus), or was not manipulated (No Responsibility Focus).[2] Subjects were then told that they could choose to see the applicant alone or with another interviewer (partner), because both conditions were needed in the study. Since some interviewers in the past had expressed curiosity about their potential partners, the experimenter would allow each "interviewer" to see how his or her previous interview experience compared to that of the potential partner.

For half of the subjects (n = 14 As; 16 Bs) in the high responsibility condition, the "randomly paired" partner was described as having "much

[1] *Because the experimenter was blind to Type (A,B) of subject, the order of tape presentation was counter-balanced across condition but not across subject Type. There were usually several of both Types in each group of subjects run. Because the order of the tapes was counter-balanced across conditions, there was no need to test for order effects.*

[2] *The high responsibility manipulation was expected to increase control concerns (even among Type As), while the low responsibility manipulation was expected to decrease control concerns (even among Type Bs). Therefore, Type As and Bs were expected to differ most under No Responsibility focus. Results showed significant differences between Type As and Bs in their work choices in the No Focus condition, but not in the High or Low Responsibility conditions. However, there was no evidence of a significant Type by Condition interaction, and these results are therefore not reported in the interests of space.*

more interview experience than you" (Superior Partner condition). For the other half (n = 12 As; 14 Bs), the partner was described as having "similar interview experience as you do" (Similar Partner condition). Subjects in the low responsibility and no focus conditions received the similar partner manipulation only (n = 26 As; 23 Bs). Since high responsibility subjects were expected to be more involved in the task, it was felt that this condition would be the best test of the internality versus minimax interpretations.[3]

Measures

Manipulation check. For the partner perception manipulation check, subjects indicated on one multiple-choice questionnaire whether they believed that their potential partner had less, similar, or more interview experience than they themselves had.

Affect. After making their work choices, subjects completed three 7-point Likert scales that measured self-ratings of competitiveness, anxiety, and importance of the situation for them personally (from 1 = "not at all" to 7 = "very").

Work choice preferences. Behavioral choice of working alone versus with the partner was the major dependent variable. Behavioral choice was measured by a forced-choice question ("If I have to choose one or the other, I'd prefer to interview the applicant: (circle one) 1. Alone; or 2. With a partner."). To examine the relative strength of that choice, subjects were also given one 31-point Likert scale (from 1 = "strongly prefer to work alone" to 31 = "strongly prefer to work with the partner").

Reasons for work choice. In order to assess how important various factors had been in making their decision, subjects completed five 7-point Likert scales asking them to rate the extent to which they believed each of the following factors had influenced their work choice ("producing the best interview possible;" "making the interview more enjoyable"; "making myself feel more comfortable or less anxious"; "having all the responsibility myself;" "being able to tell how well I am doing in the interview").

Partner helpfulness. One multiple choice question asked all subjects to indicate whether they believed that their partner would be helpful, interfering (not helpful), or neither helpful nor interfering.

Previous interview experience. A short form requested subjects to

---

3 *The design was a 2 (Type: A,B) by 4 (Conditions: No Resp. Focus-Similar Partner, Low Resp.-Similar Partner, High Resp.-Similar Partner, High Resp.-Superior Partner). The addition of a Superior Partner manipulation to the No Focus and Low Responsibility cells was not expected to yield any theoretically important results. Therefore, a fully crossed design (Type by Partner Competence by Responsibility Condition) was not used.*

estimate the number of times that they had been involved in an interview, either as an applicant or an interviewer. This information was examined to ensure that the choice of working alone was not simply due to greater previous experience with the task. It was also ostensibly used in the partner manipulation (to provide the "feedback" about the subject's experience relative to the partner's).

Suspicion probes. Following the completion of all other measures, subjects were given two open-ended questions designed to tap any suspicions about the study's actual purpose ("In your opinion, what's the purpose of the study?" and "Is there anything about the interview or the situation which you believe the experimenter didn't tell you specifically? If yes, what?").

RESULTS

Analyses for gender effects (including testing for a gender by Type interaction) revealed no significant effects on work preferences. Therefore, subsequent analyses were collapsed across gender.

Manipulation Check

A 2 (Type A/B) by 4 (experimental conditions) analysis of variance (ANOVA) on the subject's ratings of the partner's experience indicated only a main effect for condition, F (3, 95) = 49.58, $p < .001$. Post-hoc comparisons (Fisher's LSD) indicated that subjects in the Superior Partner condition (M = 1.83) rated their partner as having more experience than did subjects in any of the Similar Partner conditions (M = .96, M = .92, M = 1.00), which did not differ from each other.

Affect

Subjects were asked to indicate how important the situation was to them, and how anxious and competitive they felt. Subjects' ratings on these variables indicated that the situation was not a highly anxiety-provoking or competitive one (on 7-point scales, with low numbers indicating less feeling, anxiety M = 3.73; competitiveness M = 2.93) and was moderately important to them (M = 4.54). Thus, as intended, this was a relatively nonaversive situation. A 2 x 4 (Type x Condition) ANOVA performed on each variable indicated a main effect for Type on competitiveness, with Type As reporting greater feelings of competition than did Type Bs (Type A M = 3.46, Type B M = 2.42, F (1, 97) = 9.06, $p <$ 01). There were no other significant main effects or interactions.

Choice of Working Alone or with the Partner

Effect of Type A-B. With respect to behavioral choice, fully 73% of Type As but only 43% of Type Bs chose to work alone. An arcsin test indicated that this difference was highly significant, arcsin z = 3.17, $p <$

.01. Thus, Type As clearly chose to accomplish the task alone while Type Bs were more inclined to choose to work cooperatively. Subjects' ratings of their relative preference to work alone or with a partner yielded a similar result, with Type As (M = 13.13) indicating significantly greater desire to work alone than did Type Bs (M = 16.79: t (103) = 2.12, p < .04).

Effect of partner manipulation. An arcsin test was used to compare the choices of Type As in the Similar versus Superior Partner conditions (High Responsibility-Similar Partner, High Responsibility-Superior Partner conditions, respectively). This comparison indicated that Type As were no more willing to cooperate in the Superior, than in the Similar, Partner condition, with 67% and 79% of Type As in those two conditions choosing to work alone, respectively, $z < 1, p > .20$. Thus, the majority of Type As preferred to work alone, even when offered a superior partner. A comparable effect was obtained for Type Bs, with 43% of Similar Partner-High Responsibility subjects and 56% of Superior Partner-High Responsibility subjects choosing to work alone. It should be noted that for these two conditions (both of which led subjects to believe that they would be highly responsible for outcomes, and had therefore been expected to increase control concerns), there was also no significant difference between the percentages of Type Bs versus As who chose to work alone.[4]

Reasons for Work Choice

Subjects were asked to rate the relative importance of five factors in influencing their decision to work alone or with the partner. A series of 2 (Type) by 4 (condition) ANOVAs indicated a significant Type A-B difference in terms of how much they reported being influenced by a desire for "having all the responsibility myself," with Type As (M = 4.45) indicating that they had been more influenced by this factor than Type Bs (M = 3.53; F (1,96) = 5.60, p < .05). There were no other significant Type A-B differences.

Each of these five factors was also correlated with work preference ratings, for each Type separately. For Type As, there was a significant negative correlation between "desire to have all the responsibility" and preference ratings, r = -.44, p = .001, indicating a strong relationship between desire for responsibility and preference to work alone. There was a marginally significant correlation between Type As' preferences and "desire to produce the best interview possible," suggesting a tendency for Type As to prefer a partner when they wanted to produce the

[4] *A log-linear analysis testing for a Type A-B by Similar-Superior by Work Alone vs. Work with the Partner interaction was also run (despite the small sample size) and did not reveal any significant Type by Condition interaction.*

best outcome, $r = .25$, $p < .08$. For Type As, there was also a marginally significant, negative correlation between preference to work alone and "desire to tell how well I'm doing," $r = -.27$, $p < .06$. A different pattern of results emerged for Type Bs. In contrast to Type As, there was no evidence of a significant relationship between desire for responsibility and preference to work alone, $r = -.16$, $p > .20$. There was, however, a significant, negative correlation between preference to work alone and "desire to tell how well I'm doing," $r = -.30$, $p < .05$. There were no other correlations that approached significance.

Partner Helpfulness

Subjects had been asked to indicate how helpful they believed the partner could be to them personally. Overall, ratings of partner helpfulness were significantly correlated with preferences to work with the partner, $r = .56$, $p < .001$). Further, an arsin test indicated that significantly more Type Bs than As saw the partner as helpful (75% versus 47%; arsin $z = 2.96$, $p < .01$). This finding is consistent with their behavioral choices. Partner competence (similar vs. superior) did not affect these ratings. Despite their being less inclined than Type Bs to view the partner as helpful, it should be noted that a majority of Type As did not see the partner as actively interfering (only 25% of Type As rated the partner as interfering). Too few subjects chose the other two categories (not helpful/interfering; neither helpful nor interfering) to provide meaningful comparisons.

To better understand how partner helpfulness impacted on choice in the Similar versus Superior (High Responsibility-Similar, High Responsibility-Superior) Partner conditions, separate correlations between perceived helpfulness and preference were run for each of the two conditions. There was a highly significant positive correlation between perceived helpfulness and preference to work with the partner in both conditions, although this effect was larger in the Similar Partner condition, $r = .72$, $p < .001$, than in the Superior Partner condition, $r = .47$, $p = .005$.

Previous Interview Experience

Pearsons correlations were performed in order to assess the relationships among Type A-B scores, previous interview experience, and preference ratings for working alone versus with the partner. Results revealed no significant relationships between preference ratings and previous interview experience, $r = .02$, n.s., or between JAS scores and previous experience $r = .15$, n.s., indicating that Type As' preference for working alone could not be explained on the basis of their having greater previous experience with the task.

DISCUSSION

The results of the present study suggest that Type As chose to work alone, avoiding cooperation and thereby retaining control, significantly more often than did Type Bs. This finding is consistent with work by Miller et al. (1985) and by Strube and Werner (1985), who found a stronger desire for control among Type As than Bs when under threat. The results of the present study extend previous work in that subjects did not face explicitly aversive consequences for poor performance, nor were they exposed to any loss of control or challenge to perform well. Subjects' self-report ratings clearly indicated that although they were moderately involved with the task, this was not a highly important or anxiety-provoking situation for them. Yet, Type As were not willing to yield even partial control by cooperating with a partner on the task. The pattern of choice behaviors on the part of Type As suggests a more extensive preference for control than Glass (1977) originally outlined (see also Dembroski & MacDougall, 1979).

In contrast, a majority of Type Bs chose to work with the partner, suggesting that Type Bs may be genuinely more cooperative than Type As. These results shed new light on the control preferences of Type Bs. In previous research, Type Bs have typically been found to adopt a more cooperative than competitive stance (Gotay, 1981; Van Egeren, 1979). However, it has not been clear whether Type Bs are actually more cooperative than Type As, or whether they simply do not enjoy competition. In the present study, choosing to work with a partner did not imply an avoidance of competition. Consistent with this line of reasoning, results indicated that Type Bs felt less competitive, and were more likely to see the partner as helpful, compared with Type As.

Gender differences were neither predicted nor found. While Miller, Lack and Asroff (1985) reported gender effects, other studies on Type A and control have not (Rhodewalt & Comer, 1982; Strube, Berry & Moergen, 1985). Such differences appear to be more likely to emerge under conditions that involve an aggressive response or negative (failure) feedback about achievement. Consistent with this, the choice of retaining control was a fairly aggressive one in the Miller et al. study, because it meant risking exposing the partner (as well as oneself) to more aversive noise. Also, subjects had been negatively compared with the partner. The present study did not include either condition.

A second focus was on the underlying reasons for Type As' control concerns. Results were not consistent with a minimax explanation: that is, the hypothesis that Type As avoid yielding or sharing control mainly because they are concerned about ensuring the best outcome possible. First, although Type As did acknowledge (on the manipulation check) that the Superior Partner had more experience than they themselves had, simply knowing this did not make them more willing to work with the partner. Second, only a minority of Type As rated the partner as actively harmful or interfering, suggesting that their avoidance of the partner was not due primarily to concerns about that person's reducing the likelihood of a positive outcome. Finally, if Type As were influenced by minimax concerns, one would expect to see an inverse relationship between desire to produce the best interview possible and preference for working with the partner, given that they generally chose to work alone. Not only did this not occur, but there was actually a trend among Type As for these two factors to be positively related.

Differences in work choice between Type As and Bs were also not influenced by differential levels of anxiety, commitment to the task (as seen in subjects' ratings of the importance of the situation to them personally), desire for self-evaluation, or desire to make the task more enjoyable. The only factor that did appear to distinguish between the two Types was desire for responsibility. For Type As, there was a strong relationship between desire for responsibility and preference to work alone. For Type Bs, however, there was no evidence of a significant relationship between these two factors. These results provide some support for the view that Type As prefer control in order to attribute outcomes internally, at least when they are moderately involved in the task.

Support for an internality explanation would have been stronger had Type As not only perceived the partner as more experienced than they themselves were, but also as potentially helpful to them, and yet still chose to turn down that source of help. While it appears that the description of the partners' experience was salient (e.g., subjects later remembered it on the manipulation check), it did not appear to influence strongly perceptions of partner helpfulness. Indeed, if anything, describing the partner as superior may have made subjects more—not less—cautious about their potential utility. Consistent with this, results from within-conditions correlations between perceived helpfulness and preference to work with the partner suggest that perceived helpfulness may have been less important to subjects' choices when the partner was described as superior.

An additional, complementary, explanation for Type As' choosing to work alone might be that they simply saw no advantage in cooperating, because they did not see the partner as helpful to them. Given the strong, inverse relationship between desire to work alone and perceived partner helpfulness, this explanation seems plausible. However, it does not negate the fact that Type As appear to have been strongly influenced by a desire for responsibility. Possibly, both explanations were influential in the current context. That is, in comparison with Type Bs, Type As chose to work alone because they wished to remain in control and because they saw little advantage in having a partner help them.

It is interesting that both Type As and Bs who chose to work alone were somewhat motivated by self-evaluative concerns. In a recent study, Strube, Boland, Manfredo, and Al-Falaij (1987) found that Type As were more likely than Type Bs to seek out diagnostic information about their abilities, under conditions of uncertainty. That is, Type As appear to show such behavior in response to situational factors that increase self-doubt about their capabilities (e.g., failure, uncontrollability, and nondiagnostic feedback). Although subjects in the present study may have felt mildly uncertain about the prospective task, they did not report anxiety, nor were they exposed to failure, uncontrollability or nondiagnostic feedback. Therefore, it is not surprising that they failed to show heightened self-evaluative motives.

There are other possible explanations for the behavior of Type As. They may have chosen to work alone because they wished to avoid becoming beholden to a partner. This possibility seems unlikely, since subjects were not told to expect to have any future interactions with each other, thus eliminating any obligations. Nor does it seem likely that Type As chose to work alone due to an introverted work style, since measures of Type A have been found to be correlated with extraversion (Musante, MacDougall, Dembroski, & Van Horn, 1983). Another possibility is that Type As chose control simply out of habit, in a "mindless" or automatic fashion (e.g., Strube, Berry & Moergen, 1985). However, findings indicate that a mindless desire for control among Type As occurs mainly when the link between evaluative information about one's potential partner and control choices has not been made salient. Type As are then able to ignore evaluative information about the partner when they make their decision. This was not the case in the present study, where subjects were first given evaluative information about the partner and then immediately asked to make their work choices.

In comparing the results of Miller et al. (1985) with those of the present study, the differences in the percentages of Type As versus Bs who opted for control appear to be quite similar. In the Miller et al. study, 56% of Type As versus 22% of Type Bs preferred to exercise control instead of relinquishing it to a partner. In the present study, 76% of Type As versus 43% of Type Bs preferred to exercise control instead of sharing it with a partner. Thus, the relative strength of the difference in control preferences is significant (although not large) and consistent across aversive and nonaversive contexts as well as across total vs. partial yielding conditions.

APPLIED IMPLICATIONS

The present results may have important clinical applications. If the emphasis on self-reliance observed here is robust—and particularly if it applies to Type As identified by other, more diseased-linked, measures—it suggests that Type As may maladaptively choose to work alone, even in fairly nonchallenging situations where competent assistance is available. Indirect data suggest this. It has been found that "prospective angina candidates" rate themselves as "much more responsible than their co-workers and commonly will move in and take over a job that they see others doing less rapidly or less well than they could do it" (Jenkins, Zyzanski, & Rosenman, 1978). Similarly, in a study on young adults and coronary disease, Type As were rated as "perfectionists" who "generally chose to do the work themselves rather than delegate it to others," "taking on more responsibilities...than good judgment would dictate" (Russek & Russek, 1977).

Such a pattern of excessive self-reliance may actually increase the number and type of stresses that an individual encounters, thereby increasing feelings of pressure and work overload. It may also lead Type As to under-utilize social support, a circumstance that has been associated with increased morbidity from heart disease (Berkman, 1982; Marmot & Syme, 1976). Although Type As (versus Bs) report having larger social networks and a greater need for social support, they also report having fewer social outlets (i.e., people with whom they can socialize) as they grow older (Strube, Berry, Goza, & Fennimore, 1985). Future research will need to clarify whether or not Type As actually do under-utilize social support, and what their metacognitions are about the costs of such behavior.

Finally, individuals with a strong preference for control may be more prone than others to encounter situations where their control desires are thwarted. This, in turn, may engender greater potential for anger, now believed to be one of the more "toxic" aspects of Type A behavior, at least in terms of development of heart disease (Dembroski & Costa, 1987). Helping Type As learn to decrease their excessive control strivings and to discriminate between situations where cooperation would be more adaptive than self-reliance may increase the quality, if not the quantity, of their lives.

REFERENCES

Berkman, L.F. (1982). Social network analysis and coronary heart disease. *Advances in Cardiology, 29*, 37-49.

Burger, J. M. (1985). Desire for control and achievement-related behaviors. *Journal of Personality and Social Psychology, 48*, 1520-1533.

Dembroski, T.M., & Costa, P.T. (1987). Coronary prone behavior: Components of the Type A pattern and hostility. *Journal of Personality and Social Psychology, 55*, 211-235.

Dembroski, T.M., & MacDougall, J.M. (1978). Stress effects on affiliation preferences among subjects possessing the Type A coronary-prone behavior pattern. *Journal of Personality and Social Psychology, 36*, 23-33.

Dembroski, T.M., MacDougall, J.M., & Musante, L. (1984). Desirability of control versus locus of control: Relationship to paralinguistics in the Type A interview. *Health Psychology, 3*, 15-26.

Glass, D.C. (1977). Stress, behavior patterns, and coronary disease. *American Scientist, 65*, 177-187.

Gotay, C. (1981). Cooperation and competition as a function of Type A behavior. *Personality and Social Psychology Bulletin, 7*, 386-392.

Jenkins, C.D. (1988). Epidemiology of cardiovascular diseases. *Journal of Consulting and Clinical Psychology, 56*, 324-332.

Jenkins, C.D., Zyzanski, S.J., & Rosenman, R. H. (1971). Progress toward validation of a computer-scored test for the Type A behavior pattern. *Psychosomatic Medicine, 33*, 193-202.

Jenkins, C.D., Zyzanski, S.J., & Rosenman, R. H. (1978). Coronary-prone behavior: One pattern or several? *Psychosomatic Medicine, 40*, 25-43.

Krantz, D.S., Glass, D.C., & Snyder, M.L. (1974). Helplessness, stress level, and the coronary-prone behavior pattern. *Journal of Experimental Social Psychology, 10*, 284-300.

Marmot, M.G., & Syme, S.L. (1976). Acculturation and coronary heart disease in Japanese-Americans. *American Journal of Epidemiology, 104*, 225-247.

Miller, S.M. (1979). Controllability and human stress: Method, evidence and theory. *Behavior Research and Therapy, 17*, 287-304.

Miller, S.M. (1980). Why having control reduces stress: If I can stop the roller coaster, I don't want to get off. In J. Garber and M. Seligman (Eds.), *Human helplessness: Theory and applications* (pp. 71-95). New York: Academic Press.

Miller, S.M., Lack, E., & Asroff, S. (1985). Preference for control and the coronary-prone behavior pattern: I'd rather do it myself. *Journal of Personality and Social Psychology, 49*, 492-499.

Musante, L., MacDougall, J.M., Dembroski, T.M., & Van Horn, A.E. (1983). Component analysis of the Type A coronary-prone behavior pattern in male and female college students. *Journal of Personality and Social Psychology Bulletin, 45*, 1104-1117.

Rhodewalt, F., & Comer, R. (1982). Coronary-prone behavior and reactance: The attractiveness of an eliminated choice. *Personality and Social Psychology Bulletin, 8*, 152-158.

Russek, H.I., & Russek, L.G. (1977). Behavior patterns and emotional stress in the etiology of coronary heart disease: Sociological and occupational aspects. In D. Wheatley (Ed.), *Stress and the Heart*. New York: Raven Press.

Smith, T.W., & Brehm, S. (1981). Person perception and the Type A coronary-prone behavior pattern. *Journal of Personality and Social Psychology, 40*, 1137-1149.

Strube, M.J., Berry, J.M., Goza, B.K., & Fennimore, D. (1985). Type A, age, and psychological well-being. *Journal of Personality and Social Psychology, 49*, 203-208.

Strube, M.J., Berry, J.M., & Moergen, S. (1985). Relinquishment of control and the Type A behavior pattern: The role of performance evaluation. *Journal of Personality and Social Psychology, 49*, 831-842.

Strube, M.J., Boland, S.M., Manfredo, P.A., & Al-Falaij, M. (1987). Type A behavior pattern and the self-evaluation of abilities: Empirical tests of the self-appraisal model. *Journal of Personality and Social Psychology, 52*, 956-974.

Strube, M.J., & Werner, C.M. (1985). Relinquishment of control and the Type A behavior pattern. *Journal of Personality and Social Psychology, 48*, 688-701.

Van Egeren, L. (1979). Social interactions, communications, and the coronary-prone behavior pattern: A psychophysiological study. *Psychosomatic Medicine, 41*, 2-18.

Williams, R.B., Haney, T.L., Lee, K.L., Kong, Y-H., Blumenthal, J.A., & Whalen, R.E. (1980). Type A behavior, hostility, and coronary atherosclerosis. *Psychosomatic Medicine, 41*, 539-549.

Type A Intervention:
Where Do We Go From Here?

Ethel Roskies
Department of Psychology, University of Montreal
Box 6128, Branch A, Montreal, Quebec, Canada H3C 3J7

Twelve years ago I enthusiastically began a series of research projects evaluating different treatments for reducing the coronary risk of "healthy" Type A men. Two years ago I reluctantly called a halt to these intervention studies, not because I had found the magical cure, or even because my treatments had shown themselves to be clearly ineffective but, rather, because I was increasingly uncertain about the purposes of treatment and the methods of evaluating its effectiveness. I stopped because I strongly felt that if Type A intervention were to be anything more than another passing fad, it had to demonstrate both conceptual and methodological rigor (Roskies, 1980), but I personally could not overcome some of the conceptual and methodological problems that surfaced during my research efforts.

When I ceased doing active research on Type A, I confidently expected that I would also stop writing or even thinking about the behavior pattern. Despite my professed renunciation of interest, however, Type A still intrigues me, like a love affair that perhaps need not have ended. Hence, I could not resist this opportunity to detail the concerns that led me both to begin and to end research on Type A intervention. Perhaps some one else out there has the answers to the questions that tease me, or at least better ways of posing them.

The Initial Attraction

Although Friedman and Rosenman had begun their investigations into coronary-prone behavior in the 1950s, it was the publication of the final results of the Western Collaborative Group Study in the 1970s that brought the Type A Behavior Pattern (TABP) into the medical and psychological mainstream. In this study, healthy men categorized as Type A manifested, over an eight and a half year period, twice the incidence of heart disease compared to those in whom this behavior pattern was less

Author's Note: The work reported in this paper was supported by grants from Health and Welfare, Ottawa, Conseil en Recherche en Sante du Quebec, and CAFIR, University of Montreal.

© 1990 Select Press

prominent or absent (Type B). Moreover, the association between Type A and heart disease remained, even when other risk factors were held constant through statistical means (Rosenman et al., 1975, 1976). Thus, for the first time in the history of medicine a purely behavioral method, not tapping subclinical signs or symptoms, had successfully *predicted* the emergence of a major somatic disorder (Jenkins, 1978). Forty years of effort by Dunbar, Kemple, the Menningers, and a host of other psychosomatic workers, had finally paid off.

But if Type A established the importance of "psychological" risk factors for heart disease, it was not a psychological entity with which most psychiatrists or clinical psychologists felt either familiar or comfortable. For one thing, Type A did not fall into any of the conventional categories of psychopathology. On the contrary, Friedman and Rosenman (1974, p.67) were insistent that the Type A pattern should not be viewed as a form of neurosis, that the "chronic incessant struggle (of the Type A) to achieve more and more in less and less time" was very different from the anxiety or withdrawal of neurotics. Further evidence of the lack of fit between Type A and traditional personality categories was the relative failure of conventional personality tests, such as the MMPI or the California Psychological Inventory, to detect the presence of the pattern (Matteson & Ivancevitch, 1980).

If Type As were not clearcut psychological misfits, they were also not social deviants, at least not within the achievement-oriented North American society. In fact, after studying the relative occupational achievements and rate of promotion of Type As versus Type Bs, Mettlin (1976) concluded that "the Type A pattern is integral to the modern occupational career."

Thus, in Type A one had a behavior pattern that was not obviously psychopathological nor socially deviant, but which, nevertheless, served as an important risk factor for the number one killer disease in industrialized countries. What was there about this all-American behavior pattern that made people sick, and could its pathogenic constituents be modified without disturbing its positive elements? For a clinical psychologist interested in the newly emerging field of behavioral medicine—and more than a little Type A herself—the challenge was irresistible.

The Initial Response

At the time I began my initial intervention effort in early 1976, I knew of no other systematic effort to reduce coronary risk by changing Type A behavior. Thus, it was up to me to decide who I would treat, how I would treat them, and what would constitute the criteria of a successful outcome (Roskies, 1980).

Almost instinctively, I decided to concentrate my efforts on the population of "healthy" Type As, that is individuals manifesting the pattern but with no clinical signs of coronary heart disease. In retrospect, I recognize that it would probably have been more prudent to begin with coronary patients, as did Friedman and his associates (Friedman et al., 1984). Type A individuals who had suffered one heart attack were clearly high risk for another one, and recurrence rates could be used as a criterion for treatment success. Nevertheless, it was specifically the nonclinical population of Type As that fascinated me. After all, the Western Collaborative Group Study (WCGS) had found that 50% of their sample of asymptomatic, employed, middle aged men could be categorized as Type A. Given the widespread prevalence of this risk factor among some of the most productive members of our society, it made sense to intervene before those at risk faced the possible death and certain psychological upheaval produced by an actual heart attack.

If one were looking for challenge, furthermore, it is precisely this nonclinical population of Type As that would be hardest to reach and treat. How could apparently well functioning men be motivated to enroll and remain in a treatment program? What type of behavior change would provide the "greatest bang for the buck" in terms of maximizing coronary risk reduction while minimizing personal and social dislocation? Since the small sample and short time frame of an exploratory study made it impractical to track coronary occurrences themselves, what other criteria could be substituted to evaluate treatment effects?

The first step was to decide who to treat. If the aim was to change Type A behavior in healthy individuals at risk, it made sense to restrict the sample to the same sex (male) and same age group (39-59) for which the WCGS had established the Type A-heart disease link. To assure that the sample was truly Type A, we would recruit it at the occupational level where the behavior pattern is most prevalent (managers and professionals) and only select individuals who were categorized as extreme Type As (Type A_1) via the structured interview used in the WCGS. Finally, the "healthy" status of the sample, at least as regards heart disease, would be determined by a clinical examination and stress electrocardiogram.

The next step was to determine what to try to change and why, that is to develop a rationale for the proposed treatment. Although the behavioral characteristics of the Type A have been described repeatedly - impatience, time urgency, competitiveness, hostility towards people or things that got in the way. For treatment purposes it was still necessary to develop a conceptual model that would link these disparate behaviors into an understandable whole. The laboratory work of the Friedman group (Friedman, 1977; Friedman et al., 1958, 1975) and Glass and his associates (Glass,

1977; Glass et al., 1980) suggested that Type As are somehow deficient in their reactions to stress. Yet, paradoxically, Type As as a group do not appear to live in unusually stressful life circumstances, nor do they manifest obvious deficiencies in coping resources for managing the stresses they do encounter. Nevertheless, the TABP can be considered a stress disorder because of the Type A's frequent states of activation produced by the *choice* of potentially arousing situations, the *disposition to see* threat or challenge where the Type B does not, and the *exaggerated reactions* to perceived threats and challenges (Smith & Anderson, 1986; Smith & Rhodewalt, 1986).

Various explanations have been offered for the Type A's tendency to continuously slay dragons, both real and imaginary. Some authors postulate a need to exert control over the environment (Glass, 1977), while other claim that Type As manifest an intense ego-involvement leading to increased emotionality (Scherwitz et al., 1978, 1983). A third view would attribute the Type A's need to continuously prove him or herself to an uncertain sense of self-worth (Price, 1982). Regardless of what causes it, however, the consequence is the same: The Type A is more often at war than at peace, repeatedly mobilizing his or her resources to confront perceived threats and challenges. A game of tennis, a difference of opinion with a colleague at work, and a too-slow elevator, all produce a stress reaction in the hypersensitive Type A.

Based on this model, therefore, it would be futile to attempt to reduce Type A behavior primarily via environmental change. Even a nonstressful environment would be perceived and reacted to as challenging by the hyperreactive Type A. There are no safe environments for the person who engages in mortal combat even during a "friendly" game of tennis! Instead, treatment must focus on showing the Type A how to reduce the cost of coping in his present environment.

This conceptualization of the Type A pattern also provided a novel way of motivating asymptomatic individuals to embark on change. Type A behavior was to be rejected not primarily because of its threat to long-term health, but because it was an *inefficient* use of energy. The analogy used was of an out-of-control engine continuously running at full speed versus one that could be speeded up or slowed down as needed. The planned intervention would not seek to change the individual's desire or capacity to accomplish, but only this undifferentiated expenditure of energy. By learning to pace himself—the promise held out by the program—the individual could actually accomplish more with less strain. Therefore, unlike concerned spouses or friends, we would not counsel the Type A person to "take it easy," but instead challenge him to work harder in learning more efficient and more effective stress responses.

An initial trial of this selling message indicated that it worked, at least in producing sufficient subjects for a pilot treatment study. A short radio interview and a newspaper article describing the study purposes and entry criteria produced 150 responses, and the first 45 interviews yielded 36 potential subjects. Eventually, 27 men were enrolled in the program.

Participants in the study were randomly assigned to one of two different treatment groups. The first, a behavior therapy group, focused on tension-regulation via increased awareness of current stress responses and the use of relaxation to control arousal during stress. Individuals were first taught how to track their tension levels during the course of the day, and subsequently a sequence of relaxation exercises designed to foster physiological self-control (Bernstein & Borkovec, 1973).

Eventually, participants reached a level of proficiency at which they both could detect early warning signs of physical tension and could relax on command. The task now became one of using these skills to maintain a comfortably low level of tension. Regularly occurring events in the daily routine (e.g., shaving, opening one's agenda book, driving the car) became signals to check tension level and adjust it if necessary. Even when unexpected or strong arousal did occur (e.g., a discourteous driver cutting in, an argument with one's superior), relaxation techniques could be used to lower the tension level.

The second treatment group was led by two psychodynamically oriented group leaders. Although we had previously rejected the possibility of using psychotherapy for nonclinical subjects, the necessity of finding a control condition that would be credible to these Type A men led us to turn to the psychotherapy unit of the hospital in which the program was carried out. But instead of simply serving as an attention-placebo condition, the therapists concerned, experienced and enthusiastic practitioners of brief psychotherapy, utilized their 14 sessions to run an active treatment program. Based on their view of Type A behavior as an initially useful solution to a conflictual family constellation in childhood, the aim of therapy became one of showing these men how their childhood perceptions and responses distorted their current behavior. The assumption here was that once the individual understood why he was behaving in a certain way, he would be free to change this automatic pattern. While there was no explicit instruction in behavior change, the male and female co-therapists did serve as role models for a more relaxed, less competitive behavior style.

The issue that did not receive much attention in this initial attempt was how to measure treatment outcome. Instead, we simply compared before and after treatment status on an assortment of psychological and physiological variables that were readily available, and had some link either to Type A behavior (perceived time pressure), heart disease (serum cholesterol and triglycerides, resting systolic and diastolic blood pressure), or general well being (psychological symptoms, state and trait anxiety and perceived life satisfaction).

The most amazing result of our initial treatment efforts is that 25 of the 27 men enrolled in the 14 week program completed it, and the participants loudly proclaimed their satisfaction with both interventions. A second, completely unexpected result was the strong group feeling that developed, with some men claiming that this was the closest relationship they had had to date with individuals outside their families. In fact, the behavior treatment group staged a banquet with diplomas for the proud graduates. Obviously, we were doing something right.

The outcome measures also showed indices of improvement: Without change of their diet, exercise and smoking habits, and while continuing to work the same hours per week and to carry the same responsibilities, men in the behavior therapy group showed significant decreases in time pressure, serum cholesterol and systolic blood pressure levels and increased life satisfaction (Roskies et al., 1978). Even more important, six months later most of these changes had been maintained (Roskies et al., 1979). However, contrary to our expectations, men in the psychotherapy group showed almost as good treatment effects immediately after treatment. Although the drop in serum cholesterol was larger and more consistent in the relaxation group, the differences between the two treatment conditions were not statistically significant. They only became so at the follow-up (Roskies et al., 1979).

Second Thoughts

The initial treatment effort had clearly indicated that we could attract the supposedly hard-to-reach occupationally successful, healthy, Type A men and, even more important, keep them in the program. Secondly, based both on the men's spontaneous evaluations and the grab bag of outcome measures used, the program appeared to do the participants some good, enough good, in fact, that benefits were observable even six months after treatment ended.

Once we had recovered from the initial euphoria produced by these results, it was time for some morning after reconsideration. The behavioral program had made the men feel better and may even have reduced their coronary risk, by lowering serum cholesterol and systolic blood pressure levels. But our aim was to reduce the risk specifically associated with the Type A behavior pattern. Since serum cholesterol and *resting* blood pressure levels are typically no higher in Type As than Type Bs, there were no grounds for believing that we had, in fact, changed Type A coronary risk. Indeed, we did not even have a measure of changes in Type A behavior per se!

By this time, via published reports and informal communications, I became aware of a number of others interested in the problem of Type A modification. Although I turned to this literature eagerly for help in improving outcome measures, I found it of little help in resolving the crucial problem of how to measure treatment success or failure. The Friedman group did have an acceptable measure - reduction in coronary recurrence and mortality - but this measure could only be used with a large sample of high risk coronary patients, rather than with my small samples of "healthy" Type As. For the rest, the studies generally contained a grab bag of measures (cholesterol, triglycerides, body weight, treadmill performance), some of which (e.g., anxiety) bore no relationship either to Type A or to heart disease. Furthermore, the only study to claim a significant change in Type A behavior itself (Blumenthal et al., 1980) was based on the self-report Jenkins Activity Survey which suffers from the double disadvantage of being a much poorer predictor of coronary risk than the Structured Interview (Booth-Kewley and Friedman, 1987) and of being open to the influence of social undesirability. Ambitious, competitive Type A participants who learned via an intervention program that the TABP was undesirable could change their responses to the JAS, rather than their behavior in real life.

In summary, although the published Type A studies universally claimed success in their endeavors, there was little consensus about what constituted successful treatment outcome (see Roskies, 1982 for a detailed critique). In fact, most researchers seemed blissfully unaware that there was even a problem. Not surprisingly, therefore, my preoccupation with improving treatment criteria was not shared by most of my co-researchers.

During this period of second thoughts, I also came to the conclusion that the treatment program itself required improvement. In spite of the fact that relaxation training had proved to be a potent treatment for regulating tension, I grew increasingly dissatisfied with its limitations as a universal, all-purpose coping technique. There were just too many stress episodes where simply relaxing muscles did not speak either to the subjective experience of the person experiencing the stress, or to the situation at hand. For instance, many group participants reported experiencing stress not simply through tense muscles, but even more through obsessive worrying, racing thoughts, anger outbursts, and so on. For these people, relaxation in itself was insufficient. As one participant put it, "My muscles are relaxed, but my thoughts still keep on racing."

There were also a large number of stress situations where effective coping meant not only reducing the immediate discomfort via relaxation, but also taking action to modify the situation itself. The manager suffering from too much to do in too little time could achieve some benefit from learning to keep his cool under time pressure. He was likely to benefit even more, however, from also learning how to allocate his time more effectively, how to refuse inopportune requests, and so on.

The problem here was not to find a more powerful coping technique to substitute for relaxation, but rather to deal with the fact that no single coping technique can adequately respond to the variety of situations in which stress is experienced and the many forms it takes. This intuitive dissatisfaction with a single technique approach to coping was strengthened by the publication just at that time of a number of reports of coping in general populations indicating that effective copers tend to use a larger variety of strategies (Folkman & Lazarus, 1980; Ilfield, 1980). To conform with this concept of effective coping, the treatment program would have to be radically redesigned. Instead of simply teaching the Type A to replace a harmful coping pattern (physiological arousal) by a less harmful one (muscle relaxation), it would be necessary to introduce a repertoire of coping strategies.

Testing the New, Improved Model

The second treatment program, launched in December, 1978, intended to improve on the first one both in the selection of outcome measures, and in the treatment offered. Almost inadvertently, it was also tested on a sample that differed considerably from the previous sample group.

In the search for improved outcome measures, it was still impractical to attempt to track changes in coronary morbidity or mortality in a small, asymptomatic group of middle-aged men. Looking at changes in the Type A behavior pattern itself was also rejected in view of the growing literature suggesting that only some Type A behaviors might be responsible for the increased risk of CHD, without any clear consensus as to which specific behaviors were to be considered the pathogenic ones (Matthews et al., 1977; Williams et al., 1980). Until the dust settled, it seemed safer to focus instead on the underlying physiological mechanisms by which, presumably, overt behaviors were transformed into increased atherosclerosis and increased risk of CHD. A second advantage of using physiological measures is that changes on these indices would probably make much more of an impression on the medical world than would purely behavioral or psychological improvements.

A number of studies appearing at that time suggested what kinds of physiological measures to use. According to these reports, the crucial differences between Type As and Type Bs do not occur when both are in a resting state, but only when they are exposed to challenge. Not only do As perceive challenge where Bs do not, but they react to it with more intense and more long-lasting rises in autonomic and neuroendocrine levels (Dembroski et al., 1978; Glass et al., 1980). Furthermore, it is this hyperreactivity that presumably increases their coronary risk because of the relationship postulated between sympathetic arousal, with its associated endocrine activity, and the development of atherosclerosis (Krantz & Manuck, 1984). Any treatment, therefore, that succeeded in reducing the frequency, intensity, or duration of episodes of arousal could also be considered to reduce the coronary risk specifically associated with the TABP (Roskies, 1979).

Just about all the studies exploring the reactivity to challenge of Type As versus Type Bs were based on measures taken within a single session. Because we wanted to measure how these stress reactions changed in response to treatment, we would have to develop methods for repeated measurements before and after treatment. Essentially, the problem was of developing a methodology for tracking change across time (pre to post intervention) in patterns of change at a given moment (autonomic and endocrine reactivity to stress situations). To further complicate matters, all of these physiological measures are sensitive to a host of other influences ranging from time of day to body posture, making it extremely difficult to isolate the effects of stress, not to speak of changes in these effects due to treatment.

I still find it embarrassing to read the ambitious measurement protocol we developed for this study. In retrospect anyhow, we were very naive about the difficulties of collecting sufficiently precise data to permit the accurate observation of possible treatment effects. In the laboratory, for instance, each participant would have two sessions, before and after treatment. During each session, the subject would be asked to play a competitive game (Prisoner's Dilemma) that had already been shown as successfully eliciting Type A reactions in susceptible individuals (Van Egeren, 1979). Measures of systolic and diastolic blood pressure, heart rate, plasma epinephrine and norepinephrine would be taken before, during and after the game. At each session, the "during" and "after" measures would be compared to the "before" ones to obtain the subject's reactivity scores within the session, and the pretreatment scores would be compared to the posttreatment ones to evaluate the effects of treatment.

The measurement objectives for the field situation were even more ambitious, with one working day per fortnight during the course of the project (a total of nine days) designated as a measuring day. During this day, four types of measures were tracked, psychological state, blood pressure, urinary catecholamines and serum cholesterol and testosterone. Participants were asked to record hourly levels of muscular tension, irritability, time pressure and performance and follow this by a blood pressure reading using an electronic machine designed for home use. Urine for the analysis of catecholamine levels was collected for 24 hours divided into three time periods: the night before the working day, the working day itself, and the evening after.

Not satisfied solely with these complex measurement plans, I also enlisted the aid of a collaborator (Jacqueline Avard) to extend and develop the treatment. Instead of simply teaching relaxation, we would now offer a comprehensive package of techniques: rational-emotive training, communication skills, problem-solving skills, stress inoculation, and relapse prevention (Roskies & Avard, 1982).

Finally, almost without being aware of it, we also changed the nature of the sample. Recruiting our new sample from lists of middle managers at three large companies, we now billed the treatment simply as a "stress management program" and, in accordance with the companies' wishes, accepted all volunteers regardless of their Type A status. As a result, in this study only about half this sample had the extreme Type A pattern (A_1) characteristic of the first sample, an additional 40% were less extreme As, while 13% were actually classified as non-As (Types B and X).

Sixty-six men volunteered during the two week recruitment period in December, 1978. Forty of these men were randomly assigned to a 13-week immediate treatment group, while 26 constituted a waiting-list control. The men in the immediate treatment group met weekly in groups of 10 for 13 one-and-a-half-hour sessions. At the completion of the initial treatment period and the posttesting, individuals in the waiting-list control condition were offered the same treatment.

As in the first study, the drop out rate in this second effort remained low (5 of 66). However, this time only 72% of the men attended at least 8 of the 13 sessions, compared to the 85% of the first sample who fulfilled the far more stringent condition of attending at least 12 of 14 sessions.

Even more important, while there were some individuals who clearly benefited from the treatment, on the whole there were no meaningful differences between the treated and the non-treated men (Brochoka, 1981; Sarrasin, 1981). All our careful planning had led us to achieve the first recorded case of treatment failure in the Type A literature!

Analyzing the Failure

This time there was no initial euphoria to delay the morning after reflections. In the attempt to improve the treatment and evaluation procedures, we had actually made them worse. What had gone wrong?

Sample Selection

By not screening for Type A behavior as an entry criterion, we had succeeded in recruiting a sample where 13% of participants were not Type A. Even more important, we had designated reduction in physiological reactivity to stress as the major criterion of treatment effectiveness, but not all these men were hyperreactive to begin with. Even within the Type A sub-group, there were wide variations in initial physiological reactivity to challenge; Type As as a group may be more reactive than Type Bs, but not every Type A manifests this characteristic. Thus, by failing to screen for the presence before treatment of the characteristics we were trying to affect, we had placed ourselves in the impossible position of trying to reduce Type A behavior in non Type As and to reduce autonomic and endocrine reactivity in individuals who were not very reactive even before treatment.

Evaluation Procedures

Although the concept of tracking changes in stress reactivity in the natural environment was an appealing one, it was simply not feasible—at least, not with the size and nature of sample required for this type of study compared to the personnel and equipment we had available. First of all, a sizeable number of participants had to miss all or part of the measurement days, because of travel, special projects and so on. Even when they did try to participate, the measurement process itself often affected the variables we were trying to track. For instance, even if an angry or upset participant remembered that it was now time to take his blood pressure, the process of taking out the machine, making the measurement, and then noting the results, was in itself likely to affect his mood and his cardiovascular functioning. It was even more unrealistic to expect men who were constantly on the move, both in and out of the city, to collect urine over a 24 hour period and then to store this urine until it was picked up. Even the provision of small-sized travelling urine bottles didn't do much to improve the situation.

It is painful to admit it, but I only tested the evaluation procedures myself after we ran into problems. Two days of trying to collect my urine and to take hourly readings of blood pressure were enough to convince me of the unfeasibility of the procedures. It was an expensive lesson in the importance of pilot testing.

The laboratory procedures, too, showed obvious deficiencies. The Prisoner's Dilemma game may be an effective way of evoking arousal, but no single stressor can be confidently expected to stress all those exposed to it. Secondly, even those who were stressed did not necessarily show it via increases in all the indices. Some people demonstrated arousal via changes in systolic blood pressure while heart rate remained relatively constant, while for others the reverse was true, and so on.... Finally, there is a very strong habituation effect, since both treated and untreated subjects showed decreases in reactivity from the first pretreatment to the second posttreatment laboratory visit. Given the complexity of individual reactivity patterns and their sensitivity to a host of extraneous influences, it was obviously going to be more of a methodological challenge than we had anticipated to show improvements in these patterns as a a result of treatment.

Treatment Protocol

Although concerns about the treatment were for a long time submerged under the multitude of measurement concerns, eventually I had to face the fact that the new, "improved" treatment program was weakening rather than strengthening our treatment impact. The extension of the behavioral treatment program from relaxation alone to a variety of coping techniques was a good idea, but it had not been well translated into practice. The program, in its current form, emphasized the teaching of techniques, with the assumption that the user would adopt those solutions for which he had an appropriate problem. However, one of the salient characteristics of the TABP is that the Type A person is often unaware that certain reactions are problematic and, consequently, sees no need to learn techniques for modifying them.

To make this program useful to Type As, it would be necessary to reverse the process, first helping a participant to identify problems and only then teaching him ways of handling them. Moreover, we would have to shift our perspective from the techniques themselves to the participants' needs, that is to become user friendly. The participant really didn't care whether he was using problem-solving skills or cognitive restructuring. What did concern him was how to handle a too demanding superior, or a discourteous sales clerk. To maintain the same relevance as the relaxation program, this more comprehensive one would have to follow the same process of first establishing agreement about where the shoe pinched and then clearly demonstrating why and how the proposed remedies would effectively relieve the pressure.

Back to the Drawing Board

Fortunately for my career as a Type A researcher, a hitter requires three strikes before being declared out. A very understanding granting agency—Health and Welfare, Ottawa—gave me the chance to try once again. I was also fortunate in being able to recruit for this final effort a research team with specific competencies in epidemiological trials (Robert Oseasohn), laboratory tests of physiological reactivity (Peter

Seraganian), analyses of plasma catecholamines (Robert Collu) and biomedical statistics (Jim Hanley). In the enthusiasm of embarking on the new project, it was almost easy to admit mea culpa for the mistakes of my previous efforts, because of my confidence that this time we would surely correct them all.

Treatment Goals

The primary goal of treatment remained essentially the same: to reduce coronary risk in susceptible Type A individuals by reducing the intensity and duration of their physiological responses to everyday stress situations. A secondary goal, added as a fail safe measure, was to reduce behavioral reactivity to stress, as measured by changes in global ratings of Type A on the structured interview and changes in the individual components of the interview: loudness, explosiveness, rapid/accelerated speech, quick latency of response, potential for hostility, and competitiveness (Rosenman, 1978; Dembroski & MacDougall, 1983).

Sample Criteria

This time we were going to be sure that we were not trying to treat people who didn't require it. As a prerequisite for entry into the program, individuals were to be screened not only for presence of Type A, but also for the presence of physiological hyperreactivity as demonstrated by increases of at least 25% above baseline to at least one of two stress tasks on at least three of five measures (systolic and diastolic blood pressure, heart rate, and plasma epinephrine and norepinephrine). In addition, the "nonclinical" nature of the sample would be assured by once more recruiting middle level managers at two large companies, and screening them for the presence of hypertension, or signs of coronary heart disease.

Evaluation Procedures

This time testing for physiological reactivity would be confined to the laboratory, but with an improved and greater variety of stress stimuli. Instead of a single stress task, a battery of six comparable ones was developed, so that participants would have two different stress tasks at each testing session. (For details on the development and verification of this methodology see Seraganian et al., 1985).

To counteract the effects of habituation, there would now be three testing sessions, one for sample selection purposes, one just prior to treatment and one immediately post treatment. Presumably participants would be habituated to the laboratory by the second session, and the differences between second and third sessions could then be used to measure treatment effects.

To permit tracking of changes in behavior, individuals would have two structured interviews, before and after treatment. These interviews would be recorded and after all treatment had been completed, would be rerecorded on new tapes randomly mixing pre and post treatment interviews. They would then be scored by interviewers who would be unaware which treatment an interviewee had received, or whether a specific interview was done before or after treatment.

Treatment Protocol

The 10-week, 20 session behavioral treatment protocol was completely revised. The basic aim became one of teaching the participants to become independent behavioral engineers, capable of both distinguishing "good" and "bad" coping strategies and of transforming the latter into the former. For this purpose the program was divided into seven modules. The first three focused on basic skill building, teaching the individual to monitor and modulate physical, behavioral and cognitive stress responses. The next two modules built on these basic skills by teaching participants how to combine and apply them, first, to anticipating and planning for predictable stress triggers - trouble shooting - and second, to regaining control when suddenly confronted by unpredictable and unexpected stress emergencies. The sixth module extended the scope of self-management to the realm of pleasures. The aim here was to teach the individual how to attain needed rest and recuperation by planning for them. The seventh and final module focused on relapse prevention. This taught the participant to anticipate reversions to old habits and the methods to use for managing these lapses (For a detailed description of the behavioral program see Roskies, 1987a, 1987b).

In the event that the behavioral treatment failed to produce the desired results, it would be important to have a comparison treatment. Aerobic exercise has often been mentioned as a possible means of reducing stress reactivity. Because one of the experimenters (Pete Seraganian) was an experienced and enthusiastic advocate of this treatment approach, a comparable 10 week (three to four sessions per week) aerobic program was developed, individually tailored to each individual's aerobic capacity at program debut. To assure that this program was carried out under optimal conditions, we were able to obtain funds to lease exclusive use at 7.30 in the morning of a private, well-appointed health club located close to the worksite. We also hired well-qualified instructors, and even to provided each participant with appropriate running shoes (For details of this and the following program, see Roskies et al., 1988).

To control for attention-placebo effects, a third intervention of weight-training was developed. There are no data in the literature indicating that weight training exercise can or should change stress responses, but the intervention has the advantage of being credible and acceptable to active, Type A managers. The format of this program was very similar to the aerobic one, except that in the central segment of the session Nautilus exercises, timed to be anaerobic, were substituted for jogging.

Theory Into Practice

Determined that all our mistakes would at least be new ones, this time the main trial was preceded by a pilot study. The results of the pilot study reassured us: It appeared that we now had a methodology that could track the changes that interested us, and that the complex process of selection, treatment and evaluation was feasible.

Out of a pool of over 400 applicants, 118 men were carefully selected for this new trial. After being stratified for age and initial physical condition, they were randomly assigned to one of the three treatment conditions. (To accommodate a sample of this size, there were three sequential treatment waves each containing one behavioral, one aerobic and one weight-training treatment group.) Although participation rules were stringent - to be entered in the data analysis participants had to attend at least 90% of the recommended sessions of their respective groups and go through the posttesting - 107 of these men successfully did so (Roskies et al., 1986). Ratings by the participants of satisfaction with treatment were similarly high for all treatment approaches. Furthermore, each of the two physical activity programs achieved their immediate goals. Participants in the aerobic program showed the expected improvements in aerobic capacity, and those in the weight training program showed increases in muscle strength.

One of the treatments, too, was successful in changing Type A behavior, at least as measured by the structured interview. Participants in the behavioral program (all three treatment groups) showed significant changes both in global Type A ratings and in the component scores. For one of the other treatments (aerobic exercise) there was no improvement. For the other (weight-training) there were only minor changes. Statistically, the behavior treatment scores were significantly different from the other two groups, who did not differ significantly from each other.

Contrary to our hopes, however, there were no meaningful changes in physiological reactivity that could be attributed to treatment. Out of the five indices initially tracked, two (plasma epinephrine and norepinephrine) had to be discarded because a check of analysis reliability (a single sample split into two for separate analyses by different technicians or at different times) showed this to be insufficient. The three remaining measures (heart rate, systolic and diastolic blood pressure) did show some small drop for all treatment groups when posttreatment results were compared to pretreatment ones. However, when these findings were juxtaposed against the first laboratory session (the selection one), it became clear that what we were seeing was probably a continuation of the habituation process. The major drop in reactivity actually occurred between the first session and the second one, before treatment had even begun.

Had we not introduced the methodological refinement of three sessions, but simply followed the usual procedure of comparing before and after results, we might have been able to delude ourselves that, in fact, we had changed reactivity. Under the circumstances, however, we were forced to conclude that none of our treatments was able to effectively modify physiological reactivity to stress, at least according to our measures.

To better understand why we had failed where others appeared to succeed, we carefully reviewed any study we could find reporting efforts to change physiological stress reactivity. Somewhat to our surprise, we found that - when this review was conducted in late 1985- there were no clearcut success stories. For instance, the apparent ability of aerobic exercise to reduce reactivity was based largely on correlational studies comparing exercisers to non-exercisers (Keller & Seraganian, 1984; Light, Obrist & James, 1984). Other reports of behavioral or exercise treatments that effectively changed reactivity had obvious methodological flaws (Jacob & Chesney, 1984). In fact, the better the methodology of the study, the more likely for the results to be negative.

Where Do We Go From Here?

After three tries, I am left with the following results. We can attract asymptomatic, occupationally successful Type A men to treatment, and provide them with programs that a large percentage of participants find helpful. One of the treatment programs we have devised - the behavioral program - can affect Type A behavior as measured by the structured interview. But none of our programs has demonstrated its ability to successfully modify physiological reactivity to stress, the presumed mechanism linking the behavior pattern to the disease end point.

A recent review of treatment for Type A behavior (Nunes, Frank and Kornfeld, 1987) indicates that others have not done substantially better. Although there are continued claims of Type A treatment success, most continue to be based on inadequate outcome measures. The one exception of successful intervention using a valid outcome measure belongs to the Friedman group (Friedman et al., 1984,) who have reported changes both in non-fatal coronary infarctions and the Videotaped Structured Interview. But it is far from clear whether the reduction in coronary risk was due to modification of the TABP *per se,* or to other aspects of their treatment program which included, among other dimensions, social support facilitation. To the best of my knowledge, they have not directly correlated changes in the TABP with changes in coronary risk.

To further complicate matters, the whole rationale for undertaking intervention - that the TABP is a major risk factor for coronary heart disease - is being increasingly questioned. Some researchers dispute the coronary risk status of the pattern *per se*. Others suggest that only specific dimensions of it, such as hostility, should be viewed as pathogenic (see Matthews and Haynes, 1986 for a review).

Before one can undertake further Type A treatment studies, therefore, it is essential that we finally confront an old but still unanswered question: What is the basic purpose of each proposed intervention? If the aim of treatment is to reduce coronary risk, then there may be better ways of approaching the problem than by global, non-specific Type A modification. Increasingly current conceptions of the coronary-prone individual no longer resemble the classical portrait of the hurried, impatient workaholic: Williams (1984) speaks of hostility, Powell and Thoresen (personal communication) include lack of social support, and a recent meta-analysis of psychological predictors of heart disease (Booth-Kewley and Friedman, 1987) claims that depression is also a potent predictor. Using samples of coronary patients, it should be possible to test whether modification of one or more of these characteristics affects disease status.

For the healthy, Type A, however, the future of intervention is much less clear. Until the coronary risk status of Type A is settled, there seems to be little point in continuing to treat Type A in healthy individuals solely for the purpose of preventing a future heart attack. As it now stands, the coronary risk of Type A is simply too ambiguous to warrant interference in the lives of apparently healthy, well-functioning individuals on this basis alone.

Nevertheless, I do see a possibility for continuing to explore and treat Type A, or selected aspects of it, because this mode of perceiving and reacting to the stresses of everyday life can have a negative effect on *current* health and well-being. If Type A is to be conceptualized and treated as a maladaptive coping pattern, however, the challenge is now to delineate which aspects of the pattern are maladaptive in what types of situations. Only then, can we develop meaningful interventions to help individuals live active, productive lives without paying an unnecessary price in terms of physical tension, mental turmoil and disturbed relations with others.

REFERENCES

Bernstein, D. A., & Borkovec, T. D. (1973). *Progressive relaxation training: A manual for the helping professions*. Champaign Ill.: Research Press.

Blumenthal, J. A., Williams, R. S., Williams, R. B. & Wallace, A. G. (1980). Effects of exercise on the Type A (coronary-prone) behavior pattern. *Psychosomatic Medicine, 42*, 289-296.

Booth-Kewley, S. & Friedman, H. S. (1987). Psychological predictors of heart disease: A quantitative review. *Psychological Bulletin, 101*, 343-362.

Brochoka, J. (1981). *Evaluation d' un traitement chez les sujets de Type A dans le milieu du travail.* Unpublished master's thesis, University of Montreal.

Dembroski, T.M., & MacDougall, J.M. (1983). Behavioral and psychophysiological perspectives on coronary-prone behavior. In T. M. Dembroski, T.H. Schmidt, & G. Blumchen (Eds.), *Biobehavioral bases of coronary heart disease* (pp. 106-129). Basel: Karger.

Dembroski, T.M., MacDougall, J. M., Shields, J.L., Pettito, J. & Lushene, R. (1978). Components of the Type A coronary-prone behavior pattern and cardiovascular responses to psychomotor challenge. *Journal of Behavioral Medicine, 1*, 159-176.

Folkman, S. & Lazarus, R.S. (1980). An analysis of coping in a middle-aged community sample. *Journal of Health and Social Behavior, 21*, 219-239.

Friedman, M. (1977). Type A behavior pattern: Some of its pathophysiological components. *Bulletin of the New York Academy of Medicine, 53*, 593-604.

Friedman, M., Byers, S.O., Diamant, J., & Rosenman, R. H. (1975). Plasma catecholamine response of coronary-prone subjects (Type A) to a specific challenge. *Metabolism, 24*, 205-210.

Friedman, M., & Rosenman R. H. (1974). *Type A behavior and your heart*. New York: Knopf.

Friedman, M., Rosenman, R. H., & Carroll, V. (1958). Changes in the serum cholesterol and blood clotting time in men subjected to cyclic variation of occupational stress. *Circulation, 17*, 852-861.

Friedman M., Thoresen C. E., Gill, J. J., Powell, L., Ulmer D., Thompson, L., Price, V. A., Rabin, D. D., Breall, W. S., Dixon, T., Levy, R. A., & Bourg, E. (1984). Alteration of type A behavior and reduction in cardiac recurrences in post-myocardial infarction patients. *American Heart Journal, 108*, 237-248.

Glass, D. C. (1977). *Behavior patterns, stress and coronary disease*. Hillsdale, NJ.: Lawrence Erlbaum Associates.

Glass, D. C., Krakoff, L. R., Contrada, R. Hilton, W. F., Kehoe, K., Mannucci, E. G., Collins, C., Snow, B., & Elting, B. (1980). Effect of harassment and competition upon cardiovascular and catecholamine responses in Type A and B individuals. *Psychophysiology, 17*, 453-463.

Ilfield, F. W. (1980). Coping styles of Chicago adults: Description. *Journal of Human Stress, 6*, 2-10.

Jacob, R. G. & Chesney, M. A. (1984). Stress management for cardiovascular reactivity. *Behavioral Medicine Update, 6*, 23-27.

Jenkins, C.D. (1978). A comparative review of the interview and questionnaire methods in the assessment of the coronary-prone behavior pattern. In T. M. Dembroski, S. M. Weiss, J. L. Shields, S. Haynes, & M. Feinleib (Eds.), *Coronary-prone behavior* (pp. 71-88). New York: Springer.

Keller, S. M. & Seraganian, P. (1984). Physical fitness level and autonomic reactivity to psychological stress. *Journal of Psychosomatic Research, 28*, 279-287.

Krantz, D. S., & Manuck, S. B. (1984). Acute psychophysiological reactivity and risk of cardiovascular disease: A review and methodologic critique. *Psychological Bulletin, 96*, 435-464.

Light, K. C., Obrist, P. A., & James, S. A. (1984). Self-reported exercise levels and cardiovascular responses during rest and stress. *SPR Abstracts, 21*, 586.

Matthews, K. A., Glass, D. C., Rosenman, R. H., & Bortner, R. W. (1977). Competitive drive, pattern A and coronary heart disease: A further analysis of some data from the Western Collaborative Group Study. *Journal of Chronic Diseases, 30*, 489-498.

Matthews, K. A. & Haynes, S. G. (1986). Type A behavior pattern and coronary disease risk: Update and critical evaluation. *American Journal of Epidemiology, 123*, 923-960.

Matteson, M., & Ivancevitch, J.M. (1980). The coronary-prone behavior pattern: A review and appraisal. *Social Science and Medicine, 14A*, 337-351.

Mettlin, C. (1976). Occupational careers and the prevention of coronary-prone behavior. *Social Science and Medicine, 10*, 367-372.

Nunes, E.V., Frank, K A., & Kornfeld, D.S. (1987). Psychologic treatment for the Type A behavior pattern and for coronary heart disease: A meta-analysis of the literature. *Psychosomatic Medicine, 49*, 159-173.

Price, V. A. (1982). *Type A behavior pattern: A model for research and practice*. New York: Academic Press.

Rosenman, R.H. (1978). The interview method of assessment of the coronary-prone behavior pattern. In T.M. Dembroski, S.M. Weiss, J.Shields, S.G. Haynes, & M. Feinleib (Eds.), *Coronary-prone behavior* (pp. 55-70). New York: Springer-Verlag.

Rosenman, R.H., Brand, R.J., Jenkins D., Friedman, M., Straus, R., & Wurm, M. (1975). Coronary heart disease in the Western Collaborative Group Study: Final follow-up experience of 8 1/2 years. *Journal of the American Medical Association, 233*, 872-877.

Rosenman, R.H., Brand, R.J., Sholtz, R.I., & Friedman, M. (1976). Multivariate prediction of coronary heart disease during 8.5 follow-up period in the Western Collaborative Group Study. *American Journal of Cardiology, 37*, 903-910.

Roskies, E. (1979). Evaluating improvement in the coronary-prone (Type A) behavior pattern. In D.J. Osborne, M.M. Gruneberg, & J.R. Eiser (Eds.), *Research in psychology and medicine, vol. 1* (pp.159- 167). New York: Academic Press.

Roskies, E. (1980). Considerations in developing a treatment program for the healthy type A manager. In P.O. Davidson & S.M. Davidson (Eds.), *Behavioral medicine: Changing health lifestyles* (pp. 299-333). New York: Brunner/Mazel.

Roskies, E. (1982). Type A intervention: Finding the disease to fit the cures. In R. Surwit, R. B. Williams, A. Steptoe, & R. Biersner (Eds.), *Behavioral treatment of disease* (pp. 71-86). New York: Plenum Press.

Roskies, E. (1987a). *Stress management for the healthy type A: Theory and practice*. New York: Guilford Press.

Roskies, E. (1987b). *Stress management for the healthy type A: A skills training program*. New York: Guilford Press.

Roskies, E., & Avard, J. (1982). Teaching healthy managers to control their coronary-prone (type A) behavior. In K. R. Blankstein & J. Polivy (Eds.), *Self-control and self-modification of emotional behavior: Advances in the study of communication and affect* (pp. 161-183). New York: Plenum Press.

Roskies, E., Kearney, H. Spevack, M., Surkis, A., Cohen, C., & Gilman, S. (1979). Generalizability and durability of treatment effects in an intervention program for coronary-prone type A managers. *Journal of Behavioral Medicine, 2,* 195-207.

Roskies, E., Seraganian, P., Oseasohn, R., Hanley, J. A., Collu, R., Martin, N., & Smilga, C. (1986). The Montreal Type A Intervention Project: Major findings. *Health Psychology, 5,* 45-69.

Roskies, E., Seraganian, P., Oseasohn, R., Smilga, C., Martin, N., & Hanley, J. (1988). Treatment of psychological stress responses in healthy Type A men. In W. J. Neufeld (Ed.), *Advances in the investigation of psychological stress* (pp. 284-304). New York: Wiley.

Roskies, E., Spevack, M., Surkis, A., Cohen, C., & Gilman, S. (1978). Changing the coronary-prone type A behavior pattern in a non-clinical population. *Journal of Behavioral Medicine, 1,* 201-216.

Sarrasin, S. (1981). *Evaluation des effets d' un traitement visant la reduction du risque coronarien chez des sujets de type A.* Unpublished master's thesis, University of Montreal.

Scherwitz, L., Berton, K., & Leventhal, H. (1978). Type A behavior, self-involvement, and cardiovascular response. *Psychosomatic Medicine, 40,* 593-609.

Scherwitz, L., McKelvain, R., Laman, C., Patterson, J., Dutton, L., Yusim, S., Lester, J., Kraft, I., Rochelle, D., & Leachman, R. (1983). Type A behavior, self-involvement, and coronary atherosclerosis. *Psychosomatic Medicine, 45,* 47-58.

Seraganian, P., Hanley, J. A., Hollander, B., Roskies, E., Smilga, C., Martin, N., Collu, R.C., & Oseasohn, R. (1985). Psychophysiological reactivity: Issues in quantification and reliability. *Journal of Psychosomatic Research, 29,* 393-405.

Smith, T.W., & Anderson, N.B. (1986). Models of personality and disease: An interactional approach to Type A behavior and cardiovascular risk. *Journal of Personality and Social Psychology, 50,* 1166-1173.

Smith, T.W., & Rhodewalt, F. (1986). On states, traits and processes: A transactional alternative to the individual difference assumptions in Type A behavior and physiological reactivity. *Journal of Research in Personality, 20,* 229-251.

Van Egeren, L.F. (1979). Social interactions, communications and the coronary-prone behavior pattern: A psychophysiological study. *Psychosomatic Medicine, 41,* 2-19.

Williams, R.B., Jr. (1984). Type A behavior and coronary heart disease: Something old, something new. *Behavioral Medicine Update, 6,* 29-33.

Williams, R.B., Jr., Haney, T.L., Lee, K.L., Kong, Y., Blumenthal, J.A., & Whalen, R.E. (1980). Type A behavior, hostility, and coronary atherosclerosis. *Psychosomatic Medicine, 42,* 529-550.

Name Index

C

H

I

J

K

S

Y

Z

Subject Index

Q

R

S

Z